STUDIA FENNICA
FOLKLORISTICA 2

The Finnish Literature Society was founded in 1831 and has from
the very beginning engaged in publishing. It nowadays publishes
literature in the fields of ethnology and folkloristics, linguistics,
literary research and cultural history.
The first volume in the Studia Fennica series appeared in 1933.
The series is nowadays divided into three thematic subseries:
Ethnologica, Folkloristica and Linguistica.
In addition to its publishing activities the Finnish Literature
Society maintains a folklore archive, a literature archive and a
library.

SONGS
BEYOND THE
KALEVALA

Transformations
of Oral Poetry

Edited by
Anna-Leena Siikala
& Sinikka Vakimo

SUOMALAISEN KIRJALLISUUDEN SEURA · HELSINKI

Translations from Finnish by Susan Sinisalo
ISBN 951-717-694-5
ISSN 1235-1946
Tammer-Paino Oy, Tampere 1994

Contents

Preface

The title of this volume refers to the tradition of rune singing which was the foundation for Elias Lönnrot's compilation of the Kalevala epic. The interest in the epic poetry chosen as the basis for the *Kalevala* both gave birth to Finnish folkloristics as well as constituted its most important area from the 18th to the beginning of the 20th century. The comparative research method created by Julius Krohn, which was perfected and formulated into the historical-geographical method by his son Kaarle Krohn, formed the foundation for Kalevala poetry research in the beginning of this century. A research method derived from evolutionist and diffusionist cultural theories sought answers to questions concerning the age and character of the poetry. These questions had a central importance in the creation of the young nation-state's cultural capital. The typological research established in the 1930s and the textual critique of the 1950s did not question these basic premises, although the theoretical centres of attention had shifted. Historical types of examination preserved their status because a rune-tradition which contained pre-Christian mythology and ancient ethnographic elements was considered to provide a glimpse into the past of the non-literate Finnish-Karelian culture.

The historical perspective was also natural in the sense that the *rune*-singing lost its value and status during the modernisation process of the 19th century. In just a few decades it became a skill possessed by only a few, a skill which had only curiosity value in the village community. The collection efforts which began in the 18th century, in which the university students' journeys to the field site played a central role, produced an enormous collection of *rune*-poems. The Folklore Archives of the Finnish Literature Society grew up around this original nucleus, broadening, in the course of the decades, into a collection dealing with an increasing diversity of folklore genres and ethnographic information. Between the years 1908 and 1948 the volume series *Suomen Kansan Vanhat Runot* 'The Ancient Poems of the Finnish People' was edited from the *rune* versions amassed up to that point. This series consists of 33 volumes, each nearly one thousand pages in length. This rich body of material is the central point of departure for Finnish folk poetry research, a powerful voice beyond the *Kalevala*, of which a single researcher could hardly ever hope to attain a thorough knowledge.

Synchronically oriented and engaged in research in living cultures, the folklore generation of the 1960s rejected historical enquiry. Instead, contextual research into individual tradition-bearers, communities of tradition and forms of traditional communication took precedence as areas of examination. At the same time that perspectives and methods diversified, the study of Kalevala poetry remained the exclusive right of a few researchers representing the classical Finnish school. In the context of modernity, living folklore was seen as easier to study in local city communities or in distant cultures in which the oral tradition had retained its vitality.

After two decades of near-silence on the subject of Kalevala poetry research, interest in this area is again on the rise in the midst of a new generation of researchers. Although one cannot conduct fieldwork in the past, it is nevertheless possible to examine a traditional *rune* in its ethnographic context. The Kalevala metric *rune*-singing, once considered difficult to approach since it is no longer a living tradition, is again being viewed as an enticing subject of research. This change in attitude has been powerfully influenced by the return of the historical perspective to both European cultural studies as well as American anthropology, two fields from which Finnish folklorists have become accustomed to borrow their theoretical foundations. Folklore research has been particularly enriched by discussions concerning textual and interpretative theory as well as interpretative anthropology. In the 1980s and 1990s, however, Kalevala poetry research has been characterised by its own diversity of perspectives. As much attention has been paid to the singers' performance as to the analysis of the contents of the songs themselves. New questions have arisen, representing an aim towards gender-specific, performance-centered, cognitivistic and ethnopoetic perspectives, among other things. At this moment discussions dealing with *tradition* are the basis for a new perception of Kalevala poetry and the birth process of the *Kalevala*. Researchers are asking, for example, why only particular poetic materials were selected as the building blocks of national identity and why a large portion of the poetic tradition remained unused, even unpublished.

From the perspective of the 1990s it appears that the scientific legacy of Julius and Kaarle Krohn deserves to be re-evaluated. Beyond a critique of ideology, it is important to distinguish historical-philosophical points of departure particular to the Finnish school during different periods, as well as analyse its methodological research principles. It is also worthwhile to survey the kinds of information associated with the objects of folk research themselves which are the product of not only folklore collectors but archaeologists and linguists as well. The accumulation of information has centrally influenced our interpretations concerning the folk poetry. Not until we reassess these issues can we see how the modes of thought belonging to the Finnish school meshes with historically-directed cultural theory and which cultural theories are central to a holistic examination of the existence of folklore.

The aim of this collection of articles is to give a picture of the discussion concerning Kalevala poetry which has taken place in recent years. At the same time it attempts to bring out aspects of the *rune*-singing tradition which have remained hidden to non-Finnish readers. This volume is comprised of new articles as well as those previously published in Finnish or in sources which may be difficult to locate. The latter have been expanded and revised to meet the needs of this volume. The perspective of the volume is introduced in Professor Anna-Leena Siikala's (University of Joensuu) article *Transformations of Kalevala Epic*, in which myth and historical relationships are considered using historical anthropology as a point of departure. The poetry is examined as a continual, processual tradition, as a dialogue between past and present in which each performance transforms the poetic tradition according to the performers and their cultural influences. Since the article's perspective incorporates the possibility of continuing the examination, concentrating as much on the performer and his/her experience and on the performance and the recontextualization as on the thematic contents of the poems themselves and an analysis of language and variation, it functions as a background for the other articles.

In the first section of the volume questions concerning *Kalevala Metre* are examined. The characteristic metre of Finnish-Karelian poetry, Kalevala metre has long been the focus of interest among both linguistic researchers and folklorists. Although the principles of the metre itself have been defined in detail, the history of its development and transformation has long remained an open topic for discussion. Interest in Kalevala metre gained new momentum particularly in the 1980s when Matti Kuusi, Pentti Leino and Mikko Korhonen published works on the subject. Although the articles by these authors or their earlier versions have been published elsewhere in Finnish, we considered it important to bring them together in order to form a more complete picture concerning what are currently the most significant view of the history of the metre, as well as the differences among these views.

In his article *Questions of Kalevala Metre*, Academician Matti Kuusi seeks the so-called homeland of the classic Kalevala metre by comparing Balto-Finnic linguistic elements, proverbs and riddles. For a long time Kuusi was almost the only researcher in Finland well-versed in the Kalevala poetry research tradition, but in this volume he has received as interlocutors two additional perspectives on this linguistic research. In his article *The Kalevala Metre and its Development,* Professor Pentti Leino (University of Helsinki) examines the structural features characteristic of Kalevala metre and the development of these features in relation to the modern Finnish language. The article by the late Professor Mikko Korhonen (University of Helsinki), *The Early History of the Kalevala Metre*, sheds new light on questions concerning the ancient development of the Kalevala metre. In his discussion he ponders the relationships between the Kalevala metre and the metre of Mordvin folk poems.

The second section of the volume, *Performance and Variation,* deals with the reproduction, performance and variation of the *runes*. The contribution by Lauri Harvilahti (Researcher at the Oral Epics Project, Academy of Finland), *The Ingrian Epic Poem and its Models* has as its background Harvilahti's doctoral dissertation (1992), in which Lordian formula analysis is combined with theory on cognitive schemas. Using linguistic concepts, Harvilahti examines the ways in which Ingrian *rune*-epics were produced as well as the changes in the form and meaning of the *rune*.

The ethnopoetic perspective, which has not been previously applied to research in Kalevala poetry, is presented here by two researchers. The article *Ethnopoetic Analysis and Finnish Oral Verse* by Pertti J. Anttonen

(Research Secretary at the Nordic Institute of Folklore) starts out by exploring the basic theses of this research tradition and at the same time critically reassesses the principles of the historical-geographical method. In examining Ingrian poetry, Anttonen applies an ethnopoetic method of analysis to his outline, and seeks the meaning and function of the text in performance. The American researcher, Associate Professor Thomas DuBois'(University of Washington, Seattle) treatment of the subject is based closely on the ethnopoetic tradition linked to the works of Dell Hymes. In his analysis of the body of poetry produced by one of the most significant of the great *rune*-singers, Arhippa Perttunen, DuBois illuminates the possibilities of the ethnopoetic method of examination as well as the problems involved in the analysis of archival materials. Jukka Saarinen's (Researcher at the Finnish Literature Society) focus is the poetry of Arhippa's son Miihkali Perttunen. His article *The Päivölä Song of Miihkali Perttunen* brings to light different forms of variation and shifts in style from one performance of the *rune* to the next.

The articles in the volume's third section, *Themes, Images and Intertextuality* represent the mythical themes of the poems, points of interest in terms of ritual associations as well as research into the cosmological features of the epic poetry and incantation material. Both researchers in religious studies as well as folklorists have long been interested in questions regarding the characteristic folk world view found in Kalevala poetry. In this section, mythical themes and images are approached from a number of different perspectives. The article by Associate Professor Satu Apo (University of Helsinki), *Ale, Spirits and Patterns of Mythical Fantasy* touches upon one of the oldest mythical subjects of Kalevala poetry. In her discussion she analyses the structure of the 'birth of hops' myth and the actors and actions associated with it. The emphasis upon the sacredness of alcoholic drinks in mythical narrative can be seen as revealing a central concern in Finnish cultural tradition.

Kalevala poetry research is not the exclusive right of Finnish or Finnish-speaking persons. In the Karelian Republic, which is part of Russia, one can still find persons skilled in *rune*-singing, and folk poetry research there has a long and distinctive tradition. Karelian researchers have, among other things, been able to clarify where the Kalevala epic poetry stands in relation to Russian folk poetry. One of the authors presented in this section, Eino Kiuru, has worked as a Senior Researcher in the Karelian Scientific Centre, Petrozavodsk. His contribution, *The Wife-Killer Theme in Karelian and Russian Songs* analyses the special features of the woman-killer song. Similar to a ballad in form, it deviates from the archaic mythical epic chosen as the basis for the *Kalevala* and belongs to the body of songs favoured by women.

In her article *Song in Ritual Context: North Karelian Wedding Songs*, Henni Ilomäki (Head Librarian at the Finnish Literature Society) draws attention to the performance of Kalevala metre material in ritual contexts. She compares two wedding traditions in Finland and at the same time points out archaic features common to both wedding and bear-killing ceremonies. Lotte Tarkka (Researcher at the Oral Epics Project, Academy of Finland) interprets the poetry of a Karelian village community from a literary research perspective in her article *Other Worlds – Symbolism, Dialogue*

10

and Gender in Karelian Oral Poetry. She draws particular attention to the intertextual features of the poetry and guides the reader through a discussion of gender representation in the poetry.

From the 1980s onward the female perspective has significantly enriched not only cultural research in general but also research on Kalevala poetry in Finland. This has meant, among other things, the foregrounding of women's emotions and perspectives in the interpretation of the poetry as well as the revival of lyric research. In the section entitled *Women's Voice*, the experience of women is dealt with from three different perspectives. In her article *The Mary of Women's Epic* Senni Timonen (Researcher at the Finnish Literature Society) examines a body of poetry with Christian themes and its central figure, the Virgin Mary. Timonen analyses the many roles of the Mary-figure and stresses the personal experiences of the performers against the background of the vitality of the Mary-poems. Professor Leea Virtanen (University of Helsinki) in her article *Women's Songs and Reality* considers the relationship between women's songs and the reality of women's lives as well as the meanings behind different ways of singing. Examples are drawn from the song cultures of Estonia, Karelia and Finland, among others. The selection of songs is indicative not only of women's song culture but of the research co-operation in which Finnish, Russian Karelian and Estonian folklorists have long been interested.

Although *rune*-singers are not the central focus of this volume, their voices can also be heard in the articles. The creative singer comes to the fore in Thomas DuBois' and Jukka Saarinen's studies of Arhippa and Miihkali Perttunen, father and son, as well as in Anneli Asplund's (Researcher at the Finnish Literature Society) portrayal of a mother-daughter *rune*-singing team. Asplund's contribution *Mother and Daughter – in the Footsteps of the Itinerant Singers* depicts the last period of *rune*-singing in Finland. The article describes a process of transition for the Kalevala song tradition, the end product of which was the on-stage artistic performance. In addition to an examination of the life history of the *rune*-singers, mother and daughter, Asplund brings to light the tensions and obstacles which independently functioning female artists come up against in the course of their lives.

Explanations are in order regarding the choice of terminology. *Kalevalainen runous* 'Kalevala poetry', is a term which researchers in the 1970s strove to avoid because it was seen to be too tightly linked to nationalistic images associated with the *Kalevala*. The name refers principally to the poems assembled as the basis for the *Kalevala*-epos; it is not a part of the folk terminology. Researchers sought to replace anachronistic concepts with other designations, such as *muinaisruno* 'ancient rune', *vanha runo* 'old rune' or *runonlaulu* '*rune*-singing'. None of these terms, however, sufficiently differentiate Kalevala metric runes or Kalevala epic from other forms of the song tradition. The term 'ancient rune', is, moreover, problematic in that it contains an assumption about an ancient origin for the poems. For this reason the designation 'Kalevala poetry' has been accepted in recent years as a technical term.

The purpose of the photographs in this volume is to bring the old Finnish-Karelian and Ingrian culture which has upheld the poetic tradition as step closer to the experience of the reader. We hope that the photographs will assist in better understanding the kind of environment in which the *runes* were actualised and in which contexts their meanings took form. The photographs are for the most part scenes of the landscape and life of the *rune*-villages as seen through the eyes of well-known Finnish ethnographer-photographers. Most of the photographs from Archangel Karelia are the products of I. K. Inha (in the year 1894), Samuli Paulaharju (1910-1915) and Axel Berner (1872); the photographs from Ingria are chiefly the work of Vihtori Alava (1892). The map at the end of the volume shows the most central localities mentioned in the articles. Place-names and areas given in the information for the photographs are also shown on the map.

Each article which has appeared in an earlier form is accompanied by the original publication information. The bulk of the challenging and often tricky problems presented by the translation of the volume from Finnish to English were solved by Susan Sinisalo. In addition, Laura Stark assisted in the final revision of the translation. Other translators have been credited within specific articles. For the translation of the poems, the translations contained in the volume *Finnish Folk Poetry: Epic* (eds. Kuusi, Bosley and Branch, 1977) have been used as a guide where possible. The above volume as well as the recently published work *The Great Bear. A Thematic Anthology of Oral Poetry in the Finno-Ugrian Languages* (eds. Honko, Timonen, Branch and Bosley, 1993) provide superb additional readings to the articles. Tuija Korhonen and Leena Waismaa-Matsi assisted in the role of sub-editors. We warmly thank everyone who has assisted in the publication of this volume.

Joensuu December 1, 1993

Anna-Leena Siikala   *Sinikka Vakimo*

Tradition: Dialogue between Past and Present

ANNA-LEENA SIIKALA

Transformations of the Kalevala Epic

Kalevala poetry has occupied a special position in studies of Finnish culture. Epic songs and charms found in the 18th and 19th centuries seemed to bear the voice of the past in their odd motifs and expressions. For a nation which lacked a written history, listening to this voice was of the utmost importance. All students of Kalevala poetry agreed on the importance of the task. But disagreement arose when scholars tried to decide from how far in the past the information had been passed on and what it told. Today we know a lot more about the nature of the Kalevala epic. Yet the age and character of this poetry are still a fascinating object of study full of questions not yet answered.

In estimating what Kalevala poetry can tell us about the people who cherished it and the cultures in which it was meaningful and important, we must examine the life of oral poetry in general. Instead of studying individual poems – as was done in the days of the Finnish historical-geographical method – we should look for the transformation of poetic tradition as a whole, the praxis and institutional contexts, the changes in metre, means of reproduction, performance and poetics, and especially the formation of meanings and the reinterpretation of the traditional contents of poems. I will here be concentrating on the last of these questions.

Interpretations in dispute

Kalevala poetry existed – like the epic poetry of non-literate cultures in general – only as oral tradition. The early collectors could already make observations on its nature in the light of parallel traditions in other peoples. Mikael Agricola in 1551, for example, obviously had some kind of idea about the nature of epic poems when he named Väinämöinen and Ilmarinen, the central figures of Kalevala poetry, gods of the peoples of Häme. Elias Lönnrot, accordingly, placed Kalevala poems on the level of the great epic poetry of Europe – *The Iliad* and *Odyssey* of Greece, *The Edda* of ancient Scandinavia, *The Niebelungenlied* of Germany and *The Beowulf* of the Anglo-Saxons – when creating the Kalevala epic. The European literary epics differ both from one another and from the epics of Asia and Africa

Songs beyond
the Kalevala
Studia Fennica
Folkloristica 2
1994

not only in content but in the way and the period they were noted down. The relationship between the finished epic and the collection of oral poems telling of the deeds of the same hero is also something of a problem. Nevertheless, there are common features in these traditions. Their special value, sacredness or cultural significance place them above all other stories. Myth and history are woven into them to form true, trusted events, so that they become mirrors of the world, the nation and its early heroes.

So far attempts to determine the nature of old Finnish epic poetry have drawn on the categorising concepts 'mythical', 'historical' or 'heroic'. The mythical and the historical interpretations have been fighting for supremacy in determining the fundamental nature of Kalevala poetry from the 18th century onwards. Similar problems have been shared by research into Homeric epic (cf. Detienne 1981, 22-24) and ancient Scandinavian poetry. In Finland this dispute had deep roots. The quest for history, for insights into the past through epic poetry, is an extremely powerful force stimulating epic research in a young state devoid of literary sources. And we can see from the trend in the historical interpretations of the Finnish epic that this force not only stimulates but also guides research in accordance with whatever national interests are dominant at the time (cf. Siikala 1992, 133-136). In contrast to this there emerged a school following the trends in mythology research of the European continent. It is surely no exaggeration to claim that the more cosmopolitan a researcher's orientation is and the wider his/her familiarity with comparative materials representing different cultures, the sharper his/her view becomes of the mythical and fictive nature of the Finnish epic.

One interesting exception to this rule is Kaarle Krohn. In his work on the history of the Kalevala poems published in 1910 he in many respects followed in the footsteps of his father (Julius Krohn) in trying to make a clear distinction between poems with mythical and poems with historical motifs. A few years later his views had changed completely: Kalevala poems told about historical events. They were originally produced in Western Finland during the Viking era and then wandered to the eastern and northern parts of the Finnish-Karelian area (Krohn 1914 and 1918).

It is not difficult to observe that the scholar's interests were guided by the times, the birth of an independent Finnish state (Hautala 1954, 254 ff.; Wilson 1976; Siikala 1986). Mere nationalism is not, however, sufficient to explain Krohn's change of direction. Elsewhere, too, study of historical heroic poetry had broadened scholars' view of the themes of the folk epic. Krohn was inspired by, among other things, research into the Russian *bylina* poems. Nor should we forget that the work entitled *"The Heroic Age"* by H. Munro Chadwick appeared for the first time in 1912. Thoughts on the heroic epic as the product of a particular type of community hovered in the air. In picking out features common to Homeric and early Teutonic poetry Chadwick had recourse to the concept 'heroic poem', whose aristocratic and military ethos, the fight for personal glory and honour, reflects the aristocratic milieu in which the poetry was born (Chadwick 1912, 325-338). Features of the Chadwickian heroic poem have their counterpart in the Finnish tradition in some of the poems about Väinämöinen of the northern regions and the *Island epic* involving Kaukamoinen and Ahti. The 'barbaric' community of the heroic era was then revealed by archaeological

In Venehjärvi, an old ritual preserved in the context of the Orthodox prayer-room was used to ensure good luck in livelihood. Village residents are gathered for a sacrificial feast. Archangel Karelia. Photo: I.K. Inha 1894 (FLS 9913).

excavations of ancient settlements in Western Finland. Weapons, treasures and costumes of the Viking and Crusade eras have provided material for scholars in tracing the socio-historical details hidden in folk poetry from Kaarle Krohn to Jalmari Jaakkola (1935) right up to the present day (cf. Klinge and 1984 and Linna 1987).

The age of Kalevala poetry

Both the mythical and the historical interpretation of Kalevala poetry in fact share a tendency to look towards the distant past. Scholars have drawn on the content of the poetry in an attempt to reveal its original meaning. One of the basic assumptions behind Finnish epic research has been the concept that individual poems and motifs have been handed down from one generation to the next as, so to speak, ossified relics of their culture of origin. The problem has been how and when this tradition was born.

Since the earliest collections are only two or three hundred years old, some researchers have claimed that it is impossible to make any conclusions concerning the age of epic poems. Väinö Kaukonen, who represents an extreme view in the age dispute, has stated that Kalevala poems flourished especially in the 17th and 18th centuries just before a start was made to collecting them, and that even some of the narrative poems descend from the Crusade era. The Kalevala poetry was mostly found in the Karelian cultural area. The lack of Kalevala poems in Central Russia, where Karelians settled during the 16th and 17th centuries, testifies according to

Kaukonen that the newcomers did not know the Kalevala tradition. So the Karelian epic poetry must have originated later (Kaukonen 1977).

Because the disappearance of tradition was followed in the western areas during the 18th and 19th centuries, when a remarkable cultural change took place in Finland, it is obvious that the lack of tradition is not a solid basis for conclusions. The cultural processes influencing the life of oral tradition have taken many forms. It is a notable fact that the poems collected during the past few centuries contain references to ancient cultural phenomena which were not known in the areas of *rune*-singing. The central vocabulary of poems is also old-fashioned and includes many expressions which are not used in everyday language (cf. Ruoppila 1967). Some of these words can be found in Western and Northern Finland; in the Karelian area they have been replaced by Russian loan words in ordinary speech. Furthermore, the closest parallels to many mythical motifs and features of Kalevala poetry can be found in ancient Scandinavian poetry and *sagas* (see, for example, Siikala 1992), which obviously represent the oral tradition of the Viking and Crusade ages even though they were written down during the 12th – 14th centuries. Similarities do not necessarily point to a common origin. In the Slavic wondertale and *bylina* tradition the same kind of features can be found. It seems that these parallel phenomena belong to the wide-spread North-European tradition of the Viking and Crusade ages. It is also obvious that the Finnish mythico-historical epic tradition is even older. Hardly any nation borrows at random, piece by piece, its central heritage, the mythic tradition. Tradition already existing can in turn assimilate new elements and be renewed by them.

Matti Kuusi, who has made a thorough study of the history of Kalevala poetry[1], considers the epic tradition to be very old. In *Finnish Folk Poetry. Epic* he divides the themes of Kalevala songs into seven categories "listed in order of antiquity":
1. Myth poetry, which describes cosmogonic acts of creation at the beginning of time, the creation of the world and of human, animal and plant life, with particular reference to those factors which condition man's relation to his environment such as the need to ensure fertility and to protect himself.
2. Magic and shaman poetry, in which the characters achieve their ends by magic, and which tell of a shaman's journey to the other world in search of a particular object or item of knowledge.
3. Adventure poetry, often about journeys in search of wives or plunder, and about escape to a place across the sea.
4. Fantasy poems, in which a wondrous animal, mermaid or small child is threatened.
5. Christian legends.
6. Ballads, narrative poetry and lyrical epic.
7. Historical war poetry. (Kuusi-Bosley-Branch 1977, 46-47).

Even though all the poems belonging to these categories are in Kalevala metre, only the first four form the basis for the *Kalevala* and are usually referred to as Kalevala epics. Christian legends, ballads and lyrical epics bear clear marks of medieval poetry; 'historical war poetry' tells about kings and rulers of the New Era and differs clearly from the ancient mythical world of *Kalevala* themes.

The earliest shoots of Kalevala tradition – mythic themes – can according to Matti Kuusi be traced back thousands of years. Some of the mythical motifs, such as *The Creation of the World* and *The Oak*, represent world-wide tradition, others, such as The Origin of the *Kantele* and *the Primeval Boat*, are known only in the Finnic-Baltic area. Matti Kuusi considers that most of these mythical themes took shape during the Proto-Finnic period (Kuusi 1977, 48). Contacts with ancient Germanic tribes altered the nature of Kalevala poetry. Kuusi assumes that heroic poetry, which tells about the deeds of Väinämöinen, a magical smith and singer, and his opponents, and also of more worldly heroes, Kaukamoinen and Ahti, emerged during the centuries before the Christian era – in what is called the Middle Kalevala period (Kuusi 1977, 48-51). During the Middle Ages the Roman Catholic Church rooted out the old ways of thinking and Christian themes were favoured both in Kalevala epics and ballads. During the first Christian contacts, a period of 'barbarian Christianity', old mythical themes were interpreted from new points of view and Christian parodies of mythic poems emerged (Kuusi 1977, 53).

Matti Kuusi constructed his picture of four periods of Kalevala poetry on the basis of poetic language, stylistic features, comparative knowledge of epic imagery and themes and archeological and linguistic information. The problem is whether we can speak of the age of individual poems or whether we should speak of the poetic tradition as a whole. Lauri Honko has pointed out that in estimating the age of Kalevala poetry we should make a distinction between the theme or motif of a poem and the poem itself. Both of them have separate histories (Honko 1978, 182). Individual motifs and features can be widely known and very old. When making up poems, folk singers use all kinds of materials at hand. On the other hand, poetic form is the best way of preserving age-old motifs and handing them down from generation to generation. This process is not, however, the simple copying of inherited texts. Matti Kuusi states quite rightly that "calculating the age of an ancient poem is ... complicated, for a folk poem rarely dates from a single period. Even the first singer to compose a specific narrative sequence almost certainly incorporated passages or lines from other poems; his version was then reshaped and modified by later singers." (Kuusi 1977, 40). Kuusi's words direct our attention towards the mechanisms of remembering in non-literate societies.

The memory of oral culture

Although the time depth of the poetry is still debated by scholars, it is clear that the life of a poetic tradition is influenced by many different aspects. Instead of concentrating on individual poems, the scholar should view the poetic tradition as a whole, its language, the devices for its production, the ways in which it was sung, the genres and motifs and transformations in their meanings. The language and mechanism of poetry constitute the cultural memory mechanism on which the poetic tradition relies. The life of a poetic tradition also depends on the vitality of the messages it transmits.

The key question in estimating the age of the poetic tradition is the history of the Kalevala metre. Not only was the Kalevala metre used by the poet as an expressive device; it was also a widely-used code for memorising texts (Kuusi 1978, 209). Its roots have been sought in the poetry of the Finno-Ugrian peoples. Heikki Paasonen among others reckoned that Kalevala metre had early ties with the eight-syllable poetic metre of Mordva (Paasonen 1897, 1911), and Mikko Korhonen posited that the foundations for the birth of Kalevala metre were not laid until the changes that took place in the vowel system of secondary syllables in the early and middle Proto-Finnic era (see pp. 82; Korhonen 1987, 182). The more distantly related Finno-Ugric languages are thus not able to throw any light on the stages in its evolution.

The view on the Baltic origin of Kalevala metre nowadays established in folklore research was put forward by A.R. Niemi in 1918. His claim has been supported by a number of early Baltic-Finnic poetic motifs. Such concepts as *kantele* 'Finnish sither' and *virsi* 'song' appearing in folk songs are also thought to be of Baltic origin (see Turunen 1979). The linguists have in recent years nevertheless thrown doubt on the Baltic theory. Korhonen points out that the Baltic origin of the words *virsi* and *kantele* cannot be regarded as certain. *Kannel* may be an indigenous expression. In Korhonen's view the words *kantele* and *kannus* denoting a shaman's drum are derivatives of the Early Proto-Finnic word *komta* meaning a lid (see p. 84; Korhonen 1987, 185). Since the *dainas* reminiscent of Kalevala poetry in metre are the poetry of Latvian, a language that has diverged more markedly than Proto-Baltic Lithuanian, it is difficult to point to a Baltic poetic metre providing a suitable model for Kalevala metre. According to Korhonen, the Baltic theory comes up against serious problems of timing and distribution, and it is more likely that Latvian poetry was influenced by Baltic-Finnic (see p. 83; Korhonen 1987, 184). In light of cultural influences such borrowings are, however, in the wrong direction. It seems more probable that the Baltic Finns, the Balts and the Germanic peoples each had their own song traditions influencing one another in different ways. The strong alliteration of Kalevala metre is, for example, reminiscent of the secret magic *galdr* poetry of the Ancient Germanic peoples, of which little is known concerning the metre.

Whatever the sources of Kalevala metre, linguists seem to be unanimous in claiming that it has a history stretching back thousands of years (see p. 56, 68 and Leino 1985, 37). If, Mikko Korhonen and Pekka Sammallahti propose, early Proto-Finnic (i.e. the joint proto-language of Baltic-Finnic and Lappish) is thought to have ended in around the year 1000 BC, the seeds of Kalevala metre must already have been sown more than a thousand years before the beginning of the Christian era. Based on his knowledge of the poetry of arctic cultures, Matti Kuusi concludes that the predecessor of the Kalevalaic poetic language was possibly a code reminiscent of lament and *joik* performance modes. He stresses the importance of Baltic influences in the birth of the Kalevala metre proper. Its roots, according to him, already existed about 600 years BC when Livonian and South Estonian broke away from Proto-Finnic. Classical Kalevala metre evolved out of this pre-Kalevala metre among the Northern Proto-Finns living along the Gulf of Finland and in Häme. The Kalevala metre took root in Ancient Karelia in the 9th century (see p. 54-55; Kuusi 1978, 223). It was in Karelia that, he claims, Kalevala metre acquired its strongest position and its finest forms. As Pentti Leino has demonstrated, melody played a significant role in the development of metre (see p. 71; Leino 1985, 38-40). According to Kuusi and Leino, the Kalevala metre developed out of a simple, rigid trochee into a flexible metre of diverse construction which also contained broken trochaic tetrameters (Kuusi 1978, Leino 1974 and 1985). This general scheme is in line with the conclusions regarding the age of poetic motifs. Kuusi's theory of stylistic eras was originally founded on the observation of correspondences between poetic motifs and metric forms. Archaic mythic motifs of widespread distribution were sung to simple trochees. By contrast, the epic more akin to the Scandinavian poetry of the Viking era in its motifs was set to richer poetic patterns. Placing individual stylistic features in some specific period in the past is of course a difficult, if not impossible task. On the other hand different cultural forms also favour different modes of expression. For example, the role of dialogue in carrying the plot is conspicuous both in the ancient Icelandic poetry attributed to the Viking era and the *Island epic* in Viking spirit describing the adventures of Kaukamoinen and Ahti.

To the modern researcher accustomed to rapid changes in culture, analysis of the thousand-year history of Kalevala metre may appear some-what hazardous, especially since conclusions must be made on so many uncertain premises. Viewed from a comparative perspective, however the venerable age of Kalevala metre is to be expected.

Anthropologists, historians and literary historians have lately become interested in the representation and communication of information in non-literate and literate cultures (cf. Goody 1977, Ong 1982, Finnegan 1988). The way of preserving and codifying information peculiar to oral cultures first became the subject of broader discussion on the basis of ideas taken from the oral formulaic theory presented by Albert B. Lord and Milman Parry (see the article of Lauri Harvilahti, p. 91 ff.). In particular the study of Homeric poetry, which was considered to have been originally oral, has taken up the question of the means of oral transmission in the poetic tradition. Walter Ong, who is interested in the differences between oral and literal cultures, stresses the importance of mnemonic patterns in oral cultures: "In a primary oral culture, to solve effectively the problem of retaining and retrieving carefully articulated thought, you have to do your thinking in mnemonic patterns, shaped for ready oral recurrence. Your thought must come into being in heavily rhythmic, balanced patterns, in repetitions or antitheses, in alliterations and assonances, in epithetic and other formular expressions, in standard thematic settings.." (Ong 1982, 34). Not only the collective memory but also thinking and expression in general are based more on patterns and formulas in oral cultures than in literal cultures. Heavy patterning and communal fixed formulas replace some of the functions of writing (Ong 1982, 36). They also influence the way in which experiences are intellectualised and memorised.

The schematisation of tradition is taken for granted in folkloristic re-search. The remembering and the reproducing of folklore items have also recently become a subject of interest among folklorists. Information is stored in the memory according to ready models, schematic structures and formulaic expressions (see the article of Lauri Harvilahti, pp. 92). Oral tradition is remembered and reproduced on the basis of familiar schematic

Houses along the river banks of Miitkala village. Uhtua. Photo: I.K. Inha 1894 (FLS 9966).

structures (cf. Siikala 1984, 1990 and Kaivola-Bregenhøj 1988). These means of expression also frame the potential for creative action. The new is based on the already known. Instead of one-way evolution or devolution, the life of oral tradition consists of complicated processes, where the poems are created and recreated according to traditional patterns. Matti Kuusi, indeed, points out that the viable folk epic is characterised by the balanced converging and diverging of poetic sequences, and emphasises the process-like nature of the life of oral tradition (Kuusi 1987, 97 ff.).

The praxis of Finnish-Karelian rune-singing

The life of oral tradition is not, however, explained by the use of formulaic patterns or the creativity of individuals. Individual singers give life to poems, maintain and renew them. Still the directions and modes of renewing oral tradition are bound to larger social and cultural phenomena and finally to the position of oral tradition as a means of communication in society. In oral cultures the thinking and processing of information are channelled through oral tradition instead of abstract concepts. Knowledge of the world is organised, stored and transmitted by means of narratives and songs describing human interests and actions. Although the oral tradition does consist of cross-culturally shared, even universal elements, it nevertheless constitutes an entity made up of the way of thinking and experiencing characteristic of the culture in question. In non-literate cultures it in fact acts precisely as a medium for communication within the community, as a medium for describing and debating matters that are considered striking and important. These means of communication differ from one culture to another in both form and content. So the life of oral epic depends on its potential for expressing crucial elements of world view and experiences of life. It represents the present even though it also bears the voice of the past. Study of the social context and performance practices of an epic provides us with information on cultural meanings, the basic elements which maintain the tradition.

The Kalevala epic existed in various institutional contexts in the Baltic-Finnic area. The poetry of the various regions differs in theme, mode of performance, context and meaning. Since the same individual poems are to be found in a number of poetry regions, insufficient allowance has been made for the differences in the social context of *rune*-singing. The social and economic systems, in fact culture as a whole, have varied greatly from one region to another. The feudal farming villages of Ingria on the southern shores of the Gulf of Finland differed sharply from the Savo and Ostrobothnian settlements of Eastern and Northern Finland subsisting on slash-and-burn cultivation and hunting. Then again, life in Karelia, which came under the influence of Slav-Orthodox culture at an early period of history, centred around hunting, fishing and trading outside the villages in addition to slash-and-burn agriculture. The men would spend long periods – as in Northern and Eastern Finland – away from home in temporary, communal lodgings. The basic unit in the social organisation of the eastern and northern regions was for a long time the family, whereas the people in the compact farming villages of Ingria were divided according to ethnic, religious and feudal factors. It is therefore only to be expected that the epic poetry of these culturally divergent regions differed and almost certainly reflected special regional trends.

The position and significance of the epic in the community affected its reproduction and interpretation. Where and how it was performed indicated to whom the poetry belonged and the contexts in which it acquired meaning. Examination of the praxis of *rune*-singing thus helps us to understand the norms for the variation in content or the meaning of the poetry from different regions.

In Finland, Kalevala *rune*-singing has the longest history in Savo, Ostrobothnia and Kainuu; the epic art vanished quickly, however, and the documents we now have date from the late 18th and early 19th centuries. The oldest record of epic *rune*-singing concerns Jacobus Petri Finno, who died in 1588 and reported that epics were sung on festive occasions and on journeys, to pass the time and as a means of entertainment, the singers competing with one another (Salminen 1934, 130). A similar entertainment function is hinted at by H.G. Porthan in his classic description of *rune*-singing published in *Dissertatio de Poesi Fennica* in 1778: epics were sung above all at feasts, where Bacchus was the bringer of pleasure, and during rests on long journeys, at the inns where dozens of travellers might come together. Porthan's well-known account is based on information from Western Finland, Savo and Ostrobothnia and undoubtedly influenced later reports too. On the other hand even before Porthan and Finno a student by the name of Gabriel Paldan had, in a letter to Johan Ervasti, already mentioned *rune*-singing in similar situations (Andersson 1969, 155). And in 1795 Jakob Tengström described singing sessions with all the vividness of an eye-witness:

> In particular one of the best entertainments at social gatherings and feasts was when, the food and drink having been served, one or more singers would perform songs to the delight of the assembled guests. The poet himself, or someone else, preferably an elderly man who could reproduce ancient or more recent songs from memory, would seat himself on a chair or a long stool, leaning towards the singer or accompanist sitting opposite him, knees touching, hand in hand. One would accompany the singing so that when the singer, at a slow, solemn pace, his body swaying to the rhythm, had almost finished singing the first line, the other would join in the last two or three syllables, which they sang together. The accompanist repeated the same line, but varying the melody slightly. While he was doing this the main singer had time to compose or recall the next line, until he again joined in the final syllables sung by the accompanist. Then he would again sing the next line alone, to be repeated by his companion. This continued until the end of the poem, when the signers were regaled and entreated to continue for the pleasure of those present. But when they came to the end of their repertoire, grew tired, or their voices became hoarse, it seldom happened that there was no one ready to take their place. All those present, young and old alike, gathered round the singers, listening with pleasure and attention to the songs that were thus handed down over the years, from one generation to the next, without their ever being written down. Since this form of entertainment appealed to the people more than any other social pastime, the singing would sometimes continue uninterrupted until late at night, being finally halted by more feasting, sleep and inebriation. (Salminen 1934, 160-161).

References to the beauty and festiveness of the singing are almost a cliché in the old descriptions. There are, however, references to the exalted inspiration of the singers in later reports, too: "..It was recalled that when the singing came to the subject of Väinämöinen, both the singers and the accompanist and all those gathered to hear the singing were moved to tears: 'it was so moving'." (Salminen 1921, 144).

Drawing on the facts presented here, certain other sources and accounts by folk singers themselves of the way in which they sang, Elsa Enäjärvi-Haavio constructed a picture of how two men would solemnly sing the heroic epics. The setting was the feast, where singing was accompanied by drinking (beer in Finland, spirits in Karelia), the journey or the fishing expedition, when the men had more idle time to spend together. A line sung by a solo singer was repeated by a second, sometimes to the accompaniment of a *kantele*. Enäjärvi-Haavio concludes: "It seems that the men's singing in pairs was chiefly bound to the life of the old Finnish heroic poetry. Both the custom and the heroic poetry covered more or less the same area: Finland and East Karelia." (Enäjärvi-Haavio 1949, 133). These conclusions seem to agree above all with observations of the performance of Kalevala epic on the Finnish side of the border.

The scale of performance in the regions of Karelia where the old epic poetry survived the longest shows greater variety. Leea Virtanen, in her work *Kalevalainen laulutapa Karjalassa* (1968) 'The Kalevalaic song tradition in Karelia', gives an account of the various situations in which poetry was sung. A very large number of reports, some from this century, link the performance of Kalevala poetry with the everyday life of the extended Karelian family. Vihtoora Lesonen, for example, reported that

The mythical origin of the bear was described in magic incantations used during hunting. A trap built to catch bears in Suurijärvi. Archangel Karelia. Photo: I.K. Inha 1894 (FLS 10 000).

her father was a keen singer who, as he wove his nets by rushlight, would sing to his children and those who gathered at his farm on long winter evenings. "There they would pose riddles, tell tales and sing poems." (Niemi 1921, 1128). Since the Kalevala metre features in songs representing different genres, the reports do not always indicate what sorts of songs were sung of an evening in between the tales. The women seem to have favoured ballads, legend songs (see the article of Senni Timonen) and epic-lyrical songs more than anything else (Virtanen 1965, 19), though they undoubtedly also knew the archaic epics.

In Karelia, too, epic poems on Kalevala themes were considered above all men's tradition (Virtanen 1968, 50-51); these would be sung on fishing expeditions, during the free moments spent in the forest *saunas*, or at the religious village festivals, the *praazniekkas*, when people sometimes travelled long distances to visit their relatives (SKS, Krohn 0071; Härkönen 1909, 36-38). Leea Virtanen has come to the conclusion that the solo-repeat mode of singing was unknown in Karelia (Virtanen 1968, 40). There are, however, some reports of two men singing together in Karelia. This custom would appear to have vanished in the first half of the 19th century.

It is surprising how often Kalevala epics in Karelia had a ritual function. Two of the most popular songs in the area of Karelia around Lake Ladoga, *Lemminkäinen's Adventures* and *Courtship of the Daughter of Hiisi*, were used by *patvaskas* or sage-matchers at weddings to provide magic protection (see the articles of Jukka Saarinen, Eino Kiuru and Henni Ilomäki). According to information obtained by Kaarle Krohn, even The *Sampo* poem was performed ritually: "During the spring and autumn sowing the people first sang the sowing spell, then the song about the forging and stealing of the Sampo and the chase by the Mistress of Pohjola (the North). The rest describes how Väinämöinen banished the frost sent by the Mistress of Pohjola." (SKS, Krohn 0072). The reference to banishing the frost indicates the reason for the ritual use of this song. The same notes by Krohn state that a number of other epic songs were performed in situations analogous with their content. The poem about fishing for *The Vellamo Maiden* was sung while fishing, mythical poems about the making of skis were sung while skiing, the poem about the wound on Väinämöinen's knee while staunching blood, and that about Kaleva's son burning the forest while clearing the forest for cultivation.

It seems that the border between the incantations that were the secret tradition of sages and the epic songs for public performance was in Karelia very vague (see the article of Lotte Tarkka, p. 250 ff.). Both have preserved ancient mythical motifs and images. These features of intertextuality may in part be the outcome of the sage's central position in Karelian culture. Collectors in search of *rune*-singers were very often told to consult the sages. A.A. Borenius in fact mentions that a singer's reputation was most often founded on his knowledge of incantations, whereas the best singers of epic poetry were often anonymous (Niemi 1904, 475). The high prestige of magic knowledge is also illustrated by the fact that many *rune*-singer families were descended from a mighty witch or sage (Virtanen 1968, 9). On the other hand the communal ritual poetry performed at village or family festivals – but nowhere else – lived on in Karelia.

In the farming communities of South Karelia and Ingria epic songs were markedly women's tradition (see the articles of Lauri Harvilahti and Leea Virtanen). Although certain records of men's epics, even of singing competitions, do exist (Enäjärvi-Haavio 1949, 144), the bulk of epic songs in Kalevala metre were women's group tradition. These would be sung as the women went about their everyday work, at meetings and festivals for the girls and women, as an accompaniment to dancing in circles and chains. Even serious epic poems were sometimes used to accompany dancing in Ingria, such as *The Sun and Moon*, which contains a mythical theme about the vanishing of the sun and the moon. Choirs of young girls would sing under the leadership of a solo singer, even in many parts.

In addition to dancing in circles and chains in the manner handed down since the Middle Ages, the Ingrian maidens would also set off on singing walks in the period between the spring sowing and the autumn harvest. Such walks were also common in Russia and elsewhere in Europe (Enäjärvi-Haavio 1949, 149-156). The girls wandering along the village lanes were dressed in their finest clothes, for having reached marriageable age they were, so to say, "on display". There was a similar chance for display at the *praazniekkas*, the local holy days, described by Törneroos and Tallqvist in Ingria as follows:

> As on all festive occasions, the girls here too first passed the time by singing and dancing, in such a manner that bands of girls walked hand in hand with garlands on their heads through the market field, singing as they went, at times coming to a halt, running giggling into a circle in which two girls at a time tripped round like the Russian women in some of their dances. This would have gone on and been quite beautiful to behold had not the miserable boys, who did not seem to have had anything better to do yesterday afternoon than drink and fool around, interrupted the girls' quiet singing and dancing

and began to behave in a coarse and uncouth manner. For they pounced on the girls in an unruly manner and dragged one girl after another from the circle. (Niemi 1904, 374).

The importance of the choirs of girls in maintaining oral culture is also evident from the fact that the girls were permitted to sing the sacrificial hymns at the joint ritual festivals, even though the men were otherwise responsible for carrying out the rites. (Haavio 1961, 56).

Local interpretations

The divergence in the institutional context of the poetry from different regions, manifested in the way these poems were performed and sung, signifies that a poem was interpreted in different ways in different areas. The same motifs may have a different meaning in different communities. On the other hand meanings may in time change even within one particular group. When a poem is lifted from one cultural context to another, its surface semantics – its references – change. Meaning takes shape by a continuing process; without it a poem would in fact cease to exist and would die out.

Oral poetry is organic, continuously reproduced folklore, so changes in meaning are evident in the ways in which motifs are handled (see the ethnopoetic approach of Pertti Anttonen and Thomas DuBois, pp. 113-179). Variation is thus the basic feature of Kalevala tradition. Poems vary not only in different areas but also in different performances (see Saarinen, p. 182-195). Precisely because of the endless sets of variations it is impossible to find "the original text", even though folklorists have tried to draw conclusions as to its nature by means of text analyses. Ideas concerning variation and its reasons have influenced folkloristic theories and divided the schools of studies (cf. Jason 1970, 285-294; Leino 1990, 31-33). Whatever the reasons for variation may be, they are connected with the meanings and interpretation of tradition.

The choral repertoire of women from the southern regions consisted of ballads, legends and all manner of epic-lyrical songs dealing with kin and family relationships. In addition to these, episodes from nature myths were also adapted to songs. Motifs telling of the deeds of mythical heroes featured far less than in the northern regions; only fragments of e.g. the Sampo epic are known in Ingria. It is significant that these motifs – where they do appear – have been adapted to the general idiom of the song tradition. A typical example is *The Golden Bride* (appended are variants translated into English by Keith Bosley from Archangel Karelia and Ingria, Kuusi-Bosley-Branch 1977, 160-166). Miihkali Perttunen (see the article of Jukka Saarinen) began singing in the regular Karelian manner by introducing his hero: "That was the smith Ilmollini, his head down, in bad spirits, helmet all askew, went to the forge of the smiths." Mythical events are described as such, without any explanation. Ilmollini the Smith, i.e. Ilmarinen the forger of the lid of the skies and Väinämöinen's companion, takes a little gold and sets his slaves to blowing the forge. Not satisfied with them, he himself takes over and produces a sword, a stallion and finally

In Ingrian villages the young girls formed a strong social group which upheld the tradition of the Kalevala metre song. Photo: Vihtori Alava 1892 (MV).

a golden bride. This poem, simple in construction, follows the scheme of the three attempts and ends with lines warning of the dangers of making a golden bride, thus proving that the mythical nature of the poem has already been blurred.

In Ingria the poem begins with a motif describing the division of lands. The main character is not introduced separately. To begin with he is just a smith; the subsequent use of the name Ismaro identifies him as Ilmarinen. Although the lines "he used his shirt as a forge, and his trousers for bellows" do contain a mythical image proving that the subject of the narrative is no ordinary smith, the poem lingers over a description of village life. The smith forges tools and trinkets for the villagers, but they do not thank him for it. So he decides to prove his competence by a rare feat of skill in his relatives' eyes, but they only mock him. The poem is in its element in describing the relatives' quarrels. The reasons for the mythical deed of forging a golden bride are given: the smith sets to work because he is jeered at for not being married. The extensive episodes concentrating on the village milieu and family relations lead to structural looseness; events are made homely and concretised throughout.

Even a cursory glance at Ingrian epic shows that *The Golden Bride* is in no way exceptional and represents the trend in the fashioning of motifs typical of Ingrian poetry as a whole. When the groups of maidens adapted the old mythical-epic poems to the repertoire for their singing walks and dancing, they handled the motifs from their own perspective. Instead of mythical heroes the subject of the song is I (see also Harvilahti, p. 97), or a close relative, a brother, sometimes Jesus, in keeping with the religious

28

frame of reference. For example, the song telling how Väinämöinen made a boat, which in the northern regions regularly begins with the line "Steadfast old Väinämöinen" or something similar, usually has a 'brother' as the hero or is adapted to begin in the first person: "I send ships a-sailing" (SKVR V:1, 1063), "I ground my axe for a day" (SKVR V:1, 1066), or it acquires an anonymous main character "Wise one, skilled one, Made a boat with his learning.." (SKVR V:1, 1065). The opening cliché introducing the hero may also be replaced, as in *The Golden Bride*, by an introductory motif, such as a description of herding. Where there are figures of the heroic epic in poems, they may be equipped with some epithet indicating worldly power, such as "Smith Ilmanrinta himself, King Ilmari himself" (SKVR I:1, 351), "Kullervoinen, man and king" (SKVR V:1, 173), "Master Ilmari himself, Smith Ilmarinen himself" (SKVR V:1, 352). Such epithets indicating power or nobility provided substance for arguing the historicality of poems (cf. Krohn 1918, 216). The appearance of heroes as representatives of secular power is not, however, total; for example, *The Oak* begins with the lines: "I hurried to God's revels, Väinämöinen's assizes, the feast of Kaleva's son" (Kuusi-Bosley-Branch 1977, 263). Our attention is also caught by the fact that although the heroic figures of the mythical motifs are usually replaced by more familiar subjects, ballads have preserved their original main characters and often begin by introducing them.

A maiden or her brother appearing as the main character in an Ingrian poem operates on home ground, doing domestic chores. The frequent repetition of herder motifs is conspicuous, as is the repeated treatment of family relations (cf. Kuusi 1958, and 1983, 177-181). Further proof of this tendency towards the familiar is that in the northern regions the ordinary mythical places in the other world, such as Pohjola (The North) and Hiitola (The Devil's Abode), are missing from the poems almost entirely, or they are replaced by the concepts of Heaven and Underworld. One interesting exception to this scheme of interpretation are the locality concepts and figures of *The Sun and Moon*. For example, the wooing theme is to be found in the poem about *The Sun Boy*, who goes to woo the maid of the Underworld. Cosmogonic and nature-myth motifs have been preserved if they naturally fit in with the worldview of the singing maidens. The dangerous Pohjola or the terrifying Hiitola as distant destinations belong to male poetry.

Framing mythical themes with motivating or explanatory verses or a direct secularisation of them shows that their significance is poetic rather than indicative of a mythical worldview. Framing lines are in most cases relatively labile and "modern" in their poetic language, whereas the mythical motif itself is more fixed in form. For example, the theme *The Great Pig*, which tells about a pig which grows until it is enormous and which the gods (often Ukko, the god of thunder) try in vain to slaughter, is framed in the secular motif:

Missä olit tämän kesosen?	Where were you this summer?
Tätilläin taivosessa.	With my aunt in heaven.
Mitä tuolla teetettiin	What did you do there?
Paimenessa käytettiin	I was sent to herd
Saksan suuri sikoja.	Big German pigs.

Mitä tuolla syötettihin?	What did you eat there?
Luut lihoista, päät kaloista	The bones from the meat, the heads from the fish
Kuoret leivistä kovista	The crust of hard bread.

Tuli Ukko tappamaan	Ukko came to slaughter
Kultasen kurikan kanssa	With a golden club.
Ukko sikaa sipasi	Ukko touched the pig,
Otsakieroa olotti.	Prodded it upon the brow.
Sika käänsi kärsäjänsä;	The pig turned its snout;
Ukko kuuseen pakohon.	Ukko escapes to a fir tree.
Ukko kuusesta toruvi:	Ukko upbraids it from his tree:
Malta, malta, posso rukka,	Wait, just wait, poor swine,
La' tuloo tuleva vuosi,	Come next year,
et tongi Tolomäkeä.	You won't be rooting at Tolomäki.
(SKVR V:1, 90)	

A se sika, jok' oli miulla,	Ah, the pig I had
Teki paljon porsahii,	Bore a lot of piglets,
Enemmän emäsikkoi,	More sows,
Kesät syötin keitoksilla,	In summer I fed it swill,
Talvet toarin viertehill.	In winter beer wort.
Tuli ukko tappamaan	Ukko came to kill it
Kultasen kurikan kanssa	With a golden club,
Hopeaisen veitsen kanssa...	With a silver knife...
(SKVR V:1, 93)	

Matin moat, Matin hevoset,	Matti's lands, Matti's horses,
Matin pellot päivä-rinnat.	Matti's sunny fields.
Matti rengiks rupes.	Matti turned to servant.
Mitäs otat palkastais?	What is your wage?
Saksan suurii sikkoi,	Big German Pigs,
Tasapäitä tallikkoi.	Dung-makers all looking alike.
Etsi nuoille tappajaista.	Seeks a slaughterer for them.
Tullo ukko tappamaan	Ukko comes to kill them
Kultase kurikan kanssa...	With a golden club...
(SKVR V:1, 94)	

The line "with my aunt in heaven" in the first example shows that the motif is still conceived of as telling about events outside this world; the other two lines "I was sent to herd Big German pigs" secularise the motif entirely.

One way of bridging the gap between ancient mythical themes and the singer's personal experience is to make them Christian, to mould a motif felt to be based on belief to fit a familiar religious frame of reference. The most common device is to make the Creator or some other such figure the main character of a poem, as in *The Sun and Moon* or *The Voyage* (See Kuusi-Bosley-Branch 1977). Christianisation is also encountered as a temporary form of variation. The only poem in the Väinämöinen epic frequently recorded in Ingria is *The Singing Match*, describing the match between Väinämöinen and Joukahainen. In one variant heroes that have become strange, but are still conceived of as sacral are replaced by the nearest possible figures: "There came two angels, And two holy men, They met on the road, One said to the other..." (SKVR V:1, 196).

In the Northern regions, where epic poems on Kalevala themes were primarily men's tradition, poems were more archaic, mythical and also more fixed in form than in the south. They were in many respects reminiscent more of the traditions of the non-European unwritten cultures than the European folk cultures. The exceptionally archaic nature of the Kalevala epic alongside the other epic poetry traditions of Europe has been a constant source of interest to researchers. As long ago as 1890s the Italian Domenico Comparetti already suggested that the hero-ideal of Kalevala poetry is more of a shamanistic sage than a swordsman. In the northern regions the main hero is Väinämöinen; woven into his figure are many motifs that go without the name in the south.

Martti Haavio described Väinämöinen has being fundamentally a mythical sage, a sort of a proto-shaman (Haavio 1950, 309). He linked the poems describing journeys to the other world with the figure of Väinämöinen and regarded them as belonging to one of the oldest strata of the Finnish epic. Matti Kuusi, who calls Lemminkäinen the most thoroughbred male shaman in Finnish narrative poetry, considers that the motifs in question represent an age-old shamanistic legacy, but in poetic form they are products of the Viking Era and of the Middle Ages (Kuusi 1963, 259-260). I have in my study of Finnish shamanism showed that the motifs in question also appeared in ancient Scandinavian poetry and saga texts (Siikala 1992). They are often linked with the figure of Odin, who, like Väinämöinen, was well versed in the magic arts, secret wisdom and song. What is significant is that the Finnish shaman motifs do not resemble their Scandinavian counterparts merely in the events they describe but in their mythical images and numerous details, too.

The tradition in question is phenomenologically shamanistic. This being the case, it in turn represents a very special form: the sage institution based on the use of sung charm wich was probably widely known in Northern Europe in the pre-Christian era. Analysis of the motifs and images in elements in the Finnish shamanic poems supports the conclusion reached by Matti Kuusi on studying the stylistic elements of the poems: although the motifs are extremely old, the poems themselves represent a more recent tradition from the Viking age (Siikala 1992).

Any differences of opinion in fact spring from the nature of the material chosen for examination. Martti Haavio concentrated primarily on the Karelian epic, which also constitutes the cornerstone of the Kalevala. Although Archangel Karelia was on the periphery, where many cultural features long preserved their ancient forms, it cannot be regarded as the "deep-frozen" cradle or "original" Finnish culture. Väinämöinen's position as the "proto-shaman" is placed in a completely different light on broader examination of the poems attached to him.

In Ostrobothnia, where epic poetry was written down at the end of the 18th and beginning of the 19th centuries, Väinämöinen is beyond all doubt a central figure. 132 variants of epic poems on Kalevala themes were collected there, and in 88 of them Väinämöinen is the main character. Most in evidence in Ostrobothnia are two broad epic entities, one of which contains the most common motifs – *Courtship of the Virgin of the Air, Making the boat, Väinämöinen's Wound* (53 variants), and the other *The Boat's Complaint, Väinämöinen's Journey by a Boat, The Origin of the*

Kantele, and *Väinämöinen's Playing* (21 variants). The Väinämöinen of the Ostrobothnian poems is a mythical hero whose father, Kave ukko, Master of Pohja 'the North', is born equipped for battle on a charger's back (SKVR XII:1, 1), whose mother, the maid of Pohja 'the North', is made pregnant by Meren Ukko 'Old man of the sea' out on the waves (SKVR XII:1, 2). Väinämöinen himself makes a boat while seeking to win a maiden sitting on the vaults of the air. Not only is he a mighty singer; he is also a skilled smith and swordsman.

What is significant is that the Väinämöinen of the Ostrobothnian poems has almost none of the features of a sage. Only one variant of *The Visit to Tuonela* (the abode of the dead) has been recorded in the region; its hero is Kaukomieli (SKVR XII:1, 69). Four variants have been recorded of the poems describing how the sacred words were fetched from the dead sage, Vipunen. In one the hero is Seppo Ilmarinen (SKVR XII:1, 70), in another Väinämöinen urges his younger brother Joukahainen to fetch the words (SKVR XII:1, 73). Only two of the variants describe Väinämöinen's journey to the dead sage, and these were recorded close to the Karelian songlands, in Sotkamo and Kainuu (SKVR XII:1, 71 and 72). The poems about Väinämöinen begin in Ostrobothnia, as in Karelia, with the lines "Old Väinämöinen himself" or "Steadfast old Väinämöinen". But what is surprising is that the additional epithet "eternal sage" of Karelia is missing completely in Ostrobothnia. Instead he is referred to as "holy hero" (e.g. SKVR XII:1, 44) or "powerful boy" (SKVR XII:1, 45).

In place of the material to do with sages the Ostrobothnian poems about Väinämöinen often have episodes about warlike deeds. For example, at the beginning of the poem describing how the *kantele* was made, Väinämöinen seeks his charger and then finds a boat, which complains, "Other boats go off to wars, they are filled up with money, their sterns are weighed down with coins, while I rot on my shavings..." (Kuusi-Bosley-Branch 1977, 167). A number of poems contain an account of Väinämöinen's journey to Pohjola (the North) in which he features as an able-bodied hero rather than a sage:

Meni Pohjolan pihalle.	Entered Pohjola's yard.
Tuleppas Pohjolan tupahan:	Came to the house at Pohjola.
Täällä miehet mettä juovat	There the men were drinking nectar
Simoa sirottelevat	Sipping away at mead.
'Mitelläänpäs miekkojamme,	'Let us measure our swords,
Katellaanpas kalpojamme.'	Let us test our blades.'
Kummank' on pitempi miekka,	Which of us has a longer sword,
Kennen kalpa kauheampi?	Whose blade is more terrible?
Sen oli iskijä eellä	Leading the fray,
Jo oli pikkusta pitempi	Just a little bit longer
Miekka Vanhan Väinämöisen...	Was the sword of Old Väinämöinen...
Siitä kuu kärestä paisto	The moon shone from its tip,
Päivä västistä välötti,	The sun from the handle
Heponen kärellä seiso,	A horse was at the tip,
Penu putkessa makasi,	A dog lay in the shaft,
Kasi nauku naulan päässä	A cat mewed on the top.
(SKVR XII:1, 67)	

I shall not attempt to argue the supremacy of either song tradition, the Ostrobothnian or the Karelian. There are other features associated with Väinämöinen, such as the link with water manifest at many levels, which would then have to be taken into account. The emphasis on the heroic features of the Väinämöinen figure in Ostrobothnia finds a natural explanation in the cultural significance of the epic. Ostrobothnia represents precisely the area where, according to H.G. Porthan and others, epic poetry was sung by men to entertain people at festivals and other gatherings. Although there are some records of epic being used in a ritual context (the poem about Väinämöinen's playing, for example, was sung while catching birds to assure a successful hunt, SKVR XII:1, 80), the function of *rune*-singing in Ostrobothnia appears from the sources that have been preserved to have been one of entertainment rather than of ritual.

Rich in poetry, Karelia is not culturally uniform, as is evident from the epic tradition. Life in the province of Archangel, until the 17th century "Novgorod Lapland", beyond the reach of the church and state authorities, was more archaic than in the area of Karelia around Lake Ladoga. Contacts with Ostrobothnia on the Finnish side of the border were firmly established and even mentioned in genealogical lore; there was little difference between the language of poetry and the language of the people. The heroic themes, such as those in the Sampo epics, link the poetry of Archangel with the Ostrobothnian epic (cf. Kuusi 1949, 329-335); the poems were, however, clearly more mythical than in Northwest Finland. In Ladoga Karelia, on the other hand, the demands of the poetic metre and the potential of the spoken language no longer corresponded to a satisfactory degree, and singers had to resort to filler words and syllables (Rausmaa 1968). In some areas the epic poems were also semantically so far removed from the spoken language that they were difficult to understand (Genetz 1870). The desire among singers to preserve the already obscure words and formulae illustrates the mythical value of the epic. It utilised an independent code of its own that was not consciously changed. On the other hand the poetry in Ladoga Karelia also adapted along lines of its own. The process of Russification that had been going on since the Middle Ages manifested itself in folklore through the features associated with the Orthodox faith and the incorporation of elements of the fairytale into the epic (cf. Rausmaa 1964).

Poetry throughout the Karelian region is marked by its accent on the sage theme. There are all manner of mythical motifs and images woven into, say, *The Lemminkäinen's Adventures* – one of the most popular songs – some of them probably once had connections with earlier fertility cults (see Siikala 1992, 263-271). This proves that the poem was continuously being transformed. It would appear that the process of loosening the original sacral link, which in Scandinavia turned certain ancient mythical songs into fairytale-like ballads (cf. Liestøl 1970, 98-103; Ohlmarks 1948, 308), in Karelia caused motifs which previously contained different meanings to merge with the sage tradition. Interpreted anew, the poems acquire meaning via concepts concerning the sage and his duties, and the line material is transformed according to this new significance. Attaching epic poems to sagedom did not threaten their mythical value, as would have been the case had they been made a mere form of entertainment.

The Kalevala metre song in Ingria was accompanied by dancing. Photo: Vihtori Alava 1892 (MV).

The same epic motifs make up corpora of tradition differing in meaning from one culture area to another. Ballad-like and fictive features predominate in the epics of the feudal farming villages of Ingria, mythical and historical features in the slash-and-burn and hunting cultures of the North. The different lines of transformation followed by poetic tradition illustrate the more common discrepancies in the cognitive structures of these different cultural regions. I refer to the unconscious mental models for observation, experience and action, the mentality of village cultures. The cognitive structures in question constitute the basis for collective representations manifest as oral genres and are at the same time a sounding board for individual reflection. Changes in the Finnish-Karelian agrarian communities were slow, but inevitable. The existence of the slow tendencies to change does not therefore conflict with observations underlining singers' desire to remain faithful to the old styles of singing, to repeat poems as they were first learnt. Nor do they limit the scope of creative individuals, or outstanding and innovative singers; on the contrary, they point the way to new ideas.

The layers of myth, history and fantasy

A concept of the past of one's own group and of the fundamental essence of the universe is one of the most basic forms of human knowledge. Before the art of writing was invented, epic poetry was the primary tool for preserving this knowledge. The controversy over the explanation of the mythical knowledge codified in poetry and narratives – evident in Finnish research as a preference for either the mythical or the historical interpretation – ultimately illustrates the difference between the concepts of history and the universe held by researchers and the supporters of the tradition studied. In traditional cultures myth and reality are not placed in different compartments as they are in western thinking. The fact that comparative religion has underlined the theological dimension of mythology has often prevented us from seeing its historical function, its position as the 'sacred' history of one's own group, even though anthropologists ever since Durkheim have been talking about this aspect.

Mythical world history is just as much the history of humans and deities as of forefathers and superhuman heroes. As parts of the same concept of reality, myths and concrete historical events have merged to form a single entity. This is, of course, a broad generalisation. The sense of history owned by different cultures is expressed by means of different genres. Similarly, matters classified under mythical consciousness are manifest in many different ways, not merely as oral epic (cf. Dumézil 1970, 3). Alongside the cyclical, ritual repetition of primeval events described, for example, by Mircea Eliade (1954; see the article of Satu Apo, p. 199, 205) we find genealogical lists stretching back for dozens of generations, as on the Cook Islands, to what are reputed to be the divine forefathers. Valerio Valeri claims that the relationship between present and past is articulated by specific cultural modes which, in Hawaiian culture, he describes as paradigmatic and syntagmatic or metonymic. The genealogies represent the latter type of relationship, in which past and present are separated by a continuing chain of events. The paradigmatic mode of describing the relationship between past and present in turn "emphasises the analogic relations between certain events of the past and certain events of the present". An analogic relationship between special events is possible by "implicit mediation of a scheme or rule common to them both which makes them comparable". (Valeri 1990).

Valeri refers to the custom of passing on the concept of social rules to new generations in the form of historical or mythical narratives. The very fact that events belong to the past, that they are unalterable, gives them a position of authority vis-à-vis the present (cf. also Hastrup 1987, 264). The use of mythical narratives in rites and even everyday situations represents the paradigmatic mode of conceiving of the relationship between past and present. The Karelian forest-clearer singing about how Kaleva's son cleared the forest, or the sower describing how Väinämöinen banished the frost sent by the Mistress of Pohjola, sets a precedent for the task or case on hand. Because the case belongs to the time when the cosmic order was irrevocably created, its rules are universally applicable even to the present day. The description of a mythical event in an epic song is not the performance of a charm (if we define charm in the European way as 'a formula of magic influence repeated word-for-word'); it is a way of introducing the authoritative influence of the sacred past into the present moment. There are, however, numerous examples in Finnish folklore of epic motifs which, through repeated use, have become recognised as charms (such as *The Väinämöinen's Wound*).

The ritual use of epic poems in Karelia proves that at least some dimensions of mythical thinking were still relevant. This is also indicated by some of the events in the poems or comments on the heroes. For example, Matro Lettijeva of Archangel Karelia is said to have believed that Väinämöinen was a hero who really did live in her own native region and who would one day return as promised (Virtanen 1968, 47). Matti Immonen, from Savo in Finland,

Rune-singers Jyrki and Ohvo Mali-nen in the oldest photograph show-ing a rune-singing performance. The position of the singers corre-sponds to the classic description published by H.G. Porthan in 1778. Photo: A. Berner 1872 (FLS 5397:2).

likewise said in 1816 that Väinämöinen was a native of Savo and brought the Mistress of Pohjola to Savo as his wife. On the same occasion he conceived of the battle between Väinämöinen and Joukahainen ("Joutavainen") as having taken place in the beginning of time (SKVR VI:1, 26). Conceiving of Väinämöinen as a hero who really did exist does not conflict with mythical thinking; in fact it is more of a manifestation of this. In just the same way Odin is described as having travelled on earth with only one eye and wearing a blue cloak, sometimes revealing his true identity on certain special occa-sions. Like Väinämöinen, he was forced to leave the earth.

In speaking of the mytho-praxis of Polynesian cultures, Marshall Sahlins stresses that in these communities the mythical structures also organise other forms of cultural representations, even observations, experiences and communal events (Sahlins 1985, 57-58). Using the cosmic order step by step to structure history and even everyday life is of course typical of Polynesian cultures and cannot as such be generalised. On the other hand Sahlins' observations are in keeping with those of George Dumézil – as the writer himself points out: "The kind of transformation between sacred myth and historic legend that Dumézil finds operating between different branches of Indo-European stock thus appears within the Maori tradi-tion."(Sahlins 1985, 47). To simplify, we may say that an existing 'sacred history', a mythical tradition, also provides models for ordering and de-scribing secular history. Since both mythical and secular history are presented using the same schemes, they easily merge to become parts of the same concept of history. In other words material telling of historical events is adapted to fit old myth formulae and mythical images are in turn used to embellish what was originally a concrete event.

On the other hand the past is always viewed from the present. Thus the heroes of (mythical) history are born as a result of the interaction between experience at the present moment and the tradition which structures observations. In this respect Chadwickian theorising is somewhat justified. A heroic stratum easily forms under certain conditions as a continuation to or as part of 'sacred history'. If, like Sahlins, we combine the heroic ethos with power vested in the individual (Sahlins 1985, 35-47), we notice that the heroic stratum is represented in Finnish-Karelian epic by *The Island Poems* and such poems as *The Väinämöinen's Journey to Pohjola*. They must have originated, as Matti Kuusi has stated (Kuusi 1963, 236), before the Middle Ages, in the pre-Christian communities of Western Finland and Karelia, where power was in the hands of, say, Faravid, the king of the Kainuu, who is mentioned in Egil's saga.

The heroic concepts were preserved in the form of separate poems, motifs and images, but after the coming of Christianity they no longer acted as the principle dominating the sense of history in the recording of poetry. Karelia, and especially Archangel, was a region only remotely influenced by the machinery of state power and church authorities, and what is more, this machinery represented an alien culture and language. Society centred around village and kin. Being isolated, the communities preserved their own sacred histories, their own myths, for a surprisingly long time, but only insofar as these served everyday life or provided pleasure. They could not be used to justify the prevailing or social order. Perhaps it was the replacing of the system of chiefs by power structures imposed from outside that raised the sage to a conspicuous position both in village life and in epic poetry.

In Ingria the Kalevala epic no longer possessed the nature of a myth or of sacred history, even though people were in certain cases aware of the link with the world of belief. Heroes were equipped not with mythical attributes but with epithets suggesting power, and the quest for personal honour became the main motive for deeds. The history of heroic epic living on as a form of female entertainment alongside the ballad is realistically secular, yet at the same time wrapped in a shining shroud of fantasy.

Kalevala poetry has preserved the layers of myth, history and fantasy until recent times. The elements of these layers can – as Matti Kuusi has done – be placed in a historical order. The myth then represents the remote past, heroic elements mirror the "barbaric" era of the Vikings and Crusades, and fantasy symbolizes the transformation of these elements into entertainment during the Middle Ages. But in actual singing traditions these elements have been intertwined together, forming in different regions differently interpreted and slowly changing entities, in which the elements had their own places and their own meanings.

The structural transformation of tradition

The great transformations of tradition are manifest in extensive changes in thematic contents, in new modes of performance and in the fading out of old interests. Such processes do not happen by chance. The life of oral poems is vitally dependent on the structural changes in culture and society. Alterations to social relations and economic structures also renew the intellectual climate and the values of a given society.

The cognitive models directing the understanding and interpretation of oral tradition change during the course of history. In a state of cultural change they are transformed into a sort of continuing dialectic process. This transformation could be compared to the views of Marshall Sahlins on the culturally oriented transformation of history (Sahlins 1985). Sahlins claims that history is culturally organised. This organisation takes different forms in different cultures and depends on the semantic schemes of cultural phenomena. On the other hand the opposite also applies. Cultural schemes are also historically organised. Cultural meanings are constantly being reassessed – on a smaller or larger scale – as they become relevant in practical life. History is thus being constantly reproduced in actions, events involving meanings conforming to inherited cultural schemes. If in a new environment these meanings do not satisfy all the demands of an event, then people amend their conventional schemes and create new ones in their place. Since the transformation of certain meanings alters the mutual relationships between cultural categories, Sahlins speaks of structural transformation. If folklore genres are regarded as cognitive categories expressing cultural consciousness, they are constantly transformed to suit the demands of new cultural situations. The changing meanings of oral poetry follow the larger patterns of cultural transformation.

Changes in tradition are not therefore mechanical or unambiguous events but complicated processes in which renewing and conserving tendencies can act at the same time, influencing each other. It must also be remembered that the more central and deeply rooted the values and customs are, the larger the changes needed in a culture as a whole to alter them. The elements of mythical worldview and religion are especially conservative and may have been maintained through different stages of culture. The meanings have not necessarily been preserved; motifs may have been interpreted and modified to suit new cultural frames of reference. On the other hand, in becoming the actual mythical themes of epic poems they may have received a new form adapted to historical conditions, and maintained these forms long after the historical moment passed. The metric and stylistic features of oral poetry preserve information better than prose. Thus the old-fashioned poems may have stored information on old customs, subjects, behaviour and social order. On the other hand – as is stated earlier – oral poems are products of their own cultures. They have meaning in their own culture and they cannot be studied without remembering their basis for existence.

NOTES

This article is based on earlier version published in Finnish under the title *Runonlaulun käytäntö ja runoston kehitys*, which appeared in *Runo, alue, merkitys*. P. Hakamies (ed.). University of Joensuu. Publications of Karelian Institute No 92. Joensuu. 1990. p. 7-28.

1. See Finnish Folk Poetry: Epic (1977) and the forthcoming publication of Matti Kuusi (Studia Fennica Folkloristica 3).

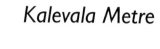
Kalevala Metre

MATTI KUUSI

Questions of Kalevala Metre

What exactly did Kalevala language signify to its users?

Some regard it simply as one poetic metre among others – and in this they are mistaken. The Kalevala tradition could undeniably be compared to the hexameter culture of Antiquity, the alexandrine or blank verse of Western Europe, the *tanka* culture of Japan or the ritual language of various religions; or we could even speak of a sociolect of Ancient Finnish. These comparisons however, fail to convey the scope of the Kalevala metre. Kalevala language is not just the language of an art or ritual. Its use was not restricted to any social community. Kalevala metre was cultivated in Finland, Karelia, Ingria, by the Votes and the Estonians. It was the dominant language of the epic, the lyric, magic, weddings, the bear and annual feasts. In addition to which, a sizable number of proverbs and riddles, and the direct speech in folk tales and legends were cast in Kalevala metre. I do not know of any other poetic metre in the world covering even approximately the same range of expression as Kalevala language.

It would in my opinion be most natural to compare Kalevala language to written language.

Kalevala metre was a code for committing texts to memory. The modern Finn wishing to ensure that his message does not get lost writes it down. Written literature is a giant store of texts that are worth remembering. "Unwritten literature" as a paraphrase for the Kalevala tradition is no mere metaphor. Our ancestors did not have any means of lasting linguistic communication apart from Kalevala language. The lament, cattle calls and prose narratives were regulated by other, looser norms. Kalevala language aimed at precise, word-for-word communication: no word could be omitted, and it was considered "better to box a man's ears than to leave a word out of a song". Naturally there were differences in the tendency towards improvisation of the different Kalevala genres. But in principle the Kalevala tradition, the Kalevala fund of memorised lore, served our forefathers in the same way as the Bible, the hymn book, the law book, the medical book, the guides to etiquette and the art of living serve people of the modern era. It was knowledge, skill and belief in crystallised, formulaic form. (See Kuusi-Bosley-Branch 1977.)

Just as the modern Finn is expected to have at least a fair command of the written language, so every respectable ancestor would have had at least

Songs beyond
the Kalevala
Studia Fennica
Folkloristica 2
1994

some command of the Kalevala code. There were experts who evinced as much respect from the ordinary folk as the editor of the local newspaper or the winner of the Nobel prize for literature today. The art of Kalevala poetry was a form of high culture arising out of folk culture, just as the written language is a form of high culture arising out of the spoken language. Marina Takalo, the last of the Finnish *rune*-singers, could neither read nor write, but she described how children in Archangel Karelia were made familiar with poetry (Pentikäinen 1978). It is no coincidence that Kalevala poetry withered and died as literacy, which had become the yardstick of children's education and human worth, spread.

The relationship of Kalevala language and written language to spoken language is, likewise, partly one of dependence, partly of independence. I use one language at home, and another for addressing a distinguished audience. I do not, however, sing my speech, I do not divide it into lines with alliteration and parallel lines in the way the Kalevala culture worker did. Like the written language, Kalevala language, too, was more archaic and less influenced by dialect than the local spoken language. "I find in them many pure Finnish words which, due to the gentle decadence of the rest of the language in these parts of the country, have since been forgotten," wrote Henrik Florinus of the language of proverbs in 1702. It is hardly likely that the archaisms and Finnicisms of the Kalevala language of Archangel Karelia emerged to facilitate the work of the Finnish collector, as has sometimes been conjectured; they are devices of elevated style such as are sometimes to be found in hymns and 'art poetry'. To the scholar of poetry they are at the same time index fossils. Like written language, Kalevala language had its own comprehension crises, but also its own give-and-take mechanisms. Only when it became 'set' as 'literature' did Kalevala language become difficult to understand.

Within the field of national disciplines Kalevala language, the age-old code of oral high culture, has long been a touchstone on which linguists, literary researchers, folklorists and musicologists have tested the validity of their methods. In 1626 Andreas Bureus stated in his atlas that the Finns "do not rhyme using similar word endings in the same way as other people but by beginning two or three words at a time in the same way, ending the line on the eighth syllable". Since then the rules of Kalevala metre have been debated by such scholars as Juslenius, Ihre, Porthan, Juteini, Renvall, v. Becker, Lönnrot, Europaeus, Ahlqvist, Genetz, Godenhjelm, the Krohns, Mikkola, Launis, Niemi, Haapanen, Väisänen, Ravila, Sadeniemi and, most recently, Pentti Leino. In particular those scholars with the character of a mathematician or a systematist and a strong tendency to see general regularities in irregularity seem to have been drawn towards cracking the nuts of the Kalevala metric system. Arvid Genetz was the first to spot the most central and the most problematic of the rules of Kalevala metre: that the syllable of the word bearing the main emphasis must in the 2nd, 3rd and 4th foot fall on the upbeat if it is long, and on the downbeat if it is short; the placing of the other syllables in the word is free. Lines where a short syllable bearing the main stress falls on the downbeat of a trochaic foot (for example, *aivo/ni a/jatte/levi*) are called broken trochaic tetrameters.

A precise image thus became established of a trochaic tetrameter operating according to highly uniform rules: of a classical Kalevala metre. The theory was substantiated so conclusively with reference to Finnish-Kare-lian material and the unique nature of the Baltic-Finnic languages that Estonian scholars for a long time accepted the same homogeneous ideal type as the basic explanation for their own *regivärss* line technique. Any deviations were usually interpreted as a secondary degeneration of classical Kalevala metre, despite the fact that there were in parts of Estonia more 'faulty' than there were 'faultless' Kalevala lines.

In late autumn 1977-1978, commissioned by the journal *Keel ja kirjan-dus*, Ülo Tedre, a leading folklorist in Tallinn, and I engaged in correspon-dence on the origin and evolution of Kalevala language. (Kuusi-Tedre 1979.) The most significant point raised in our dialogue was perhaps the doubt cast on the assumption of a uniform Kalevala-regivärss culture. Ülo Tedre began by pointing out that it would from Estonia's point of view be natural to start with the assumption of three strata of folklore; the earliest would be the pre-Kalevalaic or "*regivärss*" poetic tradition, the second the Kalevala or "*klassikaline regivärss*" and the third the rhyming song. In addition to laments and *joiks* my Tallinn colleague suggested that cattle calls and possibly also children's songs with short lines might also be pre-Kalevalaic in origin. Extremely interesting was, in his opinion, the poetic genre encountered among the Veps in recent years, characterised by alliteration and parallelism but lacking a fixed poetic metre. "The Veps poem would seem to be at a stage of development preceding Kalevala metre."

The Eesti Nõukogude Entsüklopeedia (II p. 159) crystallises the Estonian view as follows: "The predecessors of the Baltic-Finnic tribes presumably already had some kind of poetry in the manner of the laments of the Setu and other related peoples and the Lapp *joiks*. The use of parallel words and ideas, and the alliteration characteristic of our languages tied in with a sort of four-foot poetic metre. Not until about the beginning of the Christian era, or slightly earlier, did a line form emerge, chiefly in Northern Estonia, Finland and Karelia, which, drawing on these said elements, permitted verbal art of a high standard."

One of the most persistent disputes over Kalevala metre has been the relationship between classical Kalevala metre and the trochaic metre of Southern Estonia. The debate was most heated in the 1930s, when the Estonians H. Paukson and Oskar Loorits put forth the hypothesis that the Southern Estonian tetrameter based on word stress was not in fact a degeneration of classical Kalevala metre but a pre-stage. The focal point of the debate was the duality that in Northern Estonia, on the island of Kihnu, in Mulgimaa and in certain other places poems were usually sung or recited by stressing the Kalevala metre, elsewhere usually following the stress of the words. Ravila and Väisänen, among others, seconded Paukson, but Walter Anderson, the distinguished Estonian scholar, ended his stat-istical analysis with a pointed counterattack:

"It is indeed possible that, as Paukson believes, Estonian folk poetry was in ancient times unscanned. It is not in my power to refute such a hypothesis. I would nevertheless stress that the unscanned performance to be found in many places in modern Estonia is not a relic of that hypothetical primeval time but an innovation – thus not a primary but a secondary phenomenon." (Anderson 1935.)

Walter Anderson's *"Studien zur Wortsilbenstatistik"* is an admirable piece of scholarship in that it indicates precisely in what way the poems of Kolga-Jaan diverge from the norms of classical Kalevala metre. The replacement of the trochee by a dactyl, permissible in Finland and Karelia only in the first poetic foot (*vaka on vanha Väinämöinen*), is extended in the poetry of Northern Viljandi to the second and third feet, too: *Mis tuli / karates / kalda/asse*, or: *Lehm oli / laudas / laps oli / süles*. There is also another loosening of the quantitative rules of Kalevala metre: a short syllable bearing the main stress intrudes into the upbeat of the foot (*karates, süles*) and a long syllable bearing the main stress into the downbeat of the second foot: *Viiäs / se nei/du me/hele*.

The basic difference between the classical and South Estonian metres is reflected in the abundance or paucity of broken trochaic lines. The best *rune*-singers of Karelia and Ingria use trochees (in which the word stress and the poetic metre coincide (*vaka vanha Väinämöinen, ulapalla aukealla*) and broken trochaic lines in almost equal proportions (*tietäjä iänikuinen, selvällä meren selällä*). In Estonian, broken trochaic lines are used more in the north than in the south: in Virumaa almost one line in three is broken, but in Võrumaa only about one in eight. The contrast is evident from, say, the Northern and Southern Estonian versions of the poem telling of the origin of the world:

Meie koplis kolme põesast:	Meie koplis kolmi põõsast:
üks on sinine põesas,	üks oli sini, teine puna,
teine on punane põesas,	kolmas kulla karvaline.
kolmas kulla karvaline.	(Southern version, Häädemeeste)
(Northern version, Kadrina)	ERL I, p. 64
ERL I, p. 23	

Matti Sadeniemi (1951) and Pentti Leino (1970; 1974) do not commit themselves on the question of whether classical Kalevala metre developed on the basis of a more primitive trochaic metre reminiscent of the Southern Estonian one or whether the trochaic metre adhering to the Southern Estonian word stress is the result of a secondary trocheification of classical Kalevala metre. In my general treatise on unwritten literature I personally came down in favour of the latter alternative, my argument being that the centralisation of the language and the shortening of words by syncope and apocope in Western Finland and in the Salmi-Suojärvi-Säämäjärvi-Tule-majärvi area have led to a trocheification process very similar to that in Estonia. Line research into, for example, *Elinan surma* 'The death of Elina' and *Hiidestä kosinta* 'The Courtship from Hiisi' do not leave any doubt that the so-called late Kalevala metre really is of later origin than classical Kalevala metre. If the linguists refuse to accept the explanation that the alternation of a long vowel and a diphthong in the Baltic-Finnic languages derives on the one hand from an *oo > uo* and on the other hand from an *uo > oo* phonetic shift, then is it likely that an approximately similar linguistic development would have led to generalization of wordstress trochee on the northern shores, but to secondary generalization of broken trochaic lines on the southern shores of the Gulf of Finland?

This argumentation is to my mind again one balance in the scales of opposing theories. The problem is not, however, so simple as we may imagine. Ülo Tedre admits that a secondary trocheification similar to that found north of the Gulf of Finland is to be found in, say, Saaremaa. The origins of Southern Estonian metre lie elsewhere. Its characteristic features include variation in the number of syllables in one line from six to nine. So far no one has thrown any real light on the metric system of the Setu poets of Southeast Estonia.

In the course of my research I myself have several times come across a detail that does not easily fit in with my view that the trochaic metre of Southern Estonia is the product of a late development.

In the 1950s, while investigating the evolution of paraphrases connected with sunshine rain, I concluded that the oldest of the Northern European redactions that try to comment the phenomenon of simultaneous sunshine and rain was the Baltic-Ingrian-Karelian-Lapp saying that the dead are drinking at a wedding (Kuusi 1957, 52-60, 299). In Lithuania and Latvia the paraphrase usually takes the form of a *daina*, the metre of which is an ordinary four-foot trochee with a caesura: *Lietins lej / saulité / veleniesi / kazas dzer*. Among the Izhors and the Karelians the saying takes the form: *Päivää paistaa, vettä sataa, Tuonelassa häitä juodaan*, 'The sun is shining, it is raining, in Tuonela the dead are celebrating a wedding', while in different parts of Lapland the saying goes: *Peive paiste ja arvve, te jamisak häjak*. I seem to recall being bothered by the redaction known all the way from Lithuania to Norwegian Lapland with the 'late Kalevala' fourth feet – *sataa, juodaan*. I could not think of any explanation for them, so I left them unexplained. I would now say that if classical Kalevala metre was preceded by a loosish trochaic metre akin to that of Southern Estonia, then the Baltic-Finnic translation of the Baltic *daina* could well be descended from a pre-Kalevalaic pair of trochaic lines such as those.

A second, perhaps coincidental observation of detail concerns the song about the origin of the *kantele*. A corresponding song is to be found among both the Latvians and the Lithuanians, though there the instrument is a *kankles* instead of a *kantele*. Kaarle Krohn already quoted the normal forms of Pärnumaa in southwest Estonia and North Karelia:

Kusta karpi kandelele?	Mistä koppa kantelehen?
Lõhe suure lõualuusta.	Lohen leinän leukaluista.
Kusta kaela kandelele?	Mistä orsi kantelehen?
Selle teen põdra põlveluusta.	Poropeuran polviluusta.
Kusta pulgad kandelele?	Mistä naulat kantelehen?
Haui suure hamba'ista.	Hauin suuren hampahista.
Kusta keeled kandelele?	Mistä kielet kantelehen?
Hi'uksista neiu noore.	Hivuksista Hiien immen.
(Pärnumaa)	(North Karelia)

(What the kantele's sound-board?
Made from a big salmon's jawbone.
What the kantele's shaft?
Made from a reindeer's kneebone.
And what the kantele's pegs?
From the teeth of a great pike.
And what the kantele's strings?
Of hair from a demon's maid.)

The fact that the basic scheme of this section of the poem has been preserved in an identical form all the way from the Latvian border right up to the borders of Lapland, and that most of the words are even the same, is not the only striking point. The strangest thing of all is the complete adherence to normal trochaic metre, the absence of broken lines. True, supplementary broken lines do occur in Karelia: *jouhista hyvän hevosen, kuusesta kumajavasta*, etc. To give an example: Simana Sissonen of Ilomantsi in North Karelia, 40% of whose songs consisted on average of broken lines, at this point sang thirteen normal trochaic lines in succession (SKVR VII:2, 625a, 81-93). It may be that the ancient poet here stylised the text of the myth, giving it a more archaic form. But I would not reject the possibility of being able to discern a pre-Kalevalaic trochaic metre hiding beneath an Estonian-Karelian poetic petrification such as this.

Ülo Tedre writes that the pre-Christian or *regivärss* stratum interests him above all with regard to the historical division of the Baltic-Finnic tribes. Folklorists do indeed tend to be forced to subscribe to the chronological and evolutionary hypotheses of the archaeologists and linguists. Kalevala language, with its various "dialects" and possible preliminary stages, constitutes a more than usually important network of shared and unshared features. Everything we know about the distributions of different folklore genres and individual poems, riddles, etc. can always be attributed to the variability and mobility of folklore. Not so the basic norms of the metric system. That two language areas both have a common poetic metre with alliteration, rules for the mutual equivalence of parallel lines and norms for exceeding the line, etc. indicates a common cultural background in just the same way that consonant gradation or the patterns on clay pots do.

One of the most reliable index fossils to the Kalevala metre area are proverbs. The expansion of the rhyming poem has in many regions almost completely wiped out the Kalevala epic and lyric. Poetic metre was not such a strain on the proverb as to prevent the proverb cast in Kalevala metre from surviving the change in the stylistic fashion. If at some point in the distant past some community did have a Kalevala code and proverb tradition, then it will still be possible to discover a certain number of proverbs restorable to Kalevala metre. Conversely: if a community lacks a proverb tradition in Kalevala metre, it is extremely unlikely that it ever had any Kalevala tradition.

The Kalevala metric system has not attracted very much attention in the research into the loan proverbs of Northern Europe. When the proverbs of the Finno-Ugrian peoples became the object of the research project including systematic collection, publication and comparative analysis in 1963-1993, it appeared that Kalevala metre has in fact played a larger part in their development than previously assumed. The picture is more or less as follows:

Lapland lacks proverbs in Kalevala metre. In the Finnish-speaking areas they probably evenly account for around 20 per cent: though less in the southwest, more in the northeast, which is probably explained by the brisker metabolism of the areas with a faster cultural turnover. Karelia is marked by a strange pattern: about half the proverbs common in the Vuokkiniemi, Uhtua, Akonlahti and Repola songlands are either completely or partly in Kalevala metre, and 35% of the 337 proverbs collected among the Soikkola Izhors. But in Northern and Southern Archangel Karelia and at Porajärvi,

Kiestinki village, northern Archangel Karelia. Photo: I.K. Inha 1894 (FLS 10 002).

Rukajärvi, Paatene and Central Aunus, the Kalevala element is extremely rare. The percentage for the Livonians is 8, for the Ludes 2.5 and for the Veps 1.5. Yet 17 per cent of the proverbs collected by V. Alava from Tver Karelians are unquestionably Kalevala-metric, and 12 per cent of those collected by P. Virtaranta. The Kalevalaic percentage of Votic proverbs is, depending on how the criteria are interpreted, at least 5 and at most 15. Eight per cent of the normal forms of the 305 commonest proverbs in Estonia may be classified as Kalevala-metric, but the proverbs of Livonia seem to be completely devoid of classical Kalevala metre.

The percentages contain an unusual number of uncertainty factors, but though imprecise, they nevertheless bring into focus the picture created by *The Ancient Poems of the Finnish People* (SKVR) and other collections of the borders and major zones of the Kalevala language area.

In our dialogue in the Estonian journal *Keel ja kirjandus* (Kuusi-Tedre 1979) we on many occasions summarised and weighed the ethnogenetic hypotheses constructed by the archaeologists and linguists in the hope of discovering some background explanation to transition periods of Kalevala metre in the various movements taking place in the history of Baltic-Finnic language and culture. Where and when were the strong Baltic influences received? How do we explain the relative distributions of the Southern Estonian word-stress trochee and classical Kalevala language? When, and within which tribe did the latter evolve? What is the role of Votic? Why is the eastern border of Kalevala metre such as it is?

In his day Kaarle Krohn, supporting the views of A.R. Niemi (1918), assumed that the Kalevala metre emerged as a combination of the joint Finnish unfixed poetic tradition cultivating alliteration and parallelism and the more fixed poetic metre of the Baltic languages (Krohn 1924, 69). I have defined this hypothesis more closely by assuming that the broken

47

trochaic line of classical Kalevala metre is mainly derived from the free, joint Finnish metre and the trochee with caesura from the Baltic metre. The latter link is to my mind beyond dispute. The problem is that classical Kalevala metre is missing from the Balts' closest neighbours, the Livonians, and that the closer one gets to Latvia, the rarer the broken trochaic line becomes. Pekka Sammallahti's (1977) theory of Baltic influences assimilated directly from the ancient Curonians into Northern Proto-Finnic provides an excellent explanation for the origin of Kalevala language; it could perhaps be supported by a host of Latvian-Finnish folklore phenomena missing from Estonia, such as the riddle *Tuoppi tehty Tuonelassa, Vatialassa vannehdittu, tina suuhun tilkutettu, vaski pohjahan valettu,* 'A mug made in Tuonela, the hoops were cast in Vatiala, a tin tapped to the opening, a copper cast to the bottom', the answer to which is a well, in ancient times probably a sacrificial spring. Following the crushing criticism of Erkki Itkonen (1978) the direct Baltic connections to the Northern Baltic-Finns barely withstand the Kalevala strain. If Kalevala language came into being around the Gulf of Finland or further north, the missing link is presumably the Southern Estonian word-stressed trochee, which is even more markedly dependent on the Baltic metric system. Pentti Leino (1970, 1974), basing his arguments on the general theory of prosody, has defined the evolution of the Kalevala quantity rules. The shift from the Southern Estonian trochee, in which the syllables in a word are metrically either strong or weak, to classical Kalevala metre, in which only the syllables bearing the main stress are strong or weak according to quantity and all other syllables are neutral, permitted the lively rhythmical use of words with three and five syllables in particular. The first stage of the broken trochaic metre, based perhaps on the caesura line, allowed the hiding in the broken line favoured by the *daina* in lines of the type *suot sulavat, maat valuvat – sanan virkkoi, noin nimesi.* The slight modification or elimination of the compulsory caesura from every other line raised Kalevala language to a new level of expressiveness.

In Estonia the archaeologists S. Laul and V. Trummal, the philologist P. Alvre and the style scholar J. Peegel claim to have found in recent years new arguments for the old thesis put forward by Heikki Ojansuu according to which the basic distribution of Proto-Finnic was a western-eastern one. The Votes, in the archaeologists' opinion, looked towards the east, in the linguists' opinion towards the west. Unless a genetic link can be demonstrated between the Livonian – Southern Estonian trochee tradition on the one hand and the Veps – Ludic – Eastern Archangel Karelian on the other, such as a common stratum of trochaic proverbs, then it must presumably be concluded that the Eastern Proto-Finns were untouched by Baltic prosody influences.

On the other hand Ülo Tedre stresses the theory of T.-R. Viitso that the first to break away from Proto-Finnic were Ugala and Livonian. Pekka Sammallahti reckons this took place around the year 600 BC. It is unlikely that the cultivation of the pre-Kalevalaic trochee was confined solely to the southern Proto-Finns, even though it has been preserved in its purest form in Livonian and Southern Estonian.

C.F. Meinander and Terho Itkonen have, on different grounds, arrived at the conclusion that Ancient Häme already had an indigenous population even before the Roman Iron Age. These early Northern Proto-Finnic settlers represented an established arable culture and differed from the native Lapps both linguistically and anthropologically.

Conclusive proof that Ancient Häme was one of the areas of Kalevala tradition is provided by the distribution of Kalevala language in Karelia. The Häme colony established in the Hiitola-Kurkijoki region in the 9th century appears to have been a decisive factor as Ancient Karelia broke away from the descendants of the Southeast Proto-Finns, the speakers of the Ladoga proto-language and the Ancient Veps. The theory developed by Bubrih, Ariste, Virtaranta, Turunen and Terho Itkonen of a Veps substrate with, in Aunus, Karelian strata of different ages and strengths, proves to be an excellent explanation as regards the eastern periphery of Kalevala language. No longer is it necessary to yearn for a lost Kalevala land either of the "Eastern Karelians" or on the coast of Bjarmia. There is a rich Kalevala tradition wherever Ancient Karelia radiated its colonies: in Ingria, Savo-Karelia, Western Archangel Karelia, Vermlandi and Tver. The possibility that the code itself, classical Kalevala metre, was invented in Karelia, and that it travelled in the manner of numerous eastern loan words to Western Finland is dashed by the absence of Kalevalaic traits in Southeastern Proto-Finnic. It is as such illuminating that the Kalevala code did not prove capable of "migrating" even across the low Karelian-Ludic language threshold.

On which side of the Gulf of Finland should we seek the primeval home of classical Kalevala language: in the area from which the people of Ancient Häme set out, or the area to which they migrated? Has the Kalevala tradition in Estonia yielded to the word-stress trochee, or did it originate in Finland, from there making its way to an Estonia dominated by a pre-Kalevalaic metric system?

Let me try to illuminate the issue in the light of two collections of material published in 1977, Vaina Mälk's *Vadja vanasõnad eesti, soome, karjala ja vene vastetega* and the work *Arvoitukset. Finnish Riddles* by Leea Virtanen, Annikki Kaivola-Bregenhøj and Aarre Nyman. This also raises a second problem concerning Kalevala linguistic history that still remains to be solved: why were some of the proverbs and riddles, and the direct speech in folk tales and legends in the Baltic-Finnic languages cast in Kalevala metre, but the bulk of them not?

Leea Virtanen and her coworkers were not particularly concerned with making the sample variants of the different redactions of their 1248 riddle types representative in the metrical sense. The Kalevala character is, however, as a rule discernible from the material, either certain, open to interpretation or missing, and if it is not, the scholar can always consult the corresponding entries in the Folklore Archive.

It is particularly pleasing to find that the editors have given a precise account of the number of variants of each riddle type and redaction along with references to known counterparts in Karelian, Estonian, Latvian, Russian, Finnish, the Swedish spoken in Sweden, and English. The distribution of riddles within Finland has to rely on a rather imprecise system of letters; the asterisks after the frequency figures warning against textbook appearances display an excellent sense of source criticism.

The editors of *Arvoitukset. Finnish Riddles* did not, however, attempt a general introduction to the Finnish riddle tradition such as the work demands and for which all the potential exists: Leea Virtanen is content mainly to summarise earlier articles devoted to functional analysis and the history of the discipline, while Annikki Kaivola-Bregenhøj opens the heavy abracadabra door a crack on her formula-analytic doctoral thesis. The distribution and frequency apparatus of this volume of material thus remains totally unexploited and is not even provided with the statistical abstract that makes, for example, Vaina Mälk's *Vadja vanasõnad* so easy to use and stimulating.

In order to alleviate the shortcoming I now wish to list the loan riddles in the work grouped according to type of distribution (C = Karelian, E = Estonian, Fs = Finland-Swedish, L = Latvian, R = Russian, S = Swedish). I shall not be paying any attention to the English counterparts heterogeneous in origin. The numbers refer to the type numbers in the riddle publication, the numbers in italics to riddles in Kalevala metre, and the ones in italics with a question mark to riddles in which the Kalevala metre is open to interpretation.

CEFsLRS:	34 *181?* 241 574 613 633 *660* 772 1013
CEFsLR:	244 659 720 *760 1023* 1050 1105 *1172?*
CEFsLS:	707
CEFsRS:	133 224 375 433
CELRS:	*89*
CFsLRS:	620
EFsLRS:	44 96 223 267 340 *494?* 624 632 654 685 712 718 768 806 937 1002 1014 1078 1133 1197
CEFsR:	149 *466 571 759 888* 920 *1109?* 1116
CEFsS:	82
CELR:	*66?* 467 478 *570* 665 *819 858?* 904 *1084?* 1106
CERS:	*536*
CFsLR:	*606* 1087
CFsLS:	190
CFsRS:	54 1052
EFsLR:	161 275 346 374 458 *474? 582 701 731? 786? 1102 1174* 1194
EFsLS:	43 716 945
EFsRS:	*1?* 263 441 442 *456* 524 550 551 807
ELRS:	603
FsLRS:	406 549 1086
CEFs:	*527 667? 695? 1112*
CEL:	*1100?*
CER:	*403?* 420 *1058* 1195
CLR:	154 *284* 817 *861* 873 1044
EFsL:	1176
EFsR:	*238* 313 504 908 1179 1233
EFsS:	*5* 42 *138?* 140 *179* 250 251 265 298 407 425 *506?* 531 548 808 839 895 1164 1220 1226
ELR:	*94* 98 261 *285 476* 579 749 865 932 933 *1021? 1083* 1230
ERS:	68
FsLR:	587 *1024* 1224
FsLS:	1135
FsRS:	40 146 461 664 709 869 *1152* 1225
LRS:	197 *898* 960 1104
CE:	*239* 429 *446?* 534 544 566 *730* 735 814 966
CFs:	47 *360*

CR:	21 269 *322 335?* 502 567 647 708 *965* 1222
CS:	528
EFs:	15 16 52 57 *63 87* 97 147 *220* 293 307 345 354 356 365 376 404 473 *477 520* 533 *554* 558 561 565 *572 575* 655 737 804 805 823 1235
EL:	*959* 1097 *1131*
ER:	41 120 *150?* 196 221 233 257 305 309 314 *371* 432 563 *639* 800 *1059* 1101 *1144*
ES:	192 802 *803* 820 882
FsR:	*519* 843 1166
FsS:	17 46 58 64 79 126 165 178 184 235 262 *273?* 278 279 287 343 355 357 368 394 395 397 *400* 408 443 479 490 507 *511* 637 618 625 658 688 713 725 728 740 801 856 930 982 1056 1119 1171 1178 1205 1232
LR:	204 *237* 294 321 *330 419* 505 642 691 736 *762* 777 868 918 919 947 989 1043 1107 1129 1240 1245
RS:	*81* 745
C:	156 185 *286* 362 388 *489* 495 *513* 517 543 545 611 *699* 714 798 *833* 912 *952* 1048 *1071 1201*
E:	6 7 *18?* 24 30 36 37 88 112 194 *219?* 236 296 *312?* 336 341 359 *414* 418 *422* 457 462 463 471 480 503 523 564 *594?* 631 635 645 661 *662? 668 677* 680 687 *697 710 717* 723 733 734 742 *746?* 748 *750 751 752 754 757* 771 791 809 822 824 825 826 848 852 *853 863?* 875 884 905 911 *936* 950 957 *1005 1015? 1028* 1041 1042 *1047 1049* 1066 1074 *1126* 1142 1143 *1150* 1165 1169 1177 *1187?* 1192 1216 1227
Fs:	3 25 38 49 *73* 176 198 202 214 230 *255 277?* 329 377 465 591 610 653 679 702 715 724 788 837 847 903 *963?* 964 1029 1054 1070 1099 1186 1234 1239
L:	50 *401* 906 *939 958 1061 1062 1127?*
R:	83 85 86 *158* 254 256 *311* 315 349 373 *387? 412?* 431 440 449 522 535 628 689 *698 767 870 934 948* 990 993 *1006 1022?* 1026 1045 *1064* 1065 1075 *1118* 1158 *1161* 1162 1199 *1211* 1243 1248
S:	2 *28* 33 55 113 142 227 398 486 *491* 1018 1167 1196 1242 1244
(Eng:	526 532 *598* 844 1001 1203)

Of the 543 riddle types for which Finnish Riddles gives international counterparts, 117 are definitely in Kalevala metre and 38 are in a metre that could be interpreted as Kalevalaic.[1] Counting this latter category as semi-Kalevalaic, the Kalevala percentage of international riddles is 25. The corresponding figure for riddles found only in Finland is 29,5%.

There is an interesting difference between the international and Kalevala degree of the common (Finnish) and rare (local) riddles. Of the riddles with at least 100 variants, 208 are international and 46 encountered only in Finland; 32% of the former are in Kalevala metre, and 50% of the latter. But of the riddles with fewer than 100 variants, 329 are international and 665 Finnish only; the corresponding Kalevala degrees are 21% and 28%. A high number of variants thus has a positive correlation with international distribution on the one hand and Kalevalaic traits on the other.

All in all the riddle publication gives a Karelian counterpart for 109 Finnish riddle types, an Estonian for 297, a Lettish for 135, a Russian for

Man and boat. Vuonninen. Photo: Samuli Paulaharju 1915 (FLS 5429).

233, a Finland-Swedish for 249 and a Sweden-Swedish for 162. The percentages of Kalevala-metric ones are, in the same order: 33, 29, 28, 27, 16 and 10. Of those with both a Karelian and an Estonian counterpart (CE), 35 are in Kalevala metre, followed by CR 34%, CL 33, CFs 30, EL and ER 28, LR 26, EFs and FsR 21, FsL 17, CS 16, ES and RS 13, LS 9 and FsS 8%. The eastern loan riddles are thus two or three times more Kalevalaic than the western ones, which possibly reflects the early recession of the code in the west and its late preservation in the east.

Occupying a key position are the 70 definitely Kalevala-metric riddles for which the editors found counterparts in M. J. Eisen's Estonian anthology of riddles. The vast majority of the counterparts observe the "pre-Kalevalaic" four-foot word-stressed trochee; the Finnish broken trochaic line far more frequently corresponds in Estonian to a three-foot trochee-dactyl. On both sides of the Gulf of Finland only six riddles indisputably contain a broken line (94, 179, 239, 371, 754 and 803), in addition to which five have only a classical trochaic metre (477, 520, 751, 959 and 1047). A dozen or so have lines that possibly derive from a broken trochee and are open to interpretation.

Examination from the opposite perspective reveals that more than half the Estonian texts of the 297 Estonian-Finnish riddles are more or less a "pre-Kalevalaic" word-stress trochee, but of their Finnish counterparts only one in three is in classical Kalevala metre and 43% represent a word-stress trochee similar to that of Estonian.

Eisen's riddle anthology does not provide a sufficient basis for comparison in order to determine whether the surprisingly rare classical-Kalevala

Finnish-Estonianisms represent an old, receding Northern Estonian line technique or a type of cultural export heading south such as the Finnicisms of the Kuusalu poems and proverbs. What is conspicuous is the widespread use of two or three popular formulae (the numeral paradox, nominativus absolutus formula and attribute formula) and the avoidance of certain other formulae in Kalevala metre loan riddles. There is no denying that far more riddles borrowed from the south were translated into Finnish during the centuries at which Kalevala language was at its height than riddles borrowed from the west. It is better not to put forward any explanation for the 70 or so riddle types that are "pre-Kalevalaic" in Estonian but "late Kalevalaic" in Finnish until they have been subjected to stringent distribution analysis.

A sounder basis is provided for conclusions by analysing Vaina Mälk's edition of Votic proverbs. It seems from my observations that Mälk's classification of types and choice of counterparts is very careful. I have for the purpose of metrical analysis assessed the 728 proverb types given by Mälk by giving 2 points for every faultless broken trochee line, 1 point for each trochee satisfying the classical norms, 1 point for each line displaying strong alliteration and 1 point for regular parallelism between lines, giving at least 4 points as a criterion for unequivocal Kalevalaism. This raised threshold helps to eliminate the pseudo-trochaic lines from the old common Kalevalaic riddle types.

It appears that of the 728 Votic proverbs, 40 or 5% are according to the above criteria in Kalevala metre.[2] Of the 130 that are exclusively Votic 2% are in Kalevala metre, but none of the 41 Votic-Russian ones.
Of the 90 proverbs for which Mälk has found a Finnish counterpart but not an Estonian, 9 (10%) are in Kalevala metre.
Of the 327 proverbs with both a Finnish and an Estonian counterpart, 23 (7%) are in Kalevala metre.
Of the 119 proverbs with an Estonian but not a Finnish counterpart, 4 (3%) are in Kalevala metre.
Of the 192 proverbs with neither a Finnish nor an Estonian counterpart, 4 (2%) are in Kalevala metre.

Of the various distribution categories, that containing 70 Votic-Finnish-Karelian-Estonian proverbs is clearly the most Kalevalaic, its Kalevala percentage being 17. Close to them are the 7 Votic-Finnish, Votic-Finnish-Karelian and Votic-Finnish-Estonian proverbs, whose Kalevala percentage is about 13. Of the 14 proverbs for which Mälk presents an Izhor-Ingrian counterpart, three are in Kalevala metre.

If we regard Votic as a branch of Northern Estonian and Northern Estonia as the cradle of Kalevala metre, how do we explain the Finnish preponderance in Kalevala metre Votic proverbs? Where a Votic proverb has a Kalevala-metric counterpart in only one related language, that language is in four cases out of five Finnish or Karelian. The Estonian-Votic counterparts are dominated by the "pre-Kalevalaic" word-stress trochee. Considering how well Votic poetry has preserved the Kalevala metre, its proverbs are not likely to have developed in the direction of the word-stressed trochee of their own accord. That 5 per cent were probably partly loaned from the neighbouring Ingrians and partly derived from the old Gulf of Finland culture. As regards their distribution, the Votic proverbs in Kalevala metre would appear to point to the Northern Proto-Finnic origin of classical Kalevala metre.[3]

The general investigation into the borrowed proverbs of Northern Europe begun in 1964 as a joint Finnish-Soviet project seeking, among other things, to throw light on the Baltic-Finnic field of application of Kalevala language. In 1977, while going through 1,020 Livonian proverb types with Vaina Mälk, I noted a four-foot word-stressed trochee in about one in five: *mier andab, mier votab*. The proverbs found in Kalevalaic versions in Estonian and Finnish appear to be missing from Livonian; on the other hand the collective European proverbs familiar in Livonian also appear to have been cast in a non-Kalevalaic guise in Estonian and Finnish. If my first impression is correct, it might point to one reason why some of our ancient small-scale folklore has been expressed in Kalevala language, and some not. Did the collective European small-scale folklore interpreted in classical Kalevala language reach Finland or the Gulf of Finland area without passing through the Baltic area? Or did Kalevala language not spread from the epic, the lyric, the wedding and bear songs to unsung small-scale folklore and magic texts until the oldest stratum of proverbs and riddles had acquired a form other than a Kalevalaic one?[4]

I assume that the appearance of the Estonian-Finnish syncope and apocope in the 13th century, likewise of long syllables in a position other than that bearing the main stress, signified a crises in the evolution of Kalevala language that could go a long way toward explaining the different norms characteristic of the various dialect areas. Without the perspective of linguistic history, defining the boundaries of Kalevala metre – its early, middle and late forms – is merely a case of groping in the dark.

On the basis of my survey it is possible to create the following revised overall picture of the metrical development of the Kalevala tradition:

1. Towards the end of the Finnish-Volgan era, as Baltic contacts became more frequent in the 2nd millennium BC, the early Proto-Finns had, in addition to their laments, *joiks* and cattle calls, some pre-Finnish code abounding in alliteration and parallelism that was either unfixed or possibly fell into four-foot lines for the performance of mythical epics and other ritual texts. Traces of this could possibly be found in the metric systems of the Lapps and the Veps.

2. Their Baltic neighbours brought the western Proto-Finns not only *kantele*, *virsi* and numerous poetic motifs but also the fairly firmly established trochaic tetrameter with caesura closely resembling the Baltic trochee made up of two dipodies. This remained the dominant form at least in Livonian and Southern Estonian when these broke away from Proto-Finnic in about the year 600 BC. The majority of the Baltic-Baltic-Finnic songs which I attribute to the "early Kalevala" stylistic era were probably originally translated or composed on the model of the pre-Kalevalaic word-stress trochee.

3. Classical Kalevala language grew up on the basis of the pre-Kalevalaic metre among the seafarers and fishermen on the Gulf of Finland or the new Northern Proto-Finnic settlers in Häme. The opposing handling of the long and short syllable bearing the main stress became a basic metric opposition, and alternation of a normal trochee and a broken trochaic line created the potential for a new level of rhythmic artistry and the natural use of the entire

54

vocabulary in the language. The alliteration norms remained almost unchanged, but the transformation of the poetic metre was presumably accompanied by a transformation in parallelism.

4. With the Häme settlers, Kalevala language took root in the 9th century in Ancient Karelia and established its strongest position and finest forms among its subsidiary tribes. Of the five stylistic eras in the ancient Kalevala epic described by me (Kuusi 1957), the fourth, the period of the Viking Age island epic, would appear to belong chiefly within the framework of Ancient Karelia, the three preceding ones to that of the Northern Proto-Finns and Western Finns. In the division of unwritten literature into different eras, all four come under the heading of Middle Kalevala.

A number of problems remain for future scholars to solve: 1) the relationship between the trochaic metres of the various peripheries (Lappish, Ludic, Veps, Setu, Livonian) with the Kalevala tradition and each other, 2) analysis of the "metric dialects" of Estonian and Finnish and relating them to the changes and dialect borders in language history, 3) the role of Votic, 4) the age and origin of small-scale Kalevalaic folklore, 5) analysis of the parallelism and word-order norms of Kalevala language, especially its early and late forms, 6) the relating of microanalyses to the Baltic-Finnic and Northern European macroanalysis, 7) and finally a question to be solved by aesthetics and socio-linguistics: what exactly did Kalevala language signify to its users?

NOTES

This article is based on an earlier version published in Finnish under the title *Kalevalakielen kysymyksiä*, which appeared in the journal *Virittäjä*, volume *82, 1978*, p. 209-224.

1. The minimum criterion for Kalevala metre is the derivation of either the most common or of two less common redactions from classical Kalevala metre.
2. Mälk's numbers 11 24 35 51 58 150 222 225 236 270 285 291 302 308 309 315 375 376 379 384 402 416 421 445 451 510 536 546 550 599 610-614 620 625 655 675 and 716. The counterparts presented by Mälk are not always variants of the same proverb (e.g. the Finnish counterpart of 513 and the Estonian of 532). There is a slight inconsistency in combining and separating the proverbs in different redactions (e.g. 51 and 675, but 162). The Finnish counterpart of 516 is overlooked by Mälk in his statistics.

3. The most reliable detailed study of Votic folklore in the doctoral thesis of Leea Virtanen (1966, 53, 57, 96, 101-102) proves that the closest counterparts to the Votic riddle song are to be found in Setumaa (Estonia) and – Satakunta (Southwest Finland)! The ancient links between the Votes and the Setus are illustrated by the observations of H. Moora, E. Richter, A. Moora, J. Peegel, P. Alvre, H. Tampere and F. Oinas (Mälk ibid. 64-70). Väinö Salminen (1929) was already stressing the relative independence of the Votic Kalevala tradition.
4. This general investigation, *Proverbia Septentrionalia*, was published in 1985. The analytical table on pages 37-77, and especially column 7 giving a metrical definition of the 900 North European proverb types, is useful for anyone seeking an answer to the unsolved problems raised in the present study.

PENTTI LEINO

The Kalevala Metre and its Development

Elias Lönnrot published the first edition of the *Kalevala*, containing a total of 32 poems, in 1835. The longer version we know today came out in 1849. In this second edition there are 50 poems, comprising over 20,000 lines. The *Kalevala* quickly took on the status of Finland's national epic, and it is undoubtedly the most well-known work of Finnish literature abroad.

Lönnrot compiled the *Kalevala* from oral folk poetry. He combined separate poems into a single plot, thus creating a coherent whole. Lönnrot himself believed he had reconstructed an epic poem which had once actually existed and had survived only in separate fragments; but fairly early it became clear that he had, in fact, put together a number of originally independent poems. The *Kalevala* is thus Lönnrot's creation even though most of its lines originate from folk poems and only a small proportion was composed by Lönnrot himself.[1]

The Kalevala metre used in later poetry is thus based on an oral folk metre with a tradition of a thousand years, if not several thousand, behind it. A metre which is very similar to this so-called classical Kalevala metre and undoubtedly of the same origin is to be find in the folk poetry of other Baltic-Finnic peoples, at least in Votic and Estonian poetry. It is not exactly the same in all areas, but the similarities are much greater than the differences. The variation mainly concerns the strictness of the norms governing the placing of stressed syllables. It is now generally assumed that this metre dates from perhaps 2500 years ago, when the native tradition met with Baltic influences. However, conclusive evidence is lacking.[2]

Lönnrot's epic work of compilation was possible because Kalevala metre in the oral tradition was not only used in poems: sung epic, lyric, ritual verse and recited magic spells. The direct speech in prose tales and stories was often in the same metre, as were various common expressions and rhymes. Many riddles have the Kalevala metre, and also thousands of proverbs, many of which are still current in spite of the fact that folk poetry in the Kalevala metre has otherwise disappeared from the oral tradition.

In West Finland the metre was still extant in the 17th century, and in East Finland it survived to the 19th and even the present century. The reason for its decline was the appearance of new metres and new kinds of songs: the dynamic metrical system came into Finnish partly with the poetry of

Songs beyond
the Kalevala
Studia Fennica
Folkloristica 2
1994

hymns, but it developed in folk poetry at the same time, if not slightly earlier. In both cases language and cultural contacts were of paramount importance: Swedish influence in the west and Russian in the east. Nevertheless, the Kalevala metre survived alongside the new forms, not only in the oral tradition but also in written poetry, even in that of educated poets. The appearance of the Kalevala itself confirmed the status of the metre, making it an archaic but still serviceable alternative in written poetry, alongside the more modern metres of the dynamic system.

In some respects the Kalevala metre is a rather special one, and it has also aroused the interests of scholars of metrics outside Finland (see Sadeniemi 1951, Kiparsky 1968). I shall attempt to describe its characteristic features and show the covert factors underlying them. To this end, it will not suffice merely to describe the metric system of the *Kalevala*: I shall also need to refer in some detail to the metrics of modern Finnish poetry and comment on some central phonological and morphological features of Finnish.

The main components of the metre

The Kalevala metre is trochaic tetrameter: a line is comprised of four successive rises and falls.

(1) + - + - + - + -

The plus sign is used to mark the rises (i.e. stresses), and the minus marks the falls. The metre has no syntax, i.e., the lines do not combine into couplets or longer verses: a poem is made up of an optional number of independent lines. Minimal poems in this tradition are one-line proverbs, whereas the longest ones are epic songs of over 400 lines. There was no rhyme, and the fixed line did not allow an empty metrical slot at the end.

The abstract scheme given above does not suffice as a complete description of the Kalevala metre. We first need to add an account of what is known as the "winnowing" (end weight) phenomenon: longer words tend to occur towards the end of the line and shorter ones at the beginning. This is illustrated in the way lines like 2 are over ten times more frequent than lines like 3:

(2) *Laiha poika lappalainen*

(3) *Lappalainen laiha poika*

This phenomenon is a general tendency of the language and is seen in many different ways. Thus the pair of Christian name *Kalle Kustaa* is common in Finnish, as is *Karl Gustav* in Swedish, whereas the pairs *Kustaa Kalle* and *Gustav Karl* are almost unknown.[3] In the Kalevala metre the *winnowing principle* is a tendency, not an absolute requirement. It is nevertheless significant from this point of view that lines like 4 and 5 do not occur in the poems:

(4) *Laiha lappalainen poika*

(5) *Niin ylen*täköhön *nuo*li

A four-syllable word may thus occur at the end (2) or beginning (3) of a line, but not in the middle (4). This is considered to be because a pure trochaic line needs a *caesura* in the Kalevala metre, i.e. an obligatory word boundary in the middle of the line (Sadeniemi 1951, 36-39). The explanation is a natural one, since lines of widely differing metres display a tendency to split into two halves. Yet there is no clear evidence of the assumed caesura in the Kalevala metre. Neither does it prevent the oc-curence of pure trochaic lines containing a word of six syllables:

(6) *Mai*lle *ris*timät*tö*mille

And this assumption of a caesura does not suffice to explain why lines like 5 are just as strictly avoided as those like 4.

The Kalevala metre has no stanza structure, and thus no rhyme; alliteration, however, is typical. If alliteration can be said to have a metrical function, this function is a twofold one: alliteration serves to indicate word boundaries and to increase cohesion in the line (mnemonic and similar functions are no longer metrical). Alliteration is usually limited to a given line *(Itse vanha Väinämöinen / melan on merestä nosti)*, but it may sometimes extend beyond the line boundary *(Otti miekkansa omansa / kädellänsä oikealla)*; these latter cases are usually to be interpreted as statistical accidents. If a line contains two clauses these may alliterate separately *(Lepy lehto, kostu korpi)*, but other lines too may contain two alliterating pairs or series of words with the same alliteration *(Laiva lastuin lohkiella)*. Alliteration is generally free: within the line any alliterative combination is permitted, and on the other hand there does not even have to be alliteration at all.

Alliteration falls into two types. It is weak when the words begin with the same consonant followed by a different vowel *(Silloin seppo Ilmarinen)*, or when they begin with different vowels *(Ulapalla aukealla)*. The dominant form, however, is strong alliteration, where identical word-initial consonants (or a word boundary) are followed by the same vowel *(Löysi piitä pikkaraisen; Orihilla olkisella)*.

Over half the lines in Finnish folk poetry have a strong alliteration. In the epic poems about a fifth of the lines contain weak alliteration, and about the same number have no alliteration; in lyric poetry alliteration is some-what more frequent.[4] It is thus a tendency, not a rule; a poem in the Kalevala metre which contains no alliteration, however, is nevertheless an anomaly.

In addition to the winnowing principle and alliteration, parallelism is also typical of Kalevala poetry. This is a more complex phenomenon and more difficult to describe. Below is a sample from Arhippa Perttunen's *Sampo* poem, together with Keith Bosley's translation:

(7)

Silloin vanha Väinämöinen	Then the old Väinämöinen
sortui sormin lainehille,	sank with fingers to the waves
kämmenin vesille kääntyi.	turned with palms to the water:
Siellä kulki kuusi vuotta,	there he wandered for six years
seisoi seitsemän keseä,	stopped there for seven summers

kulki kuusissa hakona,	wandered as a spruce
petäjäissä pölkyn päänä.	as a log from a pine-tree.

A line may have one or even several parallels, but a repeated line itself is by no means obligatory. The third line of the above example is a repeat of the previous one: the verbs *sortui* and *kääntyi* correspond, as do *lainehille* and *vesille* and again *sormin* and *kämmenin* ('sank/turned, waves/water, fingers/palms'). In the following pair of lines *kulki* and *seisoi* correspond ('wandered/stopped'), and also the phrases *kuusi vuotta* and *seitsemän keseä* ('six years/seven summers'): *Siellä* ('there') at the beginning of the earlier line has no repeat in the Finnish. In the last pair *kuusissa* is repeated in *petäjäissä* ('spruce/pine-tree') and *hakona* in *pölkyn päänä* (not parallel in the translation); *kulki* ('wandered') is not repeated here.

The repeated line thus re-expresses the content of the main line in a particular way; Steinitz (1934) makes a semantic distinction between two main types of repetition, synonomy and analogy. Parallelism can also be classified in terms of metrical units: the repetition may be within the line, line repetition as in example 7, couplet repetition, list repetition, and so on. I bypass these and other classifications (see Kuusi 1983, 191-194), however, because parallelism remains peripheral to metrical stucture proper.

Parallelism itself is characteristic of the oral tradition in particular, as an aid to the *rune*-singer's performance and memory. In Kalevala verse, however, it has a decisive influence on the syntax of the text, as the repeated line interrupt the continuation of the clause, thus preventing the development of complex structures many lines in length. Folk poetry does not generally contain clauses longer than two or three line uninterrupted by a repeated line. In fact Kalevala poetry has a fairly simple syntax altogether: there are very few subordinate clauses, and main clauses proceed from line to line, punctuated at intervals by repeated lines.

The problem

Each rise and fall of the line is occupied by one syllable: the only exception is the first fall, which may have two and sometimes even three light syllables. The lines in example (8) are genuine Kalevala metre, from Arhippa Perttunen's *Sampo* poem. (The symbol = is used to indicate the boundary between parts of a compound word; the parts of compound word are equivalent to independent words.)

(8) Pohjan akka harva=hammas
nousi leivon lentimille.

In this respect the Kalevala metre is similar to the modern Finnish metrical system; these lines could also be from a trochaic poem in that system. But the Kalevala metre has one important requirement: a word initial syllable must be long if it is to occupy a rise. There is no such restriction in the modern trochaic metre, althoug the modern metre does tend to favour a long stressed syllable on the rise. I refer to such lines as "pure trochee lines";

they show a direct rhytmical correspondence between the basic metrical schema and its linquistic realization.

A short word-initial syllable is placed on a fall. It is this principle that differentiates sharply between the Kalevala metre and the modern metrical system. It is of crucial significance to the Kalevala metre for two reasons. In the first place, it makes it possible for the metre to use the whole vocabulary of the language in a balanced way. In the second place, it brings rhytmical variety and life to the metre in spite of the fact that it keeps strictly to the highly monotonous basic trochaic schema. I refer to lines of the kind illustrated in example (9) as "broken lines", as they break the underlying trochaic rhythm:

> (9) Sirkun siiville kohosi
> vastat siiviksi sivalti
> kokon kynkkä=luun nenille.
> Lenteä lepettelööpi
> selvällä meren selällä.

Here we have five successive broken lines. This is unusual as about half the lines of folk poetry in the Kalevala metre are pure trochee and the other half are broken lines. Typical of the broken line is that at least one of the falling positions contains a short stressed syllable (*ko*hosi, *si*valti, *ne*nille, *le*pettelööpi, *me*ren *se*lällä). Thus, it is only the first syllable of the word that is significant for the metre. If the syllable is long, it is placed on a rise; but if it is short, it must be assigned to a fall. All other syllables may be placed quite freely.

Example (9), however, does not completely adhere to these rules, for its third line begins with a short stressed syllable on the rise (*ko*kon). But this is not ummetrical and the practice is completely acceptable. The first rise of a line may have a short stressed syllable instead of a long one; correspondingly, the first fall may have a long stressed syllable instead of a short one. The line *kokon kynkkä = luun nenille* is thus correct, as are examples 10 and 11:

> (10) Jo näki tuhon tulevan
> (11) Jo tunsi tuhon tulevan

The first rise of the line shows no tendency to favour a long stressed syllable, nor is there any particular avoidance of such a syllable in the first fall. The usage is thus well established, but it only concerns the beginning of the line, for elsewhere the main rule holds: long stressed syllable on a rise, short on a fall. The beginning of the line is thus exceptional, which is also shown by the fact that only in the first falling position can there be two or – rarely – even three syllables instead of the obligatory one. But these must be light ones:

> (12) Tuopa on vanha Väinämöinen
> (13) Tuopa oli vanha Väinämöinen

Two other minor details should be mentioned with regard to the relation between the Kalevala metre and the syllables of the language. First, the line may not end with a monosyllable, so that example 14 could not occur in a Kalevala poem:

(14) Kohta pursi liikahti jo

Since Finnish has very few short monosyllables it is hard to judge whether this restriction is a purely stylistic one or whether it has a metrical motivation. The second point has to do with the monosyllabic verb form *on* ('is'):

(15) Tapasi on taskuhunsa

In line 15 *on* occurs on a fall although it is a long monosyllable. It can of course also occur on a rise, but it is fairly frequent on a fall as an insignificant filler-word completing the requisite number of syllables in the line. Line 15 must unquestionably be regarded as metrical.

Thus, the basic structural problem of the Kalevala metre is concerned with the syllables carrying primary stress and their position in the line. This is governed by three rules:

1. A long stressed syllable occurs only in a rising position in the line.
2. A short stressed syllable occurs only in a falling position.
3. These restrictions do not apply to the first rise and fall in the line; and the first fall may may comprise two syllables.

The first of these principles is not surprising: it is natural for the most prominent syllables to be placed in the rising part of the foot. The odd thing is the placing of short stressed syllables. Why is it that they cannot occur at a rise, even though all syllables that do not carry a primary stress, regardless of their length, may occur at either a rise or a fall?

A plausible explanation for this phenomenon was put forward by Paavo Ravila (1935). Ravila starts with the observation that the restrictions on the metre apply exclusively to stressed syllables. He notes that, in Proto-Finnic, long vowels occured only in the stressed syllable of a word, not elsewhere. There were minimal pairs such as *tuuli* 'wind' : *tuli* 'fire', *suuri* 'big' : *suri* '(she/he) grieved'. The same opposition in final syllables, however, appeared at a later stage in the development of Finnish: *poika* 'boy' : *poikaa* 'boy, partitive', *sata* 'a hundred' : *sataa* 'it is raining'. (These forms had three syllables in Proto-Finnic: *poikaδa, *sataβi.) In Ravila's view, Finnish could have not developed a poetic metre that would have blurred the quantity relations of the stressed syllable: the distinction between long and short vowels had to be preserveved.

The crux of Ravila's hypothesis, therefore, is this: the Kalevala metre originated during the Proto-Finnic period specifically for sung poetry. The need to maintain the distinction between the long and short vowels of stressed syllables meant that a vowel in a short stressed syllable was not "extendable". A short initial syllable therefore had to be placed on a fall. Then the listener knew immediately that if the word in its sung form sounded like *tuulii* and began on a fall, it could only be the short-syllabled *tuli*; but if it began on a rise it could only be *tuuli*. The reason why a short stressed syllable was placed on a fall was thus the need for semantic clarity, the avoidance of ambiguity. The problem of the short stressed syllable has since been regarded as solved.

Ravila's hypothesis is a simple one, and most elegant in its simplicity: a basic metrical solution is explained in terms of a single phonological feature, the quantity opposition on vowels. Yet the hypothesis is not so strong as is generally supposed.

In the first place, a metre and the performance of a poem should be kept separate. Ravila argued that Finnish could not develop a metre which would have blurred the quantity relations in stressed syllables. Yet the claim is not valid in this context, for it was not the metre that might blur the quantity opposition but the way of singing. And this has just the same effect in modern Finnish songs in the dynamic system.

In the second place, Ravila's explanation is not based on any theoretical metrical assumptions which would somehow delimit the kinds of explanations available for metrical phenomena in general. On the same grounds any phonological opposition whatsoever could be considered the cornerstone of the metrical system of the language. What we have seen concerning the dynamic system in no way supports such an approach. Ravila's explanation is really an ingeniously observed special case which fits a given metre and a given developmental stage of the language. It does not allow broader theoretical generalizations, nor does it offer a basis for the explanation of variation in the use of the metre.

Third, Ravila's hypothesis only concerns the short stressed syllable and its position on a fall. It remains an open question why such a syllable may also occur on a line-initial rise, and why a long stressed syllable may occupy the first fall of a line, although the way of singing eliminates the quantity difference in vowels in these positions as well.

Fourth, the main argument of the hypothesis is not tenable. Vowel quantity was certainly an important opposition in Proto-Finnic just as it is in modern Finnish today. Nevertheless, Ravila's hypothesis exaggerates its functional load in the interpretation of a sung poem: the explicit preservation of the long-short distinction in stressed syllables cannot have been so absolutely essential as to determine the basic principle of the whole metre. The redundancy partly created by the linguistic context, abundant parallelism, and alliteration marking word boundaries, served quite adequately to disambiguate unclear cases. Even in a sung poem difficulties of interpretation would only have occurred extremely rarely, even though the metre had not thus regulated the placing of stressed syllables (Leino 1974, 246-251). An equally good case could be made out for an explanation on aesthetic grounds; thus Krohn (1923, 344) felt that "lengthening an unstressed syllable in singing is much less disturbing than lengthening a stressed one".

It has been fairly well established that the Kalevala metre dates from the Proto-Finnic period, i.e., that it is over 2000 years old. However, it should be noted that rule 2 holds only for a part of the Baltic-Finnic area where these poems were sung. In Estonian poetry, for example, a short stressed syllable may occur quite normally at a rise in the line, and the same tendency can also be discerned fairly widely in Finnish poetry of different periods.

Even in areas where the classical Kalevala metre was used, lines breaking the correspondence rules are not unusual; below are some examples from poems sung by Arhippa Perttunen (Sadeniemi 1951, 43-45):

(16) Yhen *ka*lan kiehuessa
(17) Iso käski, *e*mo kielti
(18) Aisoilla *vaah*terisilla
(19) Kummalle menet *tyt*töni

A short stressed syllable occurs on the second rise of line 16, and again on the third rise of line 17; and on the second fall of 18 and the third of 19 the stressed syllable is a long one. The lines thus break correspondence rules 1 and 2. Lines of this type amount to 2.7 % in the poems sung by Perttunen, and in Ingrian epic poetry their proportion is from one to two per cent. In North Estonian Poetry the figure rises to 12.3 % (Kõrv 1928, 7-12) and in Southern Estonian even higher. The syllable structure rules are thus no longer rules here, but tendencies, "statistical rules" (Tedre 1965, 60). Even the North Karelian Kalevala metre came to deteriorate somewhat over a hundred years, for lines composed in the 1930's and 1940's contain over 25 % which break the correspondence rules defining the placing of syllables (Leino 1975, 43).

Deviations like examples 16 and 17 are much more common than the type in 18 and 19. In other words, a short stressed syllable comes to occupy a rise; a long stressed syllable on a fall is rarer. This reflects the tendency towards the use of pure trochee lines as opposed to broken lines, a development which would ultimately lead directly to the adoption of the dynamic system. Within the classical Kalevala metre the proportion of broken lines is nearly 50 %; in the North Karelian poetry of the 1930's and 1940's this proportion drops to 27 %. The ratio is approximately similar in Northern Estonian poetry, but the number of broken lines diminishes towards Southern Estonia to about 10 %.[5] A short stressed syllable thus occurs fairly frequently also on a rise, and hence the proportion of pure trochee lines increases.

One reason for the existence of such verses is the occurence of sound changes in the language. In Arhippa Perttunen's poems there are 47 lines with a short stressed syllable on a rise, contrary to correspondence rule 2, and the unmetricality in about half of these lines could be regarded as due to a sound change. Two examples:

(20) Tuota *i*ten tuon ikäni
(21) Meni *ko*sessa kolisten

Both these lines have a short stressed syllable on a rise, but in both cases the syllable had earlier been a long one (*iten < itken, kosessa < koskessa*). It is not necessary to assume that the lines were composed before these changes; they could also have originated in neighbouring dialects where the sound changes have not occurred. With regard to the synchronic description of the metre, however, the lines are unmetrical. Yet it is important to bear in mind that the vast majority of the lines of a given folk poem have often survived unchanged from centuries back, maybe from quite distant areas. In the poem itself they are nevertheless deviant, and when their number increases they gradually break down the basis of the metre and may ultimately lead to changes in the metrical grammar underlying the poems. The problem is not a simple one and has, in fact, led metrical theory to quite novel kinds of solutions.

Boats were an important means of transportation in the trackless wilderness. Sappuvaara canal, Archangel Karelia. Photo: I.K. Inha 1894 (FLS 9860).

Rhytmical variation

The puzzle of the Kalevala metre is its strange syllable structure rules, which cannot really be called prominence rules. Yet perhaps an even greater mystery is how this metre, with such a monotonous basic metrical schema, has been able to survive at all in Finnish – and related languages – for a thousand years or more, and moreover dominate poetry from proverbs to the epic and lyric. I think these two puzzles are linked.

To understand the nature of the Kalevala metre it will be necessary to take a brief look at the modern Finnish metrical system and its structure. (Leino 1986.) This system is essentially similar to the metrical systems of German and Swedish, for example. In modern Finnish, line and verse structures vary, and the various metres are to be numbered in thousands rather than hundreds. Alliteration has given place to rhyme, parallelism has disappeared. Syllabic metres, iambic and trochaic, are common; pure dactyl and anapest scarcely appear at all, and the paeon is also relatively rare.

Nevertheless there has been a clear change in the metric system from syllabic to asyllabic; in other words, the pure trochee and iamb have been almost completely superceded by the iamb-anapest and the trochee-dactyl. Thus there is only one syllable at a rise in the line, but at the fall there may be one or two syllables in free variation. Although this metrical system is modern one, it is not based only on lexical stress; the placing of a syllable at a rise or a fall is determined by its prominence.

By way of illustration, I shall contrast a poem in the Kalevala metre with an example of the equivalent trochaic metre in the modern Finnish metrical system. Eino Leino's poem *Ihalempi* (22) is representative of the Kalevala metre as used in written poetry, while Kaarlo Sarkia's *Unen kaivo* (23) is an example of trochaic tetrameter in the modern system. Only a section from the beginning of each poem will be analysed. This time the syllabic structure will be indicated with a numeric notation: 2 is used to mark a long stressed syllable, 1 a short stressed syllable of a polysyllabic word, and all other syllables are indicated by 0.

(22)

Tuo oli tytti päivölässä	010	20	20	00
Iha=lempi, maammon impi	10	20	20	20
mansikka hyvien maiden	20	01	00	20
Herran lehtojen hedelmä	20	20	01	00
meni karjahan kesällä	10	20	01	00
ei tullut takaisin tytti	02	01	00	20
Läksi veikko vieremähän. –	20	20	20	00
Hiidet virvoja viritti. –	20	20	01	00
"Kunne sorruit kurja sisko?"	20	20	20	20
Poika soille portahaksi.	20	20	20	00

The poem is in perfect keeping with the syllable structure rules of the Kalevala metre: a long stressed syllable (2) cannot occur on a fall, nor a short stressed one (1) on a rise; the first rise and fall of a line being exceptions. Unstressed syllables can be placed freely, but a fall, apart from the first one, can contain only one syllable. There is no stanza structure, for the boundary between the typographical "stanzas" (an empty line) can be placed between any two lines regardless of any metrical restrictions.

In Kaarlo Sarkia's poem, the lines are grouped just as loosely, which is not typical of the modern Finnish system. Although the typographical stanzas are of varying length, they do have a metrical structure: each line rhymes with one or more of the other lines in the same stanza.

(23)

Elämäni kaiken yllä	10	00	20	20
päilyt, unen kalvo syvä,	20	10	20	10
pohjastas en ylös yllä.	20	00	10	20
Sielulleni tuutu hyvä	20	00	20	10
onkin kulta=hiekkas kyllä!	20	20	20	20
Päily raunioni yllä.	20	20	00	20

In accordance with the requirements of the metrical system, each rise has a prominent syllable and each fall has an non-prominent one. This can be indirectly seen from the syllable structure indicated: a stressed syllable in the trochee, (2) or (1), is always on a rise. In the Kalevala metre, short stressed syllables are placed in falling position, and it is this that primarily increases the rhytmical variation of the lines. In the modern trochee there is a more straightforward correspondence between metre and language, and thus there is much less scope for variation in the rhythm. Furthermore, the modern trochaic metre cannot exploit the vocabulary of the language in anything approaching the balanced way in which the Kalevala metre does. The following table shows the percentage distribution of words with

varying numbers of syllables in four different text types: prose, modern
iambic metre, modern trochaic metre, and the Kalevala metre.

		Modern Finnish		
Syllables	Prose	Iamb	Trochee	Kalevala
1	17%	36%	17%	9%
2	43%	43%	71%	50%
3	28%	15%	5%	29%
4	10%	6%	7%	11%
5	2%	0%	0%	1%
Σ	100%	100%	100%	100%

As can be seen from this table, the iamb strongly favours monosyllabic
words and the trochee favours disyllabic words. Equally, the occurence of
trisyllabic words is less frequent in modern metre, particularly trochaic
metre, than in modern prose texts. The Kalevala metre is, in this respect,
more balanced.

In fact, the strict trochaic tetrameter survives in the modern metric system
only because the system allows another kind of variation: poets are not
bound to a single metre but can exploit different kinds of lines and verses.
They can switch from trochee to iamb or from a syllabic to an asyllabic
metre.

Iambic inversion in modern Finnish poetry: a poetic convention

It is the iambic line that turns out to be crucial for the understanding of the
problem associated with the Kalevala metre. In the modern Finnish iamb
and trochee the first syllable of a polysyllabic word, i.e., the syllable
receiving the main stress, is always prominent. There is only one exception
to this: an iambic line may begin with a stressed syllable. This metrical
phenomenon, iambic inversion, occurs in many languages, including English. It is quite normal in Finnish poetry, but in Estonian, for example, it is
not found at all. The reason is that, in Estonian, there are far more
monosyllabic words than in Finnish, in which there are less than a hundred.
In both Finnish and Estonian, the first syllable of a word always carries the
main stress. An iambic line must therefore begin with a monosyllabic word;
there are enough of these available in Estonian, but not in Finnish. Consequently, iambic inversion is indispensible for Finnish poetry.

Iambic inversion was introduced into the Finnish metrical system
through the translation of hymns from German and Swedish. Thus, it was
originally a loan which has since become incorporated into the system. To
describe this process, five types of iambic line will be distinquished. (The
plus sign marks the rise and the minus marks the fall in the verse.)[6]

Type							
	-	+	-	+	-	+	-
1 Te		pan -	kaa	tul -	li	kal -	lis
2 Sa -		lai -	nen	voi -	ma	pois -	taa
3 Lin -		nas -	saan	yö -	tä	päi -	vää
4 Lah -		jo -	jas	vai -	val -	lam -	me
5 Uu -		den	au -	rin -	gon	an -	taa

66

There is no inversion in type 1: the line begins with a monosyllable. In types 2, 3, and 4, there is inversion at the beginnig of the line. The line begins with a short syllable in type 2, and with a long syllable in types 3 and 4. Types 3 and 4 differ in that the following syllable is also long in type 3, whereas it is short in type 4. In type 5, inversion occurs within the line.

All five types of iambic line occur in old hymns, but there was a gradual development which resulted in either the disappearance or restructuring of inversion. Internal inversion, type 5, disappeared and so did type 4. The situation in the 1850s was that the iamb occurred only in types 1 to 3. At the beginning of the 20th century, many poets adopted the practice of accepting only types 1 and 2: a stressed syllable could occur at the beginning of a line, but it had to be short. Some poets went even further and rejected inversion altogether: their iambic lines are, without exception of the first type. The development of inversion as a whole is illustrated in the diagram below, where the numbers 1-5 refer to the line types:

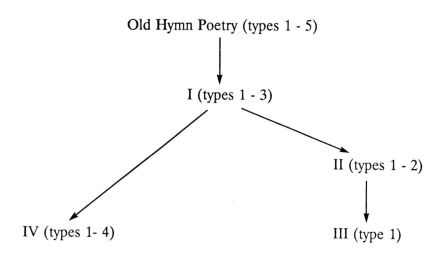

Old Hymn Poetry (types 1 - 5)

I (types 1 - 3)

II (types 1 - 2)

IV (types 1- 4)

III (type 1)

The reason for the development (I → II → III) was that the acquired loan, iambic inversion, sought to adapt itself to the language system. In these cases it is not a question of inversion proper; rather, a stressed syllable at the beginning of a line was interpreted as being non-prominent and the following syllable as prominent. From this point of view, the fairly wide-spread practice that allows only type 2 inversion is quite understandable. In fact, there are good reasons for such a practice. The intensity peak in Finnish does not always occur on the first syllable, and, in this respect, a short stressed syllable is often weaker than the following syllable. According to Sadeniemi (1949), a short stressed syllable and the following syllable generally constitute a single articulatory intensity wave with the peak usually towards the end. Lehtonen (1970) argues that the scope of stress in Finnish is not the initial syllable but the string of the first two morae (the strings CVCV, CVV and CVC(C) are dimoric), although "a Finnish person 'hears' the first short syllable as stressed even when the peaks of intonation, intensity and duration are on the second syllable of a word". On the other hand, a listener who is not bound by Finnish stress patterns hears the prominence relations differently. In Collinder's (1946) view, "a foreign speaker with a practised ear, hearing the *Sain sanat salasta ilmi* read as prose, would be inclined to regard the main stress of the word *salasta* as being on the second syllable". Collinder maintains that "in words like *salasta* the second syllable is of much greater magnitude than the first, which is only slightly more stressed, if at all".

Thus, although a Finnish speaker is accustomed to hearing word-initial syllables as prominent, the following syllable is often stronger in terms of its physical features. Prominence relations can also be heard differently, and it is this fact that underlies iambic inversion.

In other words, prominence relations in this kind of line meet the requirements of the metre. However, it is inevitable that usage is unstable, since it is based on minimally small physical differences and it is also in conflict with the perception model of a native speaker. The development has, in fact, proceeded to its logical conclusion (III), and we have now reached the position where inversion has been rejected altogether.

The other line of development (I → IV) has led in the opposite direction. There was a restructuring of metrical syntax and, consequently, iambic inversion was completely reorganized. The initial syllable of a line was no longer non-prominent but prominent; one could say that such a line began with a dactyl (previously it had begun with an ordinary iamb). Since the beginning of the 20th century, this practice has become increasingly common, and, as a result, lines of type 3 and 4 are frequently to be found in iambic verse. According to the earlier usage, then, an iambic line always began with a non-prominent syllable, either stressed or unstressed; according to the new usage the line has been restructured, and the initial syllable of the inversion line is prominent. One of the main reasons for this development is the syllable structure of the Finnish lexicon: there are too many trisyllabic words and not enough monosyllables for the requirements of the iambic line. Inversion is of crucial importance in resolving the state of tension between metre and language structure. Thus, over the centuries, iambic inversion has become a poetic convention. It would not have come into Finnish without the model of German and Swedish poetry and its present status is the result of a long developmental process.

The conventionalization of the Kalevala metre

We can assume that the Kalevala metre arose a few thousand years ago. What kind of metre was it originally?

It is evident that there was a prominent syllable at each rise of the metre. Furthermore, it is clear that the prominence relations were somewhat similar to those of modern Finnish: the most strongly prominent were long stressed syllables and these were preferred in the rise position. A short stressed syllable was weaker, but evidently its degree of prominence was also sufficient for it to occur at a rise. The metre was thus essentially similar to the modern dynamic system trochee. The following couplet would thus be in accordance with this usage:

(24)
Päivä *kuluu pilves*s*äk*in
aika *menee piik*an*ak*in.

However, since the metre was strictly syllabic, it could not have used words with an odd number of syllables at all. Allowing a short stressed syllable at a fall can be seen as a practice similar to iambic inversion, with the same linguistic justification: a short stressed syllable is not objectively stronger than the following syllable, and furthermore it was required by the structure of the lexis just as iambic inversion was. In the Kalevala metre the development of this usage was greatly facilated by the fact that the poems were sung, for in singing the correspondence requirements between metre and language are usually more lenient than in spoken poetry. Lines like the following were thus also acceptable:

(25)
Kaikki *kaunihit* ko*t*ona,
Iha*nat* is*än* maj*ass*a.

The practice which thus emerged became so far conventionalized that in some areas the convention developed over the centuries into a norm. The metre became more stable and adjusted itself to the demands of the language: polysyllables with long or short initial syllables could be placed in a balanced way throughout the line.

In modern Finnish poetry, too, there is a very marked preference for a long stressed syllable at a metric rise. About 65% of words in a prose text begin with a long syllable, but in the work of many poets as many as 90% of the syllables occurring at a rise are long (Leino 1986). This tendency is also evident in the Kalevala metre. Together with the syllabic basis of the metre and the phonological structure of the vocabulary, it led to a short stressed syllable occurring with increasing frequency in a fall position, until the tendency gradually gave rise to a new norm: a short stressed syllable could only occur at a fall.

In time, the syllable number requirements of the line were relaxed – as also in the dynamic system – as far as was possible without breaking the metre, and two syllables became permissible on the first fall. The development towards asyllabicity had begun.

In this view the Kalevala metre for centuries displayed tendencies which were also to be observed in the modern dynamic system. The most important of these was the preference for a long stressed syllable on a rise. Together with the syllabicity of the metre and the phonological structure of the lexis, this tendency led inevitably to a situation where a short stressed syllable was increasingly placed on a fall, until gradually there emerged a new norm, a new metrical convention.

The canonized syllable structure rules of the Kalevala metre are not possible for a metre with a varying number of syllables, such as the trochee-dactyl, and they would scarcely hold good even in the iambus, with its initial fall. In the trochee, too, they need a fixed tetrameter line schema. The broken line was a stylistic innovation which was the result of hundreds of years of development, and was much more significant metrically than iambic inversion: it radically increased the scope for rhytmical variation,

Varahvontta Lesonen, expert in Karelian language and culture, from Venehjärvi. Archangel Karelia. Photo: I.K. Inha 1894 (FLS 9915).

without however breaking the uniformity of the metre. In addition, it was based on the contrast between long and short syllables, i.e. a clear and linguistically significant phonological opposition, which gave it permanence. The trochaic tetrameter of the dynamic system has a much more monotonous rhythm, and it cannot exploit the vocabulary of the language to anything like the same extent. It has in fact only survived because the metrical system permits a different kind of variation: the poet is not bound to a single metre alone, but can make use of a variety of stanzas and lines, and switch from trochee to iambus or from a syllabic metre to one with a varying syllable number.

According to this reconstruction the complex relation between metre and language in the Kalevala metre is the result of a long historical process during which the metre gradually developed and established its conventions. The Kalevala metre can be described as a synchronic system, but the "understanding" of this system requires a knowledge of its historical background. This in itself is not surprising, since there are many other language phenomena of the same kind. In morphology, for example, the relation between the invariant (the morpheme) and its variants (allomorphs) may be equally conventionalized; in general, however, it can be shown that behind the complex morphophonemic correspondence relations of the modern language there lies a straightforward and natural system of an earlier date, which has gradually developed into its present form.

The decline of the Kalevala metre

The Kalevala metre began to develop its own metrical syntax, perhaps partly influenced by the tunes it was sung to. The couplet became the canonical type for proverbs, and sequences of four lines were common in lyric poems and lullabies. Yet these were simply additive combinations of lines, as the metrical system lacked the means to create a stanza structure. The fixed line did not allow the final metrical position to be occupied by a pause, nor could rhyme become a stanza-structuring factor, partly because of the syllable structure rules.

Thus, the metre was in this respect a uniform one, but the norms governing its use varied, as did the stylistic aims of individual poets. According to what is known of the metre, its usage, and its variations, it behaved in the same way as the modern Finnish metrical system. However, its internal structure made certain changes possible and others impossible, but it gradually refined itself to correspond with the structure of the language. The use of the metre has revealed tendencies and individual variations determined by both metrical considerations and language, and these have obviously been partly stylistic. The essence of the Kalevala metre was, after all, the creative use of language – poetry. And the folk poets, at least the best ones, sought to avoid automatization and looked for new ways of expression, just as their successors did in the 19th and 20th centuries.

Metrical usage varied in different areas because of linguistic differences, too, and it is fairly probable that Estonian, where words are of a shorter average length than in Finnish, never introduced into its *regivärss*, the Estonian equivalent of the Kalevala metre, a convention which would prevent a short stressed syllable from occurring on a rise. Gradual linguistic changes eroded the basis of both the Kalevala metre and *regivärss*. The process of change varied in different language and dialect areas, but, without exeption, the general direction has been the same – a drift towards the modern dynamic metre system.

The Kalevala metre became conventionalized over the centuries, and as a metrical system it grew to be unproductive. It only recognized a single actual metre and was unable to develop it further or create new ones. It was like an animal species which had evolved so far that it had become perfectly adapted to its environment. Yet it had become too specialized; when the environment changed it was no longer capable of adjusting to the changes, and so its place was taken by a new fitter species. This kind of development does not affect metrics alone, but similar cases are easy to find e.g. in morphology: an originally productive process becomes congealed and conventionalized; it is gradually displaced by a new productive process, leaving in the language only a number of irregular forms which also fade away in time.

Most of the poetry in the Kalevala metre is in the form of song. From at least the 16th century onwards, in addition to the Kalevala songs, new tunes and, with them, new rhytmical patterns began to spread. Rhyme and metrical pause at the end of a line have come to give structure to the verse. Thus, in this way, verse structure or metrical syntax has developed. The most decisive change, however, was the gradual weakening of the syllabic basis, which undermined rule 2 of the Kalevala metre. A major role has also been played by sound changes in the language, which upset the equilibrium between metre and language. In 18th and 19th century poetry written in the Kalevala metre, rule 2 has, in fact, become more relaxed: a short stressed syllable can occur at both a fall and a rise.

It is evident that a further significant factor was the change from an orally based culture to a written one. Matti Kuusi (see pp. 41; 1978, 209) argues convincingly that the language of the Kalevala was a register parallel to that of the written language. As he puts it, "Kalevala metre was a code for comitting texts to memory". The Kalevala metre contributed to the preservation of these culturally significant texts of the oral tradition, and as an mnemonic aid it had indeed developed into an optimal form. The metre helped to keep the texts alive, and the fixed texts themselves served to preserve the metre: it could not disappear or change because it was protected by tradition. Only when the written language entered the culture, with written documents replacing memorized knowledge, did the Kalevala metre lose its major function and it began to be displaced. It is scarcely a coincidence that the decline of the metre occurred during the same period that saw the birth and development of written Finnish literature; if the reasons for the decline had been no more than changes in the language itself, it would have disappeared much earlier. It was first stifled by the written culture in the more developed urban areas; it survived much longer in remote country areas, but it ultimately disappeared there as well. The Kalevala metre would have disappeared completely if Elias Lönnrot had not brought out his *Kalevala*. Its publication made the metre canonical in written poetry and established a normative rule: the placing of a short stressed syllable became a question of prescriptive grammar. It was considered incorrect to put such a syllable on a rise, it definitely had to be placed on a fall. The metre thus became an independent archaic register of 20th century Finnish metrics. It owes its existence to a long historical development: it could never have arisen spontaneously in modern Finnish poetry.

Kalevala metre and the Finnish metrical system

The Finnish metrical system cannot be traced back further than the Kalevala system with any certainty. The Kalevala system completely overturned the previously existing system (and presumably there was one). The situation may have been caused by that typical factor of language change, a loan. Either on the basis of a Baltic model, or independently, there emerged a syllabic line with a rhythm determined by the placing of stressed (prominent) syllables. It is not entirely clear what kind of prominence or syllable structure rules existed at that stage; as the language changed they did too, in various ways, and at least at the present time it is not sure whether this variation derived from a completely uniform source structure, and if so, what it looked like. One structural element in the new metre was alliteration, which increased the cohesion of the line and also served to mark word boundaries when the poems were sung.

Alongside the Kalevala metre new metres then developed, for the most part apparently based on Germanic models but also Slavonic ones in the east. They seem to have had a simple stanza structure corresponding to the tune, and the placing of syllables in metrical positions was determined by lexical stress or prominence. With this change asyllabic metres also began to emerge, with a varying syllable number on the fall and a stanza structure based on rhyme, which reduced alliteration to a mere stylistic feature (still used by many modern poets working within the dynamic system). Outside sung poetry there are also clear examples of the Kalevala and later metres in spoken poetry: proverbs, riddles, set phrases, magic spells, etc.

The modern dynamic metre system certainly did not arise from nowhere to take the place of the Kalevala system, but developed on the basis of this latter system, largely shaped by influences from outside. This view is supported by the common occurence of songs in an intermediate form in the 17th and 18th centuries (Asplund 1981, 67-68). These are obvious transitional forms between the Kalevala and dynamic systems; they are no longer the strict trochaic tetrameter of the Kalevala system, rhyme is used alongside alliteration, and many have a stanza structure. Fundamentally, then, the relation between the Kalevala and dynamic systems is a diachronic one: they represent different stages of the Finnish metrical system as a whole.[7]

A modern Finnish reader does not perceive the Kalevala metre as trochaic. Of course, the normal lines are clearly trochaic, but the "broken" lines are quite different: they contain a mixture of trochees and dactyls, and generally they have only three prominent syllables. In Eino Leino's stanza (22) five of the ten verses are pure trochee and would fit a trochaic poem in the modern Finnish metrical system, (exept the first one, which begins with a dactyl). (The symbol + marks a prominent syllable and o a non-prominent one.)

(26) Tuo oli tytti Päivölässä	+ oo + o + o + o
(27) Iha=lempi, maammon impi	+ o + o + o + o
(28) Läksi veikko vieremähän	+ o + o + o + o
(29) "Kunne sorruit kurja sisko?" –	+ o + o + o + o
(30) Poika soille portahaksi	+ o + o + o + o

The other five lines are broken ones; described in accordance with the modern system, and on the basis of speech, their prominence relations are as follows:

(31) mansikka hyvien maiden	+ oo + oo + o
(32) Herran lehtojen hedelmä	+ o + oo + o +
(33) meni karjahan kesällä	+ o + oo + o +
(34) ei tullut takaisin tytti	o + o + oo + o
(35) Hiidet virvoja viritti. –	+ o + oo + o +

On the basis of speech, lines 32, 33, and 35 ending in a short syllable could also be described as ending in a non-prominent syllable (+ o + oo + oo); the short stressed syllable at the beginning of line 33 could also be non-prominent. The examples show that the broken lines have varying rhythms: the number of prominent syllables in the line varies, the intervals may contain one or two non-prominent syllables, and the line may even begin with an unprominent syllable. The variation also extends to pure trochee lines: the first fall in a pure trochee line may be disyllabic, as in line 26.

Nevertheless, the basic trochaic nature of the metre is still evident: a stressed syllable must be long if it is the third, fifth, or seventh syllable in the line, it must be short if it is the fourth or sixth syllable in the line. (Lines with two syllables on the first fall are disregarded.) Although the lines are based on the same trochaic metre, there is a great deal of variation in their rhythm. This variation, however, is not unrestricted. With the exception on the first line quoted above, each line has eight syllables, which are by no means free to occupy any position: the placing of a stressed syllable is determined by its length. This fact has kept the Kalevala metre alive for hundreds, even thousands, of years; and it is a guarantee that the Kalevala metre will continue to maintain its special status alongside the metric system of modern Finnish.

NOTES

This article is based on a lecture given at Copenhagen University in 1985 in honour of the 150th anniversary of the *Kalevala*. The lecture is appeared in English under the title *The Structure and Development of the Kalevala Metre*, in *Det finske Kalevala. Rapport fra Kalevala-symposiet i København den 17.-18. mai 1985*. S. Kroman (ed.). København. 1985. p. 23-43.

1. A good general picture of epic folk poems in the Kalevala metre, together with their background, is to be found in the translated selection *Finnish Folk Poetry: Epic* (Kuusi - Bosley – Branch 1977), which contains a detailed commentary.
2. On the Kalevala metre and its origin see eg. Krohn 1924, 66-69; Kuusi 1963, 133-135; Kuusi 1978; Kuusi – Tedre 1979; Leino 1974; Leino 1986; Niemi 1918; Paasonen 1897, 75-78; Sadeniemi 1951.

3. For the winnowing principle and its influence in Kalevala poetry and the Finnish language in general, see Sadeniemi 1951, 30-37.
4. For detailed studies of alliteration in Kalevala poetry see Sadeniemi 1951, 79-113; Leino 1970.
5. Kõrv 1928, 15; Leino 1975, 34; Paukson 1930, 446; Sadeniemi 1951, 40-43.
6. For a more detailed description see Leino 1986, 93-105.
7. It is to be noted that Estonian, starting from the same Kalevala metre, *regivärss*, has developed exactly the same metre systems as Finnish. In written poetry *regivärss* is an archaic register, and the durational and syllabic metres survive in foreign models. In Estonian too, the productive metre in modern language is the dynamic one. See Põldmäe 1978.

74

MIKKO KORHONEN

The Early History of the Kalevala Metre

In the following article I wish to take a look at some of the problems surrounding the origin and early development of the metre used in ancient Finnish folk poetry: Kalevala metre. I shall in particular be trying to determine the relationship between Kalevala metre and the metres used in Mordvin folk poetry, the Baltic influence on the development of Kalevala metre, and the linguistic conditions for the emergence of Kalevala metre. My problems are not, therefore, new ones. Some may consider that there is nothing more to be said on the subject, that they are of no scientific interest and impossible to solve (cf. Leino 1985a, 395-396). It may on the other hand be claimed that so far research into the early history of Kalevala metre has not exploited all the linguistic-historical material that is available, to say nothing of delving deep into the history of Finnish metre as part of the development of Finnish prosody. Yet according to the widely accepted view, the metres that may be used by a given language and the suitability of a particular metre to a particular language depend primarily on the prosodic structure of the language in question. Admittedly, the further back we go in time, the more we are faced with the problem that we do not possess any direct knowledge about the prosody of the linguistic periods prior to Proto-Finnic. Scholars have, however, been able to reconstruct their phoneme system and phonotaxis right back as far as Proto-Uralic.[1] Using our knowledge of phonology, we can also draw certain conclusions regarding prosody. By applying the history of Finnish metre to the history of the Finnish language it might even be possible to obtain, if not certainty about the origin of Kalevala metre, then at least some additional arguments to add to the debate surrounding it.

The metric system of Mordvin folk poetry

Songs beyond the Kalevala
Studia Fennica
Folkloristica 2
1994

The idea of the joint origin of the Mordvin eight-syllable metre and Kalevala metre was put forward by Heikki Paasonen in a paper on Baltic-Finnic poetry, *Itäsuomalaisten kansojen runoudesta* in 1897. In addition to the eight-syllable line, the Mordvin poetry examined by Paasonen was also marked by a caesura in the middle of the line, parallelism, and a slight tendency towards alliteration. These features inevitably call to mind Kale-vala metre. Paasonen later made a second thorough analysis of the line structure of Mordvin poetry in an article entitled *Über den Versbau des mordwinischen Volkslieds* (1911). It appears from this analysis, based on a broad corpus of material, that the line in Mordvin folk songs has 7-17 syllables. The lines of one poem are, however, equal in the number of syllables. Each line is divided rhythmically into two or more parts so that, for example, 7-syllable lines are made up of two parts, the first with four and the second with three syllables. There are two types of eight-syllable lines, one with 4+4 syllables and the other with 5+3. And there are three sub-categories of, say, 12-syllable lines: 4+4+4, 4+5+3, and 5+4+3. The internal line division remains the same throughout the poem; in other words, all the lines may be of the type 5+4+3. A certain amount of deviation is, it seems, permitted both in the number of syllables in the line and in the internal division; according to my observations more so in Moksha than in Erzya, and especially in the laments and wedding songs of both dialects.

In Mordvin, the metre based on eight-syllable lines is thus just one among many and admittedly rather common, though according to Paasonen not the most common. In his assessment poems with 10-syllable lines are the most numerous.

In his article Paasonen no longer mentions the affinity between the Mordvin metres and Kalevala metre. He does, however, conclude that the Mordvin metric system is of Slavic origin. This conclusion may seem surprising in view of the fact that the Russians, who might be the most likely lenders, appear to lack a syllabic metre. Paasonen does in fact compare Mordvin poetry to Belorussian, discovering there counterparts to the majority of the Mordvin metres. He does in certain cases present a Russian parallel, too, though nevertheless admitting that they are excep-tions in this language area. Since it is highly unlikely that the Belorussians ever lived so close to the Mordvins as to influence their metres directly, Paasonen concludes that the southern Russians acted as mediators. In other words, the Belorussian syllabic metre would have spread to the southern Russians and from them to the Mordvins. According to Paasonen this would probably have taken place in the 17th century or the beginning of the 18th at the latest. His view of the Russian origin of the Mordvin metric system was later endorsed by N.S. Trubetzkoy (Trubetzkoy 1921, 187), but he considered the Belorussian influence as improbable on historical and geographical grounds.

Paasonen's loan theory calls forth certain questions. If syllabic metres were so predominant among the southern Russians that they could have engendered a corresponding metric system in Mordvin, how could they have all but vanished without trace by the end of the 19th century, i.e. in just on 200 years? If the syllabic metric system did not take root in Mordvin until the 17th century, or maybe the early 18th century, how could it already have spread evenly throughout the area in which both the main dialects were spoken by the 19th century? This seems incredible in view of the linguistic difference between Erzya and Moksha Mordvin.

The possibility of Russian influence was in fact rejected by Roman Jakobson and John Lotz in their article *Axiomatik eines Verssystems am mordwinischen Volkslied dargelegt* (1941), in which they present the

Mordvin metric system as a model example of a logical axiomatic system observing a strict structure. In their opinion such a highly-developed, regular system could not have come into existence as the result of late outside influence.

Paasonen's loan theory does not therefore sound convincing. But if the Mordvin metric system is not a Russian loan, could it after all be possible that both it and Kalevala metre have their origin in some ancient shared proto-system? Could the roots of these metres be traced back even to the Finnish-Volgan proto-language? Paavo Ravila, among others, considered the link between Kalevala metre and the 8-syllable Mordvin metre more likely than the link with the metre of Kalevala and Latvian folk songs (1935, 38).

The only features which Kalevala metre and the Mordvin metres have in common are that in both the number of syllables in the line is decisive – 8 in Kalevala metre and 7-17 in the Mordvin metres – and that they both use parallelism and alliteration, though the tendency is only slight in Mordvin. If they had a shared Baltic-Finnic/Mordvin proto-form, it would presumably be some syllabic metric system. We would then have to try to answer the question of whether the prosodic system of the Finnish-Volgan or, to be more precise, the Baltic-Finnic/Lappish/Mordvin proto-language was such that the appearance of a syllabic metric system in it could be considered likely.

The dependence of the metric system on the prosodic system of the language

Many scholars have noted that languages tend to develop and favour metric systems that suit their prosodic structure (see e.g. Sapir 1958 (1921), 230; Schmitt 1924, Sadeniemi 1949, 16-21; Lotz 1960; Leino 1982, 326-327). Metres based on the number of syllables in the line are therefore characteristic of languages in which the stress, sonority and length of the syllables are not significant, a typical example being Japanese, whereas dynamic metres are favoured by languages in which the stressed syllables are clearly distinct from the unstressed ones and in which stress is a linguistically relevant feature, as in the Germanic languages and Russian. Correspondingly, a tonal metre demands that the language has a tone system, and a durational metre can only exist in a language where the length of the syllable is relevant. Naturally the structure of certain languages may, furthermore, permit several metres, while that of others makes the use of certain metres quite impossible. The tendency to seek out the metres best suited to the language presumably applies primarily to oral folklore. Literary poets, who are as a rule more or less familiar with the structures and potentials of various metres, may consciously experiment with any number of different poetic metres. Thus all the metric systems mentioned here have been applied to modern Finnish with the exception of the tonal one (cf. Leino 1979, 304-309; 1982, 20). It may be mentioned in passing that metric typology has so far been granted little attention as a branch of linguistics. A study should be made of a broad, typologically, geographically and genetically representative selection of the world's languages to determine

The boat shore of Venehjärvi. Vuokkiniemi. Photo: Samuli Paulaharju 1915 (FLS 5440).

what metres are possible in what languages, which are the popular ones and which are impossible, with primary reference to folklore. An investigation such as this would provide a far sounder basis than at present for debating the relationship between a metric system and the other language systems, the history of poetic metres and the part played by linguistic interaction in the development of metric systems, and possibly for creating some sort of implicative hierarchy of metric systems and metres.

We can in any case regard, on the basis of the research already conducted, as obvious that syllable timed languages, i.e. languages in which the basic units in the speech rhythm are syllables, favour syllabic metres, whereas stress timed languages, in which the speech rhythm is dictated by stress maxima, tend towards dynamic metres.

Our problem is thus the relationship between Kalevala metre and the Mordvin metres. Kalevala metre is basically syllabic, but the location in the line of the syllables bearing the main stress also depends on the length of the syllables. Kalevala metre could thus be called syllabic-dynamic-durational. This system was well suited to late Proto-Finnic and to certain Baltic-Finnic dialects that followed directly from it, in which the length of the syllable bearing the main stress was relevant. On the other hand, word stress was in these language forms, as in the majority of the Baltic-Finnic languages even today, of such slight linguistic relevance that they can under no circumstances be regarded as stress timed. The syllabic basis of Kalevala metre is thus natural in the extreme.

Of the main present-day dialects of Mordvin, or of the Mordvin languages, Erzya is prosodically one of the most typical languages favouring a syllabic metric system. Word stress is grammatically totally irrelevant in it, there is no quantitative correlation between the vowels, and the syllables are prosodically equal regardless of where they occur in a word. Erzya is thus a syllable timed language, so that syllabic metres are only to be expected in it. In Moksha, by contrast, the main stress in a word is determined according to the sonorous relationships between the vowels and may appear on syllables other than the first. The stress can in principle be predicted from the vowel relations in a word. Certain vowel oppositions have become neutralised in an unstressed syllable, and the vowels of stressed syllables may seem slightly longer than those of unstressed syllables. In no way is Moksha thus a purely stress timed language in the manner of Erzya. Yet the syllabic metric system has also become established in Moksha.

As Paavo Ravila (1929) and Erkki Itkonen (1946) have demonstrated, the vowel systems of modern Erzya and Moksha are best explained by starting with the system prevailing in the final stage of Proto-Mordvin, which was prosodically closer to modern Moksha than to Erzya. Late Proto-Mordvin thus had a shifting dynamic accent with reduced vowels in the unstressed syllables. These characteristics by no means point to a purely syllable timed language. The origin of the Mordvin syllabic metres is thus anything but unproblematic. Nothing can at this stage be said about it without detailed further research. The following explanations are in the nature of working hypotheses:

1. The syllabic metric system emerged at a stage in the development of Proto-Mordvin in which even the unstressed syllables were prosodically relatively independent, i.e. the language was syllable timed or at least not purely stress timed. It is at the moment uncertain whether such an evolutionary stage can be assumed.

2. The syllabic metric system was assimilated into Mordvin from some foreign language. It is, however, presumably necessary to seek some period before the 17th-18th century, which is when Paasonen concluded that Mordvin borrowed metres from Russian.

3. The syllabic metres first developed in Erzya, which, being a syllable timed language, is naturally suited to them, and from there they were taken up by Moksha.

4. The syllabic metric system came into being even before Proto-Mordvin, i.e. at the proto-language stage to which Baltic-Finnic can be traced.

I here wish to gloss over the first three explanations and concentrate on the fourth, which is worthy of attention in trying to determine whether Kalevala metre could be akin to the Mordvin metres.

Pre-Finnic prosody

We must therefore ask whether the prosodic system of the joint Baltic-Finnic and Mordvin proto-language was such that it lent itself naturally to syllabic metres. By drawing on research into the history of phonetics, we can outline the prosodic system of this linguistic form as follows:

1. The main stress was always on the first syllable of a word. The other syllables were unstressed.

2. Phoneme opposition of the short and long vowels occurred in the syllable bearing the main stress in the cases /i/-/ī/, /u/-/ū/, /e/-/ē/ and /o/-/ō/; only short vowels occurred in other syllables.

3. Seven qualitatively different vowel phonemes occurred in the first syllable, and allowing for quantity correlation, eleven different vowel phonemes:

i	ü	u		ī	ū
e		o		ē	ō
ä	a				

It is assumed that only three different vowel phonemes occurred in the subsequent syllables:

	e				i
ä	a	or	ä	a	

Of these three, the functional load of the opposition /ä/-/a/ was, because of vowel harmony, extremely rare. In the second syllable these vowels were in opposition to one another only when the first syllable contained /i/. In the third and subsequent syllables the opposition /ä/-/a/ was always neutralised. The assumption concerning the tripartite vowel system of the subsequent syllables in principle has two weaknesses: the inverted vowel triangle and the extremely low functional load of the loose pair of vowels. It is thus justifiable to assume the opposition of two vowels in the subsequent syllables:

i

a (phonetically possibly |ə – à]

One feature of this two- or three-phoneme system is that the field of distribution of each phoneme is wide and the phonemes are realised to a greater or lesser extent as reductions.

4. It was more common for a stressed syllable than an unstressed syllable to end with a consonant. Combinations of consonants thus appeared more frequently and in greater diversity on the border between the first and second syllables than in other syllable positions.

The signs clearly point to a stress timed language. The prosody of the Baltic-Finnic/Lappish/Mordvin proto-language and its earlier predecessors seems to have been marked by a sharp contrast between the stressed and the other syllables. Secondary stress cannot be assumed to have had any linguistic relevance in this system. Bringing out the numerous vowel oppositions in the stressed syllables, the quantity correlation and the consonant combinations following the first syllable must have called for careful articulation and great articulation energy, whereas the other syllables required a minimum of articulation and energy. Although we have no direct knowledge of the prosody of these early linguistic stages, everything indicates that the linguistic forms preceding early Proto-Finnic as far away even as Proto-Uralic must have strongly favoured word stress concentrating on the first syllable. The dominant status of the first syllable in bearing the stress of the word is clearly manifest in the vowel history of the Uralic languages: the vowels in the other syllables have in most languages either been lost or reduced. They are best preserved in Baltic-Finnic and Lappish, but here too the vowel system of the subsequent syllables has undergone thorough change.

The prosodic structure of the joint Baltic-Finnic and Mordvin proto-language was thus such that it could not easily accommodate a syllabic metre founded on prosodic equality of the syllables. If there was any metric poetry in that language or in any of its predecessors, even as far away as Proto-

A family in Vuonninen. Photo: Samuli Paulaharju 1915 (FLS 5424).

Uralic, it in all probability used a dynamic metric system: always a rising syllable bearing the main stress followed by one or more falling unstressed syllables, as in the Great Russian *bylina*, for example.[2] If the joint proto-language of Finnish and Mordvin did not lend itself to syllabic metres, neither Kalevala metre nor the metres of modern Mordvin can be traced back – at least directly – to this proto-language and must be regarded as having developed independently of one another. Whatever the origin of the Mordvin metric system, it is unlikely to have emerged before Proto-Mordvin. A lot of late syncope and apocope has taken place in Moksha in particular, thereby reducing the syllable count. Despite this, the lines of songs keep very closely to the syllable count demanded by the metre. Could this possibly indicate that the metric system is only recent?

The linguistic conditions for Kalevala metre in turn probably came about in Proto-Finnic with the renewal of the vowel system in the second and subsequent syllables, as the growing vowel opposition in the second and subsequent syllables reduced the prosodic contrast between the stressed and other syllables. The first event in this evolution was probably the development of the rounded vowel in subsequent syllables out of the combination of a non-rounded vowel and *v* in early Proto-Finnic (E. Itkonen 1954), later stages included the increasing functional load of the /a/-/ä/ opposition in the second syllable as /a/ became possible after an /e/ (words such as *mela*, *kela*) and more and more frequently after /i/ in the first syllable; a further development was the oppositions /i/ – /e/, /o/ – /u/ and /u/ – /ü/ in the subsequent syllables. At the end of the late Proto-Finnic era the same short vowels appeared as phonemes in the subsequent syllables as in the first syllable, with the possible exception of /ö/. Diphthongs ending in /i/ also appeared. Articulating the later syllables now demanded more energy and care. The prosodic contrast between the syllable bearing the main stress and the other syllables was lessened. It is to the beginning of

81

this development that we can attribute the rise in secondary stress as a factor of linguistic relevance characteristic of Baltic-Finnic and Lappish. As a result of it speech fell into feet of one, two or three syllables. Words with four or more syllables consisted of two or more feet. The traces of this development appear to be very uniform in Baltic-Finnic and Lappish. Also indicating the prosodic significance of the subsequent syllables is the appearance of consonant gradation, at least as a phonetic tendency, in early Proto-Finnic already.

Baltic loan?

It may thus be assumed that the prosodic conditions for the emergence of the basically syllabic Kalevala metre were not created until the changes in early and middle Proto-Finnic outlined above. Now, did the Finns borrow any models from the Balts? Since it was pointed out by A.R. Niemi, in his exhaustive study of 1918 that the metre of Latvian folk songs and Kalevala metre resemble one another, thus leading to the conclusion that the Baltic Finns assimilated the metre of their ancient songs from the Balts, the question of the origin of Kalevala metre has generally been regarded as solved. Differences of opinion have arisen mainly over the strength of Baltic influence on the evolution of Kalevala metre. Few opposing views have been put forward. Of these, I have already mentioned the view of Ravila (1935), according to which Kalevala metre is related to the Mordvin metres rather than to those of the Balts. Pentti Leino, who was at one time (1982, 323) inclined to support the Baltic theory, has subsequently (1985, 396) adopted a skeptical attitude to the chances of verifying the origin of Kalevala metre as being either this or that. It is in my opinion nevertheless worth trying to assess the assumption of the Baltic origin of Kalevala metre on the basis of what we know from linguistic history of the contacts between the Baltic Finns and the Balts.

If the model for Kalevala metre was taken from the Balts, it would be most natural for it to coincide with the strong Baltic influence on Proto-Finnic. This would account for not only the numerous old Baltic loan words in Baltic-Finnic but also certain structural changes in Proto-Finnic, such as various phonetic changes (Posti 1953), the change in distribution of the partitive and accusative object (Kont 1963; Larsson 1981) and the birth of congruence in the adjectival attribute (Kalima 1936, 197). We may deduce from the distribution of the loan words and the phonetic changes taking place in them that the Baltic contacts probably date from just before the end of the early Proto-Finnic era and ended well before the end of the late Proto-Finnic era. The phonetic structure of the loan words indicates that the source language was Proto-Baltic or some other closely related language. Of the present Baltic languages, Lithuanian resembles the assumed source language more than Latvian, which has during its isolated history undergone more changes than Lithuanian. On the other hand Latvian alone has a poetic metre that may be conjectured as the model for Kalevala metre. In it the line consists of four two-syllable feet divided into two dipodies separated by a caesura. The second foot of the dipody may be represented by one long syllable, and the stanza usually has four lines.[3] For example

Man ka/sina // veenu / ragu. (Normal trochee: 2+2 // 2+2)
Masa/jam // kamba/ri. (2+1 // 2+1)
(Niemi 1918, 14)

The Lithuanian songs differ greatly from the Latvian. They use numerous metres, none of which are directly comparable to the metre of the Latvian *daina* quoted above (see Niemi 1913; Senkus 1957). Kazimieras Senkus assumes that the oldest stratum of Lithuanian poetry is represented by a song type in which both the metre and the number of syllables in a line is very free, and that does not adhere to any particular stanza structure (ibid. 164).

If called upon to find in the Baltic languages the poetic metre that best represented something called Proto-Baltic, it would seem natural to find it in Lithuanian, which has preserved the Proto-Baltic accentuation system and is in other respects, too, very archaistic. In Latvian, by contrast, the stress has become established on the first syllable of a word, possibly under the influence of the Baltic-Finnic languages, as has been assumed. It does not seem credible that Latvian should have preserved the Proto-Baltic prosody despite the great changes that took place in it, and so much so that Lithuanian, which is in other respects more archaistic, should have lost the old metric system. On the contrary, it would be more natural to imagine that not until the main stress became established on the first syllable could the trochaic metre emerge in Latvian. This being the case, the metre of the Latvian *daina* should be regarded as an innovation taking place during the separate evolution of the Latvian language. Could it then be possible that a relatively late and restricted innovation such as this could have been taken up by Baltic-Finnic poetry and spread across Estonia, Finland and Karelia? No other specifically Latvian feature has achieved such widespread distribution. Latvian did have a strong influence on Livonian, and a certain number of fairly recent Latvian words are to be found in Estonian, but not in the other Baltic-Finnic languages (see Kalima 1936, 49; Suhonen 1973). It seems incredible that the Latvian metric system should have crossed borders not traversed by any other linguistic structure or element.

The concept of the Baltic origin of Kalevala metre thus comes up against serious problems of timing and distribution. If we insist on seeking some kind of influence, then it would be more natural to suggest that the metre of the Latvian *daina* is of Baltic-Finnic origin. Baltic-Finnic influence is, after all, otherwise manifest in Latvian in many ways, as loan words and possibly also in prosody, namely the fixing of the stress on the first syllable of the word.

The words *virsi* and *kannel*, thought to be of Baltic origin, are regarded as indirect proof of the Baltic origin of Kalevala metre, too. Since the words for such basic concepts in Kalevala-metric poetry are borrowed, then why not the metre of the songs? The weight of these words as evidence is, however, reduced by the fact that their Baltic origin is not beyond dispute. The Finnish etymological dictionary equips both words with a question mark. According to Eino Nieminen, connecting the word *virsi* with its Baltic counterpart is sheer speculation (1945, 527; 1957, 195 note 3). What makes the etymology problematic is the fact that the Baltic word, Lithuanian *vařdas* 'name', Latvian *vàrds* 'word, speech, promise, name', Ancient

Large two-storied Karelian houses which provided shelter for cattle as well as people and which were decorated with Novgorodian traditional symbols caught the attention of the rune collectors. Photo: A. Berner 1872 (FLS 9356).

Prussian *wīrds* 'word' has of old contained an *a* in its second syllable; Baltic-Finnic *virsi* in turn has an *e*-stem. Furthermore, only Ancient Prussian has an *i* in the first syllable, Lithuanian and Latvian an *a*, which cannot be *a* counterpart to Baltic-Finnic *i*. On the other hand Jorma Koivulehto has observed that the Baltic-Finnic words with *rt* as their stem consonants are usually either loan words or old derivatives with a consonant stem (1979). This observation also supports the assumption that the word *virsi* is of foreign origin. No other etymology has been presented for the word. The Baltic-Finnic word *kannel, kantele* has in turn been regarded not only as a Baltic loan word but also as indigenous, in which case Lithuanian *kañkles*, Latvian *kuõkle* '*kantele*' could be Baltic-Finnic loans. To my mind nothing prevents us from assuming that both *kannel* and the other ancient word for an instrument, *kannus*, Lappish *govdes*, Kildinian Lappish *kūmdes* 'shaman's drum' could also be derivatives of the early Proto-Finnic word **komta* 'lid' or its extension, and thus indigenous. The words *virsi* and *kannel* are not, therefore, unproblematic Baltic loans in the sense that they may be used to draw any conclusions on the origin of Kalevala metre. And even if their Baltic origin should be confirmed, their weight of evidence in favour of Kalevala metre would be slight in view of the fact that there does not seem to be any suitable temporal or local source in the Baltic countries for Kalevala metre.

The phonetic evolution of Proto-Finnic – a condition for Kalevala metre

The birth of Kalevala metre does not to my mind require any explanation based on foreign influence. The phonetic changes in Proto-Finnic and the accompanying prosodic changes created sufficient conditions for the spontaneous emergence of a new metric system. It would seem to be impossible to determine whether the new metric system emerged alongside some old, possibly dynamic metric system, pushing it aside because it was better suited to the prosody of the language, or whether some old metre was gradually transformed. The general opinion seems to be that the oldest form of Kalevala metre is represented by the pure trochaic line of the type

> Itse / laulan / milloin / kuulen.
> Vaka / vanha / Väinä/möinen.

The broken tetrameter, likewise the rules for the length of the syllable bearing the main stress, would have developed later. (Cf. Kuusi 1978; Leino 1974, 1985a.) This order is logical if we work on the premise that the model for the Kalevala line was taken from the Baltic trochaic line. If, however, we reject, or at least strongly doubt the concept of the Baltic origin of Kalevala metre, we are then free to interpret the historical relationships of the different variants of Kalevala metre – the "dialects of Kalevala language", as Matti Kuusi would say – in a new way, and new perspectives would at the same time be opened up on the evolution of Kalevala metre itself. I should now like to propose just one alternative scenario of how Kalevala metre could have developed if it were the organic continuation of some older metric tradition.

As I have said before, if some regular poetic metre existed in Proto-Finnic or one of its preceding phases before Kalevala metre, then it was probably a falling dynamic metre with the syllable bearing the (main) stress on the rise and one or more syllables on the fall; in addition to stress, the length of the syllable and even its sonority may have been factors creating prominence. For the rhythmic regularity to be realised in performing the song, the more syllables that have to be fitted into the fall, the shorter the individual fall syllables must on average be. This "isochronous principle" is characteristic specifically of the prosody of stress timed languages and, correspondingly, of dynamic metres.[4] If the falling syllables are mainly short and do not contain any phoneme oppositions demanding careful articulation, the demand for isochronism is easy to satisfy. This was the case during the linguistic stage preceding early Proto-Finnic. But when, in Proto-Finnic, the syllables not bearing the main stress became more independent, due above all to the growth of the vowel paradigm, it was no longer as easy as it used to be to fit them all into a falling position. People could thus begin to give a song rhythm so that, if possible, there was only one syllable in each fall. The birth and strengthening of a secondary stress in the uneven syllables (except the last ones) of words with four or more syllables helped to foster the new metre. This permitted such lines consisting of two-syllable feet as

> Ruven/nenko laula/mahan.
> Sari/olan / juomin/keihin.

Making feet with one and three syllables fit into the line types demanded by the new prosody was not without its problems. Three alternatives were in principle possible:

1. Replacing the trochee if necessary by a dactyl. This is in fact what happened, on certain conditions. In "classical" Kalevala metre the first foot may contain three, sometimes even four syllables. For example

> Tuop oli / Ahti / Saare/lainen.
> Sentä ei / soita / kante/leni.

In Estonian songs this is possible in other feet, too (Andersson 1935; Kuusi 1978, 212). For example

> Mis tuli / karates / kalda/asse.
> Lehm oli /laudas / Laps oli / süles.

It would be worth investigating whether such lines could be regarded as relics of the intermediate stage when the Pre-Finnic dynamic metre was developing into Kalevala metre. Such an intermediate stage could be conjectured as a natural continuation to the fully dynamic metre, and it would further form an easy stepping stone to syllabic eight-syllable metre by also adjusting the three-syllable feet to the trochaic rhythm of *rune*-singing. This brings us to the second alternative.

2. Placing one- and three-syllable feet in an eight-syllable line and disregarding the fact that the word stress no longer follows the trochaic rhythm. For example

> Miele/ni mi/nun te/kevi.
> Suot su/lavat / maat va/luvat.

3. Replacing the four-syllable dipody if necessary by a three-syllable one, as was the case in the Latvian *daina*. This would permit such line constructions as

> Toisin / ennen, // toisin / eilen. (Normal trochee: 4+4 syllables)
> Sula/vat // sanat / suussa. (3+4 syllables)
> Sanat / suussa // sula/vat. (4+3 syllables)
> Sanat/kin // sula/vat. (3+3 syllables)

Kalevala metre did not, so far as I can see, make use of this potential, which again speaks against the Baltic origin argument. If the model had been the metre encountered in the Latvian *daina*, I would imagine that traces of it would have been found in the ancient songs of the Baltic Finns.

Against the background of the phonetic development of Proto-Finnic it is natural that the second alternative became the established practice. Due to the changes taking place in the vowels of the second and subsequent syllables, the prosodic difference between the stressed and unstressed syllables became evened out, and the statuses of the different syllables within a word became more and more equal in the prosodic sense. The language changed from being stress timed to syllable timed, or rather foot timed.[5] With this change Proto-Finnic came to favour syllabic metres. As the number of syllables in a line became fixed at eight, the only option was to fit the one- and three-syllable feet, too, into the standard-length line.

I have here dealt with only a few of the questions surrounding the early history of Kalevala metre. In my research I have come to the conclusion that the metre of the ancient songs of the Finnish people cannot have the same origin as the syllabic metres of Mordvin, that it is not of Baltic origin or the result of Baltic influence, but that it emerged as a spontaneous reaction to the phonetic and prosodic development of Proto-Finnic.

NOTES

This article is based on an earlier version in Finnish under title *Kalevalamitan varhais-historia*, which appeared in *Suomalais-ugrilaisen Seuran Aikakauskirja 81*, 1987. Helsinki. p. 175-191.

1. I shall not touch here on the reliability of these reconstructions, which I have discussed elsewhere (Korhonen 1974).
2. I cannot completely rule out the possibility that length, in addition to stress, may have influenced the metric prominence of syllables. For the syllables which we assume to have been stressed in the proto-language can be divided into several types according to vowel quantity, sonority, and whether they are open or closed. Unstressed syllables have in turn fallen into different categories according to whether they are open or closed, and their vowel sonority. Such word forms as *munan* and *mińän* (Finnish *miniän*), in which the first syllable was of the weakest possible type (a short syllable with a vowel that is short and the least sonorous possible) and a second syllable

lable of the strongest possible type (a long syllable with a vowel of the greatest sonority) may have differed greatly in their metric and prosodic status from, for example, such word forms as *sōne* (Finnish *suoni*) and *täšte* (Finnish *tähti*), in which the first syllable could not be stronger nor the second syllable weaker.
3. The Latvian metre thus differs considerably from Kalevala metre. This is the very reason why Ravila questioned the possibility of Baltic influence (1935, 38).
4. Much has been written in the literature about isochronism. Few would deny the existence of the phenomenon itself, even though its phonetic nature is a matter of controversy. For further details see, e.g. Lehiste 1977 (a good survey of recent research), 1983, 1984; Leino 1982, 278-279.
5. The term "foot timed" was used by Kalevi Wiik (in papers dealing with prosody in the Finnish language) in describing the prosodic structure of the Baltic-Finnic languages. Lappish may in the same sense be regarded as foot timed.

Performance and Variation

LAURI HARVILAHTI

The Ingrian Epic Poem and its Models

The Finnish folklorist Jouko Hautala wrote in 1945: "It is natural that the composer of a folk poem unsuspectingly and without more ado selects from his store of lines and complete verses any material that seems suited to his poem. -- Carried to extremes, this procedure means that verses can be used to construct entirely new logical entities, poems, using existing episodes like building blocks. Assisting this is the metre, which is the same for all poems." In dealing with these "existing episodes" Hautala wrote: "It is a well-known fact that there are certain stereotype poetic images that can be used in the most varied of contexts; the field covered by such images can, at least in theory, be extended to comprise all poetry."[1] Today, almost 50 years later, we might say that Hautala's concept (criticised quite heavily at the time) is quite modern.

Hautala's concept calls to mind one of the leading tenets of the oral-formulaic theory created by Milman Parry and his pupil Albert B. Lord: the performers of narrative poetry did not reproduce their poems as complete entities drawn from memory, but used instead an internalised system of poetic devices or formulaic technique providing the basic tools (formulas, themes and story patterns) for the production of folk poetry that varied from one performing situation to another (composition in performance).[2] In his study *The Singer of Tales* published in 1960 Lord presented a summary of Parry's theses and his own research.[3]

Lord's work was greeted by a mixed reception among scholars of Kalevala poetry. Some researchers have stated categorically that the formulaic technique is of no significance whatsoever to Finnish epic folk poetry[4], while others concede that formulaic thinking may well apply to some of the *Kalevala* material, and especially to lyric poetry.[5] Still others mention or present the theory of Parry and Lord but have chosen a different theoretical frame for their work and refrained from applying their theories or presenting a critique based on the analysis of materials[6], or else they have sought to launch the theory as a working hypothesis.[7]

During the thirty or more years since the work appeared, this approach, an offshoot of the research originally devoted to classical literature, has expanded into a universal school with widespread paradigms. In the late 1980s and early 1990s this approach has sought to supplement its theoretical

Songs beyond
the Kalevala
Studia Fennica
Folkloristica 2
1994

basis by exploring the potential of, among other things, folkloristic research
and cognitive science. John Miles Foley, in his bibliography *Oral-formulaic Theory and Research*, mentions over 1,800 monographs on materials
from over 90 language areas.[8] In addition to the Homeric and South Slavic
epic, the advocates of the oral-formulaic school have focused on the
Anglo-Saxon epic (Beowulf), as well as a number of other classical epics
and countless living traditions.

Within the oral-formulaic school the various definitions of the concept
of 'formula' represent a great variety of analytic levels. These levels
embrace phonetic and rhythmic, lexical, syntactic and semantic categories
and their combinations. Analyses based on limited definitions do not,
however, give an overall view of a research object but bind composition
in performance research to a system confined by formulas, themes and story
patterns.[9] The integration of various disciplines has, however, yielded some
promising results on the subject in recent years. D. Gary Miller (1987,
353-354; cf. Fry 1981) has tried to renew the theoretical basis of the
oral-formulaic school using the concepts of cognitive science, and Bruce
A. Rosenberg (1981, 447-448) has proposed that the expertise of the
socio-linguists, psycho-linguists, folklorists and cognitive psychologists
be utilized in order to solve the problems arising in the study of oral
tradition. John Miles Foley stresses the importance of each tradition's
inherent features in his comparision of Greek, South Slavic and ancient
English epic poetry. He presents an interpretative model and suggests the
factors to be borne in mind in comparing different "oral literatures" (Foley
1985, 68-70; 1988, 109-110; 1990, 5-19; 1991, 14-15). According to Foley,
formulas and story patterns function not so much as compositional conventions as cognitive immanent categories (Foley 1991, 59, 95, 252; 1992,
282). This represents a shift therefore, away from the world of grammar-like
structures and systems of compositional devices, towards a new synthesis.

The above discussion also applies to the problems arising in the study
of folkloristic variation, which has in the past few years attracted the
attention of folklorists interested in the way tradition is produced (see e.g.
Siikala 1990a, Kaivola-Bregenhøj 1985). Lauri Honko claims that the
variants in a given oral tradition were based on a functional-traditional
system (for further details see Honko 1985, 69-75; 1986, 119-120): the
background of tradition is in use and alive at the same time as the performer.
This provides a basis on which to mirror new versions. The singer does
this by drawing on her/his store of motifs within the confines of the
traditional rules and his personal competence (Harvilahti 1992, 12).

According to Lotte Tarkka the majority of poems remain within the
confines of their genre's ideal-type. On the other hand she also emphasises
the wealth of variety and the different levels of production and structuring
based on the formulaic tradition: the units in the system are not ready and
fixed but act instead as models for new ones. Referring to M. Nagler, she
underlines the associative freedom inherent in models: the formula triggers
off a network of structures based on the same model (Tarkka 1990a, 50-57).

According to my own research, epic poem production requires parallel
processing on various levels simultaneously: the activation of phonological, morphosyntactic, lexical, metrical storage and primary poetic devices.
The singer's memory is not a device for the storage of stable elements but

is a multidimensional grid.[10] The concept of formulaicity must be seen as a result of "covariation of form and meaning" (Hymes 1981, 7, 10; Briggs 1988, 10), or – representations of both surface structure and meaning structure on various levels (see Harvilahti 1992, 141-147; Foley 1991, 252; Foley 1992, 282). The following examples will, I hope, illustrate these claims. But before analysing them, let us take a quick look at the background to the Ingrian poetry tradition.

Soikkola in W. Ingria – the last intact poetic culture of narrative Kalevala poetry

Ingria is an area inhabited by Finnic groups along the southern and eastern shores of the Gulf of Finland near St. Petersburg. The Kalevala metric poems collected in Ingria in the 19th century belong to the lyrical epic tradition typically preserved and sung by women.

The account given by F.A. Saxbäck of a visit to Ingria in 1859 in order to collect poetry (see Niemi 1904, 349-350) creates a seemingly authentic, lively, and almost visual picture of the poetry collector at work. The collector was pressed for time, he toiled away in order to capture the words of his young poetess on paper with his quill pen, since shorthand was not one of the techniques known to the field worker of that day:

> Do you wish, my readers, to see two pictures of my life here? Do you see that smoke cottage over there? Let us go inside. There is a fire burning in the stove, and the room is filled with smoke. The mistress of the household is to bake some pies, for tomorrow is Sunday. Over there sits a woman rocking a sleeping child. The child sleeps in a cradle, a linen crib suspended from a supple beam by which the baby is rocked. Over on the other side are two children, wailing and crying, who will not be pacified however hard their mothers try to suppress their shouts in the way mothers do. Standing by the table are two children, a boy with his hair falling in his eyes and a girl with her finger in her mouth, stealing glances at a bag in which can be seen a couple of books and part of a picture paper. Sitting at the table is a girl of 18 with red cheeks and a red skirt, singing. Hunched over the table is a man in his shirt sleeves with a quill in his hand, frantically trying to commit to paper the words flowing from the maiden's mouth. He does so in great haste. Sweat pours from his face, but he has no time to wipe it away. Faster and faster the pen flies across the paper, until the song comes to an end, he draws breath and lays his pen aside. – The man is me.

The poetry of Ingria in Kalevala metre has been preserved almost exclusively by women. Of the 1,200 or so singers mentioned in the list of Ingrian singers by Salminen, *Inkerin runonlaulajat ja tietäjät*, there are only just over one hundred men, 32 of them from West Ingria. Men account for only some five hundred of the 15,000 or so variants recorded in Ingria, i.e. a good three per cent (Salminen 1931b, 528). Men are, however, reputed to have been skillful singers in former times, and the few male repertoires that have been recovered are impressive (See Enäjärvi-Haavio 1949, 144; Salminen 1931b, 596-598). Volmari Porkka (1886, 155) writes in his travel report:

Ingrian maidens dancing. Photo: (MV.SUK 530:316).

Such were the relative singing skills of men and women wherever I had a chance to compare them. This, too, proves in an amusing way that women preserve the legacy inherited from their forefathers far more faithfully than men, even when the latter have rejected it as being worthless and, instead of their glowing, precious pearls, idolise the glass beads brought them by outsiders.

The poetic riches of Ingria were discovered by D.E.D. Europaeus as he toured the villages of Northern and Eastern Ingria in the company of H.A. Reinholm in 1847 and 1848. In a letter addressed to M.A. Castrén and Elias Lönnrot in 1848 he stressed the importance of collecting the Ingrian Kalevala-metric folk poetry, since in his opinion it contained fuller versions of some of the poems collected earlier for the new edition of the *Kalevala*. In 1850 he underlined the poetic riches of the western parts of Ingria.

Volmari Porkka (1886, 159) gave the following opinion of the Soikkola song-lands, in which he was not merely content to praise the exalted state of the Soikkola song tradition, but also sought to find the reasons for its late flowering:

On July 1 I arrived at Uusikylä in Soikkola. It was really refreshing to hear some proper runes again after such a long time. My joy was that of the berry-picker who, having combed the dry forests and found only here and there the occasional shrivelled berry, finally sees before him tussocks ablaze with red berries. Soikkola is known all around for its rune-singing, and not without reason, for almost nowhere else can one hear so many old songs. I wish to mention a few points which, I believe, at least to some extent explain why the art of singing has been so well preserved on the Soikkola headland, though even here there are ample signs of its deterioration. When we recall that Soikkola is almost purely Izhor, and that there are over twenty Izhor villages in its small area, with a total population far exceeding that of any other Izhor group anywhere else in Ingria, it is easy to understand that the resulting community is more close-knit and better able to resist outside influence.

According to the statistics for 1848 there were 3,717 Orthodox Izhors living in Soikkola (among them the best singers in the area), 573 Lutherans, 68 Germans and 53 Russians. The Finnish Lutheran settlement was concentrated on the eastern shores of the headland.[11]

The social background to rune-singing

From 1617 to 1721 Ingria belonged to the Kingdom of Sweden. Under the Uusikaupunki accord 1721 it was annexed to Russia as part of the Government of St. Petersburg. An important factor as regards the social conditions and occupation structure was serfdom, repealed by Alexander II in 1861 despite strong resistance from the noble land owners (see Alho 1979, 10). Under the system of serfdom the people were serfs of either the private lords of the manor or of the Crown. The conditions of the Crown serfs were far better than those of the manor serfs, since the former were not required to work for the landowner but could pay their taxes in the form of money or random labour. In addition to day-labour the landowner could demand all sorts of work, taxes in kind and payments. The mobility of the serfs was limited. They could be punished with, for example, the whip or banishment to Siberia, and they had no right to appeal against their masters' behaviour. The landowner's permission was always required before a serf could marry, and marriages that would lead to the estate losing its labour were not usually permitted (Alho 1979, 11-12, Honko 1962, 32-38).

During the period of serfdom the chief occupations in Ingria were farming and stock raising, including sale of the resulting products, fishing, forestry and various cottage industries. Naturally the poorest members of the population did not benefit from the income thus obtained. The manor serfs were far worse off than the Crown serfs both economically and socially (see Anttonen 1987, 42, 45; Toiviainen 1967, 73).

During the reform following the abolition of serfdom the land was redistributed. The nobility got the best shares, the peasants got the poorest land and the average size of their lands decreased. As a result the peasants had to buy or rent meadow and forest land. The political and economic freedom brought not prosperity but poverty. Porkka (1886, 160; see also Laiho 1940, 229) explains in the account of his journey there that the people of Soikkola had little chance of being economically self-sufficient: the soil contained a high proportion of clay and the fields were small, the pasture lands poor and subject to high rents, and there was no forest. One old man told Porkka: "You see, my friend, we have to buy everything: buy corn, buy hay, buy firewood, – water we don't need to buy." The poor conditions had, according to Porkka, forced the people of Soikkola to try to earn money elsewhere, especially by herding. In actual fact their growing debts forced the peasants more and more often to seek temporary work as, for example, drivers; this fortified the migration movement that had already begun during serfdom and led more and more men, in particular, to seek work in St. Petersburg (Engman 1991, 174-175; Anttonen 1987, 46-48). Such was the situation during the widespread collection of the Ingrian rune tradition in the late 19th and early 20th century.

The Ingrian mode of singing

Ingrian group singing was characterised by movement and collectivity and can in many respects thus be compared to the women's singing tradition of Estonia, Russia or Latvia. The songs, led by solo singers, were performed in a chorus, circle or chain, dancing, playing, at the swing and out in the village streets (Simonsuuri 1972, 41-42; Niemi 1904, 290). The girls would get together, especially on holy days in spring and summer, to wander singing through the lanes, or they would gather somewhere out-of-doors. In performing the songs involving movement they either formed into free groups and processions, or into organised circles or chains. The songs were either serious poems sung in a "long" or a "soft" voice (i.e. moving slowly to a leisurely melody), such as *Ennen naidun naisen tappo* 'The Killing of the Previous Wife', *Tytärten hukuttaja* 'The Daughter Drowner' or *Laivassa surmattu veli* 'The Brother Killed on the Boat', or "quick" songs danced in pairs one behind the other. It was also common to proceed through the village singing in a chain. The girls at the head of the chain formed a gate through which the other end threaded. This was called a *kluutsa* or an *Estonian gate* (see Enäjärvi-Haavio 1949, 156-161; Simonsuuri 1972, 47-48).

The young girls and boys also met at the swings or *liekut*, mainly to sing mood songs and certain motifs of an epic-lyrical nature. Around Easter and Whitsun in particular, narrative poems performed by older women were sung around the springtime swings (Salminen 1931a, 37-39; Simonsuuri 1972, 48).

The church feast days and other festivals celebrated in honour of the patron saint of the village or on some other church festival were also occasions for singing. According to Enäjärvi-Haavio the church festivals represented the culmination of the girls' song processions and the accompanying contests. The boys were also present, and the situation carried an erotic charge, the outbreaks of which were described in disapproving terms by some song collectors (Enäjärvi-Haavio 1949, 150, 154-156; Niemi 1904, 374, 414 and Siikala 1990b, 15).

Other occasions for singing together were weddings, and many annual feasts, such as Christmas and Shrovetide. Naturally songs were also sung alone, in the course of work, while nursing a baby, and so on.

The motifs of Kalevala-metric Ingrian poetry

The words of the lyrical and lyric-epic poems sung by the women were linked to their own sphere of daily activities, family life and the immediate environment. The poems describe birth, growing up, courting, marriage, the life of a daughter-in-law, and death. Some of the songs, on the other hand, were more narrative in nature: tragic ballads, aetiological poems founded on myths, and epics on the theme of war. The mythological heroic epic is, however, missing almost entirely (cf. Siikala 1990b, 14-19). The most popular themes of Ingrian *rune*-singing thus describe the female life-span and have a special fondness for the status of the girl of marriageable age: her share of her inheritance, courting, life at her husband's home, life as a married women compared with that before. These poems often have thematic connections with wedding poems, laments and lyrics (cf. Tarkka 1990a, 37) and the narration in the first person singular indicates that the singers felt personally involved.

The ego (maiden/girl) is in many poetic motifs looked down upon or is the target of censorious activity in general. Such allegories of life – personally experienced poems – were part of a popular, productive song tradition having thematic links with the lyrical mournful, orphan and slave songs.[12] The 'I' form is a typical feature of the Ingrian epic poem and its influence spreads beyond the lyric epic proper. The songs can accordingly be divided into several categories:

1) Poems with extensive use of the 'I' form in the narrative sections, and also in the dialogues in the case of many singers. These poems are often about the position of the girl in the other home (*Myyty neito* 'The Bartered Maiden', *Oljamissa käynti* 'The Unwelcome Visitor') or a life framed by tragic events in general (*Tytärten hukuttaja* 'The Daughter Drowner', *Viron orja ja isäntä* 'The Serf and Master of Estonia'), or the fate of a close relative (*Laivassa surmattu veli* 'The Brother Killed on the Boat'). It is also common for the song to begin with a monologue introduction before later assuming the third person.

2) Poems in which the 'I' of the poem (a maiden) occupies the leading role but in which the plot is based on mythical motifs. Examples of this type are the few lyric-epic poems of mythical origin (*Iso tammi* 'The Giant Oak', *Kantelen synty* 'The Origin of the *Kantele*', *Suka mereen* 'The Currycomb in the Sea').

3) Poems in which the 'I' form appears chiefly (and sometimes exclusively) in the dialogues. These poems often fall somewhere between the lyric epic and the narrative epic proper. They include ballad-like motifs (*Ennen naidun naisen tappo* 'The Killing of the Previous Wife', *Tuurikkaisen runo* 'Tuurikkainen's Song') and lyric epics on the theme of war (*Sotasanomat* 'War News', *Sotamieheksi otto* 'The Recruiting'). Examples of songs in this category which approach the (non-lyric) mythic epic songs in tone are *Tuonelta kosinta* 'Courtship from Tuonela' and *Untamo ja Kalervo* 'Untamo and Kalervo', in which the 'I' appears only at the beginning of episodes in certain typical situations. *Hekon runo* 'Hekko's Song', which may be classified as a courting poem, also avoids the monologue-type presentation.

4) There are a few archaic themes, which in Soikkola make only slight use of direct speech or monologue (*Päivän päästö* 'The Sun's Release', *Kultaneito* 'The Golden Bride'). It is true, that also the *Golden Bride* poem is in Ingria closer to a lyrical epic dealing with everyday life than to a mythic epic (see Siikala 1990b, 16-17).

One of the main themes of the lyric-epic poems of Ingria is *the search* for something lost. In *Hanhi kadonnut* 'The Lost Goose' the main character "I" searches for a goose and finds it stewing in a pot on a strange farm. In *The brother killed on the boat* the sister looks in vain for her brother on a ship, only to hear that he has been slain. In *Oljamissa käynti* 'The Unwelcome Visitor' a young girl, after married off, goes to visit her childhood home. Her sister-in-law rejects every suggestion for entertaining her and the girl is forced to leave her former home without receiving either food or drink. Also close to this subject are the poems *Myyty neito* 'The Bartered Maiden' and *Kouluun kotoa* 'From Home to School' describing conditions in marriage or at the mother-in-law's. In *Tytärten hukuttaja* 'The Daughter Drowner' the brother returns from courting and complains that his prospective brides refuse to allow him to court them because he has too many sisters at home. His mother therefore drowns her daughters and later sets off to look for them. In *Pilviin viety neito* 'The Maiden Drawn up to the Clouds' a mother seeks her daughter, who has lost her way while travelling by water.

The concrete or symbolical searching, the allegory of doom and longing portrayed in the seeking poems lies at the core of the lyrical epic of Ingria. The themes are life conflicts, fear and being deprived of one's heritage: being given in marriage, and loss of youth, childhood home, brothers and sisters or one's own children. The 'I' form found in the seeking episodes of variants from the mythologically-inspired *Maailmansyntyruno* 'The Origin of the World', *Kantelen synty* 'The Origin of the *Kantele*' and *Iso tammi* 'The Giant Oak' is a form of adaptation prompted by the poetic system. As a result the 'I', the maiden, has an active role in the mythic poems, not only in the epic-lyric ones. She seeks her brother to fell a giant oak, or orders her three brothers to kill fighting elks in the introductory episode of *The Origin of the Kantele*, and in some variants of *The Origin of the World* takes the place of the swallow that lays the cosmic egg, thereby giving birth to the world.

The use of formulae in the Ingrian lyrical epic

Formulaic bridges

It is often possible to discern structural links in poetic motifs, references to content and recollections that illustrate the way in which similar episodes and formulae act as bridges from one poem to another.

The similarity is astonishing in the following episodes, in which the same formula is applied to the same context (question/answer); only one word is varied in the formula, which is one of the features connecting the poems. The first example is a fragment from *The Maiden Drawn up to the Clouds* performed by Olena Oussimäki, and the second is an excerpt from the variant of *The Giant Oak* performed by Kati Väärnoja.

The Maiden Drawn up to the Clouds
lines 29-32

Kelle etsoi, kulle etsoi?	For whom the search, for which the search?
Vet ei kelle, ku ei emolle;	*For whom but their mother;*
emoin etso ensimäin,	first for the mother,
muulloin muun perehen.	then for the rest of the family
(SKVR III:2, 2334)	

Houses in Kupanitsa village, Ingria. Photo: Samuli Paulaharju 1911 (MV. 3490: 1277).

The Giant Oak
lines 56-59

"kellepä hoppiiat ossat,	For whom are you buying silver,
kulle kullasi lunastat?"	for whom obtaining gold?
Velloi vaite vast[aeli]:	To which the brother replied:
"Ved ei kelle ku ei sisoille".	*"For whom but my sister".*
(SKVR III:1, 1163)	

The semantic similarities between the motifs have here guided the choice of formulae. The same formula has served to produce episodes close in meaning. This question/answer scheme is a type example of cases in which the same basic meaning can be produced by substituting whatever elements are needed in the poetic texture. There is convincing proof of the links between traditional meanings and surface structure realisations in the fact that a large proportion of the formulae used in Ingrian poetry can also be encountered in semantically similar contexts in Estonian material; consider, for example, the above question/answer scheme in the Estonian poem *The Bartered Maiden* (Eisen et al. 1926, 395-396):

"Kelle sa sineta külvad,	For whom are you sowing blue flowers,
kelle' tallad tatteraida,	for whom scattering bistort,
kelle' pillad pipparaida?"	To whom are you throwing peppers?
"Kelle' muille kui omalle!"	*"To whom but my own [sweetheart]!"*

Some of the similarities spring from precise lexical correspondence, some from phonetic and others lexical parallelism (see further Harvilahti 1992, 139).

The variants already mentioned reveal further formulaic bridges of the same type. The searching episode in Olena's *The Maiden Drawn up to the Clouds*, in which a mother seeks in vain for her daughter, corresponds to

the search for a brother generally included in *The Giant Oak* performed by
Kati in which a sister seeks her brothers to fell an oak:

The Maiden Drawn up to the Clouds
lines 42-45

Käi Suomet, käi Saaret,	*Travelled Finland, travelled the islands,*
käi Turut tunnussellen,	travelled and checked around Turku,
Moskovat molomin puolin,	both sides of Moscow,
ei saant sieltä Maijojaa.	but no sign of Maija.

(SKVR III:2, 2334)

The Giant Oak
lines 40-45

Etsin saaret, etsin Suomet,	*I searched the islands, searched Finland,*
etsin Turut tunnnustellen,	searched and looked around Turku,
Viron välit valkissellen,	had a look in Estonia,
Moskovan molemmin puolin,	both sides of Moscow.
kahen puolen Kaprioo,	either side of Kaprio,
saanut en sieltä vellojaan.	but no sign of my brother.

(SKVR III:2, 1163)

The first lines above – *Käi Suomet, käi Saaret* and *Etsin saaret, etsin Suomet*
– are, apart from the word order and minor lexical variations, identical.
There is in the Ingrian material a large number of lines of similar construction in which the unifying feature is the repetition of the verb as the first
and third word. Here is a small sample:

The Giant Oak (SKVR III:1, 1171, lines 29, 58):
Etsin Suomet, etsin saaret   I searched Finland, searched the islands

Kylpi Unto, kylpi Ventoi   Bathed Unto, bathed Vento

The Golden Bride (SKVR III:1, 1202, line 13):
Takoi niitä, takoi näitä   Forged this, forged that

Marketta's Song (SKVR III:2, 1351, line 30):
Vannoi yksi, vannoi toin   Swore one, swore another

Wedding Song (SKVR III:2 1646, line 25):
Onpa tuotu, onpa saatu   Has been brought, has been caught

The Serf and Master (SKVR III:2 1527, line 10):
Tunsin tuulet, tunsin tyynet   I knew the storm, I knew the calm

The lines do not bear any lexical similarities, and even the syntactic
structure is not necessarily identical. The two halves of the line are indeed
marked by parallelism ranging from syntactic-semantic equivalence to a
looser type of similarity. The second and fourth words in the line may be
substantives, adjectives, pronouns (used indefinitely), numerals, infinitive
forms of verbs (perfect passive participle) or adverbs.

100

The metrical mould and parallelism within the line thus combine a number of lines differing in lexical content into one single paradigm. The lines belonging to this paradigm are to be found in different types of contexts in which their job is, by using parallelism, to describe and underline the phenomenon or event portrayed. In most cases these lines illustrate the amount or duration of the action by means of e.g. synonyms and analogies (*this/ that, one /another, brought/ caught*) or antithesis (*storm/ calm*) or proper nouns (*Untoi/Ventoi*). In comparing lines, one is struck by the fact that the second and fourth words do not necessarily correspond to one another in linguistic analysis. They may represent different parts of speech and have different syntactic functions, being e.g. subjects, objects, or parts of the predicate. Lines such as those quoted above constitute a loose formulaic paradigm in which the contents of the individual lines are as a rule formulae applied to two or three poetic motifs.

Thus in *The Giant Oak* the oak is felled, the wood is used to make useful tools and the remaining splinters are jointed together in a sauna where the bathers are Unto and Vento:

The Giant Oak
lines 62-68

Mit muut muruja jäivät,	From the remaining splinters
salvoi saunan saaruelle,	he built a sauna on the island,
Kylpi Untoi, kylpi Ventoi,	*Unto bathed, Vento bathed*
kylpi viisi velvyttän'	*my five brothers bathed*
seitsemän siaruttan'.	*and my seven sisters.*
jäi Virpoi kylpömätä,	Virpi went unbathed,
Virvoin vasta hautomata.	Virpi's switch went unsoaked.
(SKVR III:2, 2289)	

A variation on the same formula is common in *The Origin of the Kantele*, the only difference being the change in verb(s) due to the different contents of the motifs. The following example was performed by the same singer as the previous one:

The Origin of the Kantele
lines 35-42

Näin mie tieltä tervaskannon;	I saw a pitchy stump on the road
siit' sain kannet kantelelle.	from it came a lid for the Kantele
Sai kannel valmiheks'.	The Kantele was completed.
Soitti untoi, soitti ventoi,	*Unto played, Vento played,*
soitti kaikk' viisi velvyttäin;	*my five brothers played.*
tantsi untoi, tantsi ventoi,	*Unto danced, Vento danced,*
tantsi viisi velvyttäin,	*my five brothers danced*
seitsemän siaruttan'.	*and my seven sisters.*
(SKVR III:2, 1969)	

The use of the same line scheme is again a consequence of the semantic similarities in the plot structures. In both cases the first person narrator goes in search of her brother(s): in *The Giant* Oak to fell the oak, in *The Elk Fight* and *The Origin of the Kantele* to kill the elks. In both myth-based poems both pieces from the oak and the elks' antlers are used to make objects or tools: barrels, spindles, tankards and a *sauna* from the oak, and a *kantele* from the elk's antlers. As a result of these similarities the formulaic sequence *V(erb) Unto, N Vento, V my five brothers and my seven sisters* applied to the plot has become fixed as a typical element of both poems (here V = active finite form of a verb in the imperfect tense, N = a noun).

In the examples given at the beginning the line *Kelle etsoi, kulle etsoi* 'For whom the search, for which the search' likewise makes use of parallelism within the line. This line is again part of a larger paradigm in which the two halves of the line are linked by the repetition of the interrogative pronoun and a noun:

The Maid Drawn up to the Clouds (SKVR III:2, 2334, line 29):
kelle etsoi, kulle etsoi   For whom the search, for which the search

The Origin of the Kantele (SKVR III:2, 1308, line 45):
mihe sarvet, kuhu sarvet   Where the horns, whither the horns

The Giant Oak (SKVR III:1, 1163, line 8):
mihe tammi, kuhu t[ammi]   Where the oak, whither the oak

Untamo and Kalervo (SKVR III:2, 1968, line 71):
mihin poikoi, kuhun poikoi   Where the boy, whither the boy

Hekko's Song (SKVR III:2, 1254, line 6):
k[elle] tyttöi, kelle poikoi   To whom a girl, tho whom a boy

The Man-Killer (SKVR III:2, 1965, line 63):
kuhun Kaise, mihin Kaise   Where Kaise, whither Kaise

Maije's Song (SKVR III:2, 1446, line 40):
mihepä Maije, kuhupa M[aije]   Where Maije, whither Maije

Currycomb in the Sea (SKVR III:1, 1186, line 36):
mistäpä miekkoi, kustapa miekkoi   From where the sword, whence the sword

We have already seen from the above examples that the formulaic processing built on parallelism within the line is not tied to any particular part of speech, nor even to syntactic structures. The same scheme thus forms the basis for an extensive family of formulae. The only factor linking manifestations of a formula is that there are four words in the line, with two in each half. Furthermore, one of the words is repeated either in exactly the same form at the beginning of each half or using some parallel word. The other components of the line halves are most often analogical or antithetical concepts, and identical repetition is quite common. Another factor often linking the line halves is alliteration.

By broadening the criteria for selection we can thus find formulae in which the conditions for correspondence can be carried beyond mere metrical, lexical or syntactical similarity. We thus find cases that extend beyond, for example, the "allomorphs" and allomorph "families" discovered by N. Nagler in Homeric poetry (Nagler 1974, 5-12). The formulaic model constitutes a large network to which strict definitions no longer apply. The following categories, for example, belong to this network:

Maidens dressed in their finest in Kallivieri village, Ingria. Photo: Lauri Laiho 1938 (MV 168a 172).

1.) Noun + verb / noun + verb

The Serf and Master (SKVR III:2, 2329, line 36):
mettä söit, mettä joit   You ate honey, you drank honey

The Serf and Master (SKVR III:2, 1967, line 65):
vettä syyä, vettä juoa   Water to eat, water to drink

The Origin of the World (SKVR III:1, 1145, line 32):
puolet söin, puolet peitin   Half I ate, half I hid

The Giant Oak (SKVR III:1, 1163, line 70):
tammen tagroi, puun piroitti   Cut the oak, lopped the tree

The Unwelcome Visitor (SKVR III:2, 1473, line 23):
läävät läikkyit, tallit taittuit   The cowsheds swayed, the stables fell down

The Unwelcome Visitor (SKVR III:2, 1477, line 24):
olut loppui, taari taittui   The beer was finished, the ale run out

The Sun's Release (SKVR III:2, 2328, line 2):
päivän peittiit, kuun sallaisiit   Covered the sun, hid the moon

Untamo and Kalervo (SKVR III:2, 1280, line 235):
lapsen katsoi, silmän kaivoi   Watched the child, rubbed the eye

2.) Adverb + noun / adverb + noun (adverb in Finnish texts, not in translations)

The Origin of the Kantele (SKVR III:2, 2315, line 33):
päältä sarvi, alta kapia   From above a horn, from below a hoof

The Serf and Master (SKVR III:2, 2329, line 3):

pahoin palkka, kurjin ruoka   Bad wages, wretched food

The Serf and Master (SKVR III:2, 2329, line 12):

suin lummee, päin vetee   On her face to the snow,
                                 head – first to the water

3.) Pronoun + verb / pronoun + verb

The Bartered Maiden (SKVR III:2, 1966, line 63):

ken möi, ken lupais   Who sold, who took vows

The Messiah (SKVR III:2, 1962, line 1):

mitä laulan, kuta laulan   What I sing, which I sing

War News (SKVR III:2, 1381, line 56):

minen annat, min avitat   What will you give, how will you help

The Maiden Drawn up to the Clouds (SKVR III:2, 2334, line 7):

mingen heitti, kungan heitti?   Which one she disowned, which one she
                                       abandoned?

The Mermaid and the Forest Groom (SKVR III:2, 2258, line 29):

itse katsoi, itse itki   She herself looked, she herself cried

There are also cases with, for example, four nouns, a numeral and a noun
or an adverb and a noun (in Finnish texts):

The Sun's Release (SKVR III:1, 1151, line 10):

k[äsin] t[ietä], sormin maata   By hand along the road, with fingers along
                                       the earth [i.e. in order to feel one's way]

The Origin of the Kantele (SKVR III:2, 1969, line 32):

kahta kantta, viittä keeltä   Two lids, five strings

The Contest with the Sun (SKVR III:2, 1410, line 32):

yyn[nä] s[yyvä], y[ynnä] j[uuva]   To eat by night, to drink by night

The category $X + X / X + X$ is thus highly varied in its morphological,
syntactical and lexical realisation. The variety of parts of speech alone
provides some sort of picture of the variation network (X = a word
belonging to any part of speech, V = verb, S = noun, A = adjective, Pr =
pronoun, Nr = numeral, Adv = Adverb):

$$X + X / X + X$$

V+V/V+V	S+S/S+S	Pr+V/Pr+V	Nr+S/Nr+S	Adv+V/Adv+V
V+S/V+V	S+V/S+V	Pr+S/Pr+S		Adv+S/Adv+S
V+S/V+S				
V+S/V+Pr				
V+A/V+A				
V+Pr/V+Pr				
V+Nr/V+Nr				
V+Adv/V+Adv				

Formula clusters

The above cases have shown that the criterion for a formula need not be lexical repetition or syntactic equivalence. In the examples dealt with the four-word construction, the division into two equal halves and the coherence caused by the parallelism existing between the two line halves is a sufficient criterion for conceiving of a large formula family. What is the significance of such a widespread category in the production of poetry, e.g. as a mnemotechnical device dividing up the flow of the narrative?

I have so far presented lines belonging to a single family taken out of their poetic context. Lines are not, however, isolated grains resembling one another to a greater or lesser extent and scattered here and there as a form of seasoning. Indeed, one criteria of formulaic technique is that the formulae act as devices to bind and shape the narrative.

An example of the effective use of the same formula family (X + X / X + X) is *Hanhi kadonnut* 'The Lost Goose', many variants of which have clusters of in-line parallelism that vary from singer to singer:

SKVR III:2, 2219
The Lost Goose, singer anonymous, Kiiskala
lines 15-61

Teen mie tarhan tanhovalle,	I make a pen in the yard,
koppelin kovalle maalle;	a cage on the hard land.
sinne paan mie vellon linnut.	There I put my brother's birds.
Mänin itse jauhamaa.	I myself went to grind flour.
Jauhon vakan, jauhon toisen,	*I ground a basket full, ground another*
jauhon kolmatta vähäisen.	*ground part of a third.*
Mänin hantta katsomaa –	I went to look at the goose
Jo oli hanheni paennut!	But my goose had already flown!
Mänin hantta etsimää.	I went to look for the goose.
Juoksin virssan, juoksin toisen,	*I ran a verst and ran another,*
juoksin kolmatta vähäisen.	*ran part of a third*
Kyntäjät pellolla kynsit,	Ploughmen were ploughing in the field
mie kyselin kyntäjilt':	I asked the ploughmen:
"Kyntäjät, kypenyveni,	"Oh my dearest ploughmen,
adran-kantajat, kanani,	Plough-bearers, my sweethearts,
näittäk miun hanhiani?"	have you seen my goose?"
"Mikä ol' merkki hanhessasi?"	"What are the markings on your goose?"
"Tina-sulka, vaski-varvas,	*"A tin feather, a brass toe,*
otsalla Otavan merkki,	a mark like the Great Bear on its brow,
päässä Päivän pyörentäinen."	the Wheel of Sun on its head."

"Täst' lensi liehutteli,	"It just fluttered over (this place),
meijen päitsen päähytteli;	Flew over our heads,
yksi siipi maata veitti,	one wing sweeping the ground,
toinen taivasta tavotti."	the other pointing to the sky."
Mänin virssa, mänin toisen.	*I went a verst and went another.*
Sotkijat joella sotkit.	Washerwomen were washing in the river.
Mie kyselin sotki'ilta:	I asked the washerwomen:
"Sotkiat, sisaruveni,	"Washerwomen, my sisters,
kartun-kantajat, kanani,	pounder-bearers, my sweethearts,
näittäk' miun hanhiani?	have you seen my goose?"
"Mikä ol' merkki hanhessasi?"	"What are the markings on your goose?"

"Tina-sulka, vaski-varvas,	*A tin feather, a brass toe,*
otsassa Otavan risti,	a cross like the Great Bear on its brow,
päässä Päivän pyörentäinen."	the Wheel of Sun on its head."
"Emmä nähneet myö, sisoni."	"We have not seen it, sister."
Mänin virssan, mänin toisen,	*I went a verst and went another*
mänin kolmatta vähäisen;	*went part of a third*
Puutun uutee kyllää,	I came to a new village,
puutun uutee talloo.	I came to a new farm.
Hano kiehu kattilass';	The goose was boiling in the pot;
välist' häntää häylyttää,	wagging its tail now and again,
välist' kääntää käpälää.	turning its leg now and again.

The lines *Mänin itse jauhamaa* 'I went myself to grind flour' and *Mänin hantta etsimää* 'I went to look for the goose' beginning the action are followed by a sequence describing the task or action based on the formula *V + N / V + "another"*. The formula recurs at various stages in the plot in describing the quantity and duration of the action embarked upon. The other formulae in the poem based on in-line parallelism have presumably been chosen under the influence of a similar process.

A formula within a poem variant may thus generate the production of variations on that formula. One formula activates other lines of the same construction or otherwise closely associated with it. This leads to clusters, to the repetition of similar formulae or parts of them within a relatively short text episode (cf. Miller 1987, 370-371; Beaugrand/Dressler 1980, § 5.12). Such clusters may accumulate as varying entities in the variants of the same song sung by a number of singers; they may also constitute structural-contentual bridges between different poetic motifs. The line structure (2+2) of the formula category discussed here is one of the most common line types not only in Ingria but in Archangel Karelia and Estonia, too.[14]

V + N / V + "another" constitutes a formula category that is put to a number of uses: in these four-word lines the first and third words are finite verbs and the fourth word is *toinen*, "another". Here is a sample from seven different motifs:

The Origin of the Kantele (SKVR III:2, 1305, line 3):
taitoin luuan, taitoin toisen   I made a broom, I made another

The Origin of the Kantele (SKVR III:3, 3426, line 5):
taittoi oksan, taittoi toisen   Broke a branch, broke another

The Bartered Maiden (SKVR III:1, 1192, line 47):
kitkin nurkan, k[itkin] toisen   I weeded a parcel, I weeded another

Seeking a Tree for a Boat (SKVR III:2, 1314, line 10):
juoksin verssan, juoksin toisen   Run a verst, run another

The Sun's Release (SKVR III:1, 1151, line 19):
ajoi virssan, ajoi toisen   Drove a verst, drove another

Hekko's Song (SKVR III:2, 1254, line 26):
kasvoi vuuen, kasvoi toisen   Grew a year, grew another

The Maiden Drawn up to the Clouds (SKVR III:3, 3465, line 27):
huusi kerran, huusi toisen   Gave a shout, gave another

Marketta's Song (SKVR III:2, 1351, line 30):
vannoi yksi, vannoi toin   One swore, swore another

The formula *V + N / V + "another"* can be applied to various motifs in describing the performance of action already embarked on, recurring, stagewise or time-consuming action or the transfer from one scene of events to another.

Formula options

As examples of the semantic links between poems and their connections with the surface-level formulaic features let us take a look at the following episodes in which the categories analysed are repeated: the opening formula *mäni X etsimään /katsomaan "went to search/look for X"* and the formula *V1 + N / V1 + "another" //V1 + "part of a third"*:

SKVR III:1, 1151
The Sun's Release
lines 15-20

Sepoil oli selvä neitoi,	The smith had a bright maid,
mäni kuuta etsimää;	*she went to seek the moon;*
otti sieran seslähää,	took a cheese upon her back,
otti kannuu olutta.	took a jug of ale.
Ajoi virssan, ajoi toisen,	*Drove a verst, drove another*
a[joi] kolmatta vähhäisen;	*drove part of a third;*

SKVR III:2, 2219
The Lost Goose, singer anonymous, Kiiskala
lines 18-25

Mänin itse jauhamaa.	*I went myself to grind flour.*
Jauhon vakan, jauhon toisen,	*I ground one basket-full, ground another*
jauhon kolmatta vähäisen.	*ground part of a third.*
Mänin hantta katsomaa –	*! went to look at the goose –*
Jo oli hanheni paennut!	but my goose had already flown!
Mänin hantta etsimää.	*I went to look for the goose.*
Juoksin virssan, juoksin toisen,	*I ran a verst, ran another,*
juoksin kolmatta vähäisen.	*ran part of a third.*

SKVR III:1, 1192
The Bartered Maiden, Kati Väärnoja
lines 39-48

mäninpä siintä katsomaa,	*I went to look at the blue flowers,*
pellavasta vaattamaa.	to check the flax.
Jo sinoi sinikukalla,	The flowers were already blue,
pellavas punakukalla;	The flax was red;
sinoi itki kitkijäistä,	the blue cried to be weeded,
pellavas puhastajaista.	the flax to be cleaned.
aloin miä kitkiä sinnooja,	I began to weed the flowers,
puhassella p[ellavasta]),	to clean the flax.
kitkin nurkan, k[itkin] toisen,	*I weeded one parcel, weeded another,*
kitkin kolmatta vähhäisen,	*weeded part of a third.*

Residents of Tarassina village, Ingria. Photo: J. Lukkarinen (MV. SUK 72: 22).

The poems *The Sun's Release*, *The Lost Goose* and *The Bartered Maiden* are linked by a sequence, the main contents of which are a departure to carry out a task/action followed by the the actual performance. In these cases the sequences use the same formulaic devices, but there were numerous other possible realisations. The action can be started by numerous alternative structures, only one of which is the formula *"went to search/look for X"*. Similarly the formula $V1 + N / V1 +$ *"another"* may be missing and replaced by other constructions. Mapu of Uusikylä uses completely different constructions and formulae to produce the searching scene in *The Sun's Release*:

SKVR III:1, 1156
The Sun's Release, Mapu of Uusikylä
lines 15-21

Sepän neitoi, neitsykkäin	The smith's maid, young virgin
noisi päivöin ets[iäksi],	*rose to be the searcher of the sun*
n[oisi] kuun tähyst[äjäksi];	*rose to be the seeker of the moon;*
käi sutena suuret metsät,	*roamed the big forests as a wolf*
karhuna kommiat korvet,	*as a bear the wild moors,*
jäniksenä järven rannat,	*as a hare the lake shores,*
matoloina maan alaitse.	*as a worm beneath the earth.*

The formula $V + X / V +$ *"another"* is not obligatory in *The Sun's Release*. The same idea can be expressed by another construction, or the descriptive episode may be missing completely, as above.[15] The use of a bear, wolf, etc. as by Mapu in the searching episode is common in *The Maiden Drawn up to the Clouds*, where a mother seeks her daughter (Kati Väärnoja's version); Mapu also uses the formula to describe the brother's search in *The Giant Oak*, further preceding this formulaic sequence by the familiar

Etsin Suomet, etsin saaret 'I searched Finland, I searched the islands' episode:[16]

SKVR III:2, 1355
The Maiden Drawn up to the Clouds
lines 45-52

Emoi kenki jalkojaa,	Mother shod herself,
yhen jalan kynnyksellä,	one foot on the threshold:
toisen Maijen kirstun päällä.	the other on Maije's chest.
Mäni etsi Maijeaa,	*Went, looked for her Maije,*
käi sutteena suuret korvet,	*roamed the big forests as a*
karhuna komeat k[orvet],	*as a bear the wild moors,*
jäniksenä järvirannat,	*as a hare the lake shores,*
oravana puijen oksat.	*as a squirrel the branches of the trees.*

SKVR III:1, 1171
The Giant Oak
lines 32-36

Mänin etsin vellojaan,	*I went, looked for my brother,*
etsin Suomet, etsin saaret,	I searched Finland, searched the islands,
Moskovat molemmin puolin,	both sides of Moscow,
etsin Turut tunnustellen.	looked around Turku.
Käin sutena suuret metsät,	*Roamed the big forests as a wolf,*
karhuna kammaalat korvet,	*as a bear the terrible moors,*
jäniksenä järven rannat,	*as a hare the lake shores,*
oravana puijen oksat,	*as a squirrel the branches of the trees,*
matokkana maan alukset;	*as a worm beneath the earth.*

Thousands more examples of this type could be quoted, but these should suffice for the following conclusions.

Conclusion

The same meaning can be expressed by devices differing greatly in their surface structures. One central semantic unit has a number of potential realisations at surface structure level. The corollary of this is that the surface structures differing in their phonological, morphological and syntactical correspondence are repeatedly used to produce poems through associative links. Thus lines that do not belong together on the basis of content may form extensive semantic networks. The links of such networks may be found in only one motif or variant, or they might join together several motifs. J.M. Foley has expressed a similar observation in the following words: "the inherent metonymic meaning of a traditional structure, while dependent on the surface denotation for a viable conduit, remains immanent, looming over the textual score and enriching it associatively" (Foley 1991, 252; 1992, 282). The devices used to produce poems constitute a multidimensional and multilevel network of inner connections and interdependences, a linguistic-poetic reproduction system based on both the surface and the semantic structure (cf. Leino 1987, 41). Proof of this are the above analyses, which are naturally able to cover only a fraction of this extensive system.

The core of formulaic composition lies not in the singer's command of crystallised expressions and established stylistic patterns. Nor can it be assumed that the generation process can be repeated over and over again. Prosody, primary poetic features, morphosyntactical, lexical and semantic interconnections, structural and contentual entities large and small are combined to form a reference network within which the singer operates. Analysis of poetic material reveals a series of replacements, transfers, additions and removals operating at many levels (cf. Miller 1987, 362-363; van Dijk 1985, 2).

It is, however, necessary to add that the choice of poetic devices is only optional within certain limits. In practice every singer establishes a number of formal devices and standard poetic content in the course of repeated performances. On the other hand the practices of other singers also affect his or her choice. The more often a poem is performed (especially in a familiar group), the easier it is for links to emerge, and singers do not necessarily deviate from the familiar paths (cf. Miller 1987, 359). The singer's expression is thus bound by a set of formulaic devices influenced by both individual and collective preferences.

NOTES

1. Hautala 1945, 15-16. In commenting on Hautala's claims Matti Kuusi stresses that some lines belong in a particular context (what he calls fixed features), while others (clichés or loose features) have no such context. Kuusi treated these categories separately in his analysis, pointing out that there are nevertheless numerous borderline cases (Kuusi 1949, 108). The concepts of Hautala and Kuusi differ widely. It should be mentioned that the Finnish epic poem chosen by Hautala for analysis was composed of an unusual number of common itinerant themes. Numerous scholars have in fact picked out contentual elements firmly attached to some poetic narrative entity and freely placed within the narrative.

2. Lord 1976a, 30, 66, 99.

3. Since this work Lord has published dozens of articles and papers examining the traditions of more and more peoples and reassessing the theoretical basis of *The singer of tales* (see Foley 1985, 403-414; Lord 1987; Lord 1990).

4. Oinas (1987, 235; 1990, 304) claims, with reference to Kiparsky (1976, 95), that the repertoires of Finnish singers consist of rather fixed structures and indicate that the different cultural role of South Slavic and Finnish poetry explains the differences in stability between the traditions. Virtanen (1968, 54-55) in turn suggests in commenting on Lord's theory on composition in performance that the reader of the Finnish material can often

say without any difficulty to what song given lines belong, and that there is always some degree of creation, variation, whatever name one chooses to give it; or that the difference between creation of the new and the variation of the old is only one of degree, and it is impossible to say where the border runs. The typologising or study of variation is on these grounds of no significance to Kalevala poetry and an invalid object for research.

5. See especially Kuusi 1970, 301-302; Kuusi 1983, 181-182. Kuusi states (1970, 302) that the lyrics of Larin Paraske and Anni Lehtonen were for the most part semi-improvised situational poetry; lyrics woven to suit the needs of the moment from traditional images and line patterns using a traditional technique of compilation.

6. See Alho 1979, 24; Saarinen 1988, 3-4.

7. According to Outi Lehtipuro (1974, 17) we should question whether our concept of the Kalevala epic as highly static in comparison with, say, the song tradition of Yugoslavia is in fact an optical illusion. This concept may prevent us from taking as a working hypothesis that, at least in the case of those singers who could go on creating new songs evening after evening, the process for producing songs was in principle the same as that familiar to us from the studies of Milman Parry and Albert B. Lord. We should, in debating this problem, remember that the epic poetry of the Southern Slavic Moslem

singers consisted of long variants often running to thousands, even tens of thousands of lines, whereas the Finnish poems were (at least during the period of the last century when they were collected) at most a few hundred lines long. The length of songs thus affects the composition process, since short songs presumably (according to Lord) tend to become increasingly crystallised the more they are sung (Lord 1976a, 100; Lord 1981, 459). Fromm (1987, 67, 71-80) nevertheless points out that compared with the songs of the Serbs, the Russian Karelian songs displayed less crystallisation in the order of their lines and their homogeneity, but more in the use of the same lines. These generalizations are supported by a few Karelian songs (SKVR I:1, 280, 280a, 362, 362a, 363, 363a, 670, SKVR I:2, 701, 758, 759, 759b, 766) some of which have been subjected to closer analysis (cf. Saarinen 1988, 5-6, 26).

8. See Foley 1985, 3-5. The bibliography mentions 13 scholars who have used Finnish material, only three of them Finns: Kaarle Krohn, whose *Kalevalastudien 1-6* (1924-1928) was included presumably because Parry uses Krohn as a source in his studies of Homeric poetic language (see M. Parry 1932, 338 (19) and 341 (22)), Tauno Mustanoja, who in one article quotes descriptions of Kalevala *rune*-singing, comparing them with those of the performance of ancient English and Germanic epics (1959, 1-11) and Elli Köngäs-Maranda, whose work *Structural Analysis of Oral Tradition* edited together with Pierre Maranda includes an article entitled *The logic of Riddles* based on Finnish material and research. One doctoral thesis has been published in Finland on oral formulaic theory, but it is based on material from the Anglo-Saxon and not the Finnish language area (Ringbom 1968). The bibliography includes D. Comparetti's *Il Kalevala; o la poesia tradizionale dei finni* because this work was of significance to Parry in developing his theory (see Foley 1985, 182 and Parry 1932, 330 (8), especially note 2). Of greater relevance among the studies based on Finnish material and mentioned by Foley are the articles and surveys by Felix Oinas (1972, 1978) and above all the paper by Paul Kiparsky (1976) entitled *Oral Poetry: Some Linguistic and Typological Considerations*. The treatise on the Baltic-Finnish epic included in Oinas' work *Heroic Epic and Saga* (1978) is the only comprehensive study of the structural and stylistic devices of Kalevala poetry to be found in Foley's bibliography. Most of the other studies based on Finnish material mentioned by Foley concentrate on some special issue and do not always fall within the confines of the research field. One group consists of studies which generalize on the basis of a number of epic poetry cultures. These include the article by S. Einarsson (1963) referring to the Kalevala mode of singing in speaking of different modes of antiphonic performance, the paper by Nabaneeta Sen (1979) seeking by means of comparison similarities and dissimilarities in the thematic structure of the epic poetry of the eastern and western worlds and quoting the *Kalevala* as one example, and the article by Arthur Hatto (1970) examining numerous epic poetry cultures by comparing the shamanistic origin of the narrative poetry of the Northern Asians. G.P. Goold (1977) presents a view opposed to the claims of the oral-formulaic school and explains that Homer was the poet of the Iliad and the Odyssey, comparable to Elias Lönnrot. Robert Kellogg (1977, 124) mentions that the *Kalevala* differs from other national epics in that its characters are not aristocratic, and that they do not possess supernatural powers; he also points out that the Finnish national epic lacks epic consecutiveness. Albert Lord (1976b) also used the *Kalevala* as a source in comparing the episode dealing with the youth of the Bulgarian hero Krali Marko with Armenian and Finnish material. Foley's bibliography covers literature appearing up to 1984 and therefore lacks such works as the paper *The Kalevala, the South Slavic Epics and Homer* presented by Lord in Dublin in 1985 (Lord 1987).

9. Formula has, among others, been described as 1) a group of words recurring in given metric environments, i.e. defined primarily on lexical-metric grounds (Parry/Lord), 2) as being based on syntactic-metric structural schemes (Notopoulos/Russo), 3) as recurring yet formally varied groups of words (Hainsworth), 4) as a quantitative category made up of recurring morphemic clusters (Peabody), and 5) as being generated on the basis of (lexically, syntactically and metrically) loosely related formulaic systems (Fry). 6) Some have abandoned the concept of formula completely and explained that poetry is produced as allomorphs on the basis of a mental model representing the surface structure at the most abstract level (Nagler), while Nagy gives an original diachronic definition explaining formulae as fixed verbal associations generated on the basis of traditional themes. The critics of the theory have, among other things, explained that a formula is more a matter of belief than a term describing some precisely defined feature of the oral tradition (Finnegan), or else they have accused the representatives of the school of formalism, of neglecting the

111

artistic-contentual aspects of the production of epic poetry (Gacak).

10. See Harvilahti 1992, 66, 141-147; Cf. e.g. Karlsson 1988, 135; Jackendoff 1985, 8-10; Miller 1987, 111 and Vikis-Freibergs 1989, 70.

11. Anttonen 1987, 39. Peter von Köppen, mentioned by Anttonen, was a member of the Russian Geographical Society, a statistician and ethnographer whom Europaeus got to know on his visit to Ingria in 1847.

12. Cf. Siikala 1990b, 16-17. Kuusi (1983, 177-178) tries to deduce the special nature and innermost aims of Maria Luukka and her singing school from the character descriptions and role relationships in the poems. He notes that Maria Luukka's most common character is *mie* 'I', dominating the lyrics, dance songs, children's lyrics and the lyrical epics. Kuusi is surprised at the popularity of the I form in the epic, too.

13. Cf. also SKVR III:1, 1045, SKVR III:2, 1571, 1572 and SKVR III:3, 2785, lines 20-61.

14. The formula analysed above also belongs to one of the commonest line schemes with regard to structure (2222); this accounted for 6.7% of the Ingrian variants analysed by Sadeniemi (1951, 20, 21, 41). The only line types to be found even more frequently than this are 224 and 233. Type 2222 is represented even more frequently in the Archangel Karelian material (Arhippa Perttunen) than in Ingria: 8.0% and in the Estonian material (*Vana kannel*) as much as 15.4%. For alliteration in four-word lines see Leino 1970, 178-179, 181-182.

15. See SKVR III:2, 1961, 31-32; SKVR III:1, 1193, 49-53; 1195,33-37.

16. SKVR III:1, 1171, 32-36; SKVR III:2, 1355, 48-52; 1356, 40-44; and 2334, 36-41.

PERTTI J. ANTTONEN

Ethnopoetic Analysis and Finnish Oral Verse

In the intersection of linguistics, anthropology, literature, and the study of folklore, ethnopoetics is an approach that focuses on the aesthetic and poetic structuring of verbal expression, especially of the kind of verbal expression that is regarded as verbal art. Its methodological and theoretical foundations lie in pragmatics, phenomenology, sociolinguistics, ethnomethodological conversation analysis, the ethnography of speaking, and the performance approach in American folklore studies.

Some of the early influences on the ethnopoetic approach are Franz Boas' studies and interlinear presentations of American Indian narratives as well as Milman Parry's and Albert B. Lord's theory of oral composition, according to which verbal art is not memorized but composed in the course of performance with audience participation (Lord 1960). Philosophically, ethnopoetics – as well as the whole performance approach in American folklore scholarship – is founded on William James' pragmatism (see Abrahams 1985 and 1992), J. L. Austin's speech act theory, Kenneth Burke's dramatism, and on the Wittgensteinian notion that language is not a passive instrument for describing a world independently constituted.

Ethnopoetics is based on the notion that songs, poems, narratives, etc. are "subtle organizations of lines and verses" (Hymes 1982, 121). Thus, these expressions are founded upon a socially constituted poetic structure that is present both in the organization of experience as well as in the organization of reports on that experience. "The lines and verses are organized in ways that are not only poetry, but also a kind of rhetoric of action in that they embody an implicit cultural schema for the organization of experience. These patterns are most finely worked out in myths but can also be found in personal narratives." (Hymes 1982, 121).

In handwriting as well as in publishing, texts are typically presented in blocks of prose, and lines are dictated by typesetting and the margins on the page. This also applies to texts that were not written to be published but have been created from recordings of oral performance. As one of its corner stones, the ethnopoetic approach emphasizes the poetic patterning of the texture, which must also be shown in the transcription. In this mode of presentation, "each line is put forth in such a manner as to render its fullest available charge of texture: rhythm, nuance, phrasing and metaphors

Songs beyond
the Kalevala
Studia Fennica
Folkloristica 2
1994

– factors which may depend partly on relation to other lines by parallelism, redundancy, grouping..." (Toelken and Scott 1981, 65). The fundamental starting point for ethnopoetic analysis is the notion that aural qualities in performance are not mere extratextual features but essential in the organization of speech, "conveying to the listener a sense of the relative importance of propositions and their connections with each other, which are essential aspects of meaning" (Mills 1991, 25).

Ethnopoetics has in the United States been divided into two 'branches', one led by Dennis Tedlock and the other by Dell Hymes, but recently such scholars as Joel Sherzer, Anthony C. Woodbury, and Charles L. Briggs have aimed at combining the two. In Tedlock's ethnopoetics, the emphasis is on the oral nature of texts and the dependence of the organization of the texts upon lines. This means that the transcription of a text is based on two factors. First, the text is organized into lines according to the pauses in the oral performance of the text. According to Tedlock, each new pause indicates the end of one line and the beginning of another. Second, the transcription shows the variation in pitch, volume, vowel length, tempo, cadence, and voice quality as used by the performer in his/her performance. They are marked in the transcription by various typographical means. For example, high pitch is shown with capital letters. The Tedlockian transcript aims to present the text as it was heard in performance – in its auditory form (see e.g. Tedlock 1983).

In his criticism of some of the principles of Tedlock's ethnopoetics, Dell Hymes points out that pauses are not necessarily a stylistic device. On the one hand, they are inevitable, and on the other, they can be accidental. "If you only have one recording, how do you know that the person would pause in the same place if he told the story again? (...) You would have to have repeated tellings of the same story to see the ways in which the patterning of pause was specific to a single story and telling, as opposed to being conventional." (Hymes 1982, 125; see also Hymes 1981, 339.) According to Hymes, the distribution of pauses may coincide with the relevant line-units, but the fundamental criterion for a line-unit is syntactic, not phonetic (Hymes 1982, 140).

One of the founding ideas in Dell Hymes' ethnopoetics is the notion that many things in narratives revolve around a pattern number or a 'sacred number', or some multiple of it. "Zuni has a pattern number, a sacred number, four. If there are going to be several people in a Zuni story who are brothers or sisters and who follow a course of action, there will be four. If the same thing is going to happen several times until it comes to a climax, it will happen four times, and so on." (Hymes 1982, 126).

According to Hymes, the patterning of 'this/then that', which is based on a culture-specific pattern number, brings rhythm to a story. In accordance with the logic of patterning, an experience is given a shape and organized into symmetrical, regular relationships. Thus, the patterning is aesthetically founded and its function is to produce a satisfying, aesthetic experience for the narrator and his/her audience. A fixed pattern arouses and satisfies expectation, as Kenneth Burke has emphasized (see Burke 1977 [1931]). The evaluation of the completeness of a narrative is based on the successful elaboration of this patterning. "Accounts are convincing not only because they may be believed in terms of the actors and actions, but also in terms of form. This form (...) is responsible for making the story seem to come out right, to be warranted in the sense of fitting a deep-seated cultural norm for the form of reported experience." (Hymes 1982, 137).

In its emphasis on the aesthetics of form as one of the guiding lines in performances, the ethnopoetic approach is in line with the Bakhtinian concept of finalization, by which is meant the constructive process whereby an utterance becomes complete (Bakhtin 1986, 76-77). Thus, the performer of an utterance, song or narrative, aims at fulfilling an internalized (but socially constituted) idea of completeness in the performance. In verse, finalization is manifested in the making of unitary structure (see e.g. Hanks 1987, 672).

Structural analysis although not structuralism

Ethnopoetic analysis focuses on the form of the performed act and its structure, that is, its composition of parts as related to the whole. It is based on the notion that within the logic of patterning performance – and reporting of experience – different segments or units in a song or narrative are linguistically and/or grammatically marked. Often the markers are initial adverbial particles, such as *meanwhile, so, and, then*, etc. Turns of speech may also count as units, and repetition of specific words or phrases (as well as initial alliteration in poetry) may also function as markers of units. The units and their markers show structure in the narrative discourse.

A narrative in ethnopoetic analysis is divided into various units which operate on a number of levels. They are lines, verses, scenes, acts, or stanzas. In Hymesian ethnopoetics, the line is the smallest unit, while in Tedlock's ethnopoetics the line is the largest unit. According to Hymes, "each change of predicate is likely to coincide with a change of line." (Hymes 1982, 140) A group of lines makes larger units such as verses, scenes, and acts or stanzas. The Hymesian transcript distinguishes these units in the overall structure with empty lines and with a varying degree of indentation. Empty lines separate succeeding units from one another, while indentation shows the relationship between units – both line-units and larger units. This relationship is based on either equality or subordination; thus it is hierarchical. The number of units in the overall structure of the text follows, according to Hymes, the culture-specific pattern number, or a multiple of it.

Hymes' ethnopoetic analysis focuses on stylistic and grammatical features in order to find the formal, poetic structure of a text, the underlying rhetorical form in the texture. This formal structure – the organization of the text into units of various kinds – is an end in itself but it is not the major goal of study. The final goal in ethnopoetic study is the meaning and function of a text in performance and communication, and this is based on the notion that interpretation is not only dependent on the referential contents of a text but also on the formal structure in which the contents are presented (see Briggs 1988, 19).

Hymes calls his ethnopoetics a structural method and an application of the elementary principle of structural linguistics, which is to look for covariation in form and meaning and patterning based upon it (Hymes 1981,

7). It is structuralist in the sense of the Prague School of Trubetzkoy and Jakobson, and the American tradition of Sapir, but it differs from Proppian and Lévi-Straussian structuralism in some fundamental ways. It is based on the pragmatic study of language, in which signs and texts are studied in terms of their use in communication. Semiotically speaking, meaning is studied in terms of the relationship between a sign and its user, and it is this approach that distinguishes ethnopoetics from formalism and structuralism.

For Propp (1968), structure is the syntagmatically patterned sequence of narrative action, or plot, which is constituted by a given set of functions. These are abstracted to represent a generic type, which is then used as a criterion for a taxonomic classification of the material. Lévi-Straussian structuralism looks for the syntagmatic and paradigmatic relationships of narrative elements as these represent fundamental oppositions in social and cultural structures. Since for Lévi-Strauss a narrative (a myth) consists, in a rather metaphysical way, of all of its 'versions', the scholar can use a composite text that consists of elements from any given performance (see Lévi-Strauss 1963, 217).[1]

In Lévi-Straussian structuralism Hymes questions especially its universalism as well as its ignorance of the linguistic organization of narratives. But the most important difference is that Lévi-Straussian structuralism excludes individual action, while the foundation of the ethnopoetic approach lies in the very act of individual performance, and its poetic patterning and rhetorical meanings. "Abstract relations among categories of plot and content are essential aspects of the understanding of myths, but aspects only. Artistry comes into view only if the text can be seen as a texture within which particular means have been chosen and deployed." (Hymes 1981, 10).

Text and its formal structure

Unlike Dennis Tedlock, Charles Briggs, and many other students of ethnopoetics who study performances that they themselves have observed, participated in and recorded, Dell Hymes analyzes texts that are available only as written documents. For this reason, although designed for the study of Native American narrative traditions, his method is perfectly applicable to the study of pre-modern Finnish tetrametric verse, which is available in archived documents only.[2] This can be studied as verbal art, although, as with the material that Hymes is using, we can hardly study the relationship between the text and its performance, its paralinguistic elements or the rhetorics and politics involved in the performance – except when information about these aspects is available, as is the case to some extent in rituals. Yet, despite these shortcomings, there are ways to do research on the material. "The gestures, voices, tunes, pauses of the original performances cannot be recovered. Still much of structure persists and can be perceived. Essential real relationships remain." (Hymes 1981, 7-8).

Most interestingly, the ethnopoetic approach takes as its starting point something that the students of Finnish oral verse have for the most part denied as existing: that is, the idea that the verse has a form and structure beyond the line unit. Representing common usage, Senni Timonen paraphrases what she calls "the so-called Kalevala metre" as "non-strophic trochaic tetrameters" (Timonen 1992, 214). Pentti Leino, a leading authority in the study of the metrical systems of Finnish oral verse, states explicitly that the syntax of the meter, the stanza structure is altogether missing (Leino 1986, 134, 146, 159). According to Leino, a song lacks a metrical syntax and thus consists of an optional number of successive independent lines (Leino 1986, 130, 132). "There is no stanza structure, for the boundary between typographical 'stanzas' (an empty line) can be placed between any two lines regardless of any metrical restrictions." (Leino 1986, 146).

Leino's categorical denial of structure in Finnish verse represents an extreme attitude in a long debate and dispute. In the early 1920s Kaarle Krohn published a collection of lyrical songs in which he arranged his material in stanzas of eight lines, or four line pairs, which he claimed to be their standard length (Krohn 1920; see also Krohn 1931, v; Haavio 1952b, 243; Hautala 1954, 372-33). This inspired Martti Haavio three decades later to look for other strophic patterns in the printed collections of lyrical songs in Finnish oral verse (SKVR), and he found material with which he argued for a three stanza structure that was comprised of either 6+6+4 lines or 5+5+5 lines (Haavio 1952b, 243-245). After taking a look at other verse material as well, he came to the conclusion that all Finnish oral verse consists of stanzas with 4, 5, 6, 7, 9, or 10 lines (Haavio 1952a, 223; Haavio 1952b, 246).

Haavio regarded these stanzas as being strict in form and of the same length in each song (Haavio 1952a, 221). Here he was led by his desire to argue that Finnish pre-modern verse was not 'primitive' and therefore 'chaotic', but instead, was highly patterned (see Haavio 1952b). Yet, he did not present any structural markers to determine these forms, except that, according to him, they followed a given number of lines. He did not discuss why the singers of oral verse in an oral culture, where the lines are not visualized in a sequence on the printed page, as they were for Haavio, should create order in their songs by structuring them on the basis of the number of lines.

Such a numerical pattern of order could possibly be determined by the musical structure of the songs, if that were based on units of a certain number of elements. However, this possibility for an explanation Haavio does not even refer to.[3] Haavio argues that the line units are also thought entities, but the example that he prints (1952a, 221-222) reveals that he must use a period – a structural marker known only in written culture – *within* a stanza, to indicate a change in its thematic contents. Moreover, he takes the liberty of omitting those lines that according to him do not fit in the structure – and explains these as "contagion from alien contact" (Haavio 1952a, 221).

Haavio called his method "structural analysis", by which he meant a perspective in which the scholar looks for thematic wholes in the texture, and "learns its shape" and "basic design" (1952b, 245-246). Within this design, there are smaller dramatic units or 'scenes' (1952a, 224). Because in most cases these lie, according to Haavio, underneath a "corrupted form" (1952b, 247), the scientific task of the scholar is to 'restore' the text and its structure to its 'uncorrupted' condition. Haavio's "structural analysis", thus, follows faithfully the theoretical and methodological premises of historic-geographic research, which aims at reconstructing a text in its supposedly original form or an abstract ideal, a 'normal form' which could be assumed as a source for the recorded document. The only difference is that in the latter the text critical method operates on the level of lines instead of 'thematic wholes'.

Haavio's stanza theory received immediate criticism because the structures that he 'found' were to a great extent his own constructions and based on his own aesthetic principles (see Kuusi 1952a). As was pointed out by Matti Kuusi, one should study the authentic recordings for possible stanzas instead of imposing a strict pattern on them, deleting those lines that do not fit in and adding those that are thought to be missing (Kuusi 1952a, 394; see also Kuusi 1952b, 257-258). Another point of criticism was that Haavio's theory, according to Kuusi, squeezed the verse into rigid moulds, albeit a variety of them. While some critics regarded it impossible that an illiterate singer would be able to think out the form of the song he was about to sing, Kuusi considered it likely that oral verse in general contains structural patterns. However, he rejected Haavio's theory and was sceptical about any signs in the texture that would show its alleged stanzaic structure (Kuusi 1952a, 393).

Twenty years later Matti Kuusi had more understanding for Haavio's attempt at finding structures in Finnish oral verse and he justified Haavio's constructions both on aesthetic grounds and on the basis of "originality" (Kuusi 1972, 133). After reading the analysis by Roman Jakobson and Claude Lévi-Strauss on Charles Baudelaire's *Les chats*, Kuusi set out to make his own "structural analytic experiment". He found a number of elements in the texture that mark cohesion and contrast both within and across the stanzas in the text. However, instead of studying a text recorded from oral tradition – as he himself had recommended in 1952 – he used a text that had received its formal structure from Haavio.

The 'structural analyses' by Krohn, Haavio and Kuusi are all based on a devolutionistic premise (see Dundes 1969), according to which the recorded songs are more or less flawed copies of 'missing original gems', which have been composed by true artists somewhere in the murky past of ancient times. This positions the performers of oral verse as 'clumsy archivists' and – to borrow an expression from a statement that speaks for the dialogic research on language – as "dupes who lack the ability to reflect meaningfully to their own communicative conduct" (Bauman and Briggs 1990, 66).

According to Lauri Honko, Haavio's "structural analysis" has nothing to do with the structuralism that received its impulse from Lévi-Strauss and Propp (Honko 1986, 58). This need not, however, be taken as a point of criticism since Haavio's approach was actually an attempt at finding poetic structure in the texture – something that neither Propp nor Lévi-Strauss was striving for. Yet, following the principles of positivistic science, Haavio's search for poetic structure was an attempt at establishing structural laws. The structures that he 'found' were those that the songs 'should have contained', had they not been 'corrupted' by the devolution of oral tradition (see also Turunen 1952).[4]

The question of formal structure in Finnish tetrametric verse has received renewed attention in the light of the theory of oral composition, which eventually came to be known as Milman Parry's and Albert B. Lord's oral formulaic theory. This first came up as early as the 1940s in the writings of Jouko Hautala, who suggested that a new song could be constructed by retrieving lines as well as sequences of lines from songs that the performer already knows (Hautala 1942, 36; see also Hautala 1945, 15-17; Hautala 1947, 40-43). Outi Lehtipuro has named Hautala's approach 'pre-Lordian' (Lehtipuro 1974, 16).[5]

Hautala emphasized how the oral composition of verse is based on a collective taste in aesthetics, as well as on the performer's and hearer's evaluation of what serves the form and cohesion of the text (Hautala 1942, 37). In this particular issue, Hautala's thinking comes close to the arguments of Väinö Kaukonen, a literary scholar who emphasized that the recorded documents of Finnish oral verse are specimens of verbal art and should be studied as such. Representing a paradigmatic difference from the 'historic-geographers' and typologists, Kaukonen insisted that instead of speculating on 'original forms' or 'normal forms', which he calls pseudohistory (Kaukonen 1982b, 85), one should regard the recorded documents as artefacts of poetic expression and performance, which can and must be studied in terms of texture as well as intertextually – both synchronically and diachronically (see e.g. Kaukonen 1979, 346-347; Kaukonen 1982a, 348, 350, 354).

Starting in the late 1980s, a new paradigm is now completely rejecting the premises of the old Finnish method. Its foundations lie in the growing tendency to focus on the living performers of oral verse, and on the social reality of the singers from whom the songs were recorded in the 19th and early 20th centuries (see e.g. Pentikäinen 1978 and 1991; Timonen 1990 and 1992). In accordance with the oral formulaic theory, Finnish oral verse is now being studied and discussed in terms of textual variation without the devolutionistic paradigm and, therefore, regarded as having been constructed, produced and reproduced in each performance by the singer's use of such elements as formulae and themes (see e.g. Saarinen 1988 and 1991; Tarkka 1989, 38, 43; Tarkka 1990, 48-57; Harvilahti 1992, 10, 141-147).

Criticizing the tendency to view and evaluate Finnish oral verse through the criteria of Western literary traditions and conventions, Lotte Tarkka points out that variation in performances or products of sung verse cannot be condemned as flaws or slips of memory on the basis of the scholars' ideal constructions of their contents (Tarkka 1989, 41, 53; see also Tarkka 1993). However, in terms of the singers' own poetic means and aesthetic goals, the songs do contain both flaws and slips of memory. Even though a performance is not based on a fixed text that is merely memorized verbatim, the singers do have an opinion about the song's completeness or incompleteness. This is supported, for example, by a quotation from Elias Lönnrot's travel descriptions, in which he depicts his encounter with the singer Martiska Karjalainen as follows: "He sang me this poem, even though, as he said, and as can be seen, it is incomplete, because he did not remember everything that he earlier had had plenty of extra time to compose." (Quoted in Tarkka 1989, 39).

To be regarded as complete, a song must express what the singer wanted to express, and contain those artistic elements which the singer wanted it to contain in order to serve his or her rhetorical purposes. Because a song's structure is based on poetic criteria, it is evaluated by the performer himself or herself as well as by the audience on the basis of how it fulfills the aesthetic criteria of form and structure – the socially constituted expectations of form and structure. Ethnopoetic analysis starts from the very idea that the recorded documents represent the aesthetic and poetic values of their performers, and for this reason the aesthetics and poetics become the main object of research.

It is obvious that not all recorded documents represent their singers' aesthetic choices and poetic ideals in their fulfillment. Communication can fail, for one reason or another, and the recordings themselves as well as the recording situations may have been unsatisfactory. Whether a document recorded a hundred years ago through oral dictation represents the singer's idea of a finalized form or not, is of course now impossible to say, unless the singer's comments to this effect have been recorded. Yet, the basic premise in the study of Finnish oral verse must be that no matter how long a history the songs may have had before the existing documents were recorded, they were not performed for antiquarian interests but for communicative purposes.

It is highly relevant for the purposes of the present article to note how, in his analysis of variation in epic verse, Jukka Saarinen emphasizes the hierarchical character of the texture (Saarinen 1988, 85; Saarinen 1991, 196, 198). According to Saarinen, the textual variation is based on this hierarchy, and therefore, variation is based on the fact that singers can omit that which is subordinated, and parallel lines with corresponding elements can change places (Saarinen 1988, 183, 186; Saarinen 1991, 205). In parallelism and other elements that are subordinate in the textual hierarchy, the ordering principle for Saarinen is thematic; that is, whether particular elements in the narrative contents can be regarded as helping the story line to proceed or whether they give 'additional' information: describe, specify or justify other parts in the text (Saarinen 1991, 196).

Saarinen's findings call for further studies on how the variation based on thematic hierarchy is related to the formal and poetic structure of the texture, since, as Roman Jakobson has pointed out, "The verse design... sets up the limits for variation" (Jakobson 1960, 364). The same applies to Lauri Harvilahti's study on the oral production of epic verse, in which the structures that he presents are thematic abstractions ('macro structures' and 'super structures') based on his own reading of the linearly progressing narrative sequence (see Harvilahti 1992, 97-140). Similar thematic abstraction is employed in Senni Timonen's study on the lyrical verse of first person narratives (Timonen 1990). In a more ethnopoetic approach, the present article aims at finding thematic units as they are founded upon actual markers in the linguistic structure of the text; in other words, in the form in which the narrative contents are set by the performer.

Parallelism as a structural marker

One of the main stylistic features in Finnish oral verse is parallelism, which may be morphological, lexical, syntactic, or semantic. Morphological

Women of Ingria. Photo: Vihtori Alava 1892 (MV).

parallelism includes case-endings as well as parts of compound words, which can also be counted as examples of lexical parallelism. It is worthy of note that even though scholars from Lönnrot (1846, 10-53) to Leino (1986, 134, 146) deny the existence of end-rhyme in Finnish oral verse, it does occur when there is morphological parallelism at the end of the line. As Hannu Launonen points out, Lönnrot as well as August Ahlqvist and others discuss rhyme in terms of sonority, instead of semantics or its position in the structure of a poem (Launonen 1984, 21).

In the following example the repetition of the phrase *illan istu* 'sat the night' represents both lexical and syntactic parallelism, while *illan istu toisen itki* 'sat the night, cried another' is syntactic parallelism. Parallelism may, thus, occur internally or between two or more lines.

> missä neito illan istu
> > illan istu, toisen itki   (SKVR III:3, 3188)
>
> where the maiden sat the night
> > sat the night, cried another

In semantic parallelism, the contents of one line are repeated in another line with different words. There is, then, correspondence either synonymically, analogically, or antithetically. According to a parallelism rule in the metrics of Finnish oral verse, the repeated line may not contain any syntactic element (object, subject, verb, etc.) which has no corresponding element in the line that it repeats (Leino 1986, 135). For example:

> Silloin vanha Väinämöinen
>
> sortui sormin lainehille
> kämmenin vesille kääntyi

121

Then the old Väinämöinen

> sank with fingers to the waves
> turned with palms to the waters

(Leino 1986, 135; translation by Andrew Chesterman)

In this example, the verbs *sortui* 'sank' and *kääntyi* 'turned' correspond, as do *lainehille* 'to the waves' and *vesille* 'to the waters' and again *sormin* 'with fingers' and *kämmenin* 'with palms'.

According to Leino, a line may have one or even several parallels, but it is by no means obligatory to have any (Leino 1986, 135). This is not, however, as accidental and random as Leino suggests, and the lines are not as independent as Leino claims them to be (Leino 1986, 130). There is a hierarchical relationship between the lines, as can be seen in the typography of the previous examples. Both the indentation and the empty line here indicate relation, while according to Leino, an empty line can be placed between any two lines regardless of any metrical restrictions (Leino 1986, 146). The following example will make the hierarchy even clearer.

Neito aitass' paoss'

> issoihe hyvvyyen pääll'
> velloin vehnä-purnun pääll'

> yheksän lukun takkaan'
>> takalukku kymmenäs

Oli enne meijen siskoi

> oli ko ori-heppoine
>> taie tamman varsukkaine

> pisyneet ei pisto-aijat
>> teko-vitsaist veräjät

> kaikk' löi rikki rinnallaa
>> halki hartiaisillaa

(SKVR III:2, 2265)

The maiden hiding in the loft

> upon her fathers' goods
> upon her brothers' wheat bin

> behind nine [outside] locks
>> inside lock the tenth

122

Our sister used to be

like a steed she used to be
or like a mare's filly

the fences didn't stay up
the withed gates

she broke all with her breast
split it with her shoulders

The semantic parallelism in this example shows that even though a line is a basic unit, a song is not structured upon a list of lines of equal rank and status. Semantic parallelism itself implies that the repeated line is secondary to the line whose contents it repeats.

This repetition can be of two kinds: first, the repeated line may contain all the same syntactic elements as the line to which it offers semantic parallelism. Second, it may contain only some of these syntactic elements. In the former case the two lines are equal in terms of their comprehensibility (which of course is socially and culturally constituted). In the latter case the repeated line is comprehensible only in its relation to the line to which it represents semantic parallelism. This is why the repeated line is here indented in relation to its preceding parallel line. Indentation marks subordination.

Together the parallel lines form a couplet, but this is not an independent unit, either syntactically or semantically. The couplet does not form an independent unit because its referential meaning is comprehensible only in relation to the line before it. This is the main line, and it is worth noting here that it has no parallel line. The main line is independent syntactically and semantically; it makes an independent statement. However, in certain cases it may also continue in the following line.

In the above example, the first main line (*Neito aitass paoss'* The Maiden Hiding in the Loft') is an independent line, and the following two couplets are its qualifiers. The second main line (*Oli enne meijen siskoi* 'Our Sister Used to be') could be interpreted as an independent statement, but most likely it must be taken as continuing in the following line, which repeats the verb and completes the comparison that is implied in the main line.

Instead of being all independent and of equal status, the lines form larger units, and parallelism itself is a proof of this, as is also pointed out by Jukka Saarinen (1988, 183, 197). In the example quoted above, the units are semantic in nature and structured upon a main line with no corresponding parallel line, as well as its qualifiers, which form couplets. As is the case in the latter part of the above example, the qualifying couplets may be hierarchically related to one another. All of this, thus, indicates an internal, finalized structure. It shows that semantic parallelism has an indexical function in the structure. The fact that some lines have parallel lines and some do not is not accidental.

Alliteration as a structural marker

Another typical feature of Finnish oral verse is alliteration, which falls into two types. In weak alliteration two or more words within one line begin with the same consonant followed by a different vowel (*silloin seppo ilmarinen*), or they begin with different vowels (*ulapalla aukealla*). In strong alliteration, which is dominant, identical word-initial consonants are followed by the same vowel (*vaka vanha Väinämöinen; löysi piitä pikkaraisen*) (Leino 1986, 134).

According to Leino, the cases in which alliteration extends beyond the line boundary "are usually to be interpreted as statistical accidents" (Leino 1986, 134). However, alliteration beyond the line unit marks a structure larger than the line unit, and this is no accident but a characteristic feature of the form-content relationship. This can be seen in an example given by Leino himself, albeit he gives it for another argument.

> Silloin vanha Väinämöinen
> sortui sormin lainehille,
> kämmenin vesille kääntyi.
> Siellä kulki kuusi vuotta,
> seisoi seitsemän keseä,
> kulki kuusissa hakona,
> petäjäissä pölkyn päänä.

The translation given by Leino is as follows:

> Then the old Väinämöinen
> sank with fingers to the waves
> turned with palms to the water:
> there he wandered for six years
> stopped there for seven summers
>   wandered as a spruce
> as a log from a pine-tree.

(Leino 1986, 135; translation by Andrew Chesterman)

Leino follows here the conventional style of transcription, but he does not explain the differences between the Finnish and the English text in punctuation, nor the indentation of the second to last line in the English text. What is more important, though, is the fact that the text is highly structured, and the structure is created not only with parallelism and the hierarchical relation of lines, but also with alliteration. This becomes evident when we first arrange the lines in accordance with their interrelations, as follows:

> Silloin vanha Väinämöinen
>
>   sortui sormin lainehille
>   kämmenin vesille kääntyi
>
> Siellä kulki kuusi vuotta
>   seisoi seitsemän keseä
>
>   kulki kuusissa hakona
>   petäjissä pölkyn päänä

124

The hierarchy that is created by parallelism and by the interrelations of lines is supported here by alliteration that extends beyond the line unit. The overall structure of two sections or scenes is made coherent and the texture receives its rhythm by having both scenes start with a line that begins with *si*. Both of the first lines are followed by a line in which the first two words relate to the initial *si* of the previous line with weak alliteration: they start with *s*. Both of these sets of words, then, relate to each other with strong alliteration: in the first scene with *so*, and in the second, with *se*. Alliteration within the line unit, both strong and weak, is met with in every line.

The example also shows obvious variation in the formal structure of the texture, which is not, therefore, based on "an optional number of successive independent lines", as suggested by Leino, nor on a rigid stanza pattern as suggested by Haavio. It is something in between, a form that has more variation than just consisting of a repetitive pattern of main line + parallel line. In the above example, as far as line parallelism is concerned, the first scene has a one + two form, while the second has a two + two form.

The second scene is further made coherent by the repetition of the verb *kulki* 'wandered', and the two occurrences are positioned in the transcription on the same vertical level. Note how the verb is in both cases joined by the homonymical word *kuusi*: first meaning a number ('six') and then a tree ('spruce'). The two occurrences of *kulki kuusi* represent lexical and phonetic parallelism but not semantic parallelism. Yet, it can be argued that the stylistic feature of having similarity in form with dissimilarity in referential meaning is itself a formal and poetic means of creating a coherent structure in the texture. Although different in meaning, the second occurrence of *kulki kuusi* becomes a marker of structural coherence by making a direct reference, by its mere occurence, to the earlier occurrence of the same linguistic signs. This follows the very function of verse: to reverse (see Launonen 1984, 31).[6]

Particles as structural markers

In addition to the relation between lines, parallelism, and alliteration, we must, in accordance with the ethnopoetic method as developed by Dell Hymes, pay attention to such linguistic elements as particles as structural markers. According to Hymes, study of the repetition of particles is one of the means of defining the structure which the performer has intended the text to disclose (Hymes 1981, 7). These particles may be sentence-initial or they may be added to the end of a word (as is customary in the Finnish language, thus: tuli*pa*, meni*pä*, toit*ko*, menit*kö*).

The above examples (except those quoted from Leino 1986) are excerpts from a wedding song which we will now look at in its entirety. The song was collected by Vihtori Alava in the village of Säätinä, on the Soikkola peninsula of Western Ingria, in 1892. The singer is an Izhor (Greek Orthodox) woman named Ol'a, and the song is in dialectal Finnish. In her comments to the song (the footnotes in the published text), the singer says that this is one of the four songs addressed to the extended family, *Sukuvirsi*, and it is performed when the bridegroom has arrived at the bride's house and sits at the table. The 'village girls', i.e. the bride's agemates and friends, sing.

(A)   Tere kuu, tere päivä

    tere kuu yli vessiin
    päivöi päältä tanvahien

        yli maien markkoi-rinta
        yli soien sormus-sormi

(B)   Toitko senen, minen lupasit?

  Toitko ait(t)ojen avvaimet?

    Neito aitass' paoss'

        issoihe hyvvyyen pääll'
        velloin vehnä-purnun pääll'

        yheksän lukun takkaan'
            takalukku kymmenäs

    Oli enne meijen siskoi

        oli ko ori-heppoine
            taie tamman varsukkaine

        pisyneet ei pisto-aijat
            teko-vitsaist veräjät

        kaikk' löi rikki rinnallaa
        halki hartiaisillaa

(C)   La nyt kysyn langoiltaan:

    Vai vävy on sivulta väärä
        vävy polvelta potteeva
        vävy on sairas santukoilta

        ku vävy istuu väärällää
            ja kovast' kossallaa?

    Vai on laavitsat lamass'
    vai on pölkyt kossallaa?

    Ei oo pölkyt kossallaa
    eik' oo laavitsas lamass'

        sill' on vävy väärällää

        jos paljo on syynt papin pappuuja
        herranvallan hernehiä

(D)   La mie kysyn langoiltaan:

        Onko teien velloistanne

            saap'ka leipää lehost'
            punakoort' koivikost'

                    (SKVR III:2, 2265)

(A)   Welcome moon, welcome sun

        welcome moon across the waters
        sun from over the plains

            across the firm land valor-breasted
            across the marshland ring-fingered

(B)   Have you brought what you promised?

     Have you brought the loft keys?

        The maiden hiding in the loft

            upon her fathers' goods
            upon her brothers' wheat bin

            behind nine [outside] locks
            inside lock the tenth

     Our sister used to be

        like a steed she used to be
        or like a mare's filly

            the fences didn't stay up
            the withed gates

            she broke all with her breast
            split it with her shoulders

(C)   So now I ask the in-laws:

        Or is the son-in-law gimpy in the side
        the son-in-law smarting in the knee
        the son-in-law sick in the crotch

            since he's sitting crookedly
            and tilting terribly?

        Or are the wall-benches warped
        or are the bench legs tilted?

The bench legs are not tilted
the wall-benches not warped

for the son-in-law [sits] crookedly

perhaps he has eaten a lot of the priest's beans
the manor lord's peas

(D)   So I ask the in-laws:

Is your brother worthy

can he make bread out of the grove
red bark from the birch forest?

The transcription of a text recorded at an oral performance is an essential theoretical and methodological question, whether one pays attention to it or not. All textual presentations by ethnographers – including folklorists – are based on a conscious or unconscious notion about the structure and other formal properties of the stretch of speech or song which they are transforming from an aural experience into writing. Most typically, scholars tend to use the established Western prose and verse formats without a second thought.

The architectural layout in the transcription of the above text is based on the following principles: First, an empty space between the lines in the vertical dimension marks the separation of the texture into both larger and smaller units. Second, these units are formed on the basis of the relations in which the lines stand to each other, and they are shown in the transcription by indentation (or lack of it).

The relation between lines is either that of subordination or of equality, except that lines in a vertical order can never be completely equal. The degree of indentation grows towards the right in correlation with the level of subordination. Thus, the lines beginning on the same vertical level have a corresponding status in the overall structure of the song, and the lines furthest to the left share the function of opening the major, thematic units. These thematic units are marked in the transcription with the letters A, B, C, and D in brackets.

The smallest unit is the independent line. It stands alone without a parallel line, and its referential contents can be understood without a reference to another line. It makes an independent statement. The next largest unit is the couplet, in which two lines are placed in immediate sequence. The couplet is based on parallelism in which the two lines have either an equal or a subordinated relationship. Indentation within a couplet indicates subordination of the latter line by the former, which is based on the fact that the referential contents of the latter line become comprehensible only in the context of the former. These are cases in which the semantic and syntactic parallelism between the two lines does not cover all of the linguistic elements in the lines.

An example of a couplet with subordination:

tere kuu yli vessiin
päivöi päältä tanhavien

welcome moon across the waters
sun from over the plains.

Whether that which is subordinated in a parallelism relationship can be omitted in different performances, as is suggested by Saarinen (1988, 183, 186), requires comparative analysis on how such omissions affect the overall formal structure of texture. Further research is, thus, due here.

In addition to subordination, the relationship between the two lines in a couplet can be equal in the sense that neither of them requires the other for comprehension, as far as referential meaning is concerned. Yet, they both may need a third line to make sense. For example, the comprehension of the parallel lines

issoihe hyvvyyen pääll'
velloin vehnä-purnun pääll'

upon her father's goods
upon her brother's wheat bin

requires the preceding line

neito aitass' paoss'

the maiden hiding in the loft

because this contains the subject and the implicit predicate. The two parrallel lines are qualifiers to this line, and therefore the three lines are semantically and structurally joined together. Note how the end-rhyme also creates structural coherence in the couplet.

Although such a couplet contains lines that are mutually correspondent in relation to a third line, they are, however, not completely equal. First of all there is hierarchy between them because one comes before the other. Whether this relation is interchangeable, as is suggested by Saarinen (1991, 205), depends on the contents and their referential meaning. Here the couplet contains a reference to two close relatives of the maiden, of which the father has obviously more status than the brother. Social hierarchy is thus directly represented – and commented upon – in the formal structure of a poetic expression. When such a comment is a confirmation, negation or contestation, and how it is marked, is not discussed here.

It is worth noting that the line to which the couplets are qualifiers – their main line – does not have a parallel line. Whether this is a stylistic and/or structural marker used more generally in Finnish oral verse, requires additional comparative analysis. However, here it forms a structural and thematic unit with the qualifying couplets, which can therefore be called a scene. The scenes are part of larger units which can be called acts or stanzas.

The overall structure in the above song consists of four acts, marked here by the letters A, B, C and D, respectively.

The division of the song into these four acts is based on the following factors. The most striking indexical sign of formal structure here is the particle *la* 'so', which occurs on two occasions: at the beginning of the opening lines for both acts C and D. They both begin an explication of an intention to make a question, and the rest of the contents in both acts discuss the theme introduced in the questions. Thus, the particle is a boundary marker which indicates a thematic change in the contents of the song in both places where it occurs. While there is formal correspondence between these acts, they consist of different thematic spaces in relation to each other.

The second act (B) does not begin with the particle *lo*, but the introduction to this act begins with a question, and thus it is syntactically similar to the opening lines of acts C and D. Moreover, both of the two opening lines of act B contain the particle *ko*, which is attached to the verb (*toit-ko* 'did you bring', 'have you brought'), and which marks a question. The lines that follow them – down to the next question beginning with the boundary marker *la* – constitute both a thematic and a structural entity in two sections or scenes, just as act C does.

But instead of focusing merely on the particle, we can notice that the question format – introduced in two cases with the same particle – is also a structural marker here. This can be regarded as formulaic. Therefore, a formula can have an essential function in the poetic structure of a song, both as a boundary marker between units and as a marker of cohesion and overall design (see also Harvilahti 1992, 57-59, 142).

Note that the two questions opening the second act are not parallel lines, and therefore there is an empty space between them in the transcription. According to the parallelism rule, the latter line cannot contain elements that do not have a correspondent in the former line (Leino 1986, 135). Here only the verb and the particle are the same, without syntactic, lexical or morphological parallelism. Yet, there is an implicit semantic correspondence that supports their positioning next to each other: a referential connection between 'what you promised' and 'the loft keys'.

Note also how the two initial question verbs in act B alliterate with the initial verb beginning the first act (A). The initial consonant *t* here represents morphological parallelism, and thus, it is a case in which alliteration beyond the line unit has an indexical function in marking units in the formal structure. Beginning a line with an initial *t* in the questions that open the second act makes a reference to the previous occurrence of the letter *t* in an initial position. The units thus separated share the same formal structure but differ in their thematic contents. Here, as elsewhere, boundary markers both separate and unite.

A finalized structure

Methodologically, when studying communication that foregrounds form, it is of the utmost importance that the thematic units or components in the syntagmatic structure of the text are not based on the scholar's intuitive reading. The division of the text into episodes, and the abstraction of these

Ingrian girls learned the art of singing within the context of the peer group. Photo: Vihtori Alava 1892 (MV).

to themes, functions, motifemes and the like, must be based on formal markers in the texture: those that create cohesion as well as those that mark boundaries. Thus, the Proppian approach to syntagmatic structure, thematic analysis that separates contents from form, must be complemented with the ethnopoetic approach.[7]

Here the first act or stanza consists of the greeting of the arriving groom, in which he is predicated with the metaphors of the moon and the sun.[8] According to the singer, he is like a person coming from abroad, from foreign lands (SKVR III:2, 2265), and indeed, he is adorned with symbols and metaphoric images that link him with the domain of the celestial bodies. Yet, he is also predicated, in metonomy, with a symbol of wealth (*markkoi-rinta* 'valor-breasted') and a symbol of marriage and union (*sormus-sormi* 'ring-fingered').

The second act discusses the bride and presents her as a challenge to the groom. In the first scene the bride is in hiding while the second scene depicts her as being difficult to tame. The first scene presents her as being protected by the symbols of wealth, which also make a reference to the exchange rate that the groom has to meet in order to marry her. In the second scene, as the singer comments, she is presented as valorous and confident (SKVR III:2, 2265), and accordingly, she is predicated with wild, young horses. As a typical trope for unmarried females in the wedding song genre, this speaks for the positioning of the female as an element of nature that the bridegroom as a man and a symbolical hunter is expected to bring into the domain of culture.

The third act discusses the groom by questioning his health and physical fitness in the first scene, and making him look politically suspicious in the second one. The implication is that the groom is incapable of meeting the challenge presented in the previous act, and the function of such a proposition is to test his and his retinue's reactions. This is in line with the custom of ridiculing a hunter – or a lover – that is met with in many cultures. In view of the fact that serfdom in Ingria was abolished in 1861 (see Kastsenko 1986), 30 years before this song was recorded, the reference to the feudal lord might seem outdated. Yet, it functions as a metaphor for the powers that be, together with the priest, and thus, speaks for both class consciousness and class solidarity. Bringing this up with reference to the groom – even if this was "just a joke" – is a discursive act upon the interests between the local people in relation to the power institutions. The metaphors of food in this comment refer to political loyalty founded upon economic dependence.

The fourth act continues to focus on the groom, but with a different approach and attitude. The singer inquires his abilities in work, and his skills in slash-and-burn cultivation. The forest metaphors relate to the ability to provide a livelihood for one's family, and thus, the social and political meaning of food is quite different here from in the previous act. According to the singer's comments, the final line refers to the clearing of new land for cultivation and marking the boundaries of that territory (SKVR III:2, 2265).

In its overall structure, the text shows elaborated symmetry. It has four acts, the first and last of which have one scene each, while the second and third both have two. It thus shows compositional finalization in form, although both the contents of the final act – a question or call – and the polarized thematic structure of the whole text create expectation of a question-response formal pattern. Indeed, the song printed in the SKVR immediately after this one, and recorded from the same singer, continues the question-response pattern (SKVR III:2, 2266). The four acts and their scenes can also be viewed as sequences of action in a plot structure. These can then be abstracted, in a Proppian manner, to the functions of initial situation (greeting), presentation of challenge, testing of the hero, and call.

Despite the highly formalized overall structure, there is variation in the smaller units. Some scenes contain couplets that are of rather equal status to their main line, while others contain varying degrees of subordination. The number of qualifying couplets can also vary, and act C has a triplet instead of a couplet. Thus, there is variation in the structure itself, not only in relation to other texts.

Formal structure signals meaning

As mentioned above, the ethnopoetic method does not merely look for the formal structure, since the motivation for structural analysis is to study how the contents receive their meanings in relation to the form in which they are expressed in performance. But in addition to the contents and their linguistic form, we must have relevant information about the culture and the social institutions, including cultural and social categories, customs, practices and values, to which the contents make references and in the context of which they receive their referential and rhetorical meanings.

The wedding ritual is characterized by the fact that it foregrounds form in communication. The ritual is a patterned sequence of events and acts, charged with symbolic meaning, and performed in a style that foregrounds formal structures, such as formalized verbal expressions. The sung verse, the wedding songs, are only a part, albeit an important one, of these formalized and poetic expressions. In terms of form, contents, and use in the ritual, the wedding song is a particular communicative genre employing particular stylistic forms, and the poetic expressions performed as songs in the ritual are related – both in performance and in their evaluation by the audience – to its generic features. In addition to the evaluations on how the songs fulfill the generic criteria of the wedding song, they are evaluated on the basis of how they are used – intentionally or unintentionally – in discussing and negotiating the social relations that are being redefined in the rite of passage.

Because the participants at any wedding ritual represent two groups – members, friends and neighbors of the bride's family vs. those of the groom – there are basically two audiences for every act and utterance. The two families are entering into a socially and economically significant relationship, and for this reason, there is motivation to find a mutual framing for successful communication. Yet, interpretations are still potentially influenced by the mutually contradictory perspectives between the two families, one of which is a wife-giver (losing a member) and the other, a wife-taker (gaining a member). It is this fundamentally inequal relationship in which the politics of the event are embedded, and as Edmund Leach points out, this inequality is "built into the structure of the local political ideology" (Leach 1976, 68). For this reason, social acts and verbal expressions are not merely referential symbols or representations of social and cultural categories, but receive their rhetorical meanings within the politics of the situation, the negotiations of social and economic relations.

One means of negotiating the mutual relationship between the two families is the dyadic exchange of formalized verbal expressions that carry the potentiality of being interpreted as either jokes or insults. This was characteristic of Ingrian weddings in pre-modern times, though by no means unique. In addition to being an authoritative rite of passage, the ritual is expected to contain a ludic and convivial atmosphere, and therefore the participants expect at least some of the wedding songs to provide sources of humor and laughter. However, because of the fundamental difference in the perspectives between the two families involved, the verbal expressions may carry or create meanings that threaten the convivial atmosphere. The genre of the verbal expressions, in terms of as a category of meaning, is thus negotiated in the interaction situation.

In view of the exchanged comments as potential jokes and insults, the ritual communication poses to its participants – as well as to its researchers – the following fundamental questions: How is the genre negotiated? How is the ludic element marked? How is the joke told from an insult?

When we focus our attention in the above text on the statement about the groom, according to which he is physically deformed – act C – we notice how it is placed in the overall structure of the text. Had we just picked out the motif and studied its contents separately, for example in comparison with other similar comments in other texts – the similarity being determined by the scholar – we would only have understood its referential meaning as an utterance that suggests the groom is deformed. This would have meant studying the utterance as an abstraction and in isolation from its cotext as well as from the discourse in which it receives both its form and its rhetorical meaning. Obviously we could not have studied it in terms of how it was performed, and how it was received by the audience, because that information is not available. Yet, we would have studied it even in isolation from its textual framing, its position in the formal structure of the song, and therefore without any information as to its genre.

Placed within a finalized structure, which creates and fulfills expectations of form, the contents metacommunicate their rhetorical meaning through this very form, and the audience makes interpretations about the contents with reference to this poetic frame – although not solely based on this.

The utterances about the groom are, first of all, expressed by the performers from the bride's side, second, in verse, and thirdly, within the same formal structure as their comments on the bride. For this reason, the comments on the groom are directly related to and contextualized with the comments on the bride. As mentioned earlier, act B praises the bride and presents her as a challenge to the groom, while act C questions the groom's competence in meeting the challenge.

The polarization of the bride and the groom is framed within the formal structure of a song, which has a particular communicative function in the particular phase of the wedding ritual in which it is performed. It is a song of welcome to the groom and his retinue when they enter the bride's native home. It is thus a song (and rite) of aggregation after the groom's passage from his home to hers within a processual structure that is itself a rite of passage.[9] Yet, it is a song that is performed on her family's territory, and addressed to the people who have entered this territory in order to take the bride to the groom's native home, where the new couple will take up residence. Thus, the situation carries a sense of contradiction and double meaning of welcoming and sending away, of joining and losing.

The song represents the dual nature of the situation by containing, within the same formal structure, both praise and scorn of the groom. For this reason, act C receives at least some of its rhetorical meaning by being contextualized with act A, in which the groom is greeted with praise. Expressed together within the same formal structure, the interpretation of the two statements, which are contradictory in their referential meaning, takes place with direct reference to each other, within the same frame and contextual realm – the realm that carries a fundamentally dual nature to the singers of this song, the relatives and friends of the bride.

The polarization of the bride and the groom in acts B and C makes a further reference to the polarized relation between the two families within the structure of the whole communicative event. The two acts within the formal structure of a wedding song are thus in a 'microcosmic' relation to the formal structure of the wedding ritual. Thus, the negotiation by the audience(s) of the meaning of the utterances about the groom in act C is in direct relationship to the negotiation of relations between the two families, both within the ritual frame and afterwards.

But even though form signals meaning, it does not determine it or guarantee it. The meaning is also influenced by the interpretation of the possible motivations and rhetorical purposes considered by the audience to be embedded in the acts and utterances. Borrowing Gregory Bateson's view of play, framing does not construct a premise 'This is a joke' but evolves the question 'Is this a joke?' (see Bateson 1972, 182). The negotiation of the genre as a category of meaning is based on 'writing' and 'reading' of signs which change from context to context, depending on what is brought into the interpretative process as relevant issues by those who participate in the communication (Briggs 1988, 15; see also Goffman 1974; Gumperz 1982). As J. L. Austin points out about ritual acts, the meaning is based on what else is said or done that is made relevant in relation to the act (Austin 1976 [1962], 69-70).

Incompetence in performance

For comparative purposes, let us finally look at an incident that took place in a wedding in the village of Loka, on the Soikkola peninsula in Western Ingria. No information is available as to when this incident occurred but it was taken down from an Izhor singer named Anni Moisef in 1938. The story refers to the custom of covering the bride's face with a veil when departing from her native home, and lifting it up at the groom's home for her display.

"It happened once in our village that the bride had only one eye when the veil was lifted. The groom had known it but others in the family had not. Then the groom's brother Miihkula started to lament and sing:

> Voi polloinen poika
> voi velloin sinnuu

> Ei ole kanallais ehk kahta silmääkää
> jo saitkii sie silmäpuolen

> Oh poor boy
> oh brother mine

> Your hen may not even have two eyes
> now you've got yourself a one-eyed one

Then the relatives took Miihkula and walked him to the loft to bed. It was not appropriate to insult the bride, even though she had only one eye." (SKS. Ulla Mannonen 7656).

Here the informant has defined the song as an insult. Yet, in terms of textual framing the utterance is finalized according to the formal properties of the wedding song genre, just as in the earlier example. In view of the available collection of wedding songs in the archives, we can also say that the theme of accusing the bride for having only one eye is in line with the traditional verse material.

Thus, a competence to adopt traditional material for verbal expressions – "to reproduce tradition" – does not guarantee a successful performance (cf. Pentikäinen 1978, 18-19; Siikala 1990, 14; Harvilahti 1992, 24, 146).

The singer in the above incident may have been competent in exploiting the formal properties of the genre in which he attempted to perform, but he did not have competence in producing an appropriate synthesis of textual and contextual realms (see Briggs 1988, 357). In that sense his 'break-through into performance' (Hymes 1975) was a failure.[10] Drunk as he seems to have been, he was walked off to bed.

Discussing a type of ritual insult called 'the sound', William Labov has pointed out how a successful 'sound' must contain an untrue statement (Labov 1972, 156-157). This indicates that the genre is negotiated, among other things, on the basis of how the contents relate to their referent. However, instead of being completely untrue, which would mean that there need not be any correspondence between the sign and the signified, the successful statement must rather be 'as if' true in order to stimulate the dyadic verbal exchange.

The statement in the above example lacked a basic comic element, because it was completely true, and this was evident to all the people present. Comedy can be created out of tragedy if this is regarded as containing an element of irony. But if there is no irony in the tragedy, it is mere tragedy. An attempt to make fun of a tragic situation will fail and create an insult.

According to the available information, the participants at the wedding did not interpret Miihkula's song as ludic, and in view of the fact that the song was an immediate response to the bride's deformity, it may be that the singer did not even intend his song to be ludic. A joker may 'hide' behind his joke and use the finalized form of the joke as a cover for a serious comment (see Basso 1979, 72).

A bride with only one eye was apparently not welcome news to the groom's family. Customarily, a great deal of attention was paid to the bride's qualities in domestic work, handicrafts, and looks, both before and during the wedding ceremony. Thus, there was deception in this marriage. But despite the obvious deception, it was not regarded as appropriate to speak out the physical defect, nor to make it a target for ridicule. Obviously, the singer's intoxication was a factor in his failure to observe this social rule. Besides, pointing out the deformity created an embarrassing situation for both the bride and the groom's family and put a finger on the social shame that the deformity as well as the deception would bring.

Despite the failure by the performer to fulfill expectations for a satisfactory synthesis of textual and contextual realms, the incident had obvious value for the narrator as an example of behavior that should be avoided. Most likely the motivation behind reporting of the incident was to make a confirmative statement about particular social boundaries that were violated here. As such a comment, the entire quotation could be analyzed in terms of how it fulfills the genre-specific expectations for a successful narrative about an embarrassing situation. In this, the ethnopoetic approach would again be most useful.

NOTES

Acknowledgment: I thank Dr. Charles Briggs and Dr. Peter Seitel, two of my teachers in the Department of Folklore & Folklife at the University of Pennsylvania in spring 1989, for invaluable criticism on the two term papers that now, after some years, have been developed into this article. Thanks are also due to Professors Roger D. Abrahams, Dan Ben-Amos, Margaret A. Mills and Robert B. St. George from the same department for their comments related to the issues discussed here. Except where otherwise stated, the verse materials have been translated into English by Dr. Tom DuBois, to whom I also wish to express my gratitude.

1. In Finnish folkloristics, structuralism has been regarded as a disappointment because it was expected to serve the taxonomic purpose of distinguishing genres from each other – or rather, to legitimate the genre system that scholars had created (see e.g. Honko 1980, 17-18; Apo 1985, 11-12; Apo 1989, 152). The present-day folkloristic research on narrative structures in Finland is to a great extent Proppian in its approach (see e.g. articles in Siikala 1989), with influences taken from, for example, psycholinguistics. Siikala 1992 paves the way for a more culture analytic approach in narrative studies.

2. I prefer to use the terms 'tetrametric verse' or 'oral verse' instead of such well-established and commonly used terms as 'oral poetry', 'Kalevala poetry' or 'Kalevala-metric poetry' for the following reasons: 1) 'verse' relates etymologically, phonetically and semantically more closely to the native term *virsi* 'song'; 2) 'poetry' obscures the musical character of the tradition; thus, the phrase 'to sing verse' sounds more appropriate than the phrase 'to sing poetry'; 3) the term 'Kalevala poetry' creates the false implication that the recorded material derives from the *Kalevala* epic, and 4) the term 'Kalevala-metric poetry' not only makes an unnecessary connection between the traditional verse and the compiled epic, as does 'Kalevala poetry', but in a rather anomalous way, it names the meter of the traditional oral verse after the literary epic that consists of material in this traditional verse (see also Kaukonen 1982b, 83-84).

3. In his criticism Matti Kuusi points out that the musical structure does not support the theory (Kuusi 1952a, 393).

4. For similar comments on a recent study by Matti Kuusi, see Nenola-Kallio 1984.

5. For the reception of the oral formulaic theory in Finland, see Harvilahti 1992, 11.

6. Hannu Launonen, a Finnish literary scholar, argues for the fundamental importance of formal structure in verse and, among other things, points to the etymology of the term. As the Latin word *versus* (from *vertere* 'to turn') implies, the poetic text forces the reader to continuously reverse, to turn back to that which precedes. The features that mark the structure, such as verse form and rhyme, make a direct reference backwards, even though the text itself proceeds (Launonen 1984, 31).

7. But as emphasized throughout this article, the ethnopoetic method does not strive for the formal linguistic structure only but aims at situating verbal art in social action, in discourse on social institutions and cultural classifications. This does not mean, however, that one uses verbal art as an instrument in studying "something else", because the point is to study verbal art in terms of how it receives both its form and its meanings in the construction of culture and society. Discourse is an embodiment of both language and culture, including both and mediating between them (Sherzer 1987, 297, 302). Emphasizing an intertextual approach in the study of Finnish oral verse, Lotte Tarkka points out that "the cultural reality is not 'around' or 'behind' its texts: cultural reality comes into being through and in the texts it produces." (Tarkka 1993, 168).

8. For predication with metaphors, see Fernandez 1986, 8 ff.

9. For a recent discussion on Ingrian and other Finnish-Karelian weddings as rites of passage, see Anttonen 1992.

10. The concept of competence in performance, as it is established by Dell Hymes (e.g. 1971, 1974, 1975) and employed in American folklore scholarship and ethnography of speaking, refers to the communicative accountability and the relative skill and effectiveness of a performer's accomplishment in producing an artistically marked act of speaking (or singing or other expressive behavior) that puts the performer and the performance on display for audience evaluation, setting up a special interpretive frame within which the act is to be understood (Bauman and Sherzer 1989, xix; see also Bauman 1986, 133). As Briggs points out, the performer directs attention to the act of performance itself as well as to its contents (Briggs 1988, 8).

THOMAS DUBOIS

An Ethnopoetic Approach to Finnish Folk Poetry: Arhippa Perttunen's Nativity[1]

In his various introductions to Finnish folk epic poetry, Matti Kuusi uses a linguistic metaphor to describe the way in which singers and composers traditionally learned their art (Kuusi 1949, 1963, 1980a; Kuusi et al. 1977, 1985). Singers acquired the ability to create and perform folk poetry in a manner similar to language acquisition: they gained a basic competence first through passive listening and then gradually developed an active competence through song performance. Folk poetry in the so-called Kalevala metre – trochaic tetrameter – was sung in many different contexts and for many different purposes: it was a frequent part of evening entertainment, wedding rituals, funerals and other communal events, and thus, its form and use varied with place and time. The traditional singer learned the "Kalevala language" (Kuusi's *kalevalakieli*) – the prosody, melodies, themes, texts, and uses – as they existed in the singer's own home region, and gradually developed a personal style and repertoire that fit the tastes and performance contexts of the community. In this article, I propose to explore a further dimension of that *kalevalakieli*: a system of esthetic values and tendencies which gave form to folk poems as artistic wholes and rendered them coherent and satisfying to an audience conversant in the tradition. This esthetic architecture – or ethnopoetics – was undoubtedly so much a part of the *kalevalakieli* that to specify its tendencies as "rules" would have seemed unnecessary. These unspoken leanings, tastes, were simply taken for granted, called into play as a "natural" part of the performance itself. They constituted the complex groundwork of esthetic values which operated within the performance to make it a success. It is these factors which ethnopoetic analysis seeks to delineate and which I will discuss in this paper.

Applying ethnopoetic theory to Finnish folk poetry requires some groundwork of its own. In the following, I will briefly explain the theory as it has been developed by Dell Hymes and other researchers in the field and demonstrate how it may be effectively applied to the songs of one of Karelia's greatest singers, Arhippa Perttunen. In so doing, I will discuss some of the methodological challenges which arise when one analyzes

Songs beyond the Kalevala
Studia Fennica
Folkloristica 2
1994

archived folk poetry from this perspective. Practical and interpretative hurdles notwithstanding, I hope to illustrate through this example the tremendous promise that lies in applying ethnopoetic analysis to folk poetry in the Kalevala metre: ethnopoetics as a research tradition offers intriguing insights into the workings of the folk poems and their creators, and the folk poems themselves – collected by diligent fieldworkers of the past and carefully preserved in archives and publications – offer tremendous potential for the international study of folk poetic systems.

Research traditions: Finland and the US

The stylistics and prosody of Finnish folk poetry have been studied for nearly as long as the folk poems have been collected. Already in Henrik Gabriel Porthan's *De poesi fennica* (1766-1778; Hautala 1969) we find references to stylistic features within the poetic system, and Elias Lönnrot devoted considerable attention to stylistics in his essays on the folk poetry he collected for his epic *Kalevala* (1836-49) and lyric anthology *Kanteletar* (1840-41). Matti Sadeniemi's study *Die Metrik des Kalevalaverses* (1951) stands as the first major exploration of the prosodic system on quantitative grounds. Sadeniemi examines systematically the same phenomena which his predecessors had observed more impressionistically: in his study, he proposes a typology for scanning poem lines, discusses primary and secondary alliteration in the poems, examines formal parallelism along lines drawn initially by Steinitz (1934), and offers an explanation for the prosodic tendency to place long words at the ends of lines. Otto Andersson (1941), Matti Kuusi (1949, 1977), Leea Virtanen (1968), and Anna-Leena Siikala (1987) explore the various formulaic, thematic, prosodic and stylistic changes that differentiate folk poems from different regions or eras. From a linguistic standpoint, Pentti Leino (1974, 1985b, 1986) examines both alliteration and metre in Finnish folk poetry. Further studies in folk poetry stylistics include Paul Kiparsky's linguistically-based inquiries (1970), Lauri Harvilahti's application of oral formulaic theory to the subject (1990), Melvin Luthy's examination of number parallelism in the *Kalevala* (1991), and my own earlier (forthcoming) application of ethnopoetics to Ingrian folk poems. As Anna-Leena Siikala has pointed out to me in a personal communication as well, Martti Haavio's experiments with poem presentation, too, could be seen as early attempts at ethnopoetic analysis (Haavio 1952a, 1952b). It would be impossible to claim, in other words, that Finnish folk poetry has been an overlooked subject within Finnish folkloristics. The abundance of research to date, however, does not preclude the possibility of offering new or different perspectives on the tradition.

Within this wealth of research, numerous studies have examined the folk poetry of Arhippa Perttunen in particular. Martti Haavio, in his classic work *Viimeiset runonlaulajat* (1943), 'The last of the *rune*-singers', summarizes the biographical and stylistic observations made by earlier folklorists, including Elias Lönnrot, M. A. Castrén, A. A. Lähteenkorva-Borenius, Julius Krohn, I. K. Inha, A. N. Setälä, A. R. Niemi, Väinö Salminen, and Samuli Pauluharju (Haavio 1943, 32-43). Lönnrot writes that Arhippa "sang his poems in good order, leaving no noticeable gaps"[2] (Haavio 1943,

35). A. A. Borenius-Lähteenkorva, in an oft-quoted appraisal of Arhippa's artistry writes: "In terms of order or form [his poems] are also excellent; one does not find mixed into the texts other poems or portions which muddle the texts of lesser singers"[3] (Haavio 1943, 40). Wolfgang Steinitz (1934) uses Arhippa's songs as the basis for his examination of formal parallelism in Finnish folk poetry in general and Matti Sadeniemi (1951) likewise uses Arhippa's singing as the basis for his study of traditional metrics. Jukka Saarinen (1988) provides a close examination of poetic variation and improvisation in different versions of Arhippa's poems, pointing to the possibility of viewing these variations from an oral formulaic perspective. In many ways, then, Arhippa's singing has become canonized as the classic performance mode of Kalevalaic folk poetry. My intention in this paper, however, is to view Arhippa's singing not as typical of the Kalevalaic tradition as a whole, but as one singer's particular adaptation of that tradition to personal and communal tastes.

Ethnopoetics as a research tradition is of a much more recent vintage, but it has proven extremely productive, particularly in the analysis of Native American oral narrative. Whereas Dennis Tedlock seeks in his seminal study *The Oral Performance and the Work of Interpretation* (1983) to discover a means of graphically representing on the printed page the complexities and nuances of an oral performance, Dell Hymes explores the structurally and linguistically encoded artistry that remains intact in previously transcribed verbatim texts (1981, 1982, 1985a, 1985b, 1986).

Working principally with Chinookan prose narrative traditions, Hymes perceives the basic unit of verbal art as the line rather than the sentence. The narratives Hymes analyzes are made up of lines of "measured verse" – something altogether different from the prose sentences familiar in literary narrative – which in turn combine to form larger groupings or verses, marked by various forms of repetition, parallelism, recurrent particles, etc. As Hymes puts it, "repetitions of particles, for example, prove to be not the limitations of a primitive mind, but the signs of an implicit structure, a structure which gives shape and point" (Hymes 1985, 15).

Further, Hymes notes that these verses are "themselves organized in terms of a rhetorical pattern, or logic, which has its roots in the pattern numbers of the community" (Hymes 1985 14). Narratives from a culture with a pattern number of three, for instance, as in the European cultural area, will tend to have structures built on groupings of three: there may be three main characters or three principle scenes, or three actions within a verse, or three repetitions of a particle, etc. This observation is quite in keeping with Axel Olrik's famous "Law of the Three" in *European Märchen narration* (Olrik 1909), but it extends its range to encompass a greater variety of fine linguistic details.

Hymes also predicts, however, that cultures which have a pattern number of three will sometimes structure verbal performance into groupings of five as well, and may create groupings of two or four for particular rhetorical significance (Hymes 1985, 55). The choice of whether to select the structural option typical of one's tradition, or to subvert audience expectations for rhetorical ends by structuring one's text in a different manner, lies with the skilled performer. That these structural tendencies may be used with cognizance as part of a rhetorical strategy is Hymes' conclusion in his analysis of Karok narratives (Hymes 1985). M. Dale Kinkade (1987) suggests in his study of an Upper Chehalis (Salishan) narrative that such a multiplicity of different patterning options may reflect changes in the culture's esthetic system (i.e. cultural change or borrowing). In the present study, I maintain that the prominence of pairing inherent in the Kalevala metre is offset, and – at least in Arhippa's performances – balanced by an affinity for groupings of three, and a specialized use of groups of five.

Applying this type of analysis to Finnish folk poetry holds much interest, since it gives us a means of understanding and appreciating each text as an entity: as an esthetically structured coherent whole. Certainly, some performances may appear better than others, and some performers more adept than their neighbors, but each text which has been collected and preserved deserves to be studied as a coherent piece. An ethnopoetic analysis helps us gain an inkling of what constituted artistic value within the tradition itself and how effectively a given text or performer handled audience expectations. Moreso than an historical-geographical, prosodic or thematic analysis, which may disintegrate the performance into its constituent parts, an ethnopoetic analysis seeks to comprehend the artistry of the text as a whole.

Applying ethnopoetic analysis to Arhippa's Nativity poem: methodological considerations

Applying ethnopoetic analysis to Finnish folk poetry entails some considerable methodological hurdles. First, it is crucial to remember that, in contrast to the prose narrative traditions which have served thus far as the basis for ethnopoetic research, Finnish folk poetry is fundamentally a genre of folk music, possessed of particular melodic and metrical features. The fact that as such the texts are overtly and emphatically poetic (instead of implicitly so, as in the case of narratives in Hymes' "measured verse") does not lessen the importance of those structuring devices which give form and rhetorical aim to the texts as wholes. It may be, as we shall see below, that rhetorical structuring within an overtly poetic genre entails the use of linguistic devices which lie outside of the formal prosody: e.g. the phatic particle *niin* 'thus', or line repetition. It may even be the case that prosodic rules are transgressed in order to accomplish rhetorical agenda: i.e., the formal parallelism usually considered typical of poetry in the Kalevala metre may be altered or abandoned in favor of structures that adhere to different esthetic principles or accomplish different rhetorical functions (e.g., groupings of three or five).

At an even more basic level, however, the accuracy of the "verbatim" texts collected at the end of the 19th century and beginning of the 20th by Finnish folklorists must be queried. It is clear that folklorists such as Elias Lönnrot, J. F. Cajan, and M. A. Castrén all desired to record their informants' songs accurately, but limitations naturally arose from the fact that they transcribed their texts by hand, without aid of any recording apparatus such as a phonograph or tape recorder. Too, informants were obliged to dictate the songs they normally sang, thereby introducing a certain element of ambiguity and artificiality into the performances themselves. The fact that the melodic portions of the performances have been lost poses a serious problem to the researcher, although it is a loss in some ways equivalent to the loss of normal verbal voice contours and stress patterns in written transcriptions of prose narrative. Analysis must proceed on the basis of the data which is preserved, keeping in mind however, that other data – such as a phonographic recording – might markedly alter the researcher's conclusions.

Further problems obtain from the nature and limitations of early field transcriptions. In the interest of saving time and paper, the folklorists whose materials I examine in this paper regularly skipped repeated passages or refrains, recording them in their texts only with shorthand ellipses, such as "etc." or "the same two more times". The kinds of fine details that may have been used to give form to the performance – a repetition of a line, the shift of a verb tense, or the addition of a particle, for example – may have been lost in that ellipticized passage. In the texts which I include from M. A. Castrén's interviews with Arhippa Perttunen, too, Castrén includes a great many lines which he records parenthetically or marginally, labelling them in Swedish *varianter*: "variants" (see text 1103b and c below). How are we to appraise such "variant" lines? Were they suggested by Arhippa after the performance, perhaps while he checked over the transcription with Castrén for accuracy? Or did Castrén judge the lines "variant" during the initial recording itself and relegate them to an artificially marginalized status (as appears to be the case with the closing lines of text 1103c, below)? Since Castrén's original fieldnotes are missing, and since the transcriptions he made differ substantively from each other, we can do little to determine exactly what Arhippa's performance contained.

Although we cannot conclusively answer these last questions, we must recognize that all analysis involves certain ambiguities, and that we are justified in relying on the data left to us – data which the folklorists who produced it must have considered at least an adequate (if not wholly satisfactory) representation of the performances they witnessed. Indeed, we can speak of a kind of linguistic or performative "overdetermination" in which one's intent is expressed and reinforced through a variety of linguistic and paralinguistic phenomena at once. As modern folklorists attuned to the nuances captured on tape and film, we tend to be intuitively aware of the contrastive relations between differing parts of the communicative apparatus: the wink that renders the serious statement a joke, for instance, or the sigh that transforms an expression of assent into one of protest. But what of the myriad ways in which propositional content is simultaneously reinforced by mechanisms of grammatical agreement, repetitions, synonyms, rephrasings, etc.? And would we not expect in the singing of a traditional folksong or other fixed form genres with elaborate metrical and melodic strictures to find features on the level of text and its form holding greater significance than the paralinguistic features more characteristic of freer discourse genres (e.g. conversational genres, prose narrative)? In other words, perhaps the highly artificed nature of Finnish folk poetry as a genre decreases the significance of the finer performance data lost to us through the limitations of early recording methods. We still have plenty of data to go on.

The Karelian villages in Archangel Karelia belonged to the sphere of the Eastern Orthodox Church."Priest and maatuska 'old woman'" in Vuonninen. Photo: Samuli Paula- harju 1915 (FLS 5422).

Discovering the "grammar" of folk poetic performances

We have stated that ethnopoetics can help us appraise individual poems as artistic entities, that we can understand the logic and artistry of a perfor- mance as it was performed. It is easy to imagine that Finnish folksingers possessed some sort of shared esthetic sensibilities with regards to the overarching structure and form of their own performances and those of others. This sensibility, acquired gradually through participation in the tradition we may label a "grammar" in accordance with what Hymes and Kuusi have written. If we were to compile such a grammar through careful analysis of numerous folk poems, then the logic behind the kinds of specific variations which occur in, say, Arhippa Perttunen's folk poems from performance to performance might emerge as regularities observable in the tradition of which he was part. Since to date no such wide ranging study of ethnopoetic features in Finnish folk poetry exists, however, we need instead to proceed in the reverse direction: i.e., to examine the variations in Arhippa's poetry for an inkling of the esthetic system that may have informed their creation. Such observations must be seen as tentative, but they remain valid as a first attempt at uncovering the grammar of Finnish folk poetic performances in general.

In the following discussion we shall examine different versions of a folk poem generally known in the Finnish research tradition as *Luojan virsi* or 'The Messiah': a corpus of poems dealing with the life of Jesus from birth to resurrection. In particular, we will examine the first poem of that cycle, one dealing with the events in Christ's life from the Annunciation to the Nativity and beyond. In fact, the poem, at least as performed by Arhippa, has more to do with the Virgin Mary than with the Messiah, and for that reason (and to distinguish it from the cycle as a whole) I refer to it here as *The Nativity*.

To gain a sense of how Arhippa varied his poem from performance to performance, let us examine the opening lines of each of the variants collected from him as they appear in *Suomen Kansan Vanhat Runot* I:2, 'Ancient Poems of the Finnish People', (hereafter SKVR).

1103 Lönnrot A II 6, n.93

Marjanen mäeltä huuti	A berry called from the hill
puna puola kankahalta:	A cranberry from the marsh:
"Tule, neiti, poimomahan,	"Come maiden and pick me
vyö vaski, valitsemahan,	copper-belt choose me
ennen kun etona syöpi	before the snail consumes
mato musta muikkoali!" (1-6)	the black worm destroys!"

1103a J. F. Cajan n.163

Kasvo marjanen meällä	A berry grows on a hill
punapuola kankahalla	a cranberry on a marsh
niin marjanen mäeltä huuti	thus the berry called from the hill
punapuola kankahalta:	the cranberry from the marsh:
"Tule neiti poimomaha	"Come maiden and pick me
vyö vaski valitsemaha	copper-belt choose me
tinarinta riipomaha	tin-breast pluck me
ennen kuin etona syöpi	before the snails consumes
mato musta muikkoavi!" (1-9)	the black worm destroys!"

1103b Castrén n.147

Marjanen mäeltä huuti	A berry called from the hill
punapuola kankahalta	a cranberry from the marsh
"Tule neiti, poimimahan	"Come maiden and pick me
(sormuskäsi suoltamahan)	(ringed-finger pickle me)
tinarinta riipomahan	tin-breast pluck me
vyövaski valitsemahan	copper-belt choose me
ennenkun etona syöpi	before the snail consumes
mato musta muikkoavi!" (1-8)	the black worm destroys!"

1103c Castrén 1204 n.1

Marjanen mäeltä huuti	A berry called from the hill
punapuola kankahalta:	a cranberry from the marsh
"Tule neiti poimimahan,	"Come maiden and pick me
tinarinta riipomahan	tin-breast pluck me
[sormuskäsi suoltamahan]	[ringed-finger pickle me]
vyövaski valitsemahan	copper-breast choose me
ennen kun etona syöpi	before the snail consumes
mato musta muikkoavi!" (1-7)	the black worm destroys!"

When we compare these short passages it becomes immediately clear that Lönnrot's transcription is both more regular and more succinct, particularly with regards to formal parallelism – the pairing of lines in terms of content and form generally seen as characteristic of the Kalevala metre tradition. The passage as recorded by Lönnrot is formed of three pairs of parallel lines, each pair of which describes a different matter, although, of course, all six lines are bound together into a clear sentence. The first pair describes the berry which calls temptingly to Mary; the second in turn describes Mary herself through the use of a clothing epithet; and the third describes the fate of the berry if Mary refuses to pick it. It is reasonable to suspect – although impossible to prove – that this marked regularity in terms of formal parallelism is due to some extent to Lönnrot's own emendations or selections while recording the poem, since the opening lines recorded by subsequent folklorists are all more variable and less tightly parallel than Lönnrot's. For example, in Cajan's transcription, we find not only an additional line pair introducing the berry (*Kasvo marjanen meällä/puna-puola kankahalla* 1-2), but also a further line added to the description of the Virgin Mary (*tinarinta riipomaha* 7).

This additional descriptive line has both stylistic and discourse analytical significance: significance which we can notice if we give Arhippa credit for performing his poem in a manner he found esthetically satisfying. First, from the standpoint of stylistics, it is evident that the additional line expands the pair into a set of three, and also breaks the possible monotony of a succession of unvaried line pairs. Indeed, sets of three lines appear to covary within Arhippa's performance with the more canonical line pairs, as is evidenced in a later passage from the same poem. Here, the line pair of Lönnrot's transcription is again replaced by a set of three lines in Cajan's:

Neitsy Maaria emonen	Virgin Mary little mother
rakas äiti armollinen	dear mother full of grace
(1103, 7-8)	

Neitsyt Maaria emonen	Virgin Mary little mother
se oli vanhin vaimoloista	she was the oldest of women
eläjien ensimäinen	the first among beings
(1103a, 10-13)	

We can imagine, then, a stylistic system in which sets of two and sets of three figure as possible alternatives, with variation between the two used to vary the texture of the poetry. The choice of a set of three lines in the description of Mary would thus stylistically compensate for the monotony that might otherwise arise through the addition of the line pair describing the berry in Cajan's transcription.

It is also possible, however, that the addition of this further descriptive line has a discourse analytical function as well. Arhippa's expansion at the beginning of the poem performed for Cajan shifts discourse time away from the balanced situation apparent in Lönnrot's transcription. The berry in Cajan's transcription receives more attention than Mary, and we may surmise that the additional line describing the Virgin helps offset this imbalance, restoring the symmetry that characterizes Lönnrot's passage.

Again, whether we see these changes as wholly stylistic in nature or partially discursive, it is likely that such choices and nuances would have been made instantaneously, as a natural and automatic part of the singer's performance. Such is the nature of a grammar of options and features underlying the performance of folk poetry.

The crucial assumption at the base of judgments such as these is that lines do not exist in isolation from each other: a modification in one part of a passage or poem may be expected to have stylistic ramifications in the rest of the text as well. The researcher should expect to find such interrelations in the songs of accomplished singers.

We may also note in comparing these initial passages, however, that sets of two and three are not the only possibilities open in Arhippa's esthetic system. In Castrén's transcription (which occurs in two different manuscript versions) a fourth line describing the Virgin Mary is included as well. In version 1103b this line (*sormuskäsi suoltamahan* 4) is written parenthetically; in version 1103c the same line was relegated to a marginal column, placed under the Swedish heading *varianter*. Although it is difficult to say for certain (since Castrén's original fieldnotes have not been preserved) we may guess that this line may have been suggested subsequently by Arhippa, as discussed above. If this line was indeed left out of Arhippa's performance itself, then, we may take its existence as evidence of the fact that Arhippa preferred pairs and sets of three to sets of four in his poetry. Arhippa could have expanded the description into a four – line sequence but chose not to – apparently for esthetic reasons.

This same aversion to sets of four is evident on a broader level in the final section of the poem. After the infant Jesus has been born, Mary hides him away. When she later returns to find him, however, the child has disappeared, and Mary must ask a succession of different natural beings whether they know anything of his whereabouts. In the transcriptions made by all three folklorists, Arhippa has Mary question three beings: the road, the moon and the sun. Each of the first two gives a reason for not wanting to divulge the secret to Mary, but finally the sun acquiesces and explains that Jesus is now in the high heavens. In Castrén's variant column, however, we find a fourth being questioned – a birch tree – whose turn at talk comes between that of the road and the moon. This fourth possibility is not merely an idle suggestion: Arhippa provided Castrén with a complete and entirely satisfactory passage devoted to the birch. For instance, when asked whether it has seen the child, the tree replies:

Jos näkisin en sanosi	If I saw him I would not tell
poikas' on miunki luonut:	your son has made me as well
pirtti puiksi pilkotahan	to be cleft into wood for a cabin
terä-rauoin rapsutahan	to be scraped by a steel blade
hakatahan halkopuiksi	to be chopped into firewood
lehti-puiksi leikatahan	into leaf trees to be cut
1103c fn 21	

The first two lines of this suggested passage parallel the lines used by the other natural beings in refusing to answer. There is little difference, indeed, between this possible turn at talk and those that are included in Arhippa's poem except that its inclusion would expand the plot structure from a series of three beings to a series of four. Arhippa had the means to structure the plot on a series of four but chose not to; clearly, the centrality of the pattern number three and its prevalence in all European folk narrative rendered the set of four an undesirable option.

We have seen so far, then, that variation occurs frequently in Arhippa's poetry, but not "freely." Even small variations occur in accordance with stylistic rules and affect adjacent lines or passages. Let us now turn to another passage from Lönnrot's transcription to further explore the range of ethnopoetic tendencies present in Arhippa's poetry. Mary's swallowing of the tempting berry is described as follows:

Tempo kartun kankahalta	She drags a pole from the marsh
senni päällä seisataksen	and standing on that
heitti marjan helmohinsa	she threw the berry into her lap
helmoiltansa vyönsä päälle	from her lap onto her belt
vyönsä päältä rinnoillensa	from her belt onto her breast
rinoiltansa huulellensa	from her breast onto her lip
huuleltansa kielellensä	from her lip onto her tongue
siitä vatsahan valahti	from there it slid into the stomach
1103, 21-28	

In this passage we can clearly note – after the initial three lines – a strictly parallel succession of five lines. Each of these lines names a place on Mary's body from which the berry moves and a place to which it proceeds. The same words, grammatical cases (ablative and allative) and possessive suffix (-nsa third person human) recur throughout the lines. The only marked difference between them occurs in the final line, in which the ablative/allative progression ("from off/onto") is replaced with an elative/illative progression ("from inside/into") accompanied by a verb (valahti 'slid') and the disappearance of the possessive suffix. These grammatical changes match the narrative shift from the berry's upward progression to its culminating downward slide. The final line is thus still parallel in many ways to the preceding line but also contrastive in the very features that seem to link all the lines together.

It is clear, however, that the closely intertwined nature of these final five lines contrasts with the lack of parallelism in the first three (21-23). These prior lines appear in a grammatically logical order, but no strict parallelism obtains between them. Now, if we wish to represent these lines on the page so that these observations would be immediately sensible to the reader, then we must learn from the example of modern poetry, using the graphic representation of the lines to its greatest advantage. If we write these lines as they might occur in a modern anthology of poetry, then we arrive at the following passage:

Tempo kartun kankahalta	She drags a pole from the marsh
senni päällä seisataksen	and standing on that
heitti marjan helmohinsa	she threw the berry into her lap
helmoiltansa vyönsä päälle	from her lap onto her belt
vyönsä päältä rinnoillensa	from her belt onto her breast

rinoiltansa huulellensa	from her breast onto her lip
huuleltansa kielellensä	from her lip onto her tongue
siitä vatsahan valahti	from there it slid into the stomach

The stepped indentation of the final five lines indicates here the existence of strict parallelism – in other words, the lines "belong" together as a group, and the singer has expressed this fact through stylistic features. The final line is written so as to denote both its being part of that group and also its somewhat distinct status: it does not simply continue the flow established in the other lines. This group of five lines is then further demarcated by the addition of a blank line before and after it. Lines which are written without such stepped indentation, as in the case of the first three lines, may belong together as a group, but are not linked together with the same kind of close parallelism that obtains in the five-line group discussed above. The important point of a textual presentation of this sort is that the reader – whether Finnish or English speaking – might not otherwise notice the esthetic qualities and variations in this passage if it were written with each line simply flush left. Through representing the poem with a modern poetic format, the researcher in ethnopoetics may present an immediately apprehensible interpretation of the poem's esthetic structure.

If we turn now to Cajan's transcription of this same passage, and represent it in the above manner, then we can glimpse further evidence of a remarkably elaborate stylistic system underlying all of Arhippa's performances. Although at first the stylistic choices made in this transcription may seem very different from those evident in Lönnrot's version, it is clear that they adhere to the same basic ethnopoetic principles.

Niin mänövi mättähälle	Thus she went to the hill	
tempo kartun kankahalta	she drags a pole from the marsh	
senki peällä seisataksen	and standing on that	25
Heitti marjan helmoillensa	She threw the berry onto her lap	
voatteille valkeille	onto the white clothes	
pätöville peäsomille	onto the worthy headdress	
Niin marja ylemä nousi	Thus the berry rose up	
polosille polvillensa	onto her dear knees	30
niin marja ylemmä nousi	thus the berry rose up	
riveille rinnoillensa	onto her nimble breast	
niin marja ylemä nousi	thus the berry rose up	
leveälle leuallehe	onto her broad chin	
leualta on huulellehe	from the chin to the lip	35
huulelta on kielellehe	from the lip to the tongue	
siitä vatsahan valahti	from there it slid into the stomach	

1103a, 23-37

In this passage the formal parallelism usually associated with Finnish folk poetry is hardly in evidence. Instead, groupings of three, carefully articulated by means of repetition, line structure, and the filler word *niin* 'thus'

A view of the famous rune-singing village, Latvajärvi. Archangel Karelia. Photo: I.K. Inha 1894 (FLS 9872).

predominate. Lines 29-34 are of particular interest, since they represent a set of three built out of three sets of two. We are dealing here not with a simple either-or situation, then, in which Arhippa chose either to conform to the tendency toward line pairs in the folk poetry tradition or chose to expand the pair into a set of three, but rather, a hierarchical relation in which both tendencies are intertwined into a single esthetically pleasing whole.

The reverse tendency (i.e., an overarching set of two built out of sets of three) is evidenced in a later passage from Cajan's transcription:

Piiletteli poiuttahen	She hid her son	
alla juoksovan jalaksen	under a running sled runner	125
alla sieklan sieklottavan	under a sieve for sifting	
alla korvon kannettavan	under a pail for carrying	
Kato pieni poikuoho	Her little son disappears	
kultane omenuosa	her golden apple	
alta juoksovan jalaksen	from under a running sled runner	130
alta korvon kannettavan	from under a pail for carrying	
alta sieklan sieklottavan	from under a sieve for sifting	

1103a, 124-132

Here we clearly find sets of three lines used to build a tightly interrelated set of two. The only difference between the parallel lines describing the infant's hiding place (besides the switch in order from runner-sieve-pail to runner-pail-sieve) is the change from the addessive preposition *alla* 'under'

149

to the ablative *alta* 'from under' so as to meet the grammatical demands made by using the verb *kato* 'disappeared'.

It is also apparent that the close parallelism obtaining between the pair of three-line passages helps set off the contrast between the other lines that occur in conjunction with them: i.e., it becomes clearer that the line *piiletteli poiuttahen* 'She hid her son' is answered by the line *Kato pieni poikuoho* 'Her little son disappeared'. And both of these lines are in turn answered by the very next line in the poem, which reads *Etsi pientä poiuttahen* 'She searched for her little son'. Thus the set of two three-line locative descriptive passages are "interlarded" between a series of three related verbs: hide/disappear/search. We find ourselves again in a situation in which sets of two and three interrelate on different levels of the poem's rhetorical structure: the closely parallel descriptive pair (*alla.../alta...*), itself made up of three parts, is used strategically to support a broader series of three verbs.

In Castrén's transcription(s) we find yet another apparently suitable stylistic option for describing the berry's passage into Mary's stomach:

Niin meni mättähälle	Thus she went to the hill	
heitti marjan helmoillehen	she threw the berry onto her lap	
helmoiltansa rinnoillehen	from her lap onto her breast	
rinnoiltansa leuoillehen	from her breast onto her chin	25
leuoiltansa huulillehen	from her chin onto her lip	
huuliltansa kielellehen	from her lip onto her tongue	
siitä vatsahan valahti	from there it slid into the stomach	

1103b, 22-28

Castrén's version is not far from that recorded by Lönnrot some five years earlier (1834 vs. 1839); the only marked difference is that the initial description of Mary's actions changes from a set of three in Lönnrot's version to a terser pair in Castrén's, indicating that Lönnrot was not as diligent in keeping out extraneous third lines from his informants' poems as I implied above.

As we compare these three different versions of the same passage, it becomes clear as well that a set of five lines was permissible in Arhippa's esthetic system. We can guess that the lengthy sets of five lines present in Lönnrot's and Castrén's transcriptions help accentuate the narrative centrality of the action they describe. This is the berry which will impregnate the Virgin, and Mary's swallowing it stands as the culmination of all the preceding lines. Thus, it stands to reason that Arhippa would choose to elaborate it in some way, either by describing it in a lengthy (but esthetically permissible) set of five lines, or by breaking it into two even more highly elaborated and parallel parts, as in Cajan's transcription.

Taking this evidence into account, we can imagine a grammar of esthetic principles operating within Arhippa's performances that called for a balance between sets of two and three, tended to avoid groupings of four, and used sets of five to accentuate key narrative moments. Rhetorical structure was expressed outside the bounds of the formal prosody by grouping choice, filler words (e.g. *niin*), and line repetition.

Ethnopoetic presentation of the texts as wholes

These observations may become clearer as we examine the poems in their entireties. I have presented all four versions of Arhippa's *Nativity* below. The groupings which I designate through the addition of blank spaces and indentation are to my mind clear, but it is possible that another researcher might interpret the same lines differently. Lines announcing turns at talk (e.g., *sanan virkko noin nimesi*, 'said a word uttered thus') have proved especially problematic, since their formulaicity renders them largely independent of neighboring lines. In the following I have written such lines separately or grouped them solely with lines which name the actor, as in the passage:

Ruma Ruotuksen emäntä	Ugly Ruotus' wife
sanan virkki noin nimesi	said a word uttered thus
1103a, 81-82	

It is clear, however, that such lines tend to act more as bridges between passages than as barriers or separate entities.

1103 Lönnrot (1834)[4]

I. The berry and Mary

Marjanen mäeltä huuti	A berry called from the hill	
puna puola kankahalta	a cranberry from the marsh:	
"Tule neiti poimomahan	"Come maiden and pick me	
vyö vaski valitsemahan	copper-belt choose me	
ennen kun etona syöpi	before the snail consumes	5
mato musta muikkoali!"	the black worm destroys!"	
Neitsy Maaria emonen	Virgin Mary little mother	
rakas äiti armollinen	dear mother full of grace	
viitisekse, vaatisekse	dresses, adorns	
pää somille suorieli	wrapped her head in a headdress	10
vaattehilla valkehilla	in clothes of white	
Läksi marjan poimentaan	She went to pick the berry	
punapuolan katsontaan	the cranberry to see to	
niin meni mäille, sano	thus she went to the hills, say,	
keksi marjasen meältä	she picked the berry on the hill	15
punapuolan kankahalta	the berry on the marsh	
On marja näkemiehen	It looks like a berry	
puola ilman luomeehen[5]	*a cranberry without interest*	
alahahko ois maasta syöä	too low to eat from the ground	
ylähähkö puuhun nosta.	too high from a tree.	20
Tempo kartun kankahalta	She drags a pole from the marsh	
senni päällä seisataksen	and standing on that	
heitti marjan helmohinsa	she threw the berry into her lap	
helmoiltansa vyönsä päälle	from her lap onto her belt	

151

vyönsä päältä rinnoillensa	from her belt onto her breast	25
rinoiltansa huulellensa	from her breast onto her lip	
huuleltansa kielellensä	from her lip onto her tongue	
siitä vatsahan valahti.	from there it slid into the stomach	

II. Mary, Piltti and Ugly Ruotus' wife

Siitä tyyty siitä täyty	Sated from that, filled from that	
siitä paksuksi panihen	grew fat from that	30
lihavaksi liittelihen	added weight	
niin kohun kovoa kanto	thus a heavy womb she carries	
vatsan täyttä vaikieta	a stomach full of trouble	
Kanto kuuta 2, 3	She carries it for months 2, 3	
3 kuuta, 4 kuuta	3 months, 4 months	35
4 kuuta 5 kuuta	4 months, 5 months	
7:n kaheksan kuuta	7, 8 months	
ympäri 9 kuuta	around 9 months	
vanhojen vaimon määriin	as old women count	
kuuta 1/2 10.	half of the tenth month	40
Niin kuulla 10:llä	Thus in the tenth month	
lyöäh kavon kipua	There strikes the pain of wives	
imen tulta tuikatah	the fire of girls sparks	
vaimon vaivaksi tuleepi	a wife's trial comes	
Sanan virkko noin nimesi:	She says a word, uttered thus	45
"Piltti pieni piikaseni	"Piltti my little servant girl	
lähe kylpyä kylästä	go find a bath in the village	
saunoa Sarajahasta	a sauna in Saraja	
jossa huono hoivan saisi	where a wretch can receive attention	
avun anke tarvitsisi."	help for the luckless one in need"	50
Piltti pieni piikojansa	Piltti her little servant girl	
hyvä kielas käskieki	good at taking orders	
kepiä kehuttuoaki	easy to persuade,	
sekä juoksi jotta joutu	both ran and rushed	
ylähäiset maat aleni	pulled down the highlands	55
alahaiset maat yleni	pulled up the lowlands	
Ruman Ruotuksen kotihin.	to Ugly Ruotus' (Herod's) home.	
Ruma Ruotus paitulainen	Ugly Ruotus shirt-sleeved one	
syöpi juopi pöyän päässä	eats, drinks at the table's head	
päässä pöyän paioillaan	at table's headinhis shirt-sleeves	60
aivin aivinaisillaan	in his clean linen	
elääpi hyvän tavalla	he lives life well	
Ruma Ruotuksen emäntä	Ugly Ruotus'wife	
liikku keski lattiella	moves about the middle of the floor	
lieho sillan liitoksella	lightly treds upon the floorjoint	65

Sano Piltti piikojansa	Says Piltti her little servant girl
"Läksin kylpyä kylästä	"I went to find a bath in the village
saunoa Sarajahasta	a *sauna* in Saraja
jossa huono hoivan saisi	where a wretch can receive attention
avun anke tarvitsisi."	help for the luckless one in need" 70
Ruma Ruotuksen emäntä	Ugly Ruotus's wife
sanan virkko noin nimesi	says a word uttered thus
"Ei ole kylpyä kylässä	"There is not a bath in the village
saunoa Sarajahassa	a *sauna* in Saraja
On talli Tapo mäellä	There is a stable on Tapo hill 75
huone hongikko koissa	a room in a fir grove house
johon portot pojan saapi	where whores go to have a son
tuulen lautat lapsen saapi."	harlots to have a child."
Piltti pieni piikojansa	Piltti her little servant girl
pian juoksi jotta joutu	soon ran and rushed 80
sano tuolta tultuaan	says once she's returned from there
"Ei ole kylpyä kylässä	"There is not a bath in the village
saunoa Sarajahassa	a *sauna* in Saraja
Ruma Ruotus paitulainen	Ugly Ruotus the shirt-sleeved
syöpi juopi pöyän päässä	eats,drinks at the table's head 85
päässä pöyän paiollaan	at table's headinhis shirt-sleeves
aivin aivinaisillaan	in his clean linen
elääpi hyvän tavalla	he lives life well
Ruma Ruotuksen emäntä	Ugly Ruotus' wife
liikku keski lattiella	moves about the middle of the floor 90
liehu sillan liitoksella	lightly treds upon the floorjoint
Mie sanon sanalla tuolla	I say these words when there
"Läksin kylpyä kylästä	"I went to find a bath in the village
saunoa Sarajahasta	a *sauna* in Saraja
jossa huono hoivan saapi	where a wretch can receive attention 95
avun anke tarvitseepi."	help for the luckless one in need."
Ruma Ruotuksen emäntä	Ugly Ruotus' wife:
"Ei ole kylpyä kylässä	"There is not a bath in the village
saunoa Sarajahassa	a *sauna* in Saraja
On talli Tapo mäellä	There is a stable on Tapo hill 100
huone hongikko keolla	a room in a fir grove house
johon portot pojan saapi	where whores go to have a son
tuulen lautat lapsen luopi."	harlots to make a child."
Vaimon vaivalle tuleepi	A wife's trial comes
Neitsy Maaria emonen	Virgin Mary little mother 105
niin sano toisen kerran	thus says a second time

"Sekä juokse jotta jouvu	"Both run and rush
mene kylpyä kylästä	go find a bath in the village
saunoa Sarajahasta	a *sauna* in Saraja
jossa huono hoivan saisi	where a wretch can receive
	attention 110
avun anke tarvitsisi."	help for the luckless one in need.
Piltti pieni piikojansa	Piltti her little servant girl
hyvä kieläs käskieki	good at taking orders
kepiä kehuttuoki	easy to persuade
sekä juoksi	both ran 115
Ruma Ruotus jotta joutu	Ugly Ruotus and rushed
alahaiset maat yleni	pulled down the highlands
ylähaiset maat aleni	pulled up the lowlands
Ruma Ruotus paitulainen	Ugly Ruotus the shirt-sleeved
syöpi juopi pöyän päässä	eats, drinks at the table's head 120
päässä pöyän paiollaan	at table's headin his shirt-sleeves
aivin aivinaisillaan	in his clean linen
elääpi hyvän tavalla	he lives life well
Sano Piltti piikojansa	Says Piltti her servant girl
"Läksin kylpyä kylästä	"I went to find a bath in the village 125
saunoa Sarajahasta	a *sauna* in Saraja
jossa huono hoivan saisi	where a wretch can receive
	attention
avun anke tarvitsisi."	help for the luckless one in need
Ruma Ruotuksen emäntä	Ugly Ruotus' wife
liikku keski lattiella	moves about the middle of the floor 130
liehu sillan liitoksella	lightly treds upon the floorjoint
sanan virkko noin nimesi	says a word utters thus
"Eule kylpyä kylässä	"There is not a bath in the village
saunoa Sarajahassa	a *sauna* in Saraja
On talli Tapomäellä	There is a stable on Tapo hill 135
huone hongikkokeolla	a room in a fir grove house
johon portot pojan saapi	where whores go to have a son
tuulen lautat lapsen luopi."	harlots to make a child."
Piltti pieni piikojansa	Piltti her little servant girl
sekä juoksi jotta joutu	both ran and rushed 140
sano tuolta tultuaan	says once she's returned from there
"Eule kylpyä kylässä	"There is not a bath in the village
saunoa Sarajahassa	a *sauna* in Saraja
Ruma Ruotuksen emäntä	Ugly Ruotus's wife
sanan virkko noin nimesi	says a word utters thus 145
"On talli Tapomeällä	"There is a stable on Tapo hill
huone hongikkokeolla	a room in a fir grove house
johon portot pojan saapi	where whores go to have a son

Finnish	English	
tuulen lautat lapsen luopi."	harlots to make a child."	
Niin sanoo mokomin."	Thus something like that she says."	150
Oli aikoa vähäsen	There was little time	
yhä tuskaksi tuleepi	still the pain comes	
painuupi pakolliseksi	presses into aches	
vaimon vaivoksi tuleepi.	a wife's trial comes	
Kohtu käänty kovaksietc.[6]	the womb turns heavy	
/vatsan täysi vaikieksi/	/the stomach full of trouble/	155
sanan virkko noin nimesi	says a word uttered thus	
"Piltti pieni piikaseni	"Piltti my little servant girl	
lähe kylpyä kylästä	go find a bath in the village	
saunoa Sarajahasta	a *sauna* in Saraja	
jossa huono hoivan saisi	where a wretch can receive attention	160
avun anke tarvitsisi."	help for the luckless one in need	
Piltti pieni piikojansa	Piltti her little servant girl	
sekä juoksi jotta joutu	both ran and rushed	
alahaiset maat yleni	pulled up the lowlands	
ylähäiset maat aleni	pulled down the highlands	165
Ruman Ruotuksen kotihin	to Ugly Ruotus' home	
Ruma Ruotus paitulainen	Ugly Ruotus the shirt-sleeved	
syöpi juopi pöyän päässä	eats, drinks at the table's head	
päässä pöyän paiollaan	at table's headinhis shirt-sleeves	
elääpi hyvän tavalla	he lives life well	170
Ruma Ruotuksen emäntä	Ugly Ruotus' wife	
liikku keski lattiella	moves about the middle of the floor	
liehu sillan liitoksella	lightly treds upon the floorjoint	
Piltti pieni piikojansa	Piltti her little servant girl	
sanan virkko noin nimesi	says a word uttered thus	175
"Läksin kylpyä kylästä	"I went to find a bath in the village	
saunoa Sarajahasta	a *sauna* in Saraja	
jossa huono hoivan saisi	where a wretch can receive attention	
avun anke tarvitsisi."	help for the luckless one in need."	
Ruma Ruotuksen emäntä	Ugly Ruotus's wife	180
sanan virkko noin nimesi	says a word uttered thus	
"Ei ole kylpyä kylässä	"There is not a bath in the village	
saunoa Sarajahassa	a *sauna* in Saraja	
On talli Tapomäelle	There is a stable on Tapo hill	
huoni hongikko keolla	a room in a fir grove house	185
johon portot pojan saapi	where whores go to have a son	
tuulen lautat lapsen luopi."	harlots to make a child."	
Piltti pieni piikosehe	Piltti her little servant girl	
sekä juoksi jotta joutu	both ran and rushed	
sano tuolta tultuaan	says once she's returned from there	190

155

"Ei ole kylpyä kylässä
saunoa Sarajahassa
jossa huono hoivan saisi
avun anke tarvitsisi

"There is not a bath in the village
a *sauna* in Saraja
where a wretch can receive attension
help for the luckless one in need

Ruma Ruotuksen emäntä
sanan virkko noin nimesi

Ugly Ruotus' wife   195
says a word uttered thus

"On talli Tapomeällä
huone hongikkokeolla
johon portot pojan saapi
tuulen lautat lapsen luopi."

"There is a stable on Tapo hill
a room in a fir grove house
where whores go to have a son
harlots to make a child."''   200

Oli aikoa vähäsen
vaimon vaivakse tulee
kohtu kääntyy kovaksi
vatsan täysi vaikieksi
Otti vassan varjoksensa
koprin helmansa kokoili
käsin kääri vaatteensa
itse noin sanoiksi virkki

There was little time
a wife's trial comes
the womb turns heavy
the stomach full of troubles
She took a *sauna*-whisk for protection 205
gathered her skirt in her fists
wound up her clothes in her hands
herself thus put in words

"Lähtie minun tuleepi
niin kun muinenki kasakan
eli orjan palkkalaisen."

"Go I must
just like a farmhand of old   210
or a serf, a hireling."

Astua taputteloo
huonehesen hongikolle
tallih on Tapomäelle
niin sano sanalla tuolla

She steps lightly
to the room in the fir grove
to the stable on Tapo hill
thus she says in words when there   215

"Hengeäs hyvä heponen
vatsan kauti vaivallisen
kyly löyly löyhähytä
sauna lämpönen lähetä
vatsan kauti vaivallisen
jossa huono hoivan saisi
avun anke tarvitsisi."

"Breathe good horse
across my troubled stomach
bathhouse heat let loose
sauna warmth send off
across my troubled stomach   220
where a wretch can receive attention
help for the luckless one in need."

Hengäsi hyvä heponen
kylyn löylyn löyähytti
saunan lämpösen lähetti
vatsan kautti vaivallisen

Breathed the good horse
bathhouse heat let loose
sauna warmth sent off   225
across the troubled stomach

Jouluna Jumala synty
paras poika pakkasella
synty heinille heposen
suora jouhen soimen päähän

On Christmas God is born
the best boy in the frost
born onto the hay of horses
into the straight-mane's manger   230

III. Mary, the Road, the Moon and the Sun

Neitsy Maria emonen
rakas äiti armollinen
piiletteli poiuttahan

Virgin Mary little mother
dear mother full of grace
she hid her son

kullaista omenoansa	her golden apple	
alla sieklan sieklottavan	under a sieve for sifting	235
alla korvon kannettavan	under a pail for carrying	
alla jouksovan jalaksen	under a running sled runner	
Kato pieni poikuoh	The little son disappears	
kultainen omenuutensa	her golden apple	
alta sieklan sieklottavan	from under a sieve for sifting	240
alta juoksevan jalaksen	from under a running sled runner	
alta korvon kannettavan	from under a pail for carrying	
Etsi pientä poiuttansa	She searched for her little son	
kullaista omenoansa	her golden apple	
kesällä kevysin pursin	in summer with a light boat	245
talvella lylyin lipein	in winter with sliding skis	
Etsittiin vain ei löytty	He was searched for but not found	
Neitsy Maaria emonen	Virgin Mary little mother	
kävi teitä asteloo	walked roads, stepped	
tiehyt vastaan tulevi	She comes upon a road	250
niin tielle kumarteleksen	thus bowing to the road	
itse noin sanoiksi virkki	herself she put in words thus	
"Tiehyöt Jumalan luoma	"Road, God's creation	
näitkö pientä poiuttani	have you seen my little son	
kullaista omenoani?"	my golden apple?"	255
Tie vastaan sanoo:	The road in response says	
"Jos tietäisin en sanoisi	"If I knew I would not say	
poikas' on minunki luonut	your son has created me as well	
ratsuilla ajettavaksi	for riding saddlehorses	
kovin kengin käytäväksi."	for using heavy shoes."	260
Neitsy Maaria emonen	Virgin Mary little mother	
rakas äiti armollinen	dear mother full of grace	
aina etsivi etemmä	ever searching onward	
kuuhut vastaan tulevi	She comes upon the moon	
niin kuulle kumarteleksen	thus bowing to the moon	265
itse noin sanoiksi virkki	*herself she put in words thus*	
"Sie kuuhut Jumalan luoma	"You, moon, God's creation	
näitkö pientä poiuttani	have you seen my little son	
kullaista omenoani?"	my golden apple?"	
Kuu se vastaan sanoo	The moon in response says	270
"Jos tietäisin en sanoisi	"If I knew I would not say	
poikais on minunki luonut	your son has created me as well	
päivällä katoamahan	to hide in the day	
yön on aian paistamahan."	to shine at nighttime."	
Aina eistyppi etemmä	Always searching onward	275

Iro, a little girl from Miinoa. Southern Archangel Karelia. Photo: I.K. Inha 1894 (FLS 9859).

Neitsy Maaria emonen	Virgin Mary little mother	
rakas äiti armollinen	dear mother full of grace	
etsi pientä poiuttansa	searched for her little son	
kullaista omenoansa	her golden apple	
päivyt vastaan tulevi	she comes upon the sun	280
päivälle kumarteleksen	bowing to the sun	
"Sie päivä Jumalan luoma	"You, sun, God's creation	
Näitkö pientä poiuttani	have you seen my little son	
kullaista omenoani?"	my golden apple?"	
Niin päivä Jumalan luoma	Thus the sun, God's creation	285
sanan virkko noin nimesi	says a word uttered thus	
"Poikas' on minunki luonut	"Your son has created me as well	
päivän ajan paistamahan	to shine in the daytime	
yön ajan lepäämähän	to rest in the nighttime	
Tuoll' on pieni poikuosi	There is you little son	290
kultainen omenasi	your golden apple	
ylisessä taivosessa	in the high heavens	
isän Jumalan sialla	in God the Father's place	
tulee sieltä tuomitsemaan."	he'll come from there to judge."	

1103a Cajan (1836)

I. The Berry and Mary

Kasvo marjanen meällä	A berry grows on a hill
punapuola kankahalla	a cranberry on a marsh

niin marjanen mäeltä huuti	thus the berry called from the hill	
punapuola kankahalta	the cranberry from the marsh	
"Tule neiti poimomaha	"Come maiden and pick me	5
vyö vaski valitsemaha	copper-belt choose me	
tinarinta riipomaha	tin-breast pluck me	
ennen kuin etona syöpi	before the snail consumes	
mato musta muikkoavi!"	the black worm destroys!"	
Neitsyt Maaria emonen	Virgin Mary little mother	10
se oli vanhin vaimoloista	she was the oldest of women	
eläjien ensimäinen	the first among beings	
viititsekse vaatiksekse	dresses, adorns	
peäsomille suoreille	in a proper headdress	
voatteille valkeille	in clothes of white	15
Läksi marjan poimentahan	She went to pick the berry	
niin meni mäen nisalle	thus she went to the hilltop	
keksi marjasen meältä	she picked the berry on the hill	
puolukkaisen kankahalta	the berry on the marsh	
On marja näkemiänsä:	It looks like a berry	20
alahahk' ois' moassa syyä	too low to eat on the ground	
ylähähkä ois' puuhun nossa	too high from a tree	
Niin mänövi mättähälle	Thus she went to the hill	
tempo kartun kankahalta	she drags a pole from the marsh	
senki peällä seisataksen	and standing on that	25
Heitti marjan helmoillensa	She threw the berry onto her lap	
voatteille valkeille	onto the clothes of white	
pätöville peäsomille	onto the worthy headress	
Niin marja ylemä nousi	Thus the berry rose up	
polosille polvillensa	onto her dear knees	30
Niin marja ylemmä nousi	Thus the berry rose up	
riveille rinnoillensa	onto her nimble breast	
Niin marja ylemä nousi	Thus the berry rose up	
leveälle leuallehe	onto her broad chin	
leualta on huulellehe	from the chin to the lip	35
huulelta on kielellehe	from the lip to the tongue	
siitä vatsahan valahti.	from there it slid into the stomach	

II. Mary, Piltti, and Ugly Ruotus' Wife

Oli aikoo vähänen	There was a little time	
jopa tuskihin tulovi	already the pain comes	
siitä tyyty siitä täyty	sated from that, filled from that	40
siitä paksuksi panihe	grew fat from that	
lihavaksi liittelihe.	added weight	
Kanto kuuta 2, 3	She carries it for months 2, 3	

kaksi, 3, 4 kuuta	two, 3, 4 months	
4 kuuta on 5 kuuta	4 months is 5 months	45
5 kuuta on 6 kuuta	5 months is 6 months	
7, 8 kuuta	7, 8 months	
ympäri 9 kuuta	around 9 months	
Niin kuulla 10:nellä	Thus in the tenth month	
vanhoin vaimo meärin	as old women count	50
lyyään on vaimon kipua	there strikes the wife's pain	
immen tulta tuikatahan	the fire of girls sparks	
Niin kuulla 10:lä	Thus in the tenth month	
vyö lapan siansa siirti	the broad belt changes place	
palin otti paikan toisen	the clasp takes another notch	55
Vaimon vaivan tullessa	as a wife's trial comes	
sanoin virkki noin nimesi	she said in words uttered thus	
"Piltti pieni piikaseni	"Piltti my little servant girl	
lähe nyt kylpyä kylästä	go find a bath in the village	
saunoa Sarajahasta	a *sauna* in Saraja	60
jossa huono hoivan saisi	where a wretch can find attention	
avun anke tarvittaisi!"	help for the luckless one in need!"	
Piltti pieni piikaseni	Piltti her little servant girl	
hyvä kielas käskeäki	good at taking orders	
kepiä kehuttoaki	easy to persuade	65
sekä juoksi jotta joutu	both ran and rushed	
ylähäiset moat aleni	pulled down the highlands	
alahaiset moat yleni	pulled up the lowlands	
Ruman Ruotuksen kotih	to ugly Ruotus' (Herod's) home	
kintahen kirvottimille	to the loosed cloth	70
Ruma Ruotus paitulainen	Ugly Ruotus shirt-sleeved one	
syöpi juopi pöyän peässä	eats, drinks at the table's head	
/päässä pöyän/ paiollah	/at table's head/ in shirt-sleeves	
aivan aivinaisillah	in his clean linen	
Ruma Ruotuksen emäntä	Ugly Ruotus' wife	75
liikku keski lattialla	moves about the middle of the floor	
liehu sillan liitoksella	lightly treds upon the floorjoint	
Piltti pieni piikasensa	Piltti her little servant girl	
sanan virkki noin nimesi	said a word uttered thus	
"Läksin kylpyä kylästä" etc.	"I went to find a bath in the village	80
/saunoa Sarajahasta/	/a *sauna* in Saraja/	
/jossa huono hoivan saisi/	/where a wretch can find attention/	
/avun anke tarvittaisi!"/	/help for the luckless one in need"/	
Ruma Ruotuksen emäntä	Ugly Ruotus' wife	
sanan virkki noin nimesi	said a word uttered thus	
"On talli Tapomäellä	"There is a stable on Tapo hill	

johon portot poian saapi	where whores go to have a son
tulen lautat lapsen tuopi."	harlots to bear a child." 85
Piltti pieni piikasensa	Piltti her little servant girl
sekä juoksi jotta joutu	both ran and rushed
sanan virkki noin nimesi	said a word uttered thus
"Ol' ei kylpyä kylässä	"There is not a bath in the village
saunoa Sarajahassa	a *sauna* in Saraja 90
jossa huono hoivan saisi	where a wretch can find attention
avun anke tarviseisi	help for the luckless one in need
Ruma Ruotuksen emäntä	Ugly Ruotus' wife
sanan virkki noin nimesi	said a word uttered thus
"On talli Tapomeällä	"There is a stable on Tapo hill 95
huone hongikkomäellä etc.	a room in a fir grove house
/johon portot poian saapi/	/where whores go to have a son/
/tulen lautat lapsen tuopi."	/harlots to bear a child.""/
Aina vaimo vaivossahin	Ever the woman in her trials
aina ajoissa pahoissa	ever in bad times
"Lähe kylpyä kylästä	"Go find a bath in the village
(siit' 2 samatse)	(ie., ll. 59-96+) (repeated twice the same)
Niin kerralla 3:nella	Thus on the third time 100
sano tuolta tultuohe	she says once she's returned
"Ol' ei kylpyä kylässä" etc.	"There is not abath in the village"etc.
/saunoa Sarajahassa/	/a *sauna* in Saraja/
/jossa huono hoivan saisi/	/where a wretch can find attention/
/avun anke tarvittaisi!"/	/help for the luckless one in need/
Neitsyt Moaria emonen	Virgin Mary little mother
rakas äiti armollinen	dear mother full of grace
käsin keäri voattehensa	wound up her clothes in her hands 105
koprin helmansa kokosi	gathered her skirt in her fists
itse noin sanoiksi virkko	herself thus put in words
otti vassan varjoksehe	took a sauna-whisk for protection
"Lähtie miun tulovi	"Go I must
niinkuin muinenki kasakan	just like a farmhand of old 110
eli korjan palkollisen."	or a serf, a hireling."
Nousovi kipumäkiä	She mounted the hill of pain
kipuvuorta kiivuoli	the mountain of pain she climbed
huonehesen honkikolle	to the room in the fir grove
tallihin Tapomeälle.	to the stable on Tapo hill. 115
Sanan virkki noin nimesi	Said a word uttered thus
"Henkiäs hyvä heponen	"Breathe good horse
vatsan kautti vaivollisen!"	across the troubled stomach!"

Henkäsi hyvä heponen	Breathed the good horse	
vatsan kautti vaivollisen	across the troubled stomach	120

Siin' siit' Jumala synty	There then God is born	
synty heinille heposen	born onto the hay of horses	
suorajouhen soimen peähän.	into the straight-mane's manger	

III. Mary, the Road, the Moon and the Sun

Piiletteli poiuttahen	She hid her son	

alla juoksovan jalaksen	under a running sled runner	125
alla sieklan sieklottavan	under a sieve for sifting	
alla korvon kannettavan	under a pail for carrying	

Kato pieni poikuoho	Her little son disappears	
kultane omenuosa	her golden apple	

alta juoksovan jalaksen	from under a running sled runner	130
alta korvon kannettavan	from under a pail for carrying	
alta sieklan sieklottavan	from under a sieve for sifting	

Etsi pientä poiuttahen	She searched for her little son	
käypi teitä astelovi	walked roads, stepped	
tiehyt vastahan tulovi	comes upon a road	135
niin tielle kumartelekse:	thus bowing to the road:	

"Sie tiehyt Jumalan luoma	"You road God's creation	
miss' on pieni poikuoni	where is my little son	
kultanen omenuoni?	my golden apple?	

Tie se varsin vastoavi	The road answers quite so:	140

"Jos tietäisin en sanoisi	"If I knew I would not say	
poikas' on miunki luonut	your son had created me as well	
kovin kenkin käytäväksi	for using heavy shoes	
ratsuilla ajettavaksi."	for riding saddlehorses."	

Aina eistyvi etemmä	Ever searching onward	145
kuuhut vastahan tulovi	she comes upon a moon	
kuulle kumartelekse	bowing to the moon	

"Sie kuuhut Jumalan luoma	"You moon God's creation	
sano miulle pieni poikuoni	tell me (of) my little son	
kultainen omenuoni!"	my golden apple!"	150

Niin kuuhut vastoavi	Thus the moon answers	
/"Jos tietäisin en sanoisi/	/"If I knew I would not say/	
poikas' on miunki luonut	your son has created me as well	
yöhön aian paistamahan	to shine at nighttime	
päivällä katoaman."	to hid in the day."	

Eistyvi etemmä	She searches onward	155
päivyt vastahan tulovi	she comes to the sun	

162

"Sano pieni poikuoni!" Niin päivyt sanoiksi virkki	"Tell (of) my little son!" Thus the sun says in words:

"Tuolla pieni poikuosi kultanen omenuosi	"There is your little son your golden apple	160

Poikas' on miunki luonut päivän aian paistamaan yön aian katoamaan.	Your son has created me as well to shine in the daytime to hide in the nighttime

Tuoll' on pieni poikuosi ylisessä taivosessa peällä taivosen 8 ilmalla 9:nnellä peällä 5 villavaipan peällä 6 kirjokannen peällä uutimen utusen."	There is your little son in the high heavens atop 8 heavens in the 9th height atop 5 woolen cloths atop 6 mottled lids atop a canopy of mist."	165 170

1103b Castrén (1839)

I. The Berry and Mary

Marjanen mäeltä huuti punapuola kankahalta "Tule neiti poimimahan (sormuskäsi suoltamahan) tinarinta riipomahan vyövaski valitsemahan ennenkun etona syöpi mato musta muikkoavi."	A berry called from the hill a cranberry from the marsh "Come maiden and pick me (ringed-finger pickle me) tin-breast pluck me copper-belt choose me before the snail consumes the black worm destroys!"	5

Neitsyt Maria emonen kuuli marjan huutavaksi viititsihin vaatitsihin pääsomeille suoreille vaatteille valkeille	Virgin Mary little mother heard the berry calling dressed, adorned in a proper headdress in clothes of white	10

Niin mäni mäen nisalle katselekse kääntelekse keksi marjasen mäeltä punapuola kankahalta	Thus she went to the hilltop she looked, turned she picked the berry on the hill the cranberry on the marsh	15

\katselovi kääntelöövi\ \soriella sormillahan\ \kaunehilla kämmelillä\[7]	\she looked, turned\ \with her pretty finger\ \with her beautiful palm\

"On marja näkömiähän puola ilmoin luomiahan alahahk' on maasta syöä ylähähk'on puuhun nosta."	"It looks like a berry a cranberry without interest too low to eat from the ground too high from a tree."	20

Niin meni mättähälle heitti marjan helmoillehen	Thus she went to the hill she threw the berry onto her lap

helmoiltansa rinnoillehen	from her lap onto her breast
rinnoiltansa leuoillehen	from her breast onto her chin
leuoiltansa huulilehen	from her chin onto her lip
huuliltansa kielellehen	from her lip onto her tongue
siitä vatsahan valahti.	from there it slid into the stomach

II. Mary, Piltti, and Ugly Ruotus' Wife

Tuosta tiity tuosta täyty	Sated from that, filled from that
tuosta paksuksi panihen	grew fat from that
lihavaksi liittelihen	added weight
Kanto kohtua kovoa	She carries a heavy womb
vatsan täyttä vaikiata	a stomach full of trouble
Kanto kuuta kaksi kolme	She carries it months two, three
kolme kuuta neljä kuuta	three months four months
neljä kuuta viisi kuuta	four months five months
viisi kuuta kuusi kuuta	five months six months
seitsemän, kaheksan kuuta	seven, eight months
ympäri yheksän kuuta	around nine months
kuuta puolen kymmenettä	half of the tenth month
(Vanhoin vaimojen tasahan)	(as old women stipulate)
Niin kuulla kymmenellä	Thus in the tenth month
vaimon vaivakse tulevi	a wife's trial comes
\panoovi panun kipuja\	\the fire of pains is kindled\
\tulta immen tuikuttaapi\	\the fire of girls sparks\
painuvi pakolliseksi	she enters the time of need
vyölapat siansa siirti	the belts changed place
palin' otti toisen paikan	the clasp takes another notch
sanan virkki noin nimesi	she said a word uttered thus
"Piltti pieni piikaseni	"Piltti my little servant girl
\Orjuoni Pilmuoni\	\my Orju my Pilmu\
\Orjani alinomani\	\my constant serf\
\rahan saatu raatajani\	\my paid laborer\
lähe kylpyä kylästä	go find a bath in the village
saunoa Sarajahasta	a *sauna* in Saraja
jossa huono hoivan saisi	where a wretch can receive attention
\pian juokse pitkät matkat\	\run quickly on the long journey\
\välien välit samua\	\wander between the spaces\
\koprin helmasi kokoa\	\gather your skirt in your fists\
\käsin kääri vaattehesi\	\wind up your clothes in your hands
avun ange tarvitseisi!"	help for the luckless one in need!"
Piltti pienin piikojansa	Piltti her little servant girl
paras palkkalaisiansa	the best of her hirelings
hyvä kielas käskiäkki	good at taking orders
kepiä kehuttoaki	easy to persuade
sekä juoksi jotta joutu	both ran and rushed
Ruman Ruotuksen kotihin	to Ugly Ruotus' (Herod's) home
Ruma Ruotus paitulainen	Ugly Ruotus shirt-sleeved one

164

syöpi juopi pöyän päässä	eats, drinks at the table's head	60
päässä pöyän paioillahan	at table's headin his shirt-sleeves	
aivin aiminaisillahan	in his clean linen	
Ruma Ruotuksen emäntä	Ugly Ruotus's wife	
liikku keski laattialla	moves about the middle of the floor	
liehu sillan liitoksella	lightly treds upon the floorjoint	65
sano Piltti pieni piika	says Piltti the little servant girl	
\Piltti pieni piikojansa\	\Piltti her little servant girl\	
\sanan virkki noin nimesi\	\said a word uttered thus\	
"Onko kylpyä kyläsä	"Is there a bath in the village	
saunoa Sarajahassa	a *sauna* in Saraja	
jossa huono hoivan saisi	where a wretch can find attention	
avun ange tarvitseisi?"	help for the luckless one in need?"	70
Ruma Ruotuksen emäntä	Ugly Ruotus' wife	
sanan virkko noin nimesi	says a word uttered thus	
"On talli Tapiomäellä	"There is a stable on Tapio hill	
huone hongikkokeolla	a room in a firgrove house	
johon portot poiat saapi	where whores go to have a son	75
tuulen lautat lapsen tuopi."	harlots to bear a child."	
Piltti pieni piikojansa	Piltti her little servant girl	
sekä juoksi jotta joutu	both ran and rushed	
sano tuolta tultuansa	says once she'd returned from there	
"Ol' ei kylpyä kyläsä	"There is not a bath in the village	80
saunoa Sarajahassa	a *sauna* in Saraja	
Ruma Ruotuksen emäntä	Ugly Ruotus' wife	
sanan virkko noin nimesi	says a word uttered thus	
"On talli Tapiomäellä	"There is a stable on Tapio hill	
huone hongikkokeolla	a room in a firgrove house	85
johon portot poiat saapi	where whores go to have sons	
tuulen lautat lapsen tuopi"	harlots to bear a child""	
Neitsyt Maaria emonen	Virgin Mary little mother	
rakas äiti armollinen	dear mother full of grace	
koprin helmansa kokosi	gathered her skirt in her fists	90
käsin kääri vaatehensa	wound up her clothes in her hands	
sanan virkki noin nimesi	says a word uttered thus	
"Lähtiä miun tulovi	"Go I must	
niinkun muinenki kasakan	just like a farmhand of old	
eli orjan palkollisen"	or a serf, a hireling"	95
Otti vastan varjoksehen	She took a sauna-whisk for protection	
kipuvuorta kiipuoovi	climbs the mountain of pain;	
mäen päälle pästyänsä	having come to the hilltop	

tallihin Tapiomäelle	to the stable on Tapio hill	
huonehesen hongikolle	to the room in the firgrove	100

sanan virkko noin nimesi	says a word uttered thus

"Henkeäs hyvä heponen	"Breathe, good horse	
\hyvä härkä höyräytä\	\good ox, bellow\	
\kylyn löylyn vassan lämmen\	\bathhouse heat stomach warmth\	
\hätähisen huutaissa\	\in this call of need\	
\pakkuisen parkuossa\	\in this poor cold\	
\(hännällähän löyhäytä)\	\(by the tail fan warmth)	
vatsan kautta vaivollisen	across the troubled stomach	
jotta huono hoivan saisi	so that a wretch can find attention	105
avun etc. /ange tarvitseisi/"	help etc./for the luckless one in need/	

Henkäsi hyvä heponen	Breathed the good horse	
vatsan kautta vaivollisen	across the troubled stomach	
kylyn löylyn löyähytti	bathhouse heat let fly	
saunan lämpösen lähetti	*sauna* warmth sent off	
vatsan kautta vaivollisen	across the troubled stomach	110

Niin meille Jumala synty	Thus to us God is born	
synty heinille heposen	born onto the hay of horses	
suorajouhen soimen päähän	into the straight-mane's manger	
Joulun Jumala synty	On Christmas God is born	
paras poika pakkasella	the best boy in the frost	115

III. Mary, the Road, the Moon and the Sun

Piilitteli poiuttansa	She hid her son	
(säilytteli lapsuetta)	(stored away her child)	
kullaista omenoansa	her golden apple	
hopiaista solkiansa	her silver brooch	

(alla leivän leivottavan)	(under a loaf for baking)	120
alla sieklan seulottavan	under a sieve for sifting	
alla korvon kannettavan	under a pail for carrying	
alla kiven jauhottavan	under a stone for milling	
alla juoksevan jalaksen	under a running sled-runner	

\Piilo päivän piilo toisen\	\Hides a day hides another\
\jo päivänä 3:ena\	\already on the third day\

(Mäni päätähän sukimahan	(She went off skiing	125
hampsiansa harjoavan	taking long strides	
korvalle tulisen kosken.)	to the edge of fiery rapids)	

kato pieni poikuensa	Her little son disappears	
kultanen omenuensa	her golden apple	
Etsi pientä poiuttansa	She searched for her little son	130
kullaista omenoansa	her golden apple	

Käypi tietä asteloopi	She walks a road, steps
niin tielle kumartelekse	thus she bows to the road

"Sie tie Jumalan luoma näitkö miun poiuttani poiuttani ainuttani kullaista omenoani hopiaista sauanvartta?"	"You road God's creation have you seen my son 135 my only son my golden apple silver skipole?"
Tie vastahan sanovi	The road in response says
"Jos näkisi en sanosi poikas on minunki luonnut kovin kengin käytäväksi ratsuin ajeltavaksi"	"If I'd seen I would not say 140 your son has created me as well for using heavy shoes for riding saddle horses"
Aina estyvi etehen \Aina eistyvi etehen\ \Koivut vastahan tulovi\	Ever searching onward \Ever searching onward\ \She comes upon a birch\
\"Oi koivut Jumalan luoma etc."\	\"Oi birch God's creation etc.\
\"Jos tietäisin etc.\ \Poikas' on minunki luonut\ \pirtti puiksi pilkotahan\ \terä rauoin rapsutahan\ \hakatahan halkopuiksi\ \lehtipuiksi leikatahan"\	\"If I knew etc.\ \Your son has created me as well\ \to be cleft into wood for a cabin\ \to be scraped by a steel blade\ \to be chopped into firewood\ \into leaf trees to be cut"\
kuuhut vastahan tulovi Hän kuulle kumartelekse	She comes upon the moon 145 She bows to the moon
"Sie kuu Jumalan luoma, etc."	"You moon God's creation, etc."
Kuuhut vastahan sanovi	The moon in response says
"Jos näkisin en sanoisi poikas' on minunki luonnut yksin yöllä kulkemahan päivällä kumottamahan" \joka paikan paistamahan\	"If I'd seen I would not say your son has created me as well 150 alone at night to wander to hide in the day \in every place to shine\
Aina eistyvi etehen päivä vastahan tulovi Päivälle kumartelekse	Ever searching onward She comes upon the sun She bows to the sun 155
"Sie päivyt Jumalan luoma, etc. näitkö pientä etc.	"You sun God's creation, etc. Have you seen the little etc.
Päivyt vastahan sanovi "Poikas on minunki luonnut päivän aian paistamahan yön aian katuomahan	The sun in response says "Your son has created me as well to shine in the daytime 160 to hide in the nighttime
Tuoll' on pieni poikuesi \Pilatuksen piinauksessa\ \pahan vallan vaivatessa\	There is your little son \being tortured by Pilate\ \being pained by powers of evil\

\kivet alla paaet päällä\   \under stones over rocks\
\somerot syäntä vasten\   \amid coarse gravel\
kultanen omenuosi   your golden apple
ylisessä taivahassa   in the high heavens
päällä taivosen kaheksan   atop eight heavens
ilmalla yheksännellä."   atop a ninth height."   166

1103c Castrén (1839)

I. The Berry and Mary

Marjanen mäeltä huuti	A berry called from the hill	
punapuola kankahalta	a cranberry from the marsh	
"Tule neiti poimimahan	"Come maiden and pick me	
tinarinta riipomahan	tin-breast pluck me	
\sormuskäsi suoltamahan\	\ringed-finger choose me\	
vyövaski valitsemahan	copper-breast choose me	5
ennen kun etona syöpi	before the snail consumes	
mato musta muikkoavi."	the black worm destroys!"	

Neitsyt Maaria emonen	Virgin Mary little mother	
kuuli marjan huutavaksi	heard the berry calling	
viititsihin vaatitsihin	got dressed, adorned	10
pääsomeille suoreille	in a proper headress	
vaatteille valkeille	in clothes of white	

Niin mäni mäen nisalle	Thus she went to the hilltop	
katselekse kääntelekse	she looked, turned	
keksi marjasen mäeltä	she picked the berry on the hill	15
punapuolan kankahalta	the cranberry on the marsh	

"On marja näkemiähän	"It looks like a berry	
puola ilmoin luomiahan	a cranberry without interest	
alahahk' on maasta syöä	too low to eat from the ground	
ylähähk' on puuhun nosta."	too high from a tree."	20

Niin mäni mättähälle	Thus she went to the hill	
heitti marjan helmoillehen	she threw the berry onto her lap	
helmoiltansa rinnoillehen	from her lap onto her breast	
rinnoiltansa leuoillehe	from her breast onto her chin	
leuoiltansa huulillehen	from her chin onto her lip	25
huuliltansa kielellehen	from her lip onto her tongue	
siitä vatsahan valahti.	from there it slipped into the stomach	

II. Mary, Piltti, and Ugly Ruotus' Wife

Tuosta tyyty tuosta täyty	Sated from that, filled from that	
tuosta paksuksi panihen	grew fat from that	
lihavaksi liittelihen	added weight	
Kanto kohtua kovoa	She carries a heavy womb	30
vatsan täyttä vaikiata	a stomach full of trouble	
Kanto kuuta kaksi kolme	She carries it for months two three	
kolme kuuta neljä kuuta	three months four months	
neljä kuuta viisi kuuta	four months five months	35

viisi kuuta kuusi kuuta	five months six months
seittemän kuuta kaheksan kuuta	seven months eight months
ympäri yheksän kuuta	around nine months
kuuta puolen kymmenettä	half of the tenth month
vanhoin vaimojen tasahan	as old women stipulate 40
Niin kuulla kymmenellä	Thus in the tenth month
vaimon vaivaksi tulevi	a wife's trial comes
panovi pakolliseksi	she enters the time of need
\panovi panun kipuja\	\the fire of pains is kindled\
\tulta immen tuikuttavi\	\the fire of girls sparks\
vyölapat siansa siirti	the belts changed place
palin otti toisen paikan	the clasp takes another notch 45
Neitsyt Maaria emonen	Virgin Mary little mother
sanan virkki noin nimesi	said a word uttered thus
"Pilti pieni piikaseni	Piltti my little servant girl
\Orjuoni Pilmuoni\	\my Orju my Pilmu\
\Orjani alinomani\	\my constant serf\
\rahan saatu raatajani\	\my paid laborer\
lähe kylpyä kylästä	go find a bath in the village
saunoa Sarajalasta	a *sauna* in Sarajala 50
jossa huono hoivan saisi	where a wretch can receive attention
avun ange tarvitseisi!	help for the luckless one in need
\pian juokse pitkät matkat\	\run quickly on the long journey\
\välien välit samua\	\wander between the spaces\
\koprin helmasi kokoa\	\gather your skirt in your fists\
\käsin kääri vaattehesi\	\wind up your clothes in your hands\
Pilti pieni piikojansa	Piltti her little servant girl
paras palkkalaisiansa	the best of her hirelings
hyvä kielas käskiäkki	good at taking orders 55
kepiä kehuttoakki	easy to persuade
sekä juoksi jotta joutu	both ran and rushed
Ruman Ruotuksen kotihin	to Ugly Ruotus' (Herod's) home
Ruma Ruotus paitulainen	Ugly Ruotus shirt-sleeved one
syöpi juopi pöyän päässä	eats, drinks at the table's head 60
päässä pöyän paioillahan	at table's headin his shirt-sleeves
aivin aiminaisillahan	in his clean linen
Ruma Ruotuksen emäntä	Ugly Ruotus' wife
liikku keski-laattialla	moves about the middle of the floor
lieho sillan liitoksella	lightly treds upon the floorjoint 65
sano Pilti pieni piika	says Piltti the little servant girl
"Onko kylpyä kylässä	"Is there a bath in the village
saunoa Sarajalassa	a *sauna* in Sarajala
jossa huono hoivan saisi	where a wretch can find attention
avun ange tarvitseisi?"	help for the luckless one in need?" 70
Ruma Ruotuksen emäntä	Ugly Ruotus' wife
sanan virkko noin nimesi	says a word utters thus

"On talli Tapiomäellä
huone hongikko-keolla
johon portot poiat saapi
tuulen lautat lapsen tuopi."

    "There is a stable on Tapio hill
    a room in a fir-grove house
    where whores go to have a son   75
    harlots to bear a child"

Pilti pieni piikojansa
sekä juoksi jotta joutu
sano tuolta tultuansa

    Piltti her little servant girl
    both ran and rushed
    says once she'd returned from there

"Ol' ei kylpyä kylässä
saunoa Sarajalassa

    "There is not a bath in the village   80
    a *sauna* in Sarajala

Ruma Ruotuksen emäntä
sanan virkko noin nimesi

    Ugly Ruotus' wife
    says a word uttered thus

"On talli Tapiomäellä
huone hongikko-keolla
johon portot poiat saapi
tuulen lautat lapsen tuopi"

    "There is a stable on Tapio hill
    a room in a fir grove house   85
    where whores go to have sons
    harlots to bear a child""

Neitsyt Maarja emonen
rakas äiti armollinen
koprin helmansa kokosi
käsin kääri vaatehensa

    Virgin Mary little mother
    dear mother full of grace
    gathered her skirt in her fists   90
    wound up her clothes in her hands

sanan virkko noin nimesi

    says a word uttered thus

"Lähteä miun tulovi
niinkun muinenki kasakan
eli orjan palkollisen"

    "Go I must
    just like a farmhand of old
    or a serf, a hireling"   95

Otti vastan varjoksehen
kipuvuorta kiipuovi
mäen päältä päästyänsä
tallihin Tapiomäelle
huonehesen hongikolle

    She took a sauna whisk for protection
    climbs the mountain of pain;
    having come to the hilltop
    to the stable on Tapio hill
    to the room in the fir grove   100

sanan virkko noin nimesi

    says a word uttered thus

"Henkeäs hyvä heponen
\Henkeäs hepovetäjä\
\hyvä härkä höyräytä\
\kylyn löylyn vassan lämmen\
\hätähisen huutaessa\
\pakkuisen parkuossa\
\(hännälläsi löyhäytä)\
vatsan kautta vaivollisen
jotta huono hoivan saisi
avun ange tarvitseisi!"
Henkäsi hyvä heponen
vatsan kautta vaivollisen
kylyn löylyn löyähytti
saunan lämpösen lähetti

    "Breathe, good horse
    \breathe draft horse\
    \good ox, bellow\
    \bathhouse heat stomach warmth\
    \in this call of need\
    \in this poor cold\
    \(by your tail fan warmth)\
    across the troubled stomach
    so that a wretch can find attention
    help for the luckless one in need!"   105
    Breathed the good horse
    across the troubled stomach
    bathhouse heat let fly
    sauna warmth sent off

Niin meille Jumala synty	Thus to us God is born	110
synty heinille heposen	born onto the hay of horses	
suorajouhen soimen päälle	into the straight-mane's manger	
Jouluna Jumala synty	On Christmas God is born	
paras poika pakkasella	the best boy in the frost	

III. Mary, the Road, the Moon and the Sun

Piiletteli poiuttansa	She hid her son	115
(säilytteli lapsuetta)	(stored away her child)	
kullaista omenoansa	her golden apple	
hopiaista solkiansa	her silver brooch	
alla leivän leivottavan	under a loaf for baking	
alla sieklan sieklottavan	under a sieve for sifting	120
alla korvon kannettavan	under a pail for carrying	
alla kiven jauhottavan	under a stone for milling	
alla juoksevan jalaksen	under a running sled-runner	
Meni päätä sukimahan	She went off skiing	
hampsiansa harjoaman	taking long strides	125
korvalle tulisen kosken.	to the edge of fiery rapids.	
\Sika on pahan tapanen\	\The pig is ill-mannered\	
\sika syyti heinät päällä\	\the pig thrashed about on the hay\	
Kato pieni poikuensa	Her little son disappears	
kultanen omenuensa	her golden apple	
Läksi Maaria etsimähän	Mary set off in search	
poiuttansa ainuttansa	of her only son	130
kullaista omenoansa	of her golden apple	
hopiaista solkiansa	of her silver brooch	
Etsi pientä poiuttansa	She searched for her little son	
puut puiten jaoten heinät	threshing trees separating hay	
katsellen kanarvan juuret	looking amid the roots of heather	135
Tiehyt vastahan tulovi	She comes upon a road	
niin tielle kumartelekse	thus she bows to the road	
"Sie tiehyt Jumalan luoma	"You road, God's creation	
näitkö pientä poiuttani	have you seen my little son	
poiuttani ainuttani	my only son	140
kullaista omenoani	my golden apple	
hopiaista solkiani?"	my silver brooch?"	
Tiehyt vastaten sanovi	The road in response says	
"Jos näkisin en sanosi	"If I'd seen I would not say	
poikas' on minunki luonut	your son has created me as well	145
kovin kengin käytäväksi	for using heavy shoes	
\joka konnan juostavaksi\	\for every bandit to run on\	
\kylmin kengin käytäväksi\	\for using cold shoes\	
ratsuin ajeltavaksi"	for riding saddle horses	

"Ole sie se ikäsi
kovin kengin käytävänä
ratsuin ajeltavana!"
\"Ole sie se ikäsi\
\alla jalan tallattava\
\sorkissa soti-heposen\
\kapehissa vaino-varsan\

"Be you that forever
for using heavy shoes
for riding saddle horses!"   150
\"Be you that forever\
\to be trodden underfoot\
\the war-horse's hooves\
\the battle-steed's hooves\

Aina eistyvi etehen
\Aina eistyvi etehen\
\Koivut vastahan tulovi\

Ever searching onward
\Ever searching onward\
\She comes upon a birch\

\"Oi koivut Jumalan luoma\
\näitkö jne."\

\"Oi birch, Cod's creation\
\have you seen etc.\

\"Jos näkisin en sanosi\
\Poikas' on miunki luonut\
\pirtti puiksi pilkotahan\
\terä-rauoin rapsutahan\
\hakatahan halkopuiksi\
\lehtipuiksi leikatahan"\

\"If I saw him I would not tell\
\your son has made me as well\
\to be cleft into wood for a cabin\
\to be scraped by a steel blade\
\to be chopped into firewood\
\into leaf trees to be cut\

Kuuhut vastahan tulovi
\katso päälle taivosehen\
Hän kuulle kumartelekse

She comes upon the moon
\looks up into the sky\
She bows to the moon

"Sie kuu Jumalan luoma
näitkö pientä poiuttani
poiuttani ainuttani?" jne.

"You moon God's creation
have you seen my little son   155
my only son etc.

Kuuhut vastaten sanovi
\Kuu varsin vastoavi\
\yläseltä taivoselta\

The moon in response says
\The moon clearly answers\
\from the sky above\

"Jos näkisin en sanosi
poikas' on miunki luonut
yksin yöllä kulkemahan
päivällä kumottamahan
joka paikan paistamahan"

"If I'd seen I would not say
your son has made me as well
alone at night to wander   160
to hide in the day
in every place to shine

"Ole ilmosen ikäsi
yksin öillä kulkemassa
päivillä kumottamassa
joka paikan paistamassa!"

"Be that way forever
alone at night to wander
to hide in the day   165
in every place to shine

Neitsyt Maaria emonen
Aina eistyvi etehen
\katso päälle taivosehen\
\aino katso aina itki\
Päivä vastahan tulovi
Päivälle kumartelekse
"Sie päivyt Jumalan luoma
näitkö jne.?"

Virgin Mary little mother
ever searching onward
\looks up into the sky\
\ever looks, ever cries\
She comes upon the sun
She bows to the sun   170
"You sun God's creation
Have you seen etc."

Päivyt vastaten sanovi	The sun in response says
"Poikas' on miunki luonut	"Your son has created me as well
päivän ajan paistamahan	to shine in the daytime 175
yön aian katoamahan	to hide in the nighttime

Tuoll' on pieni poikuesi	There is your little son
hauvattu maaemähän	buried in mother earth
\Pilatuksen piinatessa\	\being tortured by Pilate\
\pahan vallan vaivatessa\	\being pained by powers of evil\
kivet alla paaet päällä	under stones over rocks
somerot syäntä vasten	amid coarse gravel 180
vasten hieta hartioita."	up to his shoulders in sand

\(Ruots.) "Tähän lopettaa Arhippa tämän laulun seuraavilla säkeillä:\
\(In Swedish) "Here Arhippa ends this song with the following lines:\

\Tuolla on pieni poikuesi\	\"There is your little son\
\kultanen omenuosi\	\your golden apple\
\yläsessä taivosessa\	\in the high heavens\
\päällä taivosen kaheksan\	\atop eight heavens\
\ilmalla yheksännellä."\	\atop a ninth cloud"\

Further comparison of the versions

Now that the overall ethnopoetic shapes of the different versions are clearer, we may look more closely at ways they vary. A logical place to begin, of course, is by noting variation in overall length, as is tabulated in Table 1 below. Poem length is difficult to guage accurately, of course, unless we allow for lines ellipticized in the folklorists' fieldnotes. Thus, the figures presented below show "actual" numbers of lines (i.e., the number of lines actually published in SKVR) and "apparent" numbers of lines parenthetically (i.e., the actual numbers plus an estimation of the ellipticized lines). In the case of Castrén's versions, which list many lines marginally as possible variants, this parenthetical calculation must be viewed as only approximate.

Table 1. Comparison of Poem and Section Length. (Apparent length in parentheses.)

	Lönnrot (1834)		Cajan (1836)		Castrén I		Castrén II (1839)	
Act I	28		37		28	(31)	27	(28)
Act II	202	(203)	86	(180)	88	(102)	87	(101)
Act III	64		47	(48)	50	(67)	67	(98)
Total	294		170	(265)	166	(200)	181	(227)

The texts apparently vary in length from roughly 200 to 300 lines; i.e., Lönnrot's text is nearly double that of Castrén's first transcription. Despite this sizeable variation in overall length, however, the relative length of each act in relation to the other acts appears stable. Act I is always the shortest, comprising between ten and twenty percent of the total text, and

The Bogdanof family. Vuonninen. Photo: Samuli Paulaharju 1915 (FLS 5431).

Act III is always intermediate in length between Acts I and II. Act II stands as the greatest source of variability in performance length, varying from Castrén's sparing transcription of less than 100 lines to Lönnrot's extensive 202 lines.

When we compare the texts more closely, however, it becomes clear that the tremendous increase in length of Act II in Lönnrot's transcription over that recorded by later folklorists stems not from the addition of new lines but from the repetition of lines already used and common to all three folklorists' transcriptions. The description of Ugly Ruotus (Herod) for instance, is repeated four times in Lönnrot's transcription (II.58-62, 84-88, 119-123, 167-170) whereas the same description is only mentioned once in each of the other versions (Cajan's II.71-74, Castrén's II.59-62). We are dealing here, in other words, with the same tendency to selectively expand a given passage through repetition which we noted above in our discussion of the line *Niin marja ylemmä nousi* 'Thus the berry rose up' (Cajan II.29, 31, 33). Selective repetition, be it of a single line or an entire passage, thus appears a prime means of rhetorically shaping a text in Arhippa's poetic system. The very same passage, however, may not be expanded in a subsequent performance: Piltti's many journeys back and forth between Mary and Ruotus' wife are streamlined into a single trip in Castrén's transcription.

Alternatively, the expansion may take place through the insertion of other lines, such as those suggested as part of Mary's exhortation to Piltti before her departure:

lähe kylpyä kylästä	go find a bath in the village
saunoa Sarajalasta	a sauna in Sarajala
jossa huono hoivan saisi	where a wretch can receive attention
avun ange tarvitseisi!"	help for the luckless one in

	need!"
\pian juokse pitkät matkat\	\run quickly on the long journey
\välien välit samua\	\wander between the spaces
\koprin helmasi kokoa\	\gather your skirt in your fists
\käsin kääri vaattehesi\	\wind up your clothes in your hands\

1103c Castrén II.49-52 plus text fn 11

These suggested lines are partly borrowed from a later part of the poem, the moment at which Mary finally resigns herself to giving birth in the stable (1103c Castrén II.90-91), but they are also partly unique to this version of Arhippa's *Nativity*. Selective expansion in Arhippa's performance thus tends to rely on the repetition of lines usually present in the poem, but may also draw on lines from outside the poem altogether. Arhippa seems to have possessed a wealth of possible lines to insert at points where expansion was desired; note, for instance, the variation between possible further epithets by which Mary refers to her son in Castrén's two transcriptions. In his first transcription, Castrén notes the line *hopiaista sauan vartta*, 'silver skipole', which is replaced in Castrén's second transcription with the more typical *hopiaista solkiani*, 'my silver brooch'. The principle lesson which Castrén's transcriptions seem to teach is that Arhippa always knew more of his poem than he chose to perform at any given moment. Options for expansion were readily available to him, and therefore, could be used readily to give each performance its own rhetorical shape and point.

To speak only of expansion, however, is to miss two crucial aspects of Arhippa's artistry: the notion of fading explicitness and that of a balance of expansion and abbreviation, what we might call a spot-lighting effect. A comparison of the different versions of this poem make these ethnopoetic tendencies clear.

Hymes has described "fading explicitness" in his studies of Chinookan narratives (Hymes 1985, 411). In essence, this phenomenon is the tendency to ellipticize that which should be repeated, replacing a faithful repetition of lines or a passage with some marker such as "And the same thing happened two more times." Such elliptical treatment means one thing when folklorists do it (i.e., let their pens rest while their performers continue on) and quite another thing when performers themselves do it. It has been observed (e.g. in A. R. Niemi's notes concerning Arhippa in SKVR VI:2, p.1155), that Cajan was rather impatient with his informant, since Arhippa refused to perform any of the incantations, *loitsut* which were Cajan's chief interest. Cajan does indeed ellipticize a number of passages in his transcription of Arhippa's *Nativity*, but the ellipses noticeable in Mary's exhortations to the road, moon and sun appear to be Arhippa's own. Compare the different passages:

Etsi pientä poiuttahen	She searched for her little son
käypi teitä astelovi	walked roads, stepped
tiehyt vastahan tulovi	comes upon a road
niin tielle kumartelekse:	thus bowing to the road:
"Sie tiehyt Jumalan luoma	"You road God's creation

175

miss' on pieni poikuoni	where is my little son
kultanen omenuoni?"	my golden apple?"
1103a II.133-139	

Aina eistyvi etemmä	Ever searching onward
kuuhut vastahan tulovi	she comes upon a moon
kuulle kumartelekse:	bowing to the moon:

"Sie kuuhut Jumalan luoma	"You moon God's creation
sano miulle pieni poikuoni	tell me (of) my little son
kultainen omenuoni!"	my golden apple!"
1103a II.145-150	

Eistyvi etemmä	She searches onward
päivyt vastahan tulovi	she comes to the sun

"Sano pieni poikuoni!"	"Tell (of) my little son!"
1103a II.155-157	

The lines devoted to articulating Mary's search and questioning thus dwindle from a well-rounded seven lines, to a more abbreviated six, and finally to a highly abbreviated three. Indeed, the line *Sano pieni poikuoni!* (literally 'Say my little son!') makes little sense without the preceding lines to gloss it. And yet, Arhippa manages nonetheless to invoke his parallel repetitions by including enough of the essential lines to convey the parallel to the audience. This technique of narrative economy allows Arhippa to articulate a fully parallel and symmetrical set of three interrogations without spending the discourse time to do so. Fading explicitness as an ethnopoetic technique operates in the opposite direction but often for the same rhetorical purposes as the expansion techniques discussed above.

Arhippa was thus able to expand and abbreviate portions of his poems and to articulate parallel structures faithfully or through a shorthand invocation technique. Further, it is clear that Arhippa used these capabilities to spotlight certain select passages or portions of his poem in each performance, balancing that spotlighting with a concommitant downplaying of other portions. Castrén's second transcription furnishes a fine example of how the streamlining of Act II (Piltti's trips in search of a *sauna*) can be coupled with an expansion of Act III (Mary's interrogations of the road, possibly a birch tree, the moon and the sun). The curses or prophecies which Mary pronounces in response to the natural beings' refusals are built out of repetitions of the beings' own self-characterizations and expand this normally brief set of exchanges into a complex series. Observe, for example, Mary's words to the road:

Tiehyt vastaten sanovi	The road in response says

"Jos näkisi en sanosi	"If I'd seen I would not say
poikas' on minunki luonut	your son has created me as well
kovin kengin käytäväksi	for using heavy shoes
\joka konnan juostavaksi\	\for every bandit to run on\
\kylmin kengin käytäväksi\	\for using cold shoes\

ratsuin ajeltavaksi"	for riding saddle horses

"Ole sie se ikäsi	"Be you that forever
kovin kengin käytävänä	for using heavy shoes
ratsuin ajeltavana!"	for riding saddle horses!"
\"Ole sie se ikäsi\	\"Be you that forever\
\alla jalan tallattava\	\to be trodden underfoot\
\sorkissa soti-heposen\	\the war-horse's hooves\
\kapehissa vaino-varsan\	\the battle-steed's hooves\

1103c Castrén II.143-150 plus additions

Here, if we disregard the suggested variant lines for the moment, it appears clear that Mary's curse is modelled on the road's words. The only difference between road's lines 146 and 147 (*kovin kengin käytäväksi/ratsuin ajeltavaksi*, 'for using heavy shoes/for riding saddle horses') and those of Mary's response 149-150 (*kovin kengin käytävänä/ratsuin ajeltavana*, 'for using heavy shoes/for riding saddle horses') is the shift from the passive translative (here meaning "to be made into") to the passive essive (here meaning "to be used as"). Single case shifts of this sort, whether from the ablative to the allative, elative to illative, translative to essive, etc. appear a prime means of artfully repeating a line while also varying it. And regardless of how much of the suggested lines were actually included in Arhippa's performance for Castrén, it is clear that Arhippa possessed the means to spotlight this portion of the poem when he wanted to.

The above evidence all points to the notion that Arhippa's variations did not occur independently of one another: rather, Arhippa structured his performances as coherent, balanced and effective texts expanding, abbreviating, and altering in accordance with audience expectations, context, and personal taste. We may find some variation from performance to performance which appears simply haphazard, as in the case of the line *tuulen lautat lapsen saapi/luopi/tuopi*, 'harlots to have/make/bear a child'. Such variation, however, must always be scrutinized carefully, for it may in fact represent a subtle means of developing the text's rhetorical shape.

Final reflections on Finnish folk poetry research in light of the present analysis

It is clear, I believe, that Arhippa always knew more of his text than he chose to sing at any given performance. It would be misguided to search for some "original" or "most correct" version of his poem, or to create an omnibus version that would contain all the possible variations Arhippa had at his disposal. Creating such a theoretical text would be extremely difficult and would be limited by the number and accuracy of the transcriptions made by folklorists. Further, the balancing esthetic of spotlighting and abbreviation, as well as that of faithful repetition and fading explicitness would be lost. Nor should we imagine that some "core" version would be an adequate representation of Arhippa's art: it is the surface variation in content and structure that enlivens Arhippa's texts and make them truly poetic.

It is also clear that plot is not granted a more fundamental position in Arhippa's poetic system than are poetic features. The available poetic structures and the plot appear integrally and equally intertwined within the framework of an overarching ethnopoetic sensibility. As we have seen, this framework included:

1. the formal parallelism characteristic of folk poetry in the Kalevala metre;
2. a competing tendency toward groupings of three typical of most European folklore;
3. an affinity for a balance between groupings of two and three;
4. the use of groups of five at narrative highpoints or culminations;
5. various techniques for expanding or abbreviating passages;
6. selective performance through repetition or addition of certain lines in certain spotlighted passages;
7. a compensatory downplaying of passages outside of the spotlight through abbreviation or fading explicitness.

It would be worthwhile to check these observations against other poems performed by Arhippa to determine their applicability to his corpus as a whole. It would also be useful to compare this "grammar" to that observable in other poems from Arhippa's home district Latvajärvi or from Karelia as a whole. Such generalizations, however, can only be arrived at after individual texts have been analyzed as coherent wholes. The insights discussed here cannot arise from any shortcut or sampling procedure that disregards each text's individual rhetorical structure. They arise only from appreciating each text as a whole, planned and performed at a particular moment for a particular audience and context. The folk poems preserved in Finnish folklore archives thus represent a rich source of material for the study of ethnopoetics.

NOTES

1. Research for this study was funded in part by a grant from the Graduate School Research Fund of the University of Washington, Seattle. The author would like to express his thanks to Anna-Leena Siikala and Leea Virtanen for their help and encouragement in this project.
2. "Runot hän lauloi hyvässä järjestyksessä, jättämättä huomattavia aukkoja" --present author's translation.
3. "Järjestyksessä eli muotonsa puolesta olivat ne yhtä etevät, eikä niissä huomata sitä eri runojen ja runo-osien yhteensekoittamista, joka huonompien laulajien runoissa vaikuttaa hämmennystä." --present author's translation.
4. Lönnrot's transcription of Arhippa's poem is also included in Kuusi, Bosley and Branch's bilingual anthology *Finnish Folk Poetry: Epic* (Helsinki, 1977) pp. 283-291. The present author expresses his thanks to the authors of the anthology for their excellent translation and useful notes. Minor differences between the present translation and that of the 1977 anthology stem from a desire to achieve consistency in the translation of Arhippa's different versions and to create an English text that closely parallels the grammatical features of the Finnish. The present translation may suffer esthetically for its linguistic accuracy: for instance, no attempt has been made to regularize the use of present and imperfect tenses in the poem (which covary even within a single line) or to fill in semantic gaps left in the original language.
5. The asterisk (*) denotes lines ellipticized in the recorder's fieldnotes but supplied by the editors of SKVR.

6. Lines in slash brackets (/ /) were added by the present author to complete ellipses occurring in the original text and denoted by "etc." or other such demarcation. The surmised lines are taken from other passages in the same poem where the same lines appear to recur. In those cases in which the additions would become too lengthy and too conjectural I have left the ellipses in their original state.

7. Lines bracketed with the reverse slash (\ \) were listed as variants in Castren's transcriptions. They are printed as footnotes in SKVR, but are included within the text here. This inclusion, however, does not mean that that I believe these lines were necessarily part of Arhippa's actual performance; rather, I have included them in the text for ease of reference. (See discussion regarding Castren's transcriptions in the section on methodological considerations above.)

JUKKA SAARINEN

The Päivölä Song of Miihkali Perttunen

A.A. Borenius, one of the pioneers of Finnish folkloristics and the scientific collection of folk poetry, made three expeditions into Archangel Karelia in search of folk poetry, in 1871, 1872 and 1877. Of all the poetry collected in the 19th century and published in *Suomen Kansan Vanhat Runot (SKVR),* 'The Ancient Poems of the Finnish People', the thing that strikes us about Borenius's texts is his close attention to the full form and precise linguistic transcription. This polished facade is, however, only a screen for the more rugged reality richer in nuance. The texts by Borenius published in the SKVR in 1871 and 1872 are fair copies made by him of his original notes taken in the field.

To begin with, in making the fair copy, Borenius wrote out in full the words and lines abbreviated by him in his notes; he also polished the dialect transcription. His collecting technique was interesting: each of his texts was obtained by asking the singer to give two performances, one sung and the other dictated. The text obtained on the first occasion was on the second hearing expanded, and the additions and amendments indicated, either in between the lines or in the margins. (Itkonen 1936.) The fair copies are indeed very precise and faithful for field notes, but they obscure the variation in Kalevala-metric epic poetry. They are compromises between two variants.

When, in 1877, Borenius embarked on his third expedition, he took with him the notes made on his previous journeys. In collecting material from the same singers, he as a rule no longer wrote the songs down in their entirety, but compared them with his previous texts using the same technique as before: noting the additions and other amendments in between the lines and in the margins. These "comparisons" are, unlike those made in the field notes of 1871 and 1872, entered as individual variants in the SKVR. Songs not obtained by him from the same singer before were once again recorded by noting down two performances of the same song, but he no longer made fair copies of them; being more experienced by this time, he was able to make a very tidy and readable copy at the first attempt. The items in the SKVR collected in 1877 are printed straight from the field notes.

I devote some lines to the collection technique used by Borenius because it helps to throw light on the variation in the Kalevala-metric epic of Archangel Karelia. The song text presented by one singer is relatively fixed.

Songs beyond
the Kalevala
Studia Fennica
Folkloristica 2
1994

Borenius was as a rule able to include in a single recording as many as three variants presented to him without producing a chaotic copy.

This does not mean that the text of the songs was always the same, apart from a few "omissions" or "mistakes". On the contrary: there is always variation in epic poetry, and this variation conforms to its own rules and regulations.

Variation in oral tradition means that items of folklore – in the case of Kalevala-metric epic a song – that are either the same or that are felt to be the same acquire different manifestations. One idea is expressed in many ways. The concept needs adjusting somewhat by drawing a distinction between the variation revealed in the texts of different people and the variation appearing between the texts of the same person (such as a *rune*-singer) on different occasions. I here wish to use the terms *major variation* and *minor variation* to denote the two different types. Major variation is characterised by its unique, non-recurrent quality, minor variation by recurrence and constant change. This distinction is not entirely unambiguous, and I shall be returning to it at the end of the article.

Attitudes to the variation in oral tradition have varied according to the goals of the research in hand. To scholars with a diachronic orientation, such as members of the historical-geographical school, the multiplicity of variants has been a jungle in which they sought to find the one and only 'original' form of a given item of folklore. Regularities could be sought in variation (e.g. the "laws of thought", Krohn 1918) in order to arrive at the right form. Variation is a disturbance that confuses the issue and prevents the scholar from seeing the wood for the trees.

Scholars with a synchronic orientation see in variation dynamic processes of different kinds. Oral tradition is not about ready texts, their inheritance or recollection, but about the rules for producing folklore, the reproduction of a text.

The different attitudes spring from the great controversy of oral tradition: for folklore simultaneously incorporates elements both old and new, conventional and creative, static and dynamic (Kaivola-Bregenhøj 1985, 7). Research into Kalevala-metric poetry, and especially the epic, has tended towards the diachronic approach, but synchronic views have also been put forward. The problem is the difficulty of describing the rules of reproduction. The question has been approached via ready models (e.g. Fromm 1987, who bases his views on the oral-formulaic theory of Milman Parry and Albert B. Lord; Lord 1960).[1] But a ready-made model constructed by means of research into a single genre cannot possibly provide an automatic model for another genre. Each genre must be studied separately in detail, trying to extract from its texts (and contexts) its rules for reproduction. (Finnegan 1977.) I have myself studied variation in Kalevala-metric epic, taking as my material epic poetry noted down from the two Archangel Karelian *rune*-singers Miihkali Perttunen and his father Arhippa (Saarinen 1988).

The great change

We may examine variation by taking as an example *The Lemminkäinen Song* sung by Miihkali Perttunen, first noted down by Borenius in 1871

(SKVR I:2, 766; it is for the purposes of research nevertheless necessary to use the original field note, FLS. Borenius I, no. 95, which contains both the 1871 variants and the 1877 comparison). Borenius recorded it a second time in 1877, but this time his comparison technique was not quite so successful as before. The 1877 variant contained some changes of such magnitude that it proved quite impossible to jot them down in between the lines and in the margins as he had done on the previous occasions. The variant is therefore cut into two parts: the beginning is written out in full as an entry of its own (SKVR I:2, 766 b), while the end is compared with the earlier recording of *The Lemminkäinen Song* (SKVR I:2, 766 a). For the middle section it is necessary to go backwards and forwards between the note and the comparison. The result is a laboriously compiled variant that is as an entity one of the longest single Kalevala song variants ever noted down. The song known by Miihkali as *The Päivölä Song* possibly ran to some 550 lines.

The content of *The Lemminkäinen Song* as sung by Miihkali Perttunen is as follows: a feast is being prepared at Päivölä to which all except Lemminkäinen are invited. Lemminkäinen nevertheless hears of the feast and decides to attend. His mother warns him of three (or four) dangers threatening him along the way. Lemminkäinen nevertheless knows of a way of overcoming them. He travels to Päivölä. He is brought a tankard of beer seething with snakes, worms and frogs. He drinks the beer and begins to turn the guests into gold and silver trough his singing. The master of Päivölä is angry and challenges him to a sword fight. Lemminkäinen cuts the master's head off, and goes home dejected, where his mother advises him to hide on an island in the sea. Lemminkäinen escapes to the island but is once again forced to flee because of the maidens of the island. As he sails away he weeps for the maidens.[2]

The first of the major changes was that in 1877 Miihkali combined two songs he had in 1871 performed separately (though admittedly one after the other): *Oluen synty* 'The Origin of Ale' and *The Lemminkäinen Song*. *The Origin of Ale* itself has been compared to the old recording. In the 1877 manuscript *The Origin of Ale* is incorporated in *The Päivölä Song* by means of writing its opening and closing lines at the beginning of *The Päivölä Song*.

The epic songs of Archangel Karelia very often consist of narrative entities either loosely or tightly linked together; they can be regarded as songs in their own right and may be performed on their own by certain singers or in different narrative contexts. The special point in Miihkali's case is the fact that two narrative entities are performed by the same singer both separately and together. My study of the total repertoires of Arhippa and Miihkali Perttunen reveals that this is possible but not very common. Once adopted by a singer, the entities are firmly fixed. Epic songs are not performed arbitrarily, that is, sometimes together and sometimes separately.

The variation in *The Origin of Ale* and *The Lemminkäinen Song* is explained by the lability of the position of *The Origin of Ale* in the epic tradition of the entire area. It is to be found both as a song of its own and as an introduction to *The Lemminkäinen Song*. It has a complete plot, a narrative structure of its own, but at the same time the brewing of the beer

I.K. Inha's photograph of Miihkali Perttunen from Latvajärvi has helped to shape the notion of the 'ideal' classical rune-singer. Archangel Karelia. Photo: I.K. Inha 1894 (FLS 9875).

(of mythical origin) points to a festival, a feast that may be associated with the feast at Päivölä in *The Lemminkäinen Song*.

The second big change is an addition. Whereas in the 1871 variant "the crippled and lame" are simply invited to the feast at Päivölä, in 1877 Miihkali describes how invitations were sent out as follows: the first inviter to be sent out was a winter boy who blew the trees leafless. Because he was no good, a summer boy was sent, who invited the crippled and lame just as he was supposed to do.

This motif, a little episode in fact, is akin to the song about Sampsa Pellervoinen[3] and is found at the same point in *The Lemminkäinen Song* only in the versions sung by two other Archangel Karelian singers, namely Homani Ohvo and Jyrkini Iivana from the Vuonninen area (SKVR I:2, 806, 808). Immediately after it in the 1877 variant is a second addition giving instructions not to invite Lemminkäinen. This is a feature commonly encountered in Archangel Karelia. It is not in the 1871 variants; even in the variants of 1877 it is labile, and it is only amplified on Borenius's demanding an explanation for the isolated lines "Ahti lives on the island, Veitikkä upon the headlands tip, Kapo in the headlands crook".

The additions to the invitation episode answer the question of how the people were invited, of how the invitations were sent. They may be regarded as subordinate, being at a lower level in the textual hierarchy. There are in a narrative, epic poetry included, sections fulfilling different roles and with a complex relationship to one another. Some clearly occupy a subordinate status. The subordinate textual elements describe, modify, argue, specify, etc. other parts of the text. More important to the progress of the narrative are the parts at a higher hierarchical level; naturally a subordinate part cannot appear without the part it specifies. The opposite is, however, possible: a subordinate part can often be deleted without disturbing the narrative flow. This is also reflected in the variation: the deletions or additions apply particularly to the subordinate parts.

Although the seeking of the assistance of a summer or winter boy to send out invitations is a fairly extensive motif, it is a descriptive enlargement on the narrative. Lemminkäinen is in any case not invited to the feast; this can be expanded by describing how the inviters are advised and how they will recognise Lemminkäinen, which is another of Miihkali's 1877 additions; this can be carried even further by giving the reason why Lemminkäinen is not invited, because he is so quarrelsome (see e.g. FFPE, song 34, 57-59).

The difference between combining songs in longer sequences and addition is, in the final analysis, merely a question of degree. The invitation motif in Miihkali's 1877 variant is better described as an addition, because the motif is not one commonly sung on its own in the area. It is not as independent as *The Origin of Ale*. But *The Origin of Ale* could also be regarded as an enlargement, as a description adding depth to the feast motif in *The Lemminkäinen Song*.

The 1871 variants begin with the main hero: Lemminkäinen is ploughing and overhears the invitation. In the 1877 variant the order of the parts is reversed. We may put forward two reasons for this, both of which would on their own suffice to bring about a change in the order, a transfer.

Epic songs have a tendency to begin with the main hero and his name. Miihkali begins the separate rendering of *The Lemminkäinen Song* by first introducing Lemminkäinen, who is ploughing a field, and only then telling how the feast was being prepared at Päivölä. The version of *The Lemminkäinen Song* combined with *The Origin of Ale* begins more naturally with the same theme with which *The Origin of Ale* is connected: the feast at Päivölä. The narrative does not therefore proceed from Päivölä to Lemminkäinen, back to Päivölä and then back to Lemminkäinen.

The second reason ties in with the invitation motif. The narrative of Kalevala metre epic proceeds in a straight chronological order, and flashbacks are virtually unknown apart from the instances of direct speech in the songs. The order of episodes that take place simultaneously or whose temporal relationship is irrelevant may change, however.

The sending out of the invitations as related by Miihkali in 1871 takes place while Lemminkäinen is ploughing. The 1877 addition, by contrast, emphasises the events before the inviters are sent on their way, which in turn determines more closely the temporal order of the episodes.

The last major change concerns the central element in the first half of *The Lemminkäinen Song*, the broad analogy or frame repetition which I shall henceforth call *the danger sequence*. Each time it appears the frame (or incremental) repetition contains the same (but not unmodified) frame and a different analogy. The danger sequence consists of a dialogue between Lemminkäinen and his mother. The frame consists of a dialogue in which Lemminkäinen asks his mother to bring him his war-gear so that he can wear it at the feast. His mother replies with a warning that he will encounter many dangers on his journey. Lemminkäinen asks what the first (second, third, last) danger will be. Each time his mother describes in analogical terms the danger (a giant worm, a hill of poles, a fiery eagle, wolves and bears) and Lemminkäinen tells her how he intends to overcome them.

The variants of 1871 and 1877 contain two major differences in the danger sequence. Firstly, in 1877 the dialogue outlined above is coupled with a description drawing on the same analogical parts of the journey to the feast at Päivölä, *the journey sequence*: Lemminkäinen is on his journey, he encounters the very dangers of which his mother warned him and overcomes them just as he said he would. Secondly, the position of the dangers in the repetition is also different: whereas in 1871 Lemminkäinen's mother warns about four dangers, in 1877 she warns about only three. The missing danger (the worm) nevertheless turns up in the journey sequence, which in turn lacks another of the dangers (the hill of poles). In other words, all the 1871 dangers are present in 1877, but they occupy different positions.

There are points of comparison with the reshaping of the danger sequence in some of Miihkali's other texts, and among other singers. The danger sequence is a vital element of *The Lemminkäinen Song*, where it almost always appears in the variants of Archangel Karelia. The journey sequence is not quite so widespread. It should on the other hand be noted that the journey sequence is a repetition of the danger sequence. It may be interpreted as a performance repetition differing slightly from the danger sequence. In the performance repetition an order is issued in the form of direct speech and it is executed using the same line material (the same lines, line schemes and groups of lines). The journey sequence does not carry out an order issued by another; instead Lemminkäinen does what he says he will do in the danger sequence. The entire frame repetition is repeated and a new repetitive structure is formed.

One common feature, especially in the texts of Miihkali Perttunen, is that the inclusion of a mere order in the text is sufficient to express its execution, too. This also varies so that at the same point in different variants Miihkali may use either an order only or an order and its execution, in other words the performance repetition. The repeating of the danger sequence as the journey sequence may be viewed in this light: as Miihkali's way of manifesting the same narrative contents in two different ways.

Counterparts to the different placings of the analogies can also be found both in Miihkali's repertoire and in others. The analogical parts are in most cases mutually interchangeable, describing the same central contents in several different ways. It is common for analogical parts to be omitted and added. It is also common to change their order, though this does not occur in Miihkali's danger sequence. In 1871 there are four dangers in Miihkali's danger sequence. The 1877 variants are influenced by 'the Law of Three', but in using the performance repetition Miihkali manages to fit in all four dangers in his variant. Another case in which the influence of the Law of Three is visible in an unusual way is in Miihkali's song about the tasks set for the rival suitors (SKVR I:1, 472, 473, 473a, 473b). In the earlier variants there are three such tasks. With the addition of a fourth task in 1877, the number of repetitions is not raised to four as one might expect; instead Miihkali combines two analogies within one frame and thus keeps the number of times at three. The Law of Three is a strong tendency but not the sole principle of repetition in Kalevala-metric poetry.

Constant change

The ordinary variation is, however, more limited and has far less influence on the overall character of a song. Variation does not occur arbitrarily in any part of the text. Sections that are either subordinate or definitive, at a lower level in the textual hierarchy, can be omitted and added. These are not generally as extensive as the invitation motif and may be brief motifs or phrases. A transfer is possible so long as it does not disturb the chronology of the song. I now wish to take a look at four "environments" in which variation is manifest in its own way.

Repetitions

Repetitions use the same line material (the same lines, line schemes and groups of lines) several times in succession, each time being structurally related to the others. In *a frame repetition* a narrative section is repeated, part of the section remains the same (the frame) while part of it is replaced by an analogical section (the analogy). A *performance repetition* consists of a demand, order or the like and its execution using the same line material. A *reply repetition* consists of a question and answer using all or some of the same line material. In *a nucleus repetition* an event already introduced is repeated as part of the dialogue of some character in the song.

Repetition causes variation in several different ways. I have already pointed out that variation of the performance repetitions was typical of Miihkali. An order or demand is alone sufficient for the narrative to be understood, but it is in some variants accompanied by the execution of the order, that is a performance repetition. The reply repetition can be varied by either including or omitting the lines corresponding to those of the question, or in a more complicated manner: the singer has several different answers, all with parallel contents. The question put by Lemminkäinen to the Master of Päivölä "Which has a better sword, Which a foil more beautiful?" is answered in three ways: The first reply, given in 1871, provides an answer that follows a different scheme: "my sword has been chipped by bones and broken by skulls". The second time the singer uses a reply repetition, either in place of or in addition to this, "You have a better sword". In 1877 Miihkali used a line following the same scheme as the question but providing antithesis: "I have a worse sword, I have a foil more terrible", either in addition to or in place of the former.

A repetition repeats the same line material. This does not, however, mean that the repetitions are identical; they may omit, add, transfer or substitute elements. The reasons may be similar to those for variation mentioned above (textual hierarchy, etc.). But it should also be noted that due to the nature of the repetition, the comprehensibility of the text does not suffer so much if something is omitted as in the case of a text without a repetition; the omissions may thus apply to elements that would be out of the question in "normal texts".

The 1877 variant of the danger sequence has an addition applying to the third or last time only. The mother's warning "Many will be the strange things on your journey" is emphasised by the lines "Father banned, mother

Miihkali Perttunen, a member of the Old Believers' sect, ate meals separately from other family members. Latvajärvi, Archangel Karelia. Photo: I.K. Inha 1894 (FLS 9876).

ordered, a pair of witches said no, three nature-spirits forbade". This is almost word-for-word the same group of lines with which Miihkali's father Arhippa Perttunen accompanied each of the mother's warnings in his danger sequence. Could this be interpreted as a recollection of the father's song? (Fromm 1987, 75.) I rather doubt it, for the same set of lines is also to be found at Latvajärvi, Miihkali's home village, and among other singers elsewhere in the same textual context. Miihkali used the lines only on the last time, and they may be regarded as an addition designed to underline the message. Emphasising the last (in most cases the third) time in some way is common. The most common additions emphasising the last time are clichés ("Thus on the third time" or some such phrase), but Miihkali here chose another solution.

Variation can also be observed in the analogy part of the frame repetition. One way has already been revealed in the danger sequence: the changing and transferring of the analogies and the number of times. It is, however, more interesting to examine the construction of the analogies in the frame repetitions. Analogy is a fundamental concept in Kalevala-metric poetry and does not concern frame repetitions alone. The drawing of analogies was part of the *rune*-singer's competence and evident in both the major and the minor variation.

In the frame repetition, analogy in any case refers to the analogy of content, plus similarities at the level of form: the singer uses a frame in which the same lines are repeated, he presents the analogies using the same or similar constructions, partly the same lines and line schemes.

There are two contrasting tendencies in the frame repetition. One tries to carry the similarities of form as far as possible, to standardise the different repeated sections, while the other tries to present the analogical part in a manner all of its own, using line groups, lines and line schemes differing in form. It is clear that without the demand for similarity of form, the analogies can be richer in content and more freely selected. On the other hand the link between one time and the next becomes weaker. Similarity of form links the different times more closely together. Each frame repetition is in a way a compromise between these two tendencies: some repetitions stress the analogy of content, others the similarity of form. The singers themselves influence this relationship; the striving towards similarity of form is more marked among some singers than among others. The relationship is not necessarily fully established even in the repetitions of one singer, and juggling with the different tendencies constantly influences the moulding of the texts of different variants.

This is clearly visible in Miihkali's danger sequence and the journey sequence using the same analogical elements. The analogy of the danger sequence consists, like the frame, of a dialogue: the mother describes the dangers threatening Lemminkäinen on his journey and Lemminkäinen tells her how he will overcome them. In the journey sequence the frame turns into a description of how Lemminkäinen travels and in the analogy the threats foretold in the dialogue come true. In 1871 Miihkali presented the analogy parts (1-4) as follows:

(1) A   A worm lies across the road
     B   longer than the room's timbers
     C   It's eaten a hundred men
          destroyed a thousand heroes
          It will eat you too.

(2) A   There's a hill bristling with poles
          the poles are bristling with man's head
     C   One pole has been left empty
          kept for Lemminkäinen's head

(3) A   Rapids lie across the road
          amid it a fiery crag
          on the crag a fiery birch
          on the birch a fiery eagle
     C   It's eaten a hundred men
          destroyed a thousand heroes
          It will eat you too
     B   Its mouth is a hundred fathoms
          Its gullet the size of three rapids
     C   By night it sharpens its teeth
          and by day it whets its claws
          kept for Lemminkäinen's head

(4) A   The wolves are bridled ready
          the bears in iron fetters
          They've eaten a hundred men
          destroyed a thousand heroes
          They will eat you too.

There are four dangers: a giant worm (1), a hill of poles (2), an eagle (3), wolves and bears (4). The analogy parts contain lines that present the dangers (marked A), describe them in more detail (B) and in particular their danger to Lemminkäinen (C). The analogies consist of alternation between elements A and C, sometimes supported by the "extra" element B.

In order to present or name the danger (A) Miihkali uses the line scheme "---lies across the road" in speaking of the worm and the rapids where the fiery eagle is living. In 1877 he does the same with the hill: "A hill lies across the road, The hill is bristling with poles". The similarity of form between the times thus increases and the encountering of the danger along the way is thereby enhanced. As a figure of speech, however, the hill lying across the road is somewhat lame and its use is understandable only in view of its position in the repetition.

The eagle was in 1877 further described by Miihkali as "Eyes it has beneath its wings, Looking holes in the nose of a quill". Borenius's comparative technique does not indicate whether this was in place of or in addition to the old description ("Its mouth is a hundred fathoms, Its gullet the size of three rapids"). In any case they enrich the contents but reduce the similarity of form.

How the danger affects Lemminkäinen depends on what it is like. A worm, eagle, wolves and bears are animate beings, wild beasts. So the lines "It has eaten a hundred men, Destroyed a thousand heroes, And it will eat you too" can be applied to all of them. Using the same line group adds to the similarity of form. The threat of the eagle is also described in its own particular way, as the sharpening of teeth and claws. Borenius's comparison tells us only that both were used in speaking of the eagle, either in parallel or in place of one another.

Miihkali's Lemminkäinen overcomes the dangers by getting himself a "substitute" and giving it to the danger. The difference between the hill of poles and the animate dangers is clearly revealed. The hill of poles has a solution all of its own: Lemminkäinen takes a dead man's skull and sets it upon the pole. By contrast, there is one device applying to the animate dangers: by singing the hero conjures up some other being to take his place and be devoured by the beast. The same line scheme can be used to conjure up both the man of alder and the flock of sheep. Submitting to an animate danger is expressed using the same cliché-like couplet.

The way in which the hero overcomes the danger involves a wealth of similarity of form: his victorious confrontations with the worm and the eagle are even described in exactly the same way. In the journey sequence of the 1877 variant the dead man's skull takes the place of the conjuring up of the man of alder in order to overcome the giant worm. Why does Miihkali make a distinction between the wolves/bears, eagle and worm; why are the sheep sufficient for the former, the man of alder for the latter? One reason may be that wolves and bears are ordinary dangers familiar in this world, whereas a fiery eagle and a giant worm are supernatural dangers. A dead man's head is also suitable food for a supernatural being.

We can see from the danger sequence the varying influence of the tendency towards the similarity of form from one time and variant to another. Kindred dangers and overcoming them are described by similar or identical lines. There is a clear striving towards similarity of form in, for example, starting the presentation of the dangers with the "---lying across the road" scheme, which most naturally, and in accordance with tradition, belongs in a certain context (a worm). A good example of how the striving towards similarity of form is sometimes stronger than the contents is to be found in the danger sequence of Okahvie, widow of Nihvo of Latvajärvi (SKVR I:2, 767). The danger is a hill of poles, but Lemminkäinen nevertheless throws the dead man's skull into the "eater's mouth" as in connection with the second danger, the eagle. A certain tendency towards contentual richness at the cost of similarity of form can, however, be observed.

Recurring situations and clichés

Recurring situations give rise to clichés: things are expressed using similar or identical means in different textual contexts. The majority of the narrative sequences and lines in the Kalevala-metric epic nevertheless belong in a particular context in a singer's repertoire. The use of clichés and their formal variation are not revealed very clearly on examining a single song, and it is necessary to look at the singer's entire repertoire.

A general motif is a cliché consisting of a smallish narrative sequence (a motif). Miihkali Perttunen has general motifs for setting off on a journey and travelling by horse or ship, for making preparations, for being transformed and for taking flight as an eagle. *The Lemminkäinen Song* contains one instance of making preparations: his departure for the feast at Päivölä. In the variants collected of *The Lemminkäinen Song* it always seems to be of the same form, but study of other manifestations of the general motif reveals variation. The motif is an addition at the lower level in the textual hierarchy, since its inclusion can be varied. It is made up of three elements: the hero prepares himself ("dressed himself and decked himself, prettily adorned his head"), puts on his armour made of various kinds of metals, and the need for these is finally pointed out. The omission variation proceeds in the same order: the first element is always present, the second usually, the third supplements the second, but not every time.

A general motif is a typification (Harvilahti 1985, 113): the same sequence is used in kindred contexts, even though its contents may sometimes be at odds with the context. In Miihkali's songs men and women prepare themselves in the same way, whereas Arhippa Perttunen, for example, gives men and women their own ways of preparation. The first part of Miihkali's motif is attached by Arhippa to women only, as would indeed seem more natural, the others to men. Arhippa further gives other elements to these general motifs. With Miihkali both Lemminkäinen and the Virgin Mary can dress and deck themselves, they can both put on their armours of metal, and both point out their need for these.

When Lemminkäinen escapes to and from the island, another general motif is used by Miihkali. The hero lowers his boat (or ship) into the water or steps into the boat, then hoists the masts and sits himself in the stern. The general motif then normally describes the sailing of the boat through land-waters, marsh-waters and boat-waters, *venovesiä*. On escaping from the island there is no account of the journey under sail, because for as long as the island is still in sight, Lemminkäinen is too busy weeping for the maidens of the island. But it is possible that Miihkali may in 1877 have continued the weeping with a description of sailing, ending up on the shoulders of a mighty pike, thereby trying to link in with the song about *The Origin of the Kantele*. It seems that Borenius nevertheless interrupted the singer and asked him to sing the whole story of Väinämöinen's Boat Journey telling *The Origin of the Kantele*. We may note here that in 1871 Miihkali recited the episode about the escape to the island in between the songs about *Väinämöinen's Journey by Boat* and *The Origin of the Kantele*, the hero being Väinämöinen.

The use of clichés may be a source of variety: the singer has several alternative ways of expressing the same thing. Miihkali's general motifs are, with the exception of riding a horse, very limited and they do not display the richness of numerous alternative elements as, for example, those of his father. The use of alternatives appears in Miihkali's shorter clichés. He may, for example, describe travelling on foot in two ways, making use of two different couplets.

The variety of forms is manifest in the ways the characters are denoted and the start of their rejoinders expressed. The same names, and names with the same metrical qualities often appear as subjects, thereby resulting in name clichés: *lieto Lemminkäini* 'the wanton Lemminkäinen', *vanha Väinämöinen* 'the old Väinämöinen', *seppo Ilmollini* 'the smith Ilmarinen'. An epic text contains numerous examples of direct speech that can be prefaced by the same lines and line schemes: *itse tuon sanoiksi virkkoi* 'he himself put this in words', *Sano lieto Lemminkäini* 'the wanton Lemminkäinen said'. These are what I call *sanoi 'said' clichés*. There are also *addressing clichés* that are in form as a rule connected with the name clichés *Oi sie seppo Ilmollini* 'O you, the smith Ilmollini', in function with the 'said' clichés.

The name and 'said' clichés chiefly display variation in two ways. Firstly, the epic text contains situations in which they can be used: the actor (subject) changes, there is a transfer from narrative to direct speech. Singers do not always necessarily use the clichés whenever the situation presents itself. The change of actor and the transfer to direct speech is in any case obvious from the text. The style of singing of Arhippa Perttunen was marked by a certain "fullness"; he made very regular use of name and 'said' clichés. Miihkali's style was, by contrast, marked only by potentiality; he might make use of them, but he might just as well disregard them, though he tended to use them much more in 1877 than earlier. This is generally evident on comparing variants of the same song in Miihkali's epic repertoire. For some reason it is not, however, evident in the same way in all of Miihkali's songs: *The Lemminkäinen Song* is one of these and displays a minimum of variation of this kind.

The second point concerns variety. There are alternative forms with roughly the same meaning for the 'said' clichés in particular (but also for the name clichés). *Niin siitä sanuo soatto* 'so he might say', *Itse noin sanoiksi virkko* 'he himself put this in words', *Sano tuolta tultuohe* 'said he when he had come from there', *Heänp on varsin vastoauve* 'he indeed answered' are the most common separate *sanoi* whole-line clichés used by Miihkali. They can be interchanged, replacing one another. *Sano (vanha Väinämöini)*, 'Said old (Väinämöinen)', *Niin sanovi (Väinämöini)*, 'So said (Väinämöinen) (Niin Anni) sanuo soatto*, '(So Anni) might say', *(Anni)* *varsin vastoauve,* '(Anni) indeed answered', are compound 'said' cliché forms appearing in the same line as a name. Their use naturally depends on the length of the name and on the metrical qualities of the first syllable, but even so they may display variation: *Niin sanovi Väinämöini – Sano vanha Väinämöini,* 'So said Väinämöinen – Said old Väinämöinen'. A separate and combined 'said' cliché may thus be alternatives to one another, such as *Tuo lieto Lemminkäinen / sanan virkki, noin nimesi* 'The wanton Lemminkäinen / he uttered a word, spoke thus', *sano lieto Lemminkäinen* 'the wanton Lemminkäinen said'.

Parallelism

Parallelism is one of the most typical stylistic devices encountered in Kalevala metric poetry. In it a line is parallelled by one or more closely-related lines. This is manifest in both the content and the form of the line. As regards its content, a parallel line may be synonymous or in some other way analogous. In form it is above all syntactically similar: each of its phrases has a counterpart in the preceding, i.e main line; but not all the phrases in the main line necessarily have a counterpart in the parallel line. (See e.g. Leino 1986, 135). The parallel line is not often syntactically so complete that it can be understood without the main line.

The omission or addition of a parallel line is very common. For example, in the following three lines the last line is omitted in at least one of Miihkali's variants:

> The blind were rowed there in boats
> the lame driven on horseback
> the crippled dragged in sledges

A transfer is possible if the parallel line is syntactically as complete as the main line.

In the text of a song parallelism may be understood as an addition designed to repeat, expand, deepen, specify, etc. the contents of the main line in different ways. Only a small proportion of parallel lines have anything to add to the course of the narrative. As regards form, they are not independent but subordinate to the main line. Being at a lower hierarchical level in both content and form, they are very often varied by omission, addition and transfer. A certain amount of variation can be expected on comparing parallel lines.

It would perhaps be possible to interpret the prevalence of parallel line variation as deriving from the fact that the songs were sung. I refer here to the study by Ilkka Kolehmainen (1977, 23-24) on the musicological syntax of the Kalevala melody, in which he demonstrates the dependence between the text and the melody in one individual case: Textual lines and musical lines can sometimes be repeated because the singer wants both the words and the melody to end at the same time. The wealth of parallel lines and the possibility of omitting a line or of adding parallels without affecting the course of the narrative would seem to encourage the use of line parallelism in order to synchronise the textual and musical structures. Since

In June of 1872 Axel Berner met Miihkali Perttunen, a blind rune-singer from Latvajärvi who lived by begging. Miihkali sang sixteen Kalevala runes and a few of the "newer" songs as well. Vuokkiniemi. Photo: A. Berner 1872. (FLS 5398:1).

no complete melody was collected from either Arhippa or Miihkali, no firm conclusions can be drawn. In the short sample melodies of Miihkali noted down by Borenius an initial line without a parallel is repeated, or in parallel cases the second phrase of the melody corresponds to the parallel line of the text. The volume of material is, however, very slight.

Changes within lines

Variation within a line is limited by the poetic metre. The number of syllables in the line must be preserved and the word-initial syllables must be placed correctly according to their length (Leino 1986, 128-129). True, it must be remembered that poetic metre is an ideal: it has no hard-and-fast rules, only strong tendencies (Leino 1986, 151). Not all lines observe the metre exactly, but the singer does not regard deviations as in any way "erroneous".

193

The beginning of a line is susceptible to variation, because the demands of the poetic metre are not so strong as at the end of the line. The majority of lines have at the beginning short stereotyped one- or two-syllable adverbial modifiers (*jo, niin, siitä*) or pronouns (*tuo, se, ne, heän*). Their own semantic content is slight but they occupy an important role: they supplement the line to make it fit the poetic metre (very often with the help of *on* or *-pa*) and can be replaced by each other and other words. This makes it easier to transfer lines to other contexts.

As examples of variation at the beginning of a line we could take the lines *Oli – Tuo on lieto Lemminkäini* (literally: 'It was – That is the wanton Lemminkäinen') from *The Lemminkäinen Song* (the variation is bound to the position of the line; *The Lemminkäinen Song* sung separately begins with the word *oli*, 'it was'). In cases like *Ompa – Siell on suvet suitsi peässä, Tuo on – Niin on lieto Lemminkäini, Siitä – Heänp on laivaha lasekse* the meaning of the line remains the same despite the variation in the beginning of the line. It may be assumed that the lines with this kind of beginning do not occupy a fixed form in the singer's memory and they are only completed in performance. In the course of variation within a line words are also replaced by synonyms or closely-related words that are synonyms in their textual context. It should be noted that variation within lines is not limited to the line beginning only.

Since the line is a limited unit, its variation mainly consists of substitution and transfer. The most common form of substitution is the use of full or contextual synonyms. Changing the order of words in a line is also common. The poetic metre places restrictions on variation. Metre must, however, be defined slightly more loosely than usual; the rules governing word-initial syllable length are not so strict in the second or third foot as in the fourth. Alliteration may influence the choice of words, but by no means always.

The singer and his text

Variation affects different aspects of the text in different ways and to a varying extent. Each part must thus be examined separately. Variation cannot, for example, be measured by counting the number of changing lines, because a text is not a uniform mass with respect to variation. In producing epic poetry in Kalevala metre the singer has a relatively fixed text in his memory. There are, however, three things that disrupt this: 1) the different roles occupied by the elements in the textual hierarchy, 2) interchangeability, especially in frequently recurring situations, and 3) a few models for the production of text, one of the most important of which is repetitions. Ultimately the entire text is only produced in performance, and no two performances are ever exactly the same.

Variation is manifest in the comparison of two texts as omissions, additions, transfers and substitutions. There is constant minor variation backwards and forwards, and we cannot strictly speak of variation as a whole using these terms. Omission and addition are two sides of the same coin, transfer signifies a change of order, substitution interchangeability. The relationship with major variation is not completely unambiguous, since the texts of a single person also display changes that are lasting and may thus be compared to major variation.

Because variants of *The Lemminkäinen Song* sung by Miihkali Perttunen were noted down only on two occasions, there cannot be firm evidence of any permanent changes. His entire epic repertoire did, however, undergo a number of major changes between 1872 and 1877, and the permanence of some of them can be verified by comparing them with the later recordings (SKS. Varonen 1886; Karjalainen 1894). The expansion of the invitation motif would appear to be a lasting change. This and a few other additions would appear to prove that Miihkali was influenced by singers of the Vuonninen area. The start of collection in 1871 may have provided the impetus for a change. If this is so, it tells us as much about the status of the epic in Archangel Karelia in the latter half of the 19th century as about Miihkali. The epic was receding into the background and Miihkali did not have a particular reputation as a singer in his native village, because he was not known as a seer. Miihkali had learnt his songs as a young man but was perhaps no longer practised in the singing of epic songs. The regularisation of the use of name and 'said' clichés after 1872 may be a sign of a revival of his former epic competence. We also get the impression sometimes that Miihkali actively tried to assimilate new material.

There is a difference of quality between *major* and *minor* variation. The learning and adopting of a song is a process of selection, compilation and editing. Almost never is there a single source for a singer's song, but some sources may have had far more influence than others. Many of Miihkali's songs are reminiscent of his father's, but the influence of the tradition prevailing in the area is in many cases greater. Once learnt, a song becomes fixed and chiefly undergoes only minor variation, though lasting changes do still occur.

What are the factors influencing minor variation? One may be the context of performance. I do, however, consider it unlikely that a singer (at least a singer like Miihkali Perttunen) would have been able to vary his text to suit the occasion in the manner of the performer of incantations (Piela 1983). The minor variation in epics is for the most part unconscious varying of the text. It is difficult to see how the variation typical of the epic could be inspired by the situation. Only the combining of songs in long sequences and the addition of certain longish episodes could point to a striving to lengthen a song on a certain occasion. Songs were valued according to their length, which may have resulted in competition (Virtanen 1968, 14). By using line parallelism the singer could maybe make the melody and the text coincide.

The song collected by Borenius in 1871 has no title. In 1877 Miihkali called it *The Päivölä Song* after the main scene of events. The fact that it is not called *The Lemminkäinen Song* after the main character reflects the 1877 entity and the importance of the changes that had crept into the song in the intervening five years. Even so, the changes are exceptional only in their extent; they are in any case similar in nature to the hundreds of other changes appearing in the texts of Miihkali and other singers.

NOTES

This article is based on an earlier version published in Finnish under the title *Miihkali Perttusen Päivölän virsi*, which appeared in *Kolme on kovaa sanaa. Kirjoituksia kansanperinteestä*. P. Laaksonen and S.-L. Mettomäki (eds.). *Kalevalaseuran vuosikirja 71*. Helsinki. 1991. p. 193-208.

1. I do not use the word 'formula' in this article because as used by the 'oral-formulaic' school it has come to mean a specific unit of discourse for which I do not here present a very clear counterpart in Kalevala poetry.
2. FFPE songs 34-38. Note that Miihkali's father, Arhippa Perttunen, performed this same song in much the same way as Miihkali, except that his hero was Kaukamieli. See FFPE song 37, see also the comments on pp 538-542.
3. FFPE pp. 256-261.

Themes, Images and Intertextuality

SATU APO

Ale, Spirits, and Patterns of Mythical Fantasy

The origin of alcoholic beverages according to Finnish folklore[1]

The oldest stratum of Finnish folklore, i.e. the songs and poetry in Kalevala metre, includes three stories about the origin of ale. Two of them are 'obvious' myths; the third encompasses the fantasy characteristic of myths. Songs have also been composed on the origin of spirits (liquor). Compared with the poetry about ale, *The Origin of Spirits* is, however, rare and did not develop into a narrative poem.[2]

According to the classic definition, a myth is a narrative describing the origin of a natural or cultural phenomenon or its first occurrence – one of a fundamental nature and, in the narrator's opinion, one that establishes the pattern for future manifestations. The narratives set in primeval times are most readily classified as myths: they reveal that the world (at its macro- and microlevels) is not yet complete or that the scene is dominated not by man but by animals, supernatural beings or a cultural hero, who is a mediator between the everyday world of man and the supernatural.[3]

It would seem that less attention has been devoted to examining which phenomena or phenomenal categories of reality have origins crystallised in narrative. The text anthologies and reference works dealing with myth-ology demonstrate that most cultures tell of the birth of the universe, humankind, the main animal and plant species, cultural objects, institutions and customs.[4]

In the Finnish-Karelian cultural area the oldest myth themes are to be found in the old oral poetry in Kalevala metre. The best-known cosmogonic myths are about the origin of the world, the forging of the heavens, the forming of the seabed, the sowing of trees, and the growing and felling of a giant oak. The animals whose origins are reported are the bear, elk, fish and seal, and a mighty ox. The "products of nature" cultivated by man include fire, barley and hops. The cultural products fashioned by man include fishing tackle, boat, ski, knife, tar, beer, iron, *kantele* and gun. The origin of dancing has likewise been explained in poetic metre. Poems describing the origin of the gods and man seem to be missing, though concepts pointing to the birth of man are, it is claimed, to be found in an Ingrian version of *Kalevanpoika*.

Songs beyond
the Kalevala
Studia Fennica
Folkloristica 2
1994

(Kuusi 1963, 72-73, 164-165; Kuusi (Siikala) 1975, 282-292). At least two poems have, by contrast, been composed on the origin of the vagina.

There are numerous cosmogonic myths contained in incantations. The objects decribed are phenomena which are potentially harmful to man (fire, cold, stone, wood, awn, iron, bear, wolf, snake, wasp, spider, disease) or means of curing (ointment, tar, knife, spell). (Kuusi 1963, 210, 282-287; SKK 1943, 200-229.)

The later stratum of cosmogonic tales takes the form of short prose narratives, collected in Finland in the early decades of the 20th century. The subjects covered by these tales are highly varied, ranging from the structure of the universe to animal and plant species, people and their activities to ethnic groups and cultural objects.[5]

The myth as narrative

Like all folk narratives, myths are stereotypic in content. This applies both to the actions described and to the information framing and defining them.[6] Syntagmatic analysis of the narrative reveals "state" and "action" (change of state) as the most abstract categories. The components of the sequence describing the action are actor, action, object of action and result of action.[7] The basic narrative episode (the "basic event") can be thought of as comprising an initial and final state (as the result of the action) and action sequences. The states and action sequences are connected to one another temporally or temporal-causally ("thereafter and as a consequence of this"). (Ryan 1979, 138-141.)

The event structure of the myth *The origin of fishes* may be represented by the following propositions:

State: There are no fish in the world. (Thereafter and maybe also as a consequence of this:)[8]

Action: The hero picks fleas from himself. (Thereafter):

Action: The hero casts the fleas into water. (Thereafter):

Action: The fleas turn into whitefish and salmon. (Thereafter and as a consequence of this:)

State: There are fish in the world.

The events in a folk narrative are often – at their abstract level – isomorphic with actions described in other representatives of the genre. Because of these isomorphisms we can define a plot or action scheme which is characteristic of a group of narratives (e.g. a genre or sub-genre). The following action schemes and categories for the origin of a phenomenon can be abstracted from the oldest Finnish-Karelian myths:[9]

1a) An animal or plant brings about a metamorphosis (X is transformed into Y)
   – *The origin of the world*: the world and its parts spring from a waterhen's egg. (SKVR VII:1, 18)
   – *The origin of man*: a tussock or tree stump splits and from it are born or grow two baby boys. (Kuusi 1963, 72-73; Kuusi (Siikala) 1975, 248.)

1b)   A god or a hero brings about a metamorphosis (using parts of his body, his/her bodily fluids, his parasites)
   – *The origin of fish and seals*: fish are born from fleas picked from himself by a hero. (Kuusi 1963, 151.)
   – *The origin of iron*: iron springs from milk from the breasts of "a young maid" or "three virgins" on top of a cloud. (SKVR I:4, 157 and VII:3, 458.)

2)   Supernatural beings (anthropomorphic, in most cases masculine ones) act:
   – by doing creative, cosmogonic work: *Moulding the seabed, Forging the heavens*
   – by constructing a cultural object (*The origin of the kantele, The origin of the boat, The origin of the seine/net, The origin of ale*)
   – by fighting with a monstrous adversary or with one another (cf. the legend poem *Fettering the Devil*). (Haavio 1955, 7-69.)

3)   Non-anthropomorphic or zoomorphic beings act:
   – by descending from heaven (*The origin of fire, The origin of the bear*).[10]

The actors and actions of narratives are representations with a multiple semantic content. The entity consisting of all of the representations may be called the narrative world.[11]

Representations can be distinguished and defined by means of various categories. For example, the action described in the narrative may be examined. The action in the case of an origin or birth may be a metamorphosis, hunting, a fight, or building. The actors of narratives can also be defined according to their roles of action (creator, counter-creator, cf. Propp's hero and villain). The actors are, however, at the same time representatives of several semantic categories. Creators can be representatives of different animal species, plants, personified natural phenomena or gods, heroes and quasi-human fantasy figures. Actors can further be defined as representing the different sexes, age groups, etc.[12] According to the plot schemes quoted above, for example, woman plays only a very minor role as the creator of the universe and its various parts – major exceptions are the origin of iron and the Osmotar version of the origin of ale.

The relations between representations are determined firstly by the "structural" rules governing categories; they may, for example, list the features typical of the representative of a certain category and further subdivide it. If the representations are involved in action, their relations are governed by "dynamic" rules, such as those applying to causal relations. (Kamppinen 1989, 31-32).

I shall in the following be taking a look at the categories of action and actors described in mythical narratives about the origin of alcoholic beverages. I shall also examine the representations in these myths in relation to the general rules applying to the interaction between representations.

Divine ale

Two of the Finnish myths about ale – *The origin of barley and ale* and *Osmotar brews ale* – are based on series of events describing the actions of supernatural beings. In the former the gods create barley and ale without any complicating events; in the latter a (female) cultural hero is forced to seek a missing component. The third narrative telling of the origin of beer, *Barley converses with hops*, is based on personification fantasies.

In *The origin of barley and ale* Pikka (Pikki, Pekka) clears the land ready for cultivation and Ukko sows the barley and turns it into ale for the gods to drink:

Ajoi Pikka piennä kasken	Little Pikka cut the forest down
matalana maan alisti.	laid bare the land.
Jätti yhden koivahaisen	One birch he left, however,
linnuille lepämiksi	for the birds to rest on,
kokkosille istumiksi.	the eagles to sit on.
Lenti kokko halki taivon	Flew an eagle across the heavens
lintunen ylitse siiven.	winging its way onwards.
Tuli puuta katosmahan:	Stopped when it saw the birch tree.
"Mikä tarvis tuost tulevi?"	"What is that for?"
"Siksi on se jätetty,	"It has been left
linnuille lepeämäksi	for the birds to rest on,
kokkosille istumiksi."	the eagles to sit on."
Iski tulta ilman Ukko	Heavenly Ukko struck a fire
välähytti Väinämöinen.	Väinämöinen flashed the light.
Tunki kaskensa tulehen.	Cast the brushwood into the flames.
Suvituuli kasken poltti	The breeze of summer burnt the brushwood,
koillinen kalut kokosi.	the Northeast gathered the cinders together.
Onni Ukko osran kylvi.	Lucky Ukko then sowed the barley.
Kasvoi osra mieltä myöten:	The barley grew as it should:
päät on kuuella taholla	the heads six-fold and
korret kolmella solmella.	the stems long enough to make three knots.
Tuumitteli, tieusteli;	Then he pondered and he thought;
pani osraista olutta	set about brewing barley beer
tuohon Päivölän pitohin	for the feast at Päivölä,
jumalisten juominkihin.	for the gods to drink.
Kesät vettä keittelevi	Many summers the water boiled,
salot puita polttelevi	whole forests of firewood were burnt,
kuut kiviä kuumailevi.	the stones heated for months on end.
Sai olonen juotavaksi	Making ale for them to drink,
sekä aina valmeheksi.	fully brewn ale for them to taste.
(SKVR VII:1, 791)[13]	

The myth appears at first glance to be a rather dull description of how the ale was made, from growing the raw materials to the finished drink. The simple series of events has, however, been "mythified" many times over. The first mythical semantic system consists of the actors in the narrative: two gods and the bird symbolic of one of them, an eagle.

The Pikka mentioned in the opening line is Pekko (Pellonpekko), a character featuring in Finnish-Karelian and Estonian folk belief as the

202

Tea-drinking was part of festive occasions in Karelia. Jyvälahti, Archangel Karelia. Photo: I.K. Inha 1894 (FLS 9951).

guardian spirit or god of barley (the oldest cereal), or more commonly of corn and the cornfield.[14]

In the example text from Ladoga Karelia Pikka is not the guardian spirit of a regularly cultivated field but the first clearer of new land for cultivation, a field maker. The feller of trees is described in the myth as *piennä* 'little' and *matalana* 'short', a little man who does the heavy work. The mythical tree feller is just as "impossible" a hero as the tiny man who rises from the sea and fells a giant ox or a giant oak tree.[15] The small size of the tree-feller is also mentioned in three other versions of *The origin of barley and ale*:

Piennä Pikki huuhan raato:	Little Pikki toiled and laboured:
emon värttinän pituissa	no taller than his mother's spindle,
ison polven korkunaissa	no higher than his father's knee,
hoikaissa salon syteli	cleared the forest of its brushwood
matalaissa maan alaissa.	working low, close to the earth.

Raato Pekka piennä huuhan	Thus laboured Pekka, the little man,
hoikkana salon sivalti.	a thin man clearing the forest.

Lähin piennä metsälle	As a child I went to the forest
ison polven korgevussa	no higher than my father's knee
emon värttinän pituissa.	no taller than my mother's spindle
Ajoin piennä suuren kasken...	As a child I cleared a large field..
(SKVR VII:1, 812, 838, 799.)	

The exaggerated and impossible images deliberately break the cognitive rules for the structures and actions attached to the representations. The hyperbolic image of a man the size of a spindle violates the synchronic category rules: if the being is a man, he must be more than knee-high.[16] The same applies to the impossible image concerning the hero's actions: a man the height of a spindle clears a large area of trees. The mythical fantasy draws on anomalies that violate the common structures of expectation concerning reality.

Why is the god of the field, corn and ale a little man? This question is difficult to answer, because the study of the images and concepts of Finnish-Karelian myths from new, semiotic and symbolic-anthropological angles is still only in its infancy. (See e.g. Tarkka 1990b.) A hero the height of a spindle may of course be associated with a phallus and thus with ideas of the fertility of man and crops. On the other hand a little child with the strength of a grown man is an "impossible", anomalous hero appearing in many fantasy tales (cf. Hercules, Kullervo).

Is there any more precise connection between a little man and corn? The isomorphs between "man" and "corn" have been developed in, for example, riddle metaphors, where the relationship between the grain and the ear of corn may be described as the relationship between father and sons: "The boys have beards before the father is born. (Haavio – Hautala 1948, 231.) In the English narrative song *John Barleycorn* the grain of corn is a little man who rises from his grave, is killed and crushed, and who is reborn as ale.[17] The god of the field may also have been conceived of using images for the household spirit. In the western regions of Finland in particular the spirit operating within the sphere of "culture" was a little man. (Sarmela 1974, 349-351.)

The forest set aside for clearing in *The origin of barley and ale* is turned into a mythical landscape by appending to it an element of the supernatural, an eagle – the bird symbolic of the god of thunder and heaven. (Siikala 1985a, 333.) In order to court the favour of the bird, or rather its master, the tree-feller leaves a tree reaching up to heaven in the centre of the clearing.

The trees are then burnt: this too comes within the category of mythical representations, for the fallen trees are ignited by Ukko, god of heaven, thunder and rain.

The process by which the corn is sown and grows is also supranormal, for it is again watched over by Ukko, this time in his role of benefactor of the corn. He is in the words of singers either Lucky Ukko, or Ukko, the lucky sower of barley: *Onni Ukko osran kylvi, Ukko onni osran kylvi* (SKVR VII:1, 791, 812.)

The morphology of the barley described in the poem maybe corresponds more to the botanical definitions ("The heads are six fold, the stems long enough to make three knots") rather than the hyperbolical *aetas aurea* images. The harvesting is, by contrast, fantastic in two versions of *The origin of barley and ale*. The corn is harvested by birds together with special categories of men and women:

Pani lesket leikkomahan	Widows set to cutting the corn
sulhaset sitelemähän	bridegrooms to binding it,

pääskyt päitä poimimahan	swallows to gathering the heads,
kurjet kulivoitsemahan	cranes to making the stooks,
hanhet haasivoitsemahan.	geese to drying them on the frames.
(SKVR VII:1, 812.)[18]	

The process by which the ale is made, and the purpose for which the ale is used, are at odds with normal reality. The ale is intended for the feast at Päivölä, i.e. the feast of the gods. The manufacturing process is again made supranormal by using hyperbole: it takes many summers for the water to boil, whole forests of trees to heat the water and stones, and months to heat the stones.[19]

The poem refers to the primitive way of brewing beer with red-hot stones. In this process not only the water but the mass, too, is heated with glowing stones plunged into the mixture. This technique was described by Carl von Linné as early as 1732, who then went on to condemn the primitive ale as being unhealthy.[20]

The alcoholic beverage described in *The origin of barley and ale* is completely sacred or mythical. Each stage in its making is made to differ from everyday reality, either by allocating the actor roles to the chief gods of farming or by using exaggerated and impossible images. An animal mediator also features in the poem: Ukko's eagle and the tree left for it express a link between earth (the domain of Pellonpekko) and heaven (the domain of Ukko). It is tempting to see the tree as referring to the cosmic tree, the pillar of the world.[21]

The chief gods of farming, Pekko and Ukko, may have provided the models for prayers for rain addressed to the two Ingrian saints Petro and Ilja. These prayers were sung at the village festivals held on these saints' days. Ritual ale-drinking was one of the most important elements of the harvest rite attached to these saints. (Harva 1948, 111-113.)[22]

The origin of barley and ale does not appear as an independent song in the collections of poetry made in the 19th century but acts as the introduction to the popular *Lemminkäinen epic*. We can only speculate on whether this ale myth once appeared as an independent aetiological poem in connection with some agricultural rite. As regards content, it could, for example, have served as one of the ritual songs to be sung at the festival of Ukko described by Agricola in 1551:

Ia quin Keuekyluö kyluettiin,	And when the seeds were sown in the spring
silloin vkon Malia iootijn.	(then) they drank in honor of Ukko.
Sihen haetin vkon wacka,	The casket of Ukko was fetched
nin ioopui Pica ette Acka. (...)	and then both maidens and matrons got drunken. (...)
Se sis annoi Ilman ia	In this way they safeguarded good weather
Wdhen Tulon, (...)	the crops, (...)
(SKA 1963, 247-248.)	

It may be assumed that *The Lemminkäinen's Adventures* were sung in all sorts of festive contexts.[23] Later episodes of the poem describe bouts of drinking that lead to a duel, which proves that it was well-suited to an ale-drinking context and served as a masculine festive poem.

Judging from its imagery, *The origin of barley and ale* is the most archaic of the Finnish-Karelian ale myths. The chronological age of the poem is impossible to determine. The representations contained in it are in harmony with cultures in which barley was grown in fields cleared by the slash-and-burn method, ale was brewed by heating the liquid with stones, and whose beliefs embraced the concept of a male god of thunder and a male god of the fields and/or corn. Dating the poem on grounds of content is hampered by the fact that such cultures existed in the Finnish-Karelian language area from the Bronze Age right up to the 19th century.

The distribution of the myth was, according to the material in the archives, very narrow, for it was encountered only among singers in Ladoga and North Karelia.[24] It is, however, impossible to determine whether it was a late local product or a relic that had already vanished from other areas.

The cognitive model, the schema "god produces alcoholic beverage" for the origin of ale can also be discerned in the prose narratives describing the origin of spirits. The aetiological narratives about the origin of spirits and ale are, compared with the old cosmogonic poems, moralising counter-myths. The model for the divine origin of the alcoholic beverage has thus acquired a negative form: "the devil produces an alcoholic beverage". The devil is depicted as a counsellor, not the actual maker of the spirits:

> The old devil sent his sons to counsel people on all manner of vices (...). His youngest son went to several farms disguised as a human and taught the farmer how to make spirits. All fell into disorder. Befuddled by the spirits, people performed all the other wicked tricks commanded by the devil. The old devil was well pleased, named his son the Spirit Devil and made him his right-hand man.[25] (Paasio 1976, 220.)

Animal ale: Osmotar brews beer

The second story about the origin of ale, *Osmotar brews ale*, has been found over a wider area than the previous one: in Archangel Karelia, Olonets, Ladoga and North Karelia, and Savo. The central motif of the poem – obtaining the fermenting agent from the saliva of an animal – is also known in Ingria. (Krohn 1903, 516-523.)

Osmotar brews ale is constructed round a mythical lack and the way this lack is liquidated: The component vital to make the beverage is missing. The female maker manages to acquire it with the help of an animal or personally fetches it from animals. The master singer Arhippa Perttunen from Archangel Karelia described the series of events as follows:

Päivilä pitoja laati	There was to be a feast at Päivilä
Sariolan juominkihin.	a bout of drinking at Sariola.
Osmotar olosen seppä	Osmotar, maker of the beer,
Osma norosta nousi.	Osma rose from the water.
Kalevatar pani olutta:	The Kalevatar brewed ale:
oli aikoa vähänen	there was not much time
ei ota olut hapata	but the ale refused to ferment
taho taari tuuraella.	did not wish to turn into beer.
Hiero kahta kämmentänsä	The mistress rubbed her palms together,

hykerti molempiensa.	chafed both her hands together.
Hiero valkean oravan.	And a white squirrel appeared.
Siitä neuvo lintuansa	Then she told the little creature
kun kukin sukimoansa	spoke to it like to a little bird,
itse ilmon luomiansa:	conjured by her from the air:
"Oravani, lintuseni	"Oh my squirrel, little fledgling
matka juokse joutusasti	make haste upon my errand.
Pohjan peltojen perille	Run to the nothern fields,
Lapin lahtotanterille.	to the slaughtering grounds of Lapland.
Pure kuusesta käpyjä	Bite cones from a fir tree
käpy pure käyessäsi	nip a fir cone while you're there
toinen tuuo tullessasi."	and bring another home with you."
Sekä juoksi että joutu.	The squirrel sped and made good time.
Kävyn tuopi tullessansa;	Brought a fir cone home with it;
sen kanto kavon käsihin.	carried it into the woman's hands.
Kapo kanto kaljahansa	Into the ale Osmotar cast,
Osmotar olosehensa.	into the beer the fir cone.
Ei ota olut hapata	But the ale refused to ferment,
taho taari tuuraella.	did not wish to turn into beer.
Hiero kahta kämmentänsä	The mistress rubbed her palms together,
hykerti molempiensa.	chafed her hands together.
Hiero ruskean reposen.	And a brown fox appeared.
Siitä neuvo lintuansa	Then she told the little creature
kun kukin sukimoansa	spoke to it like to a little bird,
itse ilmon luomiansa:	conjured by her from the air:
"Reposeni, lintuseni!	"Oh my fox, my little fledgling!
matka juokse joutusasti	make haste upon my errand.
Pohjan peltojen perille	Run to the northern fields,
Lapin lahtotanterille.	to the slaughtering grounds of Lapland.
Siellä syyös, siellä	While you're eating,
juuos;	while you're drinking;
tuo sieltä tullessanai	bring me back when you return
tuoppa voietta vakaista	bring me ointment with a strong effect
tuo sie mettä mielehyistä."	bring me a pleasing nectar."
Sekä juoksi jotta joutu.	The fox sped and made good time.
Kävyn tuopi tullessansa;	Brought nectar home with it;
sen kanto kavon käsihin.	carried it into the woman's hands
Kapo kanto kaljahansa	Into the ale Osmotar cast,
Osmotar olosehensa.	into the beer the nectar.
Ei ota olut hapata	But the ale refused to ferment,
taho taari tuuraella.	did not wish to turn into beer.
Jo päivänä muutamena	A few days passed
huomena monikkahana	and many a morrow.
nousi aivon aikasehen	Early she rose in the morning
aivon aika huomenessa.	got up early to greet the day.
Kuuli kolkkehen merestä	Heard a knocking from the sea
lakin lyönnän laiturilta:	sounds of combat from the docks.

"Orihitko oltanehe
vai nuo miehet miekan
lyöjät?"

"Could it be the sound of horses,
or of men fighting a duel?"

Osmotar oluen seppä
sekä juoksi jotta joutu
selvälle meren selälle
ulapalle aukialle:
täällä miehet miekoin lyö
orihit tasoin panovi.
Juoksi kuona konnan suusta
kino ilkiän kiuasta
vahti vankan sieraimista.

Osmotar maker of the beer
made great haste and made her way
down to the seashore
looked out to the open sea:
here the men with swords are fighting
stallions clopping with steady tread.
Slobber ran out of the beast's mouth
saliva out of the evil beast's mouth
foam out of the strong animal's nostrils.

Osmotar oluen seppä
koprin kuonoa kokovi
käsivaattien varusti,
joka juoksi konnan suusta
siitä kanto kaljahansa
Osmonen oluen seppä.

Osmotar maker of the beer
touched the nose with her hands
used a cloth over her arm
to catch the foam from the beast's mouth
and poured it into the ale
Osmonen maker of the beer.

Oli aikoa vähänen
niin otti olut hapata
tahto taari tuuraella.

Only short a time was needed
for the ale to want to ferment
for the beer to make the foam.

Niin sanoo olut punanen:
"Kun ei tullo juojoani
juojoani, laulajani,
potin poikki vanteheni
ulos pohjani porotan."

Then spoke the russet beer:
"Where are all the drinkers then,
where the drinkers and the singers?
I will have to break the barrel
dash the bottom of the keg."

Etsittihin laulajia
laulajia, soittajia.
Etsittihin, vain ei
löytty.

A search then went out for the singers,
for the singers and for the players.
Searched and searched, but none
were found.

(SKVR I:1, 759b, Latvajärvi, Castrén 1839.)

Who was Osmotar?

According to this story the first ale was brewed by a woman called Osmotar. That she was the first to brew it is clear from the fact that she does not know where to find the fermenting agent. What makes her a fantastic hero figure, possibly with supernatural features, is her ability to command wild animals.

The ale poem quoted above is the only one in which Osmotar appears, and she remains a highly enigmatic figure to researchers. According to the system of surnames practised in Karelia, Osmotar is her patronym. In other words, the brewer of the first beer was the daughter of Osmo.[28] The etymology and meanings of the name Osmo are complex. Osmo and *osma* mean a wolverine. Since a wolverine was likened to a small bear, the word *osma* was also used to mean a bear. (Nirvi 1981, 55-69). The bear in particular is a respected, even "sacred" animal surrounded by numerous

Matro and Anni Lehtonen. Anni Lehtonen (right) was a rune-singer as well as lamenter. She was also well-versed in mythic knowledge. Vuokkiniemi. Photo: Samuli Paulaharju 1910-1915 (FLS 5412).

beliefs and rites. If Osmotar is "The Daughter of the Bear", it is easy to understand her role as the mistress of wild animals (squirrel, fox) and as the bold gatherer of a stallion's foaming saliva.

Why is the brewer of the beer a woman in most Archangel Karelian poems? Some singers see her as the mistress of Päivölä (sometimes Pohjola), the house where a feast is to be held. They also mention the master of Päivölä. In the versions of a few singers the guests are invited by the mistress, in other versions by the master. Now you will recall that the brewing of the exalted beverage in *The origin of barley and ale* was always in the hands of men. The casting of the ale-maker as a woman is probably an indication of cultural practices: women were allowed to make ale, or, rather, it was their responsibility to supervise its production. A woman is known as the leading character in the ale myth not only in Archangel Karelia but also in Olonets, Border and North Karelia, and Savo.[27] The brewer in Ingria is a masculine figure: Kalervikko, the son of God, or the birds.[28] (Krohn 1903, 525-529.)

In Finland the designation of the brewer's gender followed the cultural divide between east and west. In Eastern Finland, as in Russia and Estonia, the brewer was most often a man, in Western Finland and Scandinavia a woman. (Räsänen 1977, 29-30.)

The gender of the brewer was connected to the gender system prevailing in the community. The greater the masculine domination in the community, the more clearly the food economy was dominated by a man, too. In certain areas of Karelia it was the men who supervised the valuable foodstuffs and the making of the precious drinks (ale, spirits).[29] Some scholars have taken this as being the "original" practice, and one possibly dating back to the common Karelian era. (Nirvi 1981, 68, 73.) Another explanation may be the influence of the patriarchal Russian family system. The fact that the northern communities which made their living from hunting and fishing, slash-and-burn cultivation and peddling also sang of ale brewed by the mistress may be an indication of the relatively large authority of women within the family – as in the songs about the mistress of Pohjola who battled with men and married her daughters off. The men's mobility and the long periods spent away from home produced a variant on the agrarian patriarchy to which images of a powerful woman ruling over the homestead were admirably suited.

Another explanation could be the western roots of many Archangel Karelian singer families. Recollections of the female-dominated brewing customs in Western Finland may have contributed to the emergence of the unusual figure of Osmotar.[30]

A further model for the female brewer of the mythical ale may be found in the incantations in which the Virgin Mary brews healing ointments; the missing ingredient is then usually fetched by a bee. In one Savo version of *Osmotar brews ale* recorded in the 18th century the brewer is *neytyt måria emoinen* – the Virgin Mary. (SKVR VI:1, 60.)[31] In Arhippa Perttunen's poem Osmotar bids a fox to fetch "ointment of a strong effect, pleasant nectar from the honey-bee".

The mythical lack and its liquidation

The plot of *Osmotar brews ale* keeps very close to one of the most general myth schemes. Alan Dundes has, on the basis of the narratives of North American Indians, crystallised this as "lack – lack liquidated". (Dundes 1964, 61-64.) Many of the old Finnish poems about the origin of cultural objects adhere to this sequence of events. Väinämöinen cannot finish his boat until he has fetched the missing words needed to do so from the Underworld. The healing ointment brewed by the Virgin Mary is not ready until a bee has crossed nine seas to fetch the missing nectar or salve. These poems are concerned with a vital ingredient that is missing from a cultural object.

The mythical want may also be a lack of knowledge about how to use the object. The first *kantele* does not produce music until a skilled musician is found; naturally he is no ordinary mortal but a cultural hero or the demiurge Väinämöinen. Presumably the primitive belief world embraced the concept that a phenomenon had to have a name: it could not be assigned its place in the world, be invoked, banished or avoided unless it had a name. The missing name of the alcoholic beverage is woven into the poem about the origin of ale sung by Mateli Kuivalatar. In this poem the name of the beer is obtained from the cat warming itself on the stove. One feels tempted to ask whether the wise, authoritative cat is a parody of the seers, the experts at origins and names.

The scheme for rectifying a mythical need further incorporates concepts of the place where the missing component may be found. The component has to be fetched from beyond the borders of the everyday world, the Other World. Väinämöinen finds the missing words in *Tuonela* 'the Underworld', and the bee called upon by the Virgin Mary travels to a fantasy world nine seas away. There is also mention of a visit to Tuonela in *Osmotar brews ale*. Osmotar sends a squirrel and a fox to the north, in the direction of Tuonela and the graveyard: "Make haste to the northern fields, to the slaughtering grounds of Lapland". (cf. Tarkka 1990b, 245-246.)

The third model to be found in mythical thought for the origin of cultural objects consists of concepts concerning the nature of the components: an important object is made up of unusual components. In Finnish aetiological poems these often have their origin in the animal world. The material for a boat to be built with the help of incantations is a fish-skin, fish-scales, the teeth of a pike. The *kantele*-instrument is made from the jaw of a pike and a deer and the strings from a virgin's hair or the hairs of a horse.

The missing animal component in *Osmotar brews ale* is, according to Arhippa Perttunen, the saliva of a stallion (*ori*); other singers speak of a boar (*oronen*). The use of animal saliva as a fermenting agent may carry several meanings. In the rational interpretation put forward by scholars pig's saliva is viewed as a relic, as a reminder that the primitive fermenting agent for drinks really was, in Finland as elsewhere, animal or human saliva. (Harva 1948, 203-206; Haavio 1967, 271.) Likewise fish-skin may indeed have been used in making a boat. At symbolical level the agent obtained from an animal may reveal why ale was a "living" substance having a strong effect on people. The image of animate ale is in fact evident in Perttunen's song, in the lines describing the ale as being capable of action: the ale speaks and threatens to break down its container.

The "animal-like nature" of the first ale is further emphasised by Osmotar's helpers, the squirrel and fox.[32] The helpers are animals hunted for their fur; unlike the bear, the eagle and the giant pike they carry no strong mythical meanings. Squirrels and foxes are not common animal helpers of shamans, either. The representations of a fox and sometimes also a pine marten in the poem about Osmotar and the festive ale may have their origins in the imagery of wedding poetry: in the northern Karelian regions "little summer vixen" and "pine marten" were metaphors for the bride. (Ilomäki 1990, 228.)

The ale myth sung by Arhippa Perttunen was noted down by M.A. Castrén in 1839. The prose narratives telling about the origin of ale and recorded a hundred years later still display most of the schemes of the ancient myth, the concepts of the missing ingredient, how it was obtained from the animal kingdom, and the way the animal component functioned – again in a negative transformation:

> Noah's wife brewed some good ale and asked where she could get some ferment. The answer was: "From a boar's mouth." Then Noah built an ark, and when he drank the ale, he became drunk and cast his axe at a stone.

> That's why a drunken man grovelling in the mud, because the ale was fermented with saliva from a boar's mouth. (SKS Halikko. Kaisa Kantola 10. 1937)

The Southwest Finnish narrator presumably had not learnt about the origin of ale from the *Kalevala*, for this describes how the Mistress of Pohjola tried to brew ale from fir cones and bear's saliva, and did not succeed until a bee had fetched her some nectar. (Lönnrot 1964, 134-137.)

The aetiological legend may have drawn on knowledge of the ancient ingredient used to ferment beer and the common metaphor for a drunkard and being intoxicated: "The drunken man is a pig".

The personification and action of the ale in the *Osmotar*-poem and the aetiological legend is structured by means of metonymic (mereonymic) thinking. It all hinges on the relationships between a part and the whole. (Kamppinen 1989, 29-31; Lakoff 1987, 77-79, 114.) The boar's saliva is part of a living animal – when the saliva, i.e. the living component, becomes part of the ale, an item originally in the inanimate category, the entire drink becomes animate. The living, animal part of the drink retains the quality derived from the original entity; this is transferred to the drinker and it begins to guide the drinker's behaviour. Thus anyone drinking ale fermented with the saliva of a boar will behave like a pig and end up grovelling in the mud.

Human and spirit-like ale: Barley converses with hops

A song in which hops and barley, and sometimes water, discuss when and where they will come together and what they will then do to humans was once sung over most of the cultural areas of Finland and Karelia. This is not a myth in the narrow definition of the word: it does not tell about the first ale or events at the beginning of time. The main characters are not animals, gods or heroes.

That the poem is relatively recent is indicated by the fact that one of the basic components of the ale is hops, an ingredient not used to flavour and preserve ale until the Middle Ages.[33] (Räsänen 1977, 78-82.) Hops are not mentioned in the basic plot of *The origin of barley and ale* or *Osmotar brews ale*.

Barley converses with hops was sung at feasts, most often at Christmas and Easter, and at weddings. The simplest version of the poem dates from the 18th century and comes from Western Finland:

Humala casvoisi puusa	The hops grew in a tree,
ohra pellon pyörtänöllä.	the barley on the edge of a field.
"Cusa me yhteen tulem?"	"Where shall we come together?"
"Hyvän äitin ammeesa.	"In a good woman's bath.
Sitte me miehet juotelem	Then we'll make the men drunk
hurscat iloitelem	the pious merry
hullut tappeluttelem."	and the fools fight."
(Kuusi 1963, 140.)	

The following versions were recorded in 1887 and 1912 on the Karelian Isthmus:

Humala taposta huusi	The hops called out from the enclosure
otra pellon rinteheltä	the barley from the edge of the field and
ves kaivosta syvästä:	the water, from deep in the well:
"Millos pääsemme parriini?	"When shall we come together?
Jos ei muulloin milloinkaane,	If at no other time, then
joulun pitkinnä pyhinnä	on the long days of Christmas
pääpyhinnä pääsiäissä	on the greatest of feasts, at Easter
tammisessa tynnyrissä	in an oaken cask
koivuisen tapin toaakse."	beneath a birch stopper."
Humala taposta huusi:	The hops cried out from the enclosure:
"Jos mie parrii pääsen,	"If I can join you,

mie käytän sen oluen mi ei murra miehen päätä!" (SKVR XIII:1, 168)[34]	I'll ferment beer that doesn't break a man's head!"

Humala tapossa huus otra pellon pientariess vesi kaivossa syvässä: "Kons myö yhtehen yhymme konsa pääsemme parihin?" – "Joulun pitkinä pyhinä; siit myö pääsemme parihin, suamme toinen toisihimme yhtehen yhyttelemme. Sitt myö leikki lyötäne ja topuli piettäne joka iltasen iloks joka päivän piättimeks." (SKVR XIII:1, 170.)[35]	The hops called out from the enclosure the barley from the edge of a field and the water deep in the well: "When shall we come together, when shall we be paired together?" – "On the long days of Christmas; then we shall be paired together, we shall receive one another be joined one with another. Then we'll have some fun, and play some joyful games make merry every night at the end of every day."

The scant narrative is contained in the words spoken by the characters, in which they describe the manufacturing process and the consequences of drinking ale. The regional differences in the gender of the brewer are evident in the fact that in the western version the hops and the barley expect to meet in the vessel of a female brewer, a good woman's bath.

What is more interesting is the reliance of the poem on metaphor. The use of the metaphoric cognitive model is based on a set-up in which model X used to conceptualise being A is partly isomorphic with model Y used to conceptualise being B. Model Y is then said to structure model X. (Kamppinen et al. 1990, 5.) *Barley converses with hops* uses a model for conceptualising "ale" that is structured by a model used to conceptualise "Man" or a man-like spiritual being. In order to get speaking barley, hops and water we must use mereonymic (metonymic) thinking: the ale is divided into its components and then these are animated according to the metaphoric model.

The basic metaphor may be defined as follows: "Alcoholic drink is an animate being with a desire and ability to make humans behave in certain ways". Which, then, are the isomorphic parts of "man" or "spiritual being" and "ale"? It seems that an additional metaphor is needed, this time the model concerning the nature of the intoxication process and its consequences. The first metaphor is presumably founded on the scheme-like model of intoxication: "On drinking ale/spirits a person becomes subordinate to an alien power, which forces him to behave in an abnormal way". It is because of its latent "power", i.e. its strong effects on the drinker, that alcohol is conceptualised by models referring to "Man" and "spirit". The scheme of intoxication is thus isomorphic with the model of penetration and possession of the spirits.[36]

Alcoholic beverages and humans or spirits are animated and they have "power". In the metaphoric modelling, the isomorphism of the two counterparts allows the transfer of the non-isomorphic characteristics of the "source being" (model Y) to the "target being" (model X). According to folklore, both humans and spirits have beliefs, desires and intentions

Residents of Lapukka return from a journey to fetch flour. Vuokkiniemi. Photo: Samuli Paulaharju 1915 (FLS 5458).

concerning the world. In addition they also have the ability to communicate, to speak. In *Barley converses with hops* these characteristics are transferred to the alcoholic drink and its components. We thus arrive at barley, hops and water capable of speaking and of expressing their beliefs ("We'll come together in a good woman's bath"), their desires ("When shall we come together?" may be interpreted as a desire to come together), and their intentions ("Then we'll make the men drunk").

The intentions of the ale ingredients reflect the concepts of the state of intoxication arrived at during the feast. According to the Karelian versions, getting together, i.e. sociability (*Geselligkeit* according to Georg Simmel) is the main attraction of the feast (*päästään pariin, saadaan toinen toisi-himme*, 'being paired together, receiving one another')[37]; it is also a time for merry-making, fighting and playing – one Karelian version of the poem attaches sexual overtones to the "playing".[38] The revellers are in other words in a liminal state governed by their emotions and desires. (Cf. Falk 1983, 253-256.)

An animation metaphor for an alcoholic beverage is displayed in numerous everyday figures of Finnish speech, as in the sayings "it was the booze made him do it", "liquor excites, seduces and corrupts". Probably the best-known poetic personification metaphor is "King Alcohol". People address alcoholic beverages in both art and folk poetry: *Terve, ruskee ohranneste* 'Hail thee, rusty barley liquid' (A. Kivi), *Kules vjelä, vina kulda, vanha tuttava toveri* 'Listen, dear spirits, good old friend' (an anonymous poet of the 1820s). (SKVR VI:1, 760.) The animation may be extended to take in the vessel in which the drink is stored, as in, for example, *putelille puhelen* 'speaking to the bottle', or to the vessel in which it is made. A poem in the *Kanteletar* (1840) protesting against prohibition addresses an "imprisoned" still: *Voi sinua pannu parka! Mitä tieät tehnehesi – teitkö murhan vai varastit?* 'Oh you poor still! What did you do – did you murder or did you steal?' (Lönnrot 1966, 38.) Väinö Linna, in his novel *The unknown soldier*, calls a vessel containing fermenting beer a "boy".

The animation or personification of spirits does not at first sight fit the definition of an ontological metaphor presented by George Lakoff and Mark Johnson: an ontological metaphor is a means of perceiving a non-physical phenomenon or an entire phenomenal area as an entity or substance. A typical example is the representation of "anger" as a hot liquid in a container ("boiling with rage"). (Lakoff – Johnson 1980, 25-32; Lakoff 1987, 380-389.) As liquids, ale and spirits are highly material phenomena and easily discerned by many of the senses. What is in fact ontologised by the animation of an alcoholic beverage is presumably a more complex and more "invisible" phenomenon, namely the effect it has on man, i.e. the intoxication process and its consequences.

The need to ontologise intoxication and its effects on people is probably the main reason for producing animation and personification images for alcohol. A further explanation may be found in the process by which the drink is made. When it begins to ferment, it "lives": it bubbles, and as the bubbles burst, they make a sound.

It is difficult to find any counterparts to the strong animation of alcohol in Finnish discourse on other stimulants and foods. I would expect that tobacco and tobacco containers, or coffee and coffee pots are seldom addressed, and milk and milk jugs even less frequently.

We may indeed ask whether the animation images for alcohol had any "deeper" meanings guiding the acts of drinkers. If an alcoholic drink is imagined as a being with a will of its own, the main subject in drinking, getting intoxicated and behaving accordingly was the beer or spirits and not the drinker; this relieves the drinker of at least some of the responsibility. Like a person under the power of an evil spirit, he is not responsible for what he does.

The metamorphosis of ale

The Finnish-Karelian myths do not attach to the origin of ale any image of metamorphosis or any concept of one category being transformed into another. Metamorphosis is nevertheless manifest in the poem *The beer froth oak* containing mythical concepts. Here a maiden pours beer out of the window into her garden. Out of the froth grows a giant oak. According to Ingrian singers this is then felled by her brother, who uses the wood to make drinking vessels, spindles and a *sauna* for his sister. (See e.g. SKVR IV:2, 1851.)

Why does the beer which a maiden pours out of her window turn into a giant oak? The origin of the images may lie in wedding rites. It was sometimes the custom at Ingrian and Ladoga Karelian weddings for the bride, on her last evening at home, to sacrifice ale to the family ancestors by pouring it out of the window. (Porkka 1883, 265-266; Lukkarinen 1914, 11; Salminen 1916, 62-63; Honko 1963, 121; Konkka 1985, 181.) The purpose of the rite was to contact the dead relatives and to seek their favour in a situation where the maiden was breaking away from her father's kin and transferring to another kin for the rest of her life.

The wedding association may also explain the images in the closing episode of the poem: the vessels and spindles made by the brother may represent the bride's dowry and the *sauna* the place where the young wife will give birth to her babies.

If the singers of the poem attached the archaic meanings of a sacred tree to the oak tree, it is understandable that the ale poured down to the earth in order to bring together the two worlds – this and the other – was transformed into the cosmic tree. For this tree was thought to link the different strata of the universe: the world of humans, the kingdom of the dead, and heaven. (Siikala 1985a, 324-325.) The concept of a giant oak linking this world and the next is expressed in the Archangel Karelian poem:

Jo on tammi koatununna   Now the oak has fallen down
poikki Pohjoisen jovesta   straight across the Northern River
sillaksi ikusijahe...   as a bridge to eternity...
(SKVR I:4, 870.)

The link between the worlds is here horizontal: the fallen oak forms a bridge across the river of *Pohjola*, the North or the Underworld, *Tuonela*.

"Sacred" ale?

The Finnish-Karelian myths about the origin of beer prove that ale was regarded as a unique cultural product. It was honoured by composing a myth of its origins. Only about ten products made by human hand share this honour with ale. On top of this at least three narratives in poetic metre and, it seems, of ancient origin on the birth of ale were composed in only a small linguistic area. The same cannot be said of any other cultural product. Only the bear has three different narratives telling of its origins. (Kuusi 1963, 41-42.)

The cultural categories connected with ale in the archaic poems are momentous in the extreme: the gods and corn (*The origin of barley and ale*), domestic and game animals (*Osmotar brews ale*) and close male relatives and the dead (the maiden's beer sacrifice in *The giant oak*). Virtually no other cultural product can claim a network of associations consisting of categories of such a fundamental nature.

Alcoholic beverages were "sacred", unlike any other substance made by human hand, and were regarded metaphorically as living beings similar to a spirit, capable of entering the human body and transforming the drinker's state of consciousness and behaviour to suit their own will. The concepts of the animate nature and "power" of alcohol explain its associations with people, animals and the other world.

NOTES

The article is based on an earlier version published in Finnish under the title *Olut, viina ja myyttinen fantasia – alkoholijuomien synty suomalaisen kansanperinteen mukaan* in *Kolme kovaa sanaa. Kirjoituksia kansanperinteestä.* P. Laaksonen and S-L. Mettomäki (eds). *Kalevalaseuran vuosikirja 71.* Helsinki. 1991. p. 7-28.

1. I am grateful to Academician Matti Kuusi, Professor Anna-Leena Siikala, and Ms. Senni Timonen MA, for their comments on my article. It is a part of my ongoing study of traditional drinking in Finland. My study is financed by The Finnish Foundation for Alcohol Studies.
2. According to the poem, spirit "was born of spiky young barley, of fertile corn's lashes". The closing episode of the poem describes the effect of spirits on people: spirits feed the peasant and make men and women merry. (SKVR I:2, 1242).
3. The latest encyclopaedia definition says of myth: "*Mythos* in its meaning of 'myth' is the word for a story concerning gods and superhuman beings. A myth is an expression of the sacred in words; it reports realities and events from the origin of the world that remain valid for the basis and purpose of all there is. Consequently, a myth functions as a model for human activity, society, wisdom, and knowledge." (Bolle 1987, 261).
4. Stith Thompson's cross-cultural *Motif-Index of Folk-Literature* (Vol. 1, 1966) lists motifs concerning the origin of phenomena with a varying degrees of detail. The plots of Finnish cosmogonic narratives in prose form have been described and classified in the *Verzeichnis der Finnischen Ursprungssagen und ihrer Varianten* by Antti Aarne (1912).
5. The main text anthologies are *Suomen Kansan Vanhat Runot* 'Ancient Poems of the Finnish People (SKVR) and *Synnyt*, a work on prose narratives edited by Marja Paasio (1976).
6. "Narrative" is defined as a description of an event or sequence of events. It is concerned with the mimesis of action and structured according to the general component scheme ("the superstructure") of the narrative. The components or main categories include "setting", "complication", "resolution", and "evaluation" (expressions of the narrator's attitudes to the narrated). – See van Dijk 1980, 13-14 and Siikala 1990a, 23-26. – I prefer to add one component or category to the model, the component of "narration", i.e. the verbalisation and other "technical" solutions of the narrator (See Apo 1992, 63, 68-69).
7. James J. Liszka arrives by way of psycholinguistics and philosophical action theory (by Georg H. von Wright) at the following basic categories of the "mythemic sequence": actor, action, object, consequence. (Liszka 1989, 120.) Action theory is also referred to by Paul Ricoeur in his definition of narrative, for a narrative is in turn a mimesis of action. (Ricoeur 1984, 54-64 et passim.)
8. The state stages in a plot are not always explicated in a narrative. The listener infers them from his knowledge of the world. He also has to "fill in the gaps" in interpreting the hero's behaviour e.g. in the myth *The origin of fish*, for the elliptic myth text does not inform him of the hero's desires and intentions.
9. The plots of aetiological myths can be abstracted in a number of ways. According to Marta Weigle it is possible to discern "so-called higher or *ex nihilo* creation 'from nothing' by thought, dream, breath, spirit, laughter, and speech, and so-called lesser or elemental creation through the penetration of primal matter by earth-diver figures or parthenogenesis, cosmic hierogamy, and emergence." (Weigle 1987, 427.)
10. Compared with the cosmogonic myths of other cultures, the ancient Finnish-Karelian narrative poems seem to lack battle plots. In these stories, part of the universe emerges as a consequence of a battle between animal actors or a god/hero and a monster-like adversary.
11. The term "narrative world" has been used by e.g. René Wellek and Austin Warren (1976, 151-152).
12. I have used several levels of abstraction in describing the event structures of narratives in conjunction with my analysis of the contents of magic tales. In addition to the action sequences and roles abstracted in the manner of Propp we should also determine the means of realisation of these abstract units, in other words look to see how a "difficult task" is performed, who the "heroes" are (what categories they represent) and who the "villains" are (Apo 1986; 1990). An analytic model similar to this has been proposed for myths by James Jakób Liszka (1989, 120-128).
13. The version was collected by D.E.D. Europaeus in 1845 in Suistamo, Ladoga Karelia.
14. Martti Haavio has listed the early definitions:
    – Pellonpecko / Ohran casuon soi. (Michael Agricola 1551)
    – Hordea Pellpeckus cultis producit in arvis. Zythifer & genti creditur esse deus. (Sigfrid Aronus Forsius at the end of the 16th century).
    – Och Pellonpecko (gaf) Kornet på For. (Petrus Bång 1675).
    – Pellon pekka eller pekko, en korn-gud.

(Christfrid Ganander 1789).
– Pellonpekka, Pellonpekko, Peltopekka, åkerns skyddsande. (Elias Lönnrot 1880). (Haavio 1959, 105.)
Lines in latin: "Pellpeckus makes the barley grow in the fields. He is also believed to be a god producing ale for the people." (Harva 1948, 190.) According to Ganander, too, Pellonpekka was associated with beer: Pellonpekka brings good wort, which used to be called the milk of the field and the imbibing of which was named "tasting Pellon Pekko". (Krohn 1914a, 134.)

15. For the mythical poems about the giant oak and ox see Kuusi 1963, 73-83, 144-147, 161-165.

16. For the rules governing the relationships between representations see Kamppinen 1989, 31.

17. A man interpreted as the personification of barley also appears in the *Lokasenna* poem of the Edda. Called Byggvir, he was described as a little man small enough to hide in the straw. (Edda 1982, 146-147; Harva 1948, 196-197.)

18. There is another description of harvesting in SKVR VII:1, 800. The "impossible" image of birds taking part in the brewing of ale also appears in *The brewer tit*, which may be classified as a children's poem. Mateli Kuivalatar of North Karelia combined Osmotar and the tit: "Osmotar brew ale, Kalevatar carried water all on a summer's day. It took a month to heat the stones, the sea was dried to scoop the water; a wagtail carried the water, a redbreast chopped the wood, a tit brewed the beer – but did not know its name. (SKVR VII:2, 1314 and 1314 b. Ilomantsi, Kontiovaara. Lönnrot Ub 83 b. 1838 and Ahlqvist B 173 b).

19. A hyperbolic account of brewing is also included in some versions of *Osmotar brews ale*: "It took a summer to boil the water, it took a month to heat the stones. And Osmotar brewed ale." (SKVR I:1, 722.) The brewing of beer is also made fantastic by means of impossible images: "Osmori brewed ale in a little pan small enough to fit on his thumb, no bigger than his fingertip, from three grains of barley." (SKVR I:1, 705.)

20. For stone brewing and more recent brewing techniques see Räsänen 1977, 28, 109-110.

21. For cosmic tree images see Kuusi (Siikala) 1975, 290-291 and Siikala 1985a, 324.

22. For ale rites on the feast of Ilja see also Lukkarinen 1912, 40-47 and Mansikka 1939, 145-150, 159-160.

23. The poem about Lemmminkäinen was, according to one source, performed while the beer was brewing; there are also some references to a wedding context. According to Leea Virtanen the poem was probably performed in many contexts,

both everyday ones and ones connected with ritual singing. (Virtanen 1968, 15, 51.)

24. Seven versions of the poem have been recorded, five from Suistamo, one from Korpiselkä and one from Ilomantsi.

25. The archive reference for the narrative is SKS: Nurmes. Saul H. Viiliäinen TK 116:102, 1961.

26. See Lönnrot's Finnish-Swedish Dictionary II, 1958.

27. A female brewer (Osmotar, maiden, good woman, mistress) dominates the Karelian descriptions with the exception of Uhtua. Osmotar is also very much in evidence at Suistamo in Ladoga Karelia; at Suojärvi she appears in one version. The Ilomantsi Sissonen family of singers from North Karelia favoured Osmotar. In Olonets the brewer is most often an "islander" of no specific sex, or else the poem mentions Ahti the Islander elsewhere. Osmotar also featured in songs from Olonets, at least at Suulaansaari, Repola, Lentiera, Kolvasjärvi and Saarenpää. In the rare brewing songs from Savo Osmotar appears at Lapinlahti, Varpaisjärvi and Iisalmi.

28. In Ingria *Jumalaisen ainoi poikoi* 'God's only son' gives the festive ale the missing hops and malt. Without them the ale would not have intoxicated its drinkers. (Salminen 1917, 36.)

29. Johannes Häyhä, describing Rautjärvi on the Karelian Isthmus in the first half of the 19th century, presents the men of the extended family as the brewers of the beer and spirits. According to Väinö Salminen the wedding beer was made in Ingria by the head of the family. (Häyhä 1982, 39-40; Salminen 1916, 39-42.)

30. According to Leea Virtanen the Finnish word *olut*, meaning 'beer' or 'ale', was not used in the spoken language of Russian Karelia – the term would have been *vuassa*. (Virtanen 1968, 15.) Aleksi Konkka, Russian Karelian ethnologist, told me that beer was not used in Archangel Karelia in the 19th century.

31. Other associations connected with the Virgin Mary and beer were given by Kaarle Krohn (1903, 526-527).

32. According to the singers of Archangel Karelia Osmotar's helpers included not only a squirrel and a fox but also a pine marten and an ermine.

33. The origin of the hops is mentioned in the ancient poems in a short episode connected either with *Barley converses with hops* or *Osmotar brews ale*. In this episode the two meanings of the word *humala* are used. *Humala* means both 'intoxication' and 'hops'. According to Mateli Kuivalatar, "Humala, the son of Noise, was planted in the ground as a baby, ploughed into the earth like snakes, thrown on Osmo's field as nettles." (SKVR VII:2, 1314 a and b. Collected by

Elias Lönnrot in 1838 and August Ahlqvist in 1846.)

34. SKVR XIII:1, 168: Sung by Jerlan Vasle, aged 80 in Metsäpirtti, Vaskela 1912.

35. SKVR XIII:1, 170: Sung by Yrjänä Kotti, heard from Liisa Kotila. *Tyttölöin laulu Pääsiäisennä ja joulunna.* – Sakkola. Neovius Ad. 332. 1887.

36. The "spirit being" has in Finnish folklore often been ontologised as a being at least partly resembling a human. Animate alcoholic beverage is likened to various diseases which penetrate humans, sometimes orally, and place them in their power. Ague and pox were thought of as beings capable of speech; they asked for a ride or conversed with one another, and they had desires and intentions directed at humans (personification). On the other hand plague was ontologised as a red cock ("animalisation", zoomorphism) or as a red ball (objectification). (Simonsuuri 1975, 444-446.)

37. About drinking and Simmel's *Geselligkeit* see Partanen, 1991, 218-230.

38. The oats and barley say: "When we come together, when we begin to play, a hundred children will be born, a dozen little ones begotten". (SKVR XIII:1, 171. Pyhäjärvi. Ahlqvist A. 75. 1854). The Karelian Christmas games were above all a chance for young people of courting age to get together. The games were sometimes highly erotic. (Kuusi 1963, 412.)

EINO KIURU

The Wife-Killer Theme in Karelian and Russian Songs

The oldest recorded version of the poem *Kojosen pojan kosinta* 'The Courtship of Kojonen's Son' was published in Schröter's work *Finnische Runen* 'Finnish *runes*' in Uppsala in 1819. *Suomen Kansan Vanhat Runot* (SKVR) 'The Ancient Poems of the Finnish People' records 250 variants of it[1] and later recordings have also been published in the anthology *Karelskie epičeskie pesni* 'The Epic songs of Karelia'[2]. The plot of the poem is known from Archangel Karelia right down through Ladoga Karelia and the Karelian Isthmus to Ingria. Judging from the number of variants (c. 200), it has been most popular of all in Ingria.

The plot scheme of *Kojosen pojan kosinta* (also known as *Kojosen poika* 'The Kojonen Song', *Vävyn tuomiset* 'The Gift of Son-in-law') is as follows: Kojonen (sometimes just Kojo, Jouko, Jouto) sets out to woo a wife. Upon winning her, he sits her down beside him in his sleigh and sets off home. On their way an inexplicable argument breaks out between them, and Kojonen kills his wife, either on the way or on arriving at his home. From her flesh, most often her breasts, he makes a present (such as a filled pie) for his mother-in-law. The unsuspecting woman eats the pie and praises the present, which she believes her daughter has sent. A slave (male or female) warns her not to eat the present brought her by her son-in-law but only agrees to reveal the reason on receipt of a great reward, such as being married to the son of the house.

Generically the song qualifies as a ballad; this explains many of the special features which do not usually occur in Kalevala metric epics. Scholars have been particularly surprised at the cruel and poorly motivated murder of the innocent girl. The ballad does, however, make a clear attempt to explain the hero's barbaric act via the events preceding it. It even tries to moralise on the ruinous consequences of the deed.

Scholars have not so far succeeded in providing a natural explanation for these aspects of the plot. Ever since the song was first examined, scholars have been trying to explain away all the illogicalities as being borrowed from the Russian *bylina*. This hypothesis was presented by Julius Krohn as early as the 1870s. According to him the "Finnish version" of the song

Songs beyond
the Kalevala
Studia Fennica
Folkloristica 2
1994

was born in Ladoga Karelia and was modelled on the *bylina* Ivan Godino-vich (Krohn J. 1883-1885, 473-482). Many other Finnish scholars have addressed themselves to the song, with similar results (Krohn K. 1910, 321-324; Mansikka 1908; Mansikka 1945-1946, 178-186; Kuusi 1963, 334). Judging from the information on folklore motifs at our disposal nowadays these conjectures on the relationship between the Karelian-Finnish song and the Russian *bylina* in many respects seem erroneous and call for closer inspection.

In 1961 Matti Kuusi published an article examining the sources of the motifs of the difficult tasks performed in some versions of *Kojosen pojan kosinta* (Kuusi 1961, 195-207). In analysing the song as a whole Kuusi no longer regards it as a Finnish or a Karelian translation of the Russian *bylina*; it merely follows the same pattern. According to him, the main difference between the song and the *bylina* lies in the degree of motivation for the killing of the young wife.

Deeper analysis of the plot as a whole and its motifs led Matti Kuusi to disassociate himself from the prevailing concept that the *bylina* had been transferred to the Karelian-Finnish tradition directly. Yet he was not able to deny the basic postulation of the comparative school that any similarities observable in the motifs and figures of the folklore of different peoples are the result of borrowing. The impossible tasks set in the song were in Kuusi's opinion borrowed from Russian folklore. In the Russian songs the imposi-tion of impossible tasks by both parties does not, however, lead to one party being punished, so the loan assumption seems rather questionable, especial-ly since corresponding motifs appear in the folklore of many peoples, as Kuusi himself points out.[3]

On the one hand, even a cursory comparison of the *Kojosen pojan kosinta* song and the Russian *bylina* reveals a host of analogies. On the other hand, upon closer inspection, these analogies often prove to be very general and superficial. A clear example of this is the hero himself. In both the song and the *bylina* the hero is in most cases Ivan Godinovich (Gordinovich), i.e. the son of Iivana Kojonen. The similarity ends with the names. The *bylina* tells of a warrior, of a boyar of Vladimir, the famous Prince of Kiev, whereas the song makes no mention at all of the hero's social estate. He is neither hero, nor warrior, but "just somebody". He is unique only in what he does, but even that does not make him into a hero, because he does not do heroic deeds. The hero of the *bylina*, by contrast, performs a heroic feat such as wooing or fetching a bride from the other world, fighting an opponent from a foreign country, and even punishing a bride representing another world. (Propp-Putilov 1958, 460-461.)

Examination of the basic conflict leads to an equally false conclusion. The heroic deeds in both the *bylina* and the song would appear to be similar in content – in both of them a defenceless woman is cruelly punished. Yet the hero of the *bylina* survives and overcomes the enmity of a woman representing another world (Tchernyayeva 1981, 76), whereas Iivana Ko-jonen merely kills his wife and for some inexplicable reason seeks revenge on his mother-in-law by making her eat her daughter's flesh.

These fundamental differences between the song and the *bylina* force us to reconsider the relationship between the folklores of the two peoples involved. The loan theory clearly does not stand up to criticism. A motif that is inconceivable and makes no sense cannot be assimilated by one folklore from another. An ethnic basis must already exist for the assimilation of strange characters and plots. And it appears that in this case the ethnic basis was not ready to assimilate ideas of the type accompanying epics of a national nature. The epic of neither the Izhors nor the Karelians reached this stage because the social development of their ethnos did not attain a corresponding level. Neither the Izhors nor the Karelians achieved a nation state of their own, and even the Finns were only able to form one in the capitalist era. The epic thus remained archaic, pre-national, and was not capable of receiving the new ideas and trends manifest in the "Kiev" epic.

B.N. Putilov points out that the Russian wooing epic is characterised by the fact that the hero must not marry a girl from another world, and stresses that such a marriage causes difficulty for the hero, which he overcomes by murdering her (Putilov 1971, 130-131). Herein, according to V. Propp, lies the explanation for Ivan Godinovich's cruelty, because Avdotya personifies and bears the brunt of all the enmity of the alien tribe (Propp 1958, 134).

Karelian heroic epics in general do not condemn their heroes for marrying girls from other worlds. Their heroes travel to the North, the home of the Devil and the Underworld to fetch their brides, i.e. to exogamous tribes the names of which may even hint at the kingdom of the dead.

Since the Karelian-Finnish epic has not proved itself capable of assimilating the basic disposition of the *bylina* on the wooing theme, the question presents itself of whether Russian folklore could have had any other influence apart from lending.

The very fact that the name of the hero in the ballad song is clearly derived from the name of the *bylina* hero indicates that the Russian *bylina* was known in the Kalevalaic tradition area. On the other hand the ballad and *bylina* motifs that resemble one another in their outward characteristics differ from one another in content. In order to determine the influences and the forms they have taken, the song must be subjected to detailed analysis.

Kojosen pojan kosinta

Some forty variants of the poem *Kojosen pojan kosinta* were recorded in Archangel Karelia (the districts of Kalevala and Mujerski and the Karelian villages in Louhi district) between 1825 and 1958. The northern variant is characterised by the idiosyncratic opening in which the performer, who at a later stage in the song identifies with the heroine, laments her fate:

Jouten synnyin, jouten kasvoin	Useless born, useless I grew
jouten joukossa elin.	useless I lived with the others
Lähettih neijet illan issuntah,	The maids sent me off for the evening
peipot pesseutan pitohe.	The finches to make merry.
Sattu Jouto kuulomahe,	Jouto happened to hear this
alla seinän astumahe...	to be standing by the wall
(SKVR I:1, 554)	

The opening is interesting for the very fact that it differs in structure from the typical heroic epic. Epic heroic poems usually begin with a brief presentation of the hero and the event and do not make any reference to the singer's own fate. Similar openings were admittedly known prior to this, but they were separate exhortations to the audience to listen to what the singer had to say. In them the singer by no means attempts to identify with the hero; on the contrary, his or her aim is to stress the superiority of the epic heroes over ordinary mortals. In *Kojosen pojan kosinta*, however, the opening lines elegantly tie in with the events of the song, and the hero, who is to begin with lyrical, is equated with the epic hero whose unhappy fate reflects, as it were, the singer's own fate. Of special significance is an invitation to the girls to join in the evening's merriment, for this later provides the starting point for the unfolding of the plot.

This beginning, typical of the songs of Archangel Karelia, proves that the listeners to the song plot were quite different from those of heroic epics. The atmosphere when the girls or young people in general got together for the evening was different from the leisurely mood prevailing at the men's singing competitions such as that described by the '*rune* king' Arhippa Perttunen to Elias Lönnrot in 1834 (Pytesestvije...1985, 134-135). The heroes of the mythical epic did not provide the singer or listeners with any opportunities for identification. *Kojosen pojan kosinta* does not, however, tell of an epic hero but of the wooing of a perfectly ordinary person. It is not a feat of daring but an everyday event, even though in many variants it incorporates difficult tasks, just as in the epic wooing songs.

The figure of the bride likewise changes – in the song she becomes an active character. In the epic wooing songs the bride is glimpsed towards the beginning, but thereafter the hero deals only with her mother. The choice of prospective bridegroom remains the only active deed by the bride; in the other episodes she is merely the object of the hopes and aspirations of the bridegroom candidates.

The plot of the epic wooing songs ends with the winning of the promised bride. The plot of the ballad, by contrast, only really begins at this point, and the attention focuses specifically on the fate of the maiden who was wooed, and who went either voluntarily or was taken by force.

The custom conspicuous in the Archangel Karelian variants of concentrating on a single person is typical of the ballad as a genre. It is at the same time part of the national wedding ritual and the special occasions during which the song was performed. The invitation to the evening's merry-making is both part of real life and the theme of the song. The evening get-togethers widely arranged for young people at the time when the ballad was alive were an excellent opportunity for choosing a spouse and even marring directly by elopement (Surhasko 1977, 37-52). 'Elopement weddings' without the marriage rituals are also mentioned in the Archangel Karelian variants of *Kojosen pojan kosinta* that begin with an invitation to the event acting as the start of the tragic events.

While the performer bemoans her fate at not being wooed by Kojonen, he is in fact in the next room and can hear every word. On hearing her wish, he engages her and carries her off. From then onwards the plot proceeds without any major deviations from the predominant Karelian version.

The above episode epitomises the fatalism inherent in the ethics of ballads. The girl moves towards her fate almost against her will: in lamenting that not even Kojonen has wooed her, she invites death to carry her off. In the epic wooing songs the bride is always predestined for the hero (Putilov 1971, 126). In this ballad the situation is in a way the reverse; the groom is predestined for the bride and personifies fate, which is drawn as the bride's course in life.

This feature, typical of ballads, ties in neatly with the attempt to identify the real singer with the heroine. The identification is made easier by the use of the narrative first person singular, wich imperceptibly gives way to the third person common in epics. The lyric nature of the opening is thus enhanced and the narrative as a whole acquires a kind of lyrical tone.

The type of opening examined here to my mind best corresponds to the aesthetic demands of the ballad. Though sparing in its means, it creates a dramatic setting. It is not, however, the only type of opening. It is characteristic only of the Archangel Karelian variants and rather narrow in its distribution. Better known is the broader introduction describing not only Kojonen's proposal but sometimes the bride's 'life history' too. These openings are contaminations of the epic wooing songs.

Kaarle Krohn suggested as early as the turn of the century that the motif of the execution of difficult tasks appearing in the ballad was taken from the epic wooing songs (*Kilpakosinta* 'The Courtship', *Hiidestä kosinta* 'The Courtship from Hiisi', *Tuonelasta kosinta* 'The Courtship from Tuonela'). Matti Kuusi seconds this view, mentioning that the closest model for *Kojosen pojan kosinta* was *Tuonelasta kosinta* (Kuusi 1961, 203).

Interestingly enough, these motifs have been assimilated into the plot of the ballad in different ways. In one version they have become structural elements of the narrative, in others they are merely contamination that does not affect the logic of the plot in any way. In Archangel Karelia, for example, the execution of difficult tasks is nothing but a legacy of the epic. In them the bride is won only after the groom has passed the test. In these variants Kojonen succeeds in performing the compulsory tasks but they are immaterial to the development of the conflict. Just as in the variants in which Kojonen snatches the maid from the evening get-together without proposing to her and carries her off in his sleigh, the conflict arises out of events that have nothing to do with the wooing. This case cannot even be regarded as a veiled warning against rushing head-long into marriage.

In Aunus and Ladoga Karelia the opening to the song is expanded by contamination with the song *Laiska tyttö* 'The Lazy Girl', and supplemented with motifs on the *Monenlaiset sulhaset* 'Many Bridegrooms' theme. In the latter, suitors arrive from Estonia, the neighbouring village, from afar etc. or from the sun, the moon and the stars. Mother would give the girl to one, father to another, but the girl herself chooses a third, Kojonen.

In Ingria the song is often contaminated with *Hekon runo* 'The Hekko's Song'. In this particular contamination the ballad adds the reason for the tragic end to *Kojosen pojan kosinta*. The execution of difficult tasks is not present merely for the sake of tradition.

In this version Kojonen hides his offence at being set the impossible tasks of a groom. On returning home with his bride (sometimes actually during the journey), Kojonen orders his wife to perform impossible tasks in the same way, "to make a shirt from a single thread and a cloak from one woollen slipper" (SKVR V:1, 232, 38-41).

His wife refuses his demands, sometimes with disdain, but usually in astonishment at her husband's absurd orders. She becomes the victim of unfair treatment and tries to protest against it. The protest is against her husband's utter supremacy and is also an artistic antithesis to the epic tradition, which abounded in the execution of absurd tasks as a condition for marriage. The antithesis reflects a new level of artistic awareness and invalidates the old mythical generalisations. It is no coincidence that the word "lie" is used in the refrain as a synonym for "empty". The maiden dies the victim of false, fantastic wedding rites and an outdated social practice. In some variants the conflict ends in agreement when the wife states that Kojonen's demands are unfounded and directed at the wrong person – the groom was tormented by the mother, not the daughter. The reconciliation and the refusal to carry out the preposterous tasks are the logical conclusion to the false development of the ballad plot. Since the trials nevertheless appear only in the epic, from which they are borrowed by the ballad, the protest has no real target. The plot finds itself moving towards an impasse from the very beginning, because it is based not on reality but on the often very archaic motifs of folklore.

The heroine bride

Similar relics of archaic motifs are also to be found in the variants in which the wife is killed as revenge for being better than her husband. Another version widely known in Ingria says that Kojonen killed his wife "at Torajoki" after losing a duel with her; Hekko (his wife) had a longer sword and a superior mind.

The swordplay appears in *The Lemminkäinen Song* of the Karelian-Finnish epic. Lemminkäinen, who has arrived at the feast uninvited, has an argument with the Master of Päivölä and challenges him to a duel in which the master is killed.

The swordplay ritual in the epic provides the substance for the duel in the ballad. The woman is superior to the man and he cannot accept it. An old frame thus acquires new contents and develops in the process: instead of being a test of strength, the battle is between intellectual properties, and the swords disappear from view. In several of the Ingrian variants the Torajoki duel is one not of swords but of the duelists' personal properties: "We match our minds, we measure our miens" (SKVR III:2, 1251, 85-89).

The sword-brandishing woman of Torajoki displays relics of the female warrior, the heroine bride appearing in the folklore of various peoples. (Cf. Puhov 1962, 123.) The man must win the battle and curb the woman in order to win her as his wife. In the *bylina Dunai-kosiomies* 'The Dunai-suitor', the title character abducts the princess Afrosinya "from the golden King Orda", just as Kojonen carries Hekko off from her parents' home. Dunai's duel with the princess Nastasia is in many respects reminiscent of Kojonen's strange battle with his wife at Torajoki. It would appear that the maiden warrior of the *bylina* helped to place the sword in the hand of Kojonen's wife. What is more, the cutting of the breasts appearing in *Kojosen pojan kosinta* occurs in the same form in the duel between Dunai and Nastasia, even though in the *bylina* the motif signifies the erotic curbing

225

of the heroine and not a punishment. Dunai threatens but does not harm the maid, whereas Ivan Godinovich, in the ballad of the same name, kills his wife in the corresponding situation. Features of two *bylina* heroes thus combine in *Kojosen pojan kosinta*. The ballad further has its own conflict conception that does not justify the hero's action but reveals his low motives, since in both the versions his reasons are artificial.

The Karelian-Finnish tradition does not have a heroine figure such as that found in, for example, the *olonho* of the Yakuts, the Russian *bylina* or the Ancient Germanic epic. The heroine bride which appear in the Karelian Finnish ballad has, however, been preserved as a relic in the *olonho* of the Yakuts.

Kojonen's revenge cannot be connected as such with the heroine bride motif. All we can do is note that it exists in the Karelian-Finnish tradition, too. The swordplay with the bride is thus a synthesis of *The Lemminkäinen Song* and the Russian *bylina*.

The animal tracks motif

In a version common in the Karelian tradition Kojonen kills his wife because she has bewailed her fate without good reason and claims she would have been better off in the clutches of some beast of the forest. On the way home in Kojonen's sleigh she several times sees an animal's tracks on the road and asks what has caused them. After each answer she sighs that she would be better off on the tracks of this animal than in Kojonen's sleigh. Kojonen replies by threatening and finally punishing her. Not even the singers themselves understood why the wife sighed, nor the punishment that ensued, and sometimes changed the wife's words into more pointed attacks on her husband. In some variants she thus says that it would be better not only to be on the tracks of an animal but to be eaten by a wolf or bear. In other cases she compares the way her husband looks to a beast of prey and thus tries to offend him as deeply as possible for his conceit.

Such confusing explanations are well in keeping with the poetics of ballads as typical features of the genre. The ballad has to demonstrate Kojonen's evil intent, and there is thus sufficient motivation for the killing in the fact that the wife is wiser and more beautiful than her husband, she does not wish to perform the difficult tasks, and the compares her husband's looks to a beast of prey, and that all in all she would regard a wild animal as preferable to her husband. All the motifs in the ballad nevertheless have their roots in their own or a foreign tradition, and they are at times highly idiosyncratic interpretations of folklore motifs.

Finnish scholars have regarded the animal tracks motif as a pure Russian influence, because in the *bylina*, too, the hero returning with his bride notices an animal's tracks or hoof marks across the road. (See Krohn, J. 1883-1885, 482; Krohn, K. 1910, 321-324; Kuusi 1963, 333.) On the face of it a likeness does exist, but there the similarity between the *bylina* and *The Kojonen ballad* ends. In the ballad the animal's tracks do not only prompt the heroine to utter words of venom, it also proves that the bride in the Finnish-Karelian ballad comes from a different totemic family from the groom. In the variants of Ivan Godinovich in which the motif appears, the hero sends his companion off in pursuit of the animal's tracks in order to engage in personal battle with his opponent and to test his bride in the process. In the *bylina Dunai-kosiomies* 'the Dunai-suitor', the hero himself sets off along the hoof marks, having first entrusted the wife he has obtained for Prince Vladimir to the care of his attendants. Following the tracks, Dunai encounters a young maiden from the Poljany tribe, and after winning her in a duel takes her as his wife. The ballad contains nothing like this. It is therefore best to seek animals who leave their tracks across the road travelled by Iivana Kojonen in the epic of Karelia-Finland.

Many songs were sung in Aunus and Ladoga Karelia about courtship from the devil, *Hiidestä kosinta*, in which one of the motifs is the transformation of the bride brought home by Ilmollinen the smith into various species of animals which the groom has to chase in the form of their biological antagonists. The descriptions of these transformations greatly resemble the altercation between Kojonen and his bride. The fact that, like Kojonen's wife, the bride brought home by Ilmollinen wishes to leave her husband transformed as an animal, fish or bird is not the only thing they have in common. For in both cases the groom prevents the transformation, until he finally settles his account with his bride.

The plot of *Hiidestä kosinta* in similar in its basic scheme to the *Pohjolasta kosinta,* 'Courtship from Pohjola' song of Archangel Karelia. This latter song does, however, lack a description of the journey home of the bride and groom. On the way they get into an argument in which the bride threatens to turn herself into various animals, while the groom threatens to turn into other animals that will triumph over the incarnations of the bride. Some variants actually describe how the characters transform themselves into various animals. For example, the variant noted down by Kaarle Krohn at Suojärvi in 1884 tells how a smith, having succeeded in performing difficult tasks, began to forge a knife in order to set matters straight with the bride's father, who was beginning to get him down. At which Annikainen, daughter of Hiitola:

Mäni taivoseh täheksi	Went as a star to the sky,
seppoini haukaksi jälessä;	the smith as a hawk after her,
hän on kiiskoiksi mereh,	went as a ruff to the sea,
seppoini hauviksi jälessä;	the smith as a pike after her;
"N'ota sitä sepponi milma".	"Well, take me smith."
"Engo ota, engo lupoa,	"No, I won't promise,
siepä rannoilla radzizeego	You can chirp on the shore
luotoloilla lodzizeego	shriek on the skerries
se ilmoini ikäni".	for the rest of your life."
(SKVR VII:2, 395, 87-95)	

The conflict between the bride and the groom ends with the man reigning superior. In many variants, the song states in no uncertain terms that the groom transformed his bride into a seagull in revenge for having to perform difficult tasks, and further for having to fight with a bride who kept being transformed. In some variants the girl turned into a seagull begs to be returned to her original form, but the groom is unyielding in his decision.

This epic motif is interesting for two reasons. To begin with it provides a ready model for Iivana Kojonen's behaviour; he sought revenge on his wife because in certain cases he was forced to perform difficult tasks, while in others his bride wanted to get back her lost freedom by transforming herself into different animals, and sometimes she was simply superior to her groom. Secondly, the transformation of first the bride and then the groom into different animals which then fight each other indicates that the motif is derived from a totemic concept of different animal forms derived from mutually hostile human families. The duel between the representative of one totem (the groom) and the representative of another (the bride) would appear to be some kind of myth of a transitional rite in which the bride transfers to the groom's totem family, just at the liminal point when the old mode of marriage is being replaced by a new one. It may, for example, reflect a battle that ensued as matrilocal marriage was replaced by patrilocal. Scholars of the religion of the Siberian peoples have noted that in folk tales fights between animals always reflect fights between totemic groups (Zolotarev 1934, 18). The same appears to be true in this case.

Another interesting aspect is in that relics of totemic concepts also occur in the Russian wooing *bylina* to which, in the Finnish scholars' opinion, the ballad of Kojonen belongs. The conflict which emerges between the groom and his young wife is typologically akin to that between Iivana Kojonen and his bride. In the wooing *bylinas* (such as Mihailo Potyk, Ivan Godinovich, Dunai and Nastasia the King's daughter, Dobrynya and Marinka) the conflict ends with the death of the wife at her husband's hand. This is also what happens in the ballad of Iivana Kojonen. The heart of the conflict between Kojonen and his bride is still as mystifying as that between the smith Ilmollinen and the maid he woos, where the maiden again meets her "death" at the bridegroom's hand. Scholars are thus faced with a host of similarities and differences the mutual relationships of which are difficult to determine.

The wooing bylinas

To the modern reader, just as to the performer of the *bylinas* in the 18th and 19th centuries, the period when most of the recordings were made, there is much that remains unclear and that is simply attributed to tradition requiring neither justification nor explanation. The hero of the *bylinas* kills his wife, this being either his sole heroic deed or part of it. The *bylinas* do, however, indicate the motivation for this heroic act. Whereas in, for example, the *bylina* Mihailo Potyk all is more or less understandable and the reader (or listener) merely wonders why the hero does not get on with the job of punishing his wife, the same cannot be said of Ivan Godinovich. Here the hero goes to considerable trouble to win his bride, who, on top of everything is already engaged to another. Since, knowing this, Ivan Godinovich abducts her by force, why does he seek his revenge on her and kill her? At first it appears that the *bylina* offers a rather unique explanation for the deed – the bride not only deceives Ivan Godinovich, she even assists his opponent, an epic enemy, in a duel. However, on the other hand it is to him, Afromei Afromeyevich, tsar of Zagorsk, that Nastasia, daughter of a Chernigov merchant, is engaged. The logic of the events seems to vanish in the *bylina* for this very reason, and the bride is not won from Afromei

Kyykkä was a popular game in Archangel Karelia. Here the player takes aim. Luvajärvi. Photo: I.K. Inha 1894 (FLS 9849).

Afromeyevich until Ivan Godinovich has in practice already captured her. If he were first forced to fight a duel with his opponent, Nastasia's former betrothed, and only then won Nastasia as his wife, he would have no reason to be angry with his wife because she had helped Tsar Afromei, and the severe punishment would seem unjust.

V. Propp, in studying the wooing *bylinas*, pointed out that the marriage of the hero was acceptable in the *bylina* of the pre-national era. But during the national era the plot of *bylinas*, like those from Kiev, could not end with the hero's marriage (Propp 1958, 113, 119). The epics of the national period also feature a hero's battle with a sorceress able to turn herself into something else, this being her supernatural craft.

The realignment of the value system has led to the reassessment of a number of phenomena. Whereas the bride was previously a positive figure, she now acquires negative characteristics. Even an epithet such as a "white swan", a metaphor for beauty and purity, has become a veiled expression for a deceitful, bestial being from the other world. The bride is a werewolf, a snake intent on destroying her husband. Similar properties are attached to the wife of Ivan Godinovich who, according to certain variants, is able to turn herself into a snake. Closer examination reveals that the brutality in the female figure in the *bylina* is not just an epithet and that it ties in with the concept of the brutish origins of woman.

Potyk's wife is, as we know, from the other world, and she has the ability to return there when transformed into a snake, even though she is also capable of appearing as a pleasanter being, a white swan. Godinovich's wife has the same attributes, though slightly weaker, and she too is originally from the animal world. Commentators of the plot note that she sometimes also bears traces of a link with the mythical world: "On her head Advotya has white swans, at her feet Advotya has black ravens." (Propp – Putilov 1958, 460.)

In two cases she appears in the form of a white swan, the personification of a bride. The Archangel Karelian wooing epic also contains references to a swan in speaking of the bride. On his courting journey to Pohjola Väinämöinen answers the question put to him by Ilmarinen's sister by saying that he is going fishing (for salmon), to shoot a goose or to catch swans, "to a swan wedding". N.A. Krinichnaya has proven in studying the *Vellamo maiden* motif in Karelian-Finnish epic that the mention of animals in this context is nothing more than a "semantic equivalent" for the bride courted by Väinämöinen, and that the association of the bride with different animals is derived from the totemic concept of the unity between man and his family totem (Krinichnaya 1986, 92).

If this conclusion is correct, the Archangel Karelian poem tells of courting from an exogamous kin the totem of which was once a swan or some other figure in animal form. In the Aunus and Ladoga Karelian version of the wooing the link between the bride (and even the groom) and the totem is even clearer. This is demonstrated by the bride's attempts to turn herself back into the figure of her family totem and thus to protect herself. The Archangel Karelian poem takes a very casual attitude to the connection between the bride and the family totem, because it does not develop the theme any further. The Aunus version, by contrast, pays considerable attention to the battle with the former family totem of the bride. Not only the bride but the groom, too, is capable of turning into an animal, and the groom uses this as a means of finally bending the bride to his will. The fight between the two animals ends with victory for the groom – he turns the bride for ever into a seagull. The only thing that remains unclear is the original semantics of this victory; was it a form of revenge, or did the permanent transformation of the bride simply denote her adaptation to the family totem of the groom, her role as wife in her husband's family?

The Aunus Karelian song about the wooing and the groom's victory in the fight with the bride representing an alien totemic family does not merely depict the trend in relationships between two hostile families. It also proves that a fight such as this was conceived of as representing the incorporation of an alien totem's representative into the totem family of the groom, to which the bride was to move permanently. It is no coincidence that the entire battle is waged on the journey from the bride's home to the groom's home (or family).

The behaviour of Iivana Kojonen in seeking a reason to punish his bride and then carrying it out on the journey home corresponds to the behaviour of Ilmollinen the smith in the poem *Hiidestä kosinta*. On the other hand this model explains what appears at first sight to be the cruelty of the *bylina* hero Ivan Godinovich towards his wife, whom he had won in a battle with representatives of other totem families. The bride's hostility towards Ivan Godinovich is founded on the concept refuted by the nation state ideologies of a totemic origin in another world ruled by lowly, hostile, snake-like creatures. This is the reason why, in mutilating his wife, Godinovich tries to turn her back into a snake by cutting off everything that makes her look other than a smooth snake (Chernyayeva 1981, 276-277).

The totemic conflict

There is no doubt that familiarity with this *bylina* in the Karelian-Finnish epic area has influenced the scene in which Iivana Kojonen argues with his wife, even though the fight is not described in such gory detail as in the *bylina*. One element of this scene nevertheless acquires special significance: the cutting away of the bride's breasts and the making of a pie from them for the bride's mother. This climax is to be found in the majority of the variants. In some of them it is one of the main motifs of the ballad, according to Matti Kuusi its sensational ending. Sometimes the ballad may lack an account of the killing, but the arrival of Kojonen and his pie at his mother-in-law's is always described:

Vuota, vuota Hiitten huora!	Wait, wait, whore of Hiisi
Peäsemmä Kojosen mäellä...	we'll reach the hill of Kojonen...
kauhasetta verta juomma,	to drink blood with no ladle,
veitsetta lihoa vessämmä!	to carve meat without a knife!
Heän vei kostintsoiksi:	He took along as a present
Ol'onaisen olkaluita,	Olonja's shoulder bones,
Palakaisen peäpaloja,	bits of Palaga's head,
Moarien maitomöykkysie.	lumps of Moarie's milk
(SKVR I:1, 554, 86-94).	

This is clearly a scene that should include an account of the punishment. There is, however, no doubt what it is all about because the pie brought by the son-in-law is made from parts of the beloved daughter's body. The usual account of the punishment encountered all over the area where this song is known gives as a vital detail the cutting out of the breasts and the baking of the pie for the mother-in-law.

In studying the various motifs of *The Sampo* poems Matti Kuusi has pointed out that the cutting out of the breasts in the Iivana Kojonen song is reminiscent of the catching of a mighty pike as one of the suitor's tasks. In some variants the groom, having caught the fish, tastes it or slices off the tips of its breasts – just like the cutting out of the breasts in the song about Iivana Kojonen (Kuusi 1949, 280). It is one of the groom's tasks to catch a giant pike in the Tuonela river "to take to his mother-in-law". This motif is part of the Archangel Karelian song tradition and is not found elsewhere. The hero (Ilmarinen or Väinämöinen) wooing the maid of Pohjola turns himself into an eagle which, after a fight, conquers a mighty pike in the Tuonela river and lifts it from the water. The eagle (sometimes the groom in human form once more) nevertheless tastes the pike by nipping off the tips of its pectoral fins before taking the fish as a gift to his mother-in-law.

The slicing of a pike and certain other fish also occurs in *The Origin of Fire*, but in a different meaning. Closer to the "breast-cutting" motif is the fishing up of the maid Vellamo. A fisherman catches a strange, unrecognisable fish; it cannot be a maiden because it does not have a plait. The fisherman says he will cut his catch up for his meal, but then the fish leaps out of the boat and back into the water. When it is a safe distance from the boat, it announces that it is a maiden and that it was intending to becoming the fisherman's wife, not something for him to eat.

In the opinion of N.A. Krinichnaya there is a direct link between the maid in the form of a totemic animal and the bride in the wooing songs, even so that the suitor's task of catching a pike in the Tuonela river symbolises their betrothal (Krinichnaya 1986, 92). If this is the case, the fight between the groom disguised as an eagle and the pike in the Tuonela river is nothing but the curbing of a bride who has assumed the guise of a fish. In some of the Archangel Karelian variants of the song this motif has become a titanic battle between the representatives of two opposing natural forces, water and air. In the variant sung by Arhippa Perttunen the suitor is Väinämöinen, who, having lifted himself onto the wings of a bird, flies to the Tuonela river. Väinämöinen, disguised as an eagle, spots a great scaly pike and sinks his talons into it. The pike tries to drag him under the water and the eagle tries three times to lift the pike into the air. On the third attempt he is successful, and he flies with his prey to the top of a pine tree, where he begins to taste his catch, "to tear off the tips of its breasts" (SKVR I:1, 469, 291-317). As a whole this battle between two mighty creatures is reminiscent of the fight between Ilmollinen and his bride in various guises. As has already been mentioned, this duel is in some variants presented as one of the suitor's tasks. The only difference is that the variant from Aunus describes not a fight between two giants but the cunning and resourcefulness of two beings clever at turning themselves into something else; what is more, one of them keeps trying to eat the other, as some variants clearly state.

The duel between the eagle and the pike may well be regarded as a metaphor for the erotic curbing of the bride. This is indicated by the central motif, *riipiä, riisua, riistää rintapäitä* 'tear off, uncover, remove the tips of her breasts'. This bride-curbing motif is rather common in the archaic folklore of many peoples. One version of it is easy to observe in the section of the *Dunai bylina* already presented in which the hero intends to cut out the breasts of a maiden he has conquered, even though he ends up marrying her.

The breast-cutting motif thus clearly ties in with the concepts of curbing the bride and through it with the idea of joining her to the groom's family. On the other hand this unusual concept of initiation might in the earlier days of matrilocal marriage have been founded on the idea of incorporating the groom into the bride's totem family, because the tips of the totemic animal's breasts are eaten by the eagle, i.e. the groom. The idea of eating was presumably linked with the concept of the essence of being brought under a new totem. "Eating creates physical contact with the eaten," writes V. Propp of initiation rites. Incorporation with the totem animal and the totem family involves being eaten by it. It is not known whether the initiate himself ate a piece of the meat of the animal that had eaten him. This is always the case in myths, as we can see. "A myth narrative lives on for longer than a rite..." The myth thus contains later features, either misunderstood or distorted (Propp 1986, 229). Propp also goes on to demonstrate what kinds of new properties must be possessed by the person returning from the "womb" of the totemic animal.

The original context of quotation referring myths and rites above was rite by which boys of a certain age were initiated as men with the right to establish a family; there is no mention of a wedding rite. The ethnologists have not observed among the Karelians or other Baltic-Finnish peoples any rites such as those described by Propp, or indeed any other initiation rites, even though all groups have had numerous rites for the transition of individuals from one age and social group to another. Such rites are those attached to birth, baptism, confirmation and marriage. It is particularly significant that the wooing songs of Aunus and Ladoga Karelia have preserved faint traces of rites of transition in which the "mother of all mothers", the Mistress of Hiitola, ate the initiate. A version of wooing by Ilmollinen the smith noted down at Impilahti in 1884 describes how the mother of the bride proposes to the smith, who is in the process of carrying out difficult tasks:

Äsken annan tyttäreni	My daughter is to be given
ku astunet Hiien eukon	if you go along the few
harvoi hambahie myö.	teeth of the devil's wife.
Sitte häi astuupi	
da ajatteloo;	Then she goes and thinks;
Se akka leukahie lekahutti,	The wife moved her jaws,
sinne seppä sisäh mäni...	And in went the smith...
(SKVR VII:1, 374, 76-81.)	

The only way the smith could free himself from the mistress's womb was to build a workshop and forge a knife with which to slit open her stomach. Then at last he got his bride. There is no doubt that this motif and its variants tie in directly with the folk tale tradition, in which, according to Propp, such motifs reflect rites long since forgotten joining people to a new social group.

Ritual food plays a very significant role in the rites – especially the wedding rites – preserved right up to the present day. It is no coincidence that many of the focal points in this complex entity have to do with feasting and eating, and often with special dishes of mythological origin.

The ritual eating of a totemic animal, or certain parts of it, is reflected rather clearly in the wooing songs and even the song about the Vellamo maiden. In them the eater is the groom, who has to join his wife to his totem. In *The Kojonen Song*, by contrast, the bride's breasts are eaten by her mother. This is abnormal. The traditional motif of joining the spouse to the new family is spitefully turned upside down. At the same time the symbolic eating of the totem has in ballad-like manner turned into concrete eating, and to make it all seem even more natural, Kojonen bakes pies out of his wife's breasts. Many of the variants describe Kojonen's arrival at his mother-in-law's with the presents as the traditional visit following the wedding such as was made in real life. Even in the ballad an excuse is often trumped up for the bride's absence from the visit, where the focus was, in accordance with the prevailing custom, on feasting (Surhasko 1977, 200-201).

The closing episode of the ballad is a unique apotheosis of the hero's lack of morals. It describes how the wife's unsuspecting mother receives the presents supposedly sent her by her daughter from her new son-in-law, in keeping with the custom that prevailed right up to recent times. By feeding his mother-in-law with pies filled with her daughter's breasts Kojonen insults the family from which he has taken his bride. He presumably had evil intentions even while courting the maiden, and he has now put them into practice. The final blow is dealt the mother by the female (or male) slave who is witness to the events and who warns her mistress against eating the pies, but without revealing the reason. The mistress tries to persuade the slave to speak by promising her various rewards to solve the riddle of the mysterious food, but the slave is silent until the mistress promises to give her son as the slave's husband and half or all of the household. Only then does the slave reveal that her mistress has eaten the flesh of her own daughter.

The ballad usually ends with the revelation of Kojonen's evil act, though it sometimes goes on to describe the mother-in-law's shock, and sometimes the miscreant's punishment. Such additions clearly do not belong to the ballad and need not be discussed in the present context.

The *Kojonen ballad* is the story of a luckless girl courted by a malicious suitor only to kill her. The idea does not resemble that of the archaic wooing songs, though it does use many of their motifs. The content and meaning of the motifs change in the ballad and reflect the cruelty and immorality of the hero.

The name of the hero in the *Kojonen Song* and the basic conflict in the ballad have similarities with the name of the hero in the Ivan Godinovich *bylina* and its basic conflict, in which a wife just won is killed. Its motivation basically derives from mythic concepts of killing a witch-wife representing an alien totem family, which is quite different from the motivation of Iivana Kojonen in the Karelian-Finnish ballad.

According to Matti Kuusi this question was not understood when the conflict in the *bylina* was transferred to a new ethnic environment, the result of which is the senseless cruelty of Iivana Kojonen to his new wife. The ballad in fact represents a different form of artistic awareness from that of epics, and its themes concentrate not on the heroic deeds of the main character but on conflicts arising in everyday family life.

In Ingrian folklore the name of the hero in the ballad about the killing of the young wife has been borrowed for the hero of another, more recent ballad in which the hero kills his existing wife in order to marry a younger one. The hero is, however, severely punished – the girl refuses to come to him because he is a murderer, and so her children remain orphans. The name of Iivana Kojonen is occasionally found as that of evil-doers in other songs, too.

NOTES

This article is based on an earlier version published in Finnish under the title *Kojosen pojan kosinta ja venäläinen bylina Ivan Godinovits*, which appeared in *Kolme on kovaa sanaa. Kirjoituksia kansanperinteestä*. P. Laaksonen and S-L. Mettomäki (eds.) *Kalevalaseuran vuosikirja 71*. Helsinki. 1991. p. 49-64.

1. SKVR I:1, 551-572, SKVR II, 130-142, SKVR III-IV, around 80 in all, SKVR V:1, 46-57, 205-278, SKVR VI, 167, SKVR VII, 510-534, SKVR XIII:1, 391-423)

2. Karelskie epičeskie pesni 1950: 16, 29, 73, 87, 105; 1976: 62, 72, 77, 100, 130, 132.

3. See e.g. the folk tale *Viisas neito*, 'The Wise Maid' Andreyev's type no. 875: Sobolevski 1825, 199-201.

HENNI ILOMÄKI

Song in Ritual Context: North Karelian Wedding Songs

While journeying on foot through the Karelian songlands in 1828, Elias Lönnrot arrived at a farm at Potoskavaara in Kitee. He there postponed his departure for a couple of days, because a boy in the neighbourhood was about to be married and he was invited to join in the festivities. He later regretted that he had not witnessed the leaving ceremonies at the bride's home. He nevertheless gives a lively description of the wedding at the bridegroom's home in the account of his travels entitled *Vaeltaja* (Lönnrot 1979). It appears that the arrival ceremony began with a round of greetings, and that the marriage broker leading the accompanying guests embarked on a ritual conversation with the receivers: "How do you fare, stranger?" "In peace go we all." On inquiring of the newcomers' names and business, the broker "said he had found and captured a sizable eagle that had been running wild about his hen's nest; the hen had not tried to escape from the eagle, even though she could have freed itself from its talons. She was thought to be bewitched, and since the eagle had been captured, they wished to find out where it came from, and since it had now flown hither, they thought it must have made its home in this region, and that was what they now wished to know." Their travel papers having been inquired of, the wedding folk then sat down at the table, where the meal began with a shot of liquor. The dancing was accompanied by singing, with Lönnrot occasionally playing his pipe. The next morning it was time to distribute the gifts made by the bride, after which money was collected, first for the bride and then "to buy off the church" (Lönnrot 1979, 99-103).

To a man on his travels in the first half of the 19th century, the Kitee wedding was an experience such as he had never witnessed before. Himself a native of the little village community of Sammatti in Western Finland, Lönnrot had set out in search of a different kind of cultural milieu, and the feast he had the honour of attending was all he had hoped for.

Some sixty years later O. Relander, in the periodical *Valvoja*, published an article entitled *Nykyisestä kansanrunoudesta Itä-Suomesta* 'Contemporary Folk Poetry in Eastern Finland' (Relander 1889). In it he pours out his unscientific disappointment in somewhat indignant terms: "The winter

Songs beyond
the Kalevala
Studia Fennica
Folkloristica 2
1994

before last the grandson of Simana Sissonen was married to a girl from the village of Hattupää, and not a single poem was sung at this wedding, nor a single wedding song. At one time the village of Hattupää was by all report a real nest of wedding songs, just as Mekrijärvi is of *rune*-singing." Relander later goes on to say that the people of Ilomantsi still knew the wedding songs but did not use them (p. 403, 409).

According to the wedding customs at Taipale in Liperi noted down by J. Lukkarinen three wedding poems were "said" and "recited" as the young couple entered the wedding house (FLS, Lukkarinen 1909). An inquiry begun in 1956 produced information on a wedding at Lepolahti, Kitee in 1885 at which a man called Antti Toivonen was asked to act as the master of ceremonies and singer. By singing, he urged the people at each table to rise to their feet at the end of the meal and wished fertility on the young couple. (KO, Takala 1956). Toivonen's songs probably were not the ancient wedding songs but church hymns. The traditional wedding songs were usually sung by women. Wedding poetry in Kalevala metre was at that time still only to be found in the remote northerly regions of Archangel Karelia (Sarmela 1981, 27).

Why, then, did the wedding tradition live on in Eastern Finland right up to the beginning of the 20th century, and thereafter rapidly die away?

A wedding was not only a feast or a chance to meet new kinsfolk or to observe how all had aged. The linking of weddings with the establishment of a family was not so much a question of convention as a consequence of the social significance of marriage. The functional ties between the community and its acting unit, the family, were connected with the production of labour and ideological control, and the channelling of people's biological, psychological and socioeconomic needs (Stolte-Heiskanen 1974, 594). The place of men and women in society and the continuation of the line are integrated in the traditional model by the institution of marriage. This was not so much an agreement between two individuals as a transfer of labour from one kin to another (cf. Piha 1964, 23). The price paid for the bride was thus a justified part of the marriage deal (Harva 1941, 35). The purpose of the wedding rite was to detach the bride from the family background in which she had existed so far and to attach her to the kin community of the groom. The wedding ceremonies were a way of trying to ensure the success of the transfer and of guaranteeing the future of the new family unit as part of the kin.

Finland used to have two different wedding traditions: that of the kin community of Savo-Karelia and that of the village community of Western Finland (Sarmela 1981, 17). The rift between the marriage practices in the different regions was influenced by the trend in the economy. From the Middle Ages onwards the Church – to begin with the Roman Catholic and subsequently the Evangelical-Lutheran – also affected the emergence of the wedding rituals in Western Finland (Heikinmäki 1981, 638-639). In the latter half of the 19th century three areas emerged in the wedding traditions of Eastern Finland: many of the archaic practices lived on in Southeast Finland, whereas the Savo-Karelian area, and especially North Savo, assimilated certain new customs while the structure of the wedding remain unchanged. The Orthodox area of Border Karelia from Salmi right up to the southern Ilomantsi villages differed in its customs from the rest of the

Finnish-Karelian area. This area had its own distinctive courting and betrothal rites, the bridal *sauna*, the wedding laments belonging to the Orthodox tradition in other areas, too, the ritual reception of the wedding couple at the bridegroom's home, etc. (Heikinmäki 1981, 640-641). Two different wedding traditions thus flourished side by side in the North Karelian area of Ilomantsi: the Savo-Karelian and the Border Karelian.

Two sorts of weddings

In the Karelian kin community the preservation of the archaic wedding model based on exchange between the two kins was part of the cultural entity. Customs can be retained only if supported by the cultural structure. On the other hand appropriate variation on the practices strengthens a tradition while leaving room for creativity. It was thus possible for two wedding tradition models to exist side by side in the Karelian folklore area; while having much in common, they were to some extent suitably different in their cultural interpretations.

Even Lönnrot already noted in his diary that the wedding rites of the Karelians varied almost from parish to parish. The reason for this was, in addition to the religious background, the wealth and status of the families concerned in the village community. Descriptions of weddings have been recorded not only by scholars but by amateur collectors from the ranks of the ordinary people, too. The time at which the notes were taken to some extent undoubtedly influenced the content of the wedding descriptions. Whether the writer is describing a wedding that took place in his youth or an ordinary wedding held at the time of writing is of no minor significance. The notes do not, however, usually indicate how the wedding customs stand in relation to the time of writing. Only seldom do the notes refer to a particular wedding attended by the writer or his informant. An attempt to date the accounts of weddings is in fact evident only in the texts of reporters who do not belong to the local community. For example, the ethnologist Ilmari Manninen dates his account as applying to a wedding held in Ilomantsi in the 1910s. The description noted down by J. Lukkarinen, who made a study of the Finnish marriage institution, "concerns the customs about 50 years ago".

It can be seen from the descriptions of wedding customs in the collections of the Ethnographical Section of the National Board of Antiquities and the Folklore Archives of the Finnish Literature Society that Karelian weddings have always been in two parts, i.e. the leave-taking at the bride's home and the wedding at the groom's home (cf. Heikinmäki 1981, 306). A graphic example of the differences in the wedding festivals of Orthodox and Lutheran families is the collection sent in by A. Turunen in 1912 giving descriptions of two Ilomantsi weddings.

Of the two accounts, the fairly extensive one based on information given by people from the Huhus area represents the Lutheran marriage tradition, and the shorter text on the village of Hattuvaara the Greek Orthodox tradition. Both wedding ceremonies have certain episodes in common and comparable individual features. A church service is not a firmly established element of either. At Hattuvaara it was, according to Turunen, always performed after the wedding, at Huhus often in between the leaving ceremony and the wedding, sometimes immediately before the leaving ceremony. The events may be compared as follows:

Event	Orthodox Hattuvaara	Lutheran Huhus
inquiring after bride	father inquires after or chooses bride (agreed with son)	bride chosen from previous acquaintance, son has already sought girl's permission to propose (opinions of the *konttiämmä* village gossips also sought)
proposal	father as marriage broker, makes proposal on son's behalf, future fathers-in-law drink together, usually on a Saturday	groom and broker (seldom father) propose on a Saturday (Sunday), ritual discourse, broker offers round liquor
interim stages	son goes to see bride after father's "bear round"	bride comes to look over groom's home, day of banns decided
		banns party on first of three banns days at bride's home, liquor (later coffee) and tobacco served
		groom and broker arrive at bride's home for marriage agreement, date of leavetaking decided, payment of "head money"
leave-taking at bride's home	groom, broker and any relatives who wish arrive to fetch bride, received as guests, groom offers round liquor, meal, dancing, bride's lamenting, in the morning departure for the wedding, bride's parents stay at home	bride fetched by groom, broker (groom's brother), arrival in evening with liquor, household and bride go about their work as if nothing is happening; meal, departure for groom's home the same or the next day, bride reluctant to go, brothers, sisters and parents accompany her
wedding at groom's home	groom's parents receive them on steps with	groom's parents on the steps to receive them

Lamenting over a bride at a Vuokkiniemi wedding. On the left is the lamenter, on the right the bowing bride. Photo: I. Marttinen 1908. (FLS 5404).

bread and taper; bride bends to the ground and touches her mother-in-law's feet with her brow, meal, dancing; first night in out-building, mother-in-law prepares bed, wakes them in the morning

with bread and grain; meal, drinking, dancing, administrations of the bride's attendant, lap-boy, distribution of gifts, dancing, drinking of morning toast; bride's attendant wakes bridal couple, breakfast, food sent by bride's home

after wedding

banns read three times on same day, church ceremony, a week later bride's parents arrive to "break the oven", two weeks later couple visit bride's home to fetch the dowry

The events in these two slightly different accounts both break down into the episodes of choosing the bride, the betrothal, the leave-taking ceremony and the wedding; these are the main episodes of the Karelian wedding. The differences between the accounts possibly derive partly from the points stressed by the informants in speaking to the collector, but there are also some real differences.

The most fundamental difference lies in the role of the parents in the Hattuvaara and Huhus marriages. The role of the parents in archaic communities used to be vital in choosing the bride. The leave-taking ceremony then followed directly from the offer of marriage, or after only a short period (Sarmela 1981, 18). Betrothals, the festivities surrounding the first reading of the banns, and marriage agreements are a later addition to the chain of events making up the marriage rite. Further proof of the unstable nature of the tradition in this respect is the fact that, according to Turunen, at Huhus the proposal was also called the "engagement" and "the visit as bridegroom". This event involved ritual discourse, which in the Ilomantsi village of Melaselkä took the following form: "Before we went just as guests, now we went as the groom." "I've been waiting for a bridegroom and death to carry me off ever since a daughter was born." (KO, Manninen 1916.) There is a mention in Lutheran Liperi of 'coming to hire a serving girl'. Betrothal gifts were offered, and a promise of being "hired for life" (FLS, Lukkarinen 1909). The payment of head money regarded as binding was, according to Turunen, previously made at the leave-taking ceremony and only "at a later date" at the making of the marriage agreement. A cursory item of information was recorded in Kitee in the late 1950s according to which a 'sheath proposal' (in which the boy slipped his knife into the sheath of the girl of his choice) was also known in the locality (FLS, Eino Mähönen, KJ 41:16905. 1957). The custom is, however, better known in South Karelia.

A vital part of the leave-taking ritual was, as far as the bride was concerned, the custom of lamenting maintained among the Greek Orthodox members of the population. For her the parting then lasted several days, the entire lamenting period (FLS, Lukkarinen 1909). A Lutheran bride is also reported as having cried upon departing for the wedding at her bridegroom's home (KO, Turunen KO. 584. 1912), but ritual lamenting was not practised by the Lutherans. Shortly after the groom's people arrived, it was time to shake hands, i.e. to confirm the marriage deal, to "spread the head", i.e. to dress the girl's hair in the manner of a married woman, and to begin the feast. The serving of spirits at the leave-taking ceremony sometimes took the form of "pulling a grease sledge":

> The grease sledge is now brought in: the bride is brought inside by her kith and kin. Her head is completely covered in a large cloth or scarf called a 'cukkel'. She has a bowl in her hand and on top of it a hand towel folded into a square. They take a few steps at a time. Those inside the room urge her: "Bring, bring!" "How stiff the grease sledge is, it does not move, it must be greased!" They must be given a drink. One of the groom's relatives goes round with a bottle of spirit saying, "Grease, grease!" (KO, Manninen 1916).

The "lap-boy" practice belonging to Huhus weddings was a ritual in which a small boy was for a moment lifted into the bride's arms to ensure that the first child to be born would be a boy. The fertility rites are of archaic origin and weddings form a natural context for them. The marriage rites also incorporated a number of other magic practices, the significance of which is nevertheless thought to have increased as the wedding songs have been forgotten (Sarmela 1981, 19). The communication scheme has thus changed from verbal to symbolical.

The arrival of the bridal couple at the groom's home was a critical moment in the ritual sequence and thus prepared for in various ways. The first meeting of the in-laws and the young wife was a ritually regulated event and its significance vital to smooth relationships within the new collective. The first words might be spoken on a step covered with fur: "I sow not barley, I sow happiness" (FLS, Turunen 1932). The greeting combines the importance of grain and success; the greeters would carry a barley sowing basket, bread and a taper (KO, Manninen 1961).

The attendance of the bride's parents at the wedding in the manner of Lutheran Huhus made the archaic custom of "breaking the oven" (*pät'sin sorranda*) unnecessary (FLS, Turunen 1932). The name refers to the parents' visit to the groom's home after the wedding. At these weddings the young couple were woken by the bride's attendant and not the groom's mother, as at Hattuvaara weddings. At weddings conducted in the orthodox manner, too, the marriage broker went with the groom to fetch the bride, even though the father had acted as mediator. It is thus possible to discern several strata of wedding practices: features of archaic kin weddings and of more modern village weddings, the community orientation of which was more marked than the family (Sarmela 1981, 16). The influence of the religious orientation and with it the varying importance of the kin is evident at the level of the ritual sequence and related customs. At the verbal level, too, i.e. in the wedding poems acting as ritual texts, it is possible to observe variation, divergent interpretations within the text, and meanings that appear to be conflicting which were most likely not founded on religious background factors.

The ritual texts of the wedding drama

Wedding poems in Kalevala metre giving verbal expression to the progress of the ritual were an integral part of the wedding ceremony in Savo-Karelia. The singers were relatives of the bridal couple, women rather than men. Singing was not part of the role of either the bride or the groom, though the former was in earlier times expected to know the necessary laments.

One problem as regards source criticism of the majority of the wedding poems recorded is that the notes were not made in an "authentic" situation; persons with a command of the poems dictated them to a collector or jotted them down themselves, quite out of context. Many of the singers had a wide repertoire, and by comparing these recordings with the descriptions of wedding customs it has been possible to determine with some certainty the stages of the wedding festival at which the poems were performed. One concrete result of the wedding was from the bride's point of view the elimination of opposition between the families. This process is also manifest in the texts of the rites.

The singing part of the wedding began in the poetry of both North and Border Karelia with the groom's preparation for his journey. The lines "Are you off to be a groom, are you thinking of getting married? Leave your childhood on the *sauna* benches, your life so far on the *sauna* switch" (SKVR VII:2, 2815) demonstrate the link between the poem and the ancient practice of immediate betrothal once the proposal has been made. On setting out to make his proposal, the groom thus journeyed to a strange village or farm, and he could not be sure what sort of reception he would get. Many of the poems performed by the bride's family clearly belittle the groom;

the seeds of battle between the two kins have thus been sown. What mattered were the terms of the deal between the two families: what the bride would bring with her and the economic benefits the groom would offer her in return.

The wedding songs performed by the bride's family include numerous texts in which the proposed marriage is placed open to doubt, even though it has already been agreed upon. For example, the poems *Suostutko neito sulhoisis* 'Maiden, do you accept your betrothed?' and *Läksi kukka kulkemahan* 'Go walking, flower' invariably view the conditions in the groom's home in a negative light. The poems in the bride's repertoire often correlate with mournful poems: "I leave my marshes, leave my lands...I go forth luckless..." or "I would be better off, I would rather be in the sleigh of a running fox, embraced by a wandering bear than in the bridal sleigh of a man with a fox-skin cap". The irrevocability of the separation is reflected in the poems sung by her relatives by way of reply: "Poor girl, did you really imagine you were only going for a short time?" Three variants of the poem *Itke itke meijän neito,* 'Cry, cry, our maiden' (SKVR VII:2, 2916, 1918, 1928) have been recorded in the North Karelian songlands that stress the importance of the bride's being aware of the separation: "If you don't cry now, you will only cry the next time you come here". The words do not necessarily refer to ritual lamenting but to the necessity of grieving.

Ritual lamenting is a more recent practice than the performance of wedding songs. Lamenting was, however, such a natural part of the orthodox wedding rites that information on the survival of this practice has been recorded in fairly recent times. Lamenting by the bride is mentioned in almost every description of an orthodox wedding in North Karelia recorded at the turn of the century. Whereas the wedding songs usually deal with the relationships between the two families about to be joined through marriage, the laments regulated the relationships between the bride and the members of her own family. They were for this reason mostly performed at the leave-taking (cf. Nenola-Kallio 1981, 60).

The lamenting might begin soon after the betrothal and continue with the help of lamenters for weeks at a time (KO, Turunen 1932). According to some documents the bride visited her relatives accompanied by a lamenter with a "tear cloth" at an angle across her face, while the lamenter collected money (KO, Guseff & Reponen). In most cases, however, the lamenting centred on the bridal *sauna* and the leave-taking proper, when the bride would lament with her veil around her head (KO, Turunen 1912). In addition to pouring out her affection for members of her family, the bride would touch on the facts of her position. The words of the lament accompanying the undoing of her plait were prompted by the fact that a married woman had two plaits, an unmarried girl only one (FLS, Turunen 1932). Upon the arrival of the groom and his party the groom might be asked about life in his home and his own character in lines resembling a lament.

The emotions expressed in the wedding ritual included: longing, strangeness, and the vital need to adapt. The move to a new kin community was for the bride not without its problems, and she could not be in the least certain of striking up stable new relationships. Whereas the wedding laments were personally improvised poetry and only loosely patterned expression, the wedding poems were a genre of tradition bound

The Karelian wedding was bilocal: here the wedding party leaves the bride's home on its way to the bridegroom's farm. Photo: I.K. Inha 1894 (FLS 201).

to the community. It may be assumed that they contained information on the concepts of the singer community (cf. Holmberg-Harva 1930, 97-98). As in the wedding customs, there were regional differences in these ritual texts.

The wedding songs in relation to the community

The wedding songs touch on a number of themes and aspects of the life of the community. *Kylyvirsi* (a poem describing how the groom prepares for the wedding), *Tulovirsi* and its variations (a poem accompanying the arrival of the bridal couple at the groom's home) in the repertoire of the groom's family and *Vävyn virsi* (describing the son-in-law's arrival at the bride's home) performed by the bride's kin are examples of serious ritual poetry. The lines sung by the bride to her relatives and childhood companions on departure are, by contrast, lyrics moulded by the language of laments and personal expression in the first person singular. Some of the poetic discourse at the courting and leave-taking is reminiscent of semi-playful wrangling between the families, while in some the families really do take their measure of one another by speculating on the qualities of the bride or groom or their economic situation.

The idiom of the wedding songs and the metaphors used are to some extent those widely used in Kalevala metric poetry, but in places they are specifically tied to the ritual context. Closer examination of the ritual texts reveals a dimension that may on first hearing seem out of place in the ceremonial situation. For some of the wedding poems clearly display the impact of the economic reality on the collective worldview.

Concepts bound to the hunting culture and peasant stock raising of North Karelia feature as elements in some of the poems. *Kylyvirsi*, for example, may be examined alongside an account of preparing for a hunt. Setting off to propose to a girl was, as we have already seen, at one time a somewhat hazardous venture through which the static situation prevailing in the kin community was placed open to change. Among the central themes of *Kylyvirsi* are the real and magical preparations undertaken by the groom. In a variant sung by the widow of Jyri Solohmainen of Ryökkylä in Ilomantsi "the groom, my excellent brother" is given magic protection "so that he cannot be harmed by the darts of witches or the steel blades of seers" (SKVR VII:2, 2820). The seer or hunter would prepare himself in a similar manner. One concrete preparation was the taking of a *sauna* bath. In the words of one wedding hymn:

> This morning I rose early/I washed and cleansed myself/I wiped my little cottage/I took the rubbish out./I gathered rocks from the rapids,/firewood from the heath,/ I heated the honey-sweet *sauna*/ for the honey-sweet bather,/I soaked the *sauna* switch ready/on top of the honey-sweet stones./ I called to my groom to come and bathe.
> (SKVR VII:2, 2820)

After the *sauna* the groom was dressed in a fine linen shirt "on skin free from sweat, on body without dirt" (SKVR VII:2, 2815). The careful preparations and ritual cleansing are, at the level of expression, reminiscent of the chants accompanying the cleansing rites of the hunter. One common opening phrase in the hunting chants of Border Karelia is, for example:

> I get up early in the morning/I wash and cleanse myself (I wipe my little cottage,/ I wash my little gun,/I set off into the forest.
> (SKVR VII:5, 3218)

Preparations were made for a critical ordeal before setting off both to propose and to hunt. Protection was sought against envy and malevolence, and an attempt had to be made to ward off failure. Formally the position of the suitor was akin to that of the hunter: both were setting off to fetch something. The nature of the "catch" that would be brought home was by no means certain on departure, and the trip could well end in disaster. It has been pointed out that the archaic wedding ritual is reminiscent of a hunting drama (cf. Sarmela 1978).

The ritual texts of the wedding ceremony in places recall the poems sung at bear-killing feasts. These feasts were sometimes called "bear's weddings", at which respect was paid to the slain bear and a person of the opposite sex was dressed up as a bride or groom. Generally speaking a bear is "fetched game", like a bride. Just as the Liperi groom was asked "How did you know to come here, stupid,/your horse's muzzle found the road/to this splendid home,/ this magnificent manor" (SKVR VII:2, 2838), so the hunter is asked in the bear-feast poems by the mistress of the woods: "How did you know to come here, stupid,/your horse's muzzle found the road?" (SKVR VII:5, 3376.) The groom arriving home with his bride was further greeted in Ilomantsi with the song: "Where have you put your catch,/taken the little game you caught?/Maybe you left it on the ice/dropped it through a hole in the ice?" (SKVR VII:2, 3034). The person actually bringing home the slain bear was also asked at the bear feast: "Where have you put your catch,/taken the little game you caught?/Maybe you left it on the ice/dropped it through a hole in the ice?" (SKVR VII:5, 3399). According to the reply in the wedding poem the bride, i.e. the catch, was "carried in the elk skier's sleeve, under the bear-slayer's arm" (SKVR VII:2, 3034).

There are other parallels, too, in the ritual texts of weddings and bear feasts. The words of the son-in-law's song ask: "Can the son-in-law enter the house/without removing the ceiling beams,/without moving the walls at the side,/without upsetting the wall at the end/without removing the wall with the door,/without raising the beam o'er the door?" (SKVR VII:2, 3012). In a similar way the Nurmes bear-feast poem reckons of the bear: "Can the bear enter the house/without removing the door frame,/without raising the beam o'er the door,/without lowering the threshold?" (SKVR VII:5, 3399). Although the parallel between the catch and the groom differs from that between the bride and the game, there is nevertheless a similarity in the contexts of the songs. In both cases the songs are performed by members of the community not taking part in the trip but waiting at home, and persons living at the suitor's destination.

Although hunting incantations are as a rule men's tradition, women might also be supposed to have been waiting to receive the bear (though there are some restrictions on this). Both cases involve a fleeting visit by a member of an outside community: the groom arrives to put his suit or for the duration of the leaving-taking, and the presence of the slain bear ends with the ceremony. It seems obvious that the similarities in the elements of the poems sung at weddings and bear feasts spring from the similarity in the situations, and not from any likening of a bride to a bear. It is on the other hand clear that ritual behaviour is not purposely inexplicable or mysterious and that it is determined according to models formed on the basis of reality. Bear hunting and marriage were both undertakings of vital economic importance to the well-being of the community. Both situations were, in addition, ritually delicate, involving an element of danger brought about by a decisive change. The catch brought home from the forest and the bride transferred from one farm to another were in the same critical state in which it was deemed necessary to seek protection against harmful forces. The pressing nature of the occupational behaviour may well have acted as a model-creating factor.

Our attention is at this point caught by the fact that the lines appearing in both the wedding songs and the bear-feast poems are missing from the material from Border Karelia. This is not surprising in the sense that bear-feast poetry was not known in this area either, and nor was the bear a game animal there (cf. Sarmela 1972).

There are also other signs in the vocabulary of the poetry of the influence of hunting culture on the formation of the wedding rite texts. One of the most conspicuous spells of this is the use of game terms to refer to the bride, such as "our pine marten has been shown, our catch presented" (SKVR VII:2, 2832), "show us your pine marten" (SKVR VII:2, 3003). The girl is in the words of *Kokkovirsi* 'The Eagle Song' (according to which an eagle carries off the finest hen, goose or other bird in the flock) "fine of feather, proud of plume" (SKVR VII:2, 2882), she is exhorted to walk "with the steps of a goose", to clap "with the feet of a teal" (SKVR VII:2, 2995), and to marry as in "make an alliance, my little bird" (SKVR VII:2, 2948-2951). The tender names in a diminutive form are comparable to the words used to address game birds in the hunting spells and reflecting the respectful attitude of the hunter to his prey. Appellations of this kind are clearly more common in the wedding poetry of Archangel Karelia (e.g. Harva 1929).

Both the groom and the parents-in-law are in the bride's replies referred to as a bear or a wolf. For example, "the groom is as at home with me as a bear in the forest" (SKVR VII:2, 1246), "A bear is the master of the house, father-in-law of the manor, the mistress of the house a wolf in the kitchen" (SKVR VII:2, 2929). The groom is also described as being like a wolf: "The groom has the gums of a wolf, bear's gut under his arm" (SKVR VII:2, 2898). The attitude to the beasts of the forest expressed in these names is the opposite of what we saw above: these beasts inspire fear and represent a strange element, i.e. the forest. The parents-in-law or groom are described via the attributes of wild beasts. The gulf between the families is expressed via the unfamiliarity existing between the forest (the groom's kin community) and the village (the bride's own family).

The difference between the two attitudes is clear when we see that, for example, the groom is in the son-in-law's song compared to a bear that has been slain, and that both are treated with respect (as coming from another community). The beasts of the forest are indeed frightening creatures to be treated with enmity by the stock raiser. To the hunter the forest was a familiar element, to the stockman alien, though vital for his cattle to graze in. He sends his cows from the village out into the forest, hoping that they will return in the evening to their familiar surroundings. For him the forest was a concept outside the village, a world distinct from that around him. Associated with the forest are beasts that threaten the cattle, wolves and bears. These animals have thus acquired a negative hue in the oral tradition to do with cattle. In the wedding poetry they are overt symbols of all that is negative. By naming them it is thus possible to describe the parents-in-law in a negative way, because like the beasts, they represent an unknown element: a strange family.

The comparison of the groom to a wolf is an even more outspoken reference to the stock-raising culture. While the bride is, in accordance with the hunter's way of thinking, regarded as game, the groom is regarded as a hunter, whose attitude to his prey was one of respect. The groom-bride relationship in accordance with the stock-raising culture may be likened to the relationship between the wolf and the cattle: the groom is "the eater of bones, the biter of meat, the sucker of blood from the lamb" (SKVR VII:3, 1288). The fact that the groom has "the gums of a wolf" or that he "vanquishes the entire forest" does not suggest equality between the spouses. Compared with the role of hunter, the wolf/groom is a negative, active oppressor who is warned against chastising his young wife in public.

The wedding poetry of North Karelia displays elements illustrating the wedding customs of a stock-breeding community alongside the parallels between marriage behaviour and hunting culture. The latter stratum is naturally the more archaic. It is also to be found in the central core of wedding poetry, *Kylyvirsi* and *Vävyn virsi*, i.e. the poems performed at the most important stages in the wedding rite, the betrothal and leave-taking.

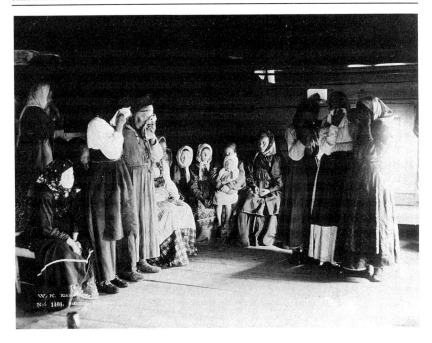

The days of an orthodoxian bride were framed by ritual lamenting. Photo: I.K. Inha 1894 (FLS 18061).

These poems are also the most constant ones for comparing the wedding poetry recorded in different regions. The poems coloured by the stockman's outlook on life are among those addressing the bride and reflect the nature of the community's control: the others, the villagers, etc. compare the groom to a wolf. It is to some extent astonishing that expressions reflecting opposing attitudes may appear at the same weddings and even in the same poems. The singers were probably not, however, aware that they were expressing different attitudes. The vocabulary of the poems was undoubtedly cliché-like, and the singers did not stop to think of the meaning of each individual expression.

We could, in order to generalise somewhat, say that the influence of hunting culture is manifest in the wedding poetry at the level of plot, whereas the stock-raising culture is mainly reflected through individual expressions. The folk economy of North Karelia was until the early decades of this century a mixed one, with hunting and fishing supplementing agriculture (Saloheimo 1970).

In order to create the overall text of the wedding rite the singers drew on the stock of expressions stored in their repertoire. A crystallised verbal composition thus acquired a new interpretation, made all the more natural by the similarity of the ritual context. Flexibility is apparent at both ritual and cultural level: the same constructions were used in the ritual texts of both bear feasts and weddings, and the poetry of the socially significant rite absorbed expressions pointing to the worldview of both a hunting culture and stock raising.

Institutional change

The reflection of cultural reality in the wedding poetry reveals the fundamental fact that the bride and groom were treated not as individuals but as part of their community, as the founders of a new family unit expected to guarantee socioeconomic continuity. The ritual control provided the limits for the roles occupied by the couple. Neither was expected to reveal his/her personality, but to behave in accordance with his/her role. On arriving at the groom's home, the bride was not therefore an individual but a person occupying the role of daughter-in-law.

The wedding song tradition has gradually died out. There are of course a number of reasons why the performing of wedding songs slowly went out of fashion, but the main one is the vanishing of the cultural background. With the change in the occupational reality, the entire worldview has been reshaped and the poems have ceased to be "real". They may have been performed for collectors as "lore", as a reference to times gone by. The performers have in fact usually been elderly people who still remember the ancient wedding practices from their youth. Following the gradual economic change, the ties of kinship surrounding marriage have become looser and there is no longer any need for a transitional rite involving the whole community. The content of the ritual texts has in the process become incomprehensible.

NOTE

This article is based on an earlier version published in Finnish under title *"Tekkä liitto lintuseni..." Häärunoista pohjoiskarjalaisissa häissä*, which appeared in *Runon ja rajan teillä*. S. Knuuttila and P. Laaksonen (eds.) *Kalevalaseuran vuosikirja 68*. Helsinki. 1989. p. 148-160.

LOTTE TARKKA

Other Worlds – Symbolism, Dialogue and Gender in Karelian Oral Poetry

The hero of the Archangel Karelian epic is male: an *uros*, a he-man and a hero. "Man... the clear stud", "old and steady" (SKVR I:1, 89, SKVR I:1, 58), is the active subject of the poetry, in relation to which women are defined as objects or as passive observers. Within the landscape of the poetry the man journeys from this world to the other: transmits and exchanges the world around him for the world beyond. He is the singer, the sage and the traveller; he seeks information, sets off to war, to woo and to hunt. He has forged the heavens from nothing, and a woman from the foam on the sea. He also has a monopoly over the prototype knowledge, the "true facts, the sacred words" (SKVR I:1, 185). The male hero's first-hand knowledge of "the starring of the skies, the setting of the air's edge" stands out in contrast to the knowledge of the ignorants: "the knowledge of children, the memory of womenfolk, not the bearded hero's" (SKVR I:1, 170).

The women in the poetry are objects or means of exchange, brides obtainable for money, but also representatives of the supranormal, associated with death or bestiality. The old woman is a mother or opponent, the young woman to be courted, caught, game. There is but one exception to the predominantly passive image of woman in the heroic epic: the Mistress of Pohjola, the matriarch of the northern otherworldly village and the demonic opponent of the positive male hero, equipped with the power to fly and addressed as a "whore" (SKVR I:1, 79). The masculinity of the heroic epics with its thematic focus on journey does not, however, reduce Kalevala-metric poetry into a reflection of patriarchal mythology produced in a language confined to the masculine (Apo 1988, 8-9; cf. Sawin 1988; Korte 1988, 80-81).

The heroic epic, and the epic in general, opens a narrow and distorted view over the cultural meanings conveyed in folklore: the texts and genres of folklore have meaning only in relation to and through one another. The same images, the same texts and fragments of texts fluctuate throughout the corpus of oral poetry, thus creating a symbolic network or intertextual space which I shall call the epic universe. The epic universe functions as

Songs beyond the Kalevala
Studia Fennica Folkloristica 2
1994

a synthetic level of the genre system. The fictive world is given its fullest elaboration and a panoramic scope in epic poems but the epic universe covers the field of themes addressed in and forms of discourse characteristic of other genres. In its polyphonic narrative structuring, the epic often contains fragments of other genres, thus making direct reference or allusions to other forms of discourse.

The concept of dialogism coined by Mikhail Bakhtin well applies to the oral epic I shall be examining: the narrative structure of Kalevala-metric epic permits a diversity of voices and points of view.[1] Here, the thematic structure of the epic universe is examined side by side with intertextuality that defines its textual essence, and the dialogue of voices and points of view portrayed in the poems. The thematic level of poetry is likewise determined by dialogism: *dia-logos* literally means 'speaking across', communication across existential or social borders.[2]

The epic world is split by a thematic border between this world and the other. Many of the poems tell about looking over or crossing the border, of joining the two worlds by symbolic means. The border is drawn most dramatically at the level of spatial description: the cosmography is visualised in the epic universe as a landscape, the worldview as a view over the world. The landscape of the epic is clearly dualistic, built on the tension between the home and the alien, village and forest, the family homestead and the mythical Pohjola. The spatialised cosmology and localised cosmography, the presentation of the otherworld and this world, chaos and cosmos, as two places between which communication (movement or speech) is possible, is nevertheless only the most obvious of the dualistic structures in the epic universe. The same opposition recurs at the different levels of the worldview represented in the epic: it provides the means for analysing the conceptual and social differences, the borders between culture and nature, self and other, subject and object, man and woman, the local community and the authorities, different religious groups, etc.

In the following, I will be examining the symbolism anchored on the other or supranormal world of Archangel Karelian poetry, and the theme of crossing its borders.[3] The heroic epics, incantations, lyric poetry, laments, wedding songs and women's epic ballads present different and complementary perspectives on the epic universe in which the heroes and heroines each have their own, culturally defined place. I hope to show that the opposition between this world and the other – and the apparent antagonism between male and female figures and universes – is merely apparent. By way of symbolic processes (metaphor and metonymy), borders are trespassed and opposition gives way to dialogue. Just as the different discourses or genres of oral poetry only make sense in terms of each other, in dialogue, the only way of making sense of this world is by way of the other.

The discussion starts with two sets of texts focusing on wooing, wedding and hunting rituals, proceeds to representations of social, symbolic, and actual death and, finally, to an analysis of the complementary imageries of parturition and cosmogony. To conclude, imagery rooted in the seemingly masculine cosmogonical myths is shown to be operative in texts that are highly subjective and autobiographical, making sense of both male and female realities.

Love, death, and difference: marriage and hunt as dialogue

The cosmological border between this world and the other also divides off the poetic world in the texts dealing at manifest level with everyday experience and social relations. Wooing is one of the central themes of epic poetry and poems dealing with courting, wooing, and seduction can be divided into two categories. The poems I call *wooing songs* are male accounts of attempts to approach a bride, and of the terms of their betrothal (*The Courtship, The Gift*). *Seduction songs* is the name I give to poems that tell from a woman's point of view of traumatic encounters in which a suitor approaches her outside the home circle (*The Suitors from the Sea, The Bartered Maiden, The Water-Carrier, The Hanged Maid*). The distinction is thus based on a supposed tendency in, or point of view determined by the voice of the poetic ego or the main actor. In practice, the distinction comes close to the generic subdivision of heroic epics and epic ballads.

The heroes of the wooing songs fail in trying to conquer the inverted and alien otherworld. The only way to conquer the women's world, the "man-eating village, the village that drowns men" is by successfully performing impossible tasks. The central figure Väinämöinen is beaten in the fight for the maiden of Pohjola, is turned down by the virgin of Tuonela, land of the dead, loses the female water spirit Vellamo who has offered to be his wife, and is disillusioned by the coldness of the Golden Bride. A woman singer from the village of Vuonninen crystallises the message: "Väinämöinen can't get married, not even by seeking a bride from the dead. He didn't get a thing from there" (FLS Väinö Kaukonen 1480).

The image of the maiden to be courted presented in wooing songs is coherent in its variability. In a poem of a Latvajärvi singer, the hero loses Vellamo, the daughter of the water spirit Väinö, and sets off to search for her in a realm displaying the many faces of otherworldliness: the water maiden lives in the village of Vuojela (a parallel name for Pohjola), in the whirlpool, "behind nine locks and nearly ten bolts", in "the stretch of blue sea, inside a speckled stone" (SKVR I:2, 758). The maid of Pohjola, the maidens of the Island, the daughters of Hiisi and Tuoni are also equipped with otherworld epithets, addressed as "children of cadaver". All are wooed from across the sea or from "the man-eating village, the village that drowns men" (SKVR I:1, 464). The maiden of Pohjola is a death-child and her body cadaverous:

Synty neiti Pohjolassa,	A maiden was born in Pohjola,
impi kylmässä kylässä,	a virgin in the cold village,
moan kuulu, vejen valivo:	known over lands, choicest of waters:
lihan läpi luu näkyvi,	her bones shine through her flesh,
luun läpi yvin näkyvi.	the marrow shines through her bones.
(SKVR I:1, 692)	

The image has been interpreted as a hyperbolic description of wan beauty and a translucent skin (e.g. Korte 1988, 90-91) even if deathly pallor and coldness was far from the ruddy and sturdy ideal of beauty in Karelia (Lukkarinen 1933, 8.) The meaning of the 'cold village' Pohjola as a concrete graveyard (Paulaharju 1924, 172) nevertheless reveals the macabre tone in the description: the girl is a *pokoiniekka*, a dead person, an inhabitant of the graveyard. The bone visible through her skin, the marrow shining through the bone indicates a body in the process of decay. The golden woman rising out of the fire and forged into a bride, and the maiden of Pohjola appearing in the incantations relating the mythological origin of fire are likewise cold and lifeless, "their skin covered with a sheet of ice" (SKVR I:4, 330):

Neiti tungekse tulesta...	A maiden pushes from the fire...
ois neiti hyvän näköni.	a maiden good to look at.
Heti öissä ensimäissä	But on the very first night
nuoren neitosen keralla	as with the young maiden
niin tuossa lepäelee...	he was having his rest...
Oli kylki kylmäämässä,	His ribs ran cold,
oli hyyksi hyytymässä,	froze as frost,
meren jääksi jäätymässä,	turned into an icy sea,
kiveksi kovoamassa.	turned hard as a stone.
(SKVR I:1, 527)	

According to Maura of Kivijärvi, Väinämöinen "tried by his cunning to forge a maiden in the smithy of the dead" (SKVR I:1, 361b). Thus the bride-to-be is not only associated with fire, ice, and decay: she may also be the product of a man's hand, an artefact. She is always defined by one or more signals of tangible otherness.

There is only one active bride in the epics centering on the hero Väinämöinen, the "watery maid" Vellamo in *The Fishing*. She, too, belongs to the otherworld: she is the daughter of the spirit and master of water, she rises from the sea, and in many poems she is associated with numerous aspects of the otherworldly. When she offers herself to Väinämöinen, she is not recognised as a human bride. She is half human, half animal, but not really either:

Siliahk' on siikaseksi,	Too smooth to be a whitefish,
haaliainen haukiseksi,	too pale to be a pike,
suomuton lohen kalaksi,	too scaleless to be a salmon,
nenätön on ihmiseksi...	too noseless to be a human being.
(SKVR I:1, 261a)	

Räpylätön hylkeheksi,	Too webless to be a seal,
pää rivaton neitoseksi,	too ribbonless to be a maiden,
vyötön Väinön tyttöseksi,	too beltless for a Väinö's daughter,
korviton kotiomaksi...	too earless to be a wife...
(SKVR I:1, 262)	

Neither human nor animal, the maid lies on the liminal zone between central conceptual classifications, among the anomalous, tabooed and the 'sacred' (Douglas 1985 (1966), 55-57; Leach 1964, 38-40; Anttonen 1992). The tension inherent in the meeting is further enhanced by hints at a sexual confrontation of man and animal, and of a kind of cannibalism: (half) an animal offers itself or herself as a man's bride, a man tries to eat a semi-human being. *The Fishing* combines the hero's roles of suitor and hunter-fisher, but Väinämöinen fails in both. The hero remains lonely and hungry and his masculinity is ridiculed: "you fool in your foolishness, feeble minded in your manliness" (SKVR I:1, 264).

The ritual relationship between man and animal is symbolically erotic and productive of prosperity and catch, and it is further articulated in the ritual texts connected with hunting, hunting incantations and bear songs. In the hunting incantations, the keepers or spirits of the forest are most often addressed as women, in affectionate terms: as "honeyed mistresses of the forest" (SKVR I:4, 1249), "white-blooded women, pure mothers of beauty" (SKVR I:4, 1110). The hunter is "the most manly of men" who sets off to court "the gals of the forest" (SKVR I:4, 1125), "to lick the kisses from a feather-maiden, with his tongue of gold" (SKVR I:4, 1250). The erotic overtones of the forest and its game are at their strongest in an incantation by Arhippa Perttunen from Latvajärvi village:

Mieleni minun tekisi,	My mind is made up,
mieli käyä Metsolassa,	I am set on going to Forestland,
metsän neittä naiakseni,	to make love to the maiden of the forest,
metsän mettä juoakseni,	to drink the honey of the forest,
lihoa lehen alaista...	flesh from under the leaves...
Metsä haisuo havulta,	The forest smells of pine,
mies haisee meen maulta.	the man smells of the taste of honey.
(SKVR I:4, 1095)	

The hunter encroaches on the territory belonging to the master of the forest to woo the game, the forest master's 'cattle' or daughters. By describing the beasts of the forest as potential partners and himself as oozing the aroma of "forest land" or "the taste of the forest" (SKVR I:4, 1091), the hunter creates by symbolical means a shared, ritual state in which the relationships between forest and man are set in motion and communication is made possible (see Ilomäki 1986, 54-59). One precondition for the creation of such a state is the perceived isomorphism of the forest community and the human community – nature and culture. In both, contracts and marriages are made, and both have masters and cattle.[4]

The landscape of seduction songs, the epic ballads reflecting the woman's point of view, is split by the border of the family circle: when confronted by a seducer or suitor, the girl is outside the domestic circle, on a journey, in the forest, on the road or the shore. In the poem *The Hanged Maid* the girl is out cutting *sauna* whisks or leaves for the cattle in the forest when she meets a man rising from moist ground, a wet hollow, a ditch, a swamp or a crack in the ground (e.g. SKVR I:1, 231a). In *The Water-Carrier* the girl goes to fetch water; she tarries on the way, spurns a "pure man" who calls to her from a boat to join him, and finally returns home. When she serves the water for her family, she is cursed as a whore and a man-seeker. In *The Bartered Maiden* the girl meets a "traveller" while she is out herding the cattle; the man is a total stranger and his qualities ambiguous, yet he presents himself as the husband to whom the girl has been sold. In *The Suitors from the Sea* the girl waits for suitors from the sea, but the men who appear out of the sea are not necessarily the longed-for "sweet-speaking bridegrooms, men to please my mind" (e.g. SKVR I:2, 1135) but "studs rising from the waves" (SKVR I:2, 1139) "one thumb's-length high" (SKVR I:2, 1142), men displaying supranormal qualities and hinting at mythic imagery:

> Pikku mies merestä nousi
> kultakelkkani perässä,
> kultakirves kelkkasessa...
> (FLS Aili Laanti 1857)

> A tiny man rose from the sea
> drawing a sledge of gold,
> an axe of gold in the sledge...

> Katso, mies merestä nousi,
> Kalevainen kassasmuasta
> Vaski suussa, vaski käässä,
> vaskikihlat kormannossa.
> (FLS Väinö Kaukonen 1551)

> See, a man rose from the sea,
> a groom from the moist ground.
> Brass in his mouth, brass in his hand,
> wedding ring of brass in his pocket.

These male characters described by extraordinary epithets belong to the cast of spirits and culture heroes familiar from incantations relating mythical origins. A man rises from the sea with a bronze helmet about his shoulders, gauntlets in his hands and a sledge behind him, e.g. in the incantation on the origin of fire (SKVR I:4, 130) and of a disease called 'the sting' (SKVR I:4, 849).

The appearance of a man from a swamp or moist ground, a "wet hollow" in *The Bartered Maiden*, is in healing incantations associated chiefly with female figures (e.g. I:4, 846), but in both the sudden entrance from a wet element emphasises the supranormal nature of the figure (see also Anttonen 1992, 65):

> Osmotar orosta nousi,
> Kalevatar kasses-maasta,
> vähän kuollutta parempi,
> kalmalaista kaunihimpi.
> (SKVR I:2, 1155)

> Osmotar rose from the wet,
> Kalevatar from the the moist ground,
> little better than a dead one,
> hardly prettier than the deathly.

The term for the groom in the seduction songs indicates his ambiguous position blurring the categories of gender, nature, and culture. *Osmo* and *Kaleva* signify a bridegroom, but the suffix *-tar* makes the name feminine; both words belong to a broader group of words linking the human groom to the animal world. *Kaleva* also signifies a man of evil intent and practising witchcraft, or a 'sturdy and strong' man, even a giant. (Nirvi 61-64, 74-78; Turunen 1979, 88.) In many senses, the 'partner' for the shepherdess is of the same, ambiguous nature as the maiden Vellamo was for the fishing man. Vellamo's initiative was in her offering of herself, whereas the semi-human grooms go a step further.

The enigmatic poem *Boat in the Cloud* or *Song of the Four Maidens* stands in opposition to the tendency characteristic of seduction songs: now it is the girl who actively sets out to find a husband. The most stable element in the poem is a multilayered vision: there is a cloud in the sky, a boat floating on a drop of water in the cloud, and finally, the "young men, unmarried men, still innocent of liquor" (SKVR I:2, 1219) – the awaited husbands – sailing in the boat. The maids sow an oak, the oak grows and stops the cloud and the boat floating in it. The poem ends with a description of the spinning of a red rope: the rope will calm the sea to make the suitors' journey easier. Through the active role of the maids and the core imagery, *Boat in the Cloud* (1) alludes to love spells (2) and the poem is also known as *Song of Love* (SKVR I:2, 1218):

1

Oli ennen neljä neittä,	Once there were four maidens,
koko kolme morsianta.	a threesome of brides.
Löyettih he lemmen lehti,	They found a leaf of love,
lemmen lehti, tammen lastu.	leaf of love, chip of oak.
Vietih maalle kasvavalle,	They brought it to fertile soil,
orolle ylenevälle.	to growing, moist ground.
Siitä kasvo kaunis tammi,	It grew into a beautiful oak,
yleni vihanta virpi.	it rose as a verdant sprig.
Lehvät ilmoille levitti,	It spread its leaves to the air,
latvat täytti taivoselle,	filled the sky with its top,
piätti pilvet juoksemasta...	stopped the clouds from running...
(SKVR I:2, 1217)	

2

Jos kylven kyllältehen...	If I bathed a plenty...
näillä koivun lehväsillä,	with these leaves of birch,
sata haaran latvasilla.	with these hundred-branched tops.
Kasvo tammi taivosalle,	An oak grew into the skies,
vesa ilmoille yleni.	a sapling rose to the air.
Siitä otin oksasia,	I cut its branches,
tavottelin varpasia,	reached for its twigs,
leikkelinp' on lehväsiä,	clipped the leaves,
josta taitan taikavastan,	for my whisk of magic:
jolla lemmen lievittelen...	with it I will soothe the love...
(SKVR I:4, 1834)	

The function of the oak is the same as that of the tree from which *sauna* whisks are made for the ritual bath increasing the girl's sexual and social desirability. For the bath, water was fetched from marshland, and the *sauna* whisks assembled from three twigs of three trees, and tied together with a red rope (SKVR I:4, 1817). The whisks and water needed also provide a hint to the interpretation of the seduction songs: when the girl returned from the forest, from making whisks or fetching water, her family accused her of man-seeking paraphrased as "pursuing the red rope" (SKVR I:2, 1196).

The course of a woman's life ensured by love magic is clear: "to the husband's place, from the husband's place to the land of the dead" (SKVR I:4, 1820), from one otherworld to another. The set-up in love spells is reminiscent of the hunting imagery of the masculine wooing songs: the girl is not resignedly waiting but active and aggressive, taking her course independently, a huntress. The red rope of the *Boat in the Cloud* and the red rope of the love bath live on as the trap wire of hunting incantations (SKVR I:4, 1181), the whisks as the "honeyed twigs" of the trap:

Lännestä lähetä pilvi...	Send a cloud from the west...
Saa nyt vettä, saa nyt mettä	Let the rain fall, a rain of honey

metisestä taivosesta.	from the honeyed skies.
Sima pilvestä pirota	Drop the honey-dew from the cloud
varvulleni keskiselle.	on my middle-twig.
Muut tässä on vihannat varvut,	Other twigs are verdant here,
vaan yksi on metinen varpu...	but only one twig is of honey...
joka on tyvin taivosehen,	the one with its root toward the sky,
latvoin laskettu lumehen,	the top laid down in the snow,
latva pihtiä pitävi...	the top holding the trap fork...
(SKVR I:4, 1183)	

The descriptions of quest for a husband and for game further assimilate the imageries of hunting (2) and love raising (1) spells:

1

Nouse, lempi, liehumah,	Rise, my love, to float,
nouse auvo astumah!	rise, my luck, onto your feet!
Tuoos miehet tuonempaata,	Bring the men from out there,
etsi miehet etempäätä,	search for men from afar,
etsi saalta saarekselta,	search from hundred islets,
linnalta yheksänneltä.	from the ninth of castles.
Miehen mieltä kääntämäh,	To turn the mind of a man,
aivoja asettamah!	to set a man's brain!
(SKVR I:4, 1822)	

2

Oles mulla oppahana,	Come and guide me,
soatappa tuolla saareksella,	come and see me to the islet,
tuolla kummulla kuleta...	take me to the hillock...
Tuuos vilja tuonnempoa,	Bring the game from out there,
etsi on etempääkin...	search for game from afar...
Poikki Pohjolan joesta	Across the Pohjola river
silkki sillaksi rapoa,	throw silk as a bridge,
punalanka portahaksi...	a red rope as a ladder...
Saata tuolla saareksella	See me to the islet,
miehen etsivän etehen,	be a guide for the searching man,
että saalis saataisihin...	for him to have his catch...
(SKVR I:4, 1135)	

The fragment of the love spell begins with an allusion to the bear song (the "luck rises to its feet" in the same words as the bear is asked to rise from its hide, e.g. SKVR I:4, 1209) and ends with a variation on the words of the trap-setter: the man's mind is "turned", like the game's head is turned towards the trap; the man's brain is "set" (*aivoja asettamah*), like the hunter's lot and hunting luck are "set" (*arvoja asettamah*) in incantations alluding to the mythical division of prosperity and luck (SKVR I:4, 1125). The woman's active search for a husband can thus be presented as a form of hunt: hunting in the actual sense of the word carries sexual and gentle overtones, and erotic manoeuvres hide aggression amounting to killing the catch.

The descriptions and addresses of game as female in hunting incantations also apply to the bear hunting songs. At the feasting rites following the

River scenery near Kiimasjärvi, southern Archangel Karelia. Photo: I.K. Inha 1894 (FLS 9835).

slaying of the bear the gender set-up is nevertheless gradually reversed. Singled out in the forest, and especially when slain, the bear is symbolically transformed into a man, and the hunter starts a dialogue 'master to master', 'man to man' (see esp. SKVR I:4, 1210). The bear feast follows the scheme of a wedding ritual, and the slain bear plays the role of the groom.[5] The women awaiting the hunters returning with their catch greet the bear: "I have awaited you as a young maiden awaits her husband, as the red-cheeked her spouse" (SKVR I:4, 1241).

In accordance with the analogy of the wedding and the bear feast, the relationship between the male hunter and the 'male' bear in the bear songs is analogous to that of the ritual relation between the *patvaska* (the ritual specialist combining the roles of a sage and match-maker) and the groom in the wedding. The hunter bargains with the spirit of the game or the "master of the forest" (e.g. SKVR I:4, 1249, SKVR I:4, 1113), and acts as mediator with the otherworld sources of prosperity, like the *patvaska* trying to bring together two families in and of this world.[6] At the bear feast the bear is thus temporarily transferred away from its natural context, the forest community, and made a member of the human community. This is, however, only a transient state: the bear feast ends with a series of rites at which the bear's skull is boiled, returned to the forest, and placed on a sacrificial tree. In the final rite the bear is once again addressed in terms of endearment and its symbolic gender reverts again to the female: back in the forest, the anonymous bear is a maiden to be courted. (Tarkka 1990a, 248-249; Ilomäki 1986, 59, 117-123.)

The relationship between woman and bear depicted in the spells and incantations for cattle breeding is opposite to that of the bear songs: the bear is no longer a hoped-for bridegroom, "the forest apple" (SKVR I:4, 1248) but the worst enemy of woman and her cattle, "the forest master's

cur" (SKVR I:4, 1441). The stock breeding theme may nevertheless encourage associations between bear, groom and seducer. One of the seduction songs, *The Bartered Maiden*, begins with a situation that would in
reality create a need for a spell to drive the bear away from the grazing
cattle. The girl is going off to tend her cattle and lets the cows out to graze
in the woods. The frame of the narrative poem and the context of situation
for the spell may be expressed word for word with the same imagery: "I
let my cows out into the grove, my hundred-horns out into the aspens"
(SKVR I:2, 1153, SKVR I:4, 1364). On the surface, *The Bartered Maiden*
appears to tell of a herder girl who meets her groom-to-be in the forest. It
is not, however, always clear whether the man in question, the 'Bridegroom'
(*Yrkä, Yrjä*), is a real man and bridegroom or a bear:

Läksin paljo paimeneen,	I went out to shepherd,
leena lehmien ajoon,	with sorrow to tend my cows,
kurja karjan katsantoon.	agonized, to look after the cattle.
Astun ma kivi kiveltä,	Step by step, stone by stone,
astun paasi paaterolta.	I placed my feet along the flags.
Yhty yrjä karjaani,	A groom joined in with my cattle,
päällemi si lehmieni.	came over my cows.
(SKVR I:2, 1151)	

The threats facing the herder in the poem and every herder girl are
intertwined: an otherworld seducer waiting outside the domestic circle, or
a bear? Some of the poems stress the humanity of the seducer (1), while
others point directly at a bear (2):

1

Yhty yrjä vastahani,	A groom joined in with me / my whisk,
lesem poika lehvihini.	a widow's son touched my leaves.
(SKVR I:1, 227)	

2

Yhty yrkä karjaani,	A groom joined in with my cattle,
lesen poika lehmiini.	a widow's son touched my cows.
(SKVR I:2, 1144)	

The former plays with shady arboreal imagery: the girl is out to tend her
cattle and cut leaves, her "leaves" are met by a man who sits at the root of
the tree, as the girl has climbed to the top of the tree. The latter needs only
slightly modifying in order to serve as a bear banishing spell: "Don't touch
my cattle, you groom – don't touch my cows, you widow's son!" (SKVR
I:4, 1495). The associations are motivated in two ways: they underline the
girl's position as the victim of a marriage deal and potential 'game', and
at the same time the erotic charge of the hunting symbolism. The dense,
assonant and parallelistic networks as well as multivalence of the names
and verbs used (*Yrkä* and *Yrjä* as 'groom' and 'bear', *yhtyä* both as 'join'
and 'have sexual intercourse', *vastahani* as both 'with / against me' and
'with my whisk') work for an allegorical reading of the intertextual
relations. The maiden's sexual purity is symbolised with the untouchability

of her cows and whisks, just like the mature woman's reproductive powers are closely linked to the productivity of her cattle, as will soon become evident.

The ambiguous relationship of the bear and women has been explained as a residue of their mythical marriage (Kuusi 1963, 50-51; Sarmela 1972, 168-169). Even if the presence of a woman was harmful to (bear) hunting and hunting weapons, she could erase a spell put upon a weapon by sexually suggestive action, e.g. by "whipping the hunter and his gun with her underskirt" (SKVR I:4, 1153). Similarly, the bear was a threat to a woman's fertility and the closely associated prosperity of her cattle, even if a woman had powers over the bear: she could, for example, drive a bear away by displaying herself and lifting up her skirt (Virtaranta 1958, 314, 160). The tabooed relation between the bear and the woman that could be reversed ritually in a symbolic marriage, or transformed into power and aggression, can also be motivated by the sexual division of labour and differentiated work spheres. In a poem about the revenge of an orphan boy sent out to shepherd, *The Orphan*, the ultimate revenge is the driving of "the cows into the forest, the milk-givers into the meadow" and "the bears to the barnyard". When the unsuspecting mistress goes to milk her cows, the bear that has invaded the domestic circle bites her "arse asunder" (SKVR I:1, 80). All the examples underline the importance of keeping apart the domestic circle and the forest, the cattle and the bear, as well as the firm link between the gender-specific livelihoods and the practitioners' reproductive powers, sexuality and fertility (Tarkka ibid. 245-248, 255-256).

The gulf between the groom's family and the bride's family conspicuous in the world of the epic is also reflected in the ritual texts of real wedding rituals, the wedding songs and laments. As in the epic, the source of a woman's alienation and alterity is in reality not only the contact with the strangeness of the groom and his kin, but also the childhood home that has "promised" and "bartered" away one of its members.

The experience of the bartered bride (as in *The Bartered Maiden*) of having been traded continues in the betrothal laments: "Do not... sell my sorrowful self, do not barter me to the soul-less strangers for brass money" (FLS Lauri Laiho 5507). The girl's separation from her childhood home established in the wedding ritual is comparable to, and symbolised as a funeral. The girl is transferred to alien territory, a strange village, "beyond far-reaching journeys", to "live with soul-less strangers, behind iron doors" (FLS Lauri Laiho 5502 & 5503). In accord with the association of hunting and courting, the strangeness of the groom's kin may be described as bestiality: the father-in-law is a "wolf in the cranny", the mother-in-law a "bear in the stall", the brother-in-law a "viper on the threshold" (SKVR I:3, 1697), the entire new family "akin to secret snakes... like bears in the woods... like forest animals" (FLS Elma Vähä-Muotia 1935, 704).

In her study on Karelian laments, Unelma Konkka stresses the isomorphism of the ritual statuses of the deceased and the young wife. The transition from a newly deceased *pokoiniekka* to a member of the ancestral community of the dead, *syntynen*, and from bride to wife, demands a liminal stage lasting six months. Unlike the deceased, a childless wife nevertheless remains 'a restless soul', an outsider in her husband's kin. (Konkka 1985, 183-185.) The woman was a stranger even in her home – she remained at the border, in between two worlds that were now both defining her as an outsider.[7] An aggravated account is provided by the poem *The Unhappy Bride* in which the husband is paraphrased as a disease demon: he "eats her flesh, bites her bones, sucks the marrow, and pours her blood into a scoop" (SKVR I:2, 1161). In the related *The Wife-Killer*, the groom "drinks blood without a scoop, slices off meat without a knife" and kills his young wife: "Puts her head as a stone in the rapid, bakes her nipples in a fish-pie" (SKVR I:1, 554, SKVR I:1, 558). Actual death can be just another image of the strangeness and aggression experienced in life. A wife might begin to wear the cap indicating widow's status even while her husband was still alive if he was "malicious and vicious" (Paulaharju ibid. 162).

The wretched and carnal imagery featuring in the most famous love poem in Finnish-Karelian folk poetry is also a variation on the theme of total, essential difference between man and woman. The two kins and genders communicating in marriage and in love are to one another as this world (living, familiar, normal, social) is to the otherworld (dead, strange, animal-like). The poem *If the One I Know Were to Come* has also been interpreted as a monologue to a dead beloved, or dialogue across the border established by the grave (Polttila 1991; Timonen 1989, 124, 133; Timonen 1992, 219):

Kunpa tuttuni tulisi,	If only the one I know came,
ennen nähtyni näkysi.	the one I've seen before showed himself.
Utuna ulos mänisin,	I would hasten to him as haze,
savuna pihalla saisin.	meet him outdoors as smoke.
Hot ois keärmis kämmenessä,	If a snake sneaked in his palm,
mie on kättä käppeäisin;	I would hold out my hand to his;
hot ois' suu suen veressä,	if his mouth were filled with wolf's blood,
mie on suuta suihkoaisin;	I would open mine to reach his kiss;
hot ois' kalma kaklan peällä,	if death were upon his neck,
mie on kakloa kapuisin.	I would fall upon his neck.
(SKVR I:3, 1434)	

The epithets used of the body of the beloved and familiar connote the unknown, snakes, death, wolves and blood. The poem is in line with the imagery of total strangeness, but it nevertheless demands communion with the embodiment of otherness: the dead body on the verge of human and non-human. The poem elaborates on conceptual categorisations and its meaningfulness is not reducible to the emotive or aesthetic levels of a "passionate gothic romance" or "openly subjective love song" with a strong erotic charge (cf. Kuusi ibid. 390-391), nor to the theme of parting and hoped-for reunion of two individuals in love. The poem is about the not least conceptual revolution or the dialogue that is essential in joining together this world and the otherworld, the familiar and the strange, the known and the unknown, the seen-before and the unforeseen, the living and the dead, man and woman. In the poem this symbolic process is founded on the macabre undoing of the contrast between the familiar and the alien, at least on the level of utopia and in the conditional: "if only..." (Timonen 1992, 217). In ritual poems, images of strangeness and otherworldliness reflecting a similar tension are elaborated as the wedding ritual moves from highlighting of the contrasting categories to the decomposing of their boundaries.

Symbolic exchange, dialogue of voices

From both the female and the male point of view the dialogues of courting take place across a symbolic border. The girl calls for sex appeal, 'love' and a groom from the otherworld, from "further away", "from beyond the stars, behind the shoulder of the Plough" (SKVR I:4, 1819). She offers her lips to a deathly lover, is harassed by a bear-like bridegroom, and, as in wedding songs, united with a husband disguised as a bird of prey and a family by marriage akin to the beasts of the forest. The groom makes a pass on "the death virgin", the "child of cadaver", or as in wedding songs, a woman whose essence is captured in tender bird metaphors likening her to a game bird. The mythical frameworks of the courting theme and the anchoring of the 'border' imagery in the cosmographic border provide a symbolic means of dealing with various concrete borders and distances: the distance between two families and two villages, between 'us' and 'them', the distance between the childhood home and the family by marriage, between the self and the other. The otherworld symbolism is a generalised, abstract way of expressing the most varied of conceptual or social differences.

The likening of the animal world to mankind and the association of hunting with seduction are not only effective as expressive devices that dramatise the change taking place in rites of passage, contrast the states before and after the transition, and value the two parties against each other. The networks of association between hunting and marriage, killing and fertility, and the sexual division of labour, and their relation to the dichotomy of nature and culture may be regarded as anthropological universals (Rosaldo Zimbalist & Monnig Atkinson 1975). It would appear at first sight that the women's sphere – the home, tending the cattle and the rituals regulating social relations, such as the wedding ritual – represents culture contrasting with the sphere of men and the beasts of the forest.

According to Sherry Ortner woman's domesticity nevertheless has the effect of symbolically placing her in the sphere in between nature and culture and making her a mediator between these. Woman is closer to nature as bearer and carer of children, she acts outside the public sphere defined as culture, transforming the raw natural resources into cultural products – children into social beings, raw materials into food, etc. (Ortner 1975, 77-80). This is precisely the logic by which a woman can be likened to an animal or a being from the otherworld by describing her as game or by using epithets derived from the animal world to describe her. The spirits of the forest acting as mediators between the forest and the human community were symbolically of the female gender, and the Vellamo maiden associated with a spirit fish was half woman. The agreement between the forest and the human community was initiated as a love affair and sealed at the 'wedding' in the bear rite, in which a human woman acted as the bride, as the symbol of the agreement and as a passive mediator.

It has by now become apparent that men, too, could represent the sphere of nature – even Ortner points out that the symbolic relations between culture and nature can also be represented by means of inversion (Ortner ibid. 85-97; cf. Boddy 1989, 69, 114-116). In hunting cultures the relationship between man and nature is ambivalent: catching game demands both identification with the forest and the forest inhabitants in order to permit communication, and being able to stand apart from it (Ilomäki ibid. 54-59). Man acts in the same way as woman, transforming the 'raw natural resources' into culture products: game into catch. Giving the catch a gender was one way of symbolically transforming the relationships between the human community and the natural resources into a manageable agreement (Ilomäki ibid. 61-63). A hunted creature was marked with the most fundamental of all social signifiers, gender: even in inversion, the association between woman and nature expresses the category of the object, as defined contextually from the point of view of the subject.

The object determined from the perspective of the ego of the song – be it a man or a woman – was associated with nature or some other sphere regarded as belonging to the otherworld. The isomorphism of nature and culture further complicates the determination of the relationship between them, and makes the projection from the gender distinction into culture-nature, and public-private relations problematic.[8] The question here is one of relations changing according to context, not of differences in substance. Furthermore, the relations were constantly transforming, either in ritual processes, or through textual strategies.

The thematic discussion on dialogue between the two 'marital' and genderised worlds was based on the assumption of two differing tendencies, points of view, and ultimately voices to be heard in the texts. The poetic ego giving the song its voice and perspective determined the interlocutor or opponent as one belonging to some of the other worlds: the realm of the dead, of animals or the supranormal. As oral poetry and as forms of discourse alive in performance only, the genres of Kalevala-metric poetry clearly point at their actual subjects, the singers. Nevertheless, the voice of the poetic ego and the point of view of the hero cannot be automatically interpreted as the voice and point of view of the singer of the song, nor to a clearly masculine of feminine view. The voice represents a rhetorical position internal to the discourse.[9] Even so, one of the reasons for the male dominance in the epic tradition of Archangel Karelia may be the incompatibility of the themes or perspective of the songs and the life experience of Karelian women. Why sing an epic that stressed one's inferior position, passivity, and alterity?[10] The gulf between the 'experienced' and the 'sung' realities is also reflected in the popularity of distinct epic poems. In the village of Vuonninen, for example, the songs in which the active main character is a woman, were sung exclusively by women, whereas male singers dominated the songs in which the active doer is a man.[11]

A number of examples may be quoted of the dialogue or fusion of male and female voices in the mind of a single singer or within the confines of a single text.[12] In August 1872 Markke Lesoni of Koivujärvi village sang two songs one after another elaborating on the wooing theme from different perspectives: *The Courtship* (SKVR I:1, 464) and *The Water-Carrier* (SKVR I:2, 1200). Both begin with the same episode: a girl is washing clothes by the shore, sees a boat approaching and guesses that it brings a suitor. There on the shore they engage in a brief dialogue. The man in *The Courtship* says he has come to court the maid "from the man-eating village", while in *The Water-Carrier* he simply asks the maid to join him in his boat: "Come, maid with me!" (SKVR I:2, 1200). Here the plots of the songs diverge and the different tendencies of the wooing and seduction songs start developing. *The Courtship* ends with victory for the man and the suitor returns "with one hand on the maiden's thigh...the other round her nipples". In *The Water-Carrier* the girl who has warded off the attempts at seduction returns home, where her family accuse her of loitering on the shore in the hope of a lover. Abused as being a "whore", the maid goes off into the forest and wards off yet another attempt at seduction, and, finally falls dead to the ground, with no explicit reason. Markke, a wealthy man and inno-vative folk poet (Niemi 1921, 1122), even mastered songs with a 'female' point of view, and wove them together with texts of opposing stance.

Female singers, too, mastered and manipulated varying gendered voices in their epics. Typically, *The Courtship* begins with a dialogue in which a maid on the shore inquires the reason for the journey of the approaching suitors. She then tells her brother, Ilmarinen the smith, of their arrival: the suitors are after the maiden of Pohjola. *The Courtship* sung by Hoto Kontratjeff (FLS Väinö Kaukonen 1542) deviates radically from the basic plot and again combines the perspectives of the wooing and seduction songs. The maid asks the smith to forge her some golden chains, but not as a reward for the information she imparts, which is the usual reason: she realises that the suitor from the waters has come to fetch her personally (not the maid of Pohjola promised to the smith) and hangs herself with the golden chains forged by her brother. Hoto Lesoni in turn sings an excep-tional version of *The Singing Match* (SKVR I:1, 183). The normal plot tells of two men who meet head-on in a narrow road and try by a test of knowledge to decide which must give way. Väinämöinen, the winner of the competition, banishes Joukahainen to the swamp by magic means, and Joukahainen promises his sister as Väinämöinen's wife. As a rule the song ends here, or briefly reveals that the future mother-in-law is pleased with her renowned son-in-law. But Hoto continues by reporting the reaction of the bartered maiden; the story to follow is the same as that sung by Hoto as an independent version, *The Water-Carrier* (SKVR I:2, 1206). The maiden in both poems, betrothed against her will or accused of independent "groom-seeking, pursuing the red rope", goes up the hill to her bridal storehouse, takes a rope from her "chest of songs" and hangs herself. Finally, even the suicide of the harassed girl in *The Hanged Maid* can be transformed into the girl's victory. In the poem sung by Iro of Kivijärvi (SKVR I:1, 216) the maid does not hang herself: out of her tears grows the giant tree that initialises the poem *Boat in the Cloud*: the victim takes the initiative.

The interweaving of typical song plots and the resulting dialogue between the different perspectives can be interpreted as deriving from the mechan-isms of song production and the limitations of poetic language. The singer produces even 'exceptional' plots by using traditional themes and thematic associations. In the epic universe songs provide the context for more songs, narratives within narratives, backgrounds and consequences for one another. The viewpoints of individual poems intersect and expand into an epic world. The dialogical nature or polyphony of the epic, both the individual epic songs and the epic universe, does not operate at random: the associations are motivated within the epic universe as a whole. So although Hoto's combination of seduction and wooing songs is exceptional, even idiosyncratic, it is still meaningful: the thematic link is the woman's lot as the object of a marriage deal, as a "bartered biddy", "bought for one hundred marks". For example, *The Singing Match* recounts from the man's point of view the events leading to the situation portrayed from the woman's point of view in *The Bartered Maiden* (the men agree on a maid's betrothal in her absence); generally, the seduction songs with a feminine tendency describe the enforced fate of the object of the marriage deal from the point of view of the girl. The apparent gender-specific tendencies in typical plot types are there only to be used to cover aspects of the epic world.

As the rhetorical structures (the person and role of the poetic ego in the text) are specific to different genres, the dialogue of voices in the texts and between the texts facilitates intergeneric dialogue. The epic universe thus engages in dialogue across its borders. The tentative definition of epic as the synthetic level of the genre system does in fact point to the ability of the epic to absorb voices from other genres, too. An epic often incorporates lyrical episodes in first person voice, either as framed or unframed quotations of the hero's speech ("he spoke thus, uttered a word..."), or as lyrical opening episodes that bridge the epic text to its singer and the present of the performance ("I'm tuning up my chest of songs..."). The tension between the ego of the song and the singer may lead to the actualisation of the lyrical voice acting as a medium between the 'experienced' and 'sung' worlds, to the intervention of the first person or subject position.[13] *The Fishing*, in which the man tries to eat the fish-woman offered to him as a bride, is an obvious challenge to the female singer, and its performers were predominantly men.[14] The interpretation of the poem by an unknown woman throws light on both the dialogue between genres and the tension between the male and female perspectives. The poem begins in lyrical mode and first person, and gradually switches through the first person plural to narration in the third person:

Enpä tiiä polonen akka,	I don't know, the poor woman,
kulla laaumma lailla,	how to sing,
kulla syyllä sylveämmä.	for what reason to chant.
Joka meitä puu purovi,	Every tree bites us,
joka lehvä leikkoavi,	all the twigs cut us,
joka sammakko sanoo,	every frog abuses us,
joka rietta riivoaa.	all the demons pursue us.
Ei auta Ahin mitänä,	Ahti can't be helped,
Ahin lapsen ainokaisen,	nor his only child,
hos häntä pyyti Väinämöinen.	if she is caught by Väinämöinen.
Myö olemma maalla matelemassa,	We are crawling on the land,
ilmoilla elelemässä.	living under the sky.
(SKVR I:1, 264)	

The song continues in traditional fashion, intermingling narration in the third person and lines framed by traditional expressions indicating *oratio recta*: Väinämöinen goes fishing, catches a fish-maiden and loses her. The three opening lines of the song present a typical example of a lyrical episode emphasising the singer: she introduces herself and paves the way for the first theme of her song, the experience of a distressed woman. The lines to follow are familiar from lyrical songs that lament the daughter-in-law's poor status in her new family. The next simile (Vellamo i.e. water spirit "Ahti's only child" and 'we', women living off the water, on land, under the sky) is the turning point in the song, forming a bridge between lyric and epic. The lyric imagery of threat in which items in nature (trees, leafy branches, frogs) metonymically stand for nature, and metaphorically for the repressing and aggressive social universe, is inverted in the epic sequel: a male representative of mankind threatens with a knife a woman transformed into a representative of the animal world, indirectly the ego of the song, the "poor woman", the "us... crawling on land". The set-up is the same as in seduction songs and, for example, the heightened expressions of strangeness used in wedding laments: the aggressive confrontation of two alien worlds. The song parallels two female fates. The first is familiar and probable to the woman of Archangel Karelia – that of the "poor woman", or the fate of the daughter-in-law, and the other of the maiden living in the waves whose potential bridegroom makes to cut her up and eat her. In its lyrical frame, the seemingly misogynistic representation of the woman (as a fish), *The Fishing* acquires an alternative, allegorical meaning. The maiden caught as a fish is an image for the powerlessness and strangeness of women in the threatening social universe. The cracking surface of the text, episodic movement from one point of view to another and the hesitating shift from one genre to another, are all indications of processes of meaning unfolding on the thematic level.

The journey and the cosmology of nostalgia

The journey in the wooing songs is only one of many: the journey to the otherworld is the great narrative of Archangel Karelian poetry. The hero makes the journey in order to acquire magical knowledge (*The Spell*), for purposes of healing (*The Wound*), looking for tools (*The Visit to Tuonela*), game or healing ointments (*The Elk*, hunting and healing spells), a bride (the wooing songs) or the 'Sampo', symbol of prosperity (*The Sampo* cycle). The ways of travelling, the vehicles and the landscape through which the journey passes indicate its supranormal nature: the token travelling man in the songs was the sage, a mediator between this and the otherworld, the keeper of magic knowledge and rite specialist. In concrete reality, too, the world of journeying was one of men. Men travelled around hunting, fishing, peddling across the national border of Finland, and working in the towns and on the shores of the White Sea, and many villages of Archangel Karelia were mostly inhabited by women for much of the year (Inha 1921 (1911), 390-391).

The other central theme of the narrative songs, singing and chanting, is comparable to the journey: casting spells, chanting incantations, is another way of communicating with the otherworld. Singing and travelling are also interwoven at the levels of plot and imagery. A person can be sent off on his journey with song or he may travel in a "sleigh of song". Distance is measured in "plots", and the words of the spell are "bends"; "mouth rivers" and "tracks" flow from the singer's mouth. Correspondingly, falling into motoric trance induced by chanting the 'sacred words' of incantations is paraphrased as diving in the form of an animal, drifting in the sea, falling into a hole on a path, sinking, or flying.[15]

The symbolism of both the incantation and the journey belong to the sage's role of the male Archangel Karelian singer. Although acting as a sage was not an institutional part of being a singer of epics, many singers were in fact famous sages. Traditional knowledge, the 'ancient truths', was encoded in the magical words of incantations, rite techniques, and epic songs (Siikala 1989a, 202) that provided a narrative meta-text for the actual, performative realisations of the knowledge. In singing of the great epic themes, the singer also sang about himself. Because of the role in common as sage, Väinämöinen was the *alter ego* of the male singer.

The otherworld landscape through which the sage or arch-sage as represented by Väinämöinen travelled was both abstract and concrete: the roots of the otherworld lie deep in the everyday landscape. The main topographical elements in the epic universe are the sea, the river, the island, the shore, the mountain, and there is an overall orientation towards the north. The otherworld is always reached through water, and most of the episodes carrying the plot along take place on the waterline. Even water itself can be interpreted as a symbol of transition, liminality, of a marginal state (Stattin 1984, 106-107). In the epics centring on the heroic deeds of Väinämöinen the sage, the generalised otherworld links the symbolisms of death and the concrete graveyard to trance symbolism, and to expressions of homesickness.

The journey, drowning and death are in poetic language symbolic equivalents and the images used for the otherworldly destination in the epic journey songs are interchangeable. Vipunen's stomach, in which Väinämöinen finds himself, may be confused with the Tuonela river (SKVR I:1, 92); in *The Sampo*, Väinämöinen, who has drifted to Pohjola, may call to the maid of Pohjola for a boat to take him across the "deep waters of Manala" (SKVR I:1, 79); in *The Wound* help is sought from the "upper house" of heaven, but simultaneously from the Tuonela river (SKVR I:4, 2145). "Drowned hero" is the epithet used of a sage in spirit possession (SKVR I:1, 92), the dead Lemminkäinen (SKVR I:2, 758) or, in lyric poetry, the dead husband of a female singer (SKVR I:3, 1388). Pohjola is the village that "drowns men", 'death' the "place where men drown" (FLS Lauri Kettunen VK 38:29).

The concrete and local land of the dead of every village, the *Kalmisto* graveyard was situated across the water, too: the Archangel Karelian graveyard was most often on an island, rising as an islet of high-growing virgin forest amid a flat landscape (Laurila 1964, 16; Paulaharju ibid. 162-163). The land of the dead is explicitly located in the village graveyard. Anni Lehtonen from the village of Vuonninen described Tuonela as an underground village, deep down in the "cold chill", a "cold village" "right there in the graveyard" (Paulaharju ibid. 172). The "cold village", "the village that eats men" is also the mythic Pohjola of the epic.

The likening of Pohjola and the graveyard also provides the key to the interpretation of its common epithet: Pohjola is called "a priestless place, unchristened land". The location of the graves in the graveyard can be read as a symbolic map of the community and the cosmos. In the Archangel Karelian graveyard each kin had its own allotted place, an area reflecting the spatial roots of the living families. At the far end, in the northwestern corner, was an area set aside for those of no status, of an alien faith, and other strangers or passers by. This plot was called 'unchristened land' or 'unchristened ground'. The relation between the graveyard and the village of the living is analogical to that between the unchristened land and the family allotted graveyard: in both instances, Pohjola can stand for death, and more specifically, for bad death.

Outsiders could be buried either totally outside the graveyard, in unhallowed land, or in the 'unchristened land' on the margins of the socially defined land of the dead. Also buried outside the graveyard were those who had died away from home, while timber floating, in the forest, in the meadows or on a journey (Paulaharju ibid. 165-168). Anyone who had to leave the community and who died there, or anyone who drowned was thus committed to "unchristened land and priestless places" – just like Väinämöinen, who drifted to the far corner of Pohjola, the northern corner of the cosmos. 'Unchristened land' as the epithet for Pohjola is in fact often to be found in the lament of the lost Väinämöinen as he drifts towards the northern waters:

Itku silmähän tulovi:	Tears come to my eyes:
mie jouvuin poloni poika,	I ended up, the poor boy,
jouvuim moalla vierahalla,	ended up on foreign land,
moalla ristimättömällä,	on unchristened land,
paikkohe papittomihin,	in priestless places,
pimiehen Pohjolah,	in the dark Pohjola,
paksuh Palehtolah,	in the thick Palehtola,
miesten syöpäh kyläh.	in the village that eats men.
Kuin oisin omilla mailla,	If I were on my own lands,
vielä kerran kellot soisi,	once more I'd hear the bells ringing,
vaskipankat vankahuisi.	the bells of brass banging.
Teälä syöpi korppi kouhkot,	Here my lungs are eaten by crows,
muun vereni musta lintu.	all my blood by the black bird.
(SKVR I:1, 83b)	

Tuonne tuuli tuuvitteli,	There, the wind lulled me,
veden henki heilutteli,	the spirit of water waved me,
pimiähän Pohjolahan,	to the dark Pohjola,
noille ouoille oville,	to those strange doors,
veräjille vieraille,	to foreign portals,
paikoille papittomille,	to priestless places,
maille ristimättömille.	to unchristened lands.
Jouvun puulle pyörivälle,	I ended up on a rolling log,
varvalle vapisevalle.	on a shaking shrub.
Jo tunnen tuhon tulevan,	I feel my fall is at hand,
hätäpäivän päälle saavan...	the day of distress dawning...
(SKVR I:1, 79a)	

Väinämöinen's laments "on Pohjola's gates, on Hiisi's doors" (SKVR I:4, 2134), "near the cold village" (SKVR I:1, 97) are traditional images of homesickness. The lamentations can be framed in the dialogue between the

Mistress of Pohjola and Väinämöinen, as lyrical responses to the question: "Would you like to go to your own lands, to those christened lands, to places with priests?" (SKVR I:1, 97, SKVR I:1, 100). Alternatively, the lyrical intermezzos can be extensions of Väinämöinen's reaction as he finds himself on Pohjola's shore: "It would be better on my own lands, to drink water from a birchbark basket, than to drink beer in pints on foreign lands" (SKVR I:1, 91). The lamentation 'performed' by the epic hero who has drifted to Pohjola is also found frequently in independent lyric songs. The following songs on the theme of finding oneself at "strange doors" are ones sung by men:

En tieä poloinen poika,	I don't know, the poor boy,
en poika polon'alainen,	me, the boy of poor luck,
miten olla, kuin eleä,	how to be, how to lead my life,
kun jouvuin omilta mailta.	as I was led from my own lands.
Jouvuin maille vierahille,	I ended up in foreign lands,
äkki ouvoille oville...	at ever strange doors...
Pääsin päälle kalliolle,	I found myself on a rock,
alasti alakivelle	naked, on a sunken stone
joka tuulen tuntemahan,	to feel every wind,
taivahan tajuamahan.	to grasp all the sky.
(SKVR I:3, 1467)	

Jouvuin puulle pyörivälle,	I ended up on a rolling log,
varvalle vapisevalle...	on a shaking shrub...
jouvuin suolle suikerrehtimahan	to meander on marshland,
palolle papattamahan...	to rattle on swidden ground...
Jo jouvuin poloinen poika,	I ended up, the poor boy
jo poika polon alainen,	me, the boy of poor luck,
jouvuin maalle vierahalle...	I ended up on foreign land...
miesten syöpihin kylihin,	in man-eating villages,
kirkon kellon kielen alle.	under the church bell's clapper.
(SKVR I:3, 1377)	

Nostalgia has a cosmic frame and profound existential grounds in the system of beliefs: in the lyrical songs the comparison of home and alien lands ties in with anxiety over the time and place of one's own death. Being homeless and dying far from home carries the fear of 'eternal death', of wandering as a dead without status. The anxiety is shared by the ego or singer of the lyrics of homesickness and the epic hero: "My mind is made up, I am set on going home to die, to the land where I used to live", states Väinämöinen in Pohjola (SKVR I:1, 97). The autobiographical *Reindeer Song* of the Archangel Karelian reindeer thief and folk poet Martiska Karjalainen is a rambling epic song recounting his adventures of reindeer theft, escape, and imprisonment. The runaway and lost soul is afraid of a lonely, sudden death not ordained by God:

Sian tieän kussa synnyn,	I know the place where I was born,
paikan kaiken kussa kasvoin.	all the place where I grew up.
Tuliko surma suutimaton,	Is this the death not ordained by God,
kesken yöllä kengimätön...	a midnight death with no shoes on...
(FLS Lönnrotiana 4:19)	

Residents from distant villages saw each other once a year at the praasniekka or village festival. People returning from the festival at Kostamus. Photo: I.K. Inha 1894 (FLS 9893).

Were the hero to die on the run, he would go on running forever, and already the journey to prison is described as an "unknown road" comparable to the "unknown", strange Pohjola (see SKVR I:2, 816). The foreign land in Väinämöinen's lament and in Martiska's *Reindeer Song* concretises and localises the otherworld: it is not an abstraction of after-life, nor a distant Hell in the far corner of the North (cf. Harva 1948, 239), but something very real and tangible in life. The borders of the 'this-worldly' cosmos are the borders of the area covered by the community; outside the community the individual is socially dead, and being dead outside the communal land of the dead is, in a sense, being doubly dead. Out of these notions grows the cosmology of nostalgia and homesickness. Home is a place to live and die in, a metonym for good life, the only entrance to, and model for existence after death.

The lyrical motifs of the *Reindeer Song* accumulate in the images of prison or alien lands. The object of nostalgia is viewed against the typical attributes of the mythical Pohjola:

Tuonne Kuusamoon kulettiin,	The road led to Kuusamo,
Oulun linnahan lujahan,	the stern castle of Oulu,
Enarihin ilkiähän.	the nasty Enari.
Siellä ei milloin päivä paista,	There the sun never shines,
eikä kuutamot kumota.	nor the moonshine shows.
Aina yhtä ajattelimma:	There was one thing on my mind:
parempi minun olisi	it would be better
vain olla omilla mailla,	to be on my own lands,
ropehesta vettä juoda,	drink water from a birchbark basket,
kuin on mailla vierahilla,	than to be in foreign lands
juoda tuopista olutta.	and drink beer in pints.

270

Kuu keritä, päivä päässä,	Lead me, moon; let me, sun;
Otava, yhä opeta	Teach me, you Plough
näiltä mailta vierahilta,	from these foreign lands,
yhä ouoilta kyliltä.	these ever strange villages.
(FLS Lönnrotiana 4:19)	

Martiska's *Reindeer Song* is virtually unique as a clearly autobiographical epic in Kalevala metre (cf. Pentikäinen ibid. 259-264). The world outside the home community, its landscape, administrative organisation, the practice of different religions, Martiska as an outlaw – all these physical and social states can be viewed in contrast to the positive home circle by means of otherworld symbolism. The otherworld was, as in F.P. Magoun's translation of the *Kalevala*, a "cold community" (Magoun 1963, 378).

There are numerous reasons for, and many manifestations of going astray and strangeness, finding oneself outside the ordered cosmos and its moral code. Iivana Malinen's version of the song *Leavetaking* (SKVR I:1, 691) tells the story of a foundling and associates the statuslessness of a person on foreign land to that of a fatherless, nameless foundling. Found in the swamp and condemned by Väinämöinen to be killed and "taken to the swamp", the foundling laments the unfair sentence on one who "found himself at strange doors, at foreign portals". A female singer from the village of Vuonninen, Malanie, places greater emphasis on the thematic link between going astray and being without social status. Her version of *Leavetaking* begins explicitly with a lyrical song framed as a lament by the foundling:

Isä heitti iljennellä,	Father threw me onto icing,
emo jeällä paljahalla!	mother onto bare ice!
Mie jäin kuin jänösem poika,	I was left like a rabbit's son,
suolla soikerrehtamah on...	to meander on marshland...
Siit on suolla löyvettihe.	There I was found, on the marshland.
(SKVR I:1, 694)	

The foundling's displacement is not only spatial ("lost" SKVR I:1, 692, found on the marsh): he is also nameless, unbaptised, statusless and to be buried on unchristened land until the priest baptises him at the end of the poem. The lost marsh-child is christened the "king of Forestland, guardian of the isle of wealth" – sometimes explicitly as a forest spirit and keeper of game (SKVR I:1, 694). The moral suspectibility of the foundling's origins is one reason for his displacement (see e.g. SKVR I:1, 694, SKVR I:1, 691). Other clearly supranormal beings out-of-place such as diseases (SKVR I:4, 910), beasts of prey (SKVR I:4, 1191), Jesus (SKVR I:2, 1116), etc. could be born as fruits of unacceptable or miraculous sexual intercourse, just as the foundling. Again, the moral community stands opposed to the otherworld.

Namelessness was one of the otherworld epithets frequently used even in aetiological incantations (e.g. SKVR I:4, 427, I:1, 342, I:4, 216). It may also be regarded as a common indicator of otherworldliness in the incantations about the origins of diseases, in which the disease is brought under control by giving it a name; a "nameless" disease "of unknown name" is born "on a nameless rock" and is christened e.g. 'rickets' (SKVR I:1, 678,

I:4, 910). Anything that is uncontrollable and undefinable, be it a place, state, person or disease, is branded as nameless, and only by giving it a name can it be brought within the confines of this world and thus under control.

The distress of the "poor boy" at "strange doors" reverberates also in descriptions of other areas of the supranormal: the epic hero "feels his fall is at hand, the day of distress dawning" in the Northern sea (SKVR I:1, 79), in Vipunen's stomach (SKVR I:1, 670), or bewitched to the swamp (SKVR I:1, 189). The same experience and expression was shared by the sage under a magic threat (SKVR I:4, 1880, I:4, 1850, I:4, 469), the shepherd wandering through the forest (SKVR I:4, 1370), and the hunter lost in a forest devoid of game (SKVR I:4, 1250, I:4, 1243). In Archangel Karelia the rich tradition around the notion of getting lost or being bewitched by the forest (metsänpeitto, or 'covered by the forest') ties in closely with the supranormal aspects of the state of being lost and astray. The otherworldly nature of the forest already discussed in connection with hunting and seduction symbolism culminated in the belief according to which man may, while out in the forest, find himself in a state in which he is concealed and invisible to other people, and from which the normal world is invisible. The spatial otherworldliness represented by the forest is interpreted in the belief as an altered state of consciousness: it is described as a timeless, dream-like state in which everything is turned upside down. In the magical procedures by which the bewitched is brought back to normality, he is called from beneath the earth, from the inside of a mountain, and from across the waters (Harva 1923), from most of the spatial frames of the otherworld.

Incantation and lamentation as 'speaking across'

The examination of the themes of journey and cosmic homesickness demonstrated how the lyrical episodes embedded in epics or intergeneric dialogue mediate the mythical images of the journey to subjective accounts of journeys, some of them clearly autobiographical. The intrusion of the ego or subject of a song into epic narrative is interesting not only as a rhetorical strategy or intertextuality, and I shall be examining its implications for the worldview represented in the epic later on. The rhetorical position of the singer also mediates the singer's experience to mythical conceptions and images in the case of another of the key themes in Archangel Karelian epics: the meta-poetic theme of the power of chanting incantations or epics. The opening up of the epic world into the world of the performer is most clearly illustrated in the generic interaction between incantations and epics often induced by thematic association or in the association of the singing mode of incantations and epics.

An incantation may be woven into an epic in many ways, the simplest of which is the historiola, the epic prologue telling of the origin of the object of the incantation. An epic may also embrace elements of incantation as embedded sequences, as lines in dialogue or as subtle associations evoked by the theme of the song. An embedded incantation is usually marked off from the narrative text by a formula designating the beginning of *oratio recta* – the same as that used to frame lyrical inserts. In *The Sampo*,

Väinämöinen can raise the wind with lines familiar from incantations invoking or calming the winds (SKVR I:1, 83b), and the creation of an islet by striking a light can bring to the surface the fire-lighting motif from the incantation on the origin of fire (SKVR I:1, 649). In the poem about a banquet in the celestial Päivölä, *Lemminkäinen*, the hero silences the dogs guarding the gateway to the otherworld with a spell used for cursing hunting dogs (SKVR I:2, 815, I:2, 850), prepares himself as a sage by dressing in "stern belts of armour" (SKVR I:2, 805, I:4, 1880) and shows off his courage and magical strength by spinning on the blade of his sword "like a dry aspen leaf" (SKVR I:2, 806). In *The Spell* the Mistress of Pohjola chases away Väinämöinen from her innards by means of a spell used to banish disease demons (FLS Lauri Kettunen VK 38:31). The Väinämöinen of *The Singing Match* beats Joukahainen with the magic words of a sage (SKVR I:1, 162), and so on.

The rupture in the epic narration may be described as a shift in the relationship between the singer and the textual universe – in other words, the form of discourse changes. In the epic the relationship with the mythical otherworld is referential or descriptive, whereas in the incantation it is direct, intentional – the singer places himself in direct contact with the mythical world by addressing and acting upon it (Howell 1986, 94-97; Jakobson 1987a, 68-70). The singer of an incantation fragment embedded in an epic poem does not address the mythical world directly, as in a ritual performance of an incantation, but indirectly places the words in the mouth of the character in the song, the sage inside the song. In the case of a long aetiological incantation and its narrative historiola, the rupture in the narrative structure is, however, lasting and the singer himself assumes the role of sage. If the song in question is a mythical epic, the incantation sequences interspersed in it may be called meta-poetic and ritual miniature performances, in which the singer's own sagedom takes over. Similar identification with a mythical model figure occurs in the general incantation motifs in which the sage boasts to speak "in a louder voice": "what flows from my mouth, flows from the mouth of the sweet God; what I drop from the tip of my tongue, drops from the tongue of Jesus" (SKVR I:4, 476).

The sagedom of the singer is activated when the plot of the song emphasises sagedom and he begins to sing not only of himself but in his own, first person voice. The thematic and generic symbiosis of epic and incantation acts as a mythical legitimation for incantation and ritual practices connected to it: it tells of a mythical sagedom whose authority radiates to the present moment of the singer through allusions to real ritual performances.[16] Unexpected and idiosyncratic incantatory embeddings can in particular be interpreted as signs of the actualisation of the singer's role of sage and thus the merging of the subject position (the ego) of the song and the real singer of the song. The singer's identification with his heroes and orientation to the supranormal reality may, for example, be enhanced by the fact that many of the tools used in Väinämöinen epics and the primary substances in the aetiological myths were among the most important magic tools and substances used by the real sage. The iconic relationship between the 'sung' and the lived-in world can thus be reinforced in many ways. The textual strategies of intervention of the subject into epic (in the cases of lyrical and incantatory inserts) are not distinct from ritual ones.

The communicative dimensions of incantations, the acts of addressing the higher and lower supranormal forces enrich the dialogical nature of the epic universe. The combinations of narrative songs and incantations used in real healing rites are hierarchical in their rhetorical structure, as in e.g. *The Wound*, which continues with a blood-staunching spell. The song (SKVR I:1, 309) begins narrating in the third person: "Once upon a time Väinämöinen" cut a wound in his knee. The next episode begins a dialogue in which Väinämöinen seeks a healer in the otherworld. The mythical healer begins to boast of his skills but then continues with a new addressing sequence. Here begins the real blood staunching spell addressing iron, but often also the supranormal helpers of the sage, "Ukko the supreme god" or the Virgin Mary (e.g. SKVR I:1, 299). Extending the role hierarchy to include the sage chanting the song in the real ritual context and his patient, the communication operates on at least three levels: the patient and healer/performer at the bottom, the wounded Väinämöinen and his mythical healer in the middle, and at the top, the ego of the incantation or the healer internal to the textual space of the incantation addressing the higher forces.

The relation of the epic sage-hero and the sage-singer to the supranormal world corresponds to that between the traveller and his destination, or the addresser and the addressee. In her ritual role of lamenter, the woman accompanies the dead on his or her journey. The lamenter's role of psychopomp may be likened to the shamanistic roles of the sage as a fetcher and mediator. The song of both is a means of crossing the border and achieving direct communication with the otherworld, and both ecstatically project themselves into another reality. The otherworld with which the woman communicates is, however, different from the more abstract *Pohjola*-Manala of the heroic sage-epic: a dirge is a means of addressing a specific dead person or the family ancestors in general, and it is directed at the concrete *Kalmisto*-Manala of the village graveyard. The meanings of homesickness and death in the heroic epic were symbolical, but death in the laments is intimate and tangible. Still, the possibility of bad or double death and its association with statuslessness and wandering as a lost soul were present in the context of lamenting: without proper dirges, the deceased remained 'travelling' in between this world and the other (Paulaharju ibid. 129).

The fact that laments stand apart from other genres has often been stressed (Nenola 1982, 79-81; cf. Ilomäki 1989, 80), but thematically they are part of a network formed by other texts, of the epic world. The epic world and laments are linked not only in the theme crossing the border between different worlds or transgression. There are narrative poems that stand in the same relationship to laments as heroic and sage epics stand to incantations. In the tradition of Archangel Karelia, *The Hanged Maid* and the *Boy and the Cloud* are examples of such meta-poems for lamentation: both tell about communication through laments with the dead.

Addressing, calling or 'raising' the dead is both the most characteristic form of discourse and a common motif in laments. The "people of death" are raised to greet a newcomer and to open the gates of Tuonela (Konkka 1985, 61): "could someone of the white ancestral-born-ones rise and meet my white cherished one?" (FLS Elma Vähä-Muotia 703). Or the lament 'raises' the deceased object of the lament to respond: "Could you not, my bearer, rise yourself onto your benumbed heels, from those dreadful seats of death one more time", "Rise and lean on your chilled elbows, and get up to lament against your poor crutches" (FLS Elma Vähä-Muotia 702, FLS Iivari Ievala 7). *The Hanged Maid* (1), *The Water-Carrier* and *The Loss* (2) also tell about raising the dead. A female relative laments and raises a daughter who has fallen dead on the ground or hanged herself:

1

Jo on Anni ammoin kuollun',	Anni died long ago,
tinarinta ripsahtane,	the tin-breast hanged herself,
riputautu rinnan kautti.	clung herself by the breast.
Läksi ämmä nostamahe,	Grandma went to raise her,
ämmä itkien mänöve:	grandma goes on crying:
"Anni tyttö, ainuo neiti,	"Anni-girl, only maiden,
nouse nuorra kuolemasta..."	rise; you're young to die..."
"Oi on kukki ämmöseni,	"O my sweet grandma,
nousisimpa, emp' on peäse,	I would rise, but I can't,
kalma kättä niin pitäve,	death so holds my one hand,
tuoni toista hallitsove..."	dying rules the other one..."
(SKVR I:2, 1206)	

2

Läksi emo ettsimäh,	Mother went searching,
kolmen vuuven oltuo.	after three years had passed.
Astu aittaseh mäjellä,	Stepped to a hill-side storehouse,
keikutteli kellarihi.	bounced to the basement.
Jo on kuollun Anni tytti.	Anni-girl is dead now.
Jo kolme jokie juoksi	Three rivers ran now
yhen emon kyynelistä;	from the tears of one mother;
kolmeh koivuh lehet kasvo	three birches came into leaf
yhen emon kyynälistä.	from the tears of one mother.
Siitä nousi Anni tytti.	Thus rose Anni-girl.
(SKVR I:1, 240)	

Although the deceased is here lamented with tears and not 'aloud', 'with words' (i.e. by a dirge), the lamentation may be interpreted as a spontaneous dirge – the girl is raised from the dead or the grave and invited to join in the dialogue (SKVR I:1, 228). Lamenting and communicating with the dead as a theme may lend an epic poem the softness and repetitiveness characteristic of lament language, just as incantation motifs could trigger the emergence of clear incantation in sage epics. The mother laments her daughter in *The Hanged Maid* performed by an unknown woman from Jyvöälahti village:

Oipa miun kallehet vetyöni,	Woe my treasured waters,
vierköä ihaloilla ihopäillä.	run on my fair skin.
Oi miun kallehet vetyöni,	O my treasured waters,
vierköä ihaloilla ihopäillä,	run on my fair skin,
kaunehilla vyöni peällä.	over my beautiful belt.
Oi miun kallehet vetyöni,	O my treasured waters,
helejillä helmoillani.	over my bright hem.
Oi miun kallehet vetyöni,	O my treasured waters,
kallehilla kantapäillä.	over my precious heels.

Oi miun kallehet vetyöni,	O my treasured waters,
kirvokkoa moa-emähe...	fall onto mother-earth...
(SKVR I:1, 237)	

Even if the style and pattern of the repetition are exceptional to an epic poem and reminiscent of laments, the girl's death and the lament raising her from the dead should not be interpreted literally. The lament episodes end a story in which a girl has got engaged, and they are associated with the separation stage of the wedding ritual, not dirges performed at funerals. Laments with the strongest emotional charge were performed to the bride as she sat on the chest containing her trousseau in the hair-dressing ceremony. At this point in the wedding ritual the bride finally took leave of her childhood home: from now onwards she was symbolically dead to her family of birth. In *The Hanged Maid*, too, the girl climbs onto her "chest" or "box" to her death; the closing episode of the song thus follows the course of the hair-dressing ceremony.

Raising the dead in laments has clear connections with trance symbolism, as in e.g. the incantations in which the sage raises his guardian spirit or the dead from the grave to help him. The sage opens the lids of the world and the grave, calling:

Nostan maasta mammojani,	I raise my mama from the ground,
kantajani kalmistosta.	my bearer from the graveyard.
Nostan ylös kalman kannet,	I raise the lids of death,
Manalan katot kohotan...	and lift up the roofs of Manala...
(SKVR I:4, 1851)	

The chest or grave described in laments, with its ceiling and lid, may be regarded as microcosms of the otherworld akin to Pohjola, which was paraphrased as a "cottage of no door, a cottage without windows" (SKVR I:1, 78).[17] Dirges treat the closing of the coffin lid as the final moment of departure: "do not... lock [him / her] behind the bolts of Tuonela to the precious ancestry... behind the thousand locks of Tuonela" (Paulaharju ibid. 119; see Mansikka 1924, 179). The lifting of lids, the opening of locks and bolts are also part of the imagery of incantations, epics and lyric poetry, of the symbolism for crossing and controlling the border.

The sage does not merely seek to enter into dialogue with the dead, but calls on them to "nurse" him, to give their "help, their mercy, their support and security" (SKVR I:4, 1850). The laments, too, indirectly tried to influence the happiness and fortune of the living. The sanctioning role of the community of the dead was in Archangel Karelian folk belief so significant that the dead may be likened to the supranormal but more impersonal spirits addressed in incantations.[18] Again, the otherworld approached by men in their ritual role shows its more abstract or symbolic character: women communicated with a concrete and physical otherworld whose temporal and spatial distance from the social reality was minimal (people who had died recently, the graveyard adjoining the village). In the wedding ritual, too, the male *patvaska* mediated social relations conceptualised as forces such as curses, *kirot* and envy, *kateet*, whereas women acted upon the people whose status in the network of social relations was in transition.[19]

276

Laments occupy two landscapes: one the landscape of the supranormal journey to the land of the dead, the other the earthly landscape through which the dead is taken to the graveyard (see e.g. Konkka ibid. 59-60; Paulaharju ibid. 105-112). The lament acts as a commentator and companion on both journeys, and both lead to another world: through the gate away from the home yard to the graveyard, and through the gateways of Tuonela. The landscape of the deceased's journey to Tuonela is greatly reminiscent of the topography of the otherworld in the epic: in laments the deceased sinks, subsides beneath the earth to somewhere cold and dark, the road to which is "unknown" and where "neither the sun shines nor the moon glows" (see Mansikka ibid. 161, 169; cf. Harva 1932, 482). The imagery for the border between the worlds is also the same as in the epic: clearing the way, opening the gates to Tuonela, soothing the dogs guarding the gate, and calling for a boat to cross the Tuonela river.

Although laments, epics and incantations differ from one another as forms of discourse, the network of meanings in each of the genres is made clearest when viewed against each other. In many places the genres engage in dialogue with one another, both in their narrative techniques (rhetorically) and in expanding the networks of meanings (thematically). At thematic level the complementary nature of genres is obvious: the death symbolism in epic and incantation, the communicative factors (addressing, raising), the plot types dominated by journeys and communication, etc., are characteristic features even of the lament and among its central themes. As members of the same symbolic system or intertextual universe, the levels of reality dealt with by different genres touch upon one another. The concrete death of laments, the symbolic death of incantations, wedding laments and journey epics, the social death of songs of homesickness all derive their expressive force from one another. In the end, the intertextual epic universe opens through discourse into the lived-in world of the singers.

The otherworld embodied, the world en-gendered

In bringing a human being to life, he is brought from the void of 'that air', *tuonilmanen* to this world and under 'this air', *tämänilmanen*. This transformation or transfer is depicted and brought about by incantations of childbirth that were to be found in the repertoires of both female midwives and male sages. In the incantations, the place from which man is born, "warm flesh", "the chest of flesh" (SKVR I:4, 985) or "bony castle, red gate" (SKVR I:4, 981) belonged to the symbolism of the otherworld. A child is called a "travelling man" whose journey in birth is described using imagery familiar from sage epics. Childbirth is a transition in which the otherworld is brought to the light of day. The obstacles and 'landscape' along the way are mythical images embodied.

The "vein gates" holding the baby back are opened using the same image as in the opening of the fence obstructing Lemminkäinen's visionary journey in the epic: the midwife or sage "tears across" the fence, opening it from "between five withes, seven stakes" (SKVR I:4, 959). Once the baby has made his transit to this world, he is surrounded by a new, symbolic fence to protect him from the otherworld forces as well as social malevolence. The fence is described as being made of iron and steel (SKVR I:4, 967) and bound together with snakes (SKVR I:4, 973), just like the obstacle encountered by Lemminkäinen and the fence protecting the *patvaska* and the wedding couple (SKVR I:2, 721, I:4, 1877, I:4, 490). The border which was momentarily opened had to be closed stage by stage, first by 'encircling' the baby with the magic fence, then by blessing the mother, and finally by baptising the child. The child's liminal state between the other-worldly and social existence is of the same length as that of the mother, the bride and the deceased, six weeks. (Paulaharju ibid. 29-30, 34-35, 41, 168; Nenola 1986, 143-144; Konkka ibid. 183-184.)

In his birth, the baby rises "to the ground of berry sprays, to the ground to crawl as man, to grow under the air", "on land", "to the meadow" or "to the yard", as if from water (SKVR I:4, 979, I:4, 973, I:4, 974). Alternatively or simultaneously, the child comes "from beyond the stars, behind the shoulder of the Plough" (SKVR I:4, 972), and birth may be described as falling from heaven:

Pilvet rakosi pirtin päällä,	The clouds parted over the cottage,
taivas rakosi tallin päällä;	the sky cracked over the stable;
putosi puhas omena,	out fell the pure apple,
puhki puisten porstuvien...	piercing the wooden porches...
(SKVR I:4, 943)	

The darkness and absence of sunlight in the otherworldly Pohjola and in any foreign village (SKVR I:1, 93, FLS Lönnrotiana 4:19) are similes for the darkness of the prenatal otherworld – the unborn child is likewise helped to "admire the air, to watch the sun" (SKVR I:4, 951). Some of the images depicting man's difficult start in life found in childbirth incantations are the same as those used to represent the cosmic homesickness on the borders of the world. The newborn "travelling man", "the one with little fingers" is lost in the otherworld and wanders from one "strange door" to another, being "poor to find his way, strange to know his course" (SKVR I:4, 981). The imagery of foreign lands and losing one's way exists in both childbirth incantations (1) and songs of homesickness (2):

1

Kuu keritä, päivyt päästä,	Lead me, moon; let me, sun;
Otava yhä opeta,	Teach me, you Plough,
miestä ouvoilta ovilta,	the man from strange doors,
veräjiltä viimmesiltä,	from the last portals,
näiltä pieniltä pesiltä,	from these small burrows,
asunnoilta ahtahilta.	out of these close quarters.
(SKVR I:4, 976)	

2

Läksisin omille maille,	I would leave for lands of my own,
pois on mailta vierahilta.	out of these foreign lands.
Siellä vuottais mun isoni,	There would my father wait for me,
valkuttelis vanhempani...	there would my parents lull me...
Lähes, kuu, kulettajaksi,	Rise, you moon, to walk along,
Lähes, päivä, päästäjäksi,	Rise, you sun, to let me,

Otava, matkan osaksi.	You, the Plough, to show the way.
(SKVR I:3, 1377)	

The adult man projects his mythical homesickness on his father and mother, his cradlers waiting at home, while the baby about to be born is a man, already on his journey. Again, the theme is associated with a liminal state and statuslessness. The child was in transit, and prematurely or still-born babies, babies dying during childbirth or before name-giving remained statusless: they were buried in 'unchristened land', some even without a coffin (Paulaharju ibid. 168).

Since the child is locked in a "fleshy" or "bony chest", the central theme of childbirth magic is that of lubricating the "mouth of rucksack" or "tongue of knapsack" with "foam of whale, slime of burbot" (SKVR I:4, 973) and opening the locks of the "chest". The doors are opened using the same images as the supranormal doors and apertures in epics – the locks are lubricated and the door is forced open:

Avaan lihasen arkun,	I will open the chest of flesh,
arkun luisen longottelen,	force the bony chest open,
päästän maille matkamiehen,	and let travelling man rise on land,
pieni sormisen pihoille.	the one with little fingers on the yard.
Jos siit' ei apua liene,	If it will not be of help,
perse pelloksi repäse,	tear the arse to be wide as a field,
vittu ilman ikkunaksi,	the cunt to be the air's window,
taivahan avarueksi,	as wide as the sky,
maailman kokoseksi.	the size of the world.
(SKVR I:4, 960)	

Tuo viikate Virosta,	Bring me a scythe of Estonia,
heinärauta Helvetistä...	a hayfork of Hell...
millä katkon kannaksia,	to cut the necks of land,
lukut luiset lonkuttelen,	to force the bony locks open,
suoni-portit pois porotan!	to burn away the gates of veins!
(SKVR I:4,948)	

Potkoas ovia porton,	Kick at the whore's doors,
kamahuta kammaria,	bang at the chamber,
lukut luiset lonkottele,	force the bony locks open,
pihtipuoliset pirota,	loosen the doorjambs,
takasalvat pois porota!	burn away the locking lever!
(SKVR I:4, 973)	

In epic poetry, the theme of freeing a child from a closed space and chest is found in the legend poem *The Messiah*. The episode of Mary's search for her baby belongs to the legend according to which the infant Jesus was taken straight from his mother's arms to the cross and to the grave. The Virgin Mary tries to persuade the sun to melt the locks holding the door to the burial chamber of the infant Jesus; the sun shines hotly, the soil "melts as salt", the stones "run as foam", and Mary, Mother of God, "finds her son, her boy, her little one, her golden apple" (FLS Aili Laanti 1896). The search by the Virgin for her child is the only example in the epic tradition of an active journey by a woman to the otherworld, and Marianic themes

Timber blockings in the cemetery signified the abodes of the dead. Vuonninen. Photo: Samuli Paulaharju 1915 (FLS 5423).

or 'interventions' can well be regarded as the central mythic tradition of women in Karelian oral poetry. (Timonen 1987, Timonen 1990b).

The direct link between the birth and death of Jesus exists in symbiosis with the images of the childbirth incantations – the infant Jesus is freed from the grave, "from between two rocks" and "from under a stone slab" (SKVR I:2, 1119), while the human child is freed "from a fleshy chest" or "coffin", breaking away in the heat of the *sauna* "from the woman's loins...like a stone loosened from the sauna stove", "like plaster crumbling off the wall", "through the stove of stones" (SKVR I:4, 966, I:4, 963, I:4, 949). In both the active doer, the subject of the quest episode in *The Messiah* and the main figure of strength in the childbirth incantations, is the Virgin Mary, "oldest of women, first of dams", "the closest of doctors" (SKVR I:4, 963, I:4, 941), and both could be called "Mary's chants" (SKVR I:4, 945, I:2, 1115). Alternatively named as the "Saviour's birth chant", *The Messiah* describes at length the Virgin's impregnation, pregnancy, childbirth and birth pangs: the "hardened womb", "difficult stomach", "compulsion" and "maiden's burning" (SKVR I:2, 1103; see also SKVR I:4, 960, I:4, 963). As Mary was turned away from the sauna traditionally used for childbirth, she is repeatedly asked to enter the birthgiving-saunas of Karelia: "Step in the sauna secretly, hiding, to the maidens' room!" (SKVR I:4, 963). Mary's role as the mythical model woman and ritual protector helps us to understand why her fight in the rebirth of her own son could at symbolical level be actualised in the birthgiving rituals of every woman.[20] Mary was both a model midwife and a mother, and in the birth of every child, the "pure apple" was seen falling from heaven to the site of Jesus's mythical birth (SKVR I:4, 943).

The infant Jesus is not the only person or value confined behind otherworld locks in epics. The Sampo, chained to the stony hill of Pohjola, is freed by lubricating the locks with slimy flesh, butter and pork (SKVR I:1,

91), or like Jesus, with the heat of the sun (SKVR I:1, 84b). The freeing of the baby can be likened to the release of the sun from behind the other-worldly northern locks (1). The theme of releasing the sun from the rocky mountain of Pohjola is a rare theme in the songs of Archangel Karelia, but it appears metaphorically in a subjective song by the male singer Ohvo Homanen as an image for redemption or freeing the distressed (2):

1

Päästit päivän pohjasesta,	You released the sun from the north,
päästä maille matkamiestä,	so let the travelling man rise on land,
pikkusormista pihalle,	the one with little fingers on the yard,
näkemähän näitä maita,	to see these lands,
ilmoja ihahumahan.	to feel about this air.
(SKVR I:4, 948)	

2

Päivän peästi, kuun keritti	He released the sun, set the moon free
yheksän lukun takova,	from behind nine locks,
lukku-puolen kymmenettä.	half-a-dozen locks.
Miksik' ei minuvo peästä,	Why not release me,
kuks' ei kurjova pelasta?	why not save the miserable?
Heitit kurjin kuolemaha,	You threw me to die miserably,
vaivasin häviemähä.	to disappear in desolation.
(SKVR I:1, 680)	

The sun and the moon are set free from the otherworld in order to shine; the ego of the song is freed from misery and redeemed from death; the child's "head is freed, its spirit redeemed" (SKVR I:4, 954, I:4, 958) from the womb "to admire this air, to learn the Plough, to watch the sun" (SKVR I:4, 951). The otherworldly attributes of darkness and night were used metaphorically as images of the human lot and mortality and they are contrasted with daylight and being born into light. Even the hero Väinä-möinen shares the existential dilemma with the distressed and the baby. He has drifted to the close quarters of Pohjola, "the cottage of no door" or "the place of no return" and asks the Mistress of Pohjola to set him free. The epic hero's plea is identical to Ohvo Homanen's lyric:

Itse noin sanoiksi virkko:	He himself put it into words:
"... Kuun peässit,	"... You released the moon,
päivän peässit	released the sun
yheksän lukun takoata,	from behind nine locks,
miks' et minuo peästän...?	why not release me...?
Heitit kurjan kuolomah..."	You threw the miserable to die..."
(SKVR I:1, 78)	

The chain of associations continues in the poem *The Boy and Cloud*. The boy named like the infant Jesus "little boy, golden apple" gets lost on a forest journey to the "rabbit's tracks" and is raised to heaven. As he is called back to earth, he replies:

Pilvet päätäni pitävät,	The clouds hold my head,
hattarat hivuksiani,	the cloudlets hold my hair,

vipu toista jalkoani.	the forks trap my other foot.
Päästä päätä, Päivän poika,	Release the head, son of the sun,
silmiä, hyvä sikiä:	the eyes, you good child:
silmät tähtiä lukevi,	my eyes read the stars,
sääret honkia hosuvi.	my legs hit the pines.
Kuu kulta, jumalan luoma,	Moon of gold, god's creature,
lähes päätä päästämähän,	come and release the head,
syötä Karjalan kaloja,	feed with fish of Karelia,
Kuvetjärven kuorehia.	the smelts of Kuvetjärvi.
(SKVR I:2,1171)	

The images of rising from the dead and being (re-)born are not therefore intermingled only in the parallel between the Christian legend (fetching the infant Jesus from the grave) and the childbirth incantation (fetching the child from its prenatal state), but in the otherworld images associated with heaven and forest, too. In *The Water-Carrier*, the reply of the girl whom female relatives try to raise from the dead might also associate the heavenly otherworld and the chtonic underworld of the dead:

Pihet jalkoja pitää,	The forks hold my feet,
pihet alla, paaet päällä.	the forks under, the stones over.
Pilvi päätäni pitää,	The cloud holds my head,
tuoni toista jalkoani,	death my other foot,
kalma kattaa käteni.	the cadaver covers my hand.
(SKVR I:2, 1199)	

From the easing of birth to communication with the dead, the states and sites of existence before and after life were alike. The network of the otherworld's potential qualities expresses and engenders a worldview that need not be interpreted as cyclical, but as one in which the unknown void is filled with comprehensible, concrete and coherent images.

Man can also incorporate the otherworld in the songs describing his inner space as a source of knowledge. In the sage songs wisdom and messages are brought from Tuonela, Pohjola, or Vipunen's inside – his mouth, breast, stomach, liver, or lungs. Vipunen the proto-sage swallows Väinämöinen, but the traveller manages to return from the "grimacing gums, squelching jaws", bringing with him words of wisdom (SKVR I:1, 420). The link between Vipunen the proto-sage and mother figures is obvious: the proto-sage and the sage's guardian spirits are associated both with the inner space of the body and with caring. The sage, the "poor boy", the "only son" or "young man" "calls for care" from his heavenly father and his worldly mother (SKVR I:4, 1869, I:4, 1850), and raises his mother to help him (1). The image is the same as that used of Vipunen (2):

1

Kauan on maammo maassa	Long has my mother
maannut,	lain in the ground,
nukkununna nurmen alla.	slept under the grass.
Kasvo haavat hampahilta,	Aspens have grown from her teeth,
lepät suuret leukaluilta,	tall alders from her jaws,
isot kolvet konkervosta,	great, old pines from her rear,
lakkapäät petäjät päästä.	flat-topped pines from her head.
(SKVR I:4, 469)	

2

Viikoist' on Vipunen kuollun,	For weeks has Vipunen been dead,
kauvon on Ankervo katonun.	long has Ankervo been lost.
Kuus' on kulmista kohonnun,	A spruce has risen from his brows,
koiv' on kasvan kanta-päistä,	a birch has grown from his heels,
hoap' on kasvan hartijesta,	an aspen has grown from his shoulder,
lepp' on kasvan leukaluista,	an alder has grown from the jaws,
paju-pehko peällä parran.	a bush of willows on the beard.
(SKVR I:1, 419)	

Vipunen is not, however, the hero's only guardian spirit or helper charac-terised by maternality. In the poem about Lemminkäinen's fall, the hero's relationship with his mother corresponds to that between the shaman and his spirit helpers. The mother guides her son on the road to the otherworld and equips him with armour, the mother collects the remains of her son from the Tuonela river and brings him back to life – in vain, because her son is just like the "drowned male" Vipunen, who spent too long in a death-like trance (SKVR I:1, 383a, I:1, 398, I:2, 758). Lemminkäinen's mother is the same "dam, the woman, my bearer" to which the sage from Archangel Karelia turned on his own journey (SKVR I:2, 740).

Vipunen typically represents the male embodiment of the otherworld in the epic and the mother giving birth the female embodiment of the other-world in incantations. Even the Mistress of Pohjola may act as a female embodiment of the otherworld and offer her body as the landscape for the sage's journey. In *The Courtship*, a poem popular in North Karelia, the Mistress of Pohjola swallows her daughter's suitor and vomits him up again. The roles of Vipunen the proto-sage and the mother-mistress of Pohjola intersect in an Archangel Karelian poem in which the mistress of Pohjola eats up Väinämöinen:

Tuop' on Pohjolan emäntä	The mistress of Pohjola herself
söip' on miehen suolinehe...	ate the man into her intestines...
Tuop on vanha Väinämöine	The old Väinämöine himself
pani paitansa pajakse...	raised his shirt as a smithy...
pikkusormensa pihikse,	his little finger as a fork,
polvensa alasimeksi...	his knee as an anvil...
takuo taputtelovi...	he forged, he hammered...
vatsassa Vipusev vaimon.	in the stomach of Vipunen's wife.
Sano Pohjolan emäntä:	The mistress of Pohjola uttered:
"Jo olen syönyn sata miestä,	"I have eaten a hundred men,
tuhat urosta tuhonnun,	a thousand heroes have I destroyed,
en ole vielä moista syönyn,	but never have I eaten one like this,
syömp' on tuiskavi tulena,	my heart whirls like fire,
palau vatsa pakkulina..."	my belly burns like gnarled birchwood..."
(FLS Lauri Kettunen VK 38:31)	

To kill the pain, the mistress utters a curse banishing a disease demon, opens her jaws and out jumps Väinämöinen with the missing knowledge. The "traveller" beats at the stomach of the mistress with his little fingers, elbows, and knee, like the "little-fingered" baby "kicks under the breast" of her mother (SKVR I:4, 983). The "burning belly" and "cramping stomach" of birthgiving incantations (SKVR I:4, 974) as well as their release further bind *The Spell*'s imagery to that of birthgiving.

The images of swallowing and eating fellow humans spin around the twin themes of birth-giving and life-taking. Once the child has been born, the mother or midwife bites off the umbilical cord and protects the child against rickets addressed as "the eater":

Syön syöjät, puren purijat	I eat the eaters, bite the biters
omastahi lapsestani.	away from my own child.
Vain en syö syntynyttä,	But I will not eat the born one,
kaottele kasvanutta.	destroy the growing one.
Jo olen syönyt sataki miestä,	I have eaten a hundred men,
tuhonnut tuhat urosta.	destroyed a thousand heroes.
(SKVR I:4, 957)	

The various aspects of the otherworld are well presented in the states and sites which the child is born from. Even the "man-eating" Pohjola (SKVR I:1, 78), the archetype of the otherworld has a part to play in the cartography of parturition. In childbirth incantations Pohjola features as a place to which the 'evils' obstructing the birth or threatening the new-born babe are banished:

Mänkää huuteh helvettiih,	Go screaming to hell,
parkuuh pahaah kylääh...	crying to the bad village...
pimieeh pohjoseeh,	to the dark north,
ihmisten syöjääh sijaah!	the man-eating site!
Siell' on hällä	There you will have
luutonta lihoa,	boneless flesh,
kieletöntä pohkiota...	stringless leg...
(SKVR I:4, 985)	

In this context, as in the mistress of Pohjola's role of "man-eater" examined above, Pohjola offers a symmetrical counter-image for the womb, "a man-eating village", "the man-eating site", and a container of non-differentiated organic material: organs and flesh that are good-to-eat for the demon or decomposed (e.g. SKVR I:4, 610e). In the incantation, the womb is the site for the inverse process and epithets: the emerging "travelling man" is guided "through the warm holes, through bony locks, through warm flesh", in the opposite direction to the disease demon's course.

The images of death and birth, eating and escape, the womb and the grave become even further interwoven when the evil obstructing the birth is sent back to its potential place of origin: death, the womb of a corpse and the grave (1). The power substance of death, *kalma*, was perceived of as one of the most typical causes of diseases and it, too, was sent back to the chtonic insides (2):

1

Jos olet kuolijan kohusta,	If you come from a dying one's womb,
sata lauvan lappiosta,	from a hundred-boarded roof,
tuhat malkosten majoista,	from a hut of thousand ridge beams,
kirkkomaijen kinteriltä,	from the heels of church-yards,

männös kuolian kohtuhun,	go to the womb of the dying one,
kirkkomaijen kinterille,	to the heels of church-yards,
vaikka vanhohon lihohon!	even to old flesh!
(SKVR I:4, 960)	

2

...Kun ollet kuollehen kohusta,	If you are from a dead one's womb,
iki männehen ihosta,	from the skin of a gone-for-good one,
sata-lauvan lappaluista,	from shoulder-blades of the
märännehen mua emästä,	hundred-boarded,
siä mäne kuollehen kotih...	from the rotten mother earth,
märännehen mua emäh,	you go to the home of a dead one...
kalmalaisen kantapiäh!	to the rotten mother earth,
(SKVR I:4, 601)	to the heel of the dead one!

Both grave and womb were microcosms symbolised as houses or homes: the synthesising vision, a metaphor connecting the body with a house, grows out of chains of parallel images playing with assonance (*kuollehen koti/kohtu* – 'a dying one's home/womb'; *satalauvan lappio/lappaluu* – 'hundred-boarded roof/shoulder blade'; *kirkkomaijen kinner/kalmalaisen kantapiä* – 'heel of/next to the churchyard/heel of the dead one'). The stress on opening the doors and locks of the womb finds its parallel in the great care for the proper building of the coffin and the miniature house built on the mound (see Paulaharju ibid. 86): all had to be equipped with at least symbolic doors and windows to facilitate communication and transition.

The association of womb and grave, birth and death is rooted in the belief system and ritual practices. The power substance of death had a certain sympathy with the womb: during pregnancy the woman and embryo were particularly vulnerable to contamination by *kalma* (Paulaharju ibid. 22). Birth and death meet once again in the woman's set of ritual roles. The lamenter woman accompanied the dead to 'that air', the midwife the child to 'this air'. The relationship between the birth-giving mother, the new-born child and the midwife continued beyond death: they helped their midwife across the Tuonela river. Another of the woman's ritual roles also reflects her journey across the Tuonela river: the dead whose bodies the woman washed when she was alive help her across the river. The rituals of life and death thus displayed symmetry, and a woman had to assist in ritual baths at three births and three laying outs: "washing three to this air, three to the death" (Paulaharju ibid. 173, 74).

The causal connection of the birth-giving role of woman and 'female suffering', the specific relation of women to death and mourning, thematised in women's studies (Nenola ibid. 133-135, 143-145, 152-154; Caraveli-Chaves 1981, 146) is not, however, reflected as such in the symbolism of Karelian oral poetry. Even the difficulties facing men, in a forest that refused to yield game, in strange lands, in prison and on the waters of the mythical Pohjola, are met in suffering and symbolically equivalent to death. Yet there is a difference between the sufferings: the man suffers as the subject of his journey, the woman as an escort releasing someone on a journey.

The most interesting difference nevertheless lies in the otherworlds as seen from the male and female perspective. It has already been noted that the otherworld approached by women was more concrete than the symbolic otherworld approached by men. The ritual poetry of women was discourse addressed to the dead, whereas that of men spoke of symbolic or social death. The difference can be clarified by comparing the two embodiments of the otherworld represented in the poems. The vaginal 'trip' or 'journey' (*retki* or *reissu*; Pelkonen 1931, 72) from the mythical landscape of the womb was travelled by a little human body – the midwife helped to fetch the human from the otherworld. In *The Spell*, in which the mythical sage-hero travels in Vipunen's body, "rowing from one end of the vein to another" (Karelskie epičeskie pesni 34), abstract symbols – words and knowledge – are fetched from the body of the male proto-sage.

The imagery of childbirth incantations and of the maternal figures and embodiments connected with sagedom opens up a new perspective on the male heroism of the epic universe, and places the otherworldliness of women in an increasingly wide symbolic field. Woman is not just the Other (an object, a beast, deathly) but the bearer or embodiment of the otherworld: she who bears and gives birth to humans and inside whom the male subject makes his first journey. The baby to be born is without exception depicted as male: as the travelling man, a boy, or as a "pure apple" (SKVR I:4, 943) – a common epithet for a bear, Jesus and a bridegroom. The woman does not only engage in exchange between the otherworld and this world like the male hunter does; with her body, she transforms elements of the otherworld into beings of this world. The opening in the female body is an opening toward the otherworld, for others to become humans and the this-worldly to be engendered. The strong taboos and rituals surrounding the woman's inner space, the opening and closing of the "gate of flesh" guard this world from the invasion of the uncontrolable.[21]

The symbolism of childbirth incantations carries a mythology all of its own backed by the Marianic themes: it is a concrete feminine counterpart to the androcentric cosmogony, the myths on the origin of the world and culture. According to feminist criticism both the study of myths and mythologies themselves regard parturition as the devalued opposite of aetiological myths. Giving birth is perceived of as a process or deed of this world, biological and non-symbolical. In aetiological myths the male creates existence with a word, with his spirit, out of nothing; culture heroes bringing forth culture from nature are also men. (Weigle 1987, 427, 433; Fox 1987; cf. Howe & Hirschfeld 1981, 322.). This contrast between the symbolic and the concrete, the abstract and the worldly corresponds to the distinction between the gender-specific otherworlds and acts of creation described in Kalevala-metric poetry (cf. Sawin ibid. 206). In the poetry of Archangel Karelia, male aetiological myths are represented by e.g. *The Creation* and the episode *Formation of the Seabed* opening *The Sampo* cycle. Väinämöinen creates the world with words, using a bird's egg as his material and moulds the seabed into rocks, skerries and graves of fish with the movements of his body. Competing for the role of the most important culture heroes are Väinämöinen and Ilmarinen the smith, the "forger of the heavens" and the forger of the Golden Maiden. If and when a woman creates, she does so by giving birth or suckling. The Mistress of Pohjola is fertilised by the wind and gives birth to diseases and beasts of prey (SKVR I:4, 910, I:4, 1085, I:4, 1164) and a maiden milks iron from her breasts to be tempered and forged by a male smith (SKVR I:4, 137). The Virgin Mary is impregnated with a berry and gives birth to Jesus – sometimes even to the moon, sun, and the stars (SKVR I:2, 1098).

Nevertheless, the networks of birth, real death, and symbolic death in one corpus of poetry demonstrate that despite their differentiation, the concrete and symbolic are complementary and merge with one another in the poetic language. The border that was concretely crossed in ritual texts of childbirth was depicted by the same mythical images as the border zones and transgressions in male heroic poetry and incantations. On the level of poetic imagery, the landscapes were identical: the direction was from heaven, close quarters and enclosures, the sea, darkness, and the strange land to life on earth, under the open skies, the light, one's own yard, one's own cottage, "to eat the fish of Karelia" (SKVR I:4, 972).

The female inner space was, potentially, "as wide as the sky" and "the size of the world".[22] In the panoramic representations of women, oppositions of activity and passivity, subject and object again show their relative quality. Was it the travelling man or the 'landscape' that was moving and acting in the incantations? As a form of discourse not based on narrative, the question is difficult to answer – the actors in the incantations were more likely the addressed or even extratextual helpers, and the performers themselves. Be it as it may, the delineation between action and non-action depends on the point of view, and ultimately on the genre.

Forgers of this world

Much of the seemingly male bias of the heroic epic and aetiological mythology is crystallised in the motif stressing the male identity of the demiurge. In *The Sampo* (1) and *The Singing Match* (2) the males boasting of the creation of the world and the forging of the heavens are Ilmarinen and Väinämöinen:

1

Katso itä, katso länsi,	Look eastwards, look westwards,
katso pitkin pohjan ranta,	look along the northern shore,
katso taivaskin peän peältä.	look to the sky above your head.
Onko oikein otava,	Is the Plough in the right way,
tähet taivon taitavasti?	stars in the sky laid with skill?
Mie olen taivoni takon,	It was me who forged the sky,
ilman koaret kalkutellun.	I did hammer the firmament.
(SKVR I:4, 2134)	

2

Olin mieki miessä siellä,	I was a man at hand,
urohona kolmantena,	the third among the heroes,
seitschemäntenä urossa,	the seventh among the heroes,
kaarta taivon kantaissa,	when the firmament was raised,
pieltä ilmon pistäissä,	when the air's edge was set,

taivoista tähittäissä,   when the sky was starred,
Otavaa ojentamassa.   when the Plough was straightened.
(SKVR I:1, 185)

The heaven's forger motif of "I was one of the men / heroes when the sky was raised" is varied in epics, lyrics and incantations. In its most fixed form, attached to the creation of the world and clearly boasting in tone, the heaven's forger motif underlines the presence of the mythical hero at the time and place of creation: "I was one of the men", there and then. In lyric poems the motif is used metaphorically: the omnipotence of the heaven's forger in the mythical beginning of time is contrasted with the powerlessness of the ego of the lyric in the present: "Once I was a man, too" (SKVR I:3, 1291, I:1, 680). A similar nostalgic structure, this time directed at both time and place, was reflected in the lyrics of mythical homesickness: the olden days, at home, were better. In hunting incantations the heaven's forger motif is applied to describe the absence of game:

Olin mieki miessä ennen,   Once I was a man, too,
olin miessä kuudentena,   the sixth among the men,
seitsemäntenä urosna,   the seventh among the heroes,
joako joi jaettaessa,   when the shares were distributed,
ilman pieltä pisteässä.   when the air's edge was set.
Olin mieki miessä ennen,   Once I was a man, too,
olin mie ohon ovilla,   I was at the doors of the bear,
veräjillä vierahilla...   at foreign portals...
(SKVR I:4, 1250)

The hunter indicates that he was there in the mythical beginning of time, to distribute the catch and lot, the game and human fates, both luck in general and specific fortunes in individual occupations (Haavio 1955, 140, 446-458). Because the ego of the incantation was present at the mythical distribution of the catch, 'once' in the beginning, he had a right to his share of luck 'now', in the forest. The "doors of the bear, foreign portals" which the hunter boasts of having visited may refer either to former, luckier hunting trips or to the place where the mythical catch was shared out, the mythical primeval forest, in other words the mythical Pohjola conceived of as the store of all game (e.g. SKVR I:4, 1135, I:2, 874). The idea of the regulation of fortune as a whole in primeval times also motivated lyrical uses of the heavens-forging motif: the subject of the lyric was present at the beginning of time, when fortune and fates were handed out, so his lack of fortune was an offence against the world order.

 The structure of the heaven's forger motif can be reduced to two contrasts, temporal and spatial: 'the olden days', the mythical beginning of time or the more fortunate past is contrasted with the present times of want; 'there', the scene of the mythic creation, with the 'here' of the present-day world. In the context of incantations, both contrasts erupt in the ritual act; in the lyric they place individual life histories within the cosmic order of things and synchronise times mythical and historical.

 There is a metaphorical relationship between the lyrical uses of the heaven's forger motif and the use of the motif in the context of incantations. Incantatory and lyrical singing are in poetic language parallels to one another and the opening words of the lyric singer are woven into the boasts of the sage. As an example of the dialogue between incantation and lyric let us take a look at the use of the heaven's forger motif in a lyrical, autobiographically motivated The *Widow's Song*. Despite its masculinity, the motif also accommodates to the personal lyric of Anni Lehtonen from the village of Vuonninen as she sings of the death of her husband, leaving her a widow with six children:

Aina sitä ammusta elävi,	Living is easy in the morning,
vain illasta on kovin ikävä,	but the evenings make one longing,
kuin on kuollut kumppalini,	since my companion has died,
vaipun' on vaippani alaini.	the one under my mantle has sunken.
Ei ole miestä mennehestä,	The one who has passed away is no man,
urohosta uponnehesta.	the drowned one is no hero.
Oi miun poikia poloisen,	Woe, the sons of poor me,
oi miun laiton lapsosieni.	woe, the children of the sad one.
Mont' on tuulta tuulovata,	There is many a wind to blow,
mont' on saapuva sajetta	there is many a rain to fall
lakittoman peälajella,	over the head uncapped,
kintahittoman käsillä.	on the hands unmittened.
Kyllä se voipi voipa Luoja,	Yes, the able Creator can,
soattavi sulo Jumala	the sweet God knows
ylentää aletun mielen,	how to lift the sunken spirit,
nostaa lasketun kypärän,	how to raise the lowered helmet,
notkot nostaa, vaarat painaa,	raise the valleys, lower the hills,
notkot nostaa, vaarat painaa,	raise the valleys, lower the hills,
emännästä orjan soaha,	turn the mistress into a serf,
piijasta talon pitäjän.	the maiden into a head of the house.
Olin mieki miessä ennen,	Once I was a man, too,
uurohona kuuventena	the sixth among the heroes
ilman pieltä pistämässä,	I was there to set the air's edge,
taivoista tähittämässä.	there, to star the sky.
(SKVR I:3, 1388)	

The song begins with a statement of grief: the husband, the one closest to her skin lies dead. The powerlessness of the dead husband is expressed by alluding to symbolism usually connected to the epic hero's drifting to the otherworld or trance: the man is a "drowned hero" (e.g. SKVR I:1, 92). His death has left both the widow and their children unprotected. This lack of protection is likewise represented by images familiar from sage symbolism: the widow is capless, mittenless, and has lowered her helmet like the sage deprived of and seeking his magic support, "without a belt, without clothes, with hands unmittened, head uncapped" (SKVR I:4, 1880). Being 'capless' for a woman referred both to the unmarried status and to the social insecurity of the widow or the ill-treated woman: generally speaking, a capless woman was a woman without the cap a married woman wore (Paulaharju ibid. 162). In the context of incantations, the sage's cap is the symbol of his supranormal power and the most important of his magic attributes (Paulaharju 1929, 178-180). "Helmet awry" or "lowered" is throughout the genres an image for grief, loss or powerlessness; in the concrete world, the helmet was a headdress worn in slash-and-burn farming, on journeys and in laying out the dead (Manninen 1932, 394-395). The images for social and supranormal insecurity were identical – and widowhood can be regarded as a form of social death (Nenola ibid. 154-157; Caraveli-Chaves ibid. 137-138).

But the widowed mother continues. The lyrical poem is not content merely to describe her want; it is also a strategy for overcoming it.[23] With the help of the "sweet God" she may become the equal of a man, a master and the keeper of her own house. Her appeal (1) is identical to that used by a sage ordering back-up from the spirits in performing his ritual tasks (2):

1

Kyllä se voipi voipa Luoja,	Yes, the able Creator can,
soattavi sulo Jumala	the sweet God knows
ylentää aletun mielen,	how to lift the sunken spirit,
nostaa lasketun kypärän...	how to raise the lowered helmet...

2

Sie Ukko ylinen luoja,	You, Ukko the high creator,
voari vanha taivahaine,	the old father in the sky,
taivahallin Jumala,	the heavenly God,
ylennä alettu mieli,	lift the sunken spirit,
nossa laskettu kypärä!	raise the lowered helmet!
(SKVR I:4, 1880)	

Even the apparent differences of tone and mood between the spell and the lyric are superficial. The imperative of the spell is relieved by the lines preceding the quoted passage, "I trust in my creator, I throw myself in the hands of my god", while the resignation in The *Widow's Song* is negated by the bold crescendo of the heaven's forger motif. The widow's vision of the servant maiden's promotion to the status of mistress of the household presents an inversion of central social roles: the first becomes the last, and the last becomes the first. The unprotected widow acquires the status of her lost husband, to become a mistress of the household providing security for her children. The aspiration towards male competence and status leads the woman singer to make the masculine boast of the demiurge, "I too was a man...".

The basic emphasis in the journey symbolism and homesickness of travelling men and male sages was the social or symbolic death lurking along the way, but for women a journey meant something different. The *Widow's Song* functions rhetorically as a rite of passage in which the social liminality of the widow is broken by a masculine spirit-raising spell. The widow prepares to break the norm according to which a woman remained within the family circle. In reality, poverty drove the widow and many of her sisters in Archangel Karelia to beg, to become 'travelling men' (Haavio 1985 (1943), 26). In the new roles of master and traveller a woman could present a utopian image of herself on a par with the hero of creation: with the intermingling tones of lyrics and incantations, the rhetorical potency and magical power of words paved the way for a survival that was more than an emotional one. According to Barbara Babcock, inversions such as "mistress into a serf, maiden into a head of the house" are a common feature in utopian discourse, changes in the accustomed and normative role behaviour and rites of passage.[24] The *Widow's Song* was all of these.

Women of Vuokkiniemi. Photo: Samuli Paulaharju 1915 (FLS 5421).

The song is structured as a series of contrasts on many levels and the flow of inversions leading to the heaven's forger motif is impressive. God can raise the "lowered helmet" of the song's subject or give her back her social power; God can raise the valleys and lower the hills, i.e. negate the work of the creator hero, the topography. Finally God can turn the hierarchical structure of society upside down. The last of the tensions is released in defiant inversion that has no respect for the cultural gender distinction or the order of the universe: the widow is the forger of the world, she is equal to a man, and at least the forger of her own fortunes. The hero, manly man and traveller may also be a woman.

The series of inversions culminating in the heaven's forger motif draws a parallel between the two dimensions of God's omnipotence, the ordering of human fates and the creation of the world. The real living conditions and the fortunes laid down at the beginning of time also motivate the use of the heaven's forger motif in the hunting incantation discussed above. The potentials and shortcomings in the human lot were expressed by motifs in which the singer claims to have been one of the first when fortune was handed out. At manifest level the motif speaks in a masculine voice and points to cosmogonical acts, but its uses and implications for the worldview are not confined to the obvious. Through a masculine aetiological myth the heaven's forger motif develops metaphorical expressions for the human lot, the right to a good life and a good catch, in both the concrete and the abstract sense. Once again, representations embedded in an epic portraying women as passive objects were voiced differently when filtered through the intertextual relations within and between the genres.

Epilogue

Notions and biases concerning gender as well as gender stereotypes have been built into the ideological foundations of folkloristics of the Romantic era and after (see e.g. Fox 1987; Nenola ibid. 92-93). Martti Haavio describes laments performed by the singer of The *Widow's Song* analysed above as "lyrical, gentle, polished almost to a degree of decadence", while "the sturdy voices of men and the clashing of weapons" rang out from the heroic epics of male singers (Haavio ibid. 31; see also Tarkiainen ibid. 98-99). Filtered through the totality of the epic universe, the voice of the heroic epics resonates softly, the uncompromising sages of incantations confess to being their mothers' distressed sons, and the gentleness of laments and lyrics gives way to the imperative. The voices or perspectives of men and women intermingle in the process: simple object-subject relationships become ambiguous.

Although the songs can at thematic level be conceived of as descriptions of the border between two worlds, the symbolic network of the poetic language links together both the worlds in question (e.g. at the level of plot) and the different levels of the otherworld (e.g. through a common set of epithets). The borders in songs are meant to be crossed in symbolic processes of metaphor and metonymy.

The border between two worlds is not just a line on the cosmographic map of the epic universe: it also coincides with the borders of the concrete, lived-in space, the home circle, the gender-specific working spheres, the village and the graveyard, and the sauna. In rituals the numerous rites performed at thresholds and gates point to the same border and its crossing. The ritual time-space can also be created within a text, by a visual description in which the place indicated by the incantation assumes an iconic relationship with the place where it is performed (Tarkka 1990a, 325-327). Supranormal or marked social states are in songs described in spatial terms, as places or landscapes. Correspondingly, ritual transitions from one sphere or state to another can be described as journeys. The travel plots of epics may be regarded as portraying a dramatisation of a rite of transition, even though the poems in question were not performed in ritual context.[25] The birth of a child from nothing is reflected in the "mythical anatomy" (Lévi-Strauss 1963a, 193-195) of the landscape of the journey from the womb and in the same journey structure as the journey of the sage and the deceased to the unknown. The border between the genders and kins actualised in courting is described as the border between two worlds; the states before and after the betrothal are divided off like those of life and death. The human life span is projected onto a landscape that expands into a cosmology.

The interchangeability of otherworld images springs partly from the nature of the poetic language (stereotyping, formulaicity, parallelism) and it generates a complicated network of meanings. The otherworlds presented in the songs constitute a paradigmatic series in which different aspects of the otherworld acquire meaning only as part of their series: all the otherworlds are comparable but not identical. Pohjola, the womb, the tomb, graveyard, the state of being lost in and hidden by the forest, the Underworld, a strange village and a foreign land are points of reference through which tradition organises the temporality and spatiality of this world, dramatising social states into metaphysically and spatially separate ones, or concretising a change as a movement in time from one place to another.

The paradigmatic series of the otherworld is contrasted with the familiar at a number of conceptual levels. Each representative of this paradigm is in principle described by negative means: as an inversion of the familiar, normal and organised world, or as the absence of the features characteristic of it. The otherworld is a doorless cottage, a fireless stove, a treeless yard, a nameless village, beyond the reach of the sun; the one from the otherworld is "too noseless to be a human". The oppositions between the otherworld and this world are relationships by which the subject of the comparison, the individual or community, defines itself in relation to others felt to be contrasting or alien. The acts of communication built on the tension of identity and otherness are essentially acts of self-understanding.

A symbolic system such as this functions by creating identities on different levels of classification: the living, humans, the home village, one's own kin, the ego. This network of conceptual or symbolic relations forms the worldview[26] represented in the epic universe. It is by nature a system of meanings made up of metonymic and metaphorical relations.[27] The basic oppositions constituting the epic world could be illustrated as follows:

this world	-	otherworld
social cosmos	-	Pohjola
the living	-	the dead
culture	-	nature
visible reality	-	the inner space of the body
the village	-	the forest
the village	-	the graveyard
the graveyard	-	unchristened land
the yard	-	the shore/forest
the house	-	the tomb
the local community	-	administrative centres

The horizontal relations between the pairs of opposites, such as between the village and the forest, are both metaphorical and metonymic. The village and the forest represent separate conceptual spheres: they are likened to one another because of their shared attributes and contrasted because of their mutual differences. The forest community was sometimes described as the metaphorical counterpart or isomorph of the human community, being 'akin to a village', constructed according to the social relationships of the human community but representing a different reality.

The relationship between the village and the forest is at the same time unavoidably metonymic. Pairs of opposites can be regarded as metonymic e.g. in a ritual process in which opposing spheres are subjected to shared and common social intercourse, as in hunting rites, in which the communication between the forest and human communities is made possible through manipulation of the parties' symbolic statuses. Metonymy thus acts in the symbolic system of ritual poetry or epics dealing with ritual transitions as the factor breaking down the border or opposition between two separate, incompatible, metaphorically related spheres: opposition or similarity gives way to continuity, the separateness dissolves into communion.[28] Metonymy occupies a central role in the analysis of the epic universe, because narrative poetry has in particular been regarded as constructed on metonymic relationships, in other words, the syntagmatic level: on the combination of elements of the same conceptual order into a sequence.[29] As abstract concepts derived from the plots, communication and transition act as mediators between opposing categories. This mediation or dialogue on the thematic level is by nature metonymic. Thus, for example, the plot of the journey to the otherworld can be viewed as a metonymic elaboration on the relationship between the otherworld and this world.

The oppositions at different levels, such as the social and cosmological ones, in turn fall into an analogic series in relation to one another (e.g. village:forest :: village:graveyard :: ordered social cosmos:the North :: visible social reality:inner space of the body, etc.) The vertical relationships within the columns are in principle metaphorical: they lead from one conceptual frame or domain to another. The relationships forming this paradigmatic level project, for example, mythical images to social differences and vice versa (the administrative centre in otherworldly darkness, etc.). On the other hand, the paradigmatic series representing this world observes the principle of synecdoche:[30] it is a series of concentric circles around the ego in which the ego adapts its identity to broader frames of reference. Basically the individual has his place as a part in many larger totalities: he belongs to his own home yard, his village, his local community, to culture, and lastly but transiently to visible reality.

In symbolic systems (as represented in individual songs, genres or systems of genres) metaphor and metonymy are not therefore mutually exclusive. On the contrary: in poetic and ritual discourses meaning arises out of the interaction of metaphorical and metonymical relations.[31] The symbols of otherness and the otherworld serve both ritual and poetic texts dealing with the basic distinctions in a culture; in both the symbols serve to accentuate and elaborate on the cultural meanings instead of designating closed and stable messages.[32] Distance – difference and otherness – is foregrounded by metaphoric means, but it is also traversed and transgressed as a journey or in the dialogue. The symbolism of the otherworld is what James Fernandez calls a "play of tropes" in which continuities and discontinuities, similarities and oppositions are constantly played against each other and reworked (Fernandez 1986; Fernandez 1991, 6-7; Willis ibid. 7).

The otherworld of songs is not only contrasted with the present world: the only way to control the unknown is to give it attributes derived from the known world. In other words, metaphorical relations are based on perceived, e.g. structural similarities as well as differences. Just as the otherworld orders this world by acting as its border, mirror and opposite, so this world structures the otherworld, dialogically.[33] Without its opposite this world remains mute and faceless: paradoxically the otherworld of the epic universe always has a name and epithets, but the heroes' homeland goes unnamed. It is assumed to be familiar, but often only depicted as absence, in terms of nostalgia. Lönnrot's treatment of the epic universe in his literary epos parted radically from the logic of the original poems. To balance the wealth of names of the otherworldly Pohjola, he named the home of the heroes and the epos after a male hero seldom found in a hero's role: Kaleva (see e.g Kaukonen 1956, 425-428). The decontextualised literary epos had to name a substantial poetic and national ego for itself, and the relational structure of the symbolism of otherworld was decomposed.

Dialogue that has been treated on the level of thematic abstraction is embedded in the intertextual nature of the epic universe.[34] However, the intertextual networks connecting themes and images into chains of paradigmatic association are not the only textual strategy creating coherence: the epic universe is ultimately made meaningful through its relation to the world experienced by the singers. This relation is not one of reflection or mimesis, but one acted out and created in performance, on the level of discourse. The various levels of experiencing the otherworld – and through it this world – meet in the dialogue between genres, voices, and points of view anchored in the concrete voices of the singers (see Tarkka 1993). The intrusion of the poetic ego into the epic narrative and the organic link between e.g. incantations and lyrics manifest and permit the meeting of levels of the worldview: the conflicts and crises of the social reality, and the ways they are solved, are embedded in the mythic strata of the worldview and vice versa. The texts of the central transitional rites and the conceptual complexes associated with them together create a coherent picture of the world via the otherworld: the otherworld is a negation, a mirror and a metaphor for this world.[35] Its symbolism is, to borrow Janice Boddy's concept, an antilanguage: a language built on the tension between quotidian and extraordinary realities, a language with a vast potential for counterhegemonic usage (Boddy ibid. 156-159; see also Ilomäki 1989). At base, it is linked with utopian discourse, as the etymology of utopia as 'no place' or a 'good place' hints (The Encyclopedia of Religion, 159; see e.g. Timonen 1992).

How does the seeming otherness of women in the epic universe relate to the generalised symbolism of the otherworld? The relationship between men and women does not simply slot into the network of otherworld symbolism. The limitations of the schematic opposition model are at the same time revealed in the interpretation of real symbolic systems. The model is not a system of substantial differences; it illustrates relations between concepts, categories or states tied to context and perspective (see also Anttonen 1992, 72). Nor are the differences between different conceptual spheres or levels stable: they are open to interpretation and made to be crossed. Coherence is achieved not so much by means of dissection and separation of categories as by the dialectics of separation and association of the categories within the system of classification.

From the analyst's point of view, there is only one possible consciouss subject in the symbolic system of the epic world: the present world, 'we' the humans. The scheme is hierarchical and clearly determines only the this-world identity.[36] Nevertheless, not even the 'voiceless', animals, the dead, etc. are the real others in the system. If the belief system in which the symbolism and ritual dialogue are embedded is taken seriously, the voiceless do answer: that which is classified as being of the otherworld may act as a subject and generate its own meanings. The question is to a great extent one of 'belief' – of the ontological status ascribed by the interpreter to the supranormal reality localised by him, to its representations and the dialogues with it. The (ritual) communication which the present writer regards as symbolical or metaphorical may have been, for its agents, communication between two equally real or equally symbolical realities, in other words metonymic. The metaphorical movement from the time of mythical origins to the ritual present may have been conceived of as one, continuous duration – as history (Hastrup 1987, 263).[37] The voices of the otherworld agents nevertheless remain implicit in this corpus and do not appear in subject position, as definers of their own identity. Their historical presence is framed in forms of discourse that subdue their autonomy as subjects, and their existence seems to be conditional on the acts of communication initiated by agents of this world.[38]

One aspect of otherworldliness in the symbolic system of Archangel Karelian poetry was crystallised in the centres of administration and the administrative authorities. The administrators belonged to the dominant Finnish or Russian cultures, which were antagonistic towards especially the religious practices of Karelian folk culture. It was to this dominant culture that the song collectors belonged. The literate culture had its own discourse of otherness, and it was largely projected toward Karelia. The ideology of the song collectors and writers of travel accounts is likewise a symbolic system that construed identities in opposition to cultural others. Karelia was likened to nature, the Karelians to animals or exotic flowers, their character to naive but "death-like" joyfulness and their songs to the unconscious forces of nature (Sihvo 1973, 270; Tarkka 1989b). This widest ideological and methodological context does not only offer the most obvious example of the reciprocal or relative nature of otherness: it also says something about the basic premises of anthropological discourse. The Romantic projection of otherness onto folk culture and folklore is an undercurrent even to the tendency of reading the worldview of the cultural other metaphorically, seeking and seeing allegorical configurations and coherence. This process of 'othering' or exoticising is, as was learned from the themes of dialogue in Karelian oral poetry, basic to the acts of communication and understanding.

NOTES

The inspiration for this article is an earlier work published in Finnish under the title *Tuonpuoleiset, tämänilmanen ja sukupuoli. Raja vienankarjalaisessa kansanrunoudessa* in *Louhen sanat. Kirjoituksia kansanperinteen naisista.* A. Nenola – S. Timonen (eds.). Helsinki. 1990. Pp. 238-259.

1. According to Bakhtin (1981, esp. p. 13-40), dialogism is a feature of both literature and forms of discourse in general, but to him epic, contrary to the view put forward here, is monological, a form of discourse determined by one authoritative voice and closed meanings. However, Bakhtin stresses the dialogical nature of folklore, and thus oral epics (ibid. 38). For an interpretation of Kalevala-metric epics and the *Kalevala* as essentially monological, see Sawin ibid. 194-195.

2. According to Dennis Tedlock (1983, 322-323), dialogism of this type is a typical feature of anthropological understanding

and the ordering of cultural difference or otherness. For Bakhtinian dialogism and otherness, see Todorov 1984, 94-112.

3. The interpretations put forward in this article are partly based on my licentiate thesis examining symbolism of the otherworld in texts collected since 1825 in the Archangel Karelian village of Vuonninen – see Tarkka 1990. The main material for the article is from Vuonninen and the surrounding parish of Vuokkiniemi.

4. On the isomorphic relationship between the forest and the human community in Finnish-Karelian tradition see Ilomäki ibid. 61, 130; Köngäs-Maranda 1967, 87-92; Tarkka ibid. 246, 265, 319-321, 350-352.

5. On the isomorphism of weddings and bear feasts see Kuusi 1963, 50-51; Sarmela 1978, 273; cf. Harva 1933, 275-279. 18. See e.g. I:4,1207; on the role of the *patvaska* see Sarmela 1981, 30; Inha 1921 (1911), 146.

6. See e.g. SKVR I:4, 1207; on the role of the *patvaska* see Sarmela 1981, 30; Inha 1921 (1911), 146.

7. On the otherness of women in Karelian culture and poetry see Voionmaa 1969 (1915), 503-507; Nenola ibid. 145-148; Tarkiainen 1911, 91-96. For the same theme in lyrics of North Karelia see Timonen 1989, 17-18.

8. Symbolic relations of men and women or public and private and their representations in the epic universe are rooted in power relations within the 'public' of the village community, and ultimately situated in the wider configuration of the village community's standing in opposition to the 'public' of centres of administration.

9. A corresponding notion of the relationship between the poetic ego, the voice and the person of the singer is presented in e.g. Cruz 1988 and Kay 1990, 94-103, 174-175. On the voices of poetic subjects and real singers in folkloric discourse see Tarkka, 1993.

10. On the relationship of life experience and Kalevala-metric narrative poetry see Timonen 1990b; Pentikäinen 1987, 246-249; on the uneasy relationship of the female point of view, subject position, and tradition dominated by a "misogynistic fantasy" see Kay ibid. 102.

11. The statistics naturally only provide information on the gender distribution of the folklore that has been collected, and the collection was clearly biased for certain heroic epics. For the differing genre profiles of men and women in Archangel Karelia and the variation in popularity within the epic corpus see Tarkka 1990, 29-31, 113, appendix 39-40; see also Timonen 1990b, 137. The statistics given by Leea Virtanen (1968, 49-51) support the observations in other Finnish-Karelian culture areas, too. On the overlapping repertoires of men and women see Apo ibid. 7.

12. On the voice or perspective of women in folklore texts see e.g. Mark 1987; on the gendered voices, points of view and the 'authors' genders in the Finnish-Karelian ballad tradition see Apo ibid. 8-13.

13. On the rhetorical position of the subject as a factor contextualising oral poetry and as a mediator of the 'experienced' and the 'sung' realities see Tarkka, 1993. On 'Marianic interventions' and 'female subjects' voices in *The Messiah* see Timonen 1990b, 137-143. Patricia Sawin's (ibid. 195) interpretation of Kalevala-metric poetry as monological is based on the assumption that there is a stable, authoritative narrator, who determines a fixed point of view for the epic, and frames the lines in order to keep the narrative under his control. The analysis is not sensitive to the epic as discourse, and to its potential for interventions by the singers themselves, but it catches the logic of Lönn-

rot's manipulation of this potential.

14. In Archangel Karelia 79% of the singers of *The Fishing* are known to be men, in the village of Vuonninen the rate is 74% (Virtanen ibid. 50; Tarkka 1990, appendix 39-40). The male bias of the poem is not unambiguous, however, since elements parodying the male hero can also be heard in it – see Kuusi 1963, 326-327.

15. For an analysis of Karelian sagedom and trance-related phenomena see Siikala 1980 & 1986 & 1986.

16. Similar cases have been reported and discussed in e.g. Tedlock & Tedlock 1985 (fusion of narrating and divination) and Hamayon 1978, Hatto 1970, Boyer 1982, 28-30 and Mastromattei 1985 (fusion of the role of shaman, the epic hero, and the singer of the epic). When discussing the Ob-Ugrian epics narrated in the first person, Cushing (1980, 217, 226) stresses the mythological and ritual nature of such fusions: the narrator identifies himself with a supernatural being. Most of the examples are connected to religious practices involving possession. Lars Lönnroth (1979) calls this phenomenon the 'double-scene of performance'. On the 'double scene' as a strategy binding the textual to the extratextual, see also Tarkka 1990, 152-171; Tarkka, 1993.

17. More precisely, Pohjola's representation as a building without apertures connects up with the idea of Pohjola as a site of 'bad death', like in its epithet of a 'place without priest': proper coffins and miniature houses built on the grave had to have doors and windows for the dead and the living to communicate through (Paulaharju ibid. 86.).

18. On the status of the dead family members and kin in folk belief see e.g. Konkka ibid. 38-40, 79-80; Mansikka 1924; Harva 1948, 510-511; Paulaharju ibid. 174-175.

19. The generalisation is not all-embracing: the *patvaska* also negotiated the pacts between the kingroups. Cf., however, the roles of the lamenter and the *patvaska* in the wedding ritual as portrayed in Konkka ibid. 104-107, Niemi 1921, 1091 and Inha ibid. 146, 248-249.

20. On the relationship of the Virgin Mary with the life experience of Karelian women and the ritual manifestation of this relationship see Timonen 1987, 112-113, 115-117; Timonen 1990b, 137-146.

21. The ambivalent sympathy easily turning into antagonism between the female inside and otherworld was not confined to the forces of death. The relation between forest nature, especially the bear, and the woman, especially her womb, was already hinted at in the context of hunting incantations: at the bear feast, women were taught to "beware of their bellies, take care of their wombs" (SKVR I:4, 1247) as the dead bear entered the house – see Paulaharju ibid. 22.

22. On the body as a symbol for the community see e.g. Douglas ibid. 115, 121-122; on the female body, especially the womb and the vagina as symbols for the community, microcosms and embodiments of communal values see Boddy 1989, 74-75, 252. According to Timonen (1990b, 126), the vision of the female inner space as "as wide as the sky", can be traced back to Orthodox hymns, and to the virginal body of the Virgin Mary.

23. The notion of lyric poetry as a concrete strategy corresponds to Senni Timonen's analysis on the utopian structures in Kalevala-metric lyric poetry – see Timonen 1989; Timonen 1992.

24. See Babcock 1978, 16-21. A more pessimistic interpretation of similar inversions as *adynatons*, tropes of the impossible, in Greek tradition is put forward in Herzfeld 1981a, 128-130.

25. On the ritual nature of the journey plot see e.g. Lord 1974 (1960), 109; Ricoeur 1976, 62. On the transformations of time, place and status in lament texts see Caraveli-Chaves ibid. 141-142, 144; see also Howe & Hirschfeld ibid. 313-314. On the journey symbolism in rites of passage in general see van Gennep 1960, 18-20; and on marked social states, their boundaries and spatial representation in Finnish and Ob-Ugrian traditions see Anttonen ibid.

26. On worldview as a multilayered system of conceptual, social and spatial distinctions see Hastrup 1981, 65, 72, 74-75; Hastrup 1985, 143, 147-151, 240; see also Herzfeld 1989 (1987), 154-155.

27. I here use the distinction between metaphor and metonymy (or paradigmatic and syntagmatic association) derived from the concepts of Roman Jakobson (e.g. Jakobson 1977) introduced into anthropological discourse by Lévi-Strauss (e.g. 1989 (1962), 75-105, 135-161). Metaphor refers to a symbolic relationship in which the parties concerned ('target' and 'source' domains) are perceived in terms of their similarity or comparability even if they belong to different conceptual domains – metonymy indicates continuity or contiguity between the domains united in the trope. See e.g. Fernandez 1986, 43-48; Durham & Fernandez 1991, 191-192; Leach 1976, 14-15.

28. On the part played by metonymy in the ritual process see e.g. Turner 1991, 147-149; Isbell 1985. See also Fernandez ibid. 39-46; Needham 1979, 28-29. Cf. the analysis by Caraveli-Chaves (ibid. 141-142) of Greek laments as a system of constructing and deconstructing symbolic oppositions.

29. See e.g. Jakobson 1987b, 310. Restoration of the metonymic relationships (or the syntagmatic level) and narrativity into the theoretical core of myth analysis is central in e.g. Turner's (1985, 53-55) critique of Lévi-Strauss.

30. Synecdoche here refers to relationships that are similar to that between a whole and its constituent parts.

31. See Jakobson's (1987a) theorem of the poetic function; in symbolic anthropology the corresponding dynamics of metaphor and metonymy is stressed in e.g. Fernandez 1991, 6-7. Durham & Fernandez ibid. 193-198; Turner 1991, 135-149, 152-155; Willis 1990, 7. On the transformations of oppositions see Needham 1979, 31-43.

32. Similar processual notions of metaphor and ritual are put forward in e.g. Fernandez 1986, 39-46 and Turner ibid. 149. See also Isbell 1985; Keesing 1985, 211-212.

33. For a discussion on the relationship between 'factual reality' and the 'anti-world' of magic and / or nature in the language of incantations see Ilomäki ibid. 82-86. On the otherworld as a generator of meanings and as the symbolic antithesis to this world see Zaleski 1987, 74.

34. On the link between worldview, metaphor and intertextuality in oral poetry see Herzfeld 1981b, 53, 56; Rosaldo 1975, 178, 198-200; Tarkka, 1993.

35. On coherence in worldview and the textual, symbolic, and ritual strategies producing it see Colby 1987; Fernandez 1982, 532-564; Eliade 1959, 99-100. On negation as a principle of cultural self-analysis see Boon 1982, 232 and on metaphor as negativity see Burke 1966, 452, 476.

36. For the hierarchical nature of systems of symbolic oppositions see Needham 1987, 18, 103, 120-21 – and for a critique based on it see Herzfeld 1989 (1987), 95-99. The symbolic system of Kalevala-metric poetry does not, however, brand the otherworld as being exclusively negative. In other words, the negativity of the otherworld was structural, not an evaluation: if this world was a world of scarcity and want, the mythical Pohjola of the songs and the otherworld generally was a potential source of prosperity, spouses, medicines and knowledge – see Tarkka 1990, 279, 291-293, 305-310.

37. On the problem of anthropological interpretation, metaphor, and metaphysical assumptions of the concept of belief see Keesing ibid. and Sandor 1986, 102-103. The interpretations put forward here do not consider whether the dialogue was 'real' or not – the analysis keeps to the level of symbolic representations and within the confines of the epic, textual universe. On the difference between the epic representation of dialogue with the supranormal and the dialogue experienced as 'real' see Mastromattei 1985.

38. Analysis of popular dream interpretations, experiences of spirit encounters, praying by an icon, or even memorates might suggest a different picture of the otherworldly agents' active participation in the dialogue.

Women's Voice

SENNI TIMONEN

The Mary of Women's Epic

> His mother looked down at Him and said:
> "Tell me, my child, how the seed was planted in me and how it grew in me.
> I behold Thee, merciful One, and I wonder..."
>
> (Kontakion on the Nativity of Christ, Romanos 1970, 4)

Karelian culture is highly complex in its religious folklore. Lying on the northern border between the religions of East and West, it looks in two directions. From the Middle Ages onwards Finland and western Karelia came, first, under the Roman Catholic Church and, later during the Reformation, under the Lutheran Church, while the eastern parts of Karelia were firmly tied to the Orthodox faith and the Russian way of life.

Between two Christian expanding worlds, meeting and to some extent merging on its territory, Karelia preserved elements of an indigenous non-Christian belief-system for much longer than neighbouring regions in Finland. This can probably be explained by its peripheral location far from both the spiritual and secular authorities. Karelia thus developed a strong local religion combining elements both familiar and alien to which the term syncretic is customarily applied. Numerous examples of this religion in Karelian – above all in the form of prayers, spells and narrative poems recorded from oral tradition – are to be found in the Karelia volumes of *Suomen Kansan Vanhat Runot* ('Ancient Poems of the Finnish People', hereafter SKVR).

Woven into many thousands of lines of poetry is evidence of the religious experience of the Karelians and the diversity of its expression. The form and meaning of these texts depend on the researcher and the particular Karelian group in question: the Karelians of the Middle Ages, of the nineteenth century or of the present day; citizens of Finland, Russia or the Soviet Union; Lutherans or Russian Orthodox; women or men.

Certain features occur in poetry throughout Karelia. The Virgin Mary, for example, is everywhere. She has, however, acquired sharply contrasting interpretations in the differing traditions of the Church and people. The distinctive features of the official – church – traditions can be described as follows: according to the Roman Catholic Church Mary, Queen of Heaven,

Songs beyond
the Kalevala
Studia Fennica
Folkloristica 2
1994

was born free of sin; she entered the world as a divine being and thus stands far above the everyday world of mortals. According to the Russian Orthodox faith Mary, Mother of God, was conceived in human fashion, but through the will of God and her own wish became divine in the course of her life on earth; in changing from being a receiver to being a giver of grace, she is identified with both mankind and God. In the Lutheran interpretation, Mary is an exemplary person, humble and devout: she is merely an instrument of God, and hence excessive worship of her is idolatry.

All the canonical images of the Virgin Mary have existed in Karelia, side-by-side, overlapping, merging and at times quite separate from one another; in their numerous transformations they have passed into popular belief. These manifestations throughout the area appear, at least quantitatively, to reflect the importance attached to the figure of Mary by the Church. Although the Reformation ended worship of the Virgin in western and Finnish North Karelia in the course of the seventeeth century, numerous indications of her medieval glory can be identified even in the twentieth century. In Orthodox Karelia and Ingria, further south, popular worship of Mary survived uninterrupted alongside the official faith from the Middle Ages until the present century; in places it continued until the Second World War.

Study of the Karelian material, most of which was collected in the nineteenth century, reveals two main types of tradition associated with the Virgin, one recorded among Orthodox believers, the other among Lutherans. In both traditions – as indeed further west in Finland and among Swedish-speaking Finns – healers invoked the Virgin's help. Indeed spells and prayer incantations are among the basic sources of Marian folk belief (cf. Krohn 1914, 215-225; Haavio 1935, 189-191; Kuusi 1966; Knuts 1974). According to one estimate (probably on the low side), the name of Mary occurs some 1500 times in incantations recorded in SKVR (Vilkuna 1966, 373) and is mentioned more than any other person in the surviving texts.

In western Finland, Marian spells are short and refer to her from a relative distance, as a memory only: they tell how she once stanched Jesus's bleeding or healed a wounded animal; or they refer to her metaphorically by reference to her ancient acts. Further east, Marian themes and motifs increase in variety and number. In Savo and especially in Karelia – even more so in Orthodox Karelia – the narrative episodes and metaphors are joined by direct appeals, prayers and pleas to the Virgin Mary. She is no longer just a memory, she is present in person.

Marian themes and motifs proliferate in incantations and prayers. Some of them are pre-Christian, subsequently attached to the Virgin Mary, others are part of common Christian tradition, Western or Orthodox in origin. Mary carrying ointment in a cup on her back or providing milk from hundreds of nipples has been interpreted as a Christian variant of the ancient mother goddess; the concept of the healing power of Mary's milk is in itself a popular Christian motif (Haavio 1928, 209, 230). The Marian themes and motifs are, however, generally regarded primarily as a relic of medieval Roman Catholic culture which has survived on its eastern periphery.

Marian motifs classifiable as Western may on closer examination, nevertheless, prove to be of Orthodox origin. An example could be the veil motif which is widespread in the Karelian prayer chants: Mary's fiery, waxy or golden veil is sought as protection for humans or animals. Iconographic study of this motif, linked through folklore with Western tradition (Kaukonen 1942), has shown it to be one of the Marian motifs that seem to have a clear link with Russian and through it with Byzantine tradition (Jääskinen 1969). In Byzantine tradition, the motif is connected with a miracle thought to have taken place in Constantinople in 626 during the Muslim siege; the Virgin Mary was seen to appear in the Temple of Blachernae spreading her protective veil over the faithful. (Wellesz 1949, 163-164.) The *Pokrova* (Russian pokrov 'veil, protection') feast held on 1 October in memory of the event was the most popular celebration of Mary in Karelia. An integral part of everyday life, it marked the return of livestock from summer grazing grounds for the winter in the byre and was watched over by the Mother of God. (Mansikka 1941, 295-299.) On that day the church and popular traditions came close to merging (Jääskinen 1969; Selinheimo 1970, 88-94). The Kontakion of the feast says: "the Virgin now stands in the church"; in the Troparion the faithful turned to the Virgin saying: "Looking at your holy image we devoutly recite: protect us with your holy covering..." As they drove the cattle into the cowshed the people would say: "Weave for me a golden cloth, full a copper cloak, with which I'll cover my herd, protect my dung-shanks!" (translated by Keith Bosley in Timonen 1987, 104.)

The prayer motifs are, *prima facie*, similar in Lutheran and Orthodox Karelia. Specifically Orthodox features are to be seen more in the overall approach, the style – intimate tone, sense of proximity and presence, personal relationship with the Virgin – rather than in the origin of individual motifs. The tradition of Orthodox Karelia draws a more conscious and more direct parallel between the supplicant and the person addressed: you too have given birth, you know what it involves, so please come and help me! Various chronological levels and the sacred and the profane are intermixed.

Another typical feature of incantations addressed to the Virgin Mary in Orthodox Karelia is the focus on the world of women: childbirth, sexual arousal, care of children and livestock, tending wounds. The prayers and incantations prompt to ask whether Mary was regarded specifically as a guardian of women, and whether worship of the Virgin Mary was primarily a female tradition. The role of protector and helper, while not confined to one sex alone, is also one of Mary's church roles, explicit in the hymns sung on the *Pokrova* feast (cf. Selin 1973, 89-91). There is one difference, however. Whereas the appeals to the Virgin in prayers and hymns performed in church are theological and abstract in content (seeking her protection in general and her intercession on behalf of the soul), folk prayers are always clearly defined, relating directly to practical concerns and anxieties of women; they beseech the Virgin to appear as a living person to help them overcome the problem. And she really is thought to appear in person, transcending time and space, milk flowing from her breasts, swaddling clothes in her hands and water from the River Jordan in her bucket.

A Messiad or a 'Mariad'?

The placing on the same level of the mundane and the sublime, the past and the present, the Virgin and the ordinary woman in Orthodox Karelian prayers to the Virgin reflects the fact that at the time of collection these prayers were still founded in a living faith. In both its church and its popular forms this faith manifests – in and through the Virgin – the existence of the sacred in everyday life. This feature emerges powerfully not only in the prayer incantations but also in rites and myths: in annual feasts in the Virgin's memory and in epic songs telling about her. 'Marian culture' in this strict sense was in Karelia restricted to the Orthodox regions of Archangel and Olonets Karelia, and Ingria in Russia, and Ladoga Karelia in Finland.

Of all the popular Marian traditions closest to those of the official church were the annual feasts to the Virgin (see Mansikka 1941; Selin 1973; Tarvasaho 1986) celebrated in Karelia as special village festivals, *praaz-niekkas* (from Russian prazdnik) if the village church was dedicated to a particular feast. In nineteenth-century Orthodox Karelia and Ingria, there appear to have been more than a hundred churches or chapels dedicated to the Virgin Mary (Sarmela 1969, 70-85; Sauhke 1971). In practice, there-fore, more than a hundred annual village feasts were dedicated in this region specifically to the memory of the Virgin. *Pokrova* was the most common, celebrated in thirty three villages and seeking the protection of the Mother of God on October 1. The popularity in Karelia and Russia of the *Pokrova* festival, which does not rank among the great Marian feasts officially celebrated by the Orthodox Church, is evidence of the need for protection, the theme of the feast, from the human point of view. The most popular of the official Marian feasts in Karelia were those in honour of the Dormition of the Mother of God, known in Karelia as *Emänpäivä* (Mother's Day) or *Uspenja* (Russian Uspenie) on 15 August (celebrated in thirty-two vil-lages), the Nativity of the Mother of God, known in Karelia as the Great Praasniekka or *Bogorotsa* (Russian bogoroditsa, god-bearer) on 8 Septem-ber (fourteen villages), the Annunciation, known in Karelia as *Blahosenja* or *Plahvesenna* (Russian blagoveščenie) on 25 March (eight villages) and the Presentation of the Mother of God in the Temple, Karelian *Vedennä* (Russian Vedenie vo khram) on 21 November 21 (five villages). Other smaller feasts to the Virgin Mary were held here and there.

The act of worship on the feasts to the Virgin concentrated on a topical event in the life of Mary and was illustrated by the icons brought out for the occasion and church hymns in elaboration of the specific theme.

It is legitimate to ask what understanding the illiterate Karelians had of events related in Church Slavonic. Earlier research often argues that the Karelians' knowledge of religion was superficial, or non-existent (cf. Genetz 1870a, 202; 1870b, 102-103). This is attributed not only to the language problem but also to the drunkenness and poor education of the Karelian priests. There are, however, reasons, most often overlooked in this connection, to the contrary. Bilingualism was, for examle, relatively common in the Karelian-Russian border areas and was reinforced by the existence there of Old Believer refugees and the fact that the Old Belief took firm root in parts of Karelia: it became the religion of many Karelians, and acquired a spirituality which exceeded that of the official church (cf. Pentikäinen 1971, 128-149). Secondly, a literal understanding of language is not essential. The liturgical and spiritual life of Orthodox believers draws as much on experience as on fact, operating to a great extent through paintings, colours, melodies, scents, movement and physical touch. Such 'wordless' elements – images, sensations, experiences of sharing, presence of holiness – conveyed religious knowledge, values and attitudes to the Karelians more naturally and more forcefully than the spoken word.

The image of the Virgin Mary, or the Mother of God, understood either with or without words and further enhanced in the believer's own mind, finds expression in the narrative songs about Mary.

Researchers have usually understood these songs as stories about the life of Christ, not Mary. While it is true that first known versions were published under the heading of *Marian virsi*,'The Song of Mary' in 1831 and 1840 (following the practice of the singers), the addenda and notes supplied by the editors – Zachris Topelius (1831) and Elias Lönnrot (1840) – show that they believed the singers to have been in error about the subject of these stories. The sub-heading added by Topelius – "Easter story dating from Papal era" – is indicative of their attitude. According to his commentary, the title had no justification in the Bible and only went to show just how vague their knowledge of God and redemption was. "Fortunate is the present day, in which the light of God's word has dispelled the idle chatter of darkness!" he concluded (SKVR I:2, 1120). Lönnrot, too, writes that "almost the whole song is but an empty tale". He justifies the inclusion of the text in his *Kanteletar* as follows: "Wrong and unfounded as this song may on the one hand be, it is, on the other, moving and beautiful in its verbal construction, from which we can see that content and verbal expression are different things, even though the uneducated may not always distinguish between them." (Foreword to book III of the *Kanteletar*, cited by J. Krohn and K. Krohn 1901, 197.) Later, such scholars as Arvid Genetz wrote after visiting Karelia (1870a, 202) that "trifling verses such as *The The Virgin Mary's song* in the *Kanteletar*, in which the most sacred truths of the Christian faith are even distorted, are sung and believed...".

Subsequent research has rejected the name *The Song of Mary*. The adoption of *The Creator's Song* or *The Messiah* has been justified on the grounds that the song is specifically about the life of Christ (Borenius 1886, 59; J. Krohn and K. Krohn 1901, 417). This interpretation applies, however, to only some of the material. The treatment of such versions as the canon reflects two factors: the researchers' own Protestant, male worldview in which Mary and women's experiences have no place, and the concept – for so long characteristic of the discipline – of the 'authentic', 'original' poem from which all later variants were thought to derive.

The Creator's Song or *The Song of Mary*, as the poem is called by the singers, is not in fact a poem but an extensive concatenation of interlinking poems; in many places, it grows into a miniature epic and for this reason has also been regarded as 'epic' and been called 'the Finnish Messiad'. (Haavio 1935, 67; Kuusi 1963, 292.) Most variants, which comprise many separate poems, usually run to about two hundred lines and have three, sometimes even four themes or separate poems. The longest variants are more than three hundred lines in length and concatenate relatively more poems.

The essence and evolution of this epic as a whole have not yet been explained by researchers, although certain parts have been analysed and the epic as whole has been dealt with only at a general level. Like Topelius,

Women from Miinoa washing clothes on the shore, in southern Archangel Karelia. Photo: I.K. Inha 1894 (FLS 9858).

the first scholars to consider the epic mainly traced the motifs back to the Roman Catholic legend tradition of Western Europe (Borenius 1886; J. Krohn and K. Krohn 1901; Haavio 1935, 66-77). However, the comparative approach has later demonstrated that the closest counterparts are almost without exception to be found in the legend songs and apocryphal sources popular among speakers of Slavic languages (Oinas 1969; Haavio 1955, 7-120; Kuusi 1963, 295). Although *The Messiah* is nowadays thought to be mainly Slavic in origin, it has adapted naturally to the Karelian verse form and milieu (Kuusi 1963, 292-298; 1980, 233-234; Kirkinen 1986, 18-20; 1988, 110-113). Estimates of its age vary. The poems may be relics of the early missionary work of the Eastern Church (Kuusi), they may date from the late Middle Ages (Kirkinen) or – because of their narrow distribution – may not have emerged until the early Modern Period in the seventeenth century (Pertti Virtaranta, oral communication).

So far I have discovered 334 texts that can be classified as variants of the epic. They date from the period between the 1820s and the 1980s, with the majority from the nineteenth century. Since both the structure and focus of the poems vary, each component poem and even each variant have to be examined separately to determine whether the main protagonist is Mary or Jesus. Marian themes occur in most variants.

I shall examine below the parts of the epic which I regard as Marian poems. The title *The Messiah* must therefore be abandoned, similarly the traditional division into five parts (*The Berry, Search for a Sauna, Search for the Lost Child, Resurrection* and *Shackling the Devil's Smith*). First, certain prominent poems about Mary have not regarded by research as important parts of the epic but as later accretions (see, however, J. Krohn and K. Krohn 1901, 44-46, 114-115; cf. Kuusi 1963, 294). However, the fact that the singers chose to include them in their renderings implies that they considered them important. Secondly, many unexpected variations in *The Messiah* will be shown to acquire significance. In such cases, a poem that is usually only about Christ (e.g. *Resurrection*) gives Mary an active role. Scholars have either regarded these sections of *Resurrection* as 'unnatural' or 'corrupt' (cf. J. Krohn and K. Krohn 1901, 105), or they have ignored them. From the point of view of the Mary theme, however, they are manifestations of the strength and creativity of the culture and I shall call them henceforth 'Marian interventions'.

The aspect that particularly concerns me here is creativity, the strength which the image of Mary inspires in the poems. How did the singers envisage Mary? Which of her usual roles dominates the poems: virgin, mother, protector, intercessor, heavenly queen, or leader of the heavenly forces? Were the performers of the narrative songs about her life men or women? What points in her life did the singers concentrate on? The large corpus of songs, their variety and the intense way in which they approach their subject show that their content was of vital importance to the singers. It should, therefore, be possible to find in the poems evidence of significant meanings and affinities with the singers' own reality.

Each of the component songs forcefully highlights a turning point in Mary's life which the singers, for one reason or another, understood as being of fundamental importance. The songs as a whole are also characterized by a certain inner approach: at the core is not only the event itself, but Mary's attitude to it. The whole series of poems may in this respect be reduced to a single question: How did Mary live? This question and its variations unlock many of the hidden messages concealed in *The Messiah*: in other words, Mary's experience as the singers might, through their own lives and culture, have understood it.

Impregnation: the berry miracle

The story of how Mary was fertilized by a berry or an apple is one of the key themes in the poems about the Virgin. Of the 120 variants, eighty-six were recorded from women, twelve from men, the rest from anonymous singers. It is thus clearly a women's poem. It was most popular in Archangel Karelia, *Viena* and Northern Olonets, *Aunus* but was also clearly known in Southern Olonets, Ladoga Karelia and Ingria.

The poem varies in length from seven to fifty-five lines, depending on whether the singer simply makes a statement or goes into detail. The latter cases, of which there are many, are vital to the interpretation of the Marian image. They are already active interpretations in themselves and thus indicate how the singers might in general have understood this basic theme.

Some singers stress Mary's virginity, insisting that she did not "sit in a sleigh drawn by a stallion, or drink the milk of a cow followed by bulls" (SKVR I:2, 1113). The description of virginity is, however, more dominant in other contexts, as in the poem about the maiden Iro who gives birth to three heroes. In the Marian poems it remains – at least as the guiding definition – in the background. Singers concentrate on the actual event, the dramatic present: Mary and the berry.

The setting is sometimes a peaceful, everyday interior: Mary is sweeping the living room. The chain of events is set in motion outside. While taking the sweepings outside, Mary hears a berry calling, shouting, screaming to her from the forest: "Come, maid, and pick me, copper-belted one, choose me...!" (FFPE 1977, 283). Sometimes the berry tells her why she must hurry: "...before the slug devours me and the black worm gobbles me!" (FFPE 1977, 283)

The poems indicate through finely-turned yet precise images that the call of the berry creates a turmoil in Mary. She cannot ignore it, she must leave the house and yard and go off into the forest. Her departure is given further significance by the accounts of how she dresses and prepares herself, thereby making her into a female counterpart of the male hero of mythical epic songs. Before setting out on a dangerous journey, the seer puts on a metal belt (SKVR I:3, 14), an iron shirt and a steel belt (SKVR I:3, 473); Ilmarinen setting off to woo and the bridegroom departing for his wedding gird themselves with iron bands and metal belts (SKVR I:1, 473; see also SKVR I:1, 494; Tarkka 1990a, 109-10, 201-19). In the same way Mary "dressed herself and decked herself, prettily adorned her head" (FFPE 1977, 283), with tin buttons on her breast, with copper bands and tin belts (SKVR I:2, 1120). All the preparations lead up to the verb "went"; its permanence amid all the variations indicates that the singers were all agreed on Mary's activeness and the irresistible call of the berry. Another indication of the significance of the departure is the fact that at this point the singer sometimes shifts to the first person singular: "I went to pick the berry" (SKVR II, 320).

The sudden, frenzied nature of departure is emphasized. "She snatched up the basket" (SKVR II, 325a), "she threw a silk kerchief round her head" (SKVR II, 323). The journey may be of immeasurable length and proceeds in giant steps: "Moved her feet: she was on the third hill. Moved them a second time: she was on the sixth hill. Moved them a third time: she was on the ninth hill" (SKVR I:2, 1111). The mountains bend under her feet (SKVR II, 329). On reaching the berry-hill, Mary finds that things are not so simple. It is too high: it has climbed a tree (SKVR I:2, 1118), it is between the earth and the sky (SKVR I:2, 1117). Thereupon Mary snatches a stick from the woods (SKVR I:2, 1118) or strips a marsh pine (SKVR I:2, 1117) and with it knocks the berry to the ground.

The berry is now before her. But how does she eat it? Some singers say that she simply "took the berry from the hill" (SKVR I:2, 1128), "took the berry in her fingers, from her fingers to her lips, her lips to her tongue..." (SKVR II, 322), or, in the first person, "I took the berry in my fingers" (SKVR II, 320). Others, however, emphasize her ecstatic state by making her even more active and determined. Her desire to obtain the berry is so great that she addresses it with lines from spells designed to rouse a man's sexual desire and potency. The ecstatic commands of the love spells in the same regions demand, for example: "Rise up love and burst into flame, rise up happiness to step on, rise up penis, stand up smith, grow up, cunt-hammer!" (SKVR I:4, 1822 + manuscript, KRA) or "Rise up penis, stand up smith ... rise unlifted, stiffen untouched, stand up like a haypole, enter like an iron rod this maid's crack, this child's buttocks" (SKVR I:4, 1815 + manuscript, KRA). Mary in turn addresses the berry: "Rise up rise up, my little berry, roll up on my bright hems! Rise up rise up my berry on the tips of my brass belt, on to my fair breasts, my silver lips, my golden tongue!" (SKVR I:2, 1116). Another singer describes the event as the immediate alternation of the words and their consequences: "'Rise up, berry, on the balls of my feet!' The berry rose up on the balls of her feet. 'Rise up, berry, on my belt!' The berry rose up on her belt. 'Rise up, berry, on my lips.' The berry rose up on her lips, and slid down into the belly." (SKVR I:2, 1109)

There is also another, though inverse mythical parallel for the rising of the berry that has been regarded as its model (J. Krohn and K. Krohn 1901, 62; Kuusi 1963, 295-296): the tears of Väinämöinen and Aino's mother, who order them to roll down: "Roll, roll my tears ...". Out of the berry rising into Mary is born a baby, while the tears flowing from their eyes grow into a river, pearls or trees. The metamorphosis of the tears is sometimes unexpectedly linked with Mary in the poem about Aino. For Aino is then "the Virgin mother" Mary who in the forest loses her virginity: on returning home she does not, as Aino usually does, hang herself. Instead her tears roll to the ground and turn into strawberries and an oak tree that unleashes a sea along which suitors sail to woo the maidens (Tarkka 1990a, 118-19). Mary thus appears here, as Tarkka shows, "as an active husband-seeker", contrary to the usual situation in the poems about loss of virginity which stress the passive, sacrificial status of women. Another interpretation may be that Mary is regarded here as the helper and protector of all who actively seek a husband: as the creator of berries and opener of the road to marriage.

In Ingria the fertilization drama is in its basics similar to the Archangel Karelian one already cited. On the surface, it is more idyllic – lacking the direct myth-poem allusions – but it is inwardly on a scale just as grand as the northern version. It opens with Mary already on the road, dressed in clean silk clothes, her skirts sweeping the ground as she searches. She comes to a barley field. In the middle of it she sees a tree full of apples and nuts: "Took an apple from the bough, took the nut from off the tree, put the apple to her lips, from her lips on to her tongue, from her tongue into her throat" (FFPE 1977, 301).

The slipping of the berry into Mary's stomach ends the dramatic climax in the poem about the miraculous berry. Sometimes Mary goes on to describe the goodness of the berry: "Many have I picked, many plucked, many fingered, but never one so good!" (SKVR I:2, 1098). The epilogue is always calm: "She was fulfilled, she was filled by it, grew thickset from it, put on flesh from it." (FFPE 1977, 283)

What was Mary seeking on the berry hill? God? A husband? Or both? A berry or an apple growing on a tree has been remotely connected with, for example, the imagery of Eve and the apple tree (J. Krohn and K. Krohn 1901, 62-63; Haavio 1935, 67; Kuusi 1963, 295). It may be assumed that this is for the singers an active, significant re-interpretation, a correct, profound understanding, and that the berry hill is, like the barley field of apple trees, a paradise image.

Is the poem dominated by Christian (Eve and the apple tree, Mary and Gabriel) or pre-Christian (the archetype theme of the immaculate conception) beliefs, a hero-myth (journey descriptions), women's daily work (cleaning, berry-picking) or erotic and sexual fantasies? Or does it incorporate elements of all of these?

"Today there come glad tidings of joy: it is the feast of the Virgin. Things below are joined to things above," says an Aposticheron of the day of the Annunciation (FM, 445). Mary is at this moment both a "height hard to climb for the thoughts of men" and a "depth hard to scan even for the eyes of angels". (Akathistos Hymn, LT, 423.) According to the teachings of the Orthodox Church, the heights and the depths might be joined on this day because a human being (i.e. Mary) willingly received the divine being, sought to "know what passes knowledge" and thus made "the unapproachable" approachable: "He who cannot be contained is contained in a womb." (FM, 443; LT, 422; Selin 1973, 74-79.)

The singers develop the combination of the heights and the depths in Mary according to their own personal concepts. As they see it, Mary did not simply meekly accept the berry. Once aware of its existence, she could not live without it; she sought it in immeasurable forests, on the distant mountain, in the middle of paradise, she knocked it down from the border of heaven with a stick and cast it with spells into the depths of her being.

How she wanted to die: the rapids miracle

Mary returns home from the forest. A poem from northern Olonets favoured and presumably also composed by women (ten variants, six by women and one by a man) recalls that Mary had in fact gone out to pick berries. On returning home she offers everyone her berries: "Eat, mother, of my berries!" (SKVR II, 329). The mother's reaction – "You were not, you whore, picking berries: you were looking for a husband!" (SKVR II, 325a) – suddenly and glaringly brings out the themes of cruelty and suffering. The mother's accusation is taken up by the other members of the family, with the exception of the grandmother. The grandmother does not, however, hold any authority. The logical consequence of being branded a whore is that the family drives out its former favourite; the banishment is often spoken by the strongest, i.e. the father: "Away, away, bringer of disgrace, Be gone, whore!" (SKVR II, 323)

Mary tries to defend herself. She reminds them of her chaste way of life through powerful hyperbole ("I've sat in no horse's sledge that has been among stallions, I have eaten no hen's eggs mounted by a cockerel!" FFPE 1977, 298). In conclusion, she tells them of the mighty significance of her own state: "This is the Creator's work, begotten by holy God!" (FFPE 1977, 298).

No one listens, and soon she finds herself outside, alone. Now begin the laments on her path through life, which she expresses in the lines of mournful, lyrical songs: "Woe is me, poor whore" (SKVR II, 322). With her heart full of despair – and guilt, for she even calls herself a whore! – she approaches a river intending to leap into it. "She would drown herself in the rapids for shame", as one of the performers of the poem explained (SKVR II, 323). Mary prays, "Take me, stream! Lift me, rapids!" (FFPE 1977, 298). It appears in some versions that the rapids are understood as the river of the otherworld, Tuonela.

Mary's weakness is turned by a miracle into a strength. The rapids gush forth words: "No, the stream will not take you, nor will the rapids lift you:

Mending fishing-nets in Akonlahti. Archangel Karelia. Photo: I.K. Inha 1894 (FLS 9864).

you'll have a boy on your knees, the Lord Christ upon your lap" (FFPE 1977, 298). The rapids' monologue introduces a strong Christian element into the epic, possibly based on apocryphal literature or some other tradition outside the Bible in which Mary's virginity is constantly doubted (by Joseph and others) and in which she is also accused of being a whore. (Cf. AE, 18; Kuusi 1980, 233.) But as in the berry miracle, this poem as a whole draws equally on elements of ancient poetry and Orthodox tradition, grafting them on to the same world. A parallel to Mary's return from berry-picking is an old song performed by women about a girl who lingers while fetching water and is driven to her death by the same accusations of being a whore (SKVR II, 390, SKVR I:2, 1195-1210; cf. Tarkka 1990a, 117-20). The chastity hyperboles are the same as those describing Iro, mother of Väinämöinen (SKVR VII:1, 100-131). The border between this world and the next is the same Tuonela river on the banks of which the male heroes in their own songs call for the ferryman to carry them over (*Väinämöinen's Journey to Tuonela*).

Is it woman's lot to seek death where the male hero seeks the words to give him strength? Are Mary's thoughts of suicide an earthly feature borrowed from poems about girls who hanged themselves in the barn and the women who longed for death in their plaints? The interpretation of Mary in this poem is fundamentally radical: the holy Mary cannot proceed through life in perfection and humility, carrying out her purpose, for she also experiences moments of great weakness and needs help from outside in order to overcome them. This is a very human view, yet basically not one opposed to the Orthodox interpretation of Mary. In the central Marian Akathistos hymn, for example, the Holy Virgin appears in the scene with Gabriel as possessed by doubts (LT, 423) and openly gives voice to her feelings: "Strange seem thy words and hard for my soul to accept. From a conception without seed how dost thou speak of childbirth, crying: Alleluia!"

How she gave birth: the miracle of the stable

The nativity poem, which scholars call The *Search for a Sauna*, is highly developed in Archangel Karelia, northern Olonets and Ingria, and is also known in Ladoga Karelia. Of the eighty-two recordings, fifty-seven were performed by women and nine by men. They all convey the same overall view, both of Mary's existential loneliness and of the cosmic overtones of the event, but vary in the way the scenes are presented and in imagery.

With slow solemnity and careful precision and using lines from poems about the pregnancy of other mythical mothers who give birth alone, such as of Loveatar, the mother of diseases (J. Krohn and K. Krohn 1901, 70; Tarkka 1990a, 95), the poem describes the progress of Mary's pregnancy, from the growing of the "hard womb" until the tenth month, "when the belt had to be let out, the clasp moved to another place" (SKVR I:2, 1103c). As the time of birth approaches, as "the girl's fire was kindled" (FFPE 1977, 284), Mary is portrayed in her most characteristic state, alone on the road, asking: "Where shall I go, where turn my steps? Who can I ask, from whom to seek help?" (SKVR I:2, 1106).

In Archangel Karelia and Olonets Mary seeks, often having already given birth to her baby in a porch, a *sauna* in which to bathe him; in Ladoga Karelia she seeks "a warm room", "a room for a woman's suffering". Sometimes the singer assumes the first person: "I sought a *sauna* in the village" (AKNC Mäkelä 1958, 80/67). The answer to her request is the same everywhere. "Has the whore got a baby son?" (SKVR I:2, 1099), the whole world cries, sometimes through the mouths of the villagers, though most often it is Mary's own mother (SKVR I:2, 1100). The Ingrian Mary is completely estranged from her own village circle and "travels from village to village, from house to house" far away to the north. There she often seeks her child, inquiring of the wind, the moon and the sun: "Have you seen the holy son, the blessed fruit?" (SKVR IV, 2050). Finally, exhausted and unsuccessful in her search, she asks for "a bed for the night", "a humble room" where she might rest. An unknown woman drives her to "the stable on the hill" (SKVR IV, 2050). The hill is also the location of the stable in the poems of singers further north where, in the terminology of the persecutors, are other "whores", "murderers" and "evil-doers" and towards which Mary makes her way, saying she must go like "a serf of old, or a hired labourer" (SKVR I:2, 1103).

Mary treads the path of suffering, "the hill of pain", "the mountain of pain" (SKVR I:2, 1103a-b), weeping tears of blood (SKVR I:2, 1099, 1101). But on reaching the hill and on placing "a son on her knee, a child on her hip" (SKVR I:2, 1109) she forgets her sorrows. The singer may also express the event in the first person: "Now I have a son on my knee, a child on my hip" (SKVR I:2, 1128). And a miracle occurs. Having given birth to the baby in the stable, Mary says to the horse: "Breathe, good horse, through your stomach on me poor wretch!" (SKVR I:2, 1103). The horse breathes, and "it is like the steam in the *sauna* bath"; the horse whisks its tail, and "it is like the whisk in the *sauna*" (SKVR I:1, 1118). In this *sauna* she washes her baby until he is "clean" and "beautiful" (SKVR II, 332).

The miracle transforms the whole environment. According to north Olonets tradition the child is "the dawn", "God's sunlight", whose birth makes the forest surrounding the hill acquire light. This occurs in many colours: "Red trees, blue lands, fir trees with golden boughs, pine trees with silver belts." (SKVR II, 323).

Like the impregnation poem, the nativity poem exists at the intersection of many levels of meaning. It is one of the core Marian poems, and hence a variation on it – i.e. the interpretation process involving the place, time and life history of the individual singer – is rich and lively.

Through her loneliness and outsider status, Mary is connected with the ego of the old plaints. In the Bible, the apocrypha, the Akathistos hymn and other Christian traditions she stands, in spite of everything, alongside Joseph. The Mary of the Karelian poems lacks any kind of security. She wanders through the same landscape as the ego of the lyric plaints: outside, along the road. In the same way as the one who "has a *sauna*, a cottage" roars at the lyric singer: "Out, shelterless from the cottage...out in the wilds your home shall be..." (SKVR VII:2, 2133), Mary is driven away the moment she dares to approach another's threshold. Like the lyric poet who sings: "My father threw me on to the ice, my mother to barren lands, threw me like a horse's droppings, left me like a rabbit's pellets" (SKVR I:3, 1370), Mary feels she has been deserted by her nearest and dearest, and left to tramp the roads.

The experience of being an outsider is further enhanced by allusions to incantation poetry. The landscape through which Mary wanders is also the Pohjola or the North of invocations, the place to which the worst diseases are sent to join the "other murderers" and "evil-doers" (comment by Lotte Tarkka; cf. Brummer 1908, 48). Mary is now in every respect outside the bounds of the human world. But even there, in the dark North – according to the versions of Ingrian singers – she retains her confidence and has the strength to seek her child. This idea, thought by some commentators of *The Messiah* to be 'unnatural', since she seeks the child even before its birth (J. Krohn and K. Krohn 1901, 44, 85), may run contrary to common sense, yet it has an inner logic. For surely people seek precisely what they know to exist but which they do not yet possess? In 1961, Oskar Groundstroem pressed the Ingrian singer Olena Pavlovna on this point: "In reply to my question how she could seek a God that was not yet born she said: 'Indeed, she must have had a presentiment that she would give birth to a holy man...'" (SKVR IV:1, 1344).

The landscape is thus more consciously mythical than that of the lyric. It combines old and new images of this world and the otherworld, re-ordering the universe but having points of contact with all that is familiar. The hill, the "mountain of pain" where the stable stands, is simultaneously the place to which diseases are exorcized, the stony hill of Pohjola, the cosmic mountain, the berry hill where impregnation took place, and Golgotha. It is also the cave of the church hymns which the "land offers to the untouchable" and which the Christmas icons depict in clear strokes (cf. Jääskinen 1983). The nascent child could be any child which, through birth prayers invoking the exemplary mother and with her help is brought into the world through an opening the size of "the space of the heavens" created through prayer (cf. e.g. I 4 960; Tarkka 1990b, 250). But he is also the Son of God, and his mother's womb is praised in the church hymns as being "more spacious than the heavens" (FM, 263). The birth in question is the first one, a sacred model to which all subsequent births can be traced. The light shed on the milieu as a result of the birth points to the light symbolism of the nativity icons of Christ, the Christmas church songs and the Akathistos Hymn, within which Mary is "the star causing the Sun to shine", "bright dawn of the mystical Day", "a lamp of living light", "a lightning-flash that shines upon our souls", and her child "a star much brighter than this star which just appeared, for He is the maker of stars" (LT, 423, 425, 435; Romanos 1970, 5). But it is at the same time firmly linked with an old 'wonderland' theme, and from this it draws its colourful visions and forms of expression. 'Wonderland' is a place where "the trees shine red, the land blue, the pine boughs silver, the tips of the heather golden" (SKVR VII:2, 2417). In ancient poetry, this land of miraculous colour is conjured up in very different contexts: hunting chants (SKVR II, 967, cf. J. Krohn and K. Krohn 1901, 69; Haavio 1952, 353), children's songs (SKVR II, 609), and lyric songs (SKVR VII:2, 2417, 2723). Despite all the diversity, the perceived land always lies in the same direction: it is a utopian state and space, a place in which man's anxiety, enmity and want fall away and in which it is good to live.

The 'wonderland' is usually somewhere else. Part of its essence is the remoteness of its other reality, far away and inaccessible. It is that other land which I see in my mind but which I cannot reach (SKVR VII:2, 2147); it is the homeland when I am far from home (SKVR V:1, 285); it is the land of death where my beloved has been taken (SKVR IV, 123). It is a utopia that exists only in the mind and in poetry.

The nativity poem is an exception. Having delivered her baby, Mary sees the wonderland as being there, near at hand, all around her, as a light that pierces and transforms reality.

How she fled from her child's persecutors: the sowing miracle

"I am about to go to Egypt, and flee with Thee, for Thee, my Guide, my Son," says Mary to her son at the end of the Christmas Kontakion. (Romanos 1970, 11.) The flight has been a powerful source of inspiration for the popular imagination, and has points of contact with one of the poems in Karelian Marian epics. The poem about the sowing miracle is part of the local tradition of Ladoga Karelia and southern Olonets (Haavio 1955, 76-81). There are ten recordings, nine sung by women.

Once again Mary prepares for her journey like a man setting off for war: "dressed for war, put on her armour". This time she is not preparing herself against evil or for a feast, but for an active confrontation. In her lap she nurses a baby, at her heels is a host of enemies: "great bands of pagans, a large host of Devil's folk". She marches or skis across the fields and marshes, in some versions defined more specifically as being in the otherworld: "Devil's heaths". Once again she is drawn towards a hill. There she meets a sower, a church builder and a calf herder, and greets them warmly despite her haste: "God bless the sower". In order to escape she begs the men she encounters to tell her pursuers that they saw her when they were sowing in the field, were building the church, when the cow was a calf. When her persecutors arrive a few minutes later, a miracle has occurred: the sower is cutting the corn, the church is old and the calf is a cow. Thus Mary escapes. But sometimes the poem continues: "her pursuers caught up with her..."

The song relives Mary's situation – persecuted, fleeing from an enemy, having to fight – through evocative images. In Karelia, the apocryphal-Christian sowing stage incorporates fairytale motifs (Haavio 1955, 81-83), and the images of the persecutors are a mixture of the devil, Judas and pre-Christian spirits. Mary is on skis, the figure of Mary is a mixture of the traditional warrior hero as he departs for battle and the Mary praised in the Akathistos Hymn – "our leader in battle", "the thunder that brings terror to our enemies" (LT, 422, 435). The otherworld forest has traits of the landscape of Tuonela. The poem prepares us for a nightmare, catastrophe and battle.

How she sought her lost child: the sun miracle

The story of how Mary lost her child and set off to seek him is another of the core poems in the Marian epic. This is reflected in the large number of recordings (111 variants, eighty-two sung by women and nine by men); in its significance the theme is akin to the berry and stable miracles. The poem was known in Archangel Karelia, northern Olonets and Ingria but is completely lacking in Ladoga Karelia and southern Olonets, where its place is taken by the sowing miracle.

Right at the very outset, the poem introduces the persecution theme. The momentary light of the 'wonderland' has gone out and its place is taken by dark oppression. For fear of losing her child, Mary never lets him out of her sight, whatever she does and wherever she goes, she keeps him hidden, using the same expressions as any anxious mother, even Loveatar, the mother of evil (J. Krohn and K. Krohn 1901, 91): "kept her offspring in hiding beneath the siftable sieve, beneath the portable tub, the sledge-runner as it ran" (FFPE 1977, 289). The theme incorporates numerous familiar images drawn from a woman's life: "beneath the bread a-baking", "beneath the heel a-stepping, beneath the cowlstaff a-carrying", "beneath the folds of the wifely wimple" (SKVR I:2, 1098-1099, 1113). The everyday tasks continue until the fateful moment when Mary combs her hair, her child upon her knee; the combing is sometimes accompanied by an adaptation of the fiery-river motif in incantations (SKVR I:2, 1103b, c). Inevitably she lets go of the child and he vanishes. Sometimes the comb or one of its teeth falls to the ground. Mary bends to pick it up and the child falls or is taken from her lap: "The boy fell from her lap" (SKVR I:2, 1108); "the boy was taken from her lap" (SKVR I:4, 1118). Its disappearance may be the consequence of Mary's falling asleep. Sometimes the child vanishes from the crib on the hill (SKVR I:2, 1099). The singer may make a point of saying on finishing the nativity song that "then the child should have been taken from her" (SKVR II, 322), or: "While she was looking for the *sauna*, the boy was taken from her" (SKVR II, 324). Another singer may adopt the first person: "At that point I began to weep" (SKVR I:2, 1129).

Now follows a new journey, a nightmare mirror image of the berry trip redolent of joy and mystery. Once again Mary "dressed herself and decked herself" and "dons her best, her most beautiful clothes" (SKVR I:2, 1096). Sometimes the singer again performs in the first person: "I set off in search of my son" (SKVR II, 320). Mary makes a careful search, "creeping through the ground, parting the hay stalks, examining the heather roots" (SKVR I:2, 1101). According to an Ingrian version (SKVR IV, 2055), her horse turns into a snake, whereas in an Archangel-Karelian version she herself leaps "as a stoat in the cranny of a stone, as a squirrel across the boughs" (SKVR I:2, 1109, 1113). But she does not confine herself to nooks and crannies, but once again – this time in the first person – strides ahead with giant steps: "The hills are booming as I go, the mountains bend as I ascend" (SKVR II, 324). Again she is the parallel to the mythical male hero, seer and shaman, despite her moments of weakness: "She is wailing with her knees on the bottom of the boat, with her arms on the bulwarks" (SKVR I:2, 1118, 1120).

As on her birth-giving journey and flight, Mary once again seeks the help of those she encounters on the way. She politely asks the road, the moon and a star, sometimes a tree and the wind, and finally the sun whether they have seen her "golden apple", her "silver buckle" (Archangel Karelia, Olonets) or her "holy son", her "blessed fruit" (Ingria). While the others give a brusque reply, the sun tells her the truth. In Archangel-Karelian poems, it reveals that the boy has been buried "in mother earth" (SKVR I:2, 1099), "nine fathoms deep", "rocks under, the slabs on top, the gravel against the heart", (FFPE 1977, 292; SKVR I:2, 1099, 1101, 1103c). He is tormented by "the devil", "evil power", "evil folk" and has rocks and hills cast on him (SKVR I:2, 1106-1107, 1109, 1115-1116).

For the Archangel Karelian singer it is the scene of the berry miracle, the miraculous birth. According to singers in Olonets, the sun says that the boy is beyond the Tuonela river (SKVR II, 322), in Ingria, under the bridge: on the stony bottom, in an iron-walled coffin fastened with tin nails, buried within the blue sea nine fathoms deep (SKVR III, 757, 1909, 1958, 2218).

Behind the grave-images we can detect the laments of the orphans and widows in traditional plaints: the "shelter" of the plaint singers – father, mother, husband or son – is beneath the rock, deep under the earth (SKVR V:2, 337), a rock is on top of a large coffin, the gravestone a pillow for his head, the rock crushed the bones of his breast, the rock presses his shoulders down (SKVR III, 296-7), on his eyes is light sand (SKVR VII: 2, 2066), he is beneath the Tuonela hill (SKVR I:3, 1806), his coffin is fastened with iron and tin nails (SKVR VII:2, 1954). Thus the singers envisaged the tomb of Mary's son as being like their own graves. (Cf. Tarkka 1990a, 182.) But it is also the tomb of Christ; the lines of the poem echo the themes of church songs. "A rock covers Him who covered the heavens with glory," bewails a Holy Saturday Sticheron (LT, 652), and the one buried beneath it complains: "They laid me in a deep pit: in dark places and in the shadow of death" (the vespers of Holy Friday, LT, 614).

The source of the search for the child theme is thought to be the story in Luke of how the twelve-year-old Christ disappears and is found in the Temple (e.g. Borenius 1886; J. Krohn and K. Krohn 1901, 80; Haavio 1952, 360). As a whole, however, the search song operates at so general a level that the biblical episode seems remote. The idea of losing a child is every woman's nightmare and for this reason alone almost an archetype image; as in many other songs and legends, it acquires here mythical dimensions and the appropriate manifestations. Mary seeks Christ in exactly the same way as other mothers seek their children in Karelian songs: like Lemminkäinen's mother, who "snatched up her skirts, her clothes over her arm,... if there were stones on the road, cast them all aside, if there were branches on the road, kicked them all out of the way" (SKVR VII:1, 836-36a); like the mother of Maije, when her daughter was carried up to the clouds, roamed the forests as a wolf, the mighty moors as a bear (SKVR III, 2192). Like Mary's child, death has carried off their children. In most cases they are unsuccessful in their search. "There is no man in the man gone, nor in one who is quite lost", it is often said of Lemminkäinen (FFPE 1977, 220); and Maije calls from on high: "I cannot come home, mother: a cloud is holding my head, a cloud's son my knees, a vapour my hair" (FFPE 1977, 478). In Mary's case the search for her child continues beyond the point where many a mother's search ends: beyond the present reality.

How she sought her lost child: the journey to Tuonela I

In north Olonets tradition (eleven recordings, nine by women, one by a man) Mary, on hearing that her son is beyond the Tuonela River, sets off to bring him back. She comes to the bank of the river or a fiery rapids and calls: "Bring a boat, girl of Tuoni!" (SKVR II, 324; cf. FFPE 1977, 192). She is asked the reason for her visit to Tuoni; she lies and says she is looking for a spike and is carried over the river in a spruce boat. Although the end of the song is unclear – often it breaks off in the middle – the overall meaning of the motif is unambiguous: this is a radical, Marian intervention which elaborates Mary's central role in the resurrection process.

The visit-to-Tuonela motif has thematic links with the apocryphal story in which Mary is described as having visited Tuonela (cf. Pascal 1976, 57-87). The song itself, however, is made up of lines from ancient myth songs sung by Karelian men. Väinämöinen summoning a boat to carry him across the river *en route* for the otherworld is the nearest model for the scene on the Tuonela river (Kuusi 1963, 294). Once again Mary is a composite of two characters: the Christian Mother of God and the shaman hero of traditional Finnish-Karelian poetry.

How she captured her child's persecutor: the journey to Tuonela II

Another widely-known song tells how, on rising from the tomb, Christ went to the forge of the Devil's Smith (i.e. Satan) and by means of a clever trick shackled him to a rock for all eternity. The song is based partly on an ancient

Eurasian myth tradition and partly on the apocryphal Gospel of Nicodemus according to which Christ, on visiting Tuonela, overcame the prince of the Kingdom of Death. (Haavio 1955, 7-75.) The event is also referred to in church hymns, such as the Canon for Holy Saturday: "Hell was wounded in the heart when it received Him whose side was pierced by the spear ..." (LT, 650). As far as Mary is concerned, it is surprising to observe that in many parts of Karelia and Ingria (twenty-one variants, nineteen by women and one by a man) Mary has become the protagonist in this song about Christ. Sometimes the singer speaks as Mary in the first person: "I went on a little journey... I came to a river, a little house beyond the river" (SKVR II, 320). Later Mary goes to a forge, sometimes transformed into an animal, and it is she who captures the devil. When the Devil's Smith tells Mary that he is making a rope with which to strangle God, who was buried yesterday, but that he forgot to measure God's neck, Mary says: "Let me measure it!" The smith is sceptical: "You lock me in a lock." To which Mary replies: "The lock is not locked with hands" and fastens the eternal lock around the smith's neck (SKVR I:2, 1109, 1122). She also addresses the smith in gentle terms: "God help you, dear smith!" (SKVR II, 322) and tells him she knows the size of God's neck because: "I long watched the eater's mouth, the beard of who bites off, the jaws of who grinds and sifts." (SKVR I:2, 1109, cf. also FFPE 1977, 294). This scene, strange when uttered by Christ (Haavio 1955, 21), acquires an obvious logic in Mary's speech: she has naturally watched her son ("eater", "one who bites") while feeding him.

There is no sign at all of Christ in these variants. Mary acts in his place and on his behalf. The motif is often a continuation of Mary's journey to Tuonela; the singers appear, too, to have understood that the forge was in Tuonela. Mary's acts in Tuonela thus acquire cosmic proportions: victory over the otherworld enemy "unto the ages of ages".

How she freed her child from the grave: the sun miracle II

The Christ-oriented core of the 'correct' *Messiah* is *The Resurrection*. Mary is not even mentioned in the common variants. The resurrection is achieved in the song with the help of the sun. The sun melts the rocks or sends the guards outside the tomb to sleep allowing Christ to escape.

There are, however, several variants in Karelia and Ingria (thirty-one items, nineteen by women, one by a man) in which Mary is, surprisingly, the subject. This occurs in a very common structure in which the resurrection is a continuation of the search for the child. Having made friends with the sun while seeking her child, Mary asks the sun for help: "Shine, dear sun, warmly, melt the rocks into salt, make the boulders run to froth" (Timonen 1992, 220). In addition to asking the sun to melt the rocks, she asks it to send the guards to sleep: "Blaze one moment sultry, another dimly swelter, send the wicked people to sleep, oppress the pagan crowd" (SKVR I:2, 1118-1120; FFPE 1977, 293). In these variants, Mary voices the words that are spoken in the 'correct' song by Christ. In their new context, the words often acquire a qualifying phrase illustrating Mary's view: "that I may find my son" (SKVR I:2, 1109), "that my son may escape" (SKVR

Various public displays of familial relations belonged to the wedding ritual: a bride from Kiestinki bows to her mother-in-law. Northern Archangel Karelia. Photo: I.K. Inha 1894 (FLS 10 007).

I:2, 1101). The sun does as required, makes "the boulders froth" and puts the pagans to sleep.

Sometimes Mary's request to the sun includes a clear indication of resurrection: "Raise the Creator from the dead, awake the Lord from the dead ... raise him, young man, from the dead, from an untimely death, spare the one still fair from loss" (SKVR I:2, 1118-1119). Sometimes Mary addresses her son direct: "Rise, Creator, from the dead!" (SKVR I:2, 1099)

The Mary of Ingrian women is more humble. She does not command the sun direct but seeks God's intervention: "Make the sun shine, melt the tin nails, free the Creator from the dead, the Divine One from the grave" (SKVR III, 1920). And God does so.

By actively influencing the sun, Mary becomes the rescuer of her son and helps to bring about his resurrection. The enlargement of her role here is probably more in line with the church hymns of the Orthodox Church for Holy Friday and Holy Saturday, in which Mary plays a central role, than the 'correct' *Resurrection*. This may account for the greater fervour of both her anguish and her desire to see her son rise from the dead. Nor does she avoid the physical expression of her anguish: "...with a mother's love she wept and bitterly her heart was wounded. She groaned in anguish from the depth of her soul, and in her grief she struck her face and tore her heart. And, beating her breast, she cried lamenting: 'Woe is me...' (LT, 612) 'Now heal the wound of my soul, O my Child, rise and still my pain and bitter anguish.' (LT, 621) 'Arise, my Child, as Thou hast foretold.' (LT, 634) 'Tarry not, O Life, among the dead.'" (LT, 638)

The Orthodox Christian frame of reference is not, however, the only one in the sun miracle. Raising a close relative from the dead is a natural and recurring motif in women's lyric songs. Ingrian women, in particular, have developed an image of opening the grave with their own hands and lifting out the dead: "Were I but able, I would awaken my dead mother, I would lift her up with ropes, I would prop her up by the gravestone, I would bring my birth-giver home" (SKVR III, 296). Sometimes singers reject such utopian thinking and say they will take the coffin to the church roof and, like Mary, address their plea to the sun: "Shine, shine, sun of the Creator, heat, sun of God... melt the tin nails, heat the brass nails!" (SKVR IV, 133). It is nevertheless clear that the real purpose is to raise the dead from the grave: "That my mother might rise ... to see her chicks" (SKVR IV, 216). Even in epic *The Song of Mary* is not the only poem where the awakening motif is developed; it is common also in other songs about a mother's search. Thus Lemminkäinen's mother: "Rise, young one, from the dead, awake from your sleep!" (SKVR I:2, 771); the mother of the girl who lingered while fetching water: "Rise, young one from the dead, from your untimely death, beautiful one from vanishing" (SKVR I:2, 1196). These attempts to raise relatives from the dead in narrative songs are interpreted by Lotte Tarkka (1990b, 248-249) as features of lament tradition in epic and thus link Mary with the women lamenters.

The theme of fetching something of value from an otherworld is not, of course, restricted to the feminine domain. Once again Mary becomes a female parallel to the heroes of the narrative songs performed by men. The male robbers of the *Sampo* – an object which brings its owner everlasting wealth – also put to sleep the evil guardians the *Sampo*, confined behind locks nine fathoms deep (J. Krohn and K. Krohn 1901, 111; Tarkka 1990b, 249). Where Mary uses the sun, they subdue the enemy with their singing, the playing of the five-stringed *kantele* and sleep darts. The tasks and the milieu in which they are carried out is the same. Both men and women encircle the same otherworld mountain at the centre of the earth: Väinämöinen sends the *Sampo* guards to sleep at the foot of the stony hill in Pohjola; Mary does the same to those who have shut her child away beneath a stony hill. The essential difference lies in the purpose of the men's and women's acts. While the men seek the essentials of a good life, the women seek life itself.

How difficult it was for her to believe: the miracle of the grouse

The story of the dead grouse which flies up is a separate prose legend appended to the epic as a closing episode by many singers in Archangel Karelia, Olonets and Ladoga Karelia; in this particular context, it may be recast in traditional trochaic tetrameters (sixteen variants, twelve by women, two by men). Mary is in her cottage baking pasties with a grouse boiling in the pot. She receives a message that her son is alive. Sometimes the son himself appears at the door. "The pasty fell from her hand," says one singer, while another stresses the immensity of the mother's suprise: so stunned that she cannot say a word, her son reproaches her: "Do you not recognize your son?", at which she falls lifeless to the floor (SKVR I:2, 1118).

The central feature of the episode is Mary's weakness, the draining of her strength, the feeling of disbelief:

The mother did not believe it when she heard her son was coming. "I will believe it," she said, "when the grouse flies out of the pot!" The grouse flew out of the pot. The son entered the cottage. She fell to her knees. (SKVR VII:2, 1089)

The miracle once again raises Mary from weakness to strength. Such miracles are common in apocryphal literature and legend tradition. Normally, however, they are associated with less sacred characters. Joseph and Stephen are, for example, typical examples of people whose experience of disbelief is proved false by a miracle – either at the birth or resurrection of Christ. Association of the motif with Mary's experience and the attempt to highlight it at the end of the epic about her is an active interpretation that reveals something vital about the singers' image of Mary. Here, as in the rapids miracle, Mary is amazed and weak: on one occasion she has to be supported by the rapids, on another by a bird. Or by God, who speaks through the rapids and the bird.

How she recovered her child: the resurrection miracle

According to Matti Kuusi's model (1968, 5) the closing lines of songs should be examined, for they often contain the "innermost sense" of the song, the singer's "true message".

The singers of songs about Mary naturally end their epic with her son's release from the grave. They do, however, give small yet consistent indications of the one who is freed. Suprisingly, the recurring closing words are most often in prose. The singers presumably placed so much emphasis on them that the collectors noted them down. The fact that prose is used shows that they are not part of the song but represent the singers' own explanation, or an interpretation which, for some reason, they wish to present.

Three things stand out in these prose statements. First: the son is "little" (KRA: Laanti 1896; SKVR I:2, 1114, 2195). This is logical, because he was still a babe in arms when he was lost, snatched from the hay at birth or a little later from his mother's knee. Secondly: at the end of the epic he is always just "son", "apple", "fruit", "rod"; he is never Christ or God. The references to the child's divinity are limited to the berry and birth miracles. Thirdly: the direction taken by the boy. In only one song does he go to heaven: "There is your little offspring, your golden apple; in the highest heaven, in the place of God, the father; he will come from there to judge" (FFPE 1977, 290-291). It is surely no coincidence that the singer who places him in heaven is a man, Arhippa Perttunen. One woman singer also says that Mary hears her son is in Tuonela: "Next to the Creator, golden flowers in his hand, the berries of the death before him" (SKVR III, 1347). According to one interpretation, Mary finds her son in a church, where God has taken the lost child to wait for its mother (SKVR III, 1346). But the most common direction of the resurrection is simply Mary herself. The statements emphasize her as the experiencer, centre, active recoverer of her son, seeker and finder: "Then she brought the boy from there" (SKVR II, 323); "She found her son" (SKVR II, 324); "Only then she found the boy" (SKVR II, 324a); "Then she brought her boy away from there, from the grave" (SKVR I:2, 1113); "She found the boy" (SKVR I:4, 2197); "Then she brought her boy, her son" (SKVR I:2, 1109). Sometimes the child is returned to her lap, from which he was stolen: "Well, the boy came to her knees, the child alongside her hips" (PKK 6, cf. KKR 270); here the form of expression uses the same structure as in the birth poem, in which Mary also has a child on her knees, a child against her hips. Although she has forgotten the end of the poem, the singer clearly recalls what she considers to be its central message: "From where she then received the boy in her arms I do not remember" (SKVR III, 1919). Sometimes a singer associates Mary with herself: "Now my son arose" (SKVR I:2, 1117); "From there my son rose" (SKVR I:2, 1129).

This short closing statement brings Mary's search to a logical conclusion. The singers consider that evil (i.e. death) robbed Mary of her child; that Mary herself overcame evil and snatched her child back from the kingdom of death. They also understand that she saved the child for herself, placed him back on her own knee and that it did not go to God or heaven.

Mary and the singer

No single text contains all the component poems. The structures display considerable variation, both regional and individual. In some regions, the epic focuses mainly on Christ, in others it is presented from Mary's point of view. The Marian areas tend to be in Russian Karelia (i.e. Archangel and Olonets Karelia) and Ingria, the Christ areas in Finnish Karelia (i.e. Ladoga Karelia). The Christ orientation of Finnish Karelia may be a consequence of contact with the Lutheran faith. In this connection, it is interesting to note that the Russian Orthodox singers of Ilomantsi, living in close contact with Lutherans, had no knowledge at all of the Marian epic.

Local names for the epic reflect the perspective adopted in the song. In Russian Karelia, the epic is commonly known as *The Song of Mary, The Song (or Tale) of the Holy Pohrotsa* (Mother of God), *The Tale of the Virgin Mary, The Tale of Mary's Journey*. There are a few exceptions: Miihkali Perttunen, for example, sings not of Mary but of the birth of the Son of God. In Finnish Karelia, the songs focus systematically on Christ: *The Tale of God* (or the Creator), or *The Death of the Creator*.

There is also a clear difference in the gender distribution of the performances of the Marian and Christ epics. As we have seen, the Marian poems were normally performed by women. Comparing female and male singers whose names are known, women are clearly in the majority throughout: 86/12; 6/1; 57/9; 9/0; 82/9; 9/1; 19/1; 19/2; 12/2. However, the resurrection poems and those about the shackling of Satan – with Christ as the central figure – belong clearly, and in Finnish Karelia principally, to male tradition: the performers of the former include thirty-one men, of the latter thirty-five men, making a total of sixty-six, whereas the eight Marian poems were performed by only thirty-seven men in all.

The predominance of women as performers of Marian themes is so striking that there must be a significant reason for it. What does the epic contain that is of such vital importance to women? The simplest way to approach women's own interpretation is to examine their personal statements. Are there, in addition to the texts, any accounts by singers of the contexts in which they performed these songs, or the meanings they ascribed to them?

The available contextual information of performance is small and sporadic. Topelius reported that they were sung especially at Easter, at the end of the long, sad period of fasting (SKVR I:2, 1120). Later scholars have also regarded Christmas – in particular the second day of Christmas dedicated to Mary – as possible times for performance (Borenius 1886, 72; J. Krohn and K. Krohn 1901, 83; Kuusi 1963, 300). It would be tempting to add other feasts when Mary's life and significance were of topical importance, such as the Annunciation, the *Pokrova* and the Dormition of the Mother of God.

Although there is no reliable data to support such calendrical assumptions, some other ritual indications can be found. A variant recorded in Archangel Karelia bears the annotation "sung among women" (KRA: Kotaniemi KT 223:1). On the basis of this and certain other clues (KRA: Helminen 2129; Virtanen 1968, 20, 51) it may be assumed that *The Song of Mary* was regularly performed when women came together in the evenings to pass the time. These were occasions for communal activities, such as handicraft, conversation, and singing about topics of common importance. Some women said that they also sang about Mary while performing solitary tasks such as spinning or milking (Virtanen 1968, 20, 28).

Some reports indicate that *The Song of Mary* was connected with practices and rites accompanying birth and death. Berry and birth miracle texts incorporated in Ladoga-Karelian birth incantations (SKVR VII:4, 3013, 3046) suggest that the Marian epic really did act as a myth in a rite. By telling of the first impregnation and birth, its performance conveys strength to women in childbirth, likening them to Mary and at the same time leading up to the request to the "oldest of wives" and "the first among mothers" (SKVR I:4, 960, SKVR VII:4, 3051) for help. The custom of carrying an icon of Mary around the mother and the baby (SKVR I:4, 967) also indicates a link between Mary's birth and the birth that is taking place. The lines describing Mary's intercession in a birth form a natural bridge between the actual situation and her experience. The lines are often the same as or similar to those in the epic about her search for the berry and her child: "Mary, fair-skinned woman, come here ... put on your bosom a clean shirt, put under your arm a whisk made of leaves of an apple tree" (SKVR III, 4511). The association of the freeing of the child from the grave with the freeing of the baby from the womb is also common, thereby linking resurrection to birth (Tarkka 1990b, 250-251). This link is further supported by Tarkka's observation of the description of the otherworld and birth in incantations as a journey from the otherworld to this world: seen from this angle "having a baby" is the same, whether it comes from the womb or the grave.

It is also possible to identify some direct links between Marian epic and death rites. In 1944 Paraskeva Bukkiev told a collector at Tulemajärvi in Olonets Karelia that the song about Mary's search for her child was performed by the women at wakes and other funeral feasts. It was half sung, half spoken by two women together, in a slow manner, with others joining in. (KRA Helminen 2129.) Bukkiev's variant includes the sowing miracle and child-seeking themes. The idea of fetching a child from the otherworld appears to be natural in that phase of death rites when the deceased was still in the liminal state, lost to mortals but not yet in the world of the dead.

Even these isolated details of performance context indicate that Marian epic is to be understood as part of women's tradition rather than merely as something that was sung on certain feast days. Moreover, the performer-gender statistics and the basic direction of women's interests also support the former rather than the latter assumption. The epic is closely connected with major events in a woman's life – sexuality, giving birth, loss of a child – but is at the same time firmly rooted in the daily round of women's life: caring for children, cleaning, gathering berries, cooking, handiwork, tending the cattle. The third link between the song and its performer concerns the ritual roles of women as midwives, healers and lamenters (i.e. as specialists in crisis and separation rites). Like the women who sang, Mary had the dual role of one who experiences (becoming pregnant, giving birth, losing her child) and one who shares, supporting other women in the same situations (midwife, healer, lamenter).

All these aspects of a woman's life are presented in the epic as various entities, varying syntheses, in sequences which overlap from one variant to another. In the texture of these poems it should be possible to discover indicators of something other than the things themselves; in other words, the poems must give some clue of the women's interpretation of these basic matters. How did the singers construct the poem, to what did they pay special attention, in their opinion, what was Mary ultimately striving towards?

Despite the variation in the epic, a certain basic line can be seen in the overall structure. The epic comprises a series of dramatic, lifelike images. They focus on and are experienced by Mary, whose intention is consistent. Text structure suggests that the basic idea of the epic can be reduced to a single statement: a sacred story of a woman who, through her own searching and a miracle, becomes pregnant, gives birth, encounters suffering and the loss of her child, who through her own searching, struggles and miracles recovers her child. Of course, this is a simplification. The myth could equally be viewed as a cyclic, unending series, searches alternating with findings, anxious, passionate journeys and momentary, blessed interludes: births, deaths, rebirths.

The berry miracle elevates women's sexual experience to the mythical, sacred sphere. The subject is woman. Sexuality and sexual intercourse are seen from her point of view: a genuine, positive value to be worked for, a state of blessedness. Here is not a question of an object or sacrifice, as in so many of the narrative poems performed by women, or of means to something else, as in, for example, love incantations. The value experience is depicted both in the active and eager way in which the event is described and in the messages of joy, strength and mystery running through the poem. Sexual encounter is interpreted as a manifestation of the divine in the everyday world. Man is here again a stranger from another world, as in so many women's fear poems (cf. Tarkka 1990b, 42), but the otherness is now experienced and explained via the concepts of holiness. As always with

Milking cows in Lonkka village. The smoke prevented mosquitoes from irritating the cows. Vuokkiniemi. Photo: Samuli Paulaharju 1910 (FLS 5396).

myth, the possible meanings of the berry miracle are wide-ranging: true, it tells of a divine sphere through images of everyday human life, but equally well of man through images of the divine. The emphasis in the interpretation may shift from one direction to another, but both aspects are present in every version.

The rapids miracle presents a picture of female sexuality as conventionally perceived. Here the woman's own experience is belittled as akin to whoring on the basis of criteria that have no relationship to her own perception. Mary's declaration that "This is the creator's work begotten by holy God" expresses women's knowledge of their innermost being, their trust in the authenticity and value of their own personal experience. Assurances of virginity and purity are here profoundly symbolic. They reflect a woman's interpretation of sexuality as something pure as opposed to the interpretation of sexuality as something degrading. The idea is bold, refuting the Christian dichotomy of Eve and Mary. It is as if the apple in the Garden of Eden and the Holy Spirit are one and the same thing: sin ceases to exist. In contrast, however, the conventional interpretation is so aggressive and dominating that it can undermine a woman's self-determination, even destroy it. Salvation presents itself once again in a sign from the otherworld: the rapids miracle. Instead of being an account of suffering, it turns the poem into a mythical episode in Mary's journey.

Refusing Mary a place in the house and forcing her to give birth in a stable is the logical consequence, and image, of the conflict between the self and the world, and a prologue to future assaults. The theme of anguish and violence is nevertheless brought to an abrupt end by the birth on the hill: it is experienced as a miracle that creates a momentary utopian state, the experience of a new holiness and the light of paradise in the world. This is again a value experience which, in so much as it tells of the birth of a magnificent ancient God, recalls the divine aspects of the birth experience of an ordinary woman in the ordinary world, the sacred otherworldness of the child, and the mystery and wonder of childbirth in a woman's experience. The prayers to Mary in the birth incantations reiterate her otherworld tale in the present world: "Let a berry come to the earth, travel an image of God!" (SKVR III:3, 4511).

The child-persecution motif leads in turn to the theme of destruction, which the epic now sets about describing. The focal point of the epic becomes the disappearance and search. No longer does Mary run away but engages in battle with her enemies. The remaining part of the epic is an elaboration on this theme. It includes images of a woman healer, a shaman who seeks the soul of her sick child and fights the forces of the otherworld in order to recover it. Mary's mythical journeys – how she dresses for them, her giant steps, her transformation into a snake, squirrel or bird, crossing the Tuonela river, and her pleas to the sun – reflect the otherworld journeys of male seer-heroes. But while Mary is a seer-mother fighting for the soul of her sick child, she is also a lamenter-mother, the prototype of every Karelian lamenter who guides the deceased to Tuonela and – through the complex ritual process – manages to bring the deceased back, relinquished yet symbolically unrelinquished (cf. Utriainen 1989). Against this background, she is also the "pillar of fire, guiding those in darkness", the "protection of the world, wider than the cloud in the wilderness" (LT, 426), the "all-Pure" who on each Annunciation Day speaks to Gabriel of the doubts in her heart, who looks amazed on the baby she has borne every Christmas Day and who stands in the middle of every church every Holy Week and, lamenting, weeping and tearing her hair raises her child from beneath the rock.

Finally she is the singer herself, the bearer and possibly the midwife of many children, the carer and burier of many children, possibly also the lamenter of others' children. Because of all this she identifies with Mary and even becomes Mary herself in the texts: "I went out to pick berries"; "I took a berry in my fingers"; "I asked for a *sauna* in the village"; "I have a son on my knees"; "I went after my son"; "And my son arose". The boundary between Mary and the singer vanishes; their experiences are one.

Women's myth

Thus in singing of Mary's fate, women also sing of themselves. The myth is an experienced one (see Eliade 1975, 19, 139; Mann 1987, 237). The simultaneous experience of holiness and familiarity also confers value and meaning on real life. Living out the myth is no easy task, no random adjustment of the parameters of self. In one sense it is always rooted in reality. Sexual relations and childbirth are for women everywhere existential experiences that change the self and one's worldview. Statistics show why the loss of a child was such a major issue to Karelian women. In Karelia, as in other poverty-stricken areas, infant mortality was very high in the nineteenth century. The death of a child was an everyday occurrence to the singer of *The Song of Mary*, not a monstrous abnormality as it is perceived today.

In principle, however, Karelian women were no different from any other women. They, too, had feelings. In order to cope, they had to be able to control their feelings and to understand both what they possessed and their losses on a symbolic, transcendental level. The living medium of this understanding was the Marian myth. It was theirs alone, not imposed on them from outside by the Church or by men. The existence of the Marian myth is of outstanding significance in that mythical poetry has usually been men's tradition in Karelia. Oral poetry noted down from women consisted of ballads, wedding songs and secular lyrics. *The Song of Mary* is an exception. It is women's own hero myth. If a part of it did not match a woman's worldview, she altered it until it did. This explains the emergence of the Marian accretions in, for example, the rapids and grouse miracles, and the Marian interventions (visits to Tuonela, the sun miracle II).

It was through the sacred images of the Marian myth – adapted to their own experience and lives – that the women perceived the reality of being tied to a man, bearing and burying children. Mary's fate (meeting the father of her child, birth and loss of her child) and the action she took (refusal to give up her search, understanding of joy and happiness, defiant and frenzied battle against death) were for these women an interlocutor for their own lives – both a mirror and a model. By considering the acts of Mary they examined their own deeds. They changed the Mary in the poem to reflect their own experiences and attitudes and they changed themselves in the light of Mary's experiences and attitudes. Thus with her, they strove to seek life and to conquer death.

The life of an individual woman is of course only one of the many possible interpretations of the Marian epic. The epic is profound, full of life, of changing and even conflicting thoughts, visions and feelings of joy and suffering, the presence of holiness in the world and the distancing of the world from holiness. In addition to making my own interpretation, I have tried to keep my ear tuned to the endless polyphony of the epic, the allusions to manhood and womanhood, to the sublime and mundane, to this world and the otherworld, to the mythical and the Christian that are contained in the hundreds of variants and thousands of details. (cf. Knuuttila 1989, 96, 101 concerning the idea of polyphony in popular culture, and Tarkka 1990b, 249 concerning the intertextual approach which I have here tried to apply not only to different genres but also to entirely different traditions, i.e. the great and the little.) Because of its polyphony, the epic can also be viewed from an entirely different perspective. As earlier research suggests, the epic is also the story of Christ. Its interpretation as the story of Christ, however, would force us to consider a completely different set of variants from those which I have used.

The tale of Mary can also be viewed in a different light – from a greater distance, in more general terms, avoiding the down-to-earth realism. It can be conceived of as a dialogue between man (Mary) and God, in which Mary represents suffering, thoughts of suicide, doubts and searching, while God represents the miracles. In such a dialogue process Mary grows – in Orthodox terminology "becomes deified" or "attains deification" – until she is capable of working with God; the symbolic consequences of this cooperation are the findings. Irma Korte speaks of similar processes (though they are the outcome of a different tradition) in interpreting the theme of the virgin birth as a metaphor of man's inner renewal. Viewed from this perspective, Mary did not give birth to a physical child, but to a higher, more conscious self. (Korte 1988, 227-253.)

I too identify signs of such value and change experiences in the Karelian Marian poems. I cannot, however, separate them from the fundamental experiences in a woman's life. Rather, taking a pragmatic approach, I consider that the inner transformations of Mary described in the epic, the discoveries of self and the divine are somehow connected with the things they actually speak of: female sexuality, motherhood, loss. Certainly, the epic can be regarded as a feminist birth-giver myth of the type discussed by Marta Weigle (1989; cf. Tarkka 1990b, 253) alongside the male, abstract creation myths. The Karelian Marian epic is convincing proof that a woman can, as a life-giving, physically creative subject, be raised in quintessential women's genres to a high, ideal level on a par with the male creator heroes.

The Marian poems contain all these features, and more besides. The expression and breadth of vision of the epic operate at so many levels, crossing the border between this and the otherworld at so many points, that I have not hesitated here to treat it as myth. Typical of myth, the Marian epic deals with the very foundations of existence and the means of assuring its continuity, while analysing the relationships between the familiar and the unfamiliar, the normal and the supranormal (Siikala 1985b, 86); the view is so female oriented and so Christian in appearance as to be misleading. The supranormal is depicted in the Marian poems at many levels: on the one hand by the sacred and divine (berry, child, paradise, and also light; cf. the mystical light pointed out by Eliade, 1965), on the other by various terrifying and evil otherworld elements (Pohjola, Hiitola, Tuonela, devils). The destructive otherworldness sometimes seems to take over not only the community but the whole world in which Mary exists. While these different otherworld images all overlap and illuminate one another, they do not resemble one another – a criterion of true myth epic (cf. Siikala 1985b); and they also throw light from the many-layered past on the fate of Mary.

The aesthetics and the religious beliefs of the epic are – quite simply – different from those with which we are familiar. Not even Christianity can be completely separated from mythical thinking, as Mircea Eliade has pointed out (1975, 164). Christian liturgical time is in essence true myth time, the events of a great exemplary drama in the present (ibid. 168-169, 174). The myth dimensions of the Christian faith have, according to Eliade, been better understood by popular Christianity in Eastern Europe (e.g. in Orthodox Romania), where they have been associated with a broad and more physical cosmic experience, a personal understanding of the world and life. This popular Christianity "is not a new form of paganism or a pagan-Christian syncretism. Rather it is an original religious creation, in which eschatology and soteriology are given cosmic dimensions" (ibid. 172). 'Cosmic Christianity' is also the term used by scholars of Russian folk belief, emphasizing the links between Mother Earth, the heavenly bodies and the Mother of God (Pascal 1976, 8-15; cf. Smolitsch 1940-1941).

The Marian traditions of Karelian women may be seen as one manifestation of the cosmic popular Christianity of Eastern Europe. Their myth tells how Mary receives a child from another world, from the divine being, into her womb, which is as large as heaven and as deep as the cave in the cosmic mountain; it tells how she conquers otherworld forces and speaks to the sun, moon and stars. But Mary cannot be imprisoned even in heaven.

Any single interpretation is as misleading as the official Christian or the geographical-historical model which, as we have seen, conceal Mary behind Christ – the myth behind the legend, the singer behind the poem – and inhibit any deviations. The Karelians, unable to read and write, had no such inhibitions. Mary roamed freely and unconditionally through their lives and poetry.

NOTE

This article is based on an earlier version published in Finnish under the title *Karjalan naisen Maria-eepos*, which appeared in *Runo, alue, merkitys*. P. Hakamies (ed.). University of Joensuu. Publications of Karelian Institute No 92. Joensuu. 1990. p. 111-148.

LEEA VIRTANEN

Women's Songs and Reality

In Estonia, unlike in Finland, the ancient art of folk singing has survived right up to the present day, above all on the island of Kihnu and in Setumaa. In 1973, while in Tallinn, I heard the Leegajus choir perform *The Tooma-laul*, a ballad about a woman killer called Toomas (Thomas). The loud voices of the old women, and their calm bearing made an indelible impression on me. The performance was archaic and different, and one not easily forgotten. What did the songs mean to them? Did the songs tell about their own lives, or their own concepts of the reality of life?

On examining the contents of *The Toomalaul* the researcher's attention is caught by the numerous marvels deviating from everyday reality that are as a matter of course woven into the plot structure. The man, Toomas, first tries to make himself a wife out of wood, gold and silver, but his efforts fail. He then takes a living wife, but kills her in a cruel manner. She has, however, foreseen her death: her jewels weep, and wolves and bears go into the forest to await her blood. Blue-winged birds carry the news of her death to her father and brothers, who seek revenge on her innocent blood: soon Toomas is burning at the stake.

The Toomalaul gives the impression of being an original traditional ballad, but a counterpart can be found in other songs for most of its motifs and lines.

In writing of *The Toomalaul* in 1974 I proposed that the song had its own worldview, an epic reality that differs from the everyday reality of the singer (Virtanen 1974, 17). The singer does not expect her own jewels to start talking to her, but she accepts this as a matter of course in the song, though possibly as an item of secondary importance, since the important thing is the message: a wife is not made of wood, she is a living, feeling person who should not be murdered for no reason.

I have since had a chance to talk to Estonian researchers familiar with Setu culture.[1] In the 1950s Veera Pino met a woman who had performed *The Toomalaul* in the belief that the events really had happened. It was a serious, horrifying case! You never can tell what will happen in life! The woman further recalled a similar case in the neighbourhood: a man killed his wife (Virtanen 1987, 184). Many of the miracles in the song did not

Songs beyond the Kalevala Studia Fennica Folkloristica 2 1994

Ustia from Nikova, Setumaa. Photo: A.O. Väisänen 1912 (MV).

therefore surprise the singer – not even the basic message; she merely shook her head and was horrified, just as she was by the local murder.

Veera Pino, herself a native of Setumaa, mentioned that her grandmother believed in fairytales, for example in a time when the birds and the beasts could speak and be understood by humans. Generally speaking, people felt fairytales could be true, or at least they did not – contrary to what researchers sometimes assume – consider they were impossible. A similar attitude has been hinted at by Bengt Holbek, who quotes examples from different parts of Europe of fairytales being taken seriously: the further west one goes, the more people are rational and skeptical, the further east, the greater people's belief and fantasy becomes. This reflects the different social framework rather than the national character or the nature of the tradition. Above all it reflects the process of disintegration of the old village community (Holbek 1987, 196-197). The different nature of the culture also poses a problem for those of us trying to understand people's attitudes to songs.

The Estonian scholars claimed that the singers they met could on the whole be said to take the contents of the poems seriously, and earlier collectors described the attitude as "reverently serious". There are also many examples from Karelia, both in the 19th century and in the present day, of singers presenting Kalevala poetry as if the events had happened only yesterday.[2] Sandra Stepanova, a Russian Karelian folklorist, told me that the singers she had interviewed often relived the words of their songs: "Well, you see Ilmarinen's the sort of man who...", "Well that's what Väinämöinen does". The singers looked upon Väinämöinen, who was a popular character, as a wise man who once lived on the fells, helped people and vanished. One interviewee of Nina Lavonen, a Russian Karelian folklorist, told that Väinämöinen used to live in the district of Kiestinki.

The singer might identify with a song and mention that it contained elements of her own life. She might project herself into the lyrical lament, and feel with Oleksei Booze, the hero of religious songs, *Stiihu*, and his fate to such an extent that the tears would fall at the end. Sometimes, again, the singer would burst out laughing. This tendency to relive the events was also manifest among Karelian folk narrators.

What, then, are the factors contributing to the epic reality of the songs, the inner world in which the most unexpected events are accepted as possible and relevant to the singer's own life? What is the relationship between the songs and that which goes by the name of everyday reality, and how is the projection achieved within the genre?

People the world over have from time immemorial been creating parallel realities that differ from the everyday ones and that permit dimensions and deeds forbidden in the everyday world. Examples are feasts, dancing (often as part of festivities), play, catchy oral folklore, and the sensing of a supranatural presence. Various forms of entertaining and entertainment can be described as pseudoworlds in which the human being temporarily reorganises his everyday reality. They may in many cases also be described as survival mechanisms helping him to overcome opposition, the harsh everyday reality. (Virtanen 1988, 126-144.)

The singer may, in performing her songs, give expression to various feelings of breaking away from reality. True, she does not always relive the words so profoundly or even think of the words every time she sings them. Väinö Salminen found that in Ingria at the beginning of the century not all the people in the village appreciated the songs (Salminen 1934, 178-179), and the Estonian scholar Vaike Sarv summarised the same concept by saying that adapting the songs to one's own worldview is not important for everyone; even so "there are in every society people who are by nature philosophers". Singing may serve a need to give voice or to dance, but it may be concluded that the words spoken with one's own mouth always hold their own significance in the cultural milieu of the folk song.

In what way do the songs differ from the everyday world and at the same time create their own inner reality? I now wish to take a look at the women's Kalevala metre epic in regions where singing has primarily and publicly belonged to the women's domain: in Ingria, South Karelia, Estonia, and especially Setumaa.

In Archangel, Olonets and Ladoga Karelia songs were communal or solo songs performed by both men and women. Men favored the songs about Väinämöinen, Lemminkäinen and other masculine heroes for singing during fishing trips or at festive occasions. Women were interested in songs about courtship and marriage. The same singer usually had three to five melodies at his or her disposal. (Virtanen 1975.) In the Karelian Isthmus, Ingria and Estonia, women usually sang in circles, while walking to the village, while swinging and at weddings. The fore-singer sang a stanza and sometimes added a few words of their own.

The power of the singing voice

Songs are performed in a voice differing from that of speech. This may sound trivial, but one may well consider the meanings attached to the use

Kirmaski-feast at the river Werska. Photo: A.O. Väisänen 1912 (MV).

of the voice in various cultural contexts. Singing may be described as "a second vernacular" for expressing both more, and different things from ordinary speech. Singing and speech – according to Veera Pino – thus satisfy different purposes. In view of this it was, for example in Setumaa, considered important to make a clear distinction between the singing and the speaking voice. Thus, the singing was unrestrained and loud. Generally, people were unashamed of singing; it was a gift to others. The old collectors would describe the singing of Setu girls as "bellowing" and that of the Ingrians as "harsh screeching"; for these singers used a special laryngeal voice that is nowadays difficult to imitate.

In the typical women's song areas of Ingria and South Karelia the voice production was thus rather powerful. The singing at the Ritvala Whitsuntide festival is described by saying that "the lasses shouted", while Gottlund (1824) used the expression "Whit-shouting" (Enäjärvi-Haavio 1953, 91-92), which again indicates the public nature of the performance. The singing presumably came close to shouting in volume. In the areas from which the girls came, singing was a public affair, and the contents of the songs were known to all, both singers and listeners alike.

In the epic songs performed by women the chief character and identification model is usually a woman, and the songs tell about love or human relations. The personal approach and the open presentation of life's problems manifest in the songs seem to link up with the collective mode of singing in which a soloist alternated with a chorus. In North Karelia, where the mode of singing was different, the women singers often also dealt with problems in human relations; there are, however, far fewer different song motifs. (Järvinen 1989.)

The folk singer's voice is not, however, always loud, and may in certain cases be quiet. According to Sandra Stepanova it was the custom in Archangel Karelia to sing in a fairly ordinary, even voice; Väinämöinen

333

was, after all, "old and steadfast", she points out. It was also the custom to sing to children in a fairly soft voice. In Aunus, in South Karelia, the voice was not "pitied" in the same way, and people also spoke in louder voices. "Bellows enough to make your ears deaf" was a mother's complaint at the singing of a relative from Aunus while her baby was asleep.

In every case the melody and the traditional voice production distinguish singing from ordinary speech; this is a sufficient source of otherness. Karelian singers believed that the only sounds the dead could hear were laments; the lamenter's voice could thus be heard in Tuonela, the land of the dead, but not ordinary speech. (Konkka 1985, 36.) This is an excellent example of a different voice production and melodic model creating an inner world all of its own with its own rules and regulations.

The poetic guise

The verse form and metre distinguish singing from everyday speech. Modern recitation, declamation, was unknown among folk performers. Instead, the items cast in poetic metre were most often sung, with the exception of chants which were "read", for example, while holding the breath, at high speed, and sometimes greatly stressing the rhythm. The ancient metre known as Kalevala metre is also found in many riddles and proverbs. This indicates that poetic metre, the Kalevala metre, was expressly aimed at in many contexts and that it was – as Matti Kuusi points out – an admirable aid in committing lines to memory, and a means of expression beyond compare. The Kalevala tradition was a giant repository of texts worth remembering. It involved not just a given poetic metre but a source of unusual stylistic devices (alliteration and redundance) and language, "Kalevala language". (Kuusi 1978, 181-185.)

The information available on Setu singers demonstrates that a beautiful song was for them a long one. Songs were considered an important element of life, so time was set aside for them, and length increased their impact. It was in the singers' opinion important for a song to have a "second word", meaning both a parallel line and an expression using alliteration. A good singer would invent such a word or line, for without it the song was not a success. (Virtanen 1987, 176.)

The singers clearly attached certain aesthetic values to the verse form. The high esteem in which poetry was held among the different genres of folklore is, according to Pirkko-Liisa Rausmaa, proved by the fact that episodes in poetic form are to be found in folk tales and legends; the most miraculous examples are the long folk tales performed by singing. Poetic form was one to be aspired towards and carried more weight than prose, and there are virtually no examples of a poem being performed as if it were prose. The lines of poetry in a prose tale or legend speak for the strength of poetry. (Rausmaa 1968, 60.)

The belief legends describing the confrontation of the everyday and supranatural worlds often contain speech made by belief figures in poetic form. This form enhances the position of the line in the legend and stresses the weightiness of what is being said. The poetic form further indicates the supranormality of the speaker, because these crystallised lines are almost without exception uttered by supranatural beings. (Ojonen 1988.)

Two young wives from Aikova, Setu-maa. Photo: A.O. Väisänen 1912 (MV).

Poetic form may be defined as an exceptional mode of expression which – like speech in an unusual voice or melody – expresses exceptional things that stand out from the stream of normal speech and have been preserved as texts worth remembering, as Matti Kuusi said.

Also interesting is the question of the general magic origin of poetic metre to which scholars have sometimes referred. In magical thinking the unusual and exceptional involves some special 'force' that is difficult to describe, some inexplicable power. Since some of this thinking is partly subconscious and not explicitly stated in words, its consequences are difficult to specify. The magic chant aims to differ from everyday prose, says Anna-Birgitta Rooth in dealing with the dimensions of rhyme. A spell or chant thus acquires a special nature, and being special is essential to all magic. (Rooth 1965, 39.) Epic poems thus come close to magic reality in which the relationship between causes and effects are impossible to analyse.

Various forms of movement

Dance, like progression in a circle or line, is a form of movement deviating from the everyday one. Dancing and the movement akin to it are forms of symbolic behaviour and a means of expressing both ideas and emotions. Dance is a way of escaping from the everyday world. A report from Southwest Finland at the beginning of the century describes how the men and women became merry while dancing after the laborious task of bringing in the harvest: "Gone were all thoughts of poverty, of life's misfortunes, of toiling in the fields and much more besides."

Dancing may induce an altered state of consciousness in which the sense of time is lost and normal control vanishes. In the same way dancing and the singing connected with it create new, unusual forms of closeness. In the southern song regions there was a physical closeness between the girls and usually the women while dancing. The feeling of togetherness generated by the movement, likewise the unusual atmosphere of the dance, permitted a wider range of expression and, in particular, the treatment of problems faced by women in their lives. (See Virtanen 1988, 154-160).

Singing combined with movement may be described as the opposite of everyday reality. The singers may have dressed in their finest clothes; colourful garments demanding hours of hard work in the long winter evenings to make, and trinkets that were part of the identity of the unmarried girl. Even if the singers did not move about, they often took hold of one another or swayed in time to the music. The singers of the Estonian islands executed steps on the spot while singing, held on to one another, bent this way and that, and swayed like the waves on the sea, or so it has been reported. The women of the Karelian Isthmus squealed while performing the old poems, clapped their hands, squatted down, and barked or howled like wolves; they moved in unusually short steps.

The combination of a solo leader and a chorus was known throughout the Karelian Isthmus, Estonia and Ingria – the entire area where women were conspicuous as singers. The leader sang one or two lines to be taken up by the chorus, which sang the refrain, sometimes varying the words. In this area it was common to sing in circles, to move in a line of couples or a broader line. The linking of sung dancing with Kalevala metre singing is not just a question of performance but of the general nature of the singing tradition on a broader scale. How was Kalevala metre poetry sung in Finland?

The sung dance of Ingria and Karelia may, of course, be a Russian loan, and indeed some of the features of the dancing undoubtedly are. The other alternative is, according to Pirkko-Liisa Rausmaa, that the tradition of Ingria and the Isthmus is a continuation of the medieval European tradition in the same way as that of the Faeroe Islands, where the sung dance with its medieval forms has survived to the present day. Forms of dancing in a circle similar to those associated with Kalevala singing were known all over Europe in the Middle Ages, and they were used in Scandinavia as an accompaniment to ballads and narrative songs. (Rausmaa 1985.)

We may in the light of the facts known about the mode of singing ask whether Western Finland, South Savo included, could have been part of the performing tradition of Ingria and the Isthmus and at the same time of Europe as well. A strange relic in Finland are the Whitsuntide songs performed in the Sääksmäki village of Ritvala, the origin of which has been the subject of much speculation.[3] It has been suggested that the Ritvala songs might have been brought to Häme from Ingria, or more generally vice versa, that Ritvala was the home of an ancient tradition that later took root in Ingria.

The link between the mode of dancing and Kalevala metre singing in Finland is an interesting problem that requires further research. Movement, dancing and being the focus of attention clearly also affected the contents of songs.

There may, therefore, at one time have been an extensive song area not separated but joined by the Gulf of Finland in which individual songs were borrowed in both directions to such an extent that we may speak of a uniform area. But this is only a hypothesis that may be either proved or disproved by analysis of the poetry documented in Finland. Matti Kuusi speaks in his monograph on Maria Luukka of a "uniform Gulf of Finland culture" stretching from the villages of Ingria to the coast of Estonia and especially Kuusalu, and on to the Karelian Isthmus and a field of interaction bordering on Säkkijärvi-Virolahti. (Kuusi 1983, 19.)

The above passage illustrates the woman's typical performance customs and singing culture revealing a vital women's culture. What would be the case with male singers in terms of their singing customs and performance situations in these societies?

In the Setu community for example, men and women as a rule sang separately. For men, singing was something to be done in the company of men. It may happen in the home or at a festival that the women ask to hear the men sing: the male voice is *tugev* 'strong'. But generally speaking the men are familiar with the motifs and words of the women's songs, but not visa versa. The women's tradition is more public than the men's and at least to some extent directed across the sex border. The fact that men and women generally sing thematically different songs in same sex groups and in different contexts, suggests the development of different worlds of reality.

Setu folk songs are, like the old song tradition in general, firmly tied to the traditional customs and the roles of the sexes in the community. Women's studies are inspired by the observation that many scientific theories are better suited to explaining men's behaviour than women's. One of the starting points for humanistic women's research is the claim that it is impossible to view all women's actions as a result of male subordination, for they may be based on trends that differ from the male world of values. It may, for example, be that the cultural significance of women has not been rated sufficiently high in African society, and often only their economically subordinate position is described. But in Tanzania, for example, women – dispite their subordinate status – are responsible for a wealth of positive forces: joy, plenty of dancing and movement, rituals, handicrafts. We must study what women have instead of what they lack. (Swantz 1979, 73.)

The reality of the words

If, then, we define singing as a mode of presentation differing from everyday speech and expression, then what sorts of things does it put into words?

The singers did not distinguish the lyric as a genre of its own in the way that scholars do; at least no such designations have been recorded. The epic song also provided objects for emotional identification, and many of the images and motifs of the lyric are again to be found in chants. Songs may, like proverbs, be described as indirect speech strategies providing a means of clothing a personal message in a traditional and therefore depersonalised guise. (See Saville-Troike 1984, 36.) Various feelings of unrest, the laments of the homeless and orphans, a melancholic frame of mind in general, are things that could, through the lyric, be expressed in a socially acceptable form.

Women of a Saratseva family. Photo: A.O. Väisänen 1912 (MV).

The subjects of the songs are limited: they do not deal with all the sorrows in life, such as the grief felt on the death of a child. For the medium for pouring out grief on death was the lament. Songs do not weigh up the singer's relationship with the dead, spirits or belief figures in the way that legends and folk beliefs do. Nor do songs complain of hunger or a general shortage of food, because these were things that affected all members of the community and could thus be dealt with in speech. The orphan's lot, being inferior to that of others, could by contrast be put into words in song, just as the daughter-in-law might pour out her experiences in lyrical clichés.

The wedding songs of the Karelian Isthmus forbid the daughter-in-law from telling of her home life in the village: she had to say her mother-in-law gave her butter even if she only actually got butter once in the summer. This behavioural norm was embedded deep in the community, in which the family was also the basic economic unit. Even as late as the 1880s people interviewed on the Isthmus stressed that it was improper for a daughter-in-law to lament her fate ("it wasn't really the done thing, complaining", "having made the deal, there was nothing for it but to stick to it", "she had to choose better things", "you mustn't take anything from home or bring anything from the village", "people kept all their sorrows within their own four walls", etc.) (Virtanen 1984, 105-106.)

The singer does not arouse aggression in claiming that her lot is particularly hard, nor does she provide any inside information about life at home; instead she can pour out her feelings by describing the general harsh lot of mankind. It is not, however, possible to deduce from the songs whether the singer has a happy life or not, because like a diary, the songs provide an outlet for the emotions.

Many of the outbursts over the harshness of existence could just as well be sung by the lowly serving maid or the humble farm lad. The different focus of interest is manifest most clearly in epic poems, in which women choose women as their main characters and men choose men. By identifying with the main character, both genders can thus deal with the problems of their own lives. The object in the women's songs might be courtship, the problems of family life and human relations, whereas the men's songs deal with death, journeys into the unknown and the dangers that threaten them. By singing of these things, people find new courage to describe the various sides of life.

What, then, is the singer's attitude to the unreal motifs appearing in the songs? The disjointed facts at our disposal support the interpretation of *The Toomalaul* motifs given at the beginning: the singer looks on the words as true without really considering or analysing them. There is no conscious striving in all communities to distinguish between fantasy and belief, to define the limit to realistic fact, and nor is there any need to. The singer may identify with a certain character to such an extent that it is irrelevant to debate the credibility of the song.

In the Ingrian ballad *Tytärten hukuttaja*, 'The Daughter Drowner', the mother drowns her daughters because her son has difficulty in bringing home a daughter-in-law. The bride he does find does not get the work done, however, and the mother begins to regret what she has done and to miss her lost children. The singer's "own dear mother" appears before her eyes, and she debates whether she could, like the daughter drowned in the song, have said in cold blood to her mother: "You're not my mother, the sea is my mother."

As a second example we could take the song about a giant oak that grows up to heaven sung by a Setu woman born in 1928. The maiden in the song decides to climb up the oak to heaven. The moon and the sun court her, but the moon is as sharp as a sickle and the sun too hot. The maiden then decides she wants to return to earth, but the oak has broken: her mother's tears have broken the trunk of the oak. "The song tells about me myself," explained the weeping singer. How often does a girl marry and believe she is doing the right thing! But being married is no fun and there is no return.

There are also examples from Setumaa of songs with a warning or a moral. In the mythical *Kalmuneiu poem* Peeter promises to take as his wife the daughter of the graveyard, Kalmuneiu 'Grave's girl', if the seeds he has sown near the graveyard yield a good harvest. But he in fact marries a rich girl from Riga and thus breaks his promise. On his way home he meets the revenge of the graveyard folk: Peeter dies and so does his bride. Veera Pino mentions that her mother thought that "in the olden days" anything you said would come true. People should think about what they say and bear the consequences of anything they say. If you tell a lie, it will come back on you, so you should think before you speak. In *The Kalmuneiu* the suitor did not think before he spoke and was careless in his speech, so he was severely punished. When the old mother said, "times are different", she meant that times have changed and things nowadays happen that would at one time have been thought strange.

These statements reveal one level of the singers' reality: the events of the songs were in the olden days considered possible, but they are no longer thought so today, because times have changed. The same philosophy is also

Dance group Helbi from Setumaa. Photo: Pirjo Mäkilä, Tallinn 1987 (FLS).

evident in Finnish folklore, such as in the belief legends in which the strangest of events are taken for granted. Giants are thought to have existed in ancient times, when all sorts of other marvellous things took place.

The different faces of truth

Do observations such as these help us to understand and interpret songs the contents of which have not elicited a single personal assessment by any singer?

The motifs of many of the women's ballads are part of the international tradition and are treated in performance in the same way as contemporary urban legends; they are remodelled and set in the narrator's immediate environment; they are received as such, as items of news affecting the hearer. The narrators and listeners may often react to the subject matter in a very emotional way, even illogically, inspired by their own experiences and mental associations. There does not, however, always seem to be any real reason why these stories should spread, except that someone once invented them and they evoke a reaction, they capture people's interest in various life situations and milieux.

What chances have we of understanding the symbolism and the thoughts on life hidden in the songs? In the case of chants in particular there is a danger of treating relics of the past as living elements of worldview. Gösta Berg (1969) criticised the application of the model used in the natural sciences to the arts: constructing a model and then testing it to see how it fits reality. Where scholars have gone astray is that in discovering in folk tradition fossilised relics of fertility cults, sun cults, etc. they have treated them as if they were full of living content, beliefs and fantasies. Berg refers to a statement made by an old Eskimo woman to Knud Rasmussen: "In your opinion these supranatural things should have a meaning: but we don't bother our heads about this. We are content not to understand." (Berg 1969, 79.)

Narrative songs may contain fossilised relics which, if regarded as instruments of a living belief, custom or norm, would be misleading. Even the singer does not know, when asked, the meaning of certain words and symbols. The international core of the songs can, it would seem, often be compared to such a stone core that cannot always be placed in relation to the singer's life situation at that particular moment.

It is at the same time probably true to say that most of the songs known in the area were in principle familiar and clear to their singers. This is suggested by scholars acquainted at the practical level with the song tradition of both Karelia and Estonia. There are also examples indicating that the singer may understand the significance of a symbolical image and make sure that it is understood by the collector, too.[4] There are various potential receptions available in the complex cultural picture of the past.

People's attitudes to the songs poses questions that have been debated in the case of Greek poetry. Did the Greeks believe in their myths? How is it possible for people to believe in many conflicting things simulta- neously? Paul Veyne notes that instead of speaking of belief in beliefs we should speak of belief in various truths, and various truths tend far more to be historical in origin than realistic. Viewed objectively, there exists a sphere of reality on which the light of our minds is reflected, only to be reflected back on our awareness. Sometimes it is reflected directly, while at other times it is tainted by our imagination, passion or ideology. Constantly flowing through our minds are various programmes fashioned partly by truth and partly by interests; this is a vital aspect of humanity. Various truths are all true in our eyes, because we do not think about them in the same part of our brains, as Veyne points out. He admits that he has an almost neurotic fear that his dead friend will come back to haunt him, while at the same time regarding this possibility as a mere fiction. (Veyne 1988, 84-87.)

Songs open up a different world which has – in the terminology of the computer age – a different program and programming. The songs are a piece hewn out of reality, a part of life isolated from the everyday environment by a different vocal technique, tune, metre, performance, and special concepts of reality. As a result of all these factors, which we could call traditional transformers of reality, the song is true for the duration of its performance in just the same way as the modern viewer accepts a television film by tuning into the reality it presents. But this otherness, which acquires entertaining features, also consists of collectively controlled elements strictly limited in theme, and when the song is over, life returns to normal, which is again a socially accepted and as such constantly changing concept.

NOTES

This article is based on an earlier version published in Finnish under the title *Naisten laulut ja todellisuus*, which appeared in *Ai-kakirja 3*. J. Tuovinen (ed.). Valkeakosken kaupungin julkaisusarja B: 3. 1991. Valkea-koski. p. 51-61.

1. The Setu are a tribe living in the south-eastern corner of Estonia whose culture, preserved in its old traditional form,

caught the attention of scholars at an early date. At the beginning of the century there were some 20,000 Setus living in the Petser area. The Setus subscribe to the Orthodox faith and their tradition differs in many ways from that of both the other Estonians and of the surrounding Russians.

2. The term Karelia is here used to refer to the area known as Archangel Karelia, *Viena*, beyond the Finnish border where most of the epic poetry in the *Kalevala* was collected in the 19th century. The inhabitants of this area belonged to the Orthdox Church and spoke Karelian. Nowadays most of the inhabitants are Russians, but scholars from the tradition archives in Petrozavodsk have until recently been able to record ancient Karelian folklore in the area.

3. Until the 1880s the village of Ritvala in the Häme parish of Sääksmäki in Finland still celebrated a medieval festival featuring a procession of maidens. From Ascension Day until Whitsun the girls would gather at the crossroads in the middle of the village on the afternoons of holy days and wander through the fields singing three ballads. Elsa Enäjärvi-Haavio, for example, assumes that the Ritvala Whitsuntide procession is of ancient origin, though she does not take a clear stand on the Ingrian tradition.

4. Ingrid Rüütel mentioned that in a poem a singer from Soikkola used the image of "getting a red shirt". She asked whether the collector understood that it meant she got a beating.

ANNELI ASPLUND

Mother and Daughter – in the Footsteps of the Itinerant Singers

In 1985 the Finns celebrated the 150th anniversary of *The Kalevala* by arranging festivals, exhibitions, concerts, theatre performances and seminars in different parts of the country. One of the festivals was held in Varkaus in Central Finland and consisted of concerts and events associated with songs and singing, such as a seminar on the essence of peasant poetry and folk singing. To their surprise, the participants in the seminar were treated to some ancient *rune*-singing of a type no longer thought to be heard in Finland. The singer, Klaudia Vonkkanen, turned out to be the daughter of the *rune*-singer Oksenja Mäkiselkä who was famous in Finland in the 1930s and 1940s. While at the seminar, Seppo Knuuttila, a researcher at the Finnish Literature Society, got to know Klaudia Vonkkanen and embarked on a field research project that is still going on.[1]

Klaudia Vonkkanen has proved to be an excellent narrator and a tradition expert with a good memory. The bulk of her song repertoire has now been recorded at least once, along with other folklore. The research project still continues, however, since items memorised many years ago may take time to recall.

The present study is part of a larger research project. It examines Klaudia Vonkkanen from a folkloristic perspective as a singer who was for decades unable to make free use of her personal song repertoire. How has this long, enforced silence affected the retention of her repertoire? What, and how, does Klaudia Vonkkanen sing today? I concern myself with the people closest to her during her life and their influence on her role as a singer, and comparing Oksenja Mäkiselkä and Klaudia Vonkkanen – mother and daughter – as singers and performers.

Oksenja – a wandering singer from Suistamo

Songs beyond the Kalevala Studia Fennica Folkloristica 2 1994

Oksenja (Ksenia) was born into the Valokainen family in the Suistamo village of Piensara in 1878.[2] Her mother, Jelena Ignaiti's-daughter (Ignaitintytär) (1837-1892), appears to have had a rather good command of

Oksenja Mäkiselkä performing a lament at the 100th anniversary celebration of the Kalevala in 1935. Photo: Collections of the Kalevala Society.

ancient poetry, since it was from her mother that Oksenja learnt at least *Luojan virsi*, 'The Messiah'.[3] Now and then she pointed out to the collector that a particular song was not one of her mother's. This indicates that she assimilated much of her basic repertoire from her mother, who likewise passed on to her the art of lamenting.

Oksenja's parents died in consecutive years. She was only 14 when her mother died. She lived at home with her brothers and sisters for a time before going into service at Heroila Farm in the nearby village of Äimäjärvi. Here she found herself in an environment where the art of *rune*-singing was still practised. The head of the household himself, Iivana Härkönen, played the *kantele*, and his parents, the aging Iivana Heroila-Härkönen and his wife Palaga (née Sotikainen), could both sing ancient songs. Oksenja was thus able to add to her skills, and she remembered that she learnt the song telling of the adventures of Lemminkäinen from the aged Iivana.

At about that time the farm was occasionally visited by folklore collectors; the first Sortavala song festivals also coincided with her stay at Heroila. Old Iivana and his wife Palaga were invited to sing the ancient *runes* at the festivals (Haavio 1948, 211). All of this undoubtedly explains why Oksenja was so eager later in life to perform her songs in public.

While in service at Heroila Farm in the 1890s Oksenja met her future life partner, Dimitri Buljugin, alias Stjopin Miitrei, who lived not far away. The Buljugin farm was one of the wealthiest and mightiest in the region and owned some 400 hectares of land.

The young couple spent the first years of their marriage on Miitrei's farm with his brother, but as the family grew, they began to talk of dividing up the estate and building a house of their own. Oksenja and Miitrei already had a number of children by the time they were able to move into their own house sometime around 1913. They changed their Russian surname Buljugin to the Finnish Mäkiselkä in the mid-1920s, the name being taken from the place where the house was built.[4]

The family soon grew. All in all Oksenja Mäkiselkä bore 13 children, two of which died in infancy. Klaudia was the eleventh child and had a twin sister. Oksenja's strength was gradually depleted by her constant child-bearing, so that after the birth of the last pair of twins in 1920 she fell ill and was for a couple of years in such poor health that a servant had to be hired to help her run the household. As the children grew up her work load gradually became slightly easier, especially when the oldest sons married and brought their wives to the house. Later, when Oksenja set off on her "singing tours", as she called them, the reason was not want, as has sometimes been claimed. True, the money she earned did come in very useful at home, but it was not, at least according to Klaudia, the primary reason for her departure: "--- Mother reckoned there was nothing to stop her from going---. She was not driven to it by hunger---."

The impetus to set off on her travels came from Oksenja's cousin, Feodor Vuorinen (formerly Valokainen). Together with Timo Lipitsä, who was known for his *kantele* playing, Feodor had toured various parts of the country, singing and playing as he went, and he was one of the itinerant singers that travelled about Finland between the end of last century and the 1930s. There were at that time other folk artists travelling about the country, too: country folk players, fiddlers and accordion players, sellers of broadsheets going from village to village, and organ grinders who often also appeared at the markets and fairs. Long before this, in the early 19th century, peddlers from Archangel Karelia had reached even the western coast of Finland. Many of them were also singers, though their purpose was not to sing but to sell their wares. The best singers of the ancient songs did not travel out into the world but remained at home, ignorant of the world outside their native region.

Teaching at the seminary in the little town of Sortavala on the shores of Lake Ladoga in the 1880s was a man by the name of O.A. Forsström-Hainari – an ardent admirer of ancient Finnish folk culture. It was his custom to invite to his home *rune*-singers and *kantele* players from among his acquaintances to entertain his guests. These were only too pleased to oblige, since they were thankful for the small sums of money which their performances earned them. It was also a pleasure for them to bask in the glow of the gentlefolk's admiration. Some of Hainari's friends then began to follow his example by inviting singers to their homes or by arranging opportunities for them to perform. As a result, players and singers began to make their way to Sortavala from further and further afield.

It was, however, through the song festival that the Karelian *rune*-singers became known to the public at large. Song festivals began to be held in Finland in the latter half of the 19th century, and they attracted choirs and bands from all over the country. These festivals became national events fostering a patriotic spirit and emphasising the Finnish identity, for conditions in Finland at that time were becoming increasingly strained as a result of tsarist policy.

In 1896 Forsström-Hainari hit on the idea of organising a sort of ethnographical museum in conjunction with the Sortavala song festival. Karelian maidens baked Karelian pasties in a Karelian cottage. Seated on a hummock over the brow of the hill was a *kantele* player, and next to him a *rune*-singer. The tradition of including *rune*-singers, *kantele* players and later other folk musicians was later taken up by other song festivals.

The performers of the ancient lore from Border Karelia thus became accustomed to travelling further and further away from Karelia to other parts of Finland. They were to be found in the largest towns, and they were invited to agricultural shows and other events. They performed in schools and other educational establishments. The best-known of these itinerant singers was Iivana Onoila of Suistamo, who travelled the length and breadth of Finland from the beginning of the century until his death in 1924. (Haavio 1948, 202-222.)

The people of Suistamo got used to the idea of making a living by *rune*-singing and *kantele* playing. A few singers were still spending long periods on the roads as late as the 1930s. Among them was Feodor Valokainen, Oksenja's cousin. Feodor's companion, Timo Lipitsä, was by that time getting on in life and the journeying was becoming too much for him. Feodor, however, was full of enthusiasm, and since he knew his cousin Oksenja to be a good singer, persuaded her to join him. Oksenja was ready to go, for the youngest children were by that time older than ten years.

At about that time Miitrei fell into bad health, he was blind, and he did not like the idea, but Oksenja was burning to try something new. According to Klaudia, "Mother was the sort that when she once decided something, she went ahead and did it and didn't ask anyone else's opinion." Oksenja thus set off with her cousin Feodor. Klaudia guesses this was in about 1933 or 1934. At that time they confined themselves more or less to Karelia. The next time she set off, Oksenja was alone. She appeared in Helsinki in November 1934. During this trip she performed at least at the Kalevala Society and was recorded at the home of A.O. Väisänen in Meilahti. On that occasion Martti Haavio wrote down everything she could possibly sing and tell.

Naturally Oksenja was invited to perform at the Kalevala centenary then being planned, along with Ogoi Määränen and Domna Huovinen (representing ancient Finnish *rune*-singing and music), and the *kantele* players Vanja Tallas, Antero Vornanen and Antti Rantonen. Oksenja became so enthusiastic about the centenary celebrations that she decided that in autumn 1935, after the Sortavala song festival, she would set off again on a broader tour of the country, since even before the festival she had been invited to sing in many places. Her companion and support on this journey was her daughter Klaudia.[5] The journey was to prove long and eventful and it lasted nine months in all. This was to be Klaudia's only singing journey for the time being, but not her mother's. And it was during the Kalevala jubilee year that Oksenja travelled abroad – the only time in her life. The trip was arranged by A.O. Väisänen to Lübeck in Germany, where the aim was to present different aspects of the Finnish way of life.

Oksenja's life was completely disrupted by the Second World War. Her family were forced to leave Karelia, the family farm and everything on which their lives were built. Oksenja and her family suffered the same pitiful fate as tens of thousands of other Karelian evacuees. There was no alternative but to leave Karelia and to move to some other part of Finland, to try to live one day at a time in a country at war with a seemingly overwhelming adversary.

During the interim peace of 1940-1941, when Finland reclaimed the areas ceded to the Soviet Union, the older sons and their families, and with them Oksenja, moved back to the home farm in Suistamo. She wanted to go home. She felt lonely and uprooted, for her husband, Miitrei, had died shortly before the outbreak of war. When Karelia was once again lost during the Continuation War (1942-1945), Oksenja finally lost her Mäkiselkä home for good and all.

After the war she lived with her children when she was not on her travels. The money she earned from singing during the difficult years of the 1940s was far, far more precious than before the war. Performing seems to have meant much to Oksenja in other ways, too. The 1930s had been the most exciting period in her life, affording her experiences seldom enjoyed by persons of her status.

Recalling these experiences, she tried to carry on after the war in the way she had before. She was by this time nearly 70 years old, and travelling was not easy in the 1940s. Yet she always tried to sing whenever she had the opportunity. She nevertheless fell ill, suffered a stroke in autumn 1946 and had to spend weeks in hospital. When she had recovered somewhat, Klaudia took her to her home at Laihia, where she died the following May.

Describing Oksenja in his book *Viimeiset runonlaulajat*, 'The last of the *rune*-singers', Martti Haavio draws a picture of a sensitive, religious woman. He notes Oksenja's ability to take control of herself when necessary, writing: "And later, too, during the ten days she spent dictating and singing to me, I noted her reserved conduct, her complete command of her feelings, her dignity and pride. (Haavio 1948, 239-240.)

Oksenja was a born performer. She revelled in publicity. She did not get nervous, even when performing to notable dignitaries, and sang to an audience of hundreds just as naturally as to a small class of schoolchildren. Yet she did not become an itinerant *rune*-singer until the closing decade of her life. Until then life at Suistamo followed its own ordained course, with its own joys and sorrows. Within her culture Oksenja had a superb command of the ancient tradition. According to Haavio she could sing 83 songs in the old poetic metre. Admittedly some of them were very short, but others were lengthy epics. Haavio also noted down 73 incantations, 12 laments, and 8 rhyming folk songs; she could undoubtedly have sung more if pressed in the same way as with Kalevala-metric poetry. She also sang for A.O. Väisänen, who recorded her songs on parlograph cylinders and discs.[6]

Oksenja herself wished to be known to the public at large as not only a *rune*-singer but as a lamenter, too. This aspect is clear from the work of the collectors. Haavio managed to commit 12 laments by her to paper, and the majority of the items recorded by Väisänen on wax cylinders were laments. Oksenja's view of herself as a lamenter was indeed justified, for she appears to have had a supreme command of the technique of composition and performance. With her firm grasp of both the inner rules of tradition and of herself, Oksenja was able to put together laments that were

The kantele-players and rune-singers who performed at the 100th anniversary celebration of the Kalevala. Oksenja Mäkiselkä first on the right. Photo: Collections of The Kalevala Society.

both beautiful and moving. She was therefore only too pleased to display this skill both to her audiences and to researchers. One major item in Oksenja's lament repertoire seems to have been a lament about the fate of the Karelians, which she performed on many occasions in the 1940s and of which several recordings exist.[7] In it she expresses her personal sense of homelessness in a way that is quite heart-rending. With her rich experience and meetings with all kinds of people she was, like most lamenters, able to look beyond her own personal grief and in a way regarded herself as the interpreter of the sorrow felt by all evacuees.

The bulk of Oksenja's basic repertoire was captured on paper, wax cylinders and disc, but modern recording techniques would undoubtedly have yielded results of a very different calibre. There would, to begin with, be far more material. The different variants of the same song were not sufficiently documented for the scholar today to get a clear picture of her powers of variation. The fact that she was a master of lament technique naturally meant she was capable of improvisation according to certain rules. As regards her other songs, her singing seems to have displayed a considerable degree of crystallisation. She obviously sang epics without any great variation. There is virtually no variation, and the same lines follow one another in the same set pattern throughout the song. Yet many of the seemingly isolated, short lyrical variants indicate that Oksenja was also able to use the formulaic language of *rune*-singing to compose new sequences. There is, however, no proof of this such as that evident in the laments, because there are not enough recorded variants. The marked crystallisation in her songs is also an indication that *rune*-singing was no longer part of the collective tradition even of Suistamo in the 20th century, that it was the individual tradition of a few singers and more in the nature of recalling an ancient art than of a living tradition.

Oksenja Mäkiselkä at the 100th anniversary celebration of the Kalevala, sitting in the front row between folk music researcher A.O. Väisänen and rune-singer Ogoi Määränen. Photo: Collections of The Kalevala Society.

Oksenja introduced her performances herself and often explained the difficult metaphoric language of her laments and poems, since she realised that, with the exception of the Karelians, they were for the most part strange and obscure to the Finns. Her intelligence and empathy are revealed in the way she selected the programmes for different kinds of audiences. She was not just any ancient monument paraded on stage simply to perform something from the distant past; she consciously selected items herself to suit the situation and the audience in question and thus tried to control the mood of the event. Singing was, of course, of great financial significance to her – there is no denying that – but money was not the most important thing. Oksenja Mäkiselkä was above all a person with a strong need to express herself, deriving undoubtedly from ambition, but who also possessed the ability to create direct contact with her listeners and thus act as mediator between two different cultures.

Klaudia's life-story

Klaudia was born on March 20, 1916, one of the last of the many children born to Oksenja and Miitrei. She was the second of twins, to be followed later by twin brothers. Although life in Suistamo was at that time still primitive to some extent, a new era was nevertheless rapidly dawning. Life at Mäkiselkä Farm was much the same as life on other farms at that time, except that the old customs and beliefs, such as incantations and magic tradition, still lived on in the home of Oksenja and Miitrei, and the way of life was dictated by expediency. The inhabitants of a remote village had to manage on their own, 20th century or no. Klaudia remembers her mother healing a bad patch of impetigo on her head by means of spells and magic, and cleansed a two-year-old nephew of rickets with a birch switch. A

349

neighbour's wife had a reputation for being a good healer, and it was to her that Oksenja turned with a request to cure a cramp in Klaudia's leg. The wife's spells, magic and medicines cured the leg.

Work was part of the lives of the Mäkiselkä children from the time they were very small. At a very early age they were taught the necessary skills, such as cooking, baking, handwork, spinning with a distaff and spinning wheel, and looking after the cattle. By the time she was seven Klaudia was already doing responsible work outside the home, looking after the children of a neighbour a couple of kilometres away, for example. The children in her care were aged one and two. The rest of the household were out working in the fields a couple of kilometres away, and the 7-year-old was expected not only to look after the children but also to do all sorts of other chores, such as taking the cows out to graze after they had been milked in the morning, and getting a meal ready before the mother came in from the fields. By modern standards, the job was impossible for a child of that age, but it undoubtedly fostered in Klaudia a sense of responsibility and independent initiative.

One of the biggest changes in the life of children at that time was brought about by elementary school, which Klaudia attended for six years. It was a carefree time, shadowed only by the knowledge (at around the age of 10) that her family would keep her only until she was old enough to be confirmed. After that the younger children would have to go out into the world; the older brothers had agreed on this with their parents.

There were lots of young people at Mäkiselkä Farm in the 1920s and 1930s. Oksenja and Miitrei were liberal-minded, and the boys arranged local dances whenever they felt like it. Mäkiselkä Farm was far from being a remote *rune*-singer's cottage, but was instead brimming with life and young people. One of the older brothers played the accordion, another the mouth organ, and the brothers taught Klaudia to dance. She quickly picked up the fashionable dances of the times, such as the ring dances and broadsheet songs just as easily as the sacred songs sung at the prayer meetings held from time to time at the farm. Upon finishing school, she left home at the age of 15 to be a household servant with her sister's family at Kollasjoki, and stayed there for more than two years. She discovered that leaving home and supporting herself were not as frightening as she had initially imagined. After being confirmed she sought a post as a domestic servant for some time in the village of Suistamo. A brisk helper was then needed at home to help the daughter-in-law. By that time her father was an old man, her brothers were serving in the army, and the youngest brothers were not yet capable of doing men's work. So Klaudia ended up having to look after them, too. She remembers this period in her life as being the hardest of all as far as work was concerned.

Approaching the age of 20, Klaudia decided to seek work outside Suistamo and had already got a post as a household servant in Helsinki when her plans were suddenly changed. For in 1935 her mother asked her to accompany her, both for companionship and assistance, since she could neither read nor write and found it difficult to travel alone. As Klaudia a practical girl who got things done, her mother got used to her making the travel arrangements, and even to her deciding where they would go next. "I just phoned through to the next school and then walked into the staff

Weeping mother and spinning daughter. Official photograph of Oksenja Mäkiselkä and Klaudia from 1935, made into a postcard. Photo: FLS, (KRA).

room and stated my business." They usually got a good reception wherever they went. *Rune*-singing was in considerable demand in the Kalevala centenary year. One of their most memorable experiences was meeting President Svinhufvud, and their visits to the homes of Martti Haavio and Samuli Paulaharju also made a deep impression.[8] Klaudia also has warm memories of a number of other people they met on their travels and in whose homes she often baked Karelian pasties while her mother chatted in the living room.

The performances by Oksenja and Klaudia were in the nature of a two-woman show: Oksenja sang and explained the background to their performances while her daughter spun with a distaff and sang a few songs with her mother if her mother's voice began to tire. Their journeying ended in the spring, when the schools broke up. Klaudia remembers it as an exciting time rich in experience, and one to which she has repeatedly dwelt on in her memories.

During the course of their travels their plans for the future changed. At Ilmajoki, in Ostrobothnia, Oksenja talked to the principal of the local dairy school, and in the autumn Klaudia applied for a place. This school was at that time known for its strict curriculum and discipline. There was plenty of practical work, interspersed with many subjects, from mathematics to geography. "My youth soon passed," says Klaudia in recalling her school days. The school was ruled in a strict spirit of Christian chastity. For the pupils, all forms of entertainment, to say nothing of cinemas or local dances, were out of the question. Some of the girls would from time to time sneak out in secret, but never Klaudia. When her father died in 1938, she had to go into mourning for one year, and during that time it was not considered fitting to attend any form of entertainment. Her youth really was a brief one, for she had to go out to work as soon as she finished school. She wanted to become a cattle inspector, and for that one needed two year's working experience. She thus started as a milkmaid in the Porvoo region, in southeast

351

Klaudia Vonkkanen with her family in Laihia, 1945. Photo: FLS, (KRA, added in 1986).

Finland, in autumn 1939 and was there when the Winter War broke out. She spent autumn 1940 and spring 1941 at Orimattila, returning to Ilmajoki for the summer, and took her inspector's exam. She then got a job as a cattle inspector at Laihia and was there throughout the Continuation War. It was there that she met her future husband, Mikko (Mikael) Vonkkanen (born 1910), a man from Suistamo who, when she first met him, was on leave from the front.

Upon marrying Mikko Vonkkanen in 1942, Klaudia was 26 years old. She had already been working for some time and was used to leading a fairly independent life. She did not look on herself as an evacuee in the way that her mother and many of her relatives did, for she had already left Suistamo before the outbreak of war. She was nevertheless sorely grieved by the loss of her homeland. Marrying a man from Suistamo helped to reinforce the Karelian element in the family. They soon settled in Ostrobothnia, however, especially once they got to know their new neighbours. Their few bitter experiences were quickly swallowed, for there were far bigger things to worry about during the war. There was a shortage of everything, but Klaudia does not remember experiencing the stinginess for which Laihia is famous.[9] "I made lots of life-long friends there," she says.

Klaudia was 29 by the time her first child was born – quite old for a first-timer. But from then onwards came a baby every year, until there were eight in all. Three of them died in infancy. As the mother of a large family Klaudia now found herself faced with a different kind of life from the one she was used to. Her troubles and cares were no way lessened by the fact that the second child, Pirkko, suffered from an attack of angina when she was two, was unconscious for a couple of weeks and sustained permanent brain damage as a result. Her mother's illness and death also coincided with the early years of her marriage.

There were in Laihia in the late 1940s few opportunities for getting ahead, and the family thus decided to look elsewhere. Mikko went to work in a mill in Varkaus, followed by Klaudia and the children a few months later.

In the beginning Mikko worked as a frame sawyer at a blockboard mill, and he also drove a forklift truck there for a few years. He then obtained a permit to act as an independent lorry-driver and was self-employed for twenty years.

In the first few years at Varkaus Klaudia was kept busy virtually round the clock. In addition to the normal job of looking after her family she did all her own baking, made all the children's clothes, knitted socks, mittens, hats and sweaters for the whole family. In order to make a little extra money she also baked Karelian pasties for the ladies of Varkaus.

While the children were small Klaudia stayed at home, but when the youngest one started school, she began to think of getting a job. She was spurred along by the idea of making a better living for her family, and ultimately of buying their own home, which they finally did. Klaudia got a job as a painter at Ahlström's. She was a reliable worker and showed initiative in a way not commonly encountered among women at the time. This is illustrated by her story of the change she brought about at Ahlström's. At first the work had been hard and boring, stripping iron with sand-paper. Only the women did this. The men then painted the iron the women had stripped for them. After doing this for a time Klaudia could not, however, understand why the women had to do the harder and more boring work while all the men had to do was paint. Together with the foreman Klaudia managed to bring in an agreement by which all the workers stripped the iron they were to paint, men too. It was not long before the stripping was mechanised, since the men soon decided they had had enough. An appreciable improvement was thus achieved in the women's working conditions.

Klaudia was full of energy in other respects, too. She could find pleasure in anything, so long as it was meaningful and sensible. She also had the courage to stand up to the foremen if necessary, and she enjoyed the respect of both colleagues and employers.

Klaudia Vonkkanen retired from her job as a painter in 1976. As a result of having so many children and her years of hard work she has had three coronary thromboses. A serious eye complaint has completely robbed her of the sight in one eye. She was left a widow in 1984.

After her husband died, Klaudia began to find living in her own house too much for her. In spring 1989 she therefore sold the house and moved to a block of flats in the centre of Varkaus, where she lives with her daughter, Pirkko. Life for Pirkko has settled on an even keel, since Finnish society takes good care of the disabled. Some of Klaudia's other children live in Varkaus, and they help her with the heavy jobs about the house and often come to see her. She has seven grandchildren and three great-grandchildren. When asked about her life today, Klaudia replies that she has never had it so easy.

Marriage

Klaudia's marriage to Mikko Vonkkanen lasted, even though life was not always easy. As far as Klaudia was concerned, her husband's quick temper, stubbornness and old-fashioned attitudes were the cause of many problems. According to Mikko a woman's place was at home with the children, and it was a long time before he accepted the fact that his wife wanted to go out to work. Looking back, Klaudia does not, however, regard this entirely as a failing in her husband. She mentions objectively that he was partly against her going out to work because of the children. He was fond of the children and felt they should be able to stay at home as long as possible. He could not see any point in putting them in day care. Klaudia says that "Daddy" liked lulling the children to sleep by singing hymns, even though he had no singing voice to speak of and he never sang hymns at any other time.

Many positive aspects of their life together come out in the interviews, and Klaudia does not forget to mention that her husband agreed to have his ailing mother-in-law to live with them, even though the times were extremely hard. Mikko Vonkkanen always took good care of his family.

Their marriage thus went at a more or less even pace from one year to the next, though chiefly on Mikko's terms. Klaudia was not, however, afraid to open her mouth, but it was she who gave way over a number of things. Mikko's attitude to domestic appliances, for example, was typical. Only after long arguments would he agree to even the essential appliances. Little by little Klaudia learnt to bide her time and to know when she might get her way.

The thing that struck Klaudia hardest of all was, however, her husband's refusal to understand why she should want to carry on *rune*-singing like her mother. On a couple of occasions a local heritage enthusiast, Tapio Kautovaara, had persuaded Klaudia to appear on the Kuopio local radio in a programme about Oksenja. Thereafter her husband flatly refused to allow her to make any public appearance whatsoever, and nothing whatever could shift him. "There was nothing for it but to heed what he said. I had two choices, either not perform, or perform but shut the door behind me. And with the children only small, I couldn't just shut the door – and even if the children had been grown up..."

There was nothing for it but to bury any ideas she had ever entertained of going off singing on her own. She therefore answered all requests with a form 'no'. After a while no one asked her any more, and apart from Kautovaara and a few others, no one in recent years has had any idea that Klaudia came from a *rune*-singing family and could herself sing.

Why was Mikko Vonkkanen so adamant in forbidding her to sing? Was he afraid he would lose his wife if he let her appear on stage? Was he jealous, or was he envious of his wife's quick, lively nature? Was the example set by his mother-in-law so terrifying that he sought to protect his family from what he considered to be unnecessary publicity? Klaudia herself prefers not to answer these questions, though she admits being deeply hurt. But she got used to giving way in this as in so many other things affecting her everyday life. Over the years her husband's refusal to accept her singing caused a mental rift between them, though the subject was hardly ever mentioned. Klaudia always avoided a row as far as possible, because of the children.

Repertoire, reproduction and performance

A couple of years after her husband's death Klaudia was asked to perform at a local Karelian festival. She consented. There was no reason why she should not, now that her husband was dead. From then onwards the idea of singing gradually took hold in her mind. Next she went off to the Joutsa Summer Festival. And when a singing festival was being planned in Varkaus, someone remembered there was a *rune*-singer right on the doorstep. Thus began Klaudia's own singing tours, and she has sung on a number of occasions in the area where she now lives. One particularly pleasurable occasion was the Suistamo Summer Festival held in Joensuu in 1987, where she was able to sing to an audience of people from her native area and, she discovered, a number of old friends. In March 1988 she sang at the 50th anniversary festival of the Helsinki branch of the Kalevala Women's Association. Her most recent trip, in spring 1989, took her as far away as Canada.

Klaudia immediately threw herself actively into the interview study. This has been conducted a few days at a time, either with Klaudia coming to Helsinki to be recorded in conjunction with one of her 'singing trips', or with me visiting her in her home in Varkaus. I began charting her repertoire with poetry in Kalevala metre and tried to get as full a picture as possible of the tradition in her command. I have also recorded laments and more recent songs in addition to other folklore materials (folk tales, legends, spells, games, beliefs, small-scale folklore, ethnographic descriptions and reminiscences). Video films have also been made of Klaudia singing and spinning – the latter being an integral part of every performance these days. The method used has been spontaneous interviewing, and I have tried to record her main repertoire as closely as possible, and in a number of different variants. In between the interviews Klaudia has got into the habit of making notes of her own, so that songs she has recalled in her everyday life are easy to remember at the start of the next round of interviews. A number of songs have also sprung to mind during an actual recording. The result is a repertoire containing about fifty songs, many of them in more than one variant. This is not as such particularly large, but it is nevertheless unequalled in Finland today in its quality and its diversity.

In all, there are three narrative songs in Kalevala metre: a legend song called *Jumalan virsi* or *Luojan virsi*, 'The Messiah', and a ballad-type song known as *Annukkaisen virsi* 'The Song of Annukkainen' or *Meren kosijat*, 'The Suitors from the Sea', about a girl who is courted by various rich suitors but finally chooses a dependable farmer. The third of Klaudia's epic songs is *Lemminkäisen kosintalaulu*, 'The Lemminkäinen Song', as she calls Oksenja's humorous song known as *Mokoman muikkarin virsi* 'The Fine Fellow's Song' in which the suitor, having carefully prepared to court a young woman, finds he has courted a shameless hussy.[10] These were among the basic songs in her mother's repertoire, too. In the category of lyrical songs in *rune* metre there are four lullabies, in addition to which Klaudia knows two spinning songs, a milking song, a slash-and-burn song and a cattle call. All these have been part of her standard tour repertoire, as can be discovered by listening to the material recorded by Väisänen. It is interesting to note that Klaudia had in the course of her travels also assimilated formulaic elements and structural models of laments, even though she never performed laments while on her travels. Nowadays they are an integral part of her performances, and there are seven lament variants on tape.

Klaudia Vonkkanen spinning on a spinning wheel at home, October 1986. Photo: Anneli Asplund 1986 (FLS).

The ballads and broadsheet songs in more modern metre in Klaudia's repertoire include *Lunastettava neito* 'The Ransomed Bride', *Velisurmaaja* 'Brother-killer', *Petollinen morsian* 'The Untrue Bride', *Kaksi neitoa ruusulaaksossa* 'Two Maidens in the Valley of Roses' and *Vilho ja Bertta* 'Vilho and Bertta'. One of the game songs is *Prossan kylvö* 'Seeding the Buckwheat'.[11] Her ring game repertoire consists of five roundelays common all over Finland; more will undoubtedly come to light as the interviews proceed. Klaudia knows five ring songs typical of the Border Karelians, plus the odd broadsheet song that may be described as a love song. In addition to these traditional songs she knows songs learnt at elementary and dairy school, hymns and sacred songs, Christmas carols, and pop songs learnt from radio and TV.

The majority of the songs in the old metre impressed themselves on Klaudia's memory during the long journey she made with her mother in 1935. For according to her daughter, Oksenja seldom sang at home, even though Klaudia clearly remembers the occasion on which she learnt a couple of the songs. Klaudia had now and then been called upon to sing some of the old songs, especially *Annukkaisen virsi*, with her mother, but her part was mostly to spin with a distaff.

How is it possible that Klaudia was able to recall the songs relatively quickly even though so many years had passed since she last sang them? The only occasions on which she had sung any ancient *runes* since the 1930s were the couple of radio programmes made by Tapio Kautovaara in the 1950s. At home she claimed she never sang anything but a few children's songs.

It soon became evident even in the early stages of our research that the texts sung by Oksenja and noted down by Haavio had helped her in recalling the most important part of her repertoire, the Kalevala-metric songs. Klaudia herself spoke openly on the subject.[12] This at least partly explains why she was able to perform a dozen or more Kalevala-metric songs even decades later.

Of the songs inherited from her mother, Klaudia seems to keep closest to the written text in *The Messiah*. Since she had presumably never sung it on her own before, it was not part of her active repertoire – unlike, say, *The Song of Annukkainen*. Observing the scheme of a repetitive song, the latter is much easier to manage than the long *Messiah* with its numerous episodes and difficult poetic language. She is sometimes therefore forced to interrupt her singing, for a long poem demands far greater concentration than, for example, *The Song of Annukkainen* or *Lemminkäinen Song*, which she never has any problem in remembering. Like *The Song of Annukkainen*, *Lemminkäinen Song* is clearly part of her active repertoire, because in both of the recordings made of her she begins with verses that are missing from the texts sung by Oksenja to Haavio. Nor does *The Messiah* appear to have the same emotional meaning to Klaudia that it did to her mother. For Oksenja believed that *The Messiah* protected its singer against all evil, whereas Klaudia does not. Nor does *The Messiah* carry the same interest as regards its contents as *The Song of Annukkainen* and *Lemminkäinen Song*, in which the basic message, in the form of clear guiding principles for life, provide a link with true life. Klaudia is religious in her own way, but she does not observe all the rites of the Orthodox Church in the way her mother did.

Klaudia sings some of the other Kalevala-metric songs line for line exactly as her mother did, while others display certain lines that differ from her mother's variants, or the order of the lines is different. All in all the recordings support what Klaudia herself has said during the interviews: her own personal command of an ancient poem is restricted to the relatively small volume of material she learnt from her mother while on their travels and consists of a few narrative songs, spinning songs, lullabies and magic wind-raising songs. She does, however, seem to have learnt these songs so well in the 1930s that she can, when an opportunity presents itself, recall them with relative ease. She never has recourse to notes in performance, with the exception of *The Messiah*. Just how much she used written notes at the recollection stage is difficult to say precisely. She certainly did study them, because she has repeatedly pointed out that there are mistakes in Haavio's orthography and that she cannot sing the songs according to his notes.

Of course in recollecting her songs, Klaudia could have used the notes to learn completely new ones. This was not, however, the case, presumably because Klaudia closely associates the tune with the words.[13] And since she did not know the melody, she could not sing the song to another one. She gives the impression that the only traditional songs she sings are ones she learnt at home, on her travels or from other young people, mostly in her native village. She appears to have learnt the shorter Kalevala-metric songs well from the outset, and seems to have a good command of the art in that even today while singing she may diverge from Oksenja's variants. This does not apply to the other songs because Haavio did not record many of Oksenja's songs in the new metre, even though she knew some of these as well. *Lunastettava neito* 'The Ransomed Bride' is, for example, sung by Klaudia in a variant differing slightly from that of Oksenja, whose version adheres systematically to its own construction and never differs. Only in the case of *The Messiah* would Klaudia appear to have needed the notes, as she herself has indicated during the interviews.

It may be observed upon examining Klaudia's learning and singing situations that she assimilated part of her repertoire in a very exceptional manner. The performing situations on her first singing tour were quite unlike those in the community in which the songs last existed. The poetic and archaic language of the songs was alien to Oksenja's Finnish audiences, who did not always understand the message or the contents unless these were explained to them. This is undoubtedly the reason why Oksenja's tour repertoire became fixed in a set pattern and why Klaudia knew only a narrow selection of the old songs. If Oksenja had sung more at home, Klaudia would have learnt more of her mother's extensive repertoire. This was not, however, the case, because the situation in the early decades of the 20th century was already quite different from that in Oksenja's childhood. *Rune*-singing had lost its significance almost completely as a natural part of both everyday life and festive occasions. True, it was not as strange to the Border Karelians as to Oksenja's listeners further west in Finland. To them Oksenja appeared as an exotic representative of an ancient Finland who commanded respect as a rare symbol of Finnish nationalism.

The same to some extent applies to Klaudia's performances. Again, her audiences do not understand fully what the old songs are about unless the contents are explained to them. The very genre of ancient poetry, with its archaic melodies, is likewise strange and bewildering. Holding the listeners' interest seems to rely entirely on the personality of the performer. Whether or not a performance is interesting depends on factors other than the contents or musical qualities of the programme. Adding to the interest is the performer's skill at spinning and her ability to make contact with her audience by speaking to them, too. Her message would carry less weight simply as an interpretation of folk songs. Klaudia's performance is an entity in itself and conveys a message of the way of life of past generations. There is, however, a clear difference from her mother's situation. The *rune*-singer nowadays commands respect because she is a rarity, but the concept of *rune*-singing no longer carries the same national symbolic value that it did in the 1930s.

Klaudia's laments

The most interesting items in Klaudia Vonkkanen's repertoire are, from the research point of view, her laments, seven of which have so far been recorded. Six of them have been performed as thanksgiving laments to listeners, and one she sang alone while visiting her husband's grave in his remembrance.[14]

Klaudia commands the structural models of laments and to some degree their formulaic language. She is, however, realistic in pointing out that she does not have such a good command as her mother: "For me --- the words of the laments are so old-fashioned." Each lament is nevertheless in its own way controlled and personally moulded to suit the situation. Naturally Klaudia's laments do not compare with those of her mother in the diversity of their formulae and their archaism, but they nevertheless prove she possessed the technique needed to compose them. She always tells the interviewer and students what the various lament expressions mean. She also stresses that her mother always ended her performances with a lament. That is why, in her opinion, it belongs to the nature of *rune*-singing performances.

Often Klaudia begins her lament by speaking to the person to whom it is addressed, and sometimes with a question. Her thanksgiving laments observe a scheme according to which the listeners are either at or near the beginning thanked for the first time for honouring the songs of the foremothers by listening to/recording them.[15] The contents of the lament consist of two or more other thanking motifs. The recorders are thanked for seeking out the singer, for entering her humble abode to record her songs, or for bringing her to Helsinki and giving her a good reception; the students for listening with great interest; the Suistamo Summer Festival for honouring the song legacy of their joint forefathers and foremothers. She then goes on to describe her own situation, to inquire how her listener is, and finally to thank her listeners again.

The stylistic devices favoured most by Klaudia are diminutives and plurals. By contrast, she makes less use of alliteration and does not appear to strive towards it as regularly as Oksenja. The use of alliteration is in Klaudia's laments connected more systematically with fixed traditional formulae. Alliteration also appears to feature more widely in the laments performed on festive occasions, for which she was able to prepare more carefully. There is less alliteration in the looser formulae used in spontaneous singing situations. Klaudia often uses frequentative derivatives of her verbs, and parallel phrases and formulae appear now and then.

Naturally Klaudia's formulaic language is for the most part similar to that of laments in general and to Oksenja's in particular. On hearing a lament sung by Klaudia Plattonen of Suistamo some years ago at a Karelian festival, she was delighted to find she had understood every word of Plattonen's lament language.[16] During their long journey Klaudia and her mother frequently discussed laments, because they always featured on their programmes. Thus Klaudia gradually assimilated the art of lamenting, even though she did not at that time perform any. Klaudia's favourite formulae are the traditional *armahat syndyset* 'my dead loved-ones', 5, *arvonimysien akkiloitsijaiset* 'bearer of titles', 6, *ylähäisien ymmärdyrksysien pidelijäiset* 'members of the clergy', 6, *kallehet kannettuset* 'dear children I have borne', 4, *sadoin kerdaset passiboset* 'my hundred-fold thanks', 9, *tuhatkerdaset kiitoksuot* 'my thousand-fold thanks', 10. The fact that most of the laments recorded from Klaudia are ones of thanks is naturally reflected in the formulae favoured. She does, however, also have other traditional formulaic elements at her disposal, and is able to create original formulae of her own. For example, the lament dedicated to her husband contains a wealth of traditional elements. The same applies to the lament performed to the people of Suistamo. Most of these are to be found in the laments sung by Oksenja. As an example of one of Klaudia's laments, here is the one she sang at the Suistamo Summer Festival in Joensuu in 1986:

A nyt jo kyselen teil koko kuundelijakundasil
näil perinteelisil itkuviryzien sanazil:
A mihbä luaduzih syndyset teidän auteltu näil aigomusiel arvonimyzien akkiloitsijaziel
dai kunnivoinimyzien kullettelijaziel dai ristoiriizusien pidelijäziel dai kuldoi kupeliziel kandajaziel dai koko kuulijakundaziel miun synnyinsi-jaziel dai kasvinkamruatsiziel.
A miun on armahat syndyzet autellehet omille armokkahil apusil hot olen joudunut tuntemattomil asuinsijoille.
Ja yli viietkymmenet vuoduzet kallis hyväzien dai kaheksan kannettuzen keral.
A nyt jo andelen teil koko juhlayleisöl dai juhlien järjestäjäsil sadoin kerdazet passiboset tai tuhanzien kerdaset kiitoksuot, kuin kunnivoitteletto meijän esi-isäzien dai esiäitizien perindölauluzie dai kaiken luaduzie teko-siehi kurjasien eläjäzien esityksysie jo.

'I now ask you, all my listeners, in the traditional words of laments: how have your late beloved helped you, good older people, bearers of titles and those members of the clergy here today, those of you from my own native country, the people I grew up with? I have been helped by my dead loved-ones, even though I have had to travel to unknown regions with my beloved husband and eight children and have lived there for over fifty years. I now extend to you, all present at this festival and the organisers of the festival, my hundred-fold and thousand-fold thanks for respecting the songs handed down to us by our forefathers and foremothers and the performances of wretched mortals such as me.'

In Klaudia's view a personal, creative approach is in the nature of the lament. She thus makes a distinction between her own songs and laments and those of others. In speaking of the way her own laments came into being she says that she does think about the wording of a lament beforehand if she knows she is going to perform it. Sometimes she writes the words down to be on the safe side. But she cannot say precisely how the actual performance will go.

Laments are for Klaudia a genre that differs from other songs in that they are for her a channel for spontaneous creativity. She has, she says, composed many laments in her mind, but she ought to perform more often in order to keep up her compositional skills: "No wonder my mother knew her laments so well – she was always travelling round performing them." When Klaudia was younger, and often even today, she would wake up in the night and poems and songs would spring to mind. She just never got round to writing them down in the middle of the night. "I think if I'd had time when I was young, I could have made up the words for songs."

The lament is thus the musical genre through which Klaudia can express her own personal feelings most directly. As a child and a young woman, she was often present when laments were composed and performed. Her mother provided her with a model for composing laments, but she had no such model for other types of songs. Her mother mostly performed a certain basic repertoire, which did not appear to contain much variation or sequences deviating from the norm. It is only natural for Klaudia to want to express her feelings through the medium of laments. The thanking laments at the end of the performance are her way of demonstrating that the performance has for her been a positive experience, even though these laments also have the important function of rounding off the event. The thanking laments performed during interviews are likewise spontaneous proof that she values the work in progress.

The external features relating to Klaudia's lament performances conform with the message contained in them in that their emotional charge is not as a rule released in actual weeping and sobbing. Since the mood at the performances has for the most part been a positive one, the grief generally associated with laments is not very marked in Klaudia's performances.

Laments have at this stage of the research proved to be the most interesting item in Klaudia Vonkkanen's repertoire. For this is the genre that best reveals the singer's talent for personal, creative expression. Her command of the general rules of the genre permits her to create new lament variants as the opportunity arises.

Mother and daughter

Oksenja and Klaudia influenced one another both as mother and daughter and in other ways – perhaps more than is usual in mother-daughter relationships. At heart they are, it would seem, very similar: determined, capable women who have escaped from the bosom of the family in a way that is highly unusual. It takes courage and self-confidence for the ordinary person to get up on stage and perform, and an awareness that her own performance carries a certain value in others' eyes and that she has something to give her listeners.

Oksenja grew to this awareness at Suistamo, where those who, in her youth, had ventured out into the world as itinerant *rune*-singers had become famous and as a result benefited financially. While working for the Härkönens she was undoubtedly inspired by the dream of performing as a *rune*-singer – a dream that for her came true more fully than for any of her contemporaries. Oksenja's first public performances came at the best possible time. Finland was just preparing for the Kalevala centenary when she appeared on the Helsinki research horizon. For the organisers it was a stroke of luck to be suddenly presented with a singer of Kalevala poetry who could be available at a moment's notice, was fit to perform and physically up to being taken anywhere, even abroad, if necessary.

For Klaudia, performing alongside her mother was a very positive experience. On seeing how her mother's singing was valued, she eagerly assimilated her mother's repertoire, unlike her brothers and sisters, who did not have a similar opportunity, and who did not in fact appear to be interested. Throughout her life, and even after her mother's death, Klaudia inwardly cherished the idea of setting off one day on similar tours herself. There seemed to be little prospect of her being able to, however, because Klaudia's life took a completely different turn. In the years of hardship following the war she was kept more than busy looking after her large family, and later doing the strenuous physical work at the mill; the social conditions under which she lived were quite different from those of her mother when setting off on her singing tours. Klaudia also had to contend with opposition such as her mother never knew, her husband being completely different in nature from Oksenja's. And whereas Miitrei Mäkiselkä was not over-pleased at his wife's jauntings, he was a good-natured man and since by that time he was in poor health he was not in a position to object much when the time came for his wife to depart. Klaudia's husband, by contrast, would not hear of his wife going off singing. Not until after his death was Klaudia able to make her fifty-year dream of taking the stage come true. She was by that time some twenty years older than her mother at the same point in her career.

Although for many years Klaudia appeared to have no chance whatever of performing, she was nevertheless mentally prepared when the time came. How could she otherwise have recalled the songs with relative ease? After all, she had only ever actually performed a few of them. Most of the Kalevala-metric songs she knew belonged to the passive tradition.

Klaudia respected her mother, and still does. She realised that her mother's spiritual legacy was worth learning and preserving. She also regards it as one of the inherent features of her own Karelianism, which is also visible in the way her home is furnished and in her interest in traditional cooking. But Klaudia does not have a trauma about Karelianism in the same way that Oksenja or many of the evacuees of her generation have. For Oksenja, the loss of Karelia meant that her home and homeland had vanished forever. It was a blow from which she never recovered. Klaudia was lucky in that she was forced to go out into the world before the war, so that the loss of Karelia did not affect her as deeply as it did the rest of the family. She had, after all, left of her own accord and created a life for herself in another part of Finland.

Although Oksenja and Klaudia are in many ways similar, they naturally do not resemble one another in every respect. Whereas Oksenja was reserved and often even sullen, Klaudia is open, probably more outward-looking than her mother. She has, however, undoubtedly inherited from her mother her ability to see certain things systematically through to the end.

The mother-daughter relationship was not, however, without its ups and downs. Living in a large family gave rise to tensions that have gradually come to light in the course of the interviews. As a child Klaudia had the feeling that her mother did not always treat her fairly compared with her brothers and sisters. The reason was, she thought, that she did not possess features of her mother's family in the way her sisters did. The long journey did, however, help to bring mother and daughter closer together. There were, after all, just the two of them – no doubt a rare situation in a large family.

Conflicts later arose between mother and daughter because Oksenja did not consider Mikko Vonkkanen to be the right husband for her daughter. Oksenja would have liked her daughter to marry a farmer. This was understandable, in that Klaudia would have been in a far safer position than as the wife of a virtually unskilled labourer, especially during the war. For at the time they were married Mikko Vonkkanen had no real occupation. Klaudia was offended at her mother's negative attitude and took it as a personal affront. This led to some extent to a cooling, though never a break, in their relations. Klaudia presumably felt her mother dominated her too much. Her mother had, after all, virtually ordered her choice of career without so much as asking her opinion. Not until Oksenja fell ill did the situation change. Oksenja lost her hold over her daughter, who tried to help her as best she could. Any disagreements between mother and daughter faded away in the final months of Oksenja's life.

Klaudia's relationship to her own singing operates at many levels. Basically it is much the same as her mother's. Singing in public has provided opportunities for new experiences, for breaking away from the family circle, for meeting new people, for recapturing something of the most exciting experience of her youth. And like her mother, Klaudia undoubtedly has a lot of ambition. But there is more to it than that. Like her mother, she is a performer with an ability to create a living contact with her listeners. She knows she is a *rune*-singer's daughter. She is also aware of the value of her own songs and of the fact that there are not many people in Finland today with a corresponding repertoire of ancient poetry. During the 'silent' years Klaudia often toyed with the idea of how it would feel to set off on a singing tour like that of her youth. The consciousness that she had, as it were, hidden within her something that might one day be useful gave her strength in the years when she was forced to keep silent. The forbidden songs were for Klaudia a secret source of strength that helped her to overcome many difficulties.

NOTES

This article is based on an earlier version published in Finnish under the title *Klaudia Oksenjantytär – vaeltavien laulajien perinteen jatkaja*, which appeared in *Louhen sanat. Kirjoituksia kansanperinteen naisista.* A. Nenola and S. Timonen (eds.). Helsinki. 1990. p. 69-83.

1. The following material is so far to be found in the Folklore Archives of the Finnish Literature Society: SKSÄ 158-159. 1986 (Team Seppo Knuuttila – Jari Kupiainen), SKSÄ 143-147. 1986 (Team Anneli Asplund – Seppo Knuuttila – Ulla Lipponen), SKSÄ 160-166. 1986 (Team Anneli Asplund – Ulla Lipponen – Sirkka-Liisa Mettomäki – Pirkko-Liisa Rausmaa – Senni Timonen), SKSÄ 225-228. 1987 (Anneli Asplund), SKSÄ 13-21. 1988 (Anneli Asplund). I have previously published a short report of my studies of Klaudia Vonkkanen, see Asplund 1988.
2. Klaudia's brother Heikki Mäkiselkä has studied his parents' families and discovered that Oksenja's mother, Jelena Ignaitintytär, was born on 14.7.1837 and died on 1.5.1892. Oksenja's father, Grigori Feudor's-son (Feudorinpoika) Valo-

kainen, was born on 23.4.1829 and died on 27.4.1893. Klaudia's paternal grandfather was Feudor Iivan's-son (Iivaninpoika) (b. 1802) and her grandmother Jevdofia Andrei's-daughter (Andreintytär) (b. 1808). For further details of the family obtained from Klaudia Vonkkanen see Kuusi 1988, 89-91.
3. *Luojan virsi* 'The Messiah' was a legend song telling of the life of Christ. It was one of the most common songs of the Orthodox Karelians and belonged in particular to the women's repertoire. See the article by Senni Timonen and Thomas DuBois.
4. When Finland became independent in 1917 the custom spread of changing primarily Russian and Swedish surnames into Finnish ones. People identified themselves specifically as Finns. The large number of Swedish surnames was a legacy of Swedish rule. Many of the people in Karelia, and especially the Orthodox population, had Russian surnames despite their Karelian origins. The Finnicising of surnames began in the 1920s and reached its peak in the 1930s. The change from Buljugin to Mäkiselkä is a typical example of the practice at that time.

5. It is easy to follow the early stages of their journey because Klaudia still has a little blue notebook in which the organiser of a performance or their hosts where they spent the night wrote their thanks to the performers. Oksenja already had a notebook like this with her on her second visit to Helsinki.

6. According to Haavio's notes (SKS) Oksenja's repertoire also included folk tales, children's rhymes, riddles, proverbs, game songs, legends, more than a hundred beliefs and other knowledge. Väisänen's recordings are unfortunately of such poor quality that the contents are in places difficult to interpret (SKSÄ).

7. Väisänen published the lament of the fate of the Karelians, see Väisänen 1940-1941, 317-328.

8. Martti Haavio (1899-1973), Professor of Folkloristics at the University of Helsinki, was already an active folklorist in the 1930s and placed the results of his field work in the Folklore Archives of the Finnish Literature Society. Samuli Paulaharju (1875-1944) was a teacher of the deaf, but also near-professional collector of folklore. He also desposited the collections he had made over the decades in the same Folklore Archives. Paulaharju lived in Oulu.

9. The inhabitants of the parish of Laihia have a reputation in Finland akin to that of the Scots: anecdotes about their stinginess and thrift are told all over the country.

10. See e.g. Kuusi-Bosley-Branch 1977, pp. 425-427.

11. *Lunastettava neito* and *Velisurmaaja* are the Finnish counterparts of the British ballads numbered 95 and 13 by Child (The maid freed from the gallows, Edward). *Petollinen morsian, Kaksi neitoa ruusulaaksossa*, and *Vilho ja Bertta* are more recent broadside ballads. All the ballads mentioned were known virtually throughout the country, but *Prossan kylvö* was a local game song known only in Ladoga Karelia.

12. SKSÄ 158, 1986. At some stage, presumably in the 1970s, Heikki Mäkiselkä asked the Folklore Archives for a copy of the song notes made by Haavio, and this was duly supplied. In the early 1970s Klaudia's brother showed it to her, after which his wife copied the material for her, amounting to about a hundred pages in all.

13. Haavio's notes on song texts do not include the melodies.

14. Klaudia performed her first recorded lament to interviewers from the Folklore Archives at home in Varkaus in October 1986 as a model of a lament. It was a thanking lament addressed to the recorders of her lament (SKSÄ 145, 1986). She similarly performed her second lament while visiting the Folklore Archive, where several days were spent recording her (SKSÄ 160, 1986). During that same visit she on two occasions performed her songs to folklore students at the Sibelius Academy, and the final item was on both occasions a thanking lament to her young listeners (SKSÄ 161, 1986 and SKSÄ 166, 1986). Again during that same visit she performed for the interviewer the lament she had sung at her husband's grave (SKSÄ 162, 1986). A year later, again on a visit to Helsinki, she performed to the interviewer the lament she had sung the previous summer at the Suistamo festival in Joensuu (SKSÄ 226, 1987). So far the last of the laments recorded from Klaudia is one composed in conjunction with an interview in 1988 (SKSÄ 13, 1988).

15. For Baltic-Finnic lament poetry see Honko 1974 and Nenola-Kallio 1982.

16. Klaudia Plattonen was another well-known *rune*-singer from the same area, the grandchild of Matjoi Plattonen.

Map

Map of areas and peoples referred to in the articles

The symbols on the map do not differentiate localities according to population size, rather, villages and cities are indicated in the same way. The borders between states follow the modern borderlines.

There is some variation in the translation of place-names into English. In this volume the significant *rune*-singing area *Viena* is referred to as 'Archangel Karelia', a term designating a large area which extends from the western edge of the White Sea to the modern Finnish border. 'Archangel Karelia' as an adminstrative area (the government of Archangel) usually refers to a much broader region, but in this volume the term is used in a more restricted sense.

Appendix

'The Golden Bride, Kultamorsian I and II'

Translation in M. Kuusi - K. Bosley - M. Branch (eds.), *Finnish Folk Poetry, Epic.* Helsinki 1977.

Kultamorsian I	*The Golden Bride I*	
Tuo on seppä Ilmollini	'Twas the smith Ilmollini	
alla päin pahalla mielin	his head down, in bad spirits	
kaiken kallella kypärin	helmet all askew	
mäni seppojen pajahe,	went to the forge of the smiths	
otti kultia vähäsen	took a little gold	5
hopeita huopin täyven.	a felt hatful of silver.	
Pani nuoret liettšomahe	He set the young men blowing	
palkkalaiset painamahe,	the hirelings pressing	
ei orjat hyvästä lietšo	but the serfs did not blow well	
eikä paina palkkalaiset.	neither did the hirelings press.	10
Rupei itše liettšomahe:	He himself took to blowing:	
liettšo kerran leukahutti	he blew once, flapped the bellows	
liettšo toisen leukahutti	he blew twice, flapped the bellows	
jo kerralla kolmannella	now at the third time	
miekko tunkekse tulesta	a sword squeezed out of the fire	15
terä kulta kuumennosta.	a gold-bladed from the heat.	
Ois miekka hyvännäkyini	The sword might be good-looking	
vain tuli pahatapani:	but evil ways came of it:	
joka päivä miehen tappo	every day it killed a man	
kaksiki monikkahana.	even two on many days.	20
Vieläpä kultija lisäsi	He added more gold	
hopeita huopin täyven.	a felt hatful of silver.	
Pani vanhat liettšomahe,	He set the old men blowing	
ei vanhat hyvästä lietšo	but the old did not blow well	
eikä paina palkkalaiset.	neither did the hirelings press.	25
Rupei itše liettšomahe:	He himself took to blowing:	
liettšo kerran leukahutti	he blew once, flapped the bellows	
liettšo toisen leukahutti	he blew twice, flapped the bellows	
jo kerralla kolmannella	now at the third time	
orih tunkekse tulesta	a stallion squeezed from the fire	30
harja kulta kuumennosta.	a golden-maned from the heat.	
Ois orih hyvännäkyini	The stallion might have good looks	
vain tuli pahatapani:	but evil ways came of it:	
joka päivä tamman tappo	every day it killed a mare	

| kaksiki monikkahana. | even two on many days. | 35 |

Vieläpä kultija lisäsi	He added more gold	
hopeita huopin täyven,	a felt hatful of silver	
pani orjat liettšomahe	and he set the serfs blowing	
palkkalaiset painamaha,	and set the hirelings pressing	
ei orjat hyvästä lietšo	but the serfs did not blow well	40
eikä paina palkkalaiset.	neither did the hirelings press.	

Rupei itše liettšomahe:	He himself took to blowing:	
liettšo kerran leukahutti	he blew once, flapped the bellows	
liettšo toisen leukahutti	he blew twice, flapped the bellows	
jo kerralla kolmannella	now at the third time	45
neiti tunkekse tulesta	a maid squeezed out of the fire	
kassa kulta kuumennosta.	a golden-locks from the heat.	
Ois neiti hyvännäkyni	The maid might be good-looking	
vaini en tapoja tiijä.	but I do not know her ways.	

Niin on yönä ensimmäissä	And so during the first night	50
vara'atu vaippahase	he kept himself in his cloak	
turva'utu turkkihise:	he held tight in his fur coat:	
se oli kylki kyllä lämmin	that side certainly was warm	
ku oli vassen villavaippua,	which was next to the wool cloak	
se oli kylki kylmämässä	that side was freezing	55
ku oli vassen neittä vassen	which was next to the maid's side	
meren jiäkse jeätymässä	icy as ice on the sea	
kivekse kovottumassa.	and as hard as rock.	

Niin on yönä toissa yönä	So during the second night	
turvuakse turkkihise	he held tight in his fur coat	60
varuakse vaippahase:	he kept himself in his cloak:	
se on kylki kyllä lämmin	that side certainly was warm	
ku on vassen villavaippua,	which was next to the wool cloak	
se on kylki kylmämässä	that side was freezing	
ku on vassen neittä vassen.	which was next to the maid's side.	65

Niin on yönä kolmantena	And so during the third night	
varuakse vaippahase	he kept himself in his cloak	
turvuakse turkkihise:	he held tight in his fur coat:	
se oli kylki kyllä lämmin	that side certainly was warm	
ku oli vassen villavaippua,	which was next to the wool cloak	70
se oli kylki kylmämässä	that side was freezing	
ku oli vassen neittä vassen.	which was next to the maid's side.	

Elköhöt esieläjät	Let not those who come after	
elköhöt takasetkana	and let not those before them	
neittä kullasta kuvato	make a maid's likeness in gold	75
hopiesta huolitello:	finish her off in silver:	
vilun huohtavi hopie	the breath of silver is chill	
kylmän kulta kuumottauve.	and the glow of gold is cold.	

Singer Miihkali Perttunen.
Latvajärvi, Vuokkiniemi, Archangel Karelia.
A.A. Borenius, 1871.

Kultamorsian II	The Golden Bride II	
Saaren maat saroin jaettu	The Island is staked in strips	
Viron maat viipin vaapin,	Estonia criss-crossed:	
pellot on piusten mittaeltu	the fields are measured with rods	
ahot on vaaksoin arvaeltu.	the clearings reckoned with spans.	
Jäi sarka jakamatointa	There was one strip left unstaked	5
pelto piuston mittomata	one field was not rod-measured	
aho vaaksoin arvomata	one clearing not span-reckoned	
aian äärtä arvan lyömätöntä:	for one fence's bounds lots were not cast:	
tuohon seppo seisattaise	there the smith settled	
takojainen pani pajaa.	there the craftsman put his forge.	10
Teki pienoisen pajaisen	He made a very small forge	
matalaisen maatupaisen	a low hut sunk in the ground	
yhen miehen mahtuvaisen	with room for one man	
käsivarren kääntyväisen	with swingig-room for one arm	
vasaran yleneväisen.	with headroom for one hammer:	15
Pani paiaa pajaksi	he used his shirt as a forge	
kaatia liityeksi.	and his trousers for bellows.	
Seppä takoi traksutteli	The smith hammered and clattered	
orjat lietsoin liikuttiit:	the serfs were busy blowing:	
takoi niitä, takoi näitä	he hammered this, hammered that	20
takoi vallan vaarnahia	hammered pegs for the estate	
seurakunnan serppilöjä	and sickles for the parish	
maakunnan kuraksen päitä.	and knife-blades for the province	
Niin takoi Hekoille helmet	he hammered beads for Hekkoi	
markat Maien tyttärelle.	and coins for Maie's daughter.	25
Hekkoi ei kiittänt helmiään	Hekkoi did not praise her beads	
Maien tyttö ei markkojaan	nor Maie's daughter her coins	
valtakunta ei vaarnahia	nor did the estate its pegs	
seurakunta ei serppilöjä	nor the parish its sickles	
maakunta ei kuraksen päitä:	nor the province its knife-blades:	30
seppä suuttui ja vihastui	the smith grew angry and wild	
pihet pisti räystähässe	he stuck his tongs in the eaves	
vasarat vajotti maahan	dropped his hammers on the ground	
sytytti pajan tulelle	set his forge on fire	
lietsot lemenen nojaan.	left his bellows in the blaze.	35
Niin noisi rekoisepäksi	So he rose as a sledge-smith	
sai tuo saanin salvajaksi.	set up as a sleigh-builder:	
Kuunkauen teki rekoi	one month long he made a sledge	
kaksi kuuta kaupitteli,	for two months put it on sale	
aastajan pani pajuja	for a year fitted wicker	40
kissan luilla kirjutteli	adorned it with a cat's bones	
hauen hammasten keralla.	and with a pike's teeth.	
Sai tuo saani valmiheksi.	The sleigh was finished	
Meni seppo vierahisse	and the smith went visiting	
ämmilleen ja äijilleen	his grannies and his grandads	45
näpehille näälilleen.	his nimble brothers-in-law.	
Arvotteli veljilleen	He set his brothers guessing	
muistatti sisarilleen:	his sisters calling to mind:	

"Arvatkaa veljyeni muistakaa sisarueni: mill on saani kirjoitettu perä on kolju korkisteltu?"	"Guess now, my brothers call to mind now, my sisters: 50 what is the sleigh adorned with the sledge-back decorated?"
Veljet vasten vastaisiit: "Kissan luill on kirjoiteltu hauen hammasten keralla."	The brothers answering said: "It's adorned with a cat's bones and with a pike's teeth." 55
Kiistoin seppo vastattiin kiistoin halli riisuttiin kiisoin vietiin tupaan kiisoin seppoo syötettiin kiisoin seppoo juotettiin kiisoin seppoo soimattiin: "Puut kuluut, maat kuluut puut kuluvat leikatessa maat kuluvat kyntäessä, seppo naiseta kuluu emännätä vanhenoo."	They vied, answering the smith vied, unharnessing the grey vied in taking him indoors vied in giving the smith food vied in giving the smith drink 60 vied in giving the smith blame: "Trees wear out and lands wear out trees wear out by being felled lands wear out by being ploughed: a smith will wear out wifeless 65 grow old without a mistress."
Seppo suuttuu ja vihastuu seppo tuulena kotiin. Seppo takoi traksutteli orjuet liettä liekuttiit, seppo kultia tuleen hopehia lietyeen sykysyisen uukon verran talvisen karitsan verran: tunkiusi hepo tulesta kultakapia kuumehesta. Muu kaikki pere ihastui, itse Ismaro pelästyi.	The smith grew angry and wild the smith drove home like the wind the smith hammered and clattered the serfs were busy blowing 70 the smith flung gold in the fire silver into the furnace as much as an autumn ewe as much ?s a winter lamb: a horse squeezed out of the fire 75 a golden-hoof from the heat. All the other kin were charmed: Ismaro himself was scared.
Seppo kultia tuleen hopehia lietyeen, seppo takoi traksutteli orjoit lietsoit liekuttiit: tunkiusi lehmä tulesta kultasarvi kuumehesta. Muu kaikki pere ihastui, itse Ismaro pelästyi.	The smith flung gold in the fire silver into the furnace 80 the smith hammered and clattered the serfs were busy blowing: a cow squeezed out of the fire a golden-horn from the heat. All the other kin were charmed: 85 Ismaro himself was scared.
Seppo kultia tuleen hopehia lietyeen sykysyisen uukon verran talvisen karitsan verran. Seppoi takoi traksutteli orjoit lietsoit liekuttiit: tunkius sika tulesta kultaharjoi kuumehesta. Muu kaikki pere ihastui, itse Ismaro pelästyi.	The smith flung gold in the fire silver into the furnace as much as an autumn ewe as much as a winter lamb 90 the smith hammered and clattered the serfs were busy blowing: a pig squeezed out of the fire a gold-bristle from the heat. All the other kin were charmed: 95 Ismaro himself was scared.

Seppo kultia tuleen	The smith flung gold in the fire
hopehia lietyeen	silver into the furnace
sykysyisen uukon verran	as much as an autumn ewe
talvisen karitsan verran.	as much as a winter lamb 100
Seppoi takoi traksutteli	the smith hammered and clattered
orjoit lietsoit liekuttiit:	the serfs were busy blowing:
tunkiusi tyttö tulesta	a girl squeezed out of the fire
kultakassa kuumehesta.	a golden-locks from the heat.
Muu kaikki pere pelästyi,	All the other kin were scared: 105
itse Ismaro ihastui.	Ismaro himself was charmed.
Täst nyt lienee varma vastus	Now there's sure to be trouble:
viipyy vihan pitäjä!-	an enemy has moved in!-
Vietiin tyttö makaamaan	The girl was led to lie down
luuttiistiin lepäämään:	taken for a rest: 110
kumpa kylki oli kullan luona	which side was next to the gold
se oli kylki kylmä kylki,	that side was the chilly side
kumpa kylki ei ollut kullan luona	which was not next to the gold
se oli kylki suoja kylki.	that side was the thawing side.

Singer unknown.
Soikkola, Ingria.
J. Länkelä, 1858.

Name Index

Agricola, M. 15, 205
Ahlqvist, A. 121
Alava, V. 125
Alexander II 95
Alvre, P. 48
Anderson, W. 43, 44
Austin, J. L. 113, 135

Babcock, B. 290
Bakhtin, M. 115 ,251, 296
Bateson, G. 135
Berg, G. 340
Berner, A. 193
Booze, O. 332
Borenius, A. A. 26, 180-182, 191
Briggs, C. L. 114, 116, 137
Bukkiev, P. 323, 324
Buljugin, D. 344
Bureus, A. 42
Burke, K. 113, 114

Cajan, J. F. 141, 145, 148, 149,
    173, 175
Castrén, M. A. 94, 139, 141, 142,
    146, 150, 173-177, 211
Chadwick, H. M. 16, 37
Colby, B. 298
Collinder, B. 68
Comparetti, D. 31, 111

DuBois, T. 363
Dumézil, G. 36
Dundes, A. 210
Durkheim, E. 35

Einarsson, S. 111

Eisen, M. J. 52
Eliade, M. 35, 328
Enäjärvi-Haavio, E. 24, 298
Ervasti, J. 23
Europaeus D. E. D. 94, 217

Fernandez, J. W. 294, 298
Finno, J. P. 23
Florinus, H. 42
Foley, J. M. 92, 109, 111
Forsström-Hainari, O. A. 345, 346
Fromm, H. 111

Genetz, A. 42, 305
van Gennep, A. 298
Goold, G. P. 111
Gottlund, K. A. 333
Groundstroem, O. 313

Haavio, M. 31, 117, 118, 125, 139,
    217, 292, 346, 347, 357, 364
Hamayon, R. 297
Harvilahti, L. 120, 139
Hatto, A. T. 111, 297
Hautala, J. 91, 117, 119, 139
Heroila-Härkönen, I. and P. 344
Holbek, B. 331
Homanen, O. 281
Honko, L. 19, 92, 118
Huovinen, D. 346
Hymes, D. 114-116, 125, 137, 138,
    140
Härkönen, I. 344
Häyhä, J. 218

Immonen, M. 35

Inha, I. K. 139
Itkonen, E. 48
Itkonen, T. 48

Jaakkola, J. 17
Jakobson, R. 76, 116, 298
James, W. 113
Johnson, M. 215

Kaivola-Bregenhøj, A. 49, 50
Karjalainen, M. 119, 269-271
Kaukonen, V. 17, 18, 119
Kautovaara, T. 354, 356
Kinkade, D. 141
Kiparsky, P. 111, 139
Kirkinen, H. 306
Knuuttila, S. 343
Koivulehto, J. 84
Kolehmainen, I. 192
Konkka, U. 297
Kontratjeff, H. 264
Korhonen, M. 20
Korte, I. 327
Krinitsnaja, N. A. 232
Krohn, J. 16, 139, 220
Krohn, K. 16, 17, 25, 26, 47, 111, 117, 218, 224
Kuivalatar, M. 210, 218
Kuusi, M. 18, 19, 21, 22, 31, 37, 72, 85, 110, 118, 137, 138, 217, 221, 224, 231, 234, 306, 321, 334, 336
Köngäs-Maranda, E.-K. 111
von Köppen, P. 112

Labov, W. 136
Lakoff, G. 215
Larin Paraske 110
Laul, S. 48
Launonen, H. 121, 137
Lavonen, N. 331
Leach, E. 133
Lehtipuro, O. 110, 119
Lehtonen, A. 67, 110, 209, 267, 289
Lehtonen, M. 209
Leino, Eino 64
Leino, Pauli 139
Leino, Pentti 21, 44, 48, 82, 117, 121-123, 125
Lesonen, Varahvontta 70

Lesonen, Vihtoora 24
Lesoni, H. 264
Lettijeva, M. 35
Lévi-Strauss, C. 116, 118, 298
Linna, V. 215
Lipitsä, T. 345, 346
Liszka, J. J. 217
Loorits, O. 43
Lord, A. B. 21, 91, 110, 111, 113, 119, 180
Lotz, J. 76
Lukkarinen, J. 237, 238
Luukka, M. 112, 337
Lähteenkorva-Borenius, A. A. 139, 140
Lönnrot, E. 15, 56, 72, 94, 119, 121, 139, 141, 145, 147, 148, 173, 174, 218, 223, 236, 238, 297, 305
Lönnroth, L. 297

Magoun, F. P. 271
Malinen, I. 271
Malinen, O. and J. 36
Manninen, I. 238
Maranda, P. 111
Mastromattei, R. 298
Meinander, C. F. 48
Melanie of Vuonninen 271
Miihkula 135, 136
Miller, D. G. 92
Moisef, A. 135
Mustanoja, T. 111
Mäkiselkä, H. 363, 364
Mäkiselkä, M. 362
Mäkiselkä, O. 343-364
Mälk, V. 49, 50, 53, 54
Määränen, O. 346, 349

Nagler, M. 92, 102
Niemi, A. R. 20, 47, 82, 139
Nyman, A. 49

Oinas, F. J. 110, 111
Ojansuu, H. 48
Okahvie, widow of Nihvo 190
Olrik, A. 140
Ong, W. 21
Onoila, I. 346
Ortner, S. 262

Subject Index

The Finnish names of poems are italized.

Bibliography

Aarne, Antti 1912. *Verzeichnis der Finnischen Ursprungssagen und ihrer Varianten. FF Communications 8*. Helsinki.

AE = *Apokryfiset evankeliumit*. Suom. Johannes Seppälä. 1980. Joensuu.

Abrahams, Roger D. 1985. Pragmatism and a Folklore of Experience. *Western Folklore 44*: 324-332.

– 1992. The Past in the Presence: An Overview of Folkloristics in the Late 20th Century. R. Kvideland et al. (eds.) *Folklore Processed in Honour of Lauri Honko on his 60th Birthday 6th March 1992. Studia Fennica Folkloristica 1*. Helsinki.

AKNC = Archives of the Karelian Scientific Centre, Russian Academy of Sciences. Petrozavodsk.

Alho, Olli 1979. *Orjat ja isännät. Tutkimus inkeriläisistä maaorjarunoista. Suomi 123:1*. Helsinki.

Anderson, Walter 1935. *Studien zur Wortsilbenstatistik der älteren estnischen Volkslieder. ACUT (Acta et Commentationes Universitatis Tartuensis). B XXXIV:1*. Tartu.

Andersson, Otto 1941. Uprepning och parallelism. *Budkavlen 20*: 113-150.

– 1969. *Studier i musik och folklore II. Skrifter utgivna av Svenska Litteratursällskapet i Finland, Nr. 432*. Helsinki.

Anttonen, Pertti J. 1987. *Rituaalinen pilkka länsi-inkeriläisissä kylähäissä*. Unpublished manuscript: pro gradu thesis. University of Helsinki, Department of Folklore.

– 1992. The Rites of Passage Revisited: A New Look at van Gennep's Theory of the Ritual Process and Its Application in the Study of Finnish-Karelian Wedding Rituals. *Temenos Vol. 28:* 15-52.

Anttonen, Veikko 1992. Interpreting Ethnic Categories Denoting 'Sacred' in a Finnish and an Ob-Ugrian Context. *Temenos Vol. 28*.

Apo, Satu 1985. Kertomusperinteen genret ja rakenneanalyysi. M. Junnonaho (ed.) *Etiäinen 1: Folkloristiikkaa ja uskontotiedettä*. Turku: University of Turku, Department of Cultural Studies.

– 1986. *Ihmesadun rakenne*. Helsinki.

– 1988. Omat on virret oppimani. Naisten suullisesta runoudesta. *Parnasso Vol. 38 No. 1*.

– 1989. The variability and narrative structures of wondertales. A.-L. Siikala (ed.) *Studies in oral narrative. Studia Fennica 33*. Helsinki.

– 1992. Analysing the contents of narratives. Methodical and technical observations. R. Kvideland et al. (eds.) *Folklore Processed in Honour of Lauri Honko on his 60th Birthday 6th March 1992. Studia Fennica Folkloristica 1*. Helsinki.

Asplund, Anneli 1981. Riimilliset kansanlaulut. A. Asplund – M. Hako (eds.) *Kansanmusiikki*. Vaasa.

– 1988. Klaudia Vonkkanen, a recent folksinger discovery; experience of using a video in field work. *Ballads and Other Genres. Balladen und andere Gattungen. Zavod za istrazivanje folklora. Special Issue 11*. Zagreb.

Austin, J. L. 1976 (1962). *How To Do Things With Words*. J. O. Urmson – M. Sbisà (eds.) *The William James Lectures delivered at Harvard University in 1955*. Second Edition. London.

Babcock, Barbara A. 1978. Introduction. B. A. Babcock (ed.) *The Reversible World. Symbolic Inversion in Art and Society*. Ithaca & London.

Bakhtin, Mikhail 1981. *The Dialogic Imagination. Four Essays*. Austin.

– 1986. The Problem of Speech Genres. C. Emerson – M. Holquist (eds.) *Mikhail Bakhtin, Speech Genres and Other Late Essays*. Austin.

Basso, Keith H. 1979. *Portraits of "the Whiteman": Linguistic Play and Cultural Symbols among the Western Apache*. Cambridge.

Bateson, Gregory 1972. *Steps to an Ecology of Mind*. New York.

Bauman, Richard 1986. Performance and Honor in 13th-Century Iceland. *Journal of American Folklore 99*: 131-150.

Bauman, Richard – Briggs, Charles L. 1990. Poetics and Performance as Critical Perspectives on Language and Social Life. *Annual Review of Anthropology 19*: 59-88.

Berg, Gösta 1969. Kansatieteellisiä tutkimusmenetelmiä. T. Vuorela (ed.) *Kansatieteen periaateoppia*. Helsinki.

Boddy, Janice 1989. *Wombs and Alien Spirits. Women, Men, and the Zar Cult in Northern Sudan*. Madison, Wisconsin.

Bolle, Kees W. 1987. Myth. M. Eliade (ed.) *The Encyclopedia of Religion. Vol. 10*. New York.

Boon, James A. 1982. *Other Tribes, Other Scribes. Symbolic Anthropology in the Comparative Study of Cultures, Histories, Religions and Texts*. Cambridge.

Borenius, A.A. 1886. Suomen keskiaikaisesta runoudesta I. Luojan virsi. *Virittäjä*.

Boyer, Pascal 1982. Récit épique et tradition. *L'Homme Vol. XXII No. 2*.

Briggs, Charles L. 1988. *Competence in Performance. The creativity of tradition in mexicano verbal art*. Philadelphia.

Brummer, O. J. 1908. *Über die Bannungsorte der Finnischen Zauberlieder*. Helsinki.

Burke, Kenneth 1966. A Dramatistic View of the Origins of Language and Postscripts on the Negative. *Language as Symbolic Action. Essays on Life, Literature and Method*. Berkeley & Los Angeles.

– 1977 (1931). *Counter-Statement*. New York: Harcourt, Brace. Republished in 1968: Berkeley and Los Angeles, and in 1977: Chicago.

Caraveli-Chaves, Anna 1980. Bridge Between Worlds. The Greek Women's Lament as Communicative Event. *Journal of American Folklore Vol. 93 No. 368*.

Chadwick, H. Munro 1912. *The Heroic Age*. Cambridge.

Child, F. J. (ed.) *The English and Scottish Popular Ballads*. New York 1882-1898.

Colby, Benjamin 1987. Coherence in Language and Culture. R. Steele – T. Threadgold (eds.) *Language Topics. Essays in Honour of Michael Halliday Vol. II*. Amsterdam & Philadelphia.

Collinder Björn 1946. Kalevala ja Ruotsi. *Kalevalaseuran vuosikirja 25-26*.

Comparetti, Domenico 1981. *Il Kalevala; o la poesia tradizionale dei Finni*. Roma.

Cruikshank, Julie 1983. *The Stolen Women: Female Journeys in Tagish and Tutchone. National Museum of Man Mercury Series; Canadian Ethnology Service Paper No. 87*. Ottawa.

Cruz, Anne J. 1988. Genre Transformations and the Question of Gender. La Bella Malmaridada as Ballad and Play. *Zavod da istrazivanje folklora Special Issue 11: Ballads and other Genres.* Zagreb.

Cushing, G.F. 1980. Ob-Ugrian (Vogul and Ostyak). A.T. Hatto (ed.) *Traditions of Heroic and Epic Poetry. Vol. I. The Traditions.* Leeds.

de Beaugrande R. – Dressler, W.U. 1980. *Introduction to text linquistics.* London.

Detienne, Marcel 1981. *The Creation of Mythology.* Chicago and London.

van Dijk, Teun 1980. *Macrostructures. An interdisciplinary study of global structures in discourse, interaction, and cognition.* Hillsdale/ NJ.

– 1985 (ed.) *Handbook of discourse analysis vol. 2.* London.

Douglas, Mary 1985 (1966). *Purity and Danger. An Analysis of the Concepts of Pollution and Taboo.* 2nd ARK edition. Reading.

DuBois, Thomas (forthcoming). Luomisen Luominen: An Ethnopoetic Approach to a Finnish Creation Poem. D. Hymes (ed.) *Volume on cross-cultural ethnopoetics.* The Hague.

Dumézil, Georges 1970. *The Destiny of the Warrior.* Chicago.

Dundes, Alan 1964. *The morphology of North American Indian folktales. FF Communications 195.* Helsinki.

– 1969. The Devolutionary Premise in Folklore Theory. *Journal of the Folklore Institute 6:* 5-19.

Durham, Deborah – Fernandez, James W. 1991. Tropical Dominions: The Figurative Struggle over Domains of Belonging and Apartness in Africa. J. W. Fernandez (ed.) *Beyond Metaphor. The Theory of Tropes in Anthropology.* Stanford.

Edda 1982. *Eddan jumalrunot.* Helsinki.

Einarsson, Stefan 1963. Harp song heroic poetry (Chadwicks) Greek and germanic alternate singing: mantic song in Lapp legend, Eddas, sagas and sturlunga. *Budkavlen 42.*

Eisen, M.J. – Kallas, O. – Krohn, K. (eds.) 1926. *Eesti rahvalaulud Dr. Jakob Hurta ja teiste kogudest.* Esimene köide. Tartu.

Eliade, Mircea 1954. *The myth of the eternal return. Bollingen series XLVI.* Princeton, N.J.

– 1959a. Methodological Remarks on the Study of Religious Symbolism. M. Eliade – J. M. Kitagawa (eds.) *The History of Religions. Essays in Methodology.* Chicago.

– 1959b (1957). *The Sacred and the Profane. The Nature of Religion.* San Diego & New York.

– 1965. Experiences of the mystic light. M. Eliade (ed.) *The two and the one.* London.

– 1974 (1951). *Shamanism. Archaic Techniques of Ecstasy.* 2nd paperback printing. *Bollingen Series LXXVI.* Princeton, N.J.

– 1975. *Myth and reality.* New York.

The Encyclopedia of Religion Vol. 15 1987. M. Eliade (ed.). New York.

Engman, Max 1991. Pietari ja Inkeri. P. Nevalainen – H. Sihvo (eds.) *Inkeri. Historia, kansa, kulttuuri.* Pieksämäki.

Envall, Markku 1985. *Nasaretin miehen pitkä marssi. Esseitä Jeesus-aiheesta kirjallisuudessa.* Juva.

Enäjärvi-Haavio, Elsa 1949. *Pankame käsi kätehen. Suomalaisten kansanrunojen esittämistavoista.* Porvoo.

– 1953. *Ritvalan helkajuhla.* Helsinki.

ERL. *Eesti rahvalaulud.* Esimene köide 1926. Tartu.

Falk, Pasi 1983. *Humalan historia. Juomisen merkitysten historiallisuus.* Unpublished manuscript: licenciate thesis. University of Helsinki. Department of Sociology.

Fernandez, James W. 1982. *Bwiti. An Ethnography of the Religious Imagination in Africa*. Princeton, New Jersey.
– 1986. *Persuasions and Performances. The Play of Tropes in Culture*. Bloomington.
– 1991. Introduction: Confluents of Inquiry. J. W. Fernandez (ed.) *Beyond Metaphor. The Theory of Tropes in Anthropology*. Stanford.
FFPE = Kuusi, M. – Bosley, K. – Branch, M. (eds.) *Finnish Folk Poetry. Epic*. 1977. Helsinki.
FLS = Finnish Literature Society. (Suomalaisen Kirjallisuuden Seura.)
FM = *The Festal Menaion*. Translated from the Original Greek by Mother Mary and Archimandrite Kallistos Ware with an Introduction by Professor Georges Florovsky. 1969. London.
Finnegan, Ruth 1976. What is oral literature anyway. B. Stolz – R. Shannon (eds.) *Oral literature and the formula*. Ann Arbor.
– 1977. *Oral poetry: its nature, significance and social context*. Cambridge.
– 1988. *Literacy & Orality*. Oxford & New York.
Finnish Folk Poetry: Epic. (FFPE). (Eds.) M. Kuusi – K. Bosley – M. Branch. 1977. Helsinki.
Foley, John Miles 1985. *Oral-Formulaic theory and research. An introduction and annotated bibliography*. New York & London.
– 1988. *The Theory of oral composition*. Bloomington & Indianapolis.
– 1990. *Traditional oral epic. The Odyssey, Beowulf and the Serbo-Croatian return song*. Berkeley & Los Angeles.
– 1991. *Immanent art. From structure to meaning in traditional oral epic*. Bloomington & Indianapolis.
– 1992. Word-power, Performance, and tradition. *Journal of American Folklore Vol. 105 No. 417*.
Fox, Jennifer 1987. The Creator Gods. Romantic Nationalism and the Engenderment of Women in Folklore. *Journal of American Folklore Vol. 100 No. 398*.
Fromm, Hans 1987. *Esseitä Kalevalasta. Suomi 139*. Rauma.
Fry, Donald K. 1967. Old english formulas and systems. *English Studies 48*.
– 1968. Old English formulaic themes and type-scenes. *Neophilologus 52*.
– 1975. Caedmon as a formulaic poet. J.J. Duggan (ed.) *Oral literature. Seven essays*. Edinburgh & London.
– 1981. The memory of Caedmon. J.M. Foley (ed.) *Oral traditional literature: A Festschrift for Albert Bates Lord*. Ohio.
Gacak, V.M. 1983. *Osnovy ustnoj èpiceskoj poètiki slavjan. Istorija, kul'tura, etnografija i fol'klor slavjanskih narodov – IX mezdunarodny s'ezd slavistov. Doklady sovetskoj delegacii*. Moskva.
Genetz, Arvid 1870a. *Kertomus Suojärven pitäjästä ja matkustuksistani siellä v. 1867. Suomi II:8*.
– 1870b. Kuvaelmia kansan elämästä Salmin kihlakunnassa. *Koitar. Savo-karjalaisen osakunnan albumi I*. Helsinki.
van Gennep, Arnold 1960. *Rites of Passage*. Great Britain.
Goffman, Erving 1974. *Frame Analysis: An Essay on the Organization of Experience*. New York.
Goody, Jack 1977. *The Domestication of the savage mind*. Cambridge.
Goold, G.P. 1977. *The nature of Homeric composition. Illinois classical studies 2*.
The Great Bear. A Thematic Anthology of Oral Poetry in the Finno-Ugrian Languages. (Eds.) L. Honko – S. Timonen – M. Branch – M. Bosley. FLS. Helsinki. 1993.
Gumperz, John J. 1982. *Discourse Strategies*. Cambridge.
Haavio, Martti 1928. Vanhojen runojemme maailmankäsityksestä. *Kalevalaseuran vuosikirja 8*.

– 1935. *Suomalaisen muinaisrunouden maailma*. Helsinki.

– 1943. *Viimeiset runonlaulajat*. Helsinki.

– 1950. *Väinämöinen*. Helsinki. Published in English 1991 under the title *Väinämöinen Eternal Sage*. *FF Communications 144*. Helsinki.

– 1952a. *Kirjokansi. Suomen kansan kertomarunoutta*. Helsinki.

– 1952b. *Laulupuu: Suomen kansan tunnelmarunoutta*. Helsinki.

– 1955. *Kansanrunojen maailmanselitys*. Helsinki.

– 1959. *Karjalan jumalat*. Helsinki.

– 1961. *Kuolematonten lehdot. Sämpsöi Pellervoisen arvoitus*. Helsinki.

– 1967. *Suomalainen mytologia*. Helsinki.

Haavio, M. – Hautala, J. 1948. (Eds.) *Suomen kansan arvoituskirja*. Helsinki.

Hainsworth, J.B. 1964. Structure and content in epic formulae: The question of the unique expression. *Classical quarterly 14*.

Hamayon, Roberte 1978. Les Héros de Service. *L'Homme Vol. XVIII Nos. 3/4*.

Hanks, William F. 1987. Discourse Genres in a Theory of Practice. *American Ethnologist 14 (4)*: 668-692.

Harva (Holmberg), Uno 1923. Metsän peitossa. *Kalevalaseuran vuosikirja 3*.

Harva, Uno 1929. *Kauko-Karjalan häärunot. Turun yliopiston julkaisu B IX*. Turku.

– 1930. De karelska bröllopsångerna som etnologisk källa. *Rig*.

– 1932. Karjalaista kansanuskoa ja palvontaa. I. Härkönen (ed.) *Karjalan kirja*. Helsinki.

– 1933. *Altain suvun uskonto*. Helsinki.

– 1941. Naimatapojemme Historiaa. *Kalevalaseuran vuosikirja 20-21*.

– 1948. *Suomalaisten muinaisusko*. Helsinki.

Harvilahti, Lauri 1985. *Bylinat*. Helsinki.

– 1990. The Production of Finnish Epic Poetry: Fixed Wholes or Creative Compositions? *Paper delivered at the 1990 Annual Meeting of the American Folklore Society, 18-24 October*. Oakland.

– 1992. *Kertovan runon keinot. Inkeriläisen runoepiikan tuottamisesta. Suomalaisen Kirjallisuuden Seuran toimituksia 522*. Helsinki.

Hastrup, Kirsten 1981. Cosmology and Society in Medieval Iceland. *Ethnologia Scandinavica 1981*.

– 1985. *Culture and History in Medieval Iceland. An Anthropological Analysis of Structure and Change*. Oxford.

– 1987. Presenting the Past. Reflections on Myth and History. *Folk, Journal of the Danish Ethnographic Society, Vol. 29*. Copenhagen.

– 1990a (1985). Male and Female in Icelandic Culture: a Preliminary Sketch. *Island of Anthropology. Studies in Past and Present Iceland*. Viborg.

– 1990b. *Island of Anthropology. Studies in past and present Iceland*. Odense.

Hatto, A.T. 1970. *Shamanism and Epic Poetry in Northern Asia. Foundation Day Lecture. School of Oriental and African Studies, University of London*. Hertford.

Hautala, Jouko 1942. Muinaisrunojemme tutkimuksen menetelmästä ja mahdollisuuksista. *Kalevalaseuran vuosikirja 22*: 22-39. Helsinki (1943).

– 1945. *Lauri Lappalaisen runo. Vertaileva kansanrunoudentutkimus*. Helsinki.

– 1947. Über Arbeitsweise und Möglichkeiten bei der Erforschung altfinnischer Runendichtung. *Studia Fennica V (2)*: 27-45. Helsinki.

– 1954. *Suomalainen kansanrunouden tutkimus*. Helsinki.

– 1969. *Finnish Folklore Research 1828-1918*. Helsinki.

Heikinmäki, Maija-Liisa 1981. *Suomalaiset häätavat. Talonpoikaiset avioliiton solmintaperiaatteet*. Helsinki.

Herzfeld, Michael 1981a. An Indigenous Theory of Meaning and its Elicitation in Performative Context. *Semiotica Vol. 34 Nos. 1/2*.

– 1981b. Performative Categories and Symbols of Passage in Rural Greece. *Journal of American Folklore Vol. 94 No. 371.*

– 1986. Closure as Cure: Tropes in the Exploration of Bodily and Social Disorder. *Current Anthropology Vol. 27.*

– 1989 (1987). *Anthropology Through the Looking-glass. Critical Ethnography in the Margins of Europe.* Cambridge, New York & Melbourne.

Holbek, Bengt 1987. *Interpretation of Fairy Tales. FF Communications 239.* Helsinki.

Honko, Lauri 1962. *Geisterglaube in Ingermanland. FF Communications 185.* Helsinki.

– 1963. Itkuvirsirunous. M. Kuusi (ed.) *Suomen kirjallisuus I. Kirjoittamaton kirjallisuus.* Helsinki.

– 1974. Balto-Finnic Lament Poetry. *Finnish Folkloristics 1. Studia Fennica 17.* Helsinki.

– 1978a. The Ingrian Lamenter as Psychopomp. *Temenos Vol. 14.*

– 1978b. Perinnetuote, perinnelaji ja perinnealue kansanrunouden ikäämisessä. *Kalevalaseuran vuosikirja 58.* Helsinki.

– 1980. Methods in Folk Narrative Research: Their Status and Future. *Ethnologia Europaea XI (1):* 6-27

– 1985. Rethinking Tradition Ecology. *Temenos Vol. 21.*

– 1986a. Martti Haavio tutkijana. *Kotiseutu 2/1986:* 52-60.

– 1986b. Types of Comparision and Forms of Variation. *Journal of Folklore Research 23.*

Honko, Lauri et.al. (eds.) 1993. *The Great Bear. A Thematic Anthology of Oral Poetry in the Finno-Ugrian Languages.* FLS, Helsinki.

Howe, James – Hirshfeld, Lawrence A. 1981. The Star Girls' Descent: A Myth about Men, Women, Matrilocality and Singing. *Journal of American Folklore Vol. 94 No. 373.*

Howell, Signe 1986. Formal Speech Acts as one Discourse. *Man Vol. 21 No. 1.*

Hymes, Dell 1971. The Contribution of Folklore to Sociolinguistic Research. A. Paredes – R. Bauman (eds.) "Toward New Perspectives in Folklore". *Journal of American Folklore 84:* 42-50. (Reprinted in A. Paredes and R. Bauman (eds.) *Toward New Perspectives in Folklore.* Austin, as well as in Dell Hymes, *Foundations in Sociolinguistics: An Ethnographic Approach.* Philadelphia.)

– 1974. *Foundations in Sociolinguistics: An Ethnographic Approach.* Philadelphia.

– 1975. Breakthrough into Performance. D. Ben-Amos and K. Goldstein (eds.) *Folklore: Performance and Communication.* The Hague. Reprinted in Dell Hymes, *"In vain I tried to tell you": Essays in Native American Ethnopoetics.* Philadelphia.

– 1981. *"In Vain I Tried to Tell You": Essays in Native American Ethnopoetics.* Philadelphia.

– 1982. Narrative Form as a "Grammar" of Experience: Native American and a Glimpse of English. *Journal of Education 164 (2):* 121-142.

– 1985a. Some Subtleties of Measured Verse. J. Hesch (ed.) *Proceedings of the Niagara Linguistic Society, 15th Spring Conference.* Buffalo.

– 1985b. Language, memory and selective performance: Cultee's "Salmon's Myth" as twice told to Boas. *Journal of American Folklore Vol. 98 No. 390.*

– 1986. The General Epistle of James. *International Journal of the Sociology of Language 62:* 75-103.

Hämäläinen, Albert 1920. *Ihmisruumiin substanssi suomalais-ugrilaisten kansojen taikuudessa. Suomalais-ugrilaisen Seuran toimituksia XLVII.* Helsinki.

Härkönen, Iivo 1909. Piirteitä karjalaisista runonlaulajista. *Valvojan Kalevalavihko.* Helsinki.

Häyhä, Johannes 1982. *Vuodenajat. Kuvaelmia itäsuomalaisten vanhoista tavoista (1893-1899)*. Helsinki.

Ilomäki, Henni 1986. *Eläinten nimittäminen ja luontosuhde. Petojen roolit pohjois- ja rajakarjalaisissa kalevalamittaisissa runoissa.* Unpublished manuscript: licentiate thesis. University of Helsinki, Department of Folklore.

– 1989. Charms as Linguistic Expressions of Dichotomized Nature and Culture. M. Hoppál – J. Pentikäinen (eds.) *Uralic Mythology and Folklore. Ethnologia Uralica 1.* Budapest.

– 1990. "Tekeväin on meiän tetri". Näkökulmia inkeriläisen morsiamen naiseuteen. A. Nenola – S. Timonen (eds.) *Louhen sanat. Kirjoituksia kansanperinteen naisista.* Helsinki.

Inha, I.K. 1921 (1911). *Kalevalan laulumailta. Elias Lönnrotin poluilla Vienan Karjalassa.* Helsinki.

Isbell, Billie Jean 1985. The Metaphoric Process: "From Culture to Nature and Back Again". G. Urton (ed.) *Animal Myths and Metaphors in South America.* Salt Lake City.

Itkonen, Erkki 1936. *A.A. Borenius-Lähteenkorva – kansanrunouden kerääjä ja tutkija.* Helsinki.

– 1946. Zur Frage nach der Entwicklung des Vokalismus der ersten Silbe in den finnisch-ugrischen Sprachen, insbesondere im Mordwinischen. *FUF* (Finnisch-ugrische Forschungen) *29:* 222-337. Helsinki

– 1954. Uber die suffixalen Labialvokale im Lappischen und Ostseefinnischen. Scandinavica et Fenno-ugrica. *Studier tillägnade Björn Collinder den 22 juli 1954:* 183-191. Uppsala.

– 1978. Einige Gesichtspunkte zur Frühgeschichte der Lappen und des Lappischen. *SUSA (Suomalais-Ugrilaisen Seuran Aikakauskirja) 76.*

Itkonen, Terho 1972. Historiantakaiset Häme ja Suomi kielentutkijan näkökulmasta. *Hist. Aikakauskirja:* 85-112.

Jaakkola, Jalmari 1935. Suomen varhaishistoria. Heimokausi ja Kalevalakulttuuri. *Suomen historia II.* Porvoo.

Jackendoff, Ray 1985. *Semantics and cognition.* Cambridge & Massachusetts & London.

Jakobson, Roman 1960. Closing Statement: Linguistics and Poetics. T. A. Sebeok (ed.) *Style in Language.* Cambridge & New York.

– 1977. On Aphasia. J. Dolgin – D. Kemnitzer – D. Schneider (eds.) *Symbolic Anthropology. A Reader in the Study of Symbols and Meanings.* New York.

– 1987a. Linguistics and Poetics. K. Pomorska – S. Rudy (eds.) *Language and Literature.* Cambridge & Massachusetts & London.

– 1987b. Marginal Notes on the Prose of the Poet Pasternak. K. Pomorska – S. Rudy (eds.) *Language and Literature.* Cambridge & Massachusetts & London.

Jakobson, Roman – Lotz, John 1941. *Axiomatik eines Verssystems am mordwinischen Volkslied dargelegt. Thesen zu einem Vortrag im Ungarischen Institut, Stockholm, am 8:ten April 1941.* Stockholm.

Jason, Heda 1970. The Russian Criticism of the "Finnish School" in Folktale Scholarship. *Norveg 14.*

Järvinen, Irma-Riitta 1989. Pohjois-Karjalan eeppisen kansanrunouden aiheita ja laulajia. *Runon ja rajan tiellä. Kalevalaseuran vuosikirja 68.* Helsinki.

Jääskinen, Aune 1969. Uskonnollisuus kuvataiteessa. K. Justander – J. Otalahti (eds.) *Itä-Suomi on erilainen.* Mikkeli.

– 1983. Ylösnousemus ikonitaiteessa. *Scripta Historica 8.* Oulu.

Kaivola-Bregenhøj, Annikki 1985. Variaatio kansanperinteessä. Päivikki Suojanen (ed.), *Muuntelu ja kulttuuri.* Tampere.

– 1988. *Kertomus ja kerronta.* Helsinki.

Kalima, Jalo 1936. *Itämerensuomalaisten kielten balttilaiset lainasanat.* Helsinki.

388

Kamppinen, Matti 1989. *Cognitive systems and cultural models of illness. FF Communications 244*. Helsinki.

Kamppinen et al. 1990. *Kognitiiviset järjestelmät ja ympäristöriskien representaatio*. Matti Kamppinen – Hasse Karlsson – Pasi Laihonen – Seppo Sajama. Unpublished manuscript.

Karelskie epičeskie pesni 1950. V. Evseev (ed.). Moscow.

Karjalan kansan runot 1946. Tallinn.

Karlsson, Fred 1988. Kieli ja kognitio. A. Hautamäki (ed.) *Kognitiotiede*. Helsinki.

Kastsenko, S. G. 1986. Agraariolot Venäjän luoteisosissa 1800-luvun jälkipuoliskolla. R. Endén – V. Laulumaa (eds.) *Suomalais-neuvostoliittolainen historiantutkijoiden symposium – Riika 1.-7.12.1985. Historiallinen arkisto 87*. Helsinki.

Kaukonen, Väinö 1942. Maarian vakainen vaippa suomalaisissa kansanrunoissa. *Kalevalaseuran vuosikirja 22.*

– 1956. *Elias Lönnrotin Kalevalan toinen painos*. Helsinki.

– 1977. Karjalaisten varhainen henkinen kulttuuri kalevalaisen runouden valossa. *Karjalan synty. Symposio 30.6.-2.7.1976 Joensuu. Alustukset. Joensuun korkeakoulu, Monistesarja A, n:o 24 A*. Joensuu.

– 1979. Kalevala ja kirjallisuuden teoria. *Virittäjä 1979*: 343-349.

– 1982a. Folkloristiikan paradigman vaihdos runouden tutkimuksen näkökulmasta. A. Viikari (ed.) *Kirjallisuudentutkijain vuosikirja 34*. Helsinki.

– 1982b. Kansanrunous ja perinne. *Virittäjä 1982*: 347-354.

Kay, Sarah 1990. *Subjectivity in Troubadour Poetry*. Cambridge.

Keesing, Roger M. 1985. Conventional Metaphors and Anthropological Metaphysics: the Problematic of Cultural Translation. *Journal of Anthropological Research Vol. 41 No. 2.*

Kellog, Robert 1979. Varietes of tradition in medieval narrative. H. Bekker-Nielsen et.al. (eds.) *Medieval narrative: A symposium*. Odense.

KEP = *Karelskie epičeskie pesni*. V. Evseev (ed.). Moscow. 1950.

Kerewsky-Halpern, Barbara 1991 (1989). Healing with Mother Metaphors: Serbian Conjurers' Word Magic. C. S. McClain (ed.) *Women as Healers. Cross-Cultural Perspectives*. New Brunswick & London.

Kinkade, M. Dale 1987. Bluejay and His Sister. B. Swann – A. Krupat (eds.) *Recovering the word: essays on Native American literature*. Berkeley.

Kiparsky Paul 1968. Metrics and Morphophonemics in the Kalevala. *Studies presented to Professor Roman Jacobson by his students*. Cambridge.

– 1970. Metrics and Morphophonemics in the Kalevala. D.C. Freeman (ed.) *Linguistics and Literary Style*. New York.

– 1976. Some linquistic and typological considerations. B. Stolz – R. Shannon (eds.) *Oral literature and the formula*. Ann Arbor.

Kirkinen, Heikki 1976. Historische Aspekte bei der Entstehung und Überlieferung der Gesänge des Kalevala. *Nordeuropa 9*. Greifswald.

– 1986. Idän kirkon vaikutusta kalevalaisessa runoperinteessä. "*Iloitkaa Sergei ja Herman, autuaat isämme*". Pieksämäki.

– 1988. *Pohjois-Karjalan kalevalaisen perinteen juuret. Tietolipas 108*. Rauma.

Klinge, Matti 1984. *Muinaisuutemme merivallat*. Keuruu.

Knuts, Ulrika 1974. *Begreppen folkreligion, universalreligion, folktro, i belysning av föreställningar om Jungfru Maria i nordiska trollformler*. Unpublished manuscript: licentiate thesis. Åbo Akademi, Department of Folklore.

Knuuttila, Seppo 1989. Paluu nykyisyyteen. T. Korhonen – M. Räsänen (ed.) *Kansa kuvastimessa. Etnisyys ja identiteetti*. Helsinki.

KO = Museovirasto. Kansatieteen toimisto. (The Collections of Ethnographic Department in the National Board of Antiquities.)

Koivulehto, Jorma 1979. Baltisches und Germanisches im Finnischen: die finn. Stämme auf -rte und die finn. Sequenz VrtV. *Explanationes et tractationes fenno-ugricae in honorem Hans Fromm. Münchener Universitäts-Schriften.* München.

Kolehmainen, Ilkka 1977. *Kalevalasävelmän musikologista syntaksia.* Unpublished manuscript: pro gradu thesis. University of Helsinki, Department of Musicology.

Konkka, Unelma 1985. *Ikuinen ikävä.* Helsinki.

Kont, Karl 1963. *Käändsõnaline objekt läänemeresoome keeltes.* Tallinn.

Korhonen, Mikko 1974. Oliko suomalais-ugrilainen kantakieli agglutinoiva? Eli mitä kielihistoriallisista rekonstruktioista voidaan lukea ja mitä ei. *Virittäjä.*

– 1976. Suomen kantakielten kronologiaa. *Virittäjä.*

– 1987. Kalevalamitan varhaishistoriaa. *Suomalais-urgilaisen seuran aikakauskirja 81.* Helsinki.

Korte, Irma 1988. *Nainen ja myyttinen nainen.* Helsinki.

Kõrv, A. V. 1928. Värsimõõt Veske "Eesti rahvalauludes". *Acta et Commentationes Universitas Tartuensis B XIII:3.* Tartu.

KRA = Suomalaisen Kirjallisuuden Seuran Kansanrunousarkisto. (The Folklore Archives of the Finnish Literature Society.)

Krinitsnaja, N.A. 1986. *K. semantike obraza devy lososja v karelo-finskom epose.* – "Kalevala" – pamjatnik mirovoj kul'tury Petrozavodsk.

Krohn, J. 1883-85. *Suomalaisen kirjallisuuden historia.* Helsinki.

Krohn, Julius – Krohn, Kaarle 1901. *Kantelettaren tutkimuksia I.*

Krohn, Kaarle 1903-1910. *Kalevalan runojen historia.* Helsinki.

– 1914a. *Suomalaisten runojen uskonto. Suomen suvun uskonnot.* Helsinki.

– 1914b. *Kaleva und seine Sippe. Suomalais-ugrilaisen seuran aikakauskirja XXX, n:o 35.* Helsinki.

– 1918. *Kalevalankysymyksiä I-II. Suomalais-ugrilaisen seuran aikakauskirja XXXV-XXXVI.* Helsinki.

– 1920. *Muinaisrunoja laulusta – surusta – lemmestä perussäkeisiinsä palauttaa yrittänyt Kaarle Krohn. Ruususarja 6.* Helsinki.

– 1924. *Kalevalastudien I. Einleitung. FF Communications 53.* Helsinki.

– 1931. *Tunnelmarunojen tutkimuksia. I: Laulusta.* Helsinki.

Kuusi, (Siikala), Anna-Leena 1975. La mythologie finnoise. *Les peuples ouraliens. Leur culture, leurs traditions.* Publié sous la direction de Péter Hajdú. Horvarth – Roanne. Budapest & France.

Kuusi, Matti 1949. *Sampo-eepos. Suomalais-ugrilaisen seuran toimituksia XCVI.* Helsinki.

– 1952a. Kaavoitettua kansanrunoutta. *Suomalainen Suomi 1952 (7):* 391-395.

– 1952b. Kalevalaisen säkeen, säeryhmän ja runon painavoituvuudesta. *Virittäjä 1952:* 241-261.

– 1958. Omaistenvertailukertomus. *Kalevalaseuran vuosikirja 48.* Helsinki.

– 1961. Mitättömistä aineksista. *Kalevalaseuran vuosikirja 41.* Helsinki.

– 1963. (Ed.) *Suomen kirjallisuus I. Kirjoittamaton kirjallisuus.* Keuruu.

– 1966. Maria. *Kulturhistoriskt lexikon för nordisk medeltid 11.* Helsingfors.

– 1968. Muinaisrunon epimyyttejä. *Kalevalaseuran vuosikirja 58.*

– 1970. Anni Lehtosen runousoppi. *Virittäjä.*

– 1972. Manalan neiti. Strukturianalyyttinen koe. *Parnasso 3/1972:* 129-134.

– 1974. 'The bridge and the church' an anti-church legend. P. Leino (ed.) *Finnish folkloristics 2. Studia Fennica 18.* Helsinki.

– 1978. Kalevalakielen kysymyksiä. *Virittäjä 82.* Helsinki.

– 1980a. (Ed.) *Kalevalaista kertomarunoutta.* Helsinki.

– 1980b. Suomalainen tutkimusmenetelmä. O. Lehtipuro (ed.) *Perinteentutkimuksen perusteita.* Helsinki.

– 1983. *Maria Luukan laulut ja loitsut. Suomalaisen Kirjallisuuden Seuran Toimituksia 379.* Helsinki.

– 1987. Eeppiset runoketjut Kalevalan perustana. L. Honko (ed.) *Kalevala ja maailman eepokset. Kalevalaseuran vuosikirja 65.* Helsinki.

– 1988. Oksenja Mäkisen suku. *Karjalan heimo 5-6.*

– (forthcoming). Selected articles by Matti Kuusi. H. Ilomäki (ed.) *Studia Fennica Folkloristica 3.* Helsinki.

Kuusi, Matti – Anttonen, Pertti 1985. *Kalevalalipas.* Helsinki.

Kuusi, M. – Bosley, K. – Branch, M. (eds.) *Finnish Folk Poetry, Epic.* 1977. Helsinki.

Kuusi, Matti – Tedre, Ülo 1979. Regivärsilise ja kalevalamõõdulise laulutraditsiooni vahekorrast. *Keel ja Kirjandus 22:* 70-78.

Köngäs-Maranda, Elli-Kaija 1967. The Cattle of the Forest and the Harvest of Water: The Cosmology of Finnish Magic. J. Helm (ed.) *Essays on the Verbal and Visual Arts. Proceedings of the 1966 Annual Spring Meeting of the American Ethnological Society.* Seattle & London.

Köngäs-Maranda, Elli 1971. The logic of riddles. P. Maranda – E. Köngäs-Maranda (eds.) *Structural analysis of oral tradition.* Pennsylvania.

Labov, William 1972. Rules for Ritual Insults. D. Sudnow (ed.) *Studies in Social Interaction.* New York.

Laiho, Lauri 1940. Viron Inkeri kansanrunouden maana. *Virittäjä.*

Lakoff, George 1987. *Women, fire, and dangerous things. What categories reveal about the mind.* Chicago & London.

Lakoff George – Johnson Mark 1980. *Metaphors we live by.* Chicago & London.

Larsson, Lars-Gunnar 1981. *Studier i de östersjöfinska språkens partitivbruk.* Uppsala.

Launonen, Hannu 1984. *Suomalaisen runon struktuurianalyysia.* Helsinki.

Laurila, Vihtori 1964. Suomen saari ja muinaisrunon saari. *Kalevalaseuran Vuosikirja 4.*

Leach, Edmund 1964. Anthropological Aspects of Language: Animal Categories and Verbal Abuse. E. Lenneberg (ed.) *New Directions in the Study of Language.* Cambridge & Massachusetts.

– 1976. *Culture and Communication. The Logic by which Symbols are Connected.* Cambridge.

Lehiste, Ilse 1977. Isochrony reconsidered. *Journal of Phonetics 5:* 253-63.

– 1983. The role of prosody in the internal structuring of a sentence. *Proceedings of the XIIIth international congress of linguists, August 29. Sebtember 4, 1982.* Tokyo.

– 1984. The metric structure of a recited Finnish spell. *UAJb* (Uralische-Altaische Jahrbücher). *Neue Folge. 4:* 83-9.

Lehtipuro, Outi 1974. Trends in Finnish folkloristics. P. Leino (ed.) *Finnish Folkloristics 2. Studia Fennica 18.* Helsinki.

Lehtonen, Jaakko 1970. *Aspects of quantity in Standard Finnish. Studia Philologica Jyväskyläensia 6.* Jyväskylä.

Leino, Pentti 1970. *Strukturaalinen alkusointu Suomessa.* Forssa.

– 1974. Kalevalamitan ongelma. P. Virtaranta et al. (eds.) *Sampo ei sanoja puutu: Matti Kuusen juhlakirja.Kalevalaseuran vuosikirja 54.* Helsinki.

– 1975. Äidinkieli ja vieras kieli: rahvaanrunouden metriikkaa. *Kalevalaseuran vuosikirja 55.*

– 1979. Suomen kielen metriset systeemit ja mittatyypit. *Virittäjä:* 302-40.

– 1982. *Kieli, runo ja mitta. Suomen kielen metriikka.* Helsinki.

– 1985a. Metriikan anti kielentutkimukselle. *Virittäjä:* 390-407.

– 1985b. The Structure and Development of the Kalevala Metre. S. Kroman (ed.) *Det finske Kalevala. Rapport fra Kalevala-symposiet i København den 17.-18. mai 1985. Finsk afdelings skrifter. Utgivet af Finsk afdeling ved Københavns universitet.* København.

– 1986. Language and metre. Metrics and the metrical system of Finnish. *Studia Fennica 31*. Helsinki.

– 1987. Kieli ja maailman hahmottaminen. T. Hoikkala (ed.) *Kieli, kertomus, kulttuuri*. Helsinki.

– 1990. The Interpretation of Tales in Folkloristics. Anna-Leena Siikala (ed.) *Studies in Oral Narrative. Studia Fennica 33*. Helsinki.

Lévi-Strauss, Claude 1963a. The Effectiveness of Symbols. *Structural Anthropology*. New York.

– 1963b. The Structural Study of Myth. Claude Lévi-Strauss, *Structural Anthropology, Vol. 1*. New York. (Also published in *Journal of American Folklore* 68: 428-222 (1955), and in T. A. Sebeok (ed.) *Myth: A Symposium*. Bloomington (1958).)

– 1989 (1962). *The Savage Mind*. 2nd edition, 5th impression. Trowbridge, Wiltshire.

Liestøl, Knut 1970. *Den Norrøne arven. Universitetsforlaget*. Oslo.

Linna, M. 1987. (Ed.) *Muinaisrunot ja todellisuus. Suomen kansan vanhojen runojen historiallinen tausta. Historian aitta XX*. Jyväskylä.

Liszka, James Jakób 1989. *The semiotic of myth. A critical study of the symbol*. Bloomington & Indianapolis.

Lord, Albert B. 1960. *The Singer of Tales*. Cambridge.

– 1974 (1960). *The Singer of Tales*. 6th printing. Forge Village, Massachusetts.

– 1976a. *The Singer of Tales*. 7th printing. New York.

– 1976b. Studies in the Bulgarian epic tradition: Thematic parallels. *Bulgaria past and present. Proceedings of the first international conference on Bulgarian studies*. Wisconsin.

– 1981. Memory, fixity and genre in oral tradition poetries. J.M. Foley (ed.) *Oral traditional literature: A Festschrift for Albert Bates Lord*. Ohio.

– 1987. The Kalevala, the South Slavic Epics and Homer. B. Almqvist et.al (eds.) *The Heroic process. Form, Function and Fantasy in Folk Epic*. Dublin.

– 1991. *Epic Singers and Oral Tradition*. Ithaca, London.

Lotz, John 1960. Metric typology. T. A. Sebeok (ed.) *Style in language*. Cambridge, Mass.

LT = *The Lenten Triodion*. Translated from the Original Greek by Mother Mary and Archimandrite Kallistos Ware. 1977. London & Boston.

Lukkarinen, J. 1912. *Inkeriläisten praasniekoista. Suomi IV:11*. Helsinki.

– 1914. *Inkeriläisten vainajainpalveluksesta*. Helsinki.

– 1933. *Suomalaisten naimatapoja. Aineksia suomalaisten kansojen avioliiton historiaan I*. Helsinki.

Luthy, Melvin J. 1991. Number Parallelisms in Finnish and Hebrew. *Paper delivered at the 1991 Conference of the Society for the Advancement of Scandinavian Study, 3-4 May*. Amherst.

Löfgren, Orvar 1981. World-Views: A Research Perspective. *Ethnologia Scandinavica 1981*.

Lönnrot, Elias 1836-49. *Kalevala taikka vanhoja Karjalan runoja Suomen kansan muinoisista ajoista*. Helsinki.

– 1840-41. *Kanteletar taikka Suomen kansan vanhojen lauluja ja virsiä*. Helsinki.

– 1958. *Suomalais-ruotsalainen sanakirja II*. Porvoo/ Helsinki.

– 1964. *Kalevala (1849)*. Helsinki.

– 1966. *Kanteletar (1840)*. Helsinki.

– 1979. *Vaeltaja. Muistelmia jalkamatkalta Hämeestä, Savosta ja Karjalasta. 2nd p*. Helsinki.

Lönnroth, Lars 1979. The Double-scene of Arrow-Odd's Drinking Contest. H. Becker-Nielsen et. al. (eds.) *Medieval Narrative. A Symposium*. Odense.

Magoun, Francis Peabody 1963. *The Kalevala, or Poems of the Kaleva District, compiled by Elias Lönnrot.* A prose translation with foreword and appendices. Cambridge, Massachusetts.

Mann, Thomas 1987. *Totuudesta ja kauneudesta. Esseitä kirjallisuudesta ja filosofiasta.* Keuruu.

Manninen, I. 1932. Karjalaisten puvustosta. I. Härkönen (ed.) *Karjalan kirja II.* Porvoo.

Mansikka V.J. 1908. "Alesa Popovits" i "Ivan Godinovits" v Finljandii. *Etnografitseskoje obozrenije.*

– 1924. Itkujen Tuonela. *Suomalais-ugrilaisen seuran toimituksia LII.* Helsinki.

– 1939. Pyhän Iljan palvonnasta. *Kalevalaseuran vuosikirja 19.*

– 1941. Karjalais-inkeriläisiä pyhimyksiä ja juhlapäiviä. 4. Neitsyt Marian juhlapäivät. *Virittäjä.*

Mark, Vera 1987. Women and Text in Gascon Tall Tales. *Journal of American Folklore Vol. 100 No. 398.*

Mastromattei, Romano 1985. Oral Tradition and Shamanic Recitals. B. Gentili – G. Paioni (eds.) *Oralità, Cultura, Letteratura, Discorso. Quaderni Urbinati di Cultura Classica – Atti di Convegni 2.* Roma.

Melodos, Romanos 1986. *Kristuksen syntymän kontakki.* Joensuu.

Miller, Gary D. 1987. Towards a new model of formulaic composition. J.M. Foley (ed.) *Comparative research on oral traditions: A memorial for Milman Parry.* Ohio.

Mills, Margaret A. 1991. *Rhetorics and Politics in Afghan Traditional Storytelling.* Philadelphia.

Mustanoja, Tauno 1959. The Presentation of ancient germanic poetry – looking for parallels. *Neuphilologishe Mitteilungen 60.*

MV = Museovirasto. (National Board of Antiquities).

Nagler, Michael N. 1974. *Spontaneity and tradition: A study in the oral art of Homer.* Berkeley.

Nagy, Gregory 1976. Formula and meter. B. Stolz – R. Shannon (eds.) *Oral literature and the formula.* Michigan.

Needham, Rodney 1979. *Symbolic Classification.* Santa Monica, California.

– 1987. *Counterpoints.* Berkeley, Los Angeles & London.

Nenola, Aili 1986. *Miessydäminen nainen. Naisnäkökulmia kulttuuriin. Tietolipas 102.* Pieksämäki.

Nenola-Kallio, Aili 1981. Inkeriläiset itkuhäät. M. Sarmela (ed.) *Pohjolan häät.* Helsinki.

– 1982. *Studies in Ingrian Laments. FF Communications 234.* Helsinki.

– 1984. Runontutkimus ja vaskoosimenetelmä. Review of Matti Kuusi, Maria Luukan laulut ja loitsut: Tutkimus läntisimmän Inkerin suomalaisperinteestä. Helsinki 1983. *Kotiseutu 1/1984*: 40-41.

Niemi, A.R. (ed.) 1904. *Runonkerääjiemme matkakertomuksia 1830-luvulta 1880-luvulle.* Helsinki.

– 1913. *Tutkimuksia liettualaisten kansanlaulujen alalta. AASF* (Suomalaisen Tiedeakatemian Toimituksia) *B: XII.*

– 1918. *Vanhan suomalaisen runomitan synnystä. Suomi IV: 19.* Helsinki.

– 1921. Vienan läänin runonlaulajat ja tietäjät. *SKVR I:4.* Helsinki.

Nieminen, Eino 1945. Orsi, aarto ja hirsi. *Virittäjä:* 524-33.

– 1957. Itämerensuomalaisten kielten vanhimmista balttilaisperäisistä lainasanoista kuvastuvia lähdekielen ominaisuuksia. *STAEP* (Suomalaisen Tiedeakatemian esitelmät ja pöytäkirjat) *1956*: 190-209. Helsinki.

Nirvi, R.E. 1982. *Petojen nimitykset kosinta- ja hääsanastossa. Suomi 123:3.* Helsinki.

Notopoulos, J.A. 1962. The Homeric hymns as oral poetry; A study of the post-homeric oral tradition. *American Journal of Philology 83.*

Ohlmarks, Åke 1948. *Eddans guda sånger*. Tolkade och kommenterade av Åke Ohlmarks. Uppsala.

Ohnuki-Tierney, Emiko (ed.) 1990. *Culture Through Time: Anthropological Approaches*. Standford.

Oinas, Felix J. 1969. *Studies in Finnic-Slavic Folklore Relations. FF Communications 205*. Helsinki.

– 1972. Folk epic: An introduction. R. Dorson (ed.) *Folklore and folklife: an introduction*. Chigago.

– 1978. *Heroic epic and saga: an introduction to worlds great folk-epics*. Bloomington, Indiana.

– 1987. Venäläiset bylinat ja suomalainen kertomarunous. L. Honko (ed.) *Kalevala ja maailman eepokset. Kalevalaseuran vuosikirja 65*. Pieksämäki.

– 1990. Russian and Finnish epic songs. L. Honko (ed.) *Religion, myth, and folklore in the world's epics*. Berlin & New York.

Ojonen, Sinimarja 1988. *Yliluonnollisten olentojen erikoinen kielenkäyttö suomalaisissa uskomustarinoissa*. Unpublished manuscript: pro gradu thesis. University of Helsinki, Department of Folklore.

Olrik, Axel 1909. Epische Gesetze der Volksdichtung. *Zeitschrift für Deutsches Altertum 51:* 1-12. Published in English in A. Dundes (ed.) *The Study of Folklore*. 1965. Englewood Cliffs.

Ong, Walter J. 1982. *Orality and Literacy. The Technologising of the Word*. London & New York.

Ortner, Sherry B. 1975. Is Female to Male as Nature is to Culture? M. Z. Rosaldo – L. Lamphere (eds.), *Woman, Culture, and Society*. Stanford.

Paasio, Marja 1976. *Synnyt*. Helsinki.

Paasonen, Heikki 1897. Itäsuomalaisten kansojen runoudesta. *Valvoja 17:* 1-26.

– 1911. Über den Versbau des mordwinischen Volksliedes. *FUF* (Finnisch-ugrische Forschungen) *10*: 153-91. Helsinki.

Pálsson, Gísli 1990. The Idea of Fish: Land and Sea in the Icelandic World-view. R. Willis (ed.) *Signifying Animals. Human Meaning in the Natural World*. Cambridge.

Parry, Milman – Lord, Albert B. 1954. *Serbocroatian heroic songs*. I, Novi Pazar (English translations). Cambridge, Mass. & Belgrade.

Partanen, Juha 1991. *Sociability and Intoxication. Alcohol and Drinking in Kenya, Africa, and the Modern World*. Helsinki.

Pascal, Pierre 1976. *The Religion of the Russian people*. New York.

Paukson, H. 1930. Eesti rahvaluule ettekanderütmict. *Looming 8*.

Paulaharju, Samuli 1924. *Syntymä, lapsuus ja kuolema. Vienan Karjalan tapoja ja uskomuksia. Kalevalaseuran julkaisuja 2*. Porvoo.

– 1929. Vienan Karjalan tietäjistä. Anni Lehtoselta v. 1922 kirjoitettujen muistiinpanojen mukaan. *Kalevalaseuran Vuosikirja 9*.

Peabody, Berkley 1975. *The winged word*. New York.

Pelkonen, E. 1931. *Über volkstümliche Geburtshilfe in Finnland. Acta Societatis Medicorum Fennicae Duodecim Ser. B. Tom. XVI*. Helsinki.

Pentikäinen, Juha 1971. *Marina Takalon uskonto. Uskontoantropologinen tutkimus*. Helsinki. Published in English, see Pentikäinen 1978.

– 1978. *Oral Repertoire and World View. An Anthropological Study of Marina Takalo's Life History. FF Communications 219*. Helsinki.

– 1987. *Kalevalan mytologia*. Helsinki.

– 1991. *Kalevala Mythology*. Bloomington.

Piela, Ulla 1983. Muuttumaton tautiloitsu? *Kalevalaseura vuosikirja 63*. Helsinki.

– 1990. Lemmenloitsujen nainen. A. Nenola – S. Timonen (eds.) *Louhen sanat. Kirjoituksia kansanperinteen naisista*. Helsinki.

Piha, Kalevi 1964. *Suurperhe karjalaisessa työyhteisössä. Karjalainen suurperhe sosiaaliantropologian ja sosiaalipsykologian valossa. Turun yliopisto sosiologian laitos. Sarja B 6.* Turku.

PKK = Karsnopolskaya, T. (ed.) *Pesni karelskogo kraya.* 1977. Petrozavodsk.

Põldmäe, Jaak 1978. *Eesti värsiõpetus.* Tallinn.

Polttila, Brita 1991. *Lauluja rakkaudesta ja kuolemasta. Taivaan mereltä.* Helsinki.

Porkka, Volmari 1883. Inkerin itkuvirsistä. *Valvoja.*

– 1886. *Kertomus runonkeruu-matkasta, jonka v. 1883 kesällä teki Inkeriin Volmari Porkka. Suomi II:19.* Helsinki.

Porthan, Henrik Gabriel 1778. *Suomalaisesta runoudesta. Suomalaisen Kirjallisuuden Seuran Toimituksia 389.* Helsinki (1983).

Posti, Lauri 1953. From Pre-Finnic to Late Proto-Finnic. *FUF* (Finnisch-ugrische Forschungen) *31:* 1-91.

Propp, V. 1968. *Morphology of the Folktale.* Austin.

Proverbia Septentrionalia. 900 Balto-finnic Proverb Types with Russian, Baltic, German and Skandinavian Parallels. (Eds.) M. Kuusi et.al. FF Communications 236. Helsinki 1985.

Rausmaa, Pirkko-Liisa 1964. *Hiidestä kosinta. Suomi 110:4.* Helsinki.

– 1968. Runo- ja proosamuodon siirtymäilmiöitä. *Kalevalaseuran vuosikirja 48.* Helsinki.

– 1985. Kalevalaiset laulutanssit. *Kansanmusiikki 2.*

Ravila, Paavo 1929. Über eine doppelte Vertretung des urfinnisch-wolgaischen *a der nictersten Silbe im Mordwinischen. *FUF* (Finnisch-ugrische Forschungen) *20:* 83-120.

– 1935. Vanhan suomalaisen runomitan problema. *Virittäjä:* 35-44.

Relander, R.O. 1889. Nykyisestä kansanrunoudesta Itä-Suomesta. Havaintoja runonkeruuretkiltä Salmin kihlakunnassa ja Ilomantsissa. *Valvoja.*

– 1895. Itkuvirsien keräämismatkalla. *Valvoja.*

Ricoeur, Paul 1976. *Interpretation Theory: Discourse and the Surplus of Meaning.* Fort Worth.

– 1984. *Time and narrative. Vol. 1.* Chicago & London.

Romanos 1970 = Kontakia of Romanos, Byzantine Melodist. 1: *On the Person of Christ.* Translated and annotated by Marjorie Carpenter. Missouri, Columbia.

Rooth, Anna-Birgitta 1965. *Folklig diktning.* Uppsala.

Rosaldo, Michelle 1975. "It's All Uphill": The Creative Metaphors of Ilongot Magical Spells. M. Sanches – B. G. Blount (eds.) *Sociocultural Dimensions of Language Use – Language, Thought, and Culture. Advances in the Study of Cognition.* New York & London & San Francisco.

Rosaldo, Michelle Z. – Atkinson, Jane Monnig 1975. Man the Hunter and Woman. Metaphors for the Sexes in Ilongot Magical Spells. R. Willis (ed.) *The Interpretation of Symbolism.* Letchworth.

Rosenberg, Bruce 1981. Oral literature in the Middle Ages. J.M. Foley (ed.) *Oral traditional literature: A Festschrift for Albert Bates Lord.* Columbus.

Ruoppila, Veikko 1967. *Kalevala ja kansankieli. Suomalaisen Kirjallisuuden Seuran Toimituksia 284.* Helsinki.

Russo, J.A. 1963. A closer look at Homeric formulas. *Transactions of the American philological association 94.*

– 1966. The structural formula in Homeric verse. *Yale classical Studies 20.*

Ryan, Marie-Laure 1979. Linguistic models in narratology: from structuralism to generative. *Semiotica Vol. 28, Nos. 1/2.*

Räsänen, Matti 1977. *Ohrasta olutta, rukiista ryypättävää. Mietojen kansanomaisten viljajuomien valmistus Suomessa.* Jyväskylä.

Saarinen, Jukka 1988. *Variaatio Arhippa ja Miihkali Perttusen epiikassa.* Unpublished manuscript: pro gradu thesis. University of Helsinki, Department of Folklore.

– 1991. Miihkali Perttusen Päivölän virsi. P. Laaksonen – S.-L. Mettomäki (eds.) *Kolme on kovaa sanaa: Kirjoituksia kansanperinteestä. Kalevalaseuran vuosikirja 71.* Helsinki.

Sadeniemi, Matti 1949. *Metriikkamme perusteet.* Helsinki.

– 1951. *Die Metrik des Kalevala-Verses. FF Communications 139.* Helsinki.

Sahlins, Marshall 1985. *Islands of History.* Chicago.

Salminen, Väinö 1916. *Inkerin kansan häärunoelma muinaisine kosimis- ja hääseremonioineen.* Helsinki.

– 1917. *Länsi-Inkerin häärunot: synty- ja kehityshistoriaa.* Helsinki.

– 1921. Mekrijärven runolaulajia. *Kalevalaseuran vuosikirja 1.* Helsinki.

– 1929. *Tutkimus vatjalaisten runojen alkuperästä. Suomi V:7.* Helsinki.

– 1931a. Keinu l. liekku ja liekkuvirret. *Kalevalaseuran vuosikirja 11.* Helsinki.

– 1931b. Inkerin runonlaulajat ja tietäjät. *SKVR V:3.* Helsinki.

– 1934. *Suomalaisten muinaisrunojen historia I.* Helsinki.

– 1942. *Sanan voima ja laulajan intoutuminen. Suomi 101.*

Saloheimo, Veijo 1970. Pohjois-Karjala vuoteen 1617. *Kotiseutu 4.*

Sandor, Andras 1986. Metaphor and Belief. *Journal of Anthropological Research Vol. 42 No. 2.*

Sapir, Edward 1958 (1921). *Language. An introduction to the study of speech.* New York.

Sarmela, Matti 1969. *Reciprocity systems of the rural society in the Finnish-Karelian culture area. FF Communications 207.* Helsinki.

– 1972. Karhunpeijaisten arvoitus. *Kotiseutu 4-5.*

– 1974. Talonhaltijat sosiaalisessa kilpailussa. Suomalaisen haltiaperinteen alueellisista eroista. *Kalevalaseuran vuosikirja 54.*

– 1978. Vienalaiset lauluhäät. *Kalevalaseuran Vuosikirja 58.*

– 1981. Suomalaiset häät. M. Sarmela (ed.) *Pohjolan häät. Tietolipas 85.* Vaasa.

Sauhke, Niilo 1971. *Karjalan praasniekat.* Jyväskylä.

Saville-Troike, Muriel 1984. *The Etnography of Communication.* Oxford.

Sawin, Patricia 1988. Lönnrot's Brainchildren: The Representation of Women in Finland's Kalevala. *Journal of Folklore Research Vol. 25 No. 3.*

Schmitt, Alfred 1924. *Untersuchungen zur allgemeinen. Akzentlehre.* Heidelberg.

Selin, Kai 1973. Mariaanisia aiheita Suomen ortodoksisen kirkon liturgisissa teksteissä. *Ortodoksia 23.*

Selinheimo, Kai 1970. *Jumalansynnyttäjä Maria Suomen ortodoksisen kirkon liturgisissa teksteissä.* Unpublished manuscript: licenciate thesis. Åbo Akademi.

Sen, Nabaneeta D. 1979. Thematic structure of epic poems in the East and the West: A comparative study. E. Kushner – R. Srtruc (eds.) *Actes du VIIe Congrés de l'Association Internationale de Littérature Comparée. Vol 2.* Stuttgart.

Senkus, Kazimieras 1957. Die Formen der litauischen Volkslieder. *Commentationes balticae III, 4:* 119-65. Bonn.

Sherzer, Joel 1987. A Discourse-Centered Approach to Language and Culture. *American Anthropologist 89 (2):* 295-309.

Sihvo, Hannes 1973. *Karjalan kuva. Karelianismin taustaa ja vaiheita autonomian aikana.* Joensuu.

Siikala, Anna-Leena 1980. Miina Huovinen. Vienankarjalainen verbaaliekstaatikko. B. Alver et. al. (eds.) *Parantamisen taitajat.* Helsinki.

– 1984. *Tarina ja tulkinta. Suomalaisen Kirjallisuuden Seuran Toimituksia 404.* Helsinki. Published in English, see Siikala 1990a.

– 1985a. Kansanusko. *Suomen historia.* Helsinki.

- 1985b. Myyttinen Pohjola. K. Sallamaa (ed.) Kalevala 150-vuotta. *Tiede ja edistys 2.*
- 1986a. Myyttinen Pohjola. P. Laaksonen (ed.) *Kirjokannesta kipinä. Kalevala-seuran vuosikirja 66.* Helsinki.
- 1986b. Shamanistic Themes in Finnish Epic Poetry. I. Lehtinen (ed.) *Traces of the Central Asian Culture in the North. Mémoires de la société finno-ougrienne 194.* Helsinki.
- 1986c. Variation in the Incantation and Mythical Thinking: The Scope of Comparative Research. *Journal of Folklore Research Vol. 23 Nos. 2/3.*
- 1987. Myytti ja historia eeppisessä kansanrunoudessa. M. Linna (ed.) *Muinais-runot ja todellisuus. Suomen kansan vanhojen runojen historiallinen tausta. Historian aitta XX.* Jyväskylä.
- 1989a. Laululoitsu ja tietäjän toimi. *Rajamailta. Studia Carelica Humanistica I.* Joensuu.
- 1989b (Ed.) *Studies in Oral Narrative. Studia Fennica 33.* Helsinki.
- 1990a. *Interpreting Oral Narrative. FF Communications 245.* Helsinki.
- 1990b. Runolaulun käytäntö ja runoston kehitys. P. Hakamies (ed.) *Runo, alue, merkitys.* University of Joensuu. *Publications of Karelian Institute No 92.* Joensuu.
- 1992a. *Suomalainen šamanismi. Suomalaisen Kirjallisuuden Seuran Toimituk-sia 565.* Helsinki.
- 1992b. Understanding Narratives of the "Other". R. Kvideland et al. (eds.) *Folklore Processed in Honour of Lauri Honko on his 60th Birthday 6th March 1992. Studia Fennica Folkloristica I.* Helsinki.
Simonsuuri, Aili 1972. "La mie tantsin tapsuttelen, kenkiäni kuluttelen". *Vak-kanen. Kalevalaisten naisten Liiton vuosikirja.*
Simonsuuri, Lauri 1975 (1947). *Myytillisiä tarinoita.*
SKA 1963 = *Suomen kirjallisuuden antologia.* K. Laitinen – M. Suurpää (eds.). Helsinki.
SKK 1943 = *Suomen kansalliskirjallisuus III. Vanhaa kansanrunoutta julkais-tuna alkuperäisten kirjaanpanojen mukaan.* V. Tarkiainen – H. Harmas (eds.). Helsinki.
SKS = Suomalaisen Kirjallisuuden Seura. (Finnish Literature Society.)
SKSÄ = Suomalaisen Kirjallisuuden Seuran Äänitearkisto. (Sound Archive of the Finnish Literature Society.)
SKVR = *Suomen Kansan Vanhat Runot* (Ancient Poems of the Finnish People). 33 Volumes, published in 1908 – 1948. Helsinki.
Smolitsch, I. 1940-41. Die Verehrung der Gottesmutter in der russichen Fröm-michkeit und Volksreligiosität. *Kyrios 5.*
Stattin, Jochum 1984. *Näcken. Spelman eller Gränsvakt.* Stockholm.
Steinitz, Wolfgang 1934. *Der Parallelismus in der Finnish-Karelischen Volks-dictung. FF Communications 115.* Helsinki.
Stolte-Heiskanen, Veronica 1974. Social Indicators for Analysis of Family Needs Related to the Life Cycle. *Journal of Marriage and the Family.*
Suhonen, Seppo 1973. Die jungen lettischen Lehnwörter im Livischen. *SUST* (Suomalais-ugrilaisen Seuran Toimituksia) *154.* Helsinki.
Suomen kielen etymologinen sanakirja. Y.H. Toivonen (ed.). 1955. I. E.Itkonen – A. J. Joki – R. Peltola (eds.). 1978, XII. Helsinki.
Swanz, Marja-Liisa 1979. *Forskning om kvinnans ställning i utvecklingslän-derna.* Kvinneforskning i de humanistiske fag. Oslo.
Tarkiainen, Viljo 1911. *Aino ja muut Kalevalan naiset.* Porvoo.
Tarkka, Lotte 1989a. *Epiikan maailma, maailmankuva, runokuva – kylä-monografia Vuonnisen runokulttuurista.* Unpublished manuscript: pro gradu thesis. University of Helsinki, Department of Folklore.

– 1989b. Karjalan kuvaus kansallisena retoriikkana. Ajatuksia karelianismin etnografisesta asetelmasta. *Kalevalaseuran vuosikirja 68*. Helsinki.

– 1990a. *Epiikan maailma. Vienalaiskylän runokulttuuri symbolisena systeeminä.* Unpublished manuscript: licenciate thesis. University of Helsinki, Department of Folklore.

– 1990b. Tuonpuoleiset, tämänilmanen ja sukupuoli. Raja vienankarjalaisessa kansanrunoudessa. A. Nenola – S. Timonen (eds.) *Louhen sanat. Kirjoituksia kansanperinteen naisista*. Helsinki.

– 1993. Intertextuality, Rhetorics, and the Interpretation of Oral Poetry: The Case of Archived Orality. P. J. Anttonen – R. Kvideland (eds.) *Nordic Frontiers: Recent Issues in the Study of Modern Traditional Culture in the Nordic Countries. NIF Publications No. 27.* Turku.

Tarvasaho, Dimitri 1986. Neitsyt Marian juhlat ortodoksisessa kirkossa. *Ortodoksinen kulttuuri.*

Taube, E. 1984. South Siberian and Central Asian Hero Tales and Shamanistic Rituals. M. Hoppál (ed.) *Shamanism in Eurasia 2.* Göttingen.

Tedlock, Barbara – Tedlock, Dennis 1985. Text and Textile: Language and Technology in the Arts of the Quiche Maya. *Journal of Anthropological Research Vol. 41 No. 2.*

Tedlock, Dennis 1983. *The Spoken Word and the Work of Interpretation.* Philadelphia.

Tedre, Ülo 1965. Rahvalaul. *Eesti kirjanduse ajalugu I.* Tallinn.

Thompson, Stith 1966. *Motif-index of folk-literature. Vol. 1.* Bloomington & London.

Timonen, Senni 1985. Naistutkimus ja kansanrunous. *Kotiseutu No. 3.*

– 1987a. The Cult of the Virgin Mary in Karelian Popular Tradition. *Byzantium and the North. Acta Byzantina Fennica III.* Helsinki.

– 1987b. Virgin Mary in Karelian Popular Tradition. *Byzantium and the North. Acta Byzantina Fennica. III.* Helsinki.

– 1989. Pohjois-Karjalan lyriikka. *Kalevalaseuran Vuosikirja 68.*

– 1990a. Orjatar, ruhtinatar ja vapauden ongelma. Naisten omaelämäkerralliset laulut Inkerissä ja Siperiassa. A. Nenola – S. Timonen (eds.) *Louhen sanat. Kirjoituksia kansanperinteen naisista.* Helsinki.

– 1990b. Karjalan naisen Maria-eepos. P. Hakamies (ed.) *Runo, alue merkitys.* University of Joensuu. Publications of Karelian Institute No 92. Joensuu.

– 1992. 'Utopian' Ideas in Women's Poetry. R. Kvideland et al. (ed.) *Folklore Processed in Honour of Lauri Honko on his 60th Birthday 6th March 1992. Studia Fennica Folkloristica I.* Helsinki.

Todorov, Tzvetan 1984. *Mikhail Bakhtin: The Dialogical Principle. Theory and History of Literature Vol. 13.* Manchester.

Toiviainen, Seppo 1967. Nuorison seksuaalinen käyttäytyminen Inkerissä. *Sosiologia 4.*

Troubetzkoy, N. 1921. De la Valeur primitive des intonations du slave commun. *Revue des études slaves I:* 171-87.

Turner, Terence 1985. Animal Symbolism, Totemism, and the Structure of Myth. Gary Urton (ed.) *Animal Myths and Metaphors in South America.* Salt Lake City.

– 1991. "We are Parrots", "Twins are Birds": Play of Tropes as Operational Structure. J. W. Fernandez (ed.), *Beyond Metaphor. The Theory of Tropes in Anthropology.* Stanford.

Turunen, Aimo 1979. *Kalevalan sanat ja niiden taustat.* Lappeenranta.

Utriainen, Terhi 1989a. Kahta kieltä kuolemaan. *Suomen Antropologi 4.*

– 1989b. *Nimettömän nimet. Vienankarjalaisen kuolemanrituaalin tarkastelua merkityksenannon prosessina.* Unpublished manuscript: pro gradu thesis. University of Helsinki, Department of the Science of Religions.

398

Valeri, Valerio 1990. Constructive History: Genealogy and Narrative in the Legitimation of Hawaiian Kingship. E. Ohnuki-Tierney (ed.) *Culture Through Time: Anthropological Approaches.* Standford.

Varonen, Matti 1898. *Vainajainpalvelus muinaisilla suomalaisilla.* Helsinki.

Veyne, Paul 1988. *Did the Greeks believe in their myths?* USA.

VH = *Veisatkaa herralle. Otteita kirkkovuoden juhlapäivien jumalanpalveluksista. III.* Pääsiäisen mukaan liikkuvat juhlat. Pieksämäki 1981.

Vīkis-Freibergs, Vaira 1989. Text variants in the folk song corpus. V. Vīkis-Freiberg (ed.), *Linquistics and poetics of Latvian folk songs.* Kingston, Montreal.

Vilkuna, Kustaa 1966. Maria. *Kulturhistorisk lexikon för nordisk medeltid 11.* Helsingfors.

Virtanen, Leea 1966. *Suomalais-virolainen arvoitussarja.* Helsinki.

– 1968. *Kalevalainen laulutapa Karjalassa. Suomi 113:1.* Helsinki.

– 1974. Tuomaanlaulun maailmankuva. *Sampo ei sanoja puutu. Kalevalaseuran vuosikirja 54.* Helsinki.

– 1975. Über die Funktionen des Kalevala-Liedes in Karelien. *Fabula. Zeitschift für Erzählforschung 16:* 256-277.

– 1984. *Onni yksillä.* Helsinki.

– 1987. Setukaiset kertovat lauluistaan. L. Virtanen (ed.) *Viron veräjät.* Helsinki.

Virtaranta, Pertti 1958. *Vienan kansa muistelee.* Porvoo.

Voionmaa, Väinö 1969 (1915). *Suomen karjalaisen heimon historia.* Porvoo.

Väisänen, A.O. 1940 – 1941. Itkuvirsi karjalaisten kohtalosta. *Kalevalaseuran vuosikirja 20-21.*

Weigle, Marta 1987. Creation and Procreation, Cosmogony and Childbirth. Reflections on Ex Nihilo, Earth Diver, and Emergence Mythology. *Journal of American folklore, Vol. 100, No. 398.*

– 1989. *Creation and procreation. Feminist reflections on mythologies of cosmogony and parturition.* Philadelphia.

Wellek, Rene – Warren, Austin 1976 (1949). *Theory of literature.* New York.

Wellesz, Egon 1949. *A history of Byzantine music and hymnography.* Oxford.

Willis, Roy 1990. Introduction. R. Willis (ed.) *Signifying Animals. Human Meaning in the Natural World.* Cambridge.

Wilson, William A. 1976. *Folklore and nationalism in modern Finland.* Bloomington & London.

Zaleski, Carol 1987. *Otherworld Journeys. Accounts of Near-death Experience in Medieval and Modern Times.* New York.